CW01083589

Enoch, Jubilees, Jasher: Banned from the Bible

by Dr. Joseph B. Lumpkin

Enoch, Jubilees, Jasher:
Banned from the Bible

1st EDITION

Copyright © 2014 Joseph B. Lumpkin.
All rights reserved.

Printed in the United States of America. No part of this book may be used
or reproduced in any manner whatsoever without written permission
except in the case of brief quotations embodied in critical articles and
reviews.

First time or interested authors, contact Fifth Estate Publishers,
Blountsville, AL 35031.

Cover Design by An Quigley
Printed on acid-free paper

Library of Congress Control No: 2014909406

ISBN: 9781936533442

Fifth Estate, 2014

Table of Contents

Introduction

Our search for deeper understanding often leads beyond the Bible itself. Even in our attempt to fully understand the Bible we must go beyond the book. As we encounter references to social conditions, cultural practices, and even other writings mentioned within the scriptures we are called to investigate and expand our knowledge in order to fully appreciate the context, knowledge base, and cultural significance of what is being taught.

Thus, to fully understand the Bible, we are necessarily drawn to sources outside the Bible. These sources add to the historical, social, or theological understanding of Biblical times. As our view becomes more macrocosmic, we see the panoramic setting and further understand the full truth within the scriptures. Yet, in the case of Enoch, we are not going beyond THE Bible. We are simply going beyond OUR bible. The Book of Enoch is contained in the Bible of the Ethiopic Christian Church.

Popular texts among early Christians

To lead us to sources of information outside of our Protestant and Catholic Bibles we must know which books were popular and important at the time the Bible was being written. There are several books mentioned in the Bible which are not included in our Bible. They are not spiritual canon, either because they were not available at the time the canon was originally adopted, or at the time they were not considered "inspired." In cases when inspiration was questioned, one could argue that any book quoted or mentioned by a prophet or an apostle should be considered as spiritual canon; unfortunately this position would prove too simplistic.

Books and writings can fall under various categories such as civil records and laws, historical documents, or spiritual writings. A city or state census is not inspired, but it could add insight into certain areas of life. Spiritual writings which are directly quoted in the Bible serve as insights into the beliefs of the writer or what was considered acceptable by society at the time. As with any new discovery, invention, or belief, the new is interpreted based upon the structure of what came before. This was the way in the first century Christian church, as beliefs were based upon the old Jewish understanding. However, one should realize pagan beliefs were also added to the church as non-Jewish populations were converted, bringing with them the foundations of their beliefs on which they interpreted Christianity.

In the case of Jude, James, Paul, and others, the Jewish past was giving way to the Christian present, but their understanding and doctrine were still being influenced by what they had learned and experienced previously. It becomes obvious that to understand the Bible one should endeavor to investigate the books and doctrines that most influenced the writers of the Bible.

The Dead Sea Scrolls, found in the caves of Qumran, are of great interest in the venture of clarifying the history and doctrine in existence between biblical times and the fixing of canon. The scrolls were penned in the second century B.C. and were in use at least until the destruction of the second temple in 70 A.D. Similar scrolls to those found in Cave 4 within the 11 caves of Qumran were also found at the Masada stronghold which fell in 73 A.D. Fragments of every book of the Old Testament except Esther were found in the caves of Qumran, but so were many other books. Some of these books are considered to have been of equal importance and influence to the people of Qumran and to the writers and scholars of the time. Some of those studying the scrolls found in Qumran were the writers of the New Testament.

Knowing this, one might ask which of the dozens of non-canonical books most influenced the writers of the New Testament. It is possible to ascertain the existence of certain influences within the Bible context by using the Bible itself. The Bible can direct us to other works in three ways. The work can be mentioned by name, as is the Book of Jasher. The work can be quoted within the Bible text, as is the case with the Book of Enoch. The existence of the work can be alluded to, as is the case of the missing letter from the apostle Paul to the Corinthians.

Books mentioned in the Holy Bible

In the case of those books named in the Bible, one can set a list as the titles are named. The list is lengthier than one might at first suspect. Most of these works have not been found. Some have been unearthed but their authenticity is questioned. Others have been found and the link between scripture and scroll is generally accepted. Following is a list of books mentioned in the Holy Bible:

1. **The Book of Jasher:** "Also he bade them teach the children of Judah the use of the bow: behold, it is written in the Book of Jasher." *(2 Samuel 1:18)* "Is it not written in the Book of Jasher? And the sun stopped in the middle of the sky and did not hasten to go down for about a whole day." *(Joshua 10:13)*
2. **The Book of Wars of the Lord:** "Therefore it is said in the Book of the Wars of the Lord." *(Num. 21:14)*
3. **The Annals of Jehu:** "Now the rest of the acts of Jehoshaphat, first to last, behold, they are written in the annals of Jehu the son of Hanani, which is recorded in the Book of the Kings of Israel." *(2 Chronicles 20:34)*
4. **The Book of the Kings:** "As to his sons and the many oracles against him and the rebuilding of the house of God, behold, they are written in the treatise of the Book of the Kings. Then Amaziah his son became king in his place." *(2 Chronicles 24:27)*
5. **The Book of Records, Book of the Chronicles of Ahasuerus:** "Now when the plot was investigated and found to be so, they were both hanged on a gallows; and it was written in the Book of the Chronicles in the king's presence." ... "During that night the king could not sleep so he gave an order to bring the book of records, the chronicles, and they were read before the king." *(Esther 2:23, 6:1)*
6. **The Acts of Solomon:** "Now the rest of the acts of Solomon and whatever he did, and his wisdom, are they not written in the book of the Acts of Solomon?" *(1 Kings 11:41)*
7. **The Sayings of Hozai:** "His prayer also and how God was entreated by him, and all his sin, his unfaithfulness, and the sites on which he built high places and erected the Asherim and the carved images, before he humbled himself, behold, they are written in the records of the Hozai." *(2 Chronicles 33:19)*
8. **The Chronicles of King David:** "Joab the son of Zeruiah had begun to count them, but did not finish; and because of this, wrath came upon Israel, and the number was not included in the account of the Chronicles of King David." *(1 Chronicles 27:24)*
9. **The Chronicles of Samuel, Nathan, Gad**: "Now the acts of King David, from first to last, are written in the Chronicles of Samuel the seer, in the Chronicles of Nathan the prophet and in the Chronicles of Gad the seer." *(1 Chronicles 29:29)*
10. **Samuel's book:** "Then Samuel told the people the ordinances of the kingdom, and wrote them in the book and placed it before the Lord." *(1 Samuel 10:25)*
11. **The Records of Nathan the Prophet:** "Now the rest of the Acts of Solomon, from first to last, are they not written in the Records of Nathan the Prophet, and in the Prophecy of Ahijah the Shilonite, and in the Visions of Iddo the Seer concerning Jeroboam the son of Nebat?" *(2 Chronicles 9:29)*
12. **The Prophecy of Ahijah the Shilonite:** "Now the rest of the acts of Solomon, from first to last, are they not written in the Records of Nathan the Prophet, and in the Prophecy of Ahijah the Shilonite, and in the Visions of Iddo the Seer concerning Jeroboam the son of Nebat?" *(2 Chronicles 9:29)*
13. **The Treatise of the Prophet Iddo:** "Now the rest of the acts of Abijah, and his ways and his words are written in the treatise of the prophet Iddo." *(2 Chronicles 13:22)*

There are several books which have come to us entitled, "Book of Jasher." One is an ethical treatise from the Middle Ages. It begins with a section on the Mystery of the Creation of the World: It is clearly unrelated to the Biblical Book of Jasher.

Another was published in 1829, supposedly translated by Flaccus Albinus Alcuinus. It opens with the chapter 1, verse 1 reading, "While it was the beginning, darkness overspread the face of nature." It is now considered a fake.

The third and most important is by Midrash, first translated into English in 1840. It opens with chapter 1, verse 1 reading, "And God said, Let us make man in our image, after our likeness, and God created man in his own image." A comparison of Joshua 10:13 with Jasher 88:63-64 and 2 Samuel 1:18 with Jasher 56:9 makes it clear that this Book of Jasher at least follows close enough with the Bible to be the Book of Jasher mentioned in the Bible.

Missing Epistles

The existence of a lost book can be inferred even if no text is available. This is clearly seen with several missing epistles.

Paul's letter to the Church at Laodicea appears to be missing, according to some scholars. Colossians 4:16 states, "When this letter is read among you, have it also read in the church of the Laodiceans; and you, for your part, read my letter that is coming from Laodicea." Since three earlier manuscripts do not contain the words "at

Ephesus" in Ephesians 1:1, some have speculated that the letter coming from Laodicea was in fact the letter of Ephesians. Apostolic fathers also debated this possibility.

In Paul's first letter to Corinth, he predated that letter by saying: "I wrote you in my letter not to associate with immoral people" *(1 Corinthians 5:9)* This could merely be a reference to the present letter of 1 Corinthians.

Book of Enoch may be most influencial

Of all the books quoted, paraphrased, or referred to in the Bible, the Book of Enoch has influenced the writers of the Bible as few others have. Even more extensively than in the Old Testament, the writers of the New Testament were frequently influenced by other writings, including the Book of Enoch.

It is not the purpose of this work to make judgments as to the validity or worth of the Book of Enoch, but rather to simply put forth a meaningful question: *Is not the non-canonical book that most influenced the thought and theology of the writers of the New Testament worth further research and contemplation?*

Before we continue in our study of the Book of Enoch there are several questions we must keep in mind. If a book is mentioned or quoted in the Bible, is it not worthy of further study? If it is worth investigating, is this the book of which the Bible speaks? What knowledge or insight does it add to our understanding of the Bible or the men who wrote it?

The Book of Enoch was once cherished by Jews and Christians alike. It is read in certain Coptic Christian Churches in Ethiopia. Three versions of the Book of Enoch exist today.

Book of Enoch: Discovering it; dating it

Most scholars date the Book of Enoch to sometime during the second century B.C. We do not know what earlier oral tradition, if any, the book contains. Enoch was considered inspired and authentic by certain Jewish sects of the first century B.C. and remained popular for at least 500 years. The earliest Ethiopian text was apparently derived from a Greek manuscript of the Book of Enoch, which itself was a copy of an earlier text. The original was apparently written in the Semitic language, now thought to be Aramaic.

The Book of Enoch was discovered in the 18th century. It was assumed to have been penned after the beginning of the Christian era. This theory was based on the fact that it had quotes and paraphrases as well as concepts found in the New Testament. Thus, it was assumed that it was heavily influenced by writers such as Jude and Peter.

However, recent discoveries of copies of the book among the Dead Sea Scrolls found at Qumran prove the book was in existence before the time of Jesus Christ. These scrolls forced a closer look and reconsideration. *It became obvious that the New Testament did not influence the Book of Enoch; on the contrary, the Book of Enoch influenced the New Testament.* The date of the original writing upon which the second century B.C. Qumran copies were based is shrouded in obscurity. Likewise lost are the sources of the oral traditions that came to be the Book of Enoch. Slowly, over the past 60 years, we have unraveled some of the mystery.

Inspired, authentic or fake?

It has been largely the opinion of historians that the book does not really contain the authentic words of the ancient Enoch, since he would have lived several thousand years earlier than the first known appearance of the book attributed to him. However, the first century Christians accepted the Book of Enoch as inspired, if not authentic. They relied on it to understand the origin and purpose of many things, from angels to wind, sun, and stars. In fact, many of the key concepts used by Jesus Christ himself seem directly connected to terms and ideas in the Book of Enoch.

The theories regarding the authenticity of Enoch vary widely. Some believe Enoch is Midrash; that is an elaboration on a biblical story. In this case it is suggested that Enoch expands Genesis chapter 6.

Parallels between Enoch and the Holy Scriptures

Another more controversial theory has Enoch predating the Genesis story. Like the Book of Enoch, Genesis seems to have several authors with stories intertwined. One of these authors is known simply as "P," owing to the fact he was thought to be a priest. If we compare the "P" contribution of Genesis to the Book of Enoch, parallels leap out.

Enoch	P
Corrupt earth	Human way corrupt on the earth (Gen 6)
eating animals	eating animals (Gen 9)
bloodshed	bloodshed (Gen 9)
364-day year	30-day months (Gen 7)
(12 months x 30 + 4)	365-day year (Gen 5)
Enoch goes to heaven	Enoch goes to heaven (Gen 5)

There are other connections. The name "Azazel" appears in Leviticus. The scapegoat is sent into the wilderness "to Azazel," and through the ceremony of laying on of hands by the priest and people, the goat is sent away, bearing the sins of the people. This reference only makes sense if the writer believed that Azazel was responsible for all human sins and would bear the punishment for it, as the Book of Enoch declares.

In Genesis, it is Cain who bears sins into the wilderness. However, we will see that there are connections between the fallen angels and the descendants of Cain.

The problem with such a connection between Enoch and Genesis is that it does not point to the direction of the transmission. We now can be reasonably sure that Enoch and Genesis are connected, but we cannot be certain which was recorded first. The best evidence we have for the undisputed authenticity of Enoch is not the connection to Genesis, but the faith Jesus and the Apostles had in the Book of Enoch, demonstrated by various references and quotes.

How Jesus and his followers used Enoch

It is hard to avoid the evidence that Jesus not only studied the book, but also respected it highly enough to allude to its doctrine and content. Enoch is replete with mentions of the coming kingdom and other holy themes. It was not only Jesus who used phrases or ideas from Enoch, there are over 100 comments in the New Testament which find precedence in the Book of Enoch.

As we begin looking for connections between the words of or about Jesus and those of Enoch, we cannot look for exact matches. It is possible that what was originally spoken by these men was very close in wording or exact meaning, but after divergent paths of transmission and translations through various languages and cultures they arrive here in the 21st century with many alterations. Like the child's game of "telephone," exact wording has been somewhat altered. Let us look at general ideas within passages.

Jesus	Enoch
Blessed are the meek, for they shall inherit the earth. (Mat 5:5)	And all the elect shall rejoice, and there shall be forgiveness of sins, and mercy and peace and forbearance and joy. There shall be salvation for them, (like/and) a good light. (Enoch 5:7)
the Father judgeth no man, but hath committed all judgment unto the son (John 5:22).	And he sat on the throne of his glory, and the sum of judgment was given to the Son of Man. (Enoch 69:27)
Matt. 19:16 Now a man came up to Jesus and asked, "Teacher, what good thing must I do to get eternal life?" (Jesus said) And everyone who has left houses or brothers or sisters or father or mother or children or fields	…who is set over the repentance and those who hope to inherit eternal life.. (Enoch 40:9)

for my sake will receive a hundred times as much and will inherit eternal life.

"Woe unto you that are rich! for ye have received your consolation. (Luke 6:24)

Woe to you, you rich, for you have trusted in your riches, and from your riches shall you depart, because you have not remembered the Most High in the days of your riches. (Enoch 94:8)

Ye also shall sit upon twelve thrones, judging the twelve tribes of Israel. (Mat. 19:28)

And I will bring out in shining light those who have loved My holy name, and I will seat each on the throne of his honor (glory). (Enoch 108:12)

Woe unto that man through whom the Son of man is betrayed! It had been good for that man if he had not been born. (Mat. 26:24)

Where will there be the dwelling for sinners, and where the will there be a resting-place for those who have denied the Lord of spirits? It had been good for them if they had not been born. (Enoch 38:2)

between us and you there is a great gulf fixed. (Luke 16:26)

Then I asked, regarding all the hollow places (chasm): 'Why is one separated from the other?'
9 And he answered me and said to me: 'These three have been made that the spirits of the dead might be separated. (Enoch 22: 9)

Luke 1:32 He will be great and will be called the Son of the Most High. The Lord God will give him the throne of his father David, 33and he will reign over the house of Jacob forever; his kingdom will never end."
John 14:2 In my Father's house are many mansions

On that day My Elect One shall sit on the throne of glory and shall try the works of the righteous, and their places of rest shall be. (Enoch 45:3)

that ye may be called the children of light (John 12:36)

And now I will summon the spirits of the good who belong to the generation of light,... (Enoch 108:11)

the water that I shall give him shall be in him a well of water springing up into everlasting life. (John 4:14)

And in that place I saw the spring of righteousness which was inexhaustible. And around it were many springs of wisdom. And all the thirsty drank of them, and were filled with wisdom, and their dwellings were with the righteous and holy and elect. (Enoch 48:1)

Further evidence of Enoch's popularity

Other evidence of the early Christians' acceptance of the Book of Enoch was for many years buried under the King James Bible's mistranslation of Luke 9:35, describing the transfiguration of Christ: "And there came a voice out of the cloud, saying, 'This is my beloved Son. Hear him.'" Apparently the translator here wished to make this verse agree with a similar verse in Matthew and Mark. But Luke's verse in the original Greek reads, "This is my Son, the Elect One (from the Greek *ho eklelegmenos*, literally, "the elect one"). Hear him."

The "Elect One" is a most significant term (found 14 times) in the Book of Enoch. If the book was indeed known to the Apostles of Christ, with its abundant descriptions of the Elect One who should "sit upon the throne of glory" and the Elect One who should "dwell in the midst of them," then the great scriptural authenticity is justly accorded to the Book of Enoch. Then the "voice out of the cloud" tells the Apostles, "This is my Son, the Elect One,"... the one promised in the Book of Enoch.

The Book of Jude tells us in verse 14 that "Enoch, the seventh from Adam, prophesied." Jude also, in verse 15, makes a direct reference to the Book of Enoch (2:1), where he writes, "to execute judgment on all, to convict all who are ungodly." As a matter of fact, it is a direct, word-for-word quote. Therefore, Jude's reference to the Enochian prophesies strongly leans toward the conclusion that these written prophesies were available to him at that time.

Fragments of ten Enoch manuscripts were found among the Dead Sea Scrolls. The number of scrolls indicate the Essenes (a Jewish commune or sect at the time of Christ) could well have used the Enochian writings as a community prayer book or teacher's manual and study text.

Many of the early church fathers also supported the Enochian writings. Justin Martyr ascribed all evil to demons whom he alleged to be the offspring of the angels who fell through lust for women; directly referencing the Enochian writings.

Athenagoras (170 A.D.) regarded Enoch as a true prophet. He describes the angels who "violated both their own nature and their office." In his writings, he goes into detail about the nature of fallen angels and the cause of their fall, which comes directly from the Enochian writings.

Irenaeus (A.D. 180), in his work "Against Heresies," spoke of Enoch, whose translation was a prophetic view of our future rapture: "For Enoch, when he pleased God, was translated in the same body in which he did please Him, thus pointing out by anticipation the translation of the just" (Against Heresies, bk. 5).

How Enoch disappeared

Since any book stands to be interpreted in many ways, Enoch posed problems for some theologians. Instead of reexamining their own theology, they sought to dispose of that which went counter to their beliefs. Some of the visions in Enoch are believed to point to the consummation of the age in conjunction with Christ's second coming, which some believe took place in A.D. 70 (in the destruction of Jerusalem).

This being the case, it should not surprise us that Enoch was declared a fake and was rejected by Hilary, Jerome, and Augustine. Enoch was subsequently lost to Western Christendom for over 1,000 years.

However, some view the Book of Enoch as prophetic, not only as a timeline, but being a picture into what is coming to all those who believe and are obedient to God.

"By faith Enoch was translated that he should not see death; and was not found, because God had translated him: for before his translation he had this testimony, that he pleased God" *(Hebrews 11:5)*. Enoch experienced "rapture" in his time before the judgment of the Flood. What Enoch experienced is what some modern Christians believe is waiting for the church. 1 Thessalonians 4:15-17 promises that Jesus will descend from heaven with a shout, with the voice of the archangel and the trumpet of God, and the church will be taken up, or "raptured,"," to meet Him in the air.

Enoch supports Biblical endtime prophecy

The Book of Enoch may inform and prepare us for coming events. Some believe there are prophecies contained in the Book of Enoch that are as applicable as those written in the books of Daniel and Revelation.

The prophecies within Enoch are presented in several ways. There is a list of weeks, much like those of Daniel. There are a list of animals and their actions toward each other. There is a list of generations defining a timeline.

Enoch's "70 generations" was also a great problem. Many scholars thought it could not be made to stretch beyond the first century. Copies of Enoch soon disappeared. Indeed, for almost 2,000 years we knew only the references made to it in the Bible. Without having the book itself, we could not have known it was being quoted in the Bible, sometimes word for word, by Peter and Jude.

"...the Lord, having saved a people out of the land of Egypt, afterward destroyed them that believed not. And angels that kept not their own principality, but left their proper habitation, he hath kept in everlasting bonds under darkness unto the judgment of the great day. Even as Sodom and Gomorrah, and the cities about them...in like manner...are set out as examples...." *(Jude 5-7)*

"For if God spared not the angels when they sinned, but cast them down into hell, and committed them to pits of darkness, to be reserved unto judgment." *(2 Peter 2.4)*

To what extent other New Testament writers regarded Enoch as scriptural canon may be determined by comparing their writings with those found in Enoch. A strong possibility of influence upon their thought and choice of wording is evidenced by a great many references found in Enoch which remind one of passages found in the New Testament.

Famous Christians who accepted Enoch

Enoch was also referenced in other writings, such as the Book of Jubilees, which is canon in the Ethiopic Christian Church, and the Book of Giants, in which one of the fallen angels is called by the name of Gilgamesh.

The Book of Enoch seems to be a missing link between Jewish and Christian theology and is considered by many to be more Christian in its theology than Jewish. It was considered scripture by many early Christians. The literature of the church fathers is filled with references to this book. The early second century apocryphal book of the Epistle of Barnabus makes many references and quotes from the Book of Enoch. Second and third century church fathers like Justin Martyr, Irenaeus, Origen and Clement of Alexandria all seemed to have accepted Enoch as authentic. Tertullian (160-230 A.D.) even called the Book of Enoch "Holy Scripture." The Ethiopian Coptic Church holds the Book of Enoch as part of its official spiritual canon. It was widely known and read the first three centuries after Christ. This and many other books became discredited after the Council of Laodicea. And being under ban of the authorities, it gradually disappeared from circulation.

How Enoch was rediscovered

In 1773, rumors of a surviving copy of the book drew Scottish explorer James Bruce to distant Ethiopia. He found the Book of Enoch had been preserved by the Ethiopian church, which put it right alongside the other books of the Bible.

Bruce secured not one, but three Ethiopian copies of the book and brought them back to Europe and Britain. In 1773 Bruce returned from six years in Abyssinia. In 1821 Richard Laurence published the first English translation. The famous R.H. Charles edition was published in 1912.

In the following years several portions of the Greek text surfaced. Then with the discovery of Cave 4 at Qumran, seven fragmentary copies of the Aramaic text were discovered. This means the text passed from its Aramaic form into Greek, and finally into Geez, an Ethiopian tongue.

Before the discovery of the Aramaic form was uncovered, it was thought that Enoch was written after Jude and borrowed heavily from it. However, after the discovery of Enoch among the texts in Qumran, scholars had to re-examine the evidence. Enoch not only existed long before the biblical book of Jude, it is now obvious that both Jude and Peter read, believed and borrowed heavily from Enoch. This makes the Book of Enoch (1 Enoch) one of the earliest apocalyptic books.

Most apocalyptic literature was written after the destruction of the Jewish temple in Jerusalem in 70 A.D. under the feet of a Roman siege. Rome was considered by the Jews to be an ungodly nation as well as the oppressors and enemy of the Jews. The Jews considered themselves to be the chosen people of God. When the temple of God was destroyed it caused great turmoil throughout Judaism. Why would God let this happen to His chosen people and moreover, to His own house? The answer must be that the Jewish people had sinned and wandered away from the will of God. If this were true then when the Jewish nation repented and came back to God, He would avenge them by allowing the Jews to conquer and crush their enemies. The Jews would once again appear to be the victorious and chosen people they were meant to be. The return of the Jewish nation to the strict will and law of God and the battle and victory through God's help is the basis of most apocalyptic literature.

This is not the case in the first and oldest section of the Book of Enoch, written as early as the 3rd century B.C. The apocalyptic theme in the section we are calling "The Book of the Watchers" is a simple one of blessing the righteous and destroying the unrighteous beings, both human and angelic. More traditional or common apocalyptic themes can be seen in sections of Enoch written around 100 A.D.

How The First Book of Enoch is divided

The First Book of Enoch is not one manuscript. It is a composite of several manuscripts written by several authors over a period of 300 to 400 years.

The Book of Enoch is composed of six main parts. These sections can be subdivided further. It could be argued that, like the writers of the Bible itself, the various authors of Enoch did not foresee their contributions being concatenated into a single volume.

The six basic sections are as follows:

The Book of Watchers (Chapters 1-36)
Probably written: Late 3rd century or early 2nd century B.C.
Overall theme: Last judgment
This section is considered to be the most authentic and important part of the Book of Enoch.
Contents:
- Introduction (Chapters 1-5): Last judgment
- The Fall (Chapters 6-36): Fall of the angels by having sex with the women of earth; the evil of the children and the corruption of mankind

The Book of Parables (Chapters 37-71)
Probably written: 1st century A.D.
Overall theme: The Messiah and His judgment
Contents:
- 1st parable: Enoch's vision of heaven containing the righteous people, the angels and the Messiah (Chapters 38-44)
- 2nd parable: The messianic judgment (Chapters 45-57)
- 3rd parable: The Son of Man (Chapters 58-71)

The Book of Astronomy and Calendar (Chapters 72-82)
Probably written: Late 3rd or early 2nd century B.C.
Overall theme & contents: Elements of weather, movement of stars, planets, sun and moon, and the calendar

The Book of Visions (Chapters 83-90)
Probably written: 165-160 B.C. (thought to be written around the time of the revolt led by the Maccabees)
Overall theme: Judgment and history
Contents:
- 1st vision: The deluge as the first judgment (Chapters 83-84)
- 2nd vision: A history of Israel until the revolt (Chapters 85-90)

The Book of Warnings and Blessings of Enoch (Chapters 91-104)
Probably written: Early 2nd century B.C.
Overall theme: Warnings, blessings and an apocalypse
Contents:
- The prophecy of the Apocalypse of Weeks (Chapters 91 and 93)
- What will befall sinners and the righteous (Chapters 94-104)

Later Additions to the Text, Book of Noah (**Chapters 105-108**)
Probably written: 2nd century B.C.
Overall theme: Noah and Methuselah
Contents: This section of the book seems to be added as an afterthought. It consists of fragments from other books, such as the Book of Noah.

When the Book of Enoch was found along with other scrolls around the Dead Sea, the Book of Parables was not included. This was because that section was added later. In addition, the Book of Watchers and the Book of Visions were already joined and intact.

Trustworthiness of the Enochian Calendar

During the time period Enoch was written, the Jewish community was torn regarding which type of calendar to use. Enoch seems to taut a solar-based calendar that is 364 days long with a week added as needed to make up for the missing a day and a quarter (1.25). Compare 365.25 days to 364 days. The Enochian calendar began each year on a Sunday. The starting point for the calendar was the spring equinox, which occurs around March 21st or 22nd. Since the year always begins on the same day of the week, and only a full week is added when needed, the calendar is considered to be a calendar of weeks. To put this in perspective, simply assume that instead of adding a day every four years as we do, a week would be added every few years as needed to align the beginning of the years as close to the first Sunday after the equinox. Now assume New Years comes, not on January 1st, but on March 21st. Although this is a bit of an over simplification, it is basically the way the Enochian calendar functioned.

The Book of Enoch tells of the sun traversing the heavens through a number of gates. The passage through the various gates represented segments of a day. The Enochian day is not divided into 24 hours but into 18 segments of one and one-third hours each. Thus, each segment lasted 80 minutes. More detailed information on the calendar will be presented at the end of this book, when we discuss its application to the Prophecy of Daniel.

The Book of Jubilees, which was written in the same timeframe, demands and defends the use of the ancient lunar calendar. Writers of Jubilees reasoned that if one were to worship in strict compliance to the customs presented by the Torah, one had to use the same lunar calendar so one would worship at the proper times and days. The Book of Enoch does not defend the choice of a solar calendar; it simply lays out the math and astronomical movements.

The Hebrew calendar is a lunar-based system. In this system Passover occurs after sundown on the 15th day of the month Nisan. Passover is celebrated for seven days. The first Passover was in the springtime and many thought it should be keep in that period of the year. Since the calendar is based in lunar movements the Hebrew calendar is offset to the solar calendar by about 11 days a year. This meant that Passover would drift from spring, to winter, to autumn, and back again. The drift had become so annoying that in the year 359 A.D. a rabbi named Hillel II began the process of aligning the lunar calendar to the solar calendar by standardizing the lunar months to 29 or 30 days and adding a day to the month of Adar when needed to keep synchronized, just as we would add a day to our leap year.

All of this information will become important as we begin discussing prophecy. So, let's nail down what the Bible says about the first Passover and the date:

Exodus 12
1 And the LORD spake unto Moses and Aaron in the land of Egypt saying,
2 This month shall be unto you the beginning of months: it shall be the first month of the year to you.
3 Speak ye unto all the congregation of Israel, saying, In the tenth day of this month they shall take to them every man a lamb, according to the house of their fathers, a lamb for an house:
4 And if the household be too little for the lamb, let him and his neighbour next unto his house take it according to the number of the souls; every man according to his eating shall make your count for the lamb.
5 Your lamb shall be without blemish, a male of the first year: ye shall take it out from the sheep, or from the goats:
6 And ye shall keep it up until the fourteenth day of the same month: and the whole assembly of the congregation of Israel shall kill it in the evening.
7 And they shall take of the blood, and strike it on the two side posts and on the upper door post of the houses, wherein they shall eat it.

8 And they shall eat the flesh in that night, roast with fire, and unleavened bread; and with bitter herbs they shall eat it.

9 Eat not of it raw, nor sodden at all with water, but roast with fire; his head with his legs, and with the purtenance thereof.

10 And ye shall let nothing of it remain until the morning; and that which remaineth of it until the morning ye shall burn with fire.

11 And thus shall ye eat it; with your loins girded, your shoes on your feet, and your staff in your hand; and ye shall eat it in haste: it is the LORD's passover.

12 For I will pass through the land of Egypt this night, and will smite all the firstborn in the land of Egypt, both man and beast; and against all the gods of Egypt I will execute judgment: I am the LORD.

13 And the blood shall be to you for a token upon the houses where ye are: and when I see the blood, I will pass over you, and the plague shall not be upon you to destroy you, when I smite the land of Egypt.

14 And this day shall be unto you for a memorial; and ye shall keep it a feast to the LORD throughout your generations; ye shall keep it a feast by an ordinance forever.

15 Seven days shall ye eat unleavened bread; even the first day ye shall put away leaven out of your houses: for whosoever eateth leavened bread from the first day until the seventh day, that soul shall be cut off from Israel.

16 And in the first day there shall be an holy convocation, and in the seventh day there shall be an holy convocation to you; no manner of work shall be done in them, save that which every man must eat, that only may be done of you.

17 And ye shall observe the feast of unleavened bread; for in this selfsame day have I brought your armies out of the land of Egypt: therefore shall ye observe this day in your generations by an ordinance forever.

18 In the first month, on the fourteenth day of the month at even, ye shall eat unleavened bread, until the one and twentieth day of the month at even.

19 Seven days shall there be no leaven found in your houses: for whosoever eateth that which is leavened, even that soul shall be cut off from the congregation of Israel, whether he be a stranger, or born in the land.

20 Ye shall eat nothing leavened; in all your habitations shall ye eat unleavened bread.

21 Then Moses called for all the elders of Israel, and said unto them, Draw out and take you a lamb according to your families, and kill the passover.

22 And ye shall take a bunch of hyssop, and dip it in the blood that is in the bason, and strike the lintel and the two side posts with the blood that is in the bason; and none of you shall go out at the door of his house until the morning.

23 For the LORD will pass through to smite the Egyptians; and when he seeth the blood upon the lintel, and on the two side posts, the LORD will pass over the door, and will not suffer the destroyer to come in unto your houses to smite you.

24 And ye shall observe this thing for an ordinance to thee and to thy sons forever.

25 And it shall come to pass, when ye be come to the land which the LORD will give you, according as he hath promised, that ye shall keep this service.

26 And it shall come to pass, when your children shall say unto you, What mean ye by this service?

27 That ye shall say, It is the sacrifice of the LORD's passover, who passed over the houses of the children of Israel in Egypt, when he smote the Egyptians, and delivered our houses. And the people bowed the head and worshipped.

28 And the children of Israel went away, and did as the LORD had commanded Moses and Aaron, so did they.

It should be noted that when the Gregorian or Enochian calendars are applied, Passover will last for eight days since the Hebrew day starts at sundown and both the Enochian and Gregorian days start at midnight.

Now, we understand that the Hebrew lunar calendar, the Enochian calendar, and the Gregorian calendar are all slightly different. When we turn our attention to the prophecy in the Book of Daniel, called "Daniel's Weeks of Years," we can now ask the first intelligent question: "What kind of year was the prophecy based upon? You will find an in-depth explanation of the application of the Enochian calendar to prophecy in the section titled "The Calendar for Enoch's and Daniel's Prophecies," starting on page 158. For now, let us turn our attention back to the Book of Enoch.

The translations used for this work are taken from both the Richard Laurence and R.H. Charles manuscripts in addition to numerous sources and commentaries. The texts were compared and rendered for easier reading by the modern "American" English reader as some phrasing from the 18th and 19th centuries may seem somewhat clumsy to our 21st century eyes. When there are clear differences in various texts, a word is added in parentheses to show both paths of translations.

In addition to the translation notes there are Biblical references showing how the Book of Enoch contains various Old Testament sources, or how the 1 Enoch was quoted, referenced, or was possibly used as a source document for New Testament writers. These Biblical references, as well as quotes from other ancient sources, are italicized and the chapters and verses noted. Notes and commentaries from the author are kept in plain text, leaving the bold text to be the Book of Enoch.

Let us now proceed to 1 Enoch.

The First Book of Enoch

1 Enoch

The Ethiopic Book of Enoch

The First Book of Enoch

The *Book of Watchers* (Chapters 1-36):
[Chapter 1]

1 The words of the blessing of Enoch, with which he blessed the elect and righteous, who will be living in the day of tribulation, when all the wicked and godless people are to be removed (from the earth).

2 And he began his story saying: (I am) Enoch, a righteous man, whose eyes were opened by God, and who saw the vision of the Holy One in heaven, which the angels showed me. And I heard everything from them, and I saw and understood, but it was not for this generation (to know), but for a remote one which is to come.

3 As I began my story concerning the elect I said, The Holy Great One will come out from His dwelling,

4 And the eternal God will tread on the earth, (even) on Mount Sinai, and appear in the strength of His might from heaven.

5 And all shall be very afraid. The Watchers shall shake, and great fear and trembling shall seize them all the way to the ends of the earth.

6 And the high mountains shall be shaken, and the high hills shall be laid low, and shall melt like wax in the flame.

7 And the earth shall be completely torn apart, and all that is on the earth shall be destroyed, And there shall be a judgment on all.

Revelation 21: 7-8 He who overcomes will inherit all this, and I will be his God and he will be my son. 8 But the cowardly, the unbelieving, the vile, the murderers, the sexually immoral, those who practice magic arts, the idolaters and all liars – their place will be in the fiery lake of burning sulfur. This is the second death."

8 But with the righteous He will make peace; and will protect the elect and mercy shall be on them. And they shall all belong to God, and they shall prosper, and they shall be blessed. And the light of God shall shine on them.

Revelation 21:23-25 The city does not need the sun or the moon to shine on it, for the glory of God gives it light, and the Lamb is its lamp. 24 The nations will walk by its light, and the kings of the earth will bring their splendor into it. 25 On no day will its gates ever be shut, for there will be no night there.

9 And behold! He comes with ten thousand of His holy ones (saints) to execute judgment on all, and to destroy all the ungodly (wicked); and to convict all flesh of all the works of their ungodliness which they have ungodly committed, and of all the hard things which ungodly sinners have spoken against Him.

Jude 1:14-15 And Enoch also, the seventh from Adam, prophesied of these, saying, Behold, the Lord cometh with ten thousands of his saints, 15To execute judgment upon all, and to convince all that are ungodly among them of all their ungodly deeds which they have ungodly committed, and of all their hard speeches which ungodly sinners have spoken against him.

[Chapter 2]

1 Observe everything that takes place in the sky, how the lights do not change their orbits, and the luminaries which are in heaven, how they all rise and set in order each in its season (proper time), and do not transgress (defy) their appointed order.

2 Consider the earth, and understand the things which take place on it from start to finish, how steadfast they are, how none of the things on the earth change, but all the works of God appear to you.

3 Behold the summer and the winter, how the whole earth is filled with water, and clouds and dew and rain lie on it.

[Chapter 3]

1 Observe and see how (in the winter) all the trees seem as though they had withered and shed all their leaves, except fourteen trees, which do not lose their foliage but retain the old foliage from two to three years until the new comes.

[Chapter 4]

1 And again, observe the days of summer how the sun is above the earth. And you seek shade and shelter because of the heat of the sun, and the earth also burns with growing heat, and so you cannot walk on the earth, or on a rock because of its heat.

[Chapter 5]

1 Observe how the trees are covered with green leaves and how they bear fruit. Understand, know, and recognize that He that lives forever made them this way for you.

2 And all His works go on before Him from year to year forever, and all the work and the tasks which they accomplish for Him do not change, and so is it done.

3 Consider how the sea and the rivers in like manner accomplish their course but do not change because of His commandments.

4 But you, you have neither held to nor have you done the commandments of the Lord, but you have turned away and spoken proud and hard words with your unclean mouths against His greatness. Oh, you hard-hearted, you shall find no peace.

5 Therefore shall you curse your days, and the years of your life shall perish, and the years of your destruction shall be multiplied and in an eternal curse you shall find no mercy.

Deuteronomy 11: 26-28 See, I am setting before you today a blessing and a curse-- 27the blessing if you obey the commands of the LORD your God that I am giving you today; 28the curse if you disobey the commands of the LORD your God and turn from the way that I command you today by following other gods, which you have not known.

6 In those days you shall make your names an eternal curse to all the righteous, and by you shall all who curse, curse, and all the sinners and godless shall curse you forever. And for you the godless there shall be a curse.

7 And all the elect shall rejoice, and there shall be forgiveness of sins, and mercy and peace and forbearance and joy. There shall be salvation for them, (like/and) a good light. And for all of you sinners there shall be no salvation, but on you all shall abide a curse.

8 But for the elect there shall be light and joy and peace, and they shall inherit the earth.

9 And then wisdom shall be given to the elect, and they shall all live and never again sin, either through forgetfulness or through pride: But those who are given wisdom shall be humble.

10 And they shall not again transgress, Nor shall they sin all the days of their life, Nor shall they die of the anger or wrath of God, But they shall complete the number of the days of their lives. And their lives shall be increased in peace, and their years will grow in joy and eternal gladness and peace, all the days of their lives.

Isaiah 65
1 I am sought of them that asked not for me; I am found of them that sought me not: I said, Behold me, behold me, unto a nation that was not called by my name.

2 I have spread out my hands all the day unto a rebellious people, which walketh in a way that was not good, after their own thoughts;

3 A people that provoketh me to anger continually to my face; that sacrificeth in gardens, and burneth incense upon altars of brick;

4 Which remain among the graves, and lodge in the monuments, which eat swine's flesh, and broth of abominable things is in their vessels;

5 Which say, Stand by thyself, come not near to me; for I am holier than thou. These are a smoke in my nose, a fire that burneth all the day.

6 Behold, it is written before me: I will not keep silence, but will recompense, even recompense into their bosom,

7 Your iniquities, and the iniquities of your fathers together, saith the LORD, which have burned incense upon the mountains, and blasphemed me upon the hills: therefore will I measure their former work into their bosom.

8 Thus saith the LORD, As the new wine is found in the cluster, and one saith, Destroy it not; for a blessing is in it: so will I do for my servants' sakes, that I may not destroy them all.

9 And I will bring forth a seed out of Jacob, and out of Judah an inheritor of my mountains: and mine elect shall inherit it, and my servants shall dwell there.

[Chapter 6]

¹And it came to pass when the children of men had multiplied that in those days were born to them beautiful and fair daughters.

Genesis 6:1-3 And it came to pass, when men began to multiply on the face of the earth, and daughters were born unto them, ²That the sons of God saw the daughters of men that they were fair; and they took them wives of all which they chose. ³And the LORD said, My spirit shall not always strive with man, for that he also is flesh: yet his days shall be an hundred and twenty years.

2 And the angels, the sons of heaven, saw and lusted after them, and said to one another: 'Come, let us choose us wives from among the children of men

3 And have children with them.' And Semjaza, who was their leader, said to them: 'I fear you will not agree to do this deed,

4 And I alone shall have to pay the penalty of this great sin.'

5 And they all answered him and said: 'Let us all swear an oath, and all bind ourselves by mutual curses so we will not abandon this plan but to do this thing.' Then they all swore together and bound themselves by mutual curses.

6 And they were in all two hundred who descended in the days of Jared in the summit of Mount Hermon, and they called it Mount Hermon, because they had sworn and bound themselves by mutual curses on the act.

(Author's note: Jared is the Father of Enoch. Mount Hermon is located in the highest point in Israel. It covers an area of about 5,000 acres and is 2814 meters above sea level.)

Jude 1:5-6 I will therefore put you in remembrance, though ye once knew this, how that the Lord, having saved the people out of the land of Egypt, afterward destroyed them that believed not. ⁶And the angels who kept not their first estate, but left their own habitation, he hath reserved in everlasting chains under darkness unto the judgment of the great day.

7 And these are the names of their leaders: Samlazaz, their leader, Araklba, Rameel, Kokablel, Tamlel, Ramlel, Danel, Ezeqeel, Baraqijal,

(Author's note: Samlazaz could be another spelling of Semjaza, and possibly be the same entity.)

8 Asael, Armaros, Batarel, Ananel, Zaqiel, Samsapeel, Satarel, Turel, Jomjael, Sariel. These are their chiefs of

tens.

[Chapter 7]

And all of them together went and took wives for themselves, each choosing one for himself, and they began to go in to them and to defile themselves with sex with them,

Genesis 5:32-6:6 And Noah was five hundred years old: and Noah begat Shem, Ham, and Japheth. ¹ And it came to pass, when men began to multiply on the face of the earth, and daughters were born unto them, ² That the sons of God saw the daughters of men that they were fair; and they took them wives of all which they chose. ³ And the LORD said, My spirit shall not always strive with man, for that he also is flesh: yet his days shall be an hundred and twenty years. ⁴ There were giants in the earth in those days; and also after that, when the sons of God came in unto the daughters of men, and they bare children to them, the same became mighty men which were of old, men of renown. ⁵ And GOD saw that the wickedness of man was great in the earth, and that every imagination of the thoughts of his heart was only evil continually. ⁶ And it repented the LORD that he had made man on the earth, and it grieved him at his heart.

2 And the angels taught them charms and spells, and the cutting of roots, and made them acquainted with plants.

3 And the women became pregnant, and they bare large giants, whose height was three thousand cubits (ells).

Jubilees 7:21-25
²¹ Because of these three things came the flood on the earth, namely, the fornication that the Watchers committed against the law of their ordinances when they went whoring after the daughters of men, and took themselves wives of all they chose, and they made the beginning of uncleanness.
²² And they begat sons, the Naphilim (Naphidim), and they were all dissimilar, and they devoured one another, and the Giants killed the Naphil, and the Naphil killed the Eljo, and the Eljo killed mankind, and one man killed another.
²³ Every one committed himself to crime and injustice and to shed much blood, and the earth was filled with sin.
²⁴ After this they sinned against the beasts and birds, and all that moved and walked on the earth, and much blood was shed on the earth, and men continually desired only what was useless and evil.
²⁵ And the Lord destroyed everything from the face of the earth. Because of the wickedness of their deeds, and because of the blood they had shed over all the earth, He destroyed everything."

4 The giants consumed all the work and toil of men. And when men could no longer sustain them, the giants turned against them and devoured mankind.

5 And they began to sin against birds, and beasts, and reptiles, and fish, and to devour one another's flesh, and drank the blood.

6 Then the earth laid accusation against the lawless ones.

Jasher 2:19-22
¹⁹ For in those days the sons of men began to trespass against God, and to go contrary to the commandments which he had given Adam, to be prolific and reproduce in the earth.
²⁰ And some of the sons of men caused their wives to drink a mixture that would render them unable to conceive, in order that they might retain their figures and their beautiful appearance might not fade.
²¹ And when the sons of men caused some of their wives to drink, Zillah drank with them.
²² And the child-bearing women appeared abominable in the sight of their husbands and they treated them as widows, while their husbands lived with those unable to conceive and to those women they were attached.

Genesis 4:8-12
And Cain talked with Abel his brother: and it came to pass, when they were in the field, that Cain rose up against Abel his brother, and slew him. ⁹ And the LORD said unto Cain, Where is Abel thy brother? And he said, I know not: Am I my brother's keeper? ¹⁰ And he said, What hast thou done? the voice of thy brother's blood crieth unto me from the ground. ¹¹ And now art thou cursed from the earth, which hath opened her mouth to receive thy brother's blood from thy hand; ¹² When

thou tillest the ground, it shall not henceforth yield unto thee her strength; a fugitive and a vagabond shalt thou be in the earth.

[Chapter 8]

1 And Azazel taught men to make swords, and knives, and shields, and breastplates, and taught them about metals of the earth and the art of working them, and bracelets, and ornaments, and the use of antimony, and the beautifying of the eyelids, and all kinds of precious stones, and all coloring and dyes.

2 And there was great impiety; they turned away from God, and committed fornication, and they were led astray, and became corrupt in all their ways.

Matthew 5:19 (New International Version)
¹⁹Anyone who breaks one of the least of these commandments and teaches others to do the same will be called least in the kingdom of heaven, but whoever practices and teaches these commands will be called great in the kingdom of heaven.

3 Semjaza taught the casting of spells, and root-cuttings, Armaros taught counter-spells (release from spells), Baraqijal taught astrology, Kokabel taught the constellations (portents), Ezeqeel the knowledge of the clouds, Araqiel the signs of the earth, Shamsiel the signs of the sun, and Sariel the course of the moon. And as men perished, they cried, and their cry went up to heaven.

Jasher 4:18-20
¹⁸And their judges and rulers went to the daughters of men and took their wives by force from their husbands according to their choice, and the sons of men in those days took from the cattle of the earth, the beasts of the field and the fowls of the air, and taught the mixture of animals of one species with the other, in order therewith to provoke the Lord; and God saw the whole earth and it was corrupt, for all flesh had corrupted its ways on earth, all men and all animals.
¹⁹And the Lord said, I will blot out man that I created from the face of the earth, yea from man to the birds of the air together with cattle and beasts that are in the field for I repent that I made them.
²⁰And all men who walked in the ways of the Lord died in those days, before the Lord brought the evil on man which he had declared, for this was from the Lord that they should not see the evil which the Lord spoke of concerning the sons of men.

[Chapter 9]

1 And then Michael, Uriel, Raphael, and Gabriel looked down from heaven and saw much blood being shed on the earth, and all lawlessness being done on the earth.

2 And they said to each other: 'Let the cries from the destruction of earth ascend up to the gates of heaven.

3 And now to you, the holy ones of heaven, the souls of men make their petition, saying, "Bring our cause before the Most High."'

4 And they said to the Lord of the ages: 'Lord of lords, God of gods, King of kings, and God of the ages, the throne of your glory endures through all the generations of the ages, and your name holy and glorious and blessed to all the ages!

1Timothy 6:15-16 Which in his times he shall shew, who is the blessed and only Potentate, the King of kings, and Lord of lords; ¹⁶ Who only hath immortality, dwelling in the light which no man can approach unto; whom no man hath seen, nor can see: to whom be honour and power everlasting. Amen.

5 You have made all things, and you have power over all things: and all things are revealed and open in your sight, and you see all things, and nothing can hide itself from you.

6 Look at what Azazel has done, who hath taught all unrighteousness on earth and revealed the eternal secrets which were made and kept in heaven, which men were striving to learn:

7 And Semjaza, who taught spells, to whom you gave authority to rule over his associates.

8 And they have gone to the daughters of men on the earth, and have had sex with the women, and have defiled themselves, and revealed to them all kinds of sins.

Genesis 6:4 There were giants in the earth in those days; and also after that, when the sons of God came in unto the daughters of men, and they bare children to them, the same became mighty men which were of old, men of renown.

9 And the women have borne giants, and the whole earth has thereby been filled with blood and unrighteousness.

Genesis 6:5-6 And GOD saw that the wickedness of man was great in the earth, and that every imagination of the thoughts of his heart was only evil continually. ⁶And it repented the LORD that he had made man on the earth, and it grieved him at his heart.

10 And now, behold, the souls of those who have died are crying out and making their petition to the gates of heaven, and their lament has ascended and cannot cease because of the lawless deeds which are done on the earth.

11 And you know all things before they come to pass, and you see these things and you have permitted them, and say nothing to us about these things. What are we to do with them about these things?'

Revelation 6:10 (New International Version) They called out in a loud voice, "How long, Sovereign Lord, holy and true, until you judge the inhabitants of the earth and avenge our blood?"

[Chapter 10]

1 Then said the Most High, the Great and Holy One, "Uriel, go to the son of Lamech.

2 Say to him: 'Go to Noah and tell him in my name "Hide yourself!" and reveal to him the end that is approaching: that the whole earth will be destroyed, and a flood is about to come on the whole earth, and will destroy everything on it.'

Genesis 7:4 For yet seven days, and I will cause it to rain upon the earth forty days and forty nights; and every living substance that I have made will I destroy from off the face of the earth.

3 'And now instruct him as to what he must do to escape that his offspring may be preserved for all the generations of the world.'

Genesis 6:13-14 And God said unto Noah, The end of all flesh is come before me; for the earth is filled with violence through them; and, behold, I will destroy them with the earth. ¹⁴ Make thee an ark of gopher wood; rooms shalt thou make in the ark, and shalt pitch it within and without with pitch.

4 And again the Lord said to Raphael: 'Bind Azazel hand and foot, and cast him into the darkness and split open the desert, which is in Dudael, and cast him in.

5 And fill the hole by covering him with rough and jagged rocks, and cover him with darkness, and let him live there forever, and cover his face that he may not see the light.

Revelation 20: 1-3 And I saw an angel come down from heaven, having the key of the bottomless pit and a great chain in his hand. ² And he laid hold of the dragon, that old serpent, which is the Devil, and Satan, and bound him a thousand years, ³ And cast him into the bottomless pit, and shut him up, and set a seal upon him, that he should deceive the nations no more, till the thousand years should be fulfilled: and after that he must be loosed for a little season.

6 And on the day of the great judgment he shall be hurled into the fire.

Revelation 19:20 (King James Version) ²⁰ *And the beast was taken, and with him the false prophet that wrought miracles before him, with which he deceived them that had received the mark of the beast, and them that worshipped his image. These both were cast alive into a lake of fire burning with brimstone.*

7 And heal the earth which the angels have ruined, and proclaim the healing of the earth, for I will restore the earth and heal the plague, that not all of the children of men may perish through all the secret things that the Watchers have disclosed and have taught their sons.

Romans 8:18-21 For I reckon that the sufferings of this present time are not worthy to be compared with the glory which shall be revealed in us. ¹⁹ For the earnest expectation of the creature waiteth for the manifestation of the sons of God. ²⁰ For the creature was made subject to vanity, not willingly, but by reason of him who hath subjected the same in hope, ²¹ Because the creature itself also shall be delivered from the bondage of corruption into the glorious liberty of the children of God.

8 The whole earth has been corrupted through the works that were taught by Azazel: to him ascribe ALL SIN.'

9 To Gabriel said the Lord: 'Proceed against the bastards and the reprobates, and against the children of fornication and destroy the children of fornication and the children of the Watchers. Cause them to go against one another that they may destroy each other in battle: Shorten their days.

Genesis 6:7-8 And the LORD said, I will destroy man whom I have created from the face of the earth; both man, and beast, and the creeping thing, and the fowls of the air; for it repenteth me that I have made them. ⁸ But Noah found grace in the eyes of the LORD.

10 No request that (the Watchers) their fathers make of you shall be granted them on their behalf; for they hope to live an eternal life, and that each one of them will live five hundred years.'

11 And the Lord said to Michael: 'Go, bind Semjaza and his team who have associated with women and have defiled themselves in all their uncleanness.

12 When their sons have slain one another, and they have seen the destruction of their beloved ones, bind them fast for seventy generations under the hills of the earth, until the day of the consummation of their judgment and until the eternal judgment is accomplished.

(Author's note: 70 generations of 500 years = 3500 years)

13 In those days they shall be led off to the abyss of fire and to the torment and the prison in which they shall be confined forever.'

14 Then Semjaza shall be burnt up with the condemned and they will be destroyed, having been bound together with them to the end of all generations.

Fragment from the Book of Giants:
And he answered, I am a giant, and by the mighty strength of my arm and my own great strength [I can defeat] anyone mortal, and I have made war against them; but I am not [strong enough for our heavenly opponent or to be] able to stand against them, for my opponents . . . reside in Heaven, and they dwell in the holy places. And not [on the earth and they] are stronger than I. . . . The time of the wild beast has come, and the wild man calls me. Then Ohya said to him, I have been forced to have a dream and the sleep of my eyes vanished in order to let me see a vision. Now I know that on Gilgamesh [our futures rest].

15 Destroy all the spirits of lust and the children of the Watchers, because they have wronged mankind.

16 Destroy all wrong from the face of the earth and let every evil work come to an end and let (the earth be planted with righteousness) the plant of righteousness and truth appear; and it shall prove a blessing,

the works of righteousness and truth shall be planted in truth and joy forevermore.

Genesis 6:7 And the LORD said, I will destroy man whom I have created from the face of the earth; both man, and beast, and the creeping thing, and the fowls of the air; for it repenteth me that I have made them.

17 And then shall all the righteous survive, and shall live until they beget thousands of children, and all the days of their youth and their old age shall they complete in peace.

Genesis 8:22 While the earth remaineth, seedtime and harvest, and cold and heat, and summer and winter, and day and night shall not cease.

Genesis 9:1 And God blessed Noah and his sons, and said unto them, Be fruitful, and multiply, and replenish the earth.

18 And then shall the whole earth be untilled in righteousness and shall be planted with trees and be full of blessing. And all desirable trees shall be planted on it, and they shall plant vines on it.

19 And the vine which they plant shall yield fruit in abundance, and as for all the seed which is sown, each measurement (of it) shall bear a thousand, and each measurement of olives shall yield ten presses of oil.

20 You shall cleanse the earth from all oppression, and from all unrighteousness, and from all sin, and from all godlessness, and all the uncleanness that is brought on the earth you shall destroy from off the earth.

21 All the children of men shall become righteous, and all nations shall offer adoration and shall praise Me,

22 And all shall worship Me. And the earth shall be cleansed from all defilement, and from all sin, and from all punishment, and from all torment, and I will never again send another flood from this generation to all generations and forever.

[Chapter 11]
1 And in those days I will open the storehouse of blessings in heaven, and rain down blessings on the earth and over the work and labor of the children of men.

Malachi 3:10 (King James Version) Bring ye all the tithes into the storehouse, that there may be meat in mine house, and prove me now herewith, saith the LORD of hosts, if I will not open you the windows of heaven, and pour you out a blessing, that there shall not be room enough to receive it.

2 Truth and peace shall be united throughout all the days of the world and throughout all the generations of men.'

[Chapter 12]
1 Then Enoch disappeared and no one of the children of men knew where he was hidden, and where he abode;

Genesis 5:21-24 And Enoch lived sixty and five years, and begat Methuselah: ²² And Enoch walked with God after he begat Methuselah three hundred years, and begat sons and daughters: ²³ And all the days of Enoch were three hundred sixty and five years: ²⁴ And Enoch walked with God: and he was not; for God took him.

2 And what had become of him. And his activities were with the Holy Ones and the Watchers.

3 And I, Enoch, was blessing the Lord of majesty and the King of the ages, and lo! the Watchers called me, Enoch the scribe, and said to me:

4 'Enoch, you scribe of righteousness, go, tell the Watchers of heaven who have left the high heaven, the holy

eternal place, and have defiled themselves with women, and have done as the children of earth do, and have taken to themselves wives:

5 "You have done great destruction on the earth: And you shall have no peace nor forgiveness of sin:

6 Since they delight themselves in their children, They shall see the murder of their beloved ones, and the destruction of their children, and they shall lament, and shall make supplication forever, you will receive neither mercy or peace."

(Author's note: Although we are led to believe the fallen angels are loathsome and evil, they loved and adored their children according to the above. Further, it was not the angels that became the demons. It was their children, whose spirits were evil and could not be killed.)

[Chapter 13]
1 And Enoch went and said: 'Azazel, you shall have no peace: a severe sentence has been passed against you that you should be bound:

2 And you shall not have rest or mercy (toleration nor request granted), because of the unrighteousness which you have taught, and because of all the works of godlessness,

3 And unrighteousness and sin which you have shown to men.

4 Then I went and spoke to them all together, and they were all afraid, and fear and trembling seized them.

5 And they asked me to write a petition for them that they might find forgiveness, and to read their petition in the presence of the Lord of heaven. They had been forbidden to speak (with Him) nor were they to lift up their eyes to heaven for shame of their sins because they had been condemned.

6 Then I wrote out their petition, and the prayer in regard to their spirits and their deeds individually and in regard to their requests that they should obtain forgiveness and forbearance.

7 And I went off and sat down at the waters of Dan, in the land of Dan, to the southwest of Hermon: I read their petition until I fell asleep.

8 And I had a dream, and I saw a vision of their chastisement, and a voice came to me that I would reprimand (reprove) them.

9 And when I awoke, I came to them, and they were all sitting gathered together, weeping in Abelsjail, which is between Lebanon and Seneser, with their faces covered.

10 And I recounted to them all the visions which I had seen when I was asleep, and I began to speak the words of righteousness, and to reprimand the heavenly Watchers.

[Chapter 14]
1 This is the book of the words of righteousness, and of the reprimand of the eternal Watchers in accordance with the command of the Holy Great One in that vision I saw in my sleep.

2 What I will now say with a tongue of flesh and with the breath of my mouth: which the Great One has given to men to speak with it and to understand with the heart.

3 As He has created and given to man the power of understanding the word of wisdom, so has He created me also and given me the power of reprimanding the Watchers, the children of heaven.

4 I wrote out your petition, and in my vision it appeared that your petition will not be granted to you

throughout all the days of eternity, and that judgment has been finally passed on you:

5 Your petition will not be granted. From here on you shall not ascend into heaven again for all eternity, and you will be bound on earth for all eternity.

6 Before this you will see the destruction of your beloved sons and you shall have no pleasure in them, but they shall fall before you by the sword.

7 Your petition shall not be granted on their behalf or on yours, even though you weep and pray and speak all the words contained in my writings.

8 In the vision I saw clouds that invited me and summoned me into a mist, and the course of the stars and the flashes of lightning and hurried me and drove me,

9 And the winds in the vision caused me to fly and lifted me up, and bore me into heaven. And I went in until I drew near to a wall which was built out of crystals and surrounded by tongues of fire, and it began to frighten me.

10 I went into the tongues of fire and drew near a large house which was built of crystals: and the walls of the house were like a mosaic of hailstones and the floor was made of crystals like snow.

Revelation 4: 6 And before the throne there was a sea of glass like unto crystal: and in the midst of the throne, and round about the throne, were four beasts full of eyes before and behind.

Revelation 21:10-12
And he carried me away in the spirit to a great and high mountain, and shewed me that great city, the holy Jerusalem, descending out of heaven from God, 11 Having the glory of God: and her light was like unto a stone most precious, even like a jasper stone, clear as crystal; 12 And had a wall great and high, and had twelve gates, and at the gates twelve angels, and names written thereon, which are the names of the twelve tribes of the children of Israel:

11 Its ceiling was like the path of the stars and lightning flashes, and between them were fiery cherubim,

12 Their sky was clear as water. A flaming fire surrounded the walls, and its doors blazed with fire.

13 I entered that house, and it was hot as fire and cold as ice; there were no pleasures or life therein: fear covered me, and trembling got hold of me.

14 As I shook and trembled, I fell on my face.

15 And I saw a vision, And lo! there was a second house, greater than the first,

16 And all the doors stood open before me, and it was built of flames of fire. And in every respect it was splendid and magnificent to the extent that I cannot describe it to you.

17 Its floor was of fire, and above it was lightning and the path of the stars, and its ceiling also was flaming fire.

18 And I looked and saw a throne set on high, its appearance was like crystal, and its wheels were like a shining sun, and there was the vision of cherubim.

1Timothy 6:16 Who only hath immortality, dwelling in the light which no man can approach unto; whom no man hath seen, nor can see: to whom be honour and power everlasting. Amen.

19 And from underneath the throne came rivers of fire so that I could not look at it.

3 Enoch: The Holy Chayoth carry the Throne of Glory from below. Each one uses only three fingers. The length of each finger is 800,000 and 700 times one hundred, and 66,000 parasangs. And underneath the feet of the Chayoth there are seven rivers of fire running and flowing

20 And He who is Great in Glory sat on the throne, and His raiment shone more brightly than the sun and was whiter than any snow.

Matthew 25:31 When the Son of man shall come in his glory, and all the holy angels with him, then shall he sit upon the throne of his glory:

21 None of the angels could enter or could behold His face because of the magnificence and glory and no flesh could behold Him.

22 The sea of fire surrounded Him, and a great fire stood in front of Him, and no one could draw close to Him: ten thousand times ten thousand stood before Him, but He needed no holy council.

23 The most Holy Ones who were near to Him did not leave night or day.

24 And until then I had been prostrate on my face, trembling, and the Lord called me with His own mouth, and said to me:

25 'Come here, Enoch, and hear my word.' And one of the Holy Ones came to me, picked me up, and brought me to the door; and I bowed down my face.

[Chapter 15]
1 And He answered and said to me, and I heard His voice: 'Do not be afraid, Enoch, you righteous man and scribe of righteousness.

2 Approach and hear my voice. Go and say to the Watchers of heaven, for whom you have come to intercede: "You should intercede for men, and not men for you."

3 Why and for what cause have you left the high, holy, and eternal heaven, and had sex with women, and defiled yourselves with the daughters of men and taken to yourselves wives, and done like the children of earth, and begotten giants (as your) sons?

4 Though you were holy, spiritual, living the eternal life, you have defiled yourselves with the blood of women, and have begotten children with the blood of flesh, and, as the children of men, you have lusted after flesh and blood like those who die and are killed.

5 This is why I have given men wives, that they might impregnate them, and have children by them, that deeds might continue on the earth.

6 But you were formerly spiritual, living the eternal life, and immortal for all generations of the world.

7 Therefore I have not appointed wives for you; you are spiritual beings of heaven, and in heaven was your dwelling place.

Luke 20:34-36 And Jesus answering said unto them, The children of this world marry, and are given in marriage: 35 But they which shall be accounted worthy to obtain that world, and the resurrection from the dead, neither marry, nor are given in marriage: 36 Neither can they die any more: for they are equal unto the angels; and are the children of God, being the children of the resurrection.

8 And now, the giants, who are produced from the spirits and flesh, shall be called evil spirits on the earth,

9 And shall live on the earth. Evil spirits have come out from their bodies because they are born from men and from the holy Watchers; their beginning is of primal origin;

10 They shall be evil spirits on earth, and evil spirits shall they be called spirits of the evil ones. [As for the spirits of heaven, in heaven shall be their dwelling, but as for the spirits of the earth which were born on the earth, on the earth shall be their dwelling.] And the spirits of the giants afflict, oppress, destroy, attack, war, destroy, and cause trouble on the earth.

11 They take no food, but do not hunger or thirst. They cause offences but are not observed.

12 And these spirits shall rise up against the children of men and against the women, because they have proceeded from them in the days of the slaughter and destruction.'

(Author's note: These are the evil spirits and demons. They are the disembodied spirits of the offspring of angels and humans.)

The Book of Jubilees
Because of these three things came the flood on the earth, namely, the fornication that the Watchers committed against the law of their ordinances when they went whoring after the daughters of men, and took themselves wives of all they chose, and they made the beginning of uncleanness.
And they begat sons, the Naphilim (Naphidim – the fallen), and they were all dissimilar, and they devoured one another, and the Giants killed the Naphil, and the Naphil killed the Eljo, and the Eljo killed mankind, and one man killed another.
Everyone committed himself to crime and injustice and to shed much blood, and the earth was filled with sin.
After this they sinned against the beasts and birds, and all that moved and walked on the earth, and much blood was shed on the earth, and men continually desired only what was useless and evil.
And the Lord destroyed everything from the face of the earth. Because of the wickedness of their deeds, and because of the blood they had shed over all the earth, He destroyed everything. "

[Chapter 16]

1 'And at the death of the giants, spirits will go out and shall destroy without incurring judgment, coming from their bodies their flesh shall be destroyed until the day of the consummation, the great judgment in which the age shall be consummated, over the Watchers and the godless, and shall be wholly consummated.'

Matthew 8:28-29 And when he was come to the other side into the country of the Gergesenes, there met him two possessed with devils, coming out of the tombs, exceeding fierce, so that no man might pass by that way. 29 And, behold, they cried out, saying, What have we to do with thee, Jesus, thou Son of God? art thou come hither to torment us before the time?

2 And now as to the Watchers who have sent you to intercede for them, who had been in heaven before,

3 (Say to them): "You were in heaven, but all the mysteries of heaven had not been revealed to you, and you knew worthless ones, and these in the hardness of your hearts you have made known to the women, and through these mysteries women and men work much evil on earth."

4 Say to them therefore: "You have no peace."

Genesis 6:1-8
¹ And it came to pass, when men began to multiply on the face of the earth, and daughters were born unto them, ² That the sons of God saw the daughters of men that they were fair; and they took them wives of all which they chose. ³ And the LORD said, My spirit shall not always strive with man, for that he also is flesh: yet his days shall be an hundred and twenty years. ⁴ There were giants in the earth in those days; and also after that, when the sons of God came in unto the daughters of men, and they bare children to them, the same became mighty men which were of old, men of renown.
⁵ And God saw that the wickedness of man was great in the earth, and that every imagination of the thoughts of his heart was only evil continually. ⁶ And it repented the LORD that he had made man on the earth, and it grieved him at his heart. ⁷

And the LORD said, I will destroy man whom I have created from the face of the earth; both man, and beast, and the creeping thing, and the fowls of the air; for it repenteth me that I have made them. *8 But Noah found grace in the eyes of the LORD.*

[Chapter 17]

1 And they took me to a place in which those who were there were like flaming fire,

2 And, when they wished, they made themselves appear as men. They brought me to the place of darkness, and to a mountain the point of whose summit reached to heaven.

3 And I saw the lighted places and the treasuries of the stars and of the thunder and in the uttermost depths, where were

4 A fiery bow and arrows and their quiver, and a fiery sword and all the lightning. And they took me to the waters of life, and to the fire of the west, which receives every setting of the sun.

5 And I came to a river of fire in which the fire flows like water into the great sea towards the west.

6 I saw the great rivers and came to the great darkness, and went to the place where no flesh walks.

7 I saw the mountains of the darkness of winter and the place from where all the waters of the deep flow.

8 I saw the mouths of all the rivers of the earth and the mouth of the deep.

[Chapter 18]

1 I saw the storehouse of all the winds: I saw how He had adorned the whole creation with them and the firm foundations of the earth.

2 And I saw the corner-stone of the earth: I saw the four winds which support the earth and the firmament of the heaven.

3 I saw how the winds stretch out the height of heaven, and have their station between heaven and earth; these are the pillars of heaven.

4 I saw the winds of heaven which turn and bring the sky and the sun and all the stars to their setting place.

5 I saw the winds on the earth carrying the clouds: I saw the paths of the angels. I saw at the end of the earth the firmament of heaven above.

6 And I continued south and saw a place which burns day and night, where there are seven mountains of magnificent stones, three towards the east, and three towards the south.

7 And as for those towards the east, they were of colored stone, and one of pearl, and one of jacinth (a stone of healing), and those towards the south of red stone.

8 But the middle one reached to heaven like the throne of God, and was made of alabaster.

9 And the summit of the throne was of sapphire.

Ezekiel 1:22-28 And the likeness of the firmament upon the heads of the living creature was as the colour of the terrible crystal, stretched forth over their heads above.
23 And under the firmament were their wings straight, the one toward the other: every one had two, which covered on this side, and every one had two, which covered on that side, their bodies.
24 And when they went, I heard the noise of their wings, like the noise of great waters, as the voice of the Almighty, the voice of speech, as the noise of an host: when they stood, they let down their wings.

25 And there was a voice from the firmament that was over their heads, when they stood, and had let down their wings.
26 And above the firmament that was over their heads was the likeness of a throne, as the appearance of a sapphire stone: and upon the likeness of the throne was the likeness as the appearance of a man above upon it.
27 And I saw as the colour of amber, as the appearance of fire round about within it, from the appearance of his loins even upward, and from the appearance of his loins even downward, I saw as it were the appearance of fire, and it had brightness round about.
28 As the appearance of the bow that is in the cloud in the day of rain, so was the appearance of the brightness round about. This was the appearance of the likeness of the glory of the LORD. And when I saw it, I fell upon my face, and I heard a voice of one that spake.

10 And I saw a great abyss of the earth, with pillars of heavenly fire, and I saw among them fiery pillars of Heaven, which were falling,

11 And as regards both height and depth, they were immeasurable.

12 And beyond that abyss I saw a place which had no firmament of heaven above, and no firmly founded earth beneath it: there was no water on it, and no birds,

13 But it was a desert and a horrible place. I saw there seven stars like great burning mountains,

14 And an angel questioned me regarding them. The angel said: 'This place is the end of heaven and earth.

15 This has become a prison for the stars and the host of heaven. And the stars which roll over the fire are they which have transgressed the commandment of the Lord in the beginning of their rising, because they did not come out at their proper times.

16 And He was angry with them, and bound them until the time when their guilt should be consummated even for ten thousand years.'

[Chapter 19]

1 And Uriel said to me: 'The angels who have had sex with women shall stand here, and their spirits, having assumed many different forms, are defiling mankind and shall lead them astray into sacrificing to demons as gods, here shall they stand, until the day of the great judgment in which they shall be judged and are made an end of.

1 Timothy 4:1 The Spirit clearly says that in later times some will abandon the faith and follow deceiving spirits and things taught by demons.

Rev 9:20-21 The rest of mankind that were not killed by these plagues still did not repent of the work of their hands; they did not stop worshiping demons, and idols of gold, silver, bronze, stone and wood – idols that cannot see or hear or walk. 21 Nor did they repent of their murders, their magic arts, their sexual immorality or their thefts.

2 And the women also of the angels who went astray shall become sirens (other versions read 'shall become peaceful' also, another version reads, 'shall salute them').'

3 And I, Enoch, alone saw the vision, the ends of all things: and no man shall see as I have seen.

1 Peter 4:7 But the end of all things is at hand: be ye therefore sober, and watch unto prayer.

[Chapter 20]

1 These are the names of the holy angels who watch.

2 Uriel, one of the holy angels, who is over the world, turmoil and terror.

3 Raphael, one of the holy angels, who is over the spirits of men.

4 Raguel, one of the holy angels who takes vengeance on the world of the luminaries.

5 Michael, one of the holy angels, set over the virtues of mankind and over chaos.

6 Saraqael, one of the holy angels, who is set over the spirits, who sin in the spirit.

7 Gabriel, one of the holy angels, who is over Paradise and the serpents and the Cherubim.

8 Remiel, one of the holy angels, whom God set over those who rise.

[Chapter 21]

1 Then, I proceeded to where things were chaotic and void.

2 And I saw there something horrible: I saw neither a heaven above nor a firmly founded earth, but a place chaotic and horrible.

3 And there I saw seven stars of heaven bound together in it, like great mountains and burning with fire.

4 Then I said: 'For what sin are they bound, and on why have they been cast in here?'

5 Then said Uriel, one of the holy angels, who was with me, and was chief over them: 'Enoch, why do you ask, and why are you eager for the truth?

6 These are some of the stars of heaven, which have transgressed the commandment of the Lord, and are bound here until ten thousand years, the time entailed by their sins, are consummated.'

7 And I went out from there to another place, which was still more horrible than the former, and I saw a terrible thing: a great fire there which burned and blazed, and the place was cleft as far as the abyss, full of great falling columns of fire:

8 Neither its width or breadth could I see, nor could I see its source.

9 Then I said: 'I am afraid of this place and cannot stand to look at it.!' Then Uriel, one of the holy angels who was with me, answered and said to me: 'Enoch, why are you so afraid?'

10 And I answered: 'Because of this fearful place, and because of the spectacle of the pain.' And he said to me: 'This place is the prison of the angels, and here they will be imprisoned forever.'

Daniel 7:9-11 As I looked, thrones were set in place, and the Ancient of Days took his seat. His clothing was as white as snow; the hair of his head was white like wool His throne was flaming with fire, and its wheels were all ablaze. 10 A river of fire was flowing, coming out from before him. Thousands upon thousands attended him; ten thousand times ten thousand stood before him. The court was seated and the books were opened. 11 Then I continued to watch because of the boastful words the horn was speaking. I kept looking until the beast was slain and its body destroyed and thrown into the blazing fire.

[Chapter 22]

1 And I went out to another place west where there was a mountain and hard rock.

2 And there was in it four hollow places, deep and wide and very smooth. How smooth are the hollow places and looked deep and dark.

3 Then Raphael answered, one of the holy angels who was with me, and said to me: 'These hollow places have been created for this very purpose, that the spirits of the souls of the dead should be gathered here, that all the

souls of the children of men should brought together here. And these places have been made to receive them until the day of their judgment and until the period appointed, until the great judgment comes on them.'

(Author note: The idea of a gathering place of the dead is seen in the doctrine of Purgatory, where the dead are gathered and those who are "redeemable" are kept and purified until such time they might ascend to heaven.)

2 Maccabee 12: 41-45 All men therefore praising the Lord, the righteous Judge, who had opened the things that were hid,
⁴² Betook themselves unto prayer, and besought him that the sin committed might wholly be put out of remembrance. Besides, that noble Judas exhorted the people to keep themselves from sin, forsomuch as they saw before their eyes the things that came to pass for the sins of those that were slain.
⁴³ And when he had made a gathering throughout the company to the sum of two thousand drachms of silver, he sent it to Jerusalem to offer a sin offering, doing therein very well and honestly, in that he was mindful of the resurrection:
⁴⁴ For if he had not hoped that they that were slain should have risen again; it had been superfluous and vain to pray for the dead.
⁴⁵ And also in that he perceived that there was great favour laid up for those that died godly, it was an holy and good thought. Whereupon he made a reconciliation for the dead, that they might be delivered from sin.

4 I saw the spirit of a dead man, and his voice went out to heaven and made petitions.

5 And I asked Raphael the angel who was with me, and I said to him: 'This spirit which petitions,

6 Whose is it, whose voice goes up and petitions heaven?'

7 And he answered me saying: 'This is the spirit which went out from Abel, whom his brother Cain slew, and he makes his suit against him until his offspring is destroyed from the face of the earth, and his offspring are annihilated from among the children of men.'

Genesis 4:8-12 And Cain talked with Abel his brother: and it came to pass, when they were in the field that Cain rose up against Abel his brother, and slew him. ⁹ And the LORD said unto Cain, Where is Abel thy brother? And he said, I know not: Am I my brother's keeper? ¹⁰ And he said, What hast thou done? the voice of thy brother's blood crieth unto me from the ground. ¹¹ And now art thou cursed from the earth, which hath opened her mouth to receive thy brother's blood from thy hand; ¹² When thou tillest the ground, it shall not henceforth yield unto thee her strength; a fugitive and a vagabond shalt thou be in the earth.

8 Then I asked, regarding all the hollow places: 'Why is one separated from the other?'

9 And he answered me and said to me: 'These three have been made that the spirits of the dead might be separated. Divisions have been made for the spirits of the righteous, in which there is the bright spring of water.

10 And one for sinners when they die and are buried in the earth and judgment has not been executed on them in their lifetime.

11 Here their spirits shall be set apart in this great pain until the great day of judgment and punishment and torment of those who curse forever and retribution for their spirits.

2 Peter 3:7 By the same word the present heavens and earth are reserved for fire, being kept for the day of judgment and destruction of ungodly men.

12 There He shall bind them forever. And such a division has been made for the spirits of those who make their petitions, who make disclosures concerning their destruction, when they were slain in the days of the sinners.

13 Such has been made for the spirits of men who were not righteous but sinners, who were complete in

transgression, and of the transgressors they shall be companions, but their spirits shall not be destroyed in the day of judgment nor shall they be raised from here.'

14 Then I blessed the Lord of glory and said: 'Blessed be my Lord, the Lord of righteousness, who rules forever.'

[Chapter 23]

1 From here I went to another place to the west of the ends of the earth.

2 And I saw a burning fire which ran without resting, and never stopped from its course day or night but flowed always in the same way.

3 And I asked saying: 'What is this which never stops?'

4 Then Raguel, one of the holy angels who was with me, answered me and said to me: 'This course of fire which you have seen is the fire in the west and is the fire of all the lights of heaven.'

[Chapter 24]

1 And from here I went to another place on the earth, and he showed me a mountain range of fire which burned day and night.

2 And I went beyond it and saw seven magnificent mountains, all differing from each other, and their stones were magnificent and beautiful, and their form was glorious: three towards the east, one founded on the other, and three towards the south, one on the other, and deep rough ravines, no one of which joined with any other.

3 And the seventh mountain was in the midst of these, and it was higher than them, resembling the seat of a throne.

4 And fragrant trees encircled the throne. And among them was a tree such as I had never smelled, nor was any among them or were others like it; it had a fragrance beyond all fragrance, and its leaves and blooms and wood would not ever wither:

5 And its fruit is beautiful, and its fruit resembles the dates of a palm. Then I said: 'How beautiful is this tree, and fragrant, and its leaves are fair, and its blooms very delightful in appearance.'

6 Then Michael, one of the holy and honored angels who was with me, and was their leader, spoke.

[Chapter 25]

1 And he said to me: 'Enoch, why do you ask me about the fragrance of the tree, and why do you wish to learn the truth?'

2 Then I answered him saying: 'I wish to know about everything, but especially about this tree.'

3 And he answered saying: 'This high mountain which you have seen, whose summit is like the throne of God, is His throne, where the Holy Great One, the Lord of Glory, the Eternal King, will sit, when He shall come down to visit the earth with goodness.

4 And as for this fragrant tree, no mortal is permitted to touch it until the great judgment, when He shall take vengeance on all and bring everything to its completion forever.

Genesis 2:8-17 Now the LORD God had planted a garden in the east, in Eden; and there he put the man he had formed. 9 And the LORD God made all kinds of trees grow out of the ground — trees that were pleasing to the eye and good for food. In the middle of the garden were the tree of life and the tree of the knowledge of good and evil. 10 A river watering the garden flowed from Eden; from there it was separated into four headwaters. 11 The name of the first is the Pishon; it winds through *the entire land of Havilah, where there is gold. ¹² (The gold of that land is good; aromatic resin and onyx are also there.) ¹³ The name of the second river is the Gihon; it winds through the entire land of Cush. ¹⁴ The name of the third river is the Tigris; it runs along the east side of Asshur. And the fourth river is the Euphrates. ¹⁵ The LORD God took the man and put him in the Garden of Eden to work it and take care of it. ¹⁶ And the LORD God commanded the man, "You are free to eat from any tree in the garden; ¹⁷but you must not eat from the tree of the knowledge of good and evil, for when you eat of it you will surely die."*

5 It shall then be given to the righteous and holy. Its fruit shall be for food to the Elect: it shall be transplanted to the holy place, to the temple of the Lord, the Eternal King.

Revelation 22:1-3 And he shewed me a pure river of water of life, clear as crystal, proceeding out of the throne of God and of the Lamb. ² In the midst of the street of it, and on either side of the river, was there the tree of life, which bare twelve manner of fruits, and yielded her fruit every month: and the leaves of the tree were for the healing of the nations. ³ And there shall be no more curses: but the throne of God and of the Lamb shall be in it; and his servants shall serve him.

6 Then they shall rejoice and be glad, and enter into the holy place; And its fragrance shall enter into their bones, And they shall live a long life on earth, as your fathers lived. And in their days there will be no sorrow or pain or torment or toil.'

7 Then I blessed the God of Glory, the Eternal King, who has prepared such things for the righteous, and has created them and promised to give to them.

Ezekiel 47:12 (New International Version) Fruit trees of all kinds will grow on both banks of the river. Their leaves will not wither, nor will their fruit fail. Every month they will bear, because the water from the sanctuary flows to them. Their fruit will serve for food and their leaves for healing."

[Chapter 26]

1 And I went from there to the middle of the earth, and I saw a blessed place in which there were trees with branches alive and blooming on a tree that had been cut down.

(Author's note: The "hollow earth theory" has been espoused by various groups throughout history. The theory was used to create the book and movie, *Journey to the Center of the Earth*.)

2 And there I saw a holy mountain,

3 And underneath the mountain to the east there was a stream and it flowed towards the south. And I saw towards the east another mountain higher than this, and between them a deep and narrow valley.

4 In it ran a stream underneath the mountain. And to the west of it there was another mountain, lower than the former and of small elevation, and a dry, deep valley between them; and another deep and dry valley was at the edge of the three mountains.

5 And all the valleys were deep and narrow, being formed from hard rock, and there were no trees planted on them.

6 And I was very amazed at the rocks in the valleys.

[Chapter 27]

1 Then I said: 'What is the purpose of this blessed land, which is entirely filled with trees, and what is the purpose of this accursed valley between them?'

2 Then Uriel, one of the holy angels who was with me, answered and said: 'This accursed valley is for those who are cursed forever: Here shall all the accursed be gathered together who utter with their lips words

against the Lord not befitting His glory or say hard things against Him. Here shall they be gathered together, and here shall be their place of judgment.

3 In the last days there shall be the spectacle of righteous judgment on them in the presence of the righteous forever: here shall the merciful bless the Lord of glory, the Eternal King.

4 In the days of judgment they shall bless Him for the mercy in that He has shown them.'

5 Then I blessed the Lord of Glory and set out His glory and praised Him gloriously.

[Chapter 28]
1 Then, I went towards the east, into the midst of the mountain range in the desert, and I saw a wilderness.

2 And it was solitary, full of trees and plants. And water gushed out from above.

3 Rushing like a torrent which flowed towards the northwest, it caused clouds and dew to fall on every side.

[Chapter 29]
1 Then I went to another place in the desert, and approached to the east of this mountain range.

2 And there I saw aromatic trees exuding the fragrance of frankincense and myrrh, and the trees also were similar to the almond tree.

[Chapter 30]
1 Beyond these, I went far to the east,

2 And I saw another place, a valley full of water like one that would not run dry.

3 And there was a tree, the color of fragrant trees was that of mastic. And on the sides of those valleys I saw fragrant cinnamon. And beyond these I proceeded to the east.

[Chapter 31]
1 And I saw other mountains, and among them were groves of trees, and there was nectar that flowed from them, which is named Sarara and Galbanum.

2 And beyond these mountains I saw another mountain to the east of the ends of the earth, on which there were aloe trees, and all the trees were full of fruit, being like almond trees.

3 And when it was burned it smelled sweeter than any fragrant odor.

[Chapter 32]
1 And after I had smelled these fragrant odors, I looked towards the north over the mountains I saw seven mountains full of fine nard and fragrant trees of cinnamon and pepper.

2 And then I went over the summits of all these mountains, far towards the east of the earth, and passed over the Red Sea and went far from it, and passed over the angel Zotiel.

(Author's note: The angel Zoteil, whose name means, "little one of God," welcomes back those sinners who have gone astray but have repented. Based on the description of the locations, some have suggested the sphinx could be a representation, although most believe this to be unlikely.)

3 And I came to the Garden of Righteousness. I saw far beyond those trees more trees and they were numerous and large. There were two trees there, very large, beautiful, glorious, and magnificent. The tree of knowledge, whose holy fruit they ate and acquired great wisdom.

4 That tree is in height like the fir, and its leaves are like those of the Carob tree,

5 And its fruit is like the clusters of the grapes, very beautiful: and the fragrance of the tree carries far.

Isaiah 60:13 "The glory of Lebanon will come to you, the pine, the fir and the cypress together, to adorn the place of my sanctuary; and I will glorify the place of my feet.

6 Then I said: 'How beautiful is the tree, and how attractive is its look!' Then Raphael the holy angel, who was with me, answered me and said: 'This is the tree of wisdom, of which your father of old and your mother of old, who were your progenitors, have eaten, and they learned wisdom and their eyes were opened, and they knew that they were naked and they were driven out of the garden.'

[Chapter 33]
1 And from there I went to the ends of the earth and saw there large beasts, and each differed from the other; and I saw birds also differing in appearance and beauty and voice, the one differing from the other.

2 And to the east of those beasts I saw the ends of the earth where heaven rests on it, and the doors of heaven open. And I saw how the stars of heaven come out, and I counted the gates from which they came out,
3 And wrote down all their outlets, of each individual star by their number and their names, their courses and their positions, and their times and their months, as Uriel the holy angel who was with me showed me.

4 He showed me all things and wrote them down for me; also their names he wrote for me, and their laws and their functions.

[Chapter 34]
1 From there I went towards the north to the ends of the earth, and there I saw a great and glorious device at the ends of the whole earth.

2 And here I saw three gates of heaven open : through each of them proceed north winds: when they blow there is cold, hail, frost, snow, dew, and rain.

3 And out of one gate they blow for good: but when they blow through the other two gates, it is for violence and torment on the earth, and they blow with force.

[Chapter 35]
1 Then I went towards the west to the ends of the earth, and saw there three gates of heaven open such as I had seen in the east, the same number of gates, and the same number of outlets.

[Chapter 36]
1 And from there I went to the south to the ends of the earth, and saw there three open gates of heaven.

2 And from them come dew, rain, and wind. And from there I went to the east to the ends of heaven, and saw here the three eastern gates of heaven open and small gates above them.

3 Through each of these small gates pass the stars of heaven and they run their course to the west on the path which is shown to them.

4 And as often as I saw I blessed always the Lord of Glory, and I continued to bless the Lord of Glory who has done great and glorious wonders, who has shown the greatness of His work to the angels and to spirits and to men, that they might praise His work and all His creation: that they might see the power of His might and praise the great work of His hands and bless Him forever.

[Chapter 37]

The *Book of Parables* (Chapters 37-71):
1 The second vision which he saw, the vision of wisdom which Enoch the son of Jared, the son of Mahalalel,

2 The son of Cainan, the son of Enos, the son of Seth, the son of Adam, saw. And this is the beginning of the words of wisdom which I lifted up my voice to speak and say to those which dwell on earth: Hear, you men of old time, and see, you that come after, the words of the Holy One which I will speak before the Lord of spirits.

3 The words are for the men of old time, and to those that come after. We will not withhold the beginning of wisdom from this present day. Such wisdom has never been given by the Lord of spirits as I have received according to my insight, according to the good pleasure of the Lord of spirits by whom the lot of eternal life has been given to me.

4 Now three Parables were imparted to me, and I lifted up my voice and recounted them to those that dwell on the earth.

[Chapter 38]

1 The first Parable: When the congregation of the righteous shall appear, and sinners shall be judged for their sins, and shall be driven from the face of the earth;

2 And when the Righteous One shall appear before the eyes of the elect righteous ones, whose works are weighed by the Lord of spirits, light shall appear to the righteous and the elect who dwell on the earth. Where will there be the dwelling for sinners, and where the will there be a resting-place for those who have denied the Lord of spirits? It had been good for them if they had not been born.

John 1:1-5 In the beginning was the Word, and the Word was with God, and the Word was God. 2 The same was in the beginning with God. 3 All things were made by him; and without him was not any thing made that was made. 4 In him was life; and the life was the light of men. 5 And the light shineth in darkness; and the darkness comprehended it not.

3 When the secrets of the righteous shall be revealed and the sinners judged, and the godless driven from the presence of the righteous and elect,

4 From that time those that possess the earth shall no longer be powerful and mighty: And they shall not be able to look at the face of the holy ones, because the Lord of spirits has caused His light to appear on the face of the holy, righteous, and elect.

2 Corinthians 3:18 But we all, with open face beholding as in a glass the glory of the Lord, are changed into the same image from glory to glory, even as by the Spirit of the Lord.

5 Then the kings and the mighty shall be destroyed and be turned over into the hands of the righteous and holy.

6 And from then on none shall seek mercy from the Lord of spirits for themselves for their life is at an end.

[Chapter 39]

1 And it shall come to pass in those days that elect and holy children will descend from the high heaven, and their offspring will become one with the children of men.

(Author's note: Here we have a verse that can be interpreted in various ways. The holy children from the high heaven could be the spirits of the righteous dead. However, other verses seem to suggest those souls are being held until judgment. Enoch 38:1 mentions a judgment and this could be the one we seek to release the souls and make this verse mesh well.

Other theories regarding this verse have been put forward by those who believe God will give his consent to angels that they may finally freely mix with people. This seems unlikely given the previous reaction. Lastly, those involved with "UFO studies" point to this verse as an indication of contact.

Revelation 21:1-5 ¹ *Then I saw a new heaven and a new earth, for the first heaven and the first earth had passed away, and there was no longer any sea.* ² *I saw the Holy City, the new Jerusalem, coming down out of heaven from God, prepared as a bride beautifully dressed for her husband.* ³ *And I heard a loud voice from the throne saying, "Now the dwelling of God is with men, and he will live with them. They will be his people, and God himself will be with them and be their God.* ⁴ *He will wipe every tear from their eyes. There will be no more death or mourning or crying or pain, for the old order of things has passed away."* ⁵ *He who was seated on the throne said, "I am making everything new!" Then he said, "Write this down, for these words are trustworthy and true."*

2 And in those days Enoch received books of indignation and wrath, and books of turmoil and confusion. There will be no mercy for them, says the Lord of spirits.

3 And in those days a whirlwind carried me off from the earth, And set me down at the end of heaven.

4 There I saw another vision, the dwelling-places of the holy, and the resting-places of the righteous.

5 Here my eyes saw the dwelling places of His righteous angels, and the resting-places of the Holy Ones. And they petitioned and interceded and prayed for the children of men, and righteousness flowed before them like water, and mercy fell like dew on the earth: Thus it is among them forever and ever.

6 And in that place my eyes saw the Elect One of righteousness and of faith,

7 And I saw his dwelling-place under the wings of the Lord of spirits.

8 And righteousness shall prevail in his days, and the righteous and elect shall be innumerable and will be before Him forever and ever.

9 And all the righteous and elect ones before Him shall be as bright as fiery lights, and their mouth shall be full of blessing, and their lips shall praise the name of the Lord of spirits. Righteousness and truth before Him shall never fail.

10 There I wished to dwell, and my spirit longed for that dwelling-place; and thus it was decided and my portion was assigned and established by the Lord of spirits.

11 In those days I praised and exalted the name of the Lord of spirits with blessings and praises, because He had destined me for blessing and glory according to the good pleasure of the Lord of spirits.

12 For a long time my eyes looked at that place, and I blessed Him and praised Him, saying: 'Blessed is He, and may He be blessed from the beginning and forevermore. And in His presence there is no end.

13 He knows before the world was created what is forever and what will be from generation to generation.

14 Those who do not sleep bless you, they stand before your glory and bless, praise, and exalt you, saying: "Holy, holy, holy, is the Lord of spirits: He fills the earth with spirits."'

15 And here my eyes saw all those who do not sleep: they stand before Him and bless Him saying: 'Blessed be you, and blessed be the name of the Lord forever and ever.'

16 And my face was changed; for I could no longer see.

Exodus 34:29 When Moses came down from Mount Sinai with the two tablets of the Testimony in his hands, he was not aware that his face was radiant because he had spoken with the LORD.

[Chapter 40]

1 And after that I saw thousands of thousands and ten thousand times ten thousand,

2 I saw a multitude beyond number and reckoning, who stood before the Lord of spirits. And on the four sides of the Lord of spirits I saw four figures, different from those that did not sleep, and I learned their names; for the angel that went with me told me their names, and showed me all the hidden things.

3 And I heard the voices of those four presences as they uttered praises before the Lord of glory.

4 The first voice blessed the Lord of spirits forever and ever.

5 The second voice I heard blessing the Elect One and the elect ones who depend on the Lord of spirits.

6 And the third voice I heard pray and intercede for those who live on the earth and pray earnestly in the name of the Lord of spirits.

7 And I heard the fourth voice fending off the Satans (adversary or accusers) and forbidding them to come before the Lord of spirits to accuse them who dwell on the earth.

8 After that I asked the angel of peace who went with me, who showed me everything that is hidden: 'Who are these four figures which I have seen and whose words I have heard and written down?'

9 And he said to me: 'This first is Michael, the merciful and long-suffering; and the second, who is set over all the diseases and all the wounds of the children of men, is Raphael; and the third, who is set over all the powers, is Gabriel' and the fourth, who is set over the repentance and those who hope to inherit eternal life, is named Phanuel.'

10 And these are the four angels of the Lord of spirits and the four voices I heard in those days.

[Chapter 41]

1 And after that I saw all the secrets of heavens, and how the kingdom is divided, and how the actions of men are weighed in the balance.

Daniel 5:27 Thou art weighed in the balances, and art found wanting.

2 And there I saw the mansions of the elect and the mansions of the holy, and my eyes saw all the sinners being driven from there which deny the name of the Lord of spirits, and they were being dragged off; and they could not live because of the punishment which proceeds from the Lord of spirits.

John 14:2-3 In my Father's house are many mansions: if it were not so, I would have told you. I go to prepare a place for you. ³ And if I go and prepare a place for you, I will come again, and receive you unto myself; that where I am, there ye may be also.

3 And there my eyes saw the secrets of the lightning and of the thunder, and the secrets of the winds, how they are divided to blow over the earth, and the secrets of the clouds and dew,

4 And there I saw where they came from and how they saturate the dusty earth.

5 And there I saw closed storehouses out of which the winds are divided, the storehouse of the hail and winds, the storehouse of the mist, and of the clouds, and the cloud thereof hovers over the earth from the beginning of the world.

6 And I saw the storehouses of the sun and moon, where they go and where they come, and their glorious return, and how one is superior to the other, and their stately orbit, and how they do not leave their orbit, and they add nothing to their orbit and they take nothing from it, and they keep faith with each other, in accordance with the oath by which they are bound together.

7 And first the sun goes out and traverses his path according to the commandment of the Lord of spirits, and mighty is His name forever and ever. And after that I saw the invisible and the visible path of the moon, and she accomplishes the course of her path in that place by day and by night - the one holding a position opposite to the other before the Lord of spirits. And they give thanks and praise and rest not; but their thanksgiving is forever and ever.

8 For the sun makes many revolutions for a blessing or a curse, and the course of the path of the moon is light to the righteous and darkness to the sinners in the name of the Lord, who made a separation between the light and the darkness, and divided the spirits of men and strengthened the spirits of the righteous, in the name of His righteousness.

Matthew 5:44-45 But I say unto you, Love your enemies, bless them that curse you, do good to them that hate you, and pray for them which despitefully use you, and persecute you; [45] That ye may be the children of your Father which is in heaven: for he maketh his sun to rise on the evil and on the good, and sendeth rain on the just and on the unjust.

9 For no angel hinders and no power is able to hinder; for He appoints a judge for them all and He judges them all Himself.

[Chapter 42]

1 Wisdom found no place where she might dwell; then a dwelling-place was assigned her in heavens.

2 Wisdom went out to make her dwelling among the children of men, and found no dwelling-place. Wisdom returned to her place, and took her seat among the angels.

3 And unrighteousness went out from her storehouses. She found those she did not seek, and dwelt with them, (she sought no one in particular but found a place...); as rain in a desert and dew on a thirsty land.

[Chapter 43]

1 And I saw other lightning and the stars of heaven, and I saw how He called them all by their names and they obeyed Him.

2 And I saw how they are weighed in a righteous balance according to their proportions of light: I saw the width of their spaces and the day of their appearing, and how their revolution produces lightning:

3 And I saw their revolution according to the number of the angels, and how they keep faith with each other. And I asked the angel who went with me who showed me what was hidden:

4 'What are these?' And he said to me: 'The Lord of spirits has shown you their parable: these are the names of the holy who dwell on the earth and believe in the name of the Lord of spirits forever and ever.'

[Chapter 44]

1 Also another phenomenon I saw in regard to the lightning: how some of the stars arise and become lightning and cannot part with their new form.

[Chapter 45]

1 And this is the second Parable: concerning those who deny the name of the dwelling of the holy ones and the Lord of spirits.

2 They shall not ascend to heaven, and they shall not come on the earth: Such shall be the lot of the sinners

who have denied the name of the Lord of spirits, who are preserved for the day of suffering and tribulation.

3 On that day My Elect One shall sit on the throne of glory and shall try the works of the righteous, and their places of rest shall be innumerable. And their souls shall grow strong within them when they see My Elect One, And those who have called on My glorious name:

4 Then will I cause My Elect One to dwell among them. I will transform heaven and make it an eternal blessing and light,

5 And I will transform the earth and make it a blessing, and I will cause My elect ones to dwell on it. But the sinners and evil-doers shall not set foot on it.

6 For I have seen and satisfied My righteous ones with peace and have caused them to dwell before Me, but for the sinners there is judgment impending with Me, so that I shall destroy them from the face of the earth.

[Chapter 46]

1 And there I saw One whose face looked ancient. His head was white like wool, and with Him was another being whose countenance had the appearance of a man, and his face was full of graciousness, like one of the holy angels.

2 And I asked the angel who went with me and showed me all the hidden things, concerning that Son of Man, who he was, and where he came from, and why he went with the Ancient One? And he answered and said to me:

3 "This is the Son of Man who hath righteousness, with whom dwells righteousness, and who reveals all the treasures of that which is hidden, because the Lord of spirits hath chosen him, and whose lot has preeminence before the Lord of spirits in righteousness and is forever.

4 And this Son of Man whom you have seen shall raise up the kings and the mighty from their seats, and the strong from their thrones and shall loosen the reins of the strong, and break the teeth of the sinners.

Matthew 13:41 The Son of man shall send forth his angels, and they shall gather out of his kingdom all things that offend, and them which do iniquity;

5 And he shall put down the kings from their thrones and kingdoms because they do not exalt and praise Him, nor humbly acknowledge who bestowed their kingdom on them.

Matthew 19:28 And Jesus said unto them, Verily I say unto you, That ye which have followed me, in the regeneration when the Son of man shall sit in the throne of his glory, ye also shall sit upon twelve thrones, judging the twelve tribes of Israel.

6 And he shall make the strong hang their heads, and shall fill them with shame. And darkness shall be their dwelling, and worms shall be their bed, and they shall have no hope of rising from their beds, because they do not exalt the name of the Lord of spirits."

7 They raise their hands against the Most High and tread on the earth and dwell on it and all their deeds manifest unrighteousness. Their power rests on their riches, and their faith is in the gods which they have made with their hands. They deny the name of the Lord of spirits,

8 And they persecute the houses of His congregations, and the faithful who depend on the name of the Lord of Spirits.

[Chapter 47]

1 In those days the prayer of the righteous shall have ascended, and the blood of the righteous from the earth shall be before the Lord of spirits.

2 In those days the holy ones who dwell above in heavens shall unite with one voice and supplicate and pray and praise, and give thanks and bless the name of the Lord of spirits on behalf of the blood of the righteous which has been shed, that the prayer of the righteous may not be in vain before the Lord of spirits, that they may have justice, and that they may not have to wait forever.

3 In those days I saw the "Head of Days" when He seated himself on the throne of His glory, and the books of the living were opened before Him; and all His host which is in heaven above and His counselors stood before Him,

4 And the hearts of the holy were filled with joy because the number of the righteous had been offered, and the prayer of the righteous had been heard, and the blood of the righteous not been required before the Lord of spirits.

Revelation 20:11-15 Then I saw a great white throne and him who was seated on it. Earth and sky fled from his presence, and there was no place for them. 12 And I saw the dead, great and small, standing before the throne, and books were opened. Another book was opened, which is the Book of Life. The dead were judged according to what they had done as recorded in the books. 13 The sea gave up the dead that were in it, and death and Hades gave up the dead that were in them, and each person was judged according to what he had done. 14 Then death and Hades were thrown into the lake of fire. The lake of fire is the second death. 15 If anyone's name was not found written in the Book of Life, he was thrown into the lake of fire.

[Chapter 48]
1 And in that place I saw the spring of righteousness which was inexhaustible. And around it were many springs of wisdom. And all the thirsty drank of them, and were filled with wisdom, and their dwellings were with the righteous and holy and elect.

2 And at that hour that Son of Man was named in the presence of the Lord of spirits, And his name was brought before the Head of Days.

3 Even before the sun and the signs were created, before the stars of heaven were made, His name was named before the Lord of spirits.

4 He shall be a staff to the righteous and they shall steady themselves and not fall. And he shall be the light of the Gentiles, and the hope of those who are troubled of heart.

Romans 11: 11-21 I say then, Have they stumbled that they should fall? God forbid: but rather through their fall salvation is come unto the Gentiles, for to provoke them to jealousy.
12 Now if the fall of them be the riches of the world, and the diminishing of them the riches of the Gentiles; how much more their fulness?
13 For I speak to you Gentiles, inasmuch as I am the apostle of the Gentiles, I magnify mine office:
14 If by any means I may provoke to emulation them which are my flesh, and might save some of them.
15 For if the casting away of them be the reconciling of the world, what shall the receiving of them be, but life from the dead?
16 For if the firstfruit be holy, the lump is also holy: and if the root be holy, so are the branches.
17 And if some of the branches be broken off, and thou, being a wild olive tree, wert grafted in among them, and with them partakest of the root and fatness of the olive tree;
18 Boast not against the branches. But if thou boast, thou bearest not the root, but the root thee.
19 Thou wilt say then, The branches were broken off, that I might be grafted in.
20 Well; because of unbelief they were broken off, and thou standest by faith. Be not highminded, but fear:
21 For if God spared not the natural branches, take heed lest he also spare not thee.

5 All who dwell on earth shall fall down and worship before him, and will praise and bless and sing and celebrate the Lord of spirits.

6 And for this reason he has been chosen and hidden in front of (kept safe by) Him, before the creation of the

world and forevermore.

7 And the wisdom of the Lord of spirits has revealed him to the holy and righteous; For he hath preserved the lot of the righteous, because they have hated and rejected this world of unrighteousness, and have hated all its works and ways in the name of the Lord of spirits. For in his name they are saved, and according to his good pleasure and it is He who has regard to their life.

8 In these days the kings of the earth and the strong who possess the land because of the works of their hands will be shamed, because on the day of their anguish and affliction they shall not be able to save themselves. And I will give them over into the hands of My elect.

9 As straw in the fire so shall they burn before the face of the holy; as lead in the water shall they sink before the face of the righteous, and no trace of them shall be found anymore.

Malachi 4:1
For, behold, the day cometh, that shall burn as an oven; and all the proud, yea, and all that do wickedly, shall be stubble: and the day that cometh shall burn them up, saith the LORD of hosts, that it shall leave them neither root nor branch.

10 And on the day of their affliction there shall be rest on the earth (because the evil ones will be destroyed), and before Him they shall fall down and not rise again, and there shall be no one to take them with his hands and raise them up; for they have denied the Lord of spirits and His Anointed. The name of the Lord of spirits be blessed.

[Chapter 49]

l For wisdom is poured out like water, and glory will not fail before him ever.

2 For he is mighty in all the secrets of righteousness, and unrighteousness shall disappear like a shadow, and will no longer exist; because the Elect One stands before the Lord of spirits, and his glory is forever and ever, and his might for all generations.

3 In him dwells the spirit of wisdom, and the spirit which gives insight, and the spirit of understanding and of might, and the spirit of those who have fallen asleep in righteousness.

4 And he shall judge the secret things, and no one shall be able to utter a lying or idle word before him, for he is the Elect One before the Lord of spirits according to His good pleasure.

[Chapter 50]

1 And in those days a change shall take place for the holy and elect, and the light of days shall abide on them, and glory and honor shall turn to the Holy.

2 On the day of trouble, affliction will be heaped on the evil. And the righteous shall be victorious in the name of the Lord of spirits. For He will tell this to others that they may repent and turn away from the works of their hands.

3 They shall have no honor through the name of the Lord of spirits, but through His name they shall be saved, and the Lord of spirits will have compassion on them, for His mercy is great.

4 He is righteous also in His judgment, and in the presence of His glory unrighteousness also shall not stand: At His judgment the unrepentant shall perish before Him.

5 And from now on I will have no mercy on them, says the Lord of spirits.

[Chapter 51]

1 And in those days shall the earth also give back that which has been entrusted to it, and Sheol (the grave)

also shall give back that which it has received, and hell shall give back that which it owes. For in those days the Elect One shall arise,

2 And he shall choose the righteous and holy from among them. For the day has drawn near that they should be saved.

Revelation 20:12-15 And I saw the dead, small and great, stand before God; and the books were opened: and another book was opened, which is the Book of Life: and the dead were judged out of those things which were written in the books, according to their works. 13 And the sea gave up the dead which were in it; and death and hell delivered up the dead which were in them: and they were judged every man according to their works. 14 And death and hell were cast into the lake of fire. This is the second death. 15 And whosoever was not found written in the Book of Life was cast into the lake of fire.

3 And in those days the Elect One shall sit on His throne, and all the secrets of wisdom and counsel shall pour from His mouth, for the Lord of spirits hath given them to Him and has glorified Him.

4 In those days shall the mountains leap like rams, and the hills shall skip like lambs satisfied with milk, and the faces of all the angels in heaven shall be lighted up with joy.

5 And the earth shall rejoice, and the righteous shall dwell on it, and the elect shall walk on it.

[Chapter 52]

1 And after those days in that place where I had seen all the visions of that which is hidden, for I had been carried off in a whirlwind and they had borne me towards the west.

2 There my eyes saw all the secret things of heaven that shall be, a mountain of iron, and a mountain of copper, and a mountain of silver, and a mountain of gold, and a mountain of soft metal, and a mountain of lead.

3 And I asked the angel who went with me, saying, 'What things are these which I have seen in secret?'

4 And he said to me: 'All these things which you have seen shall serve the authority of His Messiah that he may be powerful and mighty on the earth.'

5 The angel of peace answered me saying: 'Wait a little while, and all secret things shall be revealed to you, things which surround the Lord of spirits.

6 And these mountains which your eyes have seen, the mountain of iron, and the mountain of copper, and the mountain of silver, and the mountain of gold, and the mountain of soft metal, and the mountain of lead, all of these shall be like wax before a fire in the presence of the Elect One. Like the water which streams down from above on those mountains, and they shall be weak under his feet.

7 And it shall come to pass in those days that none shall be saved, either by gold or by silver, and none will be able to save themselves or escape.

8 And there shall be no iron for war, nor materials for breastplates. Bronze shall be of no use, tin shall be worthless, and lead shall not be desired.

9 All these things shall be destroyed from the face of the earth, when the Elect One appears before the Lord of spirits.'

[Chapter 53]

1 There my eyes saw a deep valley with its mouth open, and all who dwell on the earth and sea and islands shall bring gifts and presents and tokens of homage to Him, but that deep valley shall not become full.

2 And their hands commit lawless deeds, and everything the righteous work at the sinners devour. The sinners shall be destroyed in front of the face of the Lord of spirits, and they shall be banished from off the face of His earth, and they shall perish forever and ever.

3 For I saw all the angels of punishment abiding there and preparing all the instruments of Satan.

4 And I asked the angel of peace who went with me: 'For whom are they preparing these instruments?'

5 And he said to me: 'They prepare these for the kings and the powerful of this earth, that they may with them be destroyed.

6 After this the Righteous and Elect One shall cause the house of His congregation to appear and from then on they shall hinder no more, in the name of the Lord of spirits.

7 And these mountains shall not stand as solid ground before His righteousness, but the hills shall be like springs of water, and the righteous shall have rest from the oppression of sinners.'

[Chapter 54]

1 And I looked and turned to another part of the earth, and saw there a deep valley with burning fire.

2 And they brought the kings and the powerful, and began to cast them into this deep valley.

Revelation 6:15-17 And the kings of the earth, and the great men, and the rich men, and the chief captains, and the mighty men, and every bondman, and every free man, hid themselves in the dens and in the rocks of the mountains;
16 And said to the mountains and rocks, Fall on us, and hide us from the face of him that sitteth on the throne, and from the wrath of the Lamb:
17 For the great day of his wrath is come; and who shall be able to stand?

3 And there my eyes saw how they made their instruments for them, iron chains of immeasurable weight.

4 And I asked the angel of peace who was with me, saying: 'For whom are these chains being prepared ?'

5 And he said to me: 'These are being prepared for the hosts of Azazel, so that they may take them and throw them into the bottom of the pit of hell, and they shall cover their jaws with rough stones as the Lord of spirits commanded.

6 And Michael, and Gabriel, and Raphael, and Phanuel shall take hold of them on that great day, and throw them into the burning furnace on that day, that the Lord of spirits may take vengeance on them for their unrighteousness in becoming servants to Satan and for leading astray those who live on the earth.'

7 And in those days punishment will come from the Lord of spirits, and he will open all the storehouses of waters above heavens, and of the fountains which are under the surface of the earth.

8 And all the waters shall be come together (flow into or be joined) with the waters of heaven (above the sky), that which is above heavens is the masculine, and the water which is beneath the earth is the feminine.

9 And they shall destroy all who live on the dry land and those who live under the ends of heaven.

(Author's note: The previous verse refers to Noah's flood.)

10 And when they have acknowledged the unrighteousness which they have done on the earth, by these they shall perish.

[Chapter 55]

1 And after that the Head of Days repented and said: 'I have destroyed all who dwell on the earth to no avail.'

2 And He swore by His great name: 'From now on I will not do this to all who dwell on the earth again, and I will set a sign in heaven: and this shall be a covenant of good faith between Me and them forever, so long as heaven is above the earth. And this is in accordance with My command.

(Author's note: The previous verse refers to the rainbow.)

3 When I have desired to take hold of them by the hand of the angels on the day of tribulation, anger, and pain because of this, I will cause My punishment and anger to abide on them, says God, the Lord of spirits.

4 You mighty kings who live on the earth, you shall have to watch My Elect One sit on the throne of glory and judge Azazel, and all his associates, and all his hosts in the name of the Lord of spirits.'

[Chapter 56]

1 And I saw there the hosts of the angels of punishment going, and they held scourges and chains of iron and bronze.

2 And I asked the angel of peace who went with me, saying: 'To whom are these who hold the scourges going?'

3 And he said to me: 'Each one to the ones they have chosen and to their loved ones, that they may be cast into the chasm of the abyss in the valley.

4 And then that valley shall be filled with ones they chose and their loved ones, and the days of their lives shall be at an end, and the days of their leading astray shall no longer be remembered (counted).

5 In those days the angels shall return and gather together and throw themselves to the east on the Parthians and Medes. They shall stir up the kings, so that a spirit of unrest and disturbance will come on them, and they shall drive them from their thrones, that they may rush out like lions from their lairs, and as hungry wolves among their flocks.

(Author's note: The names of certain countries help set the date of the manuscript. Scholars believe, based on the names of the countries mentioned in Enoch, that the book could not have been written prior to 250 B.C. since some countries did not exist before that date. One could add that the particular part of Enoch is the only section dated, since the book consists of several disjointed parts.)

6 And they shall go up and trample the lands of My elect ones, and the land of His elect ones shall be before them a threshing-floor (trampled, barren ground and a highway).

7 But the city of my righteous ones shall be a hindrance to their horses, and they shall begin to fight among themselves, and their own right hand shall be strong against themselves, and a man shall not know his brother, nor a son his father or his mother, until there will be innumerable corpses because of their slaughter, and their punishment shall be not in vain.

8 In those days hell (Sheol) shall open its jaws, and they shall be swallowed up. Their destruction shall be final. Hell (Sheol) shall devour the sinners in the presence of the elect.'

Revelation 20:1-2 And I saw an angel come down from heaven, having the key of the bottomless pit and a great chain in his hand. 2 And he laid hold on the dragon, that old serpent, which is the Devil, and Satan, and bound him a thousand years.

[Chapter 57]

1 And it came to pass after this that I saw another host of chariots, and men riding on them. They were coming

on the winds from the east, and from the west to the south.

2 The noise of their chariots was heard, and when this turmoil took place the holy ones from heaven watched it, and the pillars of the earth were shaken and moved, and the sound of it was heard from the one end of heaven to the other, in one day.

3 And all shall fall down and worship the Lord of spirits. This is the end of the second Parable.

[Chapter 58]

1 And I began to speak the third Parable concerning the righteous and elect.

2 Blessed are you, you righteous and elect, for glorious shall be your lot.

3 And the righteous shall be in the light of the sun, and the elect will be in the light of eternal life. The days of their life shall be unending, and the days of the holy will be without number.

4 And they shall seek the light and find righteousness with the Lord of spirits. Peace to the righteous in the name of the Eternal Lord!

5 And after this it shall be said to the holy in heaven that they should seek secrets of righteousness, and the destiny of faith. For it has become bright as the sun on earth, and the darkness is passed away.

6 And there shall be a light that never ends, and to a number of days they shall not come, for the darkness shall first have been destroyed, [And the light established before the Lord of spirits] and the light of righteousness established forever before the Lord of spirits.

[Chapter 59]

1 In those days my eyes saw the secrets of the lightning, and of the lights, and they judge and execute their judgment, and they illuminate for a blessing or a curse as the Lord of spirits wills.

2 And there I saw the secrets of the thunder, and how when it resounds above in heaven, the sound thereof is heard, and he caused me to see the judgments executed on the earth, whether they are for well-being and blessing, or for a curse according to the word of the Lord of spirits.

3 And after that all the secrets of the lights and lightning were shown to me, and they lighten for blessing and for satisfying.

[Chapter 60] - Noah's Vision

1 In the year 500, in the seventh month, on the fourteenth day of the month in the life of Enoch, in that parable I saw how a mighty quaking made the heaven of heavens to quake, and the host of the Most High, and the angels, a thousand thousands and ten thousand times ten thousand, were disquieted with great foreboding.

2 And the Head of Days sat on the throne of His glory, and the angels and the righteous stood around Him.

3 And a great trembling seized me, and fear took hold of me, and my legs gave way, and I melted with weakness and fell on my face.

4 And Michael sent another angel from among the holy ones and he raised me up, and when he had raised me up my spirit returned; for I had not been able to endure the look of this host, and the disturbance and the shaking of heaven.

5 And Michael said to me: 'Why are you upset with such a vision? Until this day, His mercy and long-suffering has lasted toward those who dwell on the earth.'

6 And when the day, and the power, and the punishment, and the judgment come, which the Lord of spirits hath prepared for those who worship not the righteous law, and for those who deny the righteous judgment, and for those who take His name in vain, that day is prepared. It will be a covenant for the elect, but for sinners an inquisition. When the punishment of the Lord of spirits shall rest on them, it will not come in vain, and it shall slay the children with their mothers and the children with their fathers.

7 And on that day two monsters were separated from one another, a female monster named Leviathan, to dwell in the abyss of the ocean over the fountains of the waters;

8 And the male is named Behemoth, who occupied with his breast a wasted wilderness named Duidain, on the east of the garden where the elect and righteous dwell, where my (great) grandfather was taken up, the seventh from Adam, the first man whom the Lord of spirits created.

9 And I asked the other angel to show me the might of those monsters, how they were separated on one day and thrown, the one into the abyss of the sea, and the other to the earth's desert.

10 And he said to me: ' Son of man, you wish to know what is kept secret.'

11 And the other angel who went with me and showed me what was kept secret; told me what is first and last in heaven in the sky, and beneath the earth in the depth, and at the ends of heaven, and on the foundation of heaven.

12 And the storehouse of the winds, and how the winds are divided, and how they are weighed, and how the doors of the winds are calculated for each according to the power of the wind, and the power of the lights of the moon according to the power that is fitting; and the divisions of the stars according to their names, and how all the divisions are divided.

13 And the thunder according to the places where they fall, and all the divisions that are made among the lightning that it may light, and their host that they may at once obey.

14 For the thunder has places of rest which are assigned while it is waiting for its peal; and the thunder and lightning are inseparable, and although not one and undivided, they both go together in spirit and are not separate.

15 For when the lightning flashes, the thunder utters its voice, and the spirit enforces a pause during the peal, and divides equally between them; for the treasury of their peals is like the sand (of an hourglass), and each one of them as it peals is held in with a bridle, and turned back by the power of the spirit, and pushed forward according to the many parts of the earth.

16 And the spirit of the sea is masculine and strong, and according to the might of His strength He draws it back with a rein, and in like manner it is driven forward and disperses in the midst of all the mountains of the earth.

17 And the spirit of the hoar-frost is his own angel, and the spirit of the hail is a good angel. And the spirit of the snow has forsaken his storehouse because of his strength.

18 There is a special spirit there, and that which ascends from it is like smoke, and its name is frost. And the spirit of the mist is not united with them in their storehouse, but it has a special storehouse; for its course is glorious both in light and in darkness, and in winter and in summer, and in its storehouse is an angel.

19 And the spirit of the dew has its dwelling at the ends of heaven, and is connected with the storehouse of the rain, and its course is in winter and summer; and its clouds and the clouds of the mist are connected, and the one gives to the other.

20 And when the spirit of the rain goes out from its storehouse, the angels come and open the storehouse and lead it out, and when it is diffused over the whole earth it unites with the water on the earth.

21 And whenever it unites with the water on the earth, (for the waters are for those who live on the earth), they are (become) nourishment for the earth from the Most High who is in heaven.

22 Therefore there is a measurement for the rain, and the angels are in charge of it. And these things I saw towards the Garden of the Righteous.

23 And the Angel of Peace who was with me, said to me:

24 "These two monsters, prepared in accordance with the greatness of the Lord, will feed them the punishment of the Lord. And children will be killed with their mothers, and sons with their fathers.
Job 3:8 May those who curse days curse that day, those who are ready to rouse Leviathan.

Isaiah 27:1
In that day,
the LORD will punish with his sword,
his fierce, great and powerful sword,
Leviathan the gliding serpent,
Leviathan the coiling serpent;
he will slay the monster of the sea.

[Chapter 61]

1 And I saw in those days that long cords were given to those angels, and they took to themselves wings and flew, and they went towards the north.

2 I asked the angel, saying to him: 'Why have those angels who have cords taken flight?' And he said to me: 'They have gone to take measurements.'

(Author's note: There were no tape measures in those days. Measurements were taken by a simple rope or stick. The rope may have knots placed in it. Usual measurement were based on a man's forearm, the length of an arm, or the span of the arms.) In this case, the measurements, based those of the Lord or his appointed angel, encoded secret knowledge.)

3 And the angel who went with me said to me: These shall bring the measurements of the righteous, and the cords of the righteous to the righteous, that they may rely on the name of the Lord of spirits forever and ever.'

4 The elect shall begin to dwell with the elect, and those are the measurements which shall be given to faith and which shall strengthen righteousness.

5 And these measurements shall reveal all the secrets of the depths of the earth, and those who have been destroyed by the desert, and those who have been devoured by the beasts, and those who have been devoured by the fish of the sea, that they may return and rely on the day of the Elect One. For none shall be destroyed before the Lord of spirits, and none can be destroyed.

6 And all who dwell in heaven received a command and power and one voice and one light like to fire.

7 And they blessed Him with their first words and exalted and praised Him in their wisdom. And they were wise in utterance and in the spirit of life.

8 And the Lord of spirits placed the Elect One on the throne of glory. And he shall judge all the works of the holy above in heaven, and in the balance their deeds shall be weighed.

2 Timothy 4:1 I charge thee therefore before God, and the Lord Jesus Christ, who shall judge the quick and the dead at his appearing and his kingdom;

9 And when he shall lift up his face to judge their secret ways according to the word of the name of the Lord of spirits, and their path according to the way of the righteous judgment of the Lord of spirits; then they shall all speak with one voice and bless and glorify and exalt the name of the Lord of spirits.

10 And He will summon all the host of heavens, and all the holy ones above, and the host of God, the cherubim, seraphim and ophannim, and all the angels of power, and all the angels of principalities (angels that rule over other angels), and the Elect One, and the other powers on the earth and over the water. On that day shall raise one voice, and bless and glorify and exalt in the spirit of faith, and in the spirit of wisdom, and in the spirit of patience, and in the spirit of mercy, and in the spirit of judgment and of peace, and in the spirit of goodness, and shall all say with one voice: "Blessed is He, and may the name of the Lord of spirits be blessed forever and ever."

11 All who do not sleep above in heaven shall bless Him. All the holy ones who are in heaven shall bless Him; and all the elect who dwell in the garden of life, and every spirit who is able to bless, and glorify, and exalt, and praise Your blessed name, and to the extent of its ability all flesh shall glorify and bless Your name forever and ever.

12 For great is the mercy of the Lord of spirits. He is long-suffering, and all His works and all that He has created He has revealed to the righteous and elect, in the name of the Lord of spirits.

Numbers 14:18 The LORD is longsuffering, and of great mercy, forgiving iniquity and transgression, and by no means clearing the guilty, visiting the iniquity of the fathers upon the children unto the third and fourth generation.

[Chapter 62]

1 Thus the Lord commanded the kings and the mighty and the exalted, and those who dwell on the earth, and said: 'Open your eyes and lift up your horns if you are able to recognize the Elect One.'

Psalm 24:7 Lift up your heads, O ye gates; and be ye lift up, ye everlasting doors; and the King of glory shall come in.

2 And the Lord of spirits seated Him on the throne of His glory, and the spirit of righteousness was poured out on Him, and the word of His mouth slays all the sinners, and all the unrighteous are destroyed from in front of His face.

Revelation 19:15-16 And out of his mouth goeth a sharp sword, that with it he should smite the nations: and he shall rule them with a rod of iron: and he treadeth the winepress of the fierceness and wrath of Almighty God. ¹⁶ And he hath on his vesture and on his thigh a name written, KING OF KINGS, AND LORD OF LORDS.

3 And in that day all the kings and the mighty, and the exalted and those who hold the earth shall stand up and shall see and recognize that He sits on the throne of His glory, and that righteousness is judged before Him, and no lying word is spoken before Him.

4 Then pain will come on them as on a woman in labor, and she has pain in giving birth when her child enters the mouth of the womb, and she has pain in childbirth.

Micah 4:10 Be in pain, and labour to bring forth, O daughter of Zion, like a woman in travail: for now shalt thou go forth out of the city, and thou shalt dwell in the field, and thou shalt go even to Babylon; there shalt thou be delivered; there the LORD shall redeem thee from the hand of thine enemies.

5 And one portion of them shall look at the other, and they shall be terrified, and they shall look downcast, and pain shall seize them, when they see that Son of Man sitting on the throne of His glory.

Matthew 25:31 When the Son of Man shall come in His glory, and all the holy angels with Him, then shall He sit upon the throne of His glory:

6 And the kings and the mighty and all who possess the earth shall bless and glorify and exalt Him who rules over all, who was hidden.

7 For from the beginning the Son of Man was hidden, and the Most High preserved Him in the presence of His might, and revealed Him to the elect.

8 And the congregation of the elect and holy shall be sown, and all the elect shall stand before Him on that day.

9 And all the kings and the mighty and the exalted and those who rule the earth shall fall down before Him on their faces, and worship and set their hope on that Son of Man, and petition Him and supplicate for mercy at His hands.

10 Nevertheless that Lord of spirits will so press them that they shall heavily go out from His presence, and their faces shall be filled with shame, and the darkness grows deeper on their faces.

11 And He will deliver them to the angels for punishment, to execute vengeance on them because they have oppressed His children and His elect.

12 And they shall be a spectacle for the righteous and for His elect. They shall rejoice over them, because the wrath of the Lord of spirits rests on them, and His sword is drunk with their blood.

13 The righteous and elect shall be saved on that day, and they shall never again see the face of the sinners and unrighteous.

14 And the Lord of spirits will abide over them, and they shall eat, lie down and rise up with the Son of Man forever and ever.

Revelation 21:3-4 Now the dwelling of God is with men, and he will live with them. They will be his people, and God himself will be with them and be their God. [4] He will wipe every tear from their eyes. There will be no more death or mourning or crying or pain, for the old order of things has passed away."

15 The righteous and elect shall have risen from the earth, and ceased to be downcast and they will have been clothed with garments of life.

16 And these shall be the garments of life from the Lord of spirits; they shall not wear out nor will your glory pass away from before the Lord of spirits.

[Chapter 63]

1 In those days shall the mighty and the kings who possess the earth beg Him to grant them a little respite from His angels of punishment to whom they were delivered, that they might fall down and worship before the Lord of spirits, and confess their sins before Him.

Romans 14:11-12 For it is written, As I live, saith the Lord, every knee shall bow to me, and every tongue shall confess to God. [12] So then every one of us shall give account of himself to God.

2 And they shall bless and glorify the Lord of spirits, and say: 'Blessed is the Lord of spirits and the Lord of kings, and the Lord of the mighty and the Lord of the rich, and the Lord of glory and the Lord of wisdom,

3 And every secret is revealed in front of you. Your power is from generation to generation, and your glory forever and ever. Deep and innumerable are all your secrets, and your righteousness is beyond reckoning.

4 We have now learned that we should glorify and bless the Lord of kings and He who is King over all kings.'

5 And they shall say: 'Would that we had a respite to glorify and give thanks and confess our faith before His glory!

6 And now we long for a little respite but find it not. We are driven away and obtain it not: And light has vanished from before us, and darkness is our dwelling-place forever and ever;

7 Because we have not believed in Him nor glorified the name of the Lord of spirits, but our hope was in the scepter of our kingdom, and in our own glory.

8 In the day of our suffering and tribulation He does not save and we find no respite for confession that our Lord is true in all His works, and in His judgments and His justice, and His judgments have no respect of persons.

Romans 2: 7-13 To them who by patient continuance in well doing seek for glory and honour and immortality, eternal life:
8 But unto them that are contentious, and do not obey the truth, but obey unrighteousness, indignation and wrath,
9 Tribulation and anguish, upon every soul of man that doeth evil, of the Jew first, and also of the Gentile;
10 But glory, honour, and peace, to every man that worketh good, to the Jew first, and also to the Gentile:
11 For there is no respect of persons with God.
12 For as many as have sinned without law shall also perish without law: and as many as have sinned in the law shall be judged by the law;
13 For not the hearers of the law are just before God, but the doers of the law shall be justified.

9 We pass away from before His face on account of our works, and all our sins are judged in (comparison to) righteousness.'

10 Now they shall say to themselves: 'Our souls are full of unrighteous gain, but what we have gained does not prevent us from descending from the midst of our worldly gain into the torment (burden) of Hell (Sheol).'

11 And after that their faces shall be filled with darkness and shame before that Son of Man, and they shall be driven from His presence, and the sword shall abide before His face in their midst.

12 Thus spoke the Lord of spirits: 'This is the ordinance and judgment with respect to the mighty and the kings and the exalted and those who possess the earth before the Lord of spirits.'

[Chapter 64]
1 And other forms I saw hidden in that place.

2 I heard the voice of the angel saying: 'These are the angels who descended to the earth, and revealed what was hidden to the children of men and seduced the children of men into committing sin.'

Jude 1:6 And the angels which kept not their first estate, but left their own habitation, he hath reserved in everlasting chains under darkness unto the judgment of the great day.

[Chapter 65]
1 And in those days Noah saw the earth that it had sunk down and its destruction was near.

2 And he arose from there and went to the ends of the earth, and cried aloud to his grandfather, Enoch.

3 And Noah said three times with an embittered voice: "Hear me, hear me, hear me." And I said to him: 'Tell me what it is that is falling out on the earth that the earth is in such evil plight and shaken, lest perchance I shall perish with it?'

4 And there was a great disturbance on the earth, and a voice was heard from heaven, and I fell on my face. And Enoch my grandfather came and stood by me, and said to me: 'Why have you cried to me with a bitter cry and weeping?'

5 A command has gone out from the presence of the Lord concerning those who dwell on the earth that their ruin is accomplished because they have learned all the secrets of the angels, and all the violence of the Satans (deceivers, accusers);

(Author's note: There are many meanings of the word "satan" but all indicate great negativity. It can mean one who opposes, accuses, or deceives. In this case there is some confusion as to who the satans are. We are told the fallen angels taught men to war, but we are also told that it was the children of the angels that were so destructive. We are told that the angels taught men sorcery and spells, but it was the spirits of the nephilim that went out from their bodies to destroy.)

6 And all their powers - the most secret ones - and all the power of those who practice sorcery, and the power of witchcraft, and the power of those who make molten images for the whole earth.

7 And how silver is produced from the dust of the earth, and how soft metal originates in the earth.

8 For lead and tin are not produced from the earth like the first; it is a fountain that produces them;

9 And an angel stands in it, and that angel is preeminent.' And after that my grandfather Enoch took hold of me by my hand and lifted me up, and said to me:

10 'Go, for I have asked the Lord of spirits about this disturbance on the earth. And He said to me: "Because of their unrighteousness their judgment has been determined and shall not be withheld by Me forever. Because of the sorceries which they have searched out and learned, the earth and those who dwell on it shall be destroyed."

(Author's note: Flesh and blood will drown under the waters of the flood. All those who knew the fallen angels and all those who had given birth to their children would be killed, but the angels cannot die and the spirits of the nephilim do not need a body to survive. The text indicates the spirits need no food or water and go about unseen.
)

11 And from these, they have no place of repentance forever, because they have shown them what was hidden, and they are the damned. But as for you, my son, the Lord of spirits knows that you are pure and guiltless of this reproach concerning the secrets.

12 And He has destined your name to be among the holy, and will preserve you among those who dwell on the earth; and has destined your righteous seed both for kingship and for great honors, and from your seed shall proceed a fountain of the righteous and holy without number forever.

[Chapter 66]

1 And after that he showed me the angels of punishment who are prepared to come and let loose all the powers of the waters which are beneath in the earth in order to bring judgment and destruction on all who dwell on the earth.

2 Kings 19:35 And it came to pass that night, that the angel of the LORD went out, and smote in the camp of the Assyrians an hundred fourscore and five thousand: and when they arose early in the morning, behold, they were all dead corpses.

Revelation 14:15-19 And another angel came out of the temple, crying with a loud voice to him that sat on the cloud, Thrust in thy sickle, and reap: for the time is come for thee to reap; for the harvest of the earth is ripe. 16 And he that sat on the cloud thrust in his sickle on the earth; and the earth was reaped. 17 And another angel came out of the temple which is in heaven, he

also having a sharp sickle.
¹⁸ And another angel came out from the altar, which had power over fire; and cried with a loud cry to him that had the sharp sickle, saying, Thrust in thy sharp sickle, and gather the clusters of the vine of the earth; for her grapes are fully ripe.
¹⁹ And the angel thrust in his sickle into the earth, and gathered the vine of the earth, and cast it into the great winepress of the wrath of God.

2 And the Lord of spirits gave commandment to the angels who were going out, that they should not cause the waters to rise but should hold them in check; for those angels were in charge of the forces of the waters.

3 And I went away from the presence of Enoch.

[Chapter 67]

1 And in those days the word of God came to me, and He said to me: 'Noah, your lot has come up before Me, a lot without blame, a lot of love and righteousness.

2 And now the angels are making a wooden structure, and when they have completed that task I will place My hand on it and preserve it (keep it safe), and there shall come out of it the seed of life, and a change shall set in so that the earth will not remain without inhabitants.

3 And I will establish your seed before me forever and ever, and I will spread abroad those who dwell with you; and the face of the earth will be fruitful. They shall be blessed and multiply on the earth in the name of the Lord.'

4 And He will imprison those angels, who have shown unrighteousness, in that burning valley which my grandfather Enoch had formerly shown to me in the west among the mountains of gold and silver and iron and soft metal and tin.

5 And I saw that valley in which there was a great earth quake and a tidal waves of the waters.

6 And when all this took place, from that fiery molten metal and from the convulsion thereof in that place, there was a smell of sulfur produced, and it was connected with those waters, and that valley of the angels who had led mankind astray burned beneath that ground.

7 And there were streams of fire throughout the valley, where these angels are punished who had led astray those who dwell on the earth.

8 But those waters shall in those days serve for the kings and the mighty and the exalted, and those who dwell on the earth, for the healing of the body, but for the punishment of the spirit. Their spirit is full of lust, that they will be punished in their body, for they have denied the Lord of spirits. They will see their punishment daily, and yet, they believe not in His name.

9 There will be a relationship between the punishment and change. As their bodies burn, a change will take place in their spirit forever and ever; for before the Lord of spirits none shall utter an idle word.

10 For the judgment shall come on them, because they believe in the lust of their body and deny the Spirit of the Lord.

1 John 2:16-17 (New International Version) ¹⁶ For everything in the world – the cravings of sinful man, the lust of his eyes and the boasting of what he has and does – comes not from the Father but from the world. ¹⁷ And the world passeth away, and the lust thereof: but he that doeth the will of God abideth forever.

11 And the waters will change in those days; for when those angels are punished in these waters, the springs shall change, and when the angels ascend, this water of the springs shall change their temperature and become cold.

12 And I heard Michael answering and saying: 'This judgment in which the angels are judged is a testimony for the kings and the mighty who possess the earth.'

13 Because these waters of judgment minister to the healing of the body of the kings and the lust of their bodies; therefore they will not see and will not believe that those waters will change and become a fire which burns forever.

[Chapter 68]

1 And after that my grandfather Enoch gave me the explanations of all the secrets in the Book of the Parables which had been given to him, and he put them together for me in the words of the Book of the Parables.

2 And on that day Michael answered Raphael and said: 'The power of the spirit grips me and makes me tremble because of the severity of the judgment of the secrets, and the judgment of the angels. Who can endure the severe judgment which has been executed, and before which they melt away?'

3 And Michael answered again, and said to Raphael: 'Who would not have a softened heart concerning it, and whose mind would not be troubled by this judgment against them because of those who have led them out?'

4 And it came to pass when he stood before the Lord of spirits, Michael said thus to Raphael: 'I will not defend them under the eye of the Lord; for the Lord of spirits has been angry with them because they act as if they were the Lord.

5 Therefore all that is hidden shall come on them forever and ever; for no other angel or man shall have his portion in this judgment, but they alone have received their judgment forever and ever.

Psalm 82
1 God standeth in the congregation of the mighty; he judgeth among the gods.
2 How long will ye judge unjustly, and accept the persons of the wicked? Selah.
3 Defend the poor and fatherless: do justice to the afflicted and needy.
4 Deliver the poor and needy: rid them out of the hand of the wicked.
5 They know not, neither will they understand; they walk on in darkness: all the foundations of the earth are out of course.
6 I have said, Ye are gods; and all of you are children of the most High.
7 But ye shall die like men, and fall like one of the princes.
8 Arise, O God, judge the earth: for thou shalt inherit all nations.

(Author's note: The above Bible verse is in bold because it may play one of the pivotal roles in understanding the connections between the book of Enoch and the Bible.

God stands in the congregation of the mighty; He judgeth among the gods. KJV

Another version reads:
God has taken His place in the divine council. In the midst of the gods He holds judgment. RSV

The Septuagint reads:
God stands in the assembly of gods; and in the midst of them will judge gods. How long will ye judge unrighteous, and accept the persons of sinners?

In verse one we read that God (Elohiym) is standing in the congregation of the mighty; that He ("El" or God) is judging (Shaphat: governing) the gods (elohiym). One way to easily understand this is to look at a supreme God (capital "G") judging and governing a group of "godlings."

In an early study on Psalm 82, J. A. Emerton argued that in the Targum (Aramaic translation of the Old Testament) to the Psalms, as well as in the the Peshitta (Syriac Bible), and according to the Fathers, elohim (gods) in Psalm 82 was understood by all to refer to "angels." Emerton suggests that elohim refers to superhuman beings to whom the nations were allotted, whom the Jews regarded as angels but whom the Gentiles called gods (see 1 Cor 10:20). Jesus quotes the verse in John 10:34-36.

To stand in a court setting and judge indicates there was some transgression. This adds weight to the fact that some angels committed transgressions while others did not. Thus, it is this verse that points to the fall of some angels and the judgment handed down. It also articulates the position of angels as gods. It is assumed the point of view is that of men and not God.

In our mythology we see some "gods" were evil and violent, while other "gods" were kind and gentle. There were giants, Cyclops, monsters, and those, such as Hercules, Achilles who fought alongside men. These could be various angels, but it could point back to the three types of beings coming from the union of angels and women; Giants, Nephilim, and Eljo.

With their great height and six fingers per hand, it has been speculated that Goliath, his mother (the giant of Gath), and their family were descendants of the angel-woman union. We have also speculated that the Eljo could be the "men of renown" mentioned in Genesis.

Genesis 6:4 There were giants in the earth in those days; and also after that, when the sons of God came in unto the daughters of men, and they bare children to them, the same became mighty men which were of old, men of renown.

The term, "eljo or elyo" indicates a type of godlike being. The term indicates these were humanoids with special powers or abilities, to the extent they would be remembered and placed in mythic stories so that they should not be forgotten. This leaves the Nephilim, which could be the monsters such as Cyclops, Medusa, and other creatures memorialized in mythology.

It is not suggested that these stories are totally accurate, but only that they indicate the existence of some vastly unusual being with powers or abilities that spawned stories of monsters. Together these three types of angelic offspring make up the corpus of mythology, containing gods, giants, and monsters.)

To add additional fuel to the fire of controversy over Psalm 82, Jesus quotes the verse in John 10:34-35.

John 10:31 (New International Version) Again the Jews picked up stones to stone him, 32 but Jesus said to them, "I have shown you many great miracles from the Father. For which of these do you stone me?"33 "We are not stoning you for any of these," replied the Jews, "but for blasphemy, because you, a mere man, claim to be God." 34 Jesus answered them, "Is it not written in your Law, 'I have said you are gods'? 35 If he called them 'gods,' to whom the word of God came — and the Scripture cannot be broken —

Does the word of God, if we accept and understand it, makes us gods? What power or authority does the knowledge, secrets, and words brought to us from heaven by fallen angels give us?

[Chapter 69]
1 And after this judgment I will terrify and make them tremble because they have shown this to those who dwell on the earth.

2 And behold the names of those angels: the first of them is Samjaza; the second Artaqifa; and the third Armen, the fourth Kokabe, the fifth Turael; the sixth Rumjal; the seventh Danjal; the eighth Neqael; the ninth Baraqel; the tenth Azazel; the eleventh Armaros; the twelfth Batarjal; the thirteenth Busasejal; the fourteenth Hananel; the fifteenth Turel; and the sixteenth Simapesiel; the seventeenth Jetrel; the eighteenth Tumael; the nineteenth Turel; the twentieth Rumael; the twenty-first Azazyel;

(Author's note: For more information on the heavenly names, such as the various names of the "Presence of the Lord," see the Third Book of Enoch, also called the "Hebrew Book of Enoch" or "3 Enoch."

The leader of the Watchers was Samjaza, also spelled Shemhazai. Two hundred angels made the descent to earth, at Mount Hermon. Two hundred angels were divided into group of ten, each under the leadership of chieftain or captain.

They defiled themselves with women, producing children. Their children were giants of three-thousand ells tall, which some sources say is approximately 3,420 meters in height (11,250 feet tall).

According to the Haggada (book 1, chapter 4: Punishment of the Fallen Angels), the angel Shemhazai lusted after a maiden named Istehar, however, she tricked him to reveal the Ineffable Name of God. Istehar used the name to ascend to heaven and escaped her violation by Shemhazai. God rewarded Istehar for her by commemorating her as the seven-star constellation Pleides.

In Genesis 4:22, Naamah was a daughter of Lamech and Zillah, and sister of Tubal-Cain. She was a descendant of Cain, hence a Cainite. According to the Haggada, Naamah was the opposite of Istehar, because the angel Shamdon had succeeded in sexual union with Naamah. Naamah's offspring was Asmodeus, a demon, instead of a giant. Asmodeus appeared in the apocrypha Tobit.

According to the introduction of the Zohar, it was Naamah who first deceived and seduced the angels, rather than the angel seducing Naamah. Zohar 3 mentioned the angels Aza and Azael, instead of Shamdon; they were victims of her beauty. She became mother of an unknown number of demons.

Our vampire lore may have begun with the 1 Enoch, since it states the giants consumed all the food men could produce and then began devouring people and sucking their blood, like vampires.)

3 And these are the chiefs of their angels and their names, and their leaders over hundreds, and leaders over fifties, and leaders over tens.

4 The name of the first Jeqon, that is, the one who led astray the sons of God, and brought them down to the earth, and led them astray through the daughters of men.

5 And the second was named Asbeel; he imparted to the holy sons of God evil counsel, and led them astray so that they defiled their bodies with the daughters of men.

6 And the third was named Gadreel; it is he who showed the children of men all the blows of death, and he led astray Eve, and showed the weapons of death to the sons of men; the shield and the coat of mail, and the sword for battle, and all the weapons of death to the children of men.

7 And from his hand they have proceeded against those who dwell on the earth from that day and forevermore.

8 And the fourth was named Penemue; he taught the children of men the bitter and the sweet, and he taught them all the secrets of their wisdom.

9 And he instructed mankind in writing with ink and paper, and thereby many sinned from eternity to eternity and until this day.

10 For men were not created for the purpose of confirming their good faith with pen and ink.

(Author's note: Reading and writing are considered grievous sins because they allow knowledge, and thus sin, to be propagated from generation to generation. It should be pointed out that God himself wrote the Ten Commandments on stone. It is possible that this verse may refer to the Enochian alphabet, thought to convey the original teachings of the fallen angels.

The Enochian alphabet was thought to be lost with the flood, but "re-discovered" by John Dee.

John Dee (13 July 1527–1608 or 1609) was a noted mathematician, astrologer, navigator, occultist, and a consultant to Queen Elizabeth I. According to Tobias Churton in his book *The Golden Builders*, the concept of an Angelic or pre-deluge language was common during Dee's time. If one could speak with angels, it was believed one could directly interact with them.

In 1581, Dee mentioned in his personal journals that God had sent "good angels" to communicate directly with prophets. In 1582, Dee teamed up with the seer Edward Kelley, although Dee had used several other seers previously. With Kelley's help as a scryer, Dee set out to establish lasting contact with the angels, which resulted, among other things, in the reception of the Enochian or Angelical language.

According to Dee's journals, Angelical was supposed to have been the language God used to create the world, and which was later used by Adam to speak with God and the angels, and to name all things into existence.

The alphabet codified the phonetics of the language Dee claimed could be used to summon various angels, who would dispatch knowledge or assistance. The chants used complex phonetic streams named "Angelic Calls" to name and call forth angels.

Table of Enochian Letters, Print, and Script

11 For men were created exactly like the angels, to the intent that they should continue pure and righteous; and death, which destroys everything, should not have taken hold of them, but through this their knowledge they are perishing, and through this power consumes them.

Romans 5:12 (King James Version) Wherefore, as by one man sin entered into the world, and death by sin; and so death passed upon all men, for that all have sinned:

12 And the fifth was named Kasdeja; this is he who showed the children of men all the wicked smitings (blows) of spirits and demons, and the smitings (blows) of the embryo in the womb, that it may pass away, and the smitings (blows) of the soul, the bites of the serpent, and the smitings (blows) which befall through the midday heat, the son of the serpent named Taba'et.

13 And this is the task of Kasbeel, the chief of the oath which he showed to the holy ones when he dwelt high above in glory, and its name is Biqa.

14 This (angel) requested Michael to show him the hidden name, that he might enunciate it in the oath,

15 So that those might quake before that name and oath who revealed all that was in secret to the children of men. And this is the power of this oath, for it is powerful and strong, and he placed this oath Akae in the hand of (under the control of) Michael.

(Author's note: The ineffable name of God holds the power to create, bind, and destroy. In the Lillith myth, it is said she spoke this name when she argued against God and Adam. By speaking the name she flew off and became a demon.)

16 And these are the secrets of this oath (God's promise, word) that heaven was suspended before the world was created, and forever, and they are strong through his oath (word, promise).

17 And through it the earth was founded on the water, and from the secret recesses of the mountains come beautiful waters, from the creation of the world and to eternity.

18 And through that oath the sea was created, and as its foundation He set for it the sand against the time of its anger (rage) that it dare not pass beyond it from the creation of the world to eternity.

19 And through that oath are the depths made fast (strong), and abide and stir not from their place from eternity to eternity.

20 And through that oath the sun and moon complete their course, and deviate not from their ordinance from eternity to eternity.

21 And through that oath the stars complete their course, and He calls them by their names, and they answer Him from eternity to eternity.

22 [And in like manner the spirits of the water, and of the winds, and of all kinds of spirits, and (their) paths from all the quarters of the winds respond to His command.]

(Author's note: Verse 22 is not complete in some translations.)

23 And there are preserved the voices of the thunder and the light of the lightning: and there are preserved the storehouses of the hail and the storehouses of the hoarfrost,

24 And the storehouses of the mist, and the storehouses of the rain and the dew. And all these believe and give thanks before the Lord of spirits, and glorify (Him) with all their power, and their food is in every act of thanksgiving; they thank and glorify and exalt the name of the Lord of spirits forever and ever.

25 And this oath is mighty over them and through it they are preserved and their paths are preserved, and their course is not destroyed.

26 And there was great joy among them, and they blessed and glorified and exalted because the name of that Son of Man had been revealed to them.

(Author's note: The name of a person reveals their personality and power. There remains a ceremony to this day that if a person is on his deathbed a rabbi may change the person's name to trick the Angel of Death so the person might escape his reaping, suggesting the Angel seeks by name.)

27 And he sat on the throne of his glory, and the sum of judgment was given to the Son of Man. And he caused the sinners and all those who led the world astray to pass away and be destroyed from off the face of the earth.

28 They shall be bound with chains, and shut up and imprisoned in their place of assembly, and all their works vanish from the face of the earth.

29 And from that time forward, there shall be nothing corruptible; for that Son of Man has appeared, and has seated himself on the throne of his glory. And all evil shall pass away before his face, and the word of that Son of Man shall go out and be strong before the Lord of spirits.

[Chapter 70]

1 And it came to pass after this that during His lifetime His name was raised up to the Son of Man, and to the Lord of spirits from among those who dwell on the earth.

2 And He was raised aloft on the chariots of the spirit and His name vanished among them. And from that day I was no longer numbered among them; and He placed me between the two winds, between the North and the West, where the angels took the cords to measure the place for the elect and righteous for me.

3 And there I saw the first fathers and the righteous who dwell in that place from the beginning.

[Chapter 71]

1 And it came to pass after this that my spirit was translated (carried off) and it ascended into heaven; and I saw the sons of the holy angels (sons) of God. They were walking on flames of fire; their garments were white, and their faces shone like snow.

2 And I saw two rivers of fire, and the light of that fire shone like hyacinth, and I fell on my face before the Lord of spirits.

3 And the angel Michael, one of the archangels, seized me by my right hand, and lifted me up and led me out into all the secrets, and he showed me all the secrets of righteousness.

4 And he showed me all the secrets of the ends of heaven, and all the storehouses of all the stars, and all the lights, from where they proceed before the face of the holy ones.

5 And he translated (carried) my spirit into heaven of heavens, and I saw there as it were built of crystals, and between those crystals tongues of living fire.

Revelation 21:10-11 And he carried me away in the spirit to a great and high mountain, and shewed me that great city, the holy Jerusalem, descending out of heaven from God, 11 Having the glory of God: and her light was like unto a stone most precious, even like a jasper stone, clear as crystal.

6 My spirit saw circle of fire binding around the house of fire, and on its four sides were rivers full of living fire, and they encircled that house.

7 And round about were seraphim, cherubim, and ophannim; and these are they who never sleep and they guard the throne of His glory.

8 And I saw angels who could not be counted, a thousand thousands, and ten thousand times ten thousand,

encircling that house. And Michael, and Raphael, and Gabriel, and Phanuel, and the holy angels who are in heaven above, go in and out of that house.

9 And they came out from that house, and Michael and Gabriel, Raphael and Phanuel, and many holy angels without number.

10 And with them the Head of Days, His head white and pure as wool, and His raiment indescribable.

11 And I fell on my face, and my whole body melted, and my spirit was (transformed) transfigured. And I cried with a loud voice in the spirit of power, and I blessed and glorified and exalted.

Psalm 22:14-15 I am poured out like water, and all my bones are out of joint: my heart is like wax; it is melted in the midst of my bowels.
15 My strength is dried up like a potsherd; and my tongue cleaveth to my jaws; and thou hast brought me into the dust of death.

12 And these blessings which came from my mouth were very pleasing before that Head of Days.

13 And the Head of Days came with Michael and Gabriel, Raphael and Phanuel, and thousands and ten thousands of angels without number.

14 And the angel came to me and greeted me with his voice, and said to me 'This is the Son of Man who is born to righteousness, and righteousness abides over him, and the righteousness of the Head of Days forsakes him not.'

15 And he said to me: 'He proclaims to you peace in the name of the world to come; for from there peace has proceeded since the creation of the world, and it shall be with you forever and forever and ever.

John 17:24 Father, I will that they also, whom thou hast given me, be with me where I am; that they may behold my glory, which thou hast given me: for thou lovest me before the foundation of the world.

16 And all shall walk in His ways since righteousness never forsook Him. Their dwelling-place shall be with Him and it will be their heritage, and they shall not be separated from Him forever and ever and ever.

17 And so there shall be length of days with the Son of Man, and the righteous shall have peace and an upright way in the name of the Lord of spirits forever and ever.'

Hebrews 4:3 For we which have believed do enter into rest, as he said, As I have sworn in my wrath, if they shall enter into my rest: although the works were finished from the foundation of the world.

[Chapter 72]
The Book of *Astronomy and Calendar* (Chapters 72-82):
(Author's note: Full description of the calendar and its application in prophecy are discussed in the section, "The Calendar of Enoch's and Daniel's Prophecies, starting on page 158.)

1 The book of the courses of the luminaries of heaven, the relations of each, according to their name, origin, and months (dominion and seasons) which Uriel, the holy angel who was with me, who is their guide, showed me; and he showed me all their laws (regulations) exactly as they are, and how it is with each of the years of the world and to eternity, until the new creation is accomplished which endures until eternity.

2 And this is the first law of the luminaries: the luminary the Sun has its rising in the eastern doors of heaven, and its setting in the western doors of heaven.

3 And I saw six doors in which the sun rises, and six doors in which the sun sets and the moon rises and sets

in these doors, and the leaders of the stars and those whom they lead: six in the east and six in the west, and all following each other in accurately corresponding order.

4 There were also many windows to the right and left of these doors. And first there goes out the great luminary, named the Sun, and his sphere (orbit, disc) is like the sphere (orbit, disc) of heaven, and he is quite filled with illuminating and heating fire.

5 The chariot on which he ascends, the wind drives, and the sun goes down from heaven and returns through the north in order to reach the east, and is so guided that he comes to the appropriate door and shines in the face of heaven.

6 In this way he rises in the first month in the great door, which is the fourth.

7 And in that fourth door from which the sun rises in the first month are twelve windows, from which proceed a flame when they are opened in their season.

8 When the sun rises in heaven, he comes out through that fourth door, thirty mornings in succession, and sets accurately in the fourth door in the west of the heaven.

9 And during this period the day becomes daily longer and nights grow shorter to the thirtieth morning.

10 On that day the day is longer than the night by a ninth part, and the day amounts exactly to ten parts and the night to eight parts.

11 And the sun rises from that fourth door, and sets in the fourth and returns to the fifth door of the east thirty mornings, and rises from it and sets in the fifth door.

12 And then the day becomes longer by two parts and amounts to eleven parts, and the night becomes shorter and amounts to seven parts.

13 And it returns to the east and enters into the sixth door, and rises and sets in the sixth door one-and-thirty mornings on account of its sign.

14 On that day the day becomes longer than the night, and the day becomes double the night, and the day becomes twelve parts, and the night is shortened and becomes six parts.

15 And the sun mounts up to make the day shorter and the night longer, and the sun returns to the east and enters into the sixth door, and rises from it and sets thirty mornings.

16 And when thirty mornings are accomplished, the day decreases by exactly one part, and becomes eleven parts, and the night seven.

17 And the sun goes out from that sixth door in the west, and goes to the east and rises in the fifth door for thirty mornings, and sets in the west again in the fifth western door.

18 On that day the day decreases by two parts, and amounts to ten parts and the night to eight parts.

19 And the sun goes out from that fifth door and sets in the fifth door of the west, and rises in the fourth door for one-and-thirty mornings on account of its sign, and sets in the west.

20 On that day the day becomes equal with the night in length, and the night amounts to nine parts and the day to nine parts.

21 And the sun rises from that door and sets in the west, and returns to the east and rises thirty mornings in

the third door and sets in the west in the third door.

22 And on that day the night becomes longer than the day, and night becomes longer than night, and day shorter than day until the thirtieth morning, and the night amounts exactly to ten parts and the day to eight parts.

23 And the sun rises from that third door and sets in the third door in the west and returns to the east, and for thirty mornings rises in the second door in the east, and in like manner sets in the second door in the west of heaven.

24 And on that day the night amounts to eleven parts and the day to seven parts.

25 And the sun rises on that day from that second door and sets in the west in the second door, and returns to the east into the first door for one-and-thirty mornings, and sets in the first door in the west of heaven.

26 And on that day the night becomes longer and amounts to the double of the day: and the night amounts exactly to twelve parts and the day to six.

(Author's note: If the night is 12 parts and the day is six parts, the entire 24 hour day is divided into 18 sections of 80 minutes each.)

27 And the sun has traversed the divisions of his orbit and turns again on those divisions of his orbit, and enters that door thirty mornings and sets also in the west opposite to it.

28 And on that night has the night decreased in length by a ninth part, and the night has become eleven parts and the day seven parts.

29 And the sun has returned and entered into the second door in the east, and returns on those his divisions of his orbit for thirty mornings, rising and setting.

30 And on that day the night decreases in length, and the night amounts to ten parts and the day to eight.

31 And on that day the sun rises from that door, and sets in the west, and returns to the east, and rises in the third door for one-and-thirty mornings, and sets in the west of heaven.

32 On that day the night decreases and amounts to nine parts, and the day to nine parts, and the night is equal to the day and the year is exactly as to its days three hundred and sixty-four.

33 And the length of the day and of the night, and the shortness of the day and of the night arise through the course of the sun these distinctions are separated'.

34 So it comes that its course becomes daily longer, and its course nightly shorter.

35 And this is the law and the course of the great luminary which is named the sun, and his return as often as he returns sixty times and rises, forever and ever.

36 And that which rises is the great luminary, and is so named according to its appearance, according as the Lord commanded.

37 As he rises, so he sets and decreases not, and rests not, but runs day and night, and his light is sevenfold brighter than that of the moon; but in regard to size, they are both equal.

[Chapter 73]
1 And after this law I saw another law dealing with the smaller luminary, which is named the Moon.

2 And her orbit is like the sphere (orbit, disc) of heaven, and her chariot in which she rides is driven by the wind, and light is given to her in measurement.

3 And her rising and setting change every month and her days are like the days of the sun, and when her light is uniformly (completely) full it amounts to the seventh part of the light of the sun.

4 And thus she rises. And her first phase in the east comes out on the thirtieth morning and on that day she becomes visible, and constitutes for you the first phase of the moon on the thirtieth day together with the sun in the door where the sun rises.

5 And the one half of her goes out by a seventh part, and her whole disc is empty, without light, with the exception of one-seventh part of it, and the fourteenth part of her light.

6 And when she receives one-seventh part of the half of her light, her light amounts to one-seventh part and the half thereof.

7 And she sets with the sun, and when the sun rises the moon rises with him and receives the half of one part of light, and in that night in the beginning of her morning in the beginning of the lunar day the moon sets with the sun, and is invisible that night with the fourteen parts and the half of one of them.

8 And she rises on that day with exactly a seventh part, and comes out and recedes from the rising of the sun, and in her remaining days she becomes bright in the remaining thirteen parts.

[Chapter 74]

1 And I saw another course, a law for her, and how according to that law she performs her monthly revolution.

2 And all these Uriel, the holy angel who is the leader of them all, showed to me, and their positions, and I wrote down their positions as he showed them to me, and I wrote down their months as they were, and the appearance of their lights until fifteen days were accomplished.

3 In single seventh parts she accomplishes all her light in the east, and in single seventh parts accomplishes all her darkness in the west.

4 And in certain months she alters her settings, and in certain months she pursues her own peculiar course.

5 In two months the moon sets with the sun: in those two middle doors the third and the fourth.

6 She goes out for seven days, and turns about and returns again through the door where the sun rises, and all her light is full; and she recedes from the sun, and in eight days enters the sixth door from which the sun goes out.

7 And when the sun goes out from the fourth door she goes out seven days, until she goes out from the fifth and turns back again in seven days into the fourth door and accomplishes all her light; and she recedes and enters into the first door in eight days.

8 And she returns again in seven days into the fourth door from which the sun goes out.

9 Thus I saw their positions, how the moons rose and the sun set in those days.

10 And if five years are added together the sun has an excess of thirty days, and all the days which accrue to it for one of those five years, when they are full, amount to 364 days.

11 And an excess of the sun and of the stars amounts to six days; in five years six days every year come to 30

days, and the moon falls behind the sun and stars to the number of 30 days.

12 And the sun and the stars bring in all the years exactly, so that they do not advance or delay their position by a single day to eternity; but complete the years with perfect justice in 364 days.

13 In three years there are 1,092 days, and in five years 1,820 days, so that in eight years there are 2,912 days.

(Author's note: At the end of five years a week may be added to bring the year back in line. Compare 1826.25 days of the solar year in five years to 1820 days of the Enochian calendar after five years. This leaves 6.25 days difference. Adding a week to the Enochian calendar leaves a difference of only .75 of a day. The years is adjusted in this way so that the alignment is kept very close.)

14 For the moon alone the days amount in three years to 1,062 days, and in five years she falls 50 days behind to the sum of 1,770 there is five to be added 1,000 and 62 days.

15 And in five years there are 1,770 days, so that for the moon the days six in eight years amount to 21,832 days.

16 For in eight years she falls behind to the amount of 80 days, all the days she falls behind in eight years are 80.

17 And the year is accurately completed in conformity with their world-stations and the stations of the sun, which rise from the doors through which the sun rises and sets 30 days.

[Chapter 75]

1 And the leaders of the heads of the (ten) thousands, who are in charge of the whole creation and over all the stars, have also to do with the four days of the year which are not counted in the yearly calendar, being not separated from their office, according to the reckoning of the year, and these render service on the four days which are not counted in the reckoning of the year.

2 And because of them men go wrong in them, for those luminaries truly render service to the stations of the world, one in the first door, one on the third door of heaven, one in the fourth door, and one in the sixth door, and the exactness of the year is accomplished through its separate three hundred and sixty-four stations.

3 For the signs and the times and the years and the days the angel Uriel showed to me, whom the Lord of glory hath set forever over all the luminaries of heaven, in heaven and in the world, that they should rule on the face of heaven and be seen on the earth, and be leaders for the day via the sun and the night via the moon, and stars, and all the ministering creatures which make their revolution in all the chariots of heaven.

4 In like manner, twelve doors Uriel showed me, open in the sphere (disc) of the sun's chariot in heaven, through which the rays of the sun break out; and from them is warmth diffused over the earth, when they are opened at their appointed seasons.

5 And there are openings for the wind and the spirit of dew that when they are opened, stand open in heaven at the ends of the earth.

6 As for the twelve doors in the heaven, at the ends of the earth, out of which go out the sun, moon, and stars, and all the works of heaven in the east and in the west; there are many windows open to the left and right of them,

7 And one window at its appointed season produces warmth, corresponding to the doors from which the stars come out as He has commanded them; and in which they are set, corresponding to their number.

8 And I saw chariots in heaven, running in the world, above those doors in which the stars that never set.

9 And one is larger than all the rest, and it is that that makes its course through the entire world.

[Chapter 76]

1 At the ends of the earth I saw twelve doors open to all quarters of heaven, from which the winds go out and blow over the earth.

2 Three of them are open on the face of heaven, and three in the west; and three on the right of heaven, and three on the left.

3 And the three first are those of the east, and three are of the north, and three, after those on the left, of the south, and three of the west.

4 Through four of these come winds of blessing and prosperity (peace), and from those eight come hurtful winds; when they are sent, they bring destruction on all the earth and the water on it, and on all who dwell on it, and on everything which is in the water and on the land.

5 And the first wind from those doors, called the east wind, comes out through the first door which is in the east, inclining towards the south; from it desolation, drought, heat, and destruction come out .

6 And through the second door in the middle comes what is fitting (right, correct), and there come rain and fruitfulness and prosperity and dew. And through the third door which lies toward the north comes cold and drought.

7 And after these, comes out the south winds through three doors; through the first door of them inclining to the east comes out a hot wind.

8 And through the middle door next to it there comes out fragrant smells, and dew and rain, and prosperity and health.

9 And through the third door which lies to the west dew comes out and also rain, locusts and desolation.

10 And from the seventh door in the east comes the north winds, and dew, rain, locusts and desolation.

11 And from the center door come health and rain and dew and prosperity; and through the third door in the west come cloud and hoar-frost, and snow and rain, and dew and locusts.

12 And after these came the four west winds; through the first door adjoining the north come out dew and hoar-frost, and cold and snow and frost.

13 And from the center door come out dew and rain, and prosperity and blessing.

14 And through the last door which adjoins the south, come drought and desolation, and burning and destruction. And the twelve doors of the four quarters of heaven are therewith completed, and all their laws and all their plagues and all their benefactions have I shown to you, my son Methuselah.

[Chapter 77]

1 And the first quarter is called the east, because it is the first; and the second, the south, because the Most High will descend there. From there will He who is blessed forever descend.

2 And the west quarter is named the diminished, because there all the luminaries of the heaven wane and go down.

3 And the fourth quarter, named the north, is divided into three parts: the first of them is for the dwelling of

men; and the second contains seas of water, and the abyss (deep) and forests and rivers, and darkness and clouds; and the third part contains the garden of righteousness.

4 I saw seven high mountains, higher than all the mountains which are on the earth: and from here comes hoar-frost, and days, seasons, and years pass away.

5 I saw seven rivers on the earth larger than all the rivers. One of them coming from the west pours its waters into the Great Sea.

6 And these two come from the north to the sea and pour their waters into the Erythraean Sea in the east.

7 And the remaining four come out on the side of the north to their own sea, two of them to the Erythraean Sea, and two into the Great Sea and some say they discharge themselves there into the desert.

8 I saw seven great islands in the sea and in the mainland, two in the mainland and five in the Great Sea.

[Chapter 78]

1 And the names of the sun are the following: the first Orjares, and the second Tomas.

2 And the moon has four names: the first name is Asonja, the second Ebla, the third Benase, and the fourth Erae.

3 These are the two great luminaries; their spheres (disc) are like the sphere (disc) of the heaven, and the size of the spheres (disc) of both is alike.

4 In the sphere (disc) of the sun there are seven portions of light which are added to it more than to the moon, and in fixed measurements it is transferred until the seventh portion of the sun is exhausted.

5 And they set and enter the doors of the west, and make their revolution by the north, and come out through the eastern doors on the face of heaven.

6 And when the moon rises one-fourteenth part appears in heaven, and on the fourteenth day the moon's light becomes full.

7 And fifteen parts of light are transferred to her until the fifteenth day when her light is full, according to the sign of the year, and she becomes fifteen parts, and the moon grows by an additional fourteenth parts.

8 And as the moon's waning decreases on the first day to fourteen parts of her light, on the second to thirteen parts of light, on the third to twelve, on the fourth to eleven, on the fifth to ten, on the sixth to nine, on the seventh to eight, on the eighth to seven, on the ninth to six, on the tenth to five, on the eleventh to four, on the twelfth to three, on the thirteenth to two, on the fourteenth to the half of a seventh, and all her remaining light disappears wholly on the fifteenth.

9 And in certain months the month has twenty-nine days and once twenty-eight.

10 And Uriel showed me another law: when light is transferred to the moon, and on which side it is transferred to her by the sun.

11 During all the period during which the moon is growing in her light, she is transferring it to herself when opposite to the sun during fourteen days her light is full in heaven, and when she is ablaze throughout, her light is full in heaven.

12 And on the first day she is called the new moon, for on that day the light rises on her.

13 She becomes the full moon exactly on the day when the sun sets in the west, and from the east she rises at night, and the moon shines the whole night through until the sun rises over against her and the moon is seen over against the sun.

14 On the side whence the light of the moon comes out, there again she wanes until all the light vanishes and all the days of the month are at an end, and her sphere (disc) is empty, void of light.

15 And three months she makes of thirty days, and at her time she makes three months of twenty-nine days each, in which she accomplishes her waning in the first period of time, and in the first door for one hundred and seventy-seven days.

16 And in the time of her going out she appears for three months consisting of thirty days each, and she appears for three months consisting of twenty-nine each.

17 By night she looks like a man for twenty days each time, and by day she appears like heaven, and there is nothing else in her save her light.

[Chapter 79]

1 And now, my son Methuselah, I have shown you everything, and the law of all the stars of heaven is completed.

2 And he showed me all the laws of these for every day, and for every season of every rule, and for every year, and for its going out, and for the order prescribed to it every month and every week.

3 And the waning of the moon which takes place in the sixth door, for in this sixth door her light is accomplished, and after that there is the beginning of the waning.

4 And the waning which takes place in the first door in its season, until one hundred and seventy-seven days are accomplished, calculated according to weeks, twenty-five weeks and two days.

5 She falls behind the sun and the order of the stars exactly five days in the course of one period, and when this place which you see has been traversed.

6 Such is the picture and sketch of every luminary which Uriel the archangel, who is their leader, showed to me.

(Author's note: For more information on the storehouses of heaven, the starts, gates, and luminaries, see 2 Enoch.)

[Chapter 80]

1 And in those days the angel Uriel answered and said to me: 'Behold, I have shown you everything, Enoch, and I have revealed everything to you that you should see this sun and this moon, and the leaders of the stars of heaven and all those who turn them, their tasks and times and departures.

2 And in the days of the sinners the years shall be shortened, and their seed shall be tardy on their lands and fields, and all things on the earth shall alter, and shall not appear in their time. And the rain shall be kept back, and heaven shall withhold it.

3 And in those times the fruits of the earth shall be backward, and shall not grow in their time, and the fruits of the trees shall be withheld in their time.

4 And the moon shall alter her customs, and not appear at her time.

5 And in those days the sun shall be seen and he shall journey in the evening on the extremity of the great chariot in the west and shall shine more brightly than accords with the order of light.

6 And many rulers of the stars shall transgress their customary order. And these shall alter their orbits and tasks, and not appear at the seasons prescribed to them.

7 And the whole order of the stars shall be concealed from the sinners, and the thoughts of those on the earth shall err concerning them, and they shall be altered from all their ways, they shall err and take them to be gods.

Romans 1:18-27 The wrath of God is being revealed from heaven against all the godlessness and wickedness of men who suppress the truth by their wickedness, ¹⁹ since what may be known about God is plain to them, because God has made it plain to them. ²⁰ For since the creation of the world God's invisible qualities – his eternal power and divine nature – have been clearly seen, being understood from what has been made, so that men are without excuse.
²¹ For although they knew God, they neither glorified him as God nor gave thanks to him, but their thinking became futile and their foolish hearts were darkened. ²² Although they claimed to be wise, they became fools ²³ and exchanged the glory of the immortal God for images made to look like mortal man and birds and animals and reptiles.
²⁴ Therefore God gave them over in the sinful desires of their hearts to sexual impurity for the degrading of their bodies with one another. ²⁵ They exchanged the truth of God for a lie, and worshiped and served created things rather than the Creator – who is forever praised. Amen.
²⁶ Because of this, God gave them over to shameful lusts. Even their women exchanged natural relations for unnatural ones. ²⁷ In the same way the men also abandoned natural relations with women and were inflamed with lust for one another. Men committed indecent acts with other men, and received in themselves the due penalty for their perversion.

(Author's note: Recall that many people of the time believed the stars to be angels. They worshipped the stars, believing them to have power to control fate. The scripture above tells us that God was angry because men had taken to the worship of the things God created and had forsaken the worship of Him who created those things. As an added note, we are told in other ancient texts that angels had begun taking men as lovers as well as females. Angels are always considered males in these texts.)

8 And evil shall be multiplied on them, and punishment shall come on them so as to destroy all.'

[Chapter 81]

1 And he said to me: 'Enoch, look at these heavenly tablets and read what is written on them, and mark every individual fact.'

2 And I looked at the heavenly tablets, and read everything which was written on it and understood everything, and read the book of all the deeds of mankind, and of all the children of flesh; that shall be on the earth to the end of generations.

3 And I blessed the great Lord the King of glory forever, in that He has made all the works of the world, and I exalted the Lord because of His patience, and blessed Him because of the children of men (sons of Abraham).

4 And then I said: 'Blessed is the man who dies in righteousness and goodness, concerning whom there is no book of unrighteousness written, and against whom no day of judgment shall be found.'

5 And the seven holy ones brought me and placed me on the earth before the door of my house, and said to me: 'Declare everything to your son Methuselah, and show to all your children that no flesh is righteous in the sight of the Lord, for He is their Creator.

6 For one year we will leave you with your son, until you give your last commands, that you may teach your children and record it for them, and testify to all your children; and in the second year they shall take you from their midst.

7 Let your heart be strong, for the good shall proclaim righteousness to the good; the righteous shall rejoice with the righteous, and shall wish one another well.

8 But the sinners shall die with the sinners, and the apostate shall go down with the apostate.

9 And those who practice righteousness shall die on account of the deeds of men, and be taken away on account of the deeds of the godless.'

10 And in those days they finished speaking to me, and I came to my people, blessing the Lord of the world.

[Chapter 82]

1 And now, my son Methuselah, all these things I am recounting to you and writing down for you! And I have revealed to you everything, and given you books concerning all these; so, my son Methuselah, preserve the books from your father's hand, and see that you deliver them to the generations of the world.

2 I have given wisdom to you and to your children, and those children to come, that they may give it to their children for generations. This wisdom namely that passes their understanding.

3 And those who understand it shall not sleep, but shall listen that they may learn this wisdom, and it shall please those that eat thereof better than good food.

4 Blessed are all the righteous, blessed are all those who walk in the way of righteousness and sin not as the sinners, in the numbering of all their days in which the sun traverses heaven, entering into and departing from the doors for thirty days with the heads of thousands of the order of the stars, together with the four which are within the calendar which divide the four portions of the year, which lead them and enter with them four days.

(Author's note: It is verse 4 that leads some to believe the week should begin on a Wednesday, the fourth day of the week.. The verse is unclear and seems to point more to the fact that there are four seasons and the divisions of time were created on the fourth day. All Hebrew calendars had the same week and began on Sunday, the first day of the week, no matter what the name of the day was at that time in that tongue.)

Genesis 1:14-19 And God said, "Let there be lights in the expanse of the sky to separate the day from the night, and let them serve as signs to mark seasons and days and years, 15 and let them be lights in the expanse of the sky to give light on the earth." And it was so. 16 God made two great lights — the greater light to govern the day and the lesser light to govern the night. He also made the stars. 17 God set them in the expanse of the sky to give light on the earth, 18 to govern the day and the night, and to separate light from darkness. And God saw that it was good. 19 And there was evening, and there was morning — the fourth day.

5 Owing to them men shall be at fault and not count them in the whole number of days of the year. Men shall be at fault, and not recognize them accurately.

6 For they belong to the calculations of the year and are truly recorded therein forever, one in the first door and one in the third, and one in the fourth and one in the sixth, and the year is completed in three hundred and sixty-four days.

7 And the account of it is accurate and the recorded counting thereof is exact; for the luminaries, and months and festivals, and years and days, has Uriel shown and revealed to me, to whom the Lord of the whole creation of the world hath subjected the host of heaven.

8 And he has power over night and day in heaven to cause the light to shine on men via the sun, moon, and stars, and all the powers of the heaven which revolve in their circular chariots. And these are the orders of the stars, which set in their places, and in their seasons and festivals and months.

9 And these are the names of those who lead them, who watch that they enter at their times, in their orders, in their seasons, in their months, in their periods of dominion, and in their positions.

10 Their four leaders who divide the four parts of the year enter first; and after them the twelve leaders of the orders who divide the months; and for the three hundred and sixty days there are heads over thousands who divide the days; and for the four days in the calendar there are the leaders which divide the four parts of the year.

11 And these heads over thousands are interspersed between leader and leader, each behind a station, but their leaders make the division.

12 And these are the names of the leaders who divide the four parts of the year which are ordained:

13 Milki'el, Hel'emmelek, and Mel'ejal, and Narel. And the names of those who lead them: Adnar'el, and Ijasusa'el, and 'Elome'el.

14 These three follow the leaders of the orders, and there is one that follows the three leaders of the orders which follow those leaders of stations that divide the four parts of the year. In the beginning of the year Melkejal rises first and rules, who is named Tam'aini and sun, and all the days of his dominion while he bears rule are ninety-one days.

15 And these are the signs of the days which are to be seen on earth in the days of his dominion: sweat, and heat; and calms; and all the trees bear fruit, and leaves are produced on all the trees, and the harvest of wheat, and the rose-flowers, and all the flowers which come out in the field, but the trees of the winter season become withered.

16 And these are the names of the leaders which are under them: Berka'el, Zelebs'el, and another who is added a head of a thousand, called Hilujaseph: and the days of the dominion of this leader are at an end.

17 The next leader after him is Hel'emmelek, whom one names the shining sun, and all the days of his light are ninety-one days.

18 And these are the signs of his days on the earth: glowing heat and dryness, and the trees ripen their fruits and produce all their fruits ripe and ready, and the sheep pair and become pregnant, and all the fruits of the earth are gathered in, and everything that is in the fields, and the winepress: these things take place in the days of his dominion.

19 These are the names, and the orders, and the leaders of those heads of thousands: Gida'ljal, Ke'el, and He'el, and the name of the head of a thousand which is added to them, Asfa'el: and the days of his dominion are at an end.

(Author's note: The seasons are 91 days each. There are four seasons. The years is 91 x 4 or 364 days. We are warned to calculate the years correctly in order to celebrate the holy days on the days they were meant to be honored. Descriptions of the seasons are given along with the angels who control them.)

[Chapter 83]
The *Book of Visions* (Chapters 83-90):

1 And now, my son Methuselah, I will show you all my visions which I have seen, recounting them before you.

2 I saw two visions before I got married (took a wife), and the one was quite unlike the other: the first when I was learning to write: the second before I married (took) your mother, was when I saw a terrible vision.

3 And regarding them I prayed to the Lord. I had laid down in the house of my grandfather Mahalalel, when I saw in a vision how heaven collapsed and was carried off (removed, torn down) and fell to the earth.

4 And when it fell to the earth I saw how the earth was swallowed up in a great abyss, and mountains were suspended on mountains, and hills sank down on hills, and high trees were ripped from their stems, and hurled down and sunk in the abyss.

5 And then a word fell into my mouth, and I lifted up my voice to cry aloud, and said:

6 'The earth is destroyed.' And my grandfather Mahalalel woke me as I lay near him, and said to me: 'Why do you cry so, my son, and why do you make such moaning (lamentation)?'

7 And I recounted to him the whole vision which I had seen, and he said to me: 'You have seen a terrible thing, my son. Your dream (vision) is of a grave time and concerns the secrets of all the sin of the earth: it must sink into the abyss and be totally destroyed.

8 And now, my son, arise and pray to the Lord of glory, since you are a believer, that a remnant may remain on the earth, and that He may not destroy the whole earth.

9 My son, from heaven all this will come on the earth, and on the earth there will be great destruction.

10 After that I arose and prayed and implored and besought (God), and wrote down my prayer for the generations of the world, and I will show everything to you, my son Methuselah.

11 And when I had gone out below and seen the heaven, and the sun rising in the east, and the moon setting in the west, and a few stars, and the whole earth, and everything as He had known it in the beginning, then I blessed the Lord of judgment and exalted Him because He had made the sun to go out from the windows of the east, and he ascended and rose on the face of heaven, and set out and kept traversing the path shown to it.

(Author's note: This first vision would seem to foreshadow the flood, but since the vision was of a piece of heaven breaking off and falling to earth with destructive force, it may be an end time prophecy of a meteor strike. Another, more timely interpretation is that of Satan falling to earth, which is the beginnings of sorrow.)

[Chapter 84]

1 And I lifted up my hands in righteousness and blessed the Holy and Great One, and spoke with the breath of my mouth, and with the tongue of flesh, which God has made for the children of the flesh of men, that they should speak therewith, and He gave them breath and a tongue and a mouth that they should speak therewith:

2 Blessed be you, O Lord, King, Great and mighty in your greatness, Lord of the whole creation of heaven, King of kings and God of the whole world. And your power and kingship and greatness abide forever and ever, and throughout all generations your dominion and all heavens are your throne forever, and the whole earth your footstool forever and ever.

3 For you have made and you rule all things, and nothing is too hard for you, wisdom never departs from the place of your throne, nor turns away from your presence. You know and see and hear everything, and there is nothing hidden from you for you see everything.

4 And now the angels of your heavens are guilty of trespass, and on the flesh of men abide your wrath until the great day of judgment.

5 And now, O God and Lord and Great King, I implore and beseech you to fulfill my prayer, to leave me a posterity on earth, and not destroy all the flesh of man, and make the earth without inhabitant, so that there should be an eternal destruction.

6 And now, my Lord, destroy from the earth the flesh which has aroused your wrath, but the flesh of righteousness and uprightness establish as an eternal plant bearing seed forever, and hide not your face from the prayer of your servant, O Lord.'

(Author's note: In chapter 85 and following, a series of animals is mentioned. These seem to refer to nations or ethnicities. For example, the eagles may refer to the Roman empire; the Islamic nation is represented by the asses; Egyptians are wolves; the Assyrians are lions, and so on. See Daniel 10 for other like imagery.

Other writers have attempted to be more specific. Starting with Adam and Eve, the story begins. Abraham may be a white bull, Ishmael the wild ass; Isaac the white bull, Jacob a white sheep, Esau the wild boar. There is the concept that Noah's three sons, Shem, Ham and Japheth, give rise to all the various animals or nations. The small lambs with open eyes are the Essenes; Jesus is the "sheep with the big horn," and in 90.17, the final 12 shepherds represent the Christian era and the 12 Apostles.

Notes are included within the chapters and at the end of the section. They suggest possible interpretations. As with any prophecy written in such imagery, it is impossible to know exactly what the author was trying to convey. Prophecy tends to be interpreted according to one's viewpoint. When one looks at the prophecies from a purely Jewish viewpoint it is likely that the savior of the people, represented by the sheep with a large horn, is not the Messiah at all, but a historical military figure such as Judas Maccabaeus, who led the great Maccabean revolt of 167 B.C. – 160 B.C. against Rome.

Judas Maccabeus is also described as a great horn among six others on the head of a lamb. This possibly pertains to his five brothers and Mattathias. If you take this in context of the history from Maccabeus time, the explanation of the verse may be found in 1 Maccabees 3:7 and 6:52, 2 Maccabees 6:8-14, and 1 Maccabees 7:41-42.

[Chapter 85]

1 And after this I saw another dream, and I will show the whole dream to you, my son.

2 And Enoch lifted up his voice and spoke to his son Methuselah: 'I will speak to you, my son, hear my words. Incline your ear to the dream (vision) of your father.

3 Before I married (took) your mother Edna, I saw in a vision on my bed, and behold a bull came out from the earth, and that bull was white.

4 And after it came out a heifer, and along with this later came out two bulls, one of them black and the other red.

5 And that black bull gored the red one and pursued him over the earth, and then I could no longer see that red bull. But that black bull grew and that heifer went with him, and I saw that many oxen proceeded from him which resembled and followed him.

6 And that cow, that first one, went from the presence of that first bull in order to seek that red one, but found him not, and mourned with a great lamentation and sought him.

7 And I looked until that first bull came to her and quieted (calmed) her, and from that time onward she cried no more.

8 And after that she bore another white bull, and after him she bore many bulls and black cows.

9 And I saw in my sleep that white bull likewise grew and became a great white bull, and from him proceeded many white bulls, and they resembled him. And they began to father many white bulls, which resembled them, one following another.

(Author's note: Many believe verses 1–9 represent the story of Adam, Eve, Cain, and Abel. The first white bull mentioned is Adam. The heifer is Eve. The two bulls born to them are a black one [Cain] and a red one [Abel]. Eve leaves to seek Abel and finds him. She laments his death. Adam comforts her. Cain goes on to produce many oxen. Eve produces another son and thus produces many more bulls and cows.)

[Chapter 86]

1 And again I looked with my eyes as I slept, and I saw the heaven above, and behold a star fell from heaven, and it arose and ate and pastured among those oxen (bulls).

2 And after that I saw the large and the black oxen (bulls), and behold they all changed their stalls and pastures and their heifers (cattle) , and began to live with each other.

(Author's note: The first star to fall was Satan. Then other stars fell, and these are the Watchers.. They caused the heifers, who are the women, to begin living with and having sex with the angels. Based on the previous verses it would appear that Satan and the fallen angels picked the descendents of Cain with whom to have sex.)

Second Book of Adam and Eve, Chapter 20
29 Enoch was already grown up at that time, and in his zeal for God, he stood and said, "Hear me, you large and small (young and old) sons of Seth! When you transgress the commandment of our fathers and go down from this holy mountain, you shall not come up here again forever."
30 But they rose up against Enoch and would not listen to his words, but they went down from the Holy Mountain.
31 And when they looked at the daughters of Cain, at their beautiful figures, and at their hands and feet dyed with color, and the tattoos on their faces that ornamented them, the fire of sin was set ablaze in them.
32 Then Satan made them look most beautiful before the sons of Seth, as he also made the sons of Seth appear the most handsome in the eyes of the daughters of Cain, so that the daughters of Cain lusted after the sons of Seth like ravenous beasts, and the sons of Seth lusted after the daughters of Cain until they committed disgusting and disgraceful acts with them.)

3 And again I saw in the vision, and looked towards heaven, and behold I saw many stars descend and cast themselves down from heaven to that first star, and they became bulls among those cattle and pastured with them.

4 And I looked at them and saw they all let out their private (sexual) members, like horses, and began to mount the cows of the bulls (oxen), and they all became pregnant and bore elephants, camels, and asses.

Author's note: The Book of Jubilees indicates that the offspring of the angels and women were somehow different, and they are divided into categories of the Naphidim (or Naphilim, depending or the transliteration), the Giants, and the Eljo. (Naphil are mentioned but this is the singular of Naphilim.) The word "Naphil" means "The Fallen." There is no indication as to the meaning of "Eljo *(Elyo),*" but the word would indicate these are "godlings" and are likely those referred to in the Book of Genesis as "men of renown."

5 And all the bulls (oxen) feared them and were frightened of them, and began to bite with their teeth and to devour, and to gore with their horns.

6 And, moreover, they began to devour those oxen; and behold all the children of the earth began to tremble and shake before them and to flee from them.

[Chapter 87]

1 And again I saw how they began to gore each other and to devour each other, and the earth began to cry aloud.

2 And I raised my eyes again to heaven, and I saw in the vision, and behold there came out from heaven beings who were like white men, and four went out from that place and three others with them.

3 And those three that had come out last grasped me by my hand and took me up, away from the generations of the earth, and raised me up to a high place, and showed me a tower raised high above the earth, and all the hills were lower.

4 And one said to me: 'Remain here until you see everything that befalls those elephants, camels, and asses,

and the stars and the oxen, and all of them.'

[Chapter 88]
1 And I saw one of those four who had come out first, and he seized that first star which had fallen from heaven, and bound it hand and foot and cast it into an abyss; now that abyss was narrow and deep, and horrible and dark.

2 Peter 2:4 For if God spared not the angels that sinned, but cast them down to hell, and delivered them into chains of darkness, to be reserved unto judgment...

2 And one of them drew a sword, and gave it to those elephants and camels and asses then they began to smite each other, and the whole earth shook because of them.

3 And as I was beholding in the vision one of those four who had come out stoned them from heaven, and gathered and took all the great stars whose private (sexual) members were like those of horses, and bound them all hand and foot, and threw them in an abyss of the earth.

(Author's note: One must smile at the idea of the angels having penises the size of horses. In the ancient mind, this was one reason some of the women gave in so easily. If a spiritual creature is determined to become corporeal, why not create a body that will fulfill the lust that drives one to incarnate in the first place?)

[Chapter 89]
1 And one of those four went to that white bull and instructed him in a secret, and he was terrified: he was born a bull and became a man, and built for himself a great vessel and dwelt on it.

2 And three bulls dwelt with him in the vessel and they were covered over. And again I raised my eyes towards heaven and saw a high roof, with seven water torrents on it, and those torrents flowed with much water into an enclosure. And I looked again, and behold fountains were opened on the surface of that great enclosure, and the water began to bubble and swell and rise on the surface, and I saw that enclosure until all its surface was covered with water.

3 And the water, the darkness, and mist increased on it; and as I looked at the height of that water, the water had risen above the height of the enclosure, and was streaming over the enclosure, and it stood on the earth.

4 And all the cattle of the enclosure were gathered together until I saw how they sank and were swallowed up and perished in that water.

5 But that vessel floated on the water, while all the oxen (bulls) and elephants and camels and asses sank to the bottom with all the animals, so that I could no longer see them, and they were not able to escape, but perished and sank into the depths.

6 And again I watched in the vision until those water torrents were removed from that high roof, and the chasms of the earth were leveled up and other abysses were opened.

7 Then the water began to run down into these abysses, until the earth became visible; but that vessel settled on the earth, and the darkness retired and light appeared.

8 But that white bull which had become a man came out of that vessel, and the three bulls with him, and one of those three was white like that bull, and one of them was red as blood, and one black; and that white bull departed from them.

(Author's note: Here we have the story of Noah and the flood. The flood came because of the sins of the Watchers and their offspring, who began killing everything. The flood cleansed the earth and left only the sons of Noah and their wives to repopulate. The story seems to indicate that the various races of the world (white, red, and black, began with the sons of Noah.)

9 And they began to bring out beasts of the field and birds, so that there arose different genera: lions, tigers, wolves, dogs, hyenas, wild boars, foxes, squirrels, swine, falcons, vultures, kites, eagles, and ravens; and among them was born a white bull.

10 And they began to bite one another; but that white bull which was born among them fathered a wild ass and a white bull with it, and the wild asses multiplied.

11 But that bull which was born from him fathered a black wild boar and a white sheep; and the former fathered many boars, but the sheep gave birth to twelve sheep.

(Author's note: Abraham gave birth to Ishmael (the wild ass) and Isaac (the white bull). Isaac fathered a boar (Esau) and a sheep (Jacob.) Jacob had 12 sheep, who are the 12 patriarchs and the beginning of the 12 tribes.)

12 And when those twelve sheep had grown, they gave up one of them to the asses, and the asses again gave up that sheep to the wolves, and that sheep grew up among the wolves.

(Author's note: Joseph was sold to the Midiantes or Ishaelites as a slave. They, in turn, sold him to the Egyptians. See Genesis 37:25-39.)

13 And the Lord brought the eleven sheep to live with it and to pasture with it among the wolves and they multiplied and became many flocks of sheep.

(Author's note: This begins the story of Moses and how the Egyptians oppressed the Israelites until he led them out of captivity.)

14 And the wolves began to fear them, and they oppressed them until they destroyed their little ones, and they threw their young into a deep river, but those sheep began to cry aloud on account of their little ones, and to complain to their Lord.

15 And a sheep which had been saved from the wolves fled and escaped to the wild asses; and I saw the sheep how they lamented and cried, and besought their Lord with all their might, until that Lord of the sheep descended at the voice of the sheep from a high abode, and came to them and pastured them.

16 And He called that sheep which had escaped the wolves, and spoke with it concerning the wolves that it should admonish them not to touch the sheep.

17 And the sheep went to the wolves according to the word of the Lord, and another sheep met it and went with it, and the two went and entered together into the assembly of those wolves, and spoke with them and admonished them not to touch the sheep from then on.

18 And on it I saw the wolves, and how they more harshly oppressed the sheep with all their power; and the sheep cried aloud.

19 And the Lord came to the sheep and they began to beat those wolves, and the wolves began to make lamentation; but the sheep became quiet and ceased to cry out.

20 And I saw the sheep until they departed from among the wolves; but the eyes of the wolves were blinded, and the wolves departed in pursuit of the sheep with all their power.

21 And the Lord of the sheep went with them, as their leader, and all His sheep followed Him.

22 And his face was dazzling and glorious and terrible to behold. But the wolves began to pursue those sheep

until they reached a sea of water.

23 And that sea was divided, and the water stood on this side and on that before their face, and their Lord led them and placed Himself between them and the wolves.

24 And as those wolves had not yet seen the sheep, they proceeded into the midst of that sea, and the wolves followed the sheep, and those wolves ran after them into that sea.

25 And when they saw the Lord of the sheep, they turned to flee before His face, but that sea gathered itself together, and became as it had been created, and the water swelled and rose until it covered the wolves.

26 And I watched until all the wolves who pursued those sheep perished and were drowned.

27 But the sheep escaped from that water and went out into a wilderness, where there was no water and no grass; and they began to open their eyes and to see;

28 And I saw the Lord of the sheep pasturing them and giving them water and grass, and that sheep going and leading them.

(Author's note: The Israelites escaped. They passed through the divided sea, but the Egyptians were covered by the water and drowned. Now, we begin the story of Moses and the ascent up the mountain, where God gave him the Ten Commandments.)

29 And the sheep ascended to the summit of that high rock, and the Lord of the sheep sent it to them. And after that I saw the Lord of the sheep who stood before them, and His appearance was great and terrible and majestic, and all those sheep saw Him and were afraid before His face.

30 And they all feared and trembled because of Him, and they cried to that sheep which was among them:

31 'We are not able to stand before our Lord or to behold Him.' And that sheep which led them again ascended to the summit of that rock, but the sheep began to be blinded and to wander from the way which he had showed them, but that sheep did not realize it.

(Author's note: When Moses came down from the mountain he discovered a large group of the Israelites had made a golden calf idol and were worshipping it.)

32 And the Lord of the sheep was very angry with them, and that sheep discovered it, and went down from the summit of the rock, and came to the sheep, and found the greatest part of them blinded and fallen away.

33 And when they saw it they feared and trembled at its presence, and desired to return to their folds. And that sheep took other sheep with it, and came to those sheep which had fallen away, and began to slay them; and the sheep feared its presence, and thus that sheep brought back those sheep that had fallen away, and they returned to their folds.

34 And I saw in this vision until that sheep became a man and built a house for the Lord of the sheep, and placed all the sheep in that house.

35 And I saw until this sheep which had met that sheep which led them fell asleep (died); and I saw until all the great sheep perished and little ones arose in their place, and they came to a pasture, and approached a stream of water.

36 Then that sheep, their leader which had become a man, withdrew from them and fell asleep (died), and all the sheep looked for it (sought it) and cried over it with a great crying.

37 And I saw until they left off crying for that sheep and crossed that stream of water, and there arose the two sheep as leaders in the place of those which had led them and fallen asleep.

38 And I saw until the sheep came to a good place, and a pleasant and glorious land, and I saw until those sheep were satisfied; and that house stood among them in the (green) pleasant land.

(Author's note: After Moses died and the two spies were sent into the Promised Land to bring back a report, Joshua took over and led the Israelites into the Promised Land.)

39 And sometimes their eyes were opened, and sometimes blinded, until another sheep arose and led them and brought them all back, and their eyes were opened.

40 And the dogs and the foxes and the wild boars began to devour those sheep until the Lord of the sheep raised up another sheep, a ram from their midst, which led them.

41 And that ram began to butt on either side those dogs, foxes, and wild boars until he had destroyed them all.

(Author's note: This is the succession of judges and kings leading up to David. All of them had to fight the surrounding nations.)

42 And that sheep whose eyes were opened saw that ram, which was among the sheep, until it forsook its glory and began to butt those sheep, and trampled on them, and behaved itself unseemly.

43 And the Lord of the sheep sent the lamb to another lamb and raised it to being a ram and leader of the sheep instead of that ram which had forsaken its glory.

44 And it went to it and spoke to it alone, and raised it to being a ram, and made it the prince and leader of the sheep; but during all these things those dogs oppressed the sheep.

45 And the first ram pursued the second ram, and the second ram arose and fled before it; and I saw until those dogs pulled down the first ram.

46 And that second ram arose and led the little sheep. And those sheep grew and multiplied; but all the dogs, and foxes, and wild boars feared and fled before it, and that ram butted and killed the wild beasts, and those wild beasts had no longer any power among the sheep and robbed them no more of anything.

47 And that ram fathered many sheep and fell asleep; and a little sheep became ram in its place, and became prince and leader of those sheep.

48 And that house became great and broad, and it was built for those sheep: and a high and great tower was built on the house for the Lord of the sheep, and that house was low, but the tower was elevated and high, and the Lord of the sheep stood on that tower and they offered a full table before him.

49 And again I saw those sheep that they again erred and went many ways, and forsook that their house, and the Lord of the sheep called some from among the sheep and sent them to the sheep, but the sheep began to slay them.

50 And one of them was saved and was not slain, and it sped away and cried aloud over the sheep; and they sought to slay it, but the Lord of the sheep saved it from the sheep, and brought it up to me, and caused it to live there.

(Author's note: Verse 50 could be a reference to Elijah.)

51 And many other sheep He sent to those sheep to testify to them and lament over them.

52 And after that I saw that when they forsook the house of the Lord and His tower they fell away entirely, and their eyes were blinded; and I saw the Lord of the sheep how He worked much slaughter among them in their herds until those sheep invited that slaughter and betrayed His place.

53 And He gave them over into the hands of the lions and tigers, and wolves and hyenas, and into the hand of the foxes, and to all the wild beasts, and those wild beasts began to tear in pieces those sheep.

54 And I saw that He forsook their house and their tower and gave them all into the hand of the lions, to tear and devour them, into the hand of all the wild beasts.

55 And I began to cry aloud with all my power, and to appeal to the Lord of the sheep, because the sheep were being devoured by all the wild beasts.

56 But He remained unmoved, though He saw it, and rejoiced that they were devoured and swallowed and robbed, and left them to be devoured in the hand of all the beasts.

57 And He called seventy shepherds, and gave those sheep to them that they might pasture them, and He spoke to the shepherds and their companions: 'Let each individual of you pasture the sheep from now on, and everything that I shall command you that do you.

(Author's note: The 70 are religious leaders of that time frame. In the 3 Enoch God mentions 70 nations, leading one to believe that from God's viewpoint there are only 70 true nations. All other divisions are man made and false.)

58 And I will deliver them over to you duly numbered, and tell you which of them are to be destroyed-and them you will destroy.' And He gave over to them those sheep.

59 And He called another and spoke to him: 'Observe and mark everything that the shepherds will do to those sheep; for they will destroy more of them than I have commanded them.

60 And every excess and the destruction which will be done through the shepherds, record how many they destroy according to my command, and how many according to their own caprice; record against every individual shepherd all the destruction he effects.

61 And read out before me by number how many they destroy, and how many they deliver over for destruction, that I may have this as a testimony against them, and know every deed of the shepherds, that I may comprehend and see what they do, whether or not they abide by my command which I have commanded them.

62 But they shall not know it, and you shall not declare it to them, nor admonish them, but only record against each individual all the destruction which the shepherds effect each in his time and lay it all before me.'

63 And I saw until those shepherds pastured in their season, and they began to slay and to destroy more than they were bidden, and they delivered those sheep into the hand of the lions.

64 And the lions and tigers ate and devoured the greater part of those sheep, and the wild boars ate along with them; and they burned that tower and demolished that house.

65 And I became very sorrowful over that tower because that house of the sheep was demolished, and afterwards I was unable to see if those sheep entered that house.

66 And the shepherds and their associates delivered over those sheep to all the wild beasts, to devour them, and each one of them received in his time a definite number, it was written by the other in a book how many

each one of them destroyed of them.

67 And each one slew and destroyed many more than was prescribed; and I began to weep and lament on account of those sheep.

68 And thus in the vision I saw that one who wrote, how he wrote down every one that was destroyed by those shepherds, day by day, and carried up and laid down and showed actually the whole book to the Lord of the sheep - everything that they had done, and all that each one of them had made away with, and all that they had given over to destruction.

69 And the book was read before the Lord of the sheep, and He took the book from his hand and read it and sealed it and laid it down.

(Author's note: Verses 65–69 refer to the first temple being destroyed. Verse 72 begins the story of Ezra and the return to Jerusalem to rebuild the city and temple.)

70 And I saw how the shepherds pastured for twelve hours, and behold three of those sheep turned back and came and entered and began to build up all that had fallen down of that house; but the wild boars tried to hinder them, but they were not able.

71 And they began again to build as before, and they raised up that tower, and it was named the high tower; and they began again to place a table before the tower, but all the bread on it was polluted and not pure.

72 And as touching all this the eyes of those sheep were blinded so that they saw not, and the eyes of their shepherds likewise were blinded; and they delivered them in large numbers to their shepherds for destruction, and they trampled the sheep with their feet and devoured them.

73 And the Lord of the sheep remained unmoved until all the sheep were dispersed over the field and mingled with the beasts, and the shepherds did not save them out of the hand of the beasts.

74 And this one who wrote the book carried it up, and showed it and read it before the Lord of the sheep, and implored Him on their account, and besought Him on their account as he showed Him all the doings of the shepherds, and gave testimony before Him against all the shepherds.

(Author's note: Ezra, Haggai, and Zechariah returned and wrote books of the Old Testament.)

75 And he took the actual book and laid it down beside Him and departed.

[Chapter 90]

1 And I saw until that in this manner thirty-five shepherds undertook the pasturing of the sheep, and they completed their periods as did the first; and others received them into their hands, to pasture them for their period, each shepherd in his own period.

2 And after that I saw in my vision all the birds of heaven coming, the eagles, the vultures, the kites, the ravens; but the eagles led all the birds; and they began to devour those sheep, and to pick out their eyes and to devour their flesh.

(Author's note: Now the Eagle, which is Roman, appears from among the nations.)

3 And the sheep cried out because their flesh was being devoured by the birds, and as for me I looked and lamented in my sleep over that shepherd who pastured the sheep.

4 And I saw until those sheep were devoured by the dogs and eagles and kites, and they left neither flesh nor skin nor sinew remaining on them until only their bones stood there; and their bones too fell to the earth and

the sheep became few.

5 And I saw until that twenty-three had undertaken the pasturing and completed in their many periods fifty-eight times.

(Author's note: Of the 70 appointed religious leaders throughout time, 58vhave passed. Verse 6 introduces the Essenes. Verse 8 probably refers to John The Baptist.)

6 But behold lambs were borne by those white sheep, and they began to open their eyes and to see, and to cry to the sheep.

7 They cried to them, but they did not hearken to what they said to them, but were very deaf, and their eyes were very blinded.

8 And I saw in the vision how the ravens flew on those lambs and took one of those lambs, and dashed the sheep in pieces and devoured them.

9 And I saw until horns grew on those lambs, and the ravens cast down their horns; and I saw until there sprouted a great horn of one of those sheep, and their eyes were opened.

(Author's note: According to the way in which verse 9 is interpreted, it begins the story of Jesus. The story seems to end at verse 16. The sheep with the great horn is never said to be killed. It only states that he was stopped. Another interpretation points to Judas Maccabaeus.)

10 And it looked at them and their eyes opened, and it cried to the sheep, and the rams saw it and all ran to it.

11 And notwithstanding all this, those eagles and vultures and ravens and kites kept on tearing the sheep and swooping down on them and devouring them until the sheep remained silent, but the rams lamented and cried out.

12 And those ravens fought and battled with it and sought to lay low its horn, but they had no power over it.

13 All the eagles and vultures and ravens and kites were gathered together, and there came with them all the sheep of the field, they all came together, and helped each other to break that horn of the ram.

14 And I saw that man, who wrote down the names of the shepherds and brought them up before the Lord of the sheep, came, and he helped that ram and showed it everything; its help was coming down.

15 And I looked until that Lord of the sheep came to them angry, all those who saw him ran, and they all fell into the shadow in front of Him.

16 All the eagles and vultures and ravens and kites, gathered together and brought with them all the wild sheep, and they all came together and helped one another in order to dash that horn of the ram in pieces.

17 And I looked at that man, who wrote the book at the command of the Lord, until he opened that book of the destruction that those last twelve shepherds had done. And he showed, in front of the Lord of the sheep, that they had destroyed even more than those before them had.

(Author's note: The 12 shepherds are either the Apostles, if one interprets the sheep with the large horn as Jesus, or the 12 shepherds are the leaders of the Jews joining themselves in the revolt led by Judas Maccabeus. If one goes with the apostle theory, the books refer to the New Testament, but more specifically it refers to the path of "enlightenment." I use this word since the text itself uses the terms "to be blinded" and "to have the eyes opened." It should be noted that there are books attributed to most of the Apostles, but many are not included in the Bible. This ends past events. What remains from verse 17 on is prophetic. Following the idea that Enoch is one of the first apocalyptic books, we will see in figurative language a great battle and the judgment. The stars are judged. This is the judgment of the fallen angels. The 70 Jewish religious leaders, representing the Pharisee mind set and the religious oppression of the Jewish people are judged. Then the eyes of the faithful are opened and they are brought into the Lord's house. The number of believers is so great the house overflows.)

18 And I looked and the Lord of the sheep came to them and took the Staff of His Anger and struck the Earth. And the Earth was split. And all the animals, and the birds of the sky, fell from those sheep and sank in the earth, and it closed over them.

19 And I saw until a great sword was given to the sheep, and the sheep proceeded against all the beasts of the field to slay them, and all the beasts and the birds of the heaven fled before their face. And I saw that man, who wrote the book according to the command of the Lord, until he opened that book concerning the destruction which those twelve last shepherds had wrought, and showed that they had destroyed much more than their predecessors, before the Lord of the sheep. And I saw until the Lord of the sheep came to them and took in His hand the staff of His wrath, and smote the earth, and the earth clave asunder, and all the beasts and all the birds of heaven fell from among those sheep, and were swallowed up in the earth and it covered them.

20 And I saw until a throne was erected in the pleasant land, and the Lord of the sheep sat Himself on it, and the other took the sealed books and opened those books before the Lord of the sheep.

21 And the Lord called those men, the seven first white ones, and commanded that they should bring before Him, beginning with the first star which led the way, all the stars whose private members were like those of horses, and they brought them all before Him.

22 And He said to that man who wrote before Him, being one of those seven white ones, and said to him: 'Take those seventy shepherds to whom I delivered the sheep, and who taking them on their own authority slew more than I commanded them.'

23 And behold they were all bound, I saw, and they all stood before Him.

24 And the judgment was held first over the stars, and they were judged and found guilty, and went to the place of condemnation, and they were cast into an abyss, full of fire and flaming, and full of pillars of fire.

25 And those seventy shepherds were judged and found guilty, and they were cast into that fiery abyss.

26 And I saw at that time how a like abyss was opened in the midst of the earth, full of fire, and they brought those blinded sheep, and they were all judged and found guilty and cast into this fiery abyss, and they burned; now this abyss was to the right of that house.

27 And I saw those sheep burning and their bones burning.

28 And I stood up to see until they folded up that old house; and carried off all the pillars, and all the beams and ornaments of the house were at the same time folded up with it, and they carried it off and laid it in a place in the south of the land.

29 And I saw until the Lord of the sheep brought a new house greater and loftier than that first, and set it up in the place of the first which had been folded up; all its pillars were new, and its ornaments were new and larger than those of the first, the old one which He had taken away, and all the sheep were within it.

Hebrews 13:14 For here have we no continuing city, but we seek one to come.

30 And I saw all the sheep which had been left, and all the beasts on the earth, and all the birds of heaven, falling down and doing homage to those sheep and making petition to and obeying them in every thing.

31 And thereafter those three who were clothed in white and had seized me by my hand [who had taken me up before], and the hand of that ram also seizing hold of me, they took me up and set me down in the midst of those sheep before the judgment took place.

32 And those sheep were all white, and their wool was abundant and clean.

33 And all that had been destroyed and dispersed, and all the beasts of the field, and all the birds of heaven, assembled in that house, and the Lord of the sheep rejoiced with great joy because they were all good and had returned to His house.

34 And I saw until they laid down that sword, which had been given to the sheep, and they brought it back into the house, and it was sealed before the presence of the Lord, and all the sheep were invited into that house, but it held them not.

35 And the eyes of them all were opened, and they saw the good, and there was not one among them that did not see.

36 And I saw that the house was large and broad and very full.

37 And I saw that a white bull was born, with large horns and all the beasts of the field and all the birds of the air feared him and made petition to him all the time.

(Author's note: If one assumes the previous "sheep with a large horn" was Judas Maccabaeus, then verse 37 is the birth of the Messiah.)

38 And I saw until all their generations were transformed, and they all became white bulls; and the first among them became a lamb, and that lamb became a great animal and had great black horns on its head; and the Lord of the sheep rejoiced over it and over all the oxen.

39 And I slept in their midst: And I awoke and saw everything.

40 This is the vision which I saw while I slept, and I awoke and blessed the Lord of righteousness and gave Him glory.

41 Then I wept greatly and my tears ceased not until I could no longer endure it; when I saw, they flowed on account of what I had seen; for everything shall come and be fulfilled, and all the deeds of men in their order were shown to me.

42 On that night I remembered the first dream, and because of it I wept and was troubled-because I had seen that vision.

[Author's note: At this point, the time frame and text flow becomes non sequitur. It appears the codex was not kept in sequence here. Thus, the translated pages are out of sequence. The flow of time and occurrences seems to follow the pattern listed:

91:6 to 92.1 through 92:5 then jumps to 93:1. The flow then continues from 93:1 to 93:10 and then jumps to 91:7. From 91:7 the text continues to 91:19. It then picks up again at 93:11 and continues.

If one were to attempt to put this section into a timeline, the interval would link together in some fashion resembling the following:

Ten Weeks of Judgment

WEEK 1 *Judgment & righteousness 93.3 Enoch's time Antediluvian (Ice-age - 16,000 B.C.)*	
WEEK 2 Judgment & cleansing 93.4 Noah's time and the great flood The first judgment of the world (16,000 – 10,000 B.C)	
WEEK 3 Righteousness is planted 93.5 Abraham's time (10,000 – 2000 B.C.)	
WEEK 4 Law for all generations 93.6 Moses' time WEEK 4 2000 – 1400 B.C.	
WEEK 5 House of Glory 93.7 Solomon's time 1400 – 900 B.C.	
WEEK 6 Jesus ascends, temple burned, elect scattered 93.8 Jesus' time 900 B.C – 100 A.D.	
WEEK 7 Apostate generation Judgment of Fire 93.9 - 91.11 Our time The second judgment of earth. 100 A.D. - ?	
WEEK 8 A sword 91.12–13 New house, new heaven & earth Future time	
WEEK 9 The righteous judgment revealed 91.14 The judgment time	
WEEK 10 God's power is forever 91.15-16 Eternal time	

When reading the text from this point to the end of chapter 93, one should keep this flow in mind.]

[Chapter 91]
The Book of Warnings and Blessings of Enoch (Chapters 91-104):

1 And now, my son Methuselah, call to me all your brothers and gather together to me all the sons of your mother; for the word calls me, and the spirit is poured out on me, that I may show you everything that shall befall you forever.'

2 And thereon Methuselah went and summoned to him all his brothers and assembled his relatives.

3 And he spoke to all the children of righteousness and said: 'Hear, you sons of Enoch, all the words of your father, and hearken, as you should, to the voice of my mouth; for I exhort you and say to you, beloved:

4 Love righteousness and walk in it, and draw near to righteousness without a double heart, and do not associate with those of a double heart, but walk in righteousness, my sons. And it shall guide you on good paths. And righteousness shall be your companion.'

James 1:6-8 But let him ask in faith, nothing wavering. For he that wavereth is like a wave of the sea driven with the wind and tossed. 7 For let not that man think that he shall receive any thing of the Lord. 8 A double-minded man is unstable in all his ways.

5 'For I know that violence must increase on the earth, and a great punishment will be executed on the earth, it shall be cut off from its roots, and its whole construct will be destroyed.

6 And unrighteousness shall again be complete on the earth, and all the deeds of unrighteousness and of violence and sin shall prevail a second time.

7 And when sin and unrighteousness and blasphemy and violence in all kinds of deeds increase, and apostasy and transgression and uncleanness increase; a great chastisement shall come from heaven on all these, and the holy Lord will come out with wrath and chastisement to execute judgment on earth.

2 Thessalonians 2:3 Let no man deceive you by any means: for that day shall not come, except there come a falling away first, and that man of sin be revealed, the son of perdition.

8 In those days violence shall be cut off from its roots, and the roots of unrighteousness together with deceit, and they shall be destroyed from under heaven.

9 And all the idols of the heathen shall be abandoned. And the temples burned with fire, and they shall remove them from the whole earth; and the heathen shall be cast into the judgment of fire, and shall perish in wrath and in grievous judgment forever.

10 And the righteous shall arise from their sleep, and wisdom shall arise and be given to them.

11 And after that the roots of unrighteousness and those who plan violence and those who commit blasphemy shall be cut off, and the sinners shall be destroyed by the sword.

12 And after this there will be another week; the eighth, that of righteousness, and a sword will be given to it so that the Righteous Judgment may be executed on those who do wrong, and the sinners will be handed over into the hands of the righteous.

13 And, at its end, they will acquire Houses because of their righteousness, and a House will be built for the Great King in Glory, forever.

14 And after this, in the ninth week, the Righteous Judgment will be revealed to the whole world. And all the deeds of the impious will vanish from the whole Earth. And the world will be written down for destruction and all men will look to the Path of Uprightness.

15 And, after this, in the tenth week, in the seventh part, there will be an Eternal Judgment that will be executed on the Watchers and the Great Eternal Heaven that will spring from the midst of the Angels.

16 And the First Heaven will vanish and pass away and a New Heaven will appear, and all the Powers of Heaven will shine forever, with light seven times as bright.

17 And after this, there will be many weeks without number, forever, in goodness and in righteousness. And from then on sin will never again be mentioned.

18 And now I tell you, my sons, and show you, the paths of righteousness and the paths of violence. I will show them to you again that you may know what will come to pass.

19 And now, hearken to me, my sons, and walk in the paths of righteousness, and walk not in the paths of violence; for all who walk in the paths of unrighteousness shall perish forever.'

[Chapter 92]

1 The book written by Enoch (Enoch indeed wrote this complete doctrine of wisdom, [which is] praised of all men and a judge of all the earth) for all my children who shall live on the earth. And for the future generations who shall observe righteousness and peace.

2 Let not your spirit be troubled on account of the times; for the Holy and Great One has appointed days for all things.

3 And the righteous one shall arise from sleep, (shall arise) and walk in the paths of righteousness, and all his path and conversation shall be in eternal goodness and grace.

4 He will be gracious to the righteous and give him eternal righteousness, and He will give him power so that he shall be (endowed) with goodness and righteousness. And he shall walk in eternal light.

5 And sin shall perish in darkness forever, and shall no more be seen from that day forevermore.

[Chapter 93]

(Author's note: Chapters 91–93 recount and expand on the events listed in the following weeks of prophecy. The explanations of the events are scattered in chapters 91–93; however, the list of events are stated clearly in the following list of weeks in Chapter 93.)

1 And after that Enoch both gave and began to recount from the books. And Enoch said:

2 'Concerning the children of righteousness and concerning the elect of the world, and concerning the plant of righteousness, I will speak these things. I Enoch will declare (them) to you, my sons, according to that which appeared to me in heavenly vision, and which I have known through the word of the holy angels, and have learned from heavenly tablets.'

3 And Enoch began to recount from the books and said: 'I was born the seventh in the first week, able judgment and righteousness still endured.

(Author's note: Enoch was the seventh son. He was born in the beginning of the timeline he is laying out.)

4 And after me there shall arise in the second week great wickedness, and deceit shall have sprung up; and in it there shall be the first end.

(Author's note: This is the rise of evil. The angels have fallen.)

5 And in it a man shall be saved; and after it is ended unrighteousness shall grow up, and a law shall be made for the sinners. And after that in the third week at its close a man shall be elected as the plant of righteous judgment, and his posterity shall become the plant of righteousness forevermore.

(Author's note: This is the time of Moses and the establishment of the Ten Commandments, the beginning of the law.)

6 And after that in the fourth week, at its close, visions of the holy and righteous shall be seen, and a law for all generations and an enclosure shall be made for them.

(Author's note: This is the time of David and the wars that defined the Holy Land.)

7 And after that in the fifth week, at its close, the house of glory and dominion shall be built forever.

(Author's note: This concerns the time of Solomon and the first temple.)

8 And after that in the sixth week, all who live in it shall be blinded, and the hearts of all of them shall godlessly forsake wisdom. And in it a man shall ascend; and at its close the house of dominion shall be burned with fire, and the whole race of the chosen root shall be dispersed.

(Author's note: In the sixth week Christ came to the chosen ones, but they were blinded. He ascended and the Jewish nation was scattered. In the holocaust innumerable Jews were burned. The diaspora remains scattered but has begun to gather into the new nation of Israel.)

9 And after that in the seventh week shall an apostate generation arise, and many shall be its deeds, and all its deeds shall be apostate.

(Author's note: It is assumed that we are in the seventh week of Enoch's prophecy. This aligns in a very general way to the prophecies of the churches in Revelation. At the end of the seventh week there will be a "great falling away.")

2 Thessalonians 2:3 Let no man deceive you by any means: for that day shall not come, except there come a falling away first, and that man of sin be revealed, the son of perdition;

Revelation 2

1 Unto the angel of the church of Ephesus write; These things saith he that holdeth the seven stars in his right hand, who walketh in the midst of the seven golden candlesticks;

2 I know thy works, and thy labour, and thy patience, and how thou canst not bear them which are evil: and thou hast tried them which say they are apostles, and are not, and hast found them liars:

3 And hast borne, and hast patience, and for my name's sake hast laboured, and hast not fainted.

4 Nevertheless I have somewhat against thee, because thou hast left thy first love.

5 Remember therefore from whence thou art fallen, and repent, and do the first works; or else I will come unto thee quickly, and will remove thy candlestick out of his place, except thou repent.

6 But this thou hast, that thou hatest the deeds of the Nicolaitanes, which I also hate.

7 He that hath an ear, let him hear what the Spirit saith unto the churches; To him that overcometh will I give to eat of the tree of life, which is in the midst of the paradise of God.

8 And unto the angel of the church in Smyrna write; These things saith the first and the last, which was dead, and is alive;

9 I know thy works, and tribulation, and poverty, (but thou art rich) and I know the blasphemy of them which say they are Jews, and are not, but are the synagogue of Satan.

10 Fear none of those things which thou shalt suffer: behold, the devil shall cast some of you into prison, that ye may be tried; and ye shall have tribulation ten days: be thou faithful unto death, and I will give thee a crown of life.

11 He that hath an ear, let him hear what the Spirit saith unto the churches; He that overcometh shall not be hurt of the second death.

12 And to the angel of the church in Pergamos write; These things saith he which hath the sharp sword with two edges;

13 I know thy works, and where thou dwellest, even where Satan's seat is: and thou holdest fast my name, and hast not denied my faith, even in those days wherein Antipas was my faithful martyr, who was slain among you, where Satan dwelleth.

14 But I have a few things against thee, because thou hast there them that hold the doctrine of Balaam, who taught Balac to cast a stumblingblock before the children of Israel, to eat things sacrificed unto idols, and to commit fornication.

15 So hast thou also them that hold the doctrine of the Nicolaitanes, which thing I hate.

16 Repent; or else I will come unto thee quickly, and will fight against them with the sword of my mouth.

17 He that hath an ear, let him hear what the Spirit saith unto the churches; To him that overcometh will I give to eat of the hidden manna, and will give him a white stone, and in the stone a new name written, which no man knoweth saving he that receiveth it.

18 And unto the angel of the church in Thyatira write; These things saith the Son of God, who hath his eyes like unto a flame of fire, and his feet are like fine brass;

19 I know thy works, and charity, and service, and faith, and thy patience, and thy works; and the last to be more than the first.

20 Notwithstanding I have a few things against thee, because thou sufferest that woman Jezebel, which calleth herself a prophetess, to teach and to seduce my servants to commit fornication, and to eat things sacrificed unto idols.

21 And I gave her space to repent of her fornication; and she repented not.

22 Behold, I will cast her into a bed, and them that commit adultery with her into great tribulation, except they repent of their deeds.

23 And I will kill her children with death; and all the churches shall know that I am he which searcheth the reins and hearts: and I will give unto every one of you according to your works.

24 But unto you I say, and unto the rest in Thyatira, as many as have not this doctrine, and which have not known the depths of Satan, as they speak; I will put upon you none other burden.

25 But that which ye have already hold fast till I come.

26 And he that overcometh, and keepeth my works unto the end, to him will I give power over the nations:

27 And he shall rule them with a rod of iron; as the vessels of a potter shall they be broken to shivers: even as I received of my Father.

28 And I will give him the morning star.

29 He that hath an ear, let him hear what the Spirit saith unto the churches.

Revelation 3

1 And unto the angel of the church in Sardis write; These things saith he that hath the seven Spirits of God, and the seven stars; I know thy works, that thou hast a name that thou livest, and art dead.

2 Be watchful, and strengthen the things which remain, that are ready to die: for I have not found thy works perfect before God.

3 Remember therefore how thou hast received and heard, and hold fast, and repent. If therefore thou shalt not watch, I will come on thee as a thief, and thou shalt not know what hour I will come upon thee.

4 Thou hast a few names even in Sardis which have not defiled their garments; and they shall walk with me in white: for they are worthy.

5 He that overcometh, the same shall be clothed in white raiment; and I will not blot out his name out of the Book of Life, but I will confess his name before my Father, and before his angels.

6 He that hath an ear, let him hear what the Spirit saith unto the churches.

7And to the angel of the church in Philadelphia write; These things saith he that is holy, he that is true, he that hath the key of David, he that openeth, and no man shutteth; and shutteth, and no man openeth;

8 I know thy works: behold, I have set before thee an open door, and no man can shut it: for thou hast a little strength, and hast kept my word, and hast not denied my name.

9 Behold, I will make them of the synagogue of Satan, which say they are Jews, and are not, but do lie; behold, I will make them to come and worship before thy feet, and to know that I have loved thee.

10 Because thou hast kept the word of my patience, I also will keep thee from the hour of temptation, which shall come upon all the world, to try them that dwell upon the earth.

11 Behold, I come quickly: hold that fast which thou hast, that no man take thy crown.

12 Him that overcometh will I make a pillar in the temple of my God, and he shall go no more out: and I will write upon him the name of my God, and the name of the city of my God, which is new Jerusalem, which cometh down out of heaven from my God: and I will write upon him my new name.

(Author's note: Most scholars agree that we are in the age of Laodicea)

13 He that hath an ear, let him hear what the Spirit saith unto the churches.

14 And unto the angel of the church of the Laodiceans write; These things saith the Amen, the faithful and true witness, the beginning of the creation of God;

15 I know thy works, that thou art neither cold nor hot: I would thou wert cold or hot.

16 So then because thou art lukewarm, and neither cold nor hot, I will spue thee out of my mouth.

17 Because thou sayest, I am rich, and increased with goods, and have need of nothing; and knowest not that thou art wretched, and miserable, and poor, and blind, and naked:

18 I counsel thee to buy of me gold tried in the fire, that thou mayest be rich; and white raiment, that thou mayest be clothed, and that the shame of thy nakedness do not appear; and anoint thine eyes with eyesalve, that thou mayest see.

19 As many as I love, I rebuke and chasten: be zealous therefore, and repent.

20 Behold, I stand at the door, and knock: if any man hear my voice, and open the door, I will come in to him, and will sup with him, and he with me.

21 To him that overcometh will I grant to sit with me in my throne, even as I also overcame, and am set down with my Father in his throne.

22 He that hath an ear, let him hear what the Spirit saith unto the churches.

10 And at its end shall be elected, the elect righteous of the eternal plant of righteousness shall be chosen to receive sevenfold instruction concerning all His creation.

11 For who is there of all the children of men that is able to hear the voice of the Holy One without being troubled? And who can think His thoughts? Who is there that can behold all the works of heaven?

12 And how should there be one who could behold heaven, and who is there that could understand the things of heaven and see a soul or a spirit and could tell of it, or ascend and see all their ends and think them or do like them?

13 And who is there of all men that could know what is the breadth and the length of the earth, and to whom has the measurement been shown of all of them?

14 Or is there any one who could discern the length of the heaven and how great is its height, and on what it is

founded, and how great is the number of the stars, and where all the luminaries rest?

(Author's note: In this age of space travel, we have indeed beheld the heavens and measured and numbered the stars. These are the end times.)

[Chapter 94]

1 And now I say to you, my sons, love righteousness and walk in it; because the paths of righteousness are worthy of acceptation, but the paths of unrighteousness shall suddenly be destroyed and vanish.

2 And to certain men of a generation shall the paths of violence and of death be revealed, and they shall hold themselves afar from them, and shall not follow them.

3 And now I say to you, the righteous, walk not in the paths of wickedness, nor in the paths of death, and draw not near to them, lest you be destroyed.

4 But seek and choose for yourselves righteousness and an elect life, and walk in the paths of peace, and you shall live and prosper.

5 And hold (keep) my words in the thoughts of your hearts, and permit them not to be erased from your hearts; for I know that sinners will tempt men to evilly entreat wisdom, so that no place may be found for her, and temptation will increase.

Ecclesiastes 12:13 Now all has been heard; here is the conclusion of the matter: Fear God and keep his commandments, for this is the whole duty of man. 14 For God will bring every deed into judgment, including every hidden thing, whether it is good or evil.

6 Woe to those who build unrighteousness and oppression and lay deceit as a foundation; for they shall be suddenly overthrown, and they shall have no peace.

7 Woe to those who build their houses with sin; for from all their foundations shall they be overthrown, and by the sword shall they fall. And those who acquire gold and silver shall suddenly perish in the judgment.

8 Woe to you, you rich, for you have trusted in your riches, and from your riches shall you depart, because you have not remembered the Most High in the days of your riches.

Isaiah 5:19-23 Woe to those who rise early in the morning to run after their drinks, who stay up late at night till they are inflamed with wine.
20 Woe to those who call evil good and good evil, who put darkness for light and light for darkness, who put bitter for sweet and sweet for bitter.
21 Woe to those who are wise in their own eyes and clever in their own sight.
22 Woe to those who are heroes at drinking wine and champions at mixing drinks,
23 who acquit the guilty for a bribe, but deny justice to the innocent.

9 You have committed blasphemy and unrighteousness, and have become ready for the day of slaughter, and the day of darkness and the day of the great judgment.

10 Thus I speak and tell you: He who hath created you will overthrow you, and for your fall there shall be no compassion, and your Creator will rejoice at your destruction.

11 And your righteousness shall be a reproach to the sinners and the godless in those days.

James 5:1-6 Go to now, ye rich men, weep and howl for your miseries that shall come upon you. 2 Your riches are corrupted, and your garments are moth-eaten. 3 Your gold and silver is cankered; and the rust of them shall be a witness against you, and shall eat your flesh as if it were fire. Ye have heaped treasure together for the last days. 4 Behold, the hire of the labourers who have reaped down your fields, which is of you kept back by fraud, crieth: and the cries of them which have reaped are entered into the ears of the Lord of sabaoth. ⁵ Ye have lived in pleasure on the earth, and been wanton; ye have nourished your hearts, as in a day of slaughter. ⁶ Ye have condemned and killed the just; and he doth not resist you.

(Author's note: In the above biblical verses from James, "sabaoth" is from the Hebrew, plural form of "host" or "army." The word is used almost exclusively in conjunction with the Divine name as a title of majesty: "the Lord of Hosts," or "the Lord God of Hosts.")

[Chapter 95]

1 Would that my eyes were rain clouds of water that I might weep over you, and pour down my tears as a cloud of water, that I might rest from my trouble of heart!

2 Who has permitted you to practice reproaches and wickedness? And so judgment shall overtake you, sinners.

3 You, righteous! Fear not the sinners, for again the Lord will deliver them into your hands, that you may execute judgment on them according to your desires.

4 Woe to you who speak against God (fulminate anathemas) which cannot be removed (reversed) - healing shall be far from you because of your sins.

5 Woe to you who repay your neighbor with evil; for you shall be repaid according to your works.

6 Woe to you, lying witnesses, and to those who weigh out injustice, for you shall suddenly perish.

7 Woe to you, sinners, for you persecute the righteous; for you shall be delivered up and persecuted because of injustice, and your yoke shall be heavy on you.

Luke 6:24-31 "But woe to you who are rich, for you have already received your comfort. ²⁵ Woe to you who are well fed now, for you will go hungry. Woe to you who laugh now, for you will mourn and weep. ²⁶ Woe to you when all men speak well of you, for that is how their fathers treated the false prophets. ²⁷"But I tell you who hear me: Love your enemies, do good to those who hate you, ²⁸ bless those who curse you, pray for those who mistreat you. ²⁹ If someone strikes you on one cheek, turn to him the other also. If someone takes your cloak, do not stop him from taking your tunic. ³⁰ Give to everyone who asks you, and if anyone takes what belongs to you, do not demand it back. ³¹ Do to others as you would have them do to you.

[Chapter 96]

1 Be hopeful, you righteous; for suddenly shall the sinners perish before you, and you shall have lordship over them, according to your desires.

2 And in the day of the tribulation of the sinners, your children shall mount and rise as eagles, and your nests shall be higher than the vultures'. You shall ascend as badgers and enter the crevices of the earth, and the clefts of the rock forever before the unrighteous. And the satyrs (sirens) shall sigh and weep because of you.

3 Wherefore fear not, you that have suffered, for healing shall be your portion, and a bright light shall enlighten you, and the voice of rest you shall hear from heaven.

4 Woe to you, you sinners, for your riches make you appear like the righteous, but your hearts convict you of being sinners, and this fact shall be a testimony against you for a memorial of your evil deeds.

5 Woe to you who devour the finest of the wheat, and drink wine in large bowls (the best of waters), and tread under foot the lowly (humble) with your might.

6 Woe to you who drink water from every fountain (drink water all the time), for suddenly shall you be consumed and wither away, because you have forsaken the fountain of life.

(Author's note: The above reference is a euphemism for promiscuity.)

7 Woe to you who work unrighteousness and deceit and blasphemy; it shall be a memorial against you for evil.

8 Woe to you, you mighty, who with might oppress the righteous; for the day of your destruction is coming. Many and good days shall come to the righteous in those days - in the day of your judgment.

[Chapter 97]

1 Believe, you righteous, that the sinners will become a shame and perish in the day of unrighteousness.

2 Be it known to you, you sinners, that the Most High is mindful of your destruction, and the angels of heaven rejoice over your destruction.

3 What will you do, you sinners, and where shall you flee on that day of judgment, when you hear the voice of the prayer of the righteous?

4 You shall fare like to them, against whom these words shall be a testimony: "You have been companions of sinners."

5 And in those days the prayer of the righteous shall reach to the Lord, and for you the days of your judgment shall come.

6 And all the words of your unrighteousness shall be read out before the Great Holy One, and your faces shall be covered with shame, and He will reject every work which is grounded on unrighteousness.

7 Woe to you, you sinners, who live on the middle of the ocean and on the dry land, whose remembrance is evil against you.

8 Woe to you who acquire silver and gold in unrighteousness and say: "We have become rich with riches and have possessions; and have acquired everything we have desired.

9 And now let us do what we purposed, for we have gathered silver, and many are the servants in our houses and our granaries are full to the brim as if with water."

10 Yea, and like water your lies shall flow away; for your riches shall not abide but quickly depart (go up) from you, for you have acquired it all in unrighteousness, and you shall be given over to a great curse.

[Chapter 98]

1 And now I swear to you, to the wise and to the foolish, that you shall see (have) many experiences on the earth.

2 For you men shall put on more adornments than a woman, and colored garments more than a young woman, like royalty and in grandeur and in power, and in silver and in gold and in purple, and in splendor and in food they shall be poured out as water.

3 Therefore they shall have neither knowledge nor wisdom, and because of this they shall die together with their possessions; and with all their glory and their splendor, and in shame and in slaughter and in great destitution, their spirits shall be thrown into the furnace of fire.

4 I have sworn to you, you sinners, as a mountain has not become a slave, and a hill does not become the servant of a woman, even so sin has not been sent on the earth, but man of himself has created it, and they that commit it shall fall under a great curse.

5 And barrenness has not been given to the woman, but on account of the deeds of her own hands she dies without children.

6 I have sworn to you, you sinners, by the Holy Great One, that all your evil deeds are revealed in heaven, and that none of your wrong deeds (of oppression) are covered and hidden.

7 And do not think in your spirit nor say in your heart that you do not know and that you do not see that every sin is recorded every day in heaven in the presence of the Most High.

8 From now on, you know that all your wrongdoing that you do will be written down every day, until the day of your judgment.

9 Woe to you, you fools, for through your folly you shall perish; and you do not listen to the wise so no good will come to you against the wise,

10 And so and now, know you that you are prepared for the day of destruction. Therefore do not hope to live, you sinners, but you shall depart and die; for there will be no ransom for you; because you are prepared for the day of the great judgment, for the day of tribulation and great shame for your spirits.

11 Woe to you, you obstinate of heart, who work wickedness and eat blood. Where do you have good things to eat and to drink and to be filled? From all the good things which the Lord the Most High has placed in abundance on the earth; therefore you shall have no peace.

(Author's note: The above reference to eating blood may indicate cannibalism. As a side note, The Book of Jubilees tells us that the offspring of the fallen angels drank blood.)

Genesis 9:3-6 Every moving thing that liveth shall be meat for you; even as the green herb have I given you all things. 4 But flesh with the life thereof, which is the blood thereof, shall ye not eat. 5 And surely your blood of your lives will I require; at the hand of every beast will I require it, and at the hand of man; at the hand of every man's brother will I require the life of man. 6 Whoso sheddeth man's blood, by man shall his blood be shed: for in the image of God made he man.

12 Woe to you who love the deeds of unrighteousness; wherefore do you hope for good for yourselves? You know that you shall be delivered into the hands of the righteous, and they shall cut off your necks and slay you, and have no mercy on you.

13 Woe to you who rejoice in the distress of the righteous; for no grave shall be dug for you.

14 Woe to you who say the words of the wise are empty; for you shall have no hope of life.

15 Woe to you who write down lying and godless words; for they write down their lies so that men may hear them and act godlessly towards their neighbor. Therefore they shall have no peace but die a sudden death.

[Chapter 99]

1 Woe to you who do godless acts, and praise and honor lies; you shall perish, and no happy life shall be yours.

2 Woe to them who pervert the words of righteousness, and transgress the eternal law, and count themselves as sinless. They shall be trodden under foot on the earth.

3 In those days make ready, you righteous, to raise your prayers as a memorial, and place them as a testimony before the angels, that they may place the sin of the sinners for a reminder before the Most High.

4 In those days the nations shall be stirred up, and the families of the nations shall arise on the day of

destruction.

5 And in those days the destitute shall go and throw their children out, and they shall abandon them, so that their children shall perish because of them. They shall abandon their children that are still babies (sucklings), and not return to them, and shall have no pity on their loved ones.

6 Again, I swear to you, you sinners, that sin is prepared for a day of unceasing bloodshed.

Matthew 24:6-8 And ye shall hear of wars and rumours of wars: see that ye be not troubled: for all these things must come to pass, but the end is not yet. 7 For nation shall rise against nation, and kingdom against kingdom: and there shall be famines, and pestilences, and earthquakes, in diverse places. 8 All these are the beginning of sorrows.

7 And they who worship stones, and carved images of gold and silver and wood and stone and clay, and those who worship impure spirits and demons, and all kinds of idols not according to knowledge, shall get no manner of help from them.

8 And they shall become godless by reason of the folly of their hearts, and their eyes shall be blinded through the fear of their hearts and through visions in their ambitions (dreams).

Colossians 2:16-19 Let no man therefore judge you in meat, or in drink, or in respect of an holyday, or of the new moon, or of the sabbath days:
17 Which are a shadow of things to come; but the body is of Christ.
18 Let no man beguile you of your reward in a voluntary humility and worshipping of angels, intruding into those things which he hath not seen, vainly puffed up by his fleshly mind,
19 And not holding the Head, from which all the body by joints and bands having nourishment ministered, and knit together, increaseth with the increase of God.

9 Through these they shall become godless and fearful; for they shall have done all their work with lies, and shall have worshiped a stone, therefore in an instant shall they perish.

Revelation 9:19-21 For their power is in their mouth, and in their tails: for their tails were like unto serpents, and had heads, and with them they do hurt.
20 And the rest of the men which were not killed by these plagues yet repented not of the works of their hands, that they should not worship devils, and idols of gold, and silver, and brass, and stone, and of wood: which neither can see, nor hear, nor walk: 21 Neither repented they of their murders, nor of their sorceries, nor of their fornication, nor of their thefts.

10 But in those days blessed are all they who accept the words of wisdom, and understand them, and observe the paths of the Most High, and walk in the path of His righteousness, and become not godless with the godless, for they shall be saved.

11 Woe to you who spread evil to your neighbors, for you shall be slain in Hell.

12 Woe to you who make your foundation that of deceitful (sin) and lies, and who cause bitterness on the earth; for they shall thereby be utterly consumed.

13 Woe to you who build your houses through the hard labor of others, and all their building materials are the bricks and stones of sin; I tell you, you shall have no peace.

14 Woe to them who reject the measure and eternal inheritance of their fathers and whose souls follow after idols; for they shall have no rest.

15 Woe to them who do unrighteous acts and help oppression, and kill their neighbors until the day of the great judgment, for He will throw down your glory.

16 For He shall throw down your glory, and bring affliction on your hearts, and shall arouse His fierce anger, and destroy you all with the sword; and all the holy and righteous shall remember your sins.

[Chapter 100]

1 And in those days in one place the fathers together with their sons shall kill one another and brothers shall fall in death together until the streams flow with their blood.

2 For a man shall not withhold his hand from killing his sons and his sons' sons, and the sinner shall not withhold his hand from his honored brother, from dawn until sunset they shall kill one another.

Mark 13:12 Now the brother shall betray the brother to death, and the father the son; and children shall rise up against their parents, and shall cause them to be put to death.

3 And the horse shall walk up to the breast in the blood of sinners, and the chariot shall be submerged to its height.

Revelation 14:20 And the winepress was trodden without the city, and blood came out of the winepress, even unto the horse bridles, by the space of a thousand and six hundred furlongs.

4 In those days the angels shall descend into the secret places and gather together into one place all those who brought down sin and the Most High will arise on that day of judgment to execute great judgment among sinners.

5 And over all the righteous and holy He will appoint guardians from among the holy angels to guard them as the apple of an eye, until He makes an end of all wickedness and all sin, and even if the righteous sleep a long sleep, they have nothing to fear.

6 And the wise men will seek the truth and they and their sons will understand the words of this book, and recognize that their riches shall not be able to save them or overcome their sins.

7 Woe to you sinners, on the day of strong anguish, you who afflict the righteous and burn them with fire; you shall be requited according to your works.

8 Woe to you, you obstinate of heart, who watch in order to devise wickedness; therefore shall fear come on you and there shall be none to help you.

9 Woe to you, you sinners, on account of the words of your mouth, and on account of the deeds of your hands which your godlessness has caused, in blazing flames burning worse than fire shall you burn.

2 Thessalonians 1:7-9 And to you who are troubled rest with us, when the Lord Jesus shall be revealed from heaven with his mighty angels, 8 In flaming fire taking vengeance on them that know not God, and that obey not the gospel of our Lord Jesus Christ: 9 Who shall be punished with everlasting destruction from the presence of the Lord, and from the glory of his power?

10 And now, know that the angels will ask Him in heaven about your deeds and from the sun and from the moon and from the stars they will ask about your sins because on the earth you execute judgment on the righteous.

11 And He will summon to testify against you every cloud and mist and dew and rain; for they shall all be withheld from falling on you, and they shall be mindful of your sins.

12 And now give gifts to the rain that it cease not from falling on you, nor the dew, when it has received gold and silver from you that it may fall. When the hoar-frost and snow with their chilliness, and all the snow storms with all their plagues fall on you, in those days you shall not be able to stand before them.

[Chapter 101]

1 Observe heaven, you children of heaven, and every work of the Most High, and fear Him and work no evil in His presence.

2 If He closes the windows of heaven, and withholds the rain and the dew from falling on the earth on your account, what will you do then?

3 And if He sends His anger on you because of your deeds, you cannot petition Him; for you spoke proud and arrogant words against His righteousness, therefore you shall have no peace.

4 Don't you see the sailors of the ships, how their ships are tossed back and forth by the waves, and are shaken by the winds, and are in great trouble?

5 And therefore they are afraid because all their nice possessions go on the sea with them, and they have bad feelings in their heart that the sea will swallow them and they will perish therein.

6 Are not the entire sea and all its waters, and all its movements, the work of the Most High, and has He not set limits to its actions, and confined it throughout by the sand?

7 And at His reproof it fears and dries up, and all its fish die and all that is in it; but you sinners that are on the earth fear Him not.

8 Has He not made heaven and the earth, and all that is in it? Who has given understanding and wisdom to everything that moves on the earth and in the sea?

9 Do not the sailors of the ships fear the sea? Yet you sinners do not fear the Most High.

[Chapter 102]

1 In those days if He sent a horrible fire on you, where will you flee, and where will you find deliverance? And when He launches out His Word against you will you not be shaken and afraid?

2 And all the luminaries shall be shaken with great fear, and all the earth shall be afraid and tremble and be alarmed.

3 And all the angels shall execute their commands and shall seek to hide themselves from the presence of He who is Great in Glory, and the children of earth shall tremble and shake; and you sinners shall be cursed forever, and you shall have no peace.

2 Peter 3:8-13 But, beloved, be not ignorant of this one thing, that one day is with the Lord as a thousand years, and a thousand years as one day.
9 The Lord is not slack concerning his promise, as some men count slackness; but is longsuffering to us-ward, not willing that any should perish, but that all should come to repentance.
10 But the day of the Lord will come as a thief in the night; in which the heavens shall pass away with a great noise, and the elements shall melt with fervent heat, the earth also and the works that are therein shall be burned up.
11 Seeing then that all these things shall be dissolved, what manner of persons ought ye to be in all holy conversation and godliness,
12 Looking for and hasting unto the coming of the day of God, wherein the heavens being on fire shall be dissolved, and the elements shall melt with fervent heat?
13 Nevertheless we, according to his promise, look for new heavens and a new earth, wherein dwelleth righteousness.

4 Fear you not, you souls of the righteous, and fear not you who have died in righteousness.

5 And don't grieve if your soul has descended in to the grave in grief, and that in your life you were not

rewarded according to your goodness, but wait for the day of the judgment of sinners and for the day of cursing and chastisement.

6 And when you die the sinners will say about you: "As we die, so die the righteous, and what benefit do they reap for their deeds?

7 See, even as we, so do they die in grief and darkness, and what have they more than we? From now on we are equal.

8 And what will they receive and what will they see forever? Look, they too have died, and from now on forever shall they see no light."

9 I tell you, you sinners, you are content to eat and drink, and rob and sin, and strip men naked, and acquire wealth and see good days.

10 Have you seen the righteous how their end was peace, that no violence is found in them until their death?

11 Nevertheless they died and became as though they had not been, and their spirits descended into Hell in tribulation.

Matthew 10:28 Do not be afraid of those who kill the body but cannot kill the soul. Rather, be afraid of the One who can destroy both soul and body in hell.

[Chapter 103]

1 Now, therefore, I swear to the righteous, by the glory of the Great and Honored and Mighty One who reigns, I swear to you, I know this mystery.

2 I have read the heavenly tablets, and have seen the holy books, and have found written in it and inscribed regarding them.

3 That all goodness and joy and glory are prepared for them, and written down for the spirits of those who have died in righteousness, and that much good shall be given to you in reward for your labors, and that your lot is abundant beyond the lot of the living.

4 And the spirits of you who have died in righteousness shall live and rejoice, and your spirits shall not perish, nor shall your memory from before the face of the Great One to all the generations of the world, therefore no longer fear their abuse.

5 Woe to you, you sinners, when you have died, if you die in the abundance of your sins, and woe to those who are like you and say regarding you: "Blessed are the sinners, they have seen all their days.

6 And how they have died in prosperity and in wealth, and have not seen tribulation or murder in their life; and they have died in honor, and judgment has not been executed on them during their life."

7 You know that their souls will be made to descend into Hell and they shall be wracked in great tribulation.

8 And into darkness and chains and a burning flame where there is harsh judgment your spirits shall enter, and the great judgment shall be for all the generations of the world. Woe to you, for you shall have no peace.

9 The righteous and good who are alive, do not say: "In our troubled days we have worked hard and experienced every trouble, and met with much evil and been afflicted, and have become few and our spirit small.

10 And we have been destroyed and have not found any to help us even with a word. We have been tortured

and destroyed, and not expect to live from day to day.

11 We hoped to be the head and have become the tail. We have worked hard and had no satisfaction in our labor; and we have become the food of the sinners and the unrighteous, and they have laid their yoke heavily on us.

12 They have ruled over us and hated us and hit us, and to those that hated us we have bowed our necks but they pitied us not.

13 We desired to get away from them that we might escape and be at rest, but found no place where we should flee and be safe from them.

14 We complained to the rulers in our tribulation, and cried out against those who devoured us, but they did not pay attention to our cries and would not listen to our voice.

15 And they helped those who robbed us and devoured us and those who made us few; and they concealed their oppression (wrongdoing), and they did not remove from us the yoke of those that devoured us and dispersed us and murdered us, and they concealed their murder, and did not remember that they had lifted up their hands against us."

Jeremiah 30:15-19 Why do you cry out over your wound, your pain that has no cure? Because of your great guilt and many sins I have done these things to you.
16 But all who devour you will be devoured; all your enemies will go into exile. Those who plunder you will be plundered; all who make spoil of you I will despoil.
17 But I will restore you to health and heal your wounds, declares the LORD, 'because you are called an outcast, Zion for whom no one cares.
18 This is what the LORD says: "I will restore the fortunes of Jacob's tents and have compassion on his dwellings; the city will be rebuilt on her ruins, and the palace will stand in its proper place.
19 From them will come songs of thanksgiving and the sound of rejoicing. I will add to their numbers, and they will not be decreased; I will bring them honor, and they will not be disdained."

[Chapter 104]

1 I swear to you, that in heaven the angels remember you for good before the glory of the Great One.

2 And your names are written before the glory of the Great One. Be hopeful; for before you were put to shame through sickness and affliction; but now you shall shine as the lights of heaven,

3 You shall shine and you shall be seen, and the doors of heaven shall be opened to you. And in your cry, cry for judgment, and it shall appear to you; for all your tribulation shall be visited on the rulers, and on all who helped those who plundered you.

4 Be hopeful, and do not throw away your hopes for you shall have great joy as the angels of heaven.

5 What will you have to do ? You shall not have to hide on the day of the great judgment and you shall not be found as sinners, and the eternal judgment shall not come to you for all the generations, eternally.

6 And now fear not, you righteous, when you see the sinners growing strong and prospering in their ways; do not be their companions, but keep away from their violence.

7 For you shall become companions of the hosts of heaven. And, although you sinners say, "All our sins shall not be found out and be written down," nevertheless they shall write down all your sins every day.

8 And now I show to you that light and darkness, day and night, see all your sins.

9 Do not be godless in your hearts, and do not lie and do not change the words of righteousness, nor say that the words of the Holy Great One are lies, nor praise or rely on your idols; for all your lying and all your godlessness come not from (or lead not to) righteousness but from (or lead to) great sin.

10 And now I know this mystery, that sinners will alter and pervert the words of righteousness in many ways, and will speak wicked words, and lie, and practice great deceits, and write books concerning their words.

11 But when they write down all my words truthfully in their languages, and do not change or omit any of my words but write them all down truthfully - all that I first testified concerning them.

12 Then, I know another mystery, that books will be given to the righteous and the wise to produce joy and righteousness and much wisdom.

13 And to them the books shall be given, and they shall believe them and rejoice over them, and then all the righteous who have learned from them all the paths of righteousness shall be paid back.'

[Chapter 105]
Later Additions to the Text – Book of Noah (Chapters 105-108):
1 In those days the Lord called them (the wise and righteous) to testify to the children of earth concerning their wisdom: Show it to them; for you are their guides, and a recompense over the whole earth.

2 For I and my son will be united with them forever in the paths of righteousness in their lives; and you shall have peace: rejoice, you children of righteousness. Amen.

[Chapter 106]
This section of Enoch was not originally attached. It is a fragment from the Book of Noah.

Though this book has not come down to us independently, it has in large measure been incorporated in the Ethiopic Book of Enoch, and can in part be reconstructed from it.

The Book of Noah is mentioned several times in the Book of Jubilees. The editor simply changed the name Noah in the context before him into Enoch, for the statement is based on Gen. 5: 32, and Enoch lived only 365 years. Chapters 6-11 are from the same source. They make no reference to Enoch, but bring forward Noah and mention the sin of the angels that led to the flood, and of their temporal and eternal punishment. This section is a repeat of the Semjaza and Azazel myths.

Other pieces of the Book of Noah can be found scattered throughout Enoch in chapters 6-11, 39:1-2a, 54:7-55:2, 60, 65:1-69:25, and 106-107. The fragments seem to have been written earlier than the Book of Jubilees and thus was likely written around 200 B.C.

Fragment from the Book of Noah.
1 And after some days my son Methuselah took a wife for his son, Lamech, and she became pregnant by him and bore a son. And his body was white as snow and red as the blooming of a rose, and the hair of his head and his long curls were white as wool, and his eyes beautiful.

2 And when he opened his eyes, he lit up the whole house like the sun, and the whole house was very bright.

3 And on it he levitated (arose) in the hands of the midwife, opened his mouth, and conversed with the Lord of righteousness.

4 And his father, Lamech, was afraid of him and fled, and came to his father Methuselah. And he said to him: 'I have begotten a strange son, different and unlike man, and resembling the sons of the God of heaven; and his nature is different and he is not like us, and his eyes are as the rays of the sun, and his face is glorious.

5 And it seems to me that he did not spring from me but from the angels, and I fear that in his days a wonder may be performed on the earth.

6 And now, my father, I am here to ask you and beg you that you may go to Enoch, our father, and learn from him the truth, for his dwelling-place is among the angels."

7 And when Methuselah heard the words of his son, he came to me to the ends of the earth; for he had heard that I was there, and he cried aloud, and I heard his voice and I came to him. And I said to him: 'Behold, here am I, my son, why have you come to me? '

8 And he answered and said: 'Because of a great cause of anxiety have I come to you, and because of a disturbing vision have I approached.

9 And now, my father, hear me. To Lamech, my son, there has been born a son, the like of whom there is none other, and his nature is not like man's nature, and the color of his body is whiter than snow and redder than the bloom of a rose, and the hair of his head is whiter than white wool, and his eyes are like the rays of the sun, and he opened his eyes and the whole house lit up.

10 And he levitated (arose) in the hands of the midwife, and opened his mouth and blessed the Lord of heaven.

11 And his father Lamech became afraid and fled to me, and did not believe that he was sprung from him, but that he was in the likeness of the angels of heaven; and now I have come to you that you may make known to me the truth.'

12 And I, Enoch, answered and said to him: 'The Lord will do a new thing on the earth, and this I have already seen in a vision, and make known to you that in the generation of my father Jared some of the angels of heaven violated the word of the Lord. And they commit sin and broke the law, and have had sex (united themselves) with women and committed sin with them, and have married some of them, and have had children by them.

13 And they shall produce on the earth giants not according to the spirit, but according to the flesh, and there shall be a great punishment on the earth, and the earth shall be cleansed from all impurity.

14 There shall come a great destruction over the whole earth, and there shall be a flood (deluge) and a great destruction for one year.

15 And this son who has been born to you shall be left on the earth, and his three children shall be saved with him: when all mankind that are on the earth shall die, he and his sons shall be saved.

16 And now make known to your son, Lamech, that he who has been born is in truth his son, and call his name Noah; for he shall be left to you, and he and his sons shall be saved from the destruction, which shall come on the earth on account of all the sin and all the unrighteousness, which shall be full (completed) on the earth in his days.

17 And after that (flood) there shall be more unrighteousness than that which was done before on the earth; for I know the mysteries of the holy ones; for He, the Lord, has showed me and informed me, and I have read (them) in heavenly tablets.

[Chapter 107]
1 And I saw written about them that generation after generation shall transgress, until a generation of righteousness arises, and transgression is destroyed and sin passes away from the earth, and all manner of good comes on it.

2 And now, my son, go and make known to your son Lamech that this son, which has been born, is in truth his son, and this is no lie.'

3 And when Methuselah had heard the words of his father Enoch, for he had shown to him everything in secret, he returned and showed those things to him and called the name of that son Noah; for he will comfort the earth after all the destruction.

[Chapter 108]

(Author's note: Chapter 108 was added later and was not part of the original text.)

1 Another book which Enoch wrote for his son Methuselah and for those who will come after him, and keep the law in the last days.

2 You who have done good shall wait for those days until an end is made of those who work evil; and an end of the power of the wrongdoers.

3 And wait until sin has passed away indeed, for their names shall be blotted out of the Book of Life and out of the holy books, and their (children) seed shall be destroyed forever, and their spirits shall be killed, and they shall cry and lament in a place that is a chaotic desert, and they shall be burned in the fire; for there is no earth there.

4 I saw something there like an invisible cloud; because it was so deep I could not look over it, and I saw a flame of fire blazing brightly, and things like shining mountains circling and sweeping back and forth.

5 And I asked one of the holy angels who was with me and said to him: 'What is this bright thing (shining)? For it is not heaven but there was only the flame of a blazing fire, and the voice of weeping and crying and moaning, lamenting, and agony.'

6 And he said to me: 'This place which you see are where the spirits of sinners and blasphemers, and of those who work wickedness, are cast and the spirits of those who pervert everything that the Lord hath spoken through the mouth of the prophets and even the prophecies (things that shall be).

7 For some of them are written and inscribed above in heaven, in order that the angels may read them and know that which shall befall the sinners, and the spirits of the humble, and of those who have afflicted their bodies, and been recompensed by God; and of those who have been abused (put to shame) by wicked men:

8 Who love God and loved neither gold nor silver nor any of the good things which are in the world, but gave over their bodies to torture.

9 Who, since they were born, longed not after earthly food, but regarded everything as a passing breath, and lived accordingly, and the Lord tried them much, and their spirits were found pure so that they should bless His name.

10 And all the blessings destined for them I have recounted in the books. And he has assigned them their reward, because they have been found to love heaven more than their life in the world, and though they were trodden under foot by wicked men, and experienced abuse and reviling from them and were put to shame, they blessed Me.

11 And now I will summon the spirits of the good who belong to the generation of light, and I will transform those who were born in darkness, who in the flesh were not rewarded with such honor as their faithfulness deserved.

12 And I will bring out in shining light those who have loved My holy name, and I will seat each on the throne of his honor.

Matthew 19:28 And Jesus said unto them, Verily I say unto you, That ye which have followed me, in the regeneration when the Son of Man shall sit in the throne of his glory, ye also shall sit upon twelve thrones, judging the twelve tribes of Israel.

13 And they shall shine for time without end; for righteousness is the judgment of God; because to the faithful He will give faithfulness in the habitation of upright paths.

14 And they shall see those who were born in darkness led into darkness, while the righteous shall shine. And the sinners shall cry aloud and see them shining, and they indeed will go where days and seasons are written down (prescribed) for them.'

The Calendar of Enoch's and Daniel's Prophecies

Before we proceed, let us state the obvious. As scholars, as rational people, we must understand and acknowledge the propensity of our minds. The human brain is made in such a way as to recognize patterns. This was a survival mechanism at one time. We would see movement, shape, and various patterns in such a way as to predict the object, direction, and action We also attributed patterns to sequences, shapes, and markings in an attempt to determine of an object was food, or predator. The human brain tends to look for patterns and attribute them to items or circumstances, imposing a pattern at times even if in one time occurrences or if no clear pattern exists. This is why one may see a face, animal, bird, bat, or butterfly in a cloud, or even an ink blot.

Such may be the case with the prophecy we are about to investigate. Admittedly, the Enochian calendar seems to make the prophecy of Daniel's 70 weeks fit a timeline exactly. On the other hand, we may have looked at all possible timelines and calendars until we found one that happened to fit. You, the reader, should decide for yourself if Enoch holds the key to Biblical prophecy, or if we are simply looking at a singular, amazing coincidence without an established pattern. It is my task to attempt only a clear presentation of the facts.

John Pratt and Sir Isaac Newton

I first ran across the idea of taking the Enochian Calendar and applying it to the Prophecy in the Book of Daniel after reading the work of John Pratt. He had been spurred into the project after reading the calculations of Sir Isaac Newton regarding Biblical prophecies. After combing through the math and scriptural references, I concluded there was enough coincidence to give the theory weight. It is my hope that the language and references makes this complicated study understandable.

To review: When a prophecy is uttered that is relative to a space of time, the mode of measurement must be specified. Daniel's prophecy is spoken of as 70 weeks, but it is understood that the weeks are actually years. Thus, the week of 70 years is a time span of 490 years. Now, the question becomes, "What kind of years?" Are these lunar years, solar years, or another type of year? Each type of year has a different length and over a period of 490 years the accumulative differences become significant.

There have been thousands of attempts to explain Daniel's "Weeks of Years." All seem to be rather contrived to force a predetermined solution. Most deal with future prophecies, which is always a safe way to go, seeing as how the interpreter would usually be dead before his or her theory was proven incorrect.

A new solution to Daniel's "Weeks of Years"

What if we interpret this passage differently? If we assume Daniel is speaking of a time period that begins with a ruler making peace with the Jews and ending with the bringing of everlasting righteousness?

What would happen if we applied the Enochian year, based on weeks, to solve Daniel's "Week of Years?"

The portion of 1 Enoch referred to as the Book of Astronomy is dated in the fourth to third century B.C. according to many western scholars.

This book contains descriptions of the movement of heavenly bodies as revealed to Enoch in his trips to Heaven. The book describes a solar calendar that was later described in The Book of Jubilees. The most Jews of that time used a lunar-based calendar. The use of this calendar made it impossible to celebrate the festivals simultaneously with those in the temple of Jerusalem.

The year was composed of 364 days, divided in four seasons of 91 days each. Each season was composed of three equal months of 30 days, plus an extra day at the end of the third month. The whole year was thus composed of exactly 52 weeks, and every calendar day occurred always on the same day of the week. There is some controversy as to which day of the year the calendar started on each year. Some say each year and each season started always on Wednesday, which was the fourth day of creation and the day when the lights in the sky, the seasons, the days and the years were created. Others claim the calendar began on Sunday, the first day of the week. To reconcile this calendar with the exact 365.24219 days they added a week every few years, in order to have the year always to start on Wednesday or Sunday, according to which scholar one believes.

For this exercise in Daniel, we will assume the calendar begins on a Sunday. Since the calendar of Enoch is based on weeks, it begins every year on a Sunday, and adds a week of days when needed to keep the first day of the year as near the spring equinox (usually 21 or 22 March) as possible.

Artaxerxes and Ezra Pact

Artaxerxes, king of Persia, and Ezra the prophet made a pact. The king agreed to release the Jews and permit them to return to Jerusalem and rebuild the city.

Daniel 9 (King James Version)
1 In the first year of Darius the son of Ahasuerus, of the seed of the Medes, which was made king over the realm of the Chaldeans;
2 In the first year of his reign I Daniel understood by books the number of the years, whereof the word of the LORD came to Jeremiah the prophet, that he would accomplish seventy years in the desolations of Jerusalem.
3 And I set my face unto the Lord God, to seek by prayer and supplications, with fasting, and sackcloth, and ashes:
4 And I prayed unto the LORD my God, and made my confession, and said, O Lord, the great and dreadful God, keeping the covenant and mercy to them that love him, and to them that keep his commandments;
5 We have sinned, and have committed iniquity, and have done wickedly, and have rebelled, even by departing from thy precepts and from thy judgments:
6 Neither have we hearkened unto thy servants the prophets, which spake in thy name to our kings, our princes, and our fathers, and to all the people of the land.
7 O LORD, righteousness belongeth unto thee, but unto us confusion of faces, as at this day; to the men of Judah, and to the inhabitants of Jerusalem, and unto all Israel, that are near, and that are far off, through all the countries whither thou hast driven them, because of their trespass that they have trespassed against thee.
8 O Lord, to us belongeth confusion of face, to our kings, to our princes, and to our fathers, because we have sinned against thee.
9 To the Lord our God belong mercies and forgivenesses, though we have rebelled against him;
10 Neither have we obeyed the voice of the LORD our God, to walk in his laws, which he set before us by his servants the prophets.
11 Yea, all Israel have transgressed thy law, even by departing, that they might not obey thy voice; therefore the curse is poured upon us, and the oath that is written in the law of Moses the servant of God, because we have sinned against him.
12 And he hath confirmed his words, which he spake against us, and against our judges that judged us, by bringing upon us a great evil: for under the whole heaven hath not been done as hath been done upon Jerusalem.
13 As it is written in the law of Moses, all this evil is come upon us: yet made we not our prayer before the LORD our God, that we might turn from our iniquities, and understand thy truth.
14 Therefore hath the LORD watched upon the evil, and brought it upon us: for the LORD our God is righteous in all his works which he doeth: for we obeyed not his voice.
15 And now, O Lord our God, that hast brought thy people forth out of the land of Egypt with a mighty hand, and hast gotten thee renown, as at this day; we have sinned, we have done wickedly.
16 O LORD, according to all thy righteousness, I beseech thee, let thine anger and thy fury be turned away from thy city Jerusalem, thy holy mountain: because for our sins, and for the iniquities of our fathers, Jerusalem and thy people are become a reproach to all that are about us.
17 Now therefore, O our God, hear the prayer of thy servant, and his supplications, and cause thy face to shine upon thy sanctuary that is desolate, for the Lord's sake.
18 O my God, incline thine ear, and hear; open thine eyes, and behold our desolations, and the city which is called by thy name: for we do not present our supplications before thee for our righteousnesses, but for thy great mercies.
19 O Lord, hear; O Lord, forgive; O Lord, hearken and do; defer not, for thine own sake, O my God: for thy city and thy people are called by thy name.
20 And whiles I was speaking, and praying, and confessing my sin and the sin of my people Israel, and presenting my supplication before the LORD my God for the holy mountain of my God;
21 Yea, whiles I was speaking in prayer, even the man Gabriel, whom I had seen in the vision at the beginning, being caused to fly swiftly, touched me about the time of the evening oblation.
22 And he informed me, and talked with me, and said, O Daniel, I am now come forth to give thee skill and understanding.
23 At the beginning of thy supplications the commandment came forth, and I am come to shew thee; for thou art greatly beloved: therefore understand the matter, and consider the vision.
24 Seventy weeks are determined upon thy people and upon thy holy city, to finish the transgression, and to make an end of sins, and to make reconciliation for iniquity, and to bring in everlasting righteousness, and to seal up the vision and prophecy, and to anoint the most Holy.
25 Know therefore and understand, that from the going forth of the commandment to restore and to build Jerusalem unto the

Messiah the Prince shall be seven weeks, and threescore and two weeks: the street shall be built again, and the wall, even in troublous times.
26 And after threescore and two weeks shall Messiah be cut off, but not for himself: and the people of the prince that shall come shall destroy the city and the sanctuary; and the end thereof shall be with a flood, and unto the end of the war desolations are determined.
27 And he shall confirm the covenant with many for one week: and in the midst of the week he shall cause the sacrifice and the oblation to cease, and for the overspreading of abominations he shall make it desolate, even until the consummation, and that determined shall be poured upon the desolate.

In the year 458 B.C. the first day of the Enochian year fell on Sunday, March 21st, which was the spring equinox. On Saturday, April 3, 458 B.C., the 14th day of the first month (14 Spring), which is Passover on that calendar, Ezra and the Jews departed Babylon and headed for the Holy City of Jerusalem.

Ezra 7
1 Now after these things, in the reign of Artaxerxes king of Persia, Ezra the son of Seraiah, the son of Azariah, the son of Hilkiah,
2 The son of Shallum, the son of Zadok, the son of Ahitub,
3 The son of Amariah, the son of Azariah, the son of Meraioth,
4 The son of Zerahiah, the son of Uzzi, the son of Bukki,
5 The son of Abishua, the son of Phinehas, the son of Eleazar, the son of Aaron the chief priest:
6 This Ezra went up from Babylon; and he was a ready scribe in the law of Moses, which the LORD God of Israel had given: and the king granted him all his request, according to the hand of the LORD his God upon him.
7 And there went up some of the children of Israel, and of the priests, and the Levites, and the singers, and the porters, and the Nethinims, unto Jerusalem, in the seventh year of Artaxerxes the king.
8 And he came to Jerusalem in the fifth month, which was in the seventh year of the king.
9 For upon the first day of the first month began he to go up from Babylon, and on the first day of the fifth month came he to Jerusalem, according to the good hand of his God upon him.
10 For Ezra had prepared his heart to seek the law of the LORD, and to do it, and to teach in Israel statutes and judgments.

Using Enoch's calendar: *the exact day?*
The day of the crucifixion, Friday, April 1, A.D. 33, was the day preceding Passover on the Enochian calendar. Passover always falls on a Saturday on the Enochian calendar. The Friday crucifixion completed exactly 490 years to the very day on the Enoch calendar, because the 491st year would have begun on Passover, April 2, A.D. 33. Remember, there is no year zero. The calendar goes from 1 B.C. to 1 A.D.

Thus, the interval from Ezra's departure to rebuild Jerusalem to the date Christ died was 7 x 70 or 490 years according to the Calendar of Enoch.

How do we know it was the exact day? Passover lasts seven days according to the Hebrew calendar and eight days according to the Gregorian and Enochian calendar, because the Hebrew Calendar begins the day at sundown. Out of these eight days, how do we know which day Jesus died?

Luke 22:7 Now the day of Unleavened Bread came, during which it was necessary to sacrifice the Passover lamb. And he sent out Peter and Johannes, saying, 'Go and prepare the Passover for us, so that we may eat.'....Now they went and found it just as he had told them, and they prepared the Passover.

This was the evening which began Nisan 14. Luke 22:1 indicates that the entire feast (Nisan 14-20) was called "Passover." We know that only one day is actually the specific day of Passover. Matthew uses this term indicating the week-long observance. In a while, we will examine Jesus' timeline in more detail and will see that this is the case.

Matthew 26:17 tells us that it was the evening which began the first day of the Feast of Unleavened Bread, it was the beginning of Nisan 14. Their lamb had already been slaughtered. This was done on the afternoon of the 13th of Nisan.

According to Luke 22:15, on the evening of the 14th, they were going to prepare and eat the lamb--one day earlier than normal. The accounts give no reason, but it may have been simply that Jesus wanted to eat the feast one more time before he was crucified.

Luke 22 (King James Version)

1 Now the feast of unleavened bread drew nigh, which is called the Passover.

2 And the chief priests and scribes sought how they might kill him; for they feared the people.

3 Then entered Satan into Judas surnamed Iscariot, being of the number of the twelve.

4 And he went his way, and communed with the chief priests and captains, how he might betray him unto them.

5 And they were glad, and covenanted to give him money.

6 And he promised, and sought opportunity to betray him unto them in the absence of the multitude.

7 Then came the day of unleavened bread, when the passover must be killed.

8 And he sent Peter and John, saying, Go and prepare us the passover, that we may eat.

9 And they said unto him, Where wilt thou that we prepare?

10 And he said unto them, Behold, when ye are entered into the city, there shall a man meet you, bearing a pitcher of water; follow him into the house where he entereth in.

11 And ye shall say unto the goodman of the house, The Master saith unto thee, Where is the guestchamber, where I shall eat the passover with my disciples?

12 And he shall shew you a large upper room furnished: there make ready.

13 And they went, and found as he had said unto them: and they made ready the passover.

14 And when the hour was come, he sat down, and the twelve apostles with him.

15 And he said unto them, With desire I have desired to eat this passover with you before I suffer:

16 For I say unto you, I will not any more eat thereof, until it be fulfilled in the kingdom of God.

17 And he took the cup, and gave thanks, and said, Take this, and divide it among yourselves:

18 For I say unto you, I will not drink of the fruit of the vine, until the kingdom of God shall come.

19 And he took bread, and gave thanks, and brake it, and gave unto them, saying, This is my body which is given for you: this do in remembrance of me.

20 Likewise also the cup after supper, saying, This cup is the new testament in my blood, which is shed for you.

21 But, behold, the hand of him that betrayeth me is with me on the table.

22 And truly the Son of man goeth, as it was determined: but woe unto that man by whom he is betrayed!

John tells us that it was not yet the day of the Passover when Jesus and his students had their meal. Since the term "day" is used, it points to the specific day. However, it was the day before the feast that Jesus and his students ate the meal. Both John and Luke refer to this as the "Day of Preparation." This is when the lambs were sacrificed.

Both John and Luke indicate that the day of Jesus' crucifixion preceded a Sabbath, with John providing the further detail that this was a "Great Sabbath." The Great Sabbath was the Sabbath that occurred on the feast day. In this case it was Nisan 15. *(Jn 19:14, 31, 42; Lk 23:54).*

John 19

1 Then Pilate therefore took Jesus, and scourged him.

2 And the soldiers platted a crown of thorns, and put it on his head, and they put on him a purple robe,

3 And said, Hail, King of the Jews! and they smote him with their hands.

4 Pilate therefore went forth again, and saith unto them, Behold, I bring him forth to you, that ye may know that I find no fault in him.

5 Then came Jesus forth, wearing the crown of thorns, and the purple robe. And Pilate saith unto them, Behold the man!

6 When the chief priests therefore and officers saw him, they cried out, saying, Crucify him, crucify him. Pilate saith unto them, Take ye him, and crucify him: for I find no fault in him.

7 The Jews answered him, We have a law, and by our law he ought to die, because he made himself the Son of God.

8 When Pilate therefore heard that saying, he was the more afraid;

9 And went again into the judgment hall, and saith unto Jesus, Whence art thou? But Jesus gave him no answer.

10 Then saith Pilate unto him, Speakest thou not unto me? knowest thou not that I have power to crucify thee, and have power to release thee?

11 Jesus answered, Thou couldest have no power at all against me, except it were given thee from above: therefore he that delivered me unto thee hath the greater sin.

12 And from thenceforth Pilate sought to release him: but the Jews cried out, saying, If thou let this man go, thou art not Caesar's friend: whosoever maketh himself a king speaketh against Caesar.

13 When Pilate therefore heard that saying, he brought Jesus forth, and sat down in the judgment seat in a place that is called the Pavement, but in the Hebrew, Gabbatha.
14 And it was the preparation of the passover, and about the sixth hour: and he saith unto the Jews, Behold your King!
15 But they cried out, Away with him, away with him, crucify him. Pilate saith unto them, Shall I crucify your King? The chief priests answered, We have no king but Caesar.
16 Then delivered he him therefore unto them to be crucified. And they took Jesus, and led him away.

Matthew agrees with Mark
Matthew's account does not indicate that it was the Day of Preparation during which Jesus was slain, but he does say that the next day, Sabbath/Passover, was "after the preparation" (27:62), implying that the day of Jesus' death was the same Day of Preparation mentioned by the others.
Mark 14:12 tells us that the Passover lamb was killed during the first day of the Feast of Unleavened Bread.

Mark 14:10 And Judas Iscariot, one of the twelve, went unto the chief priests, to betray him unto them.
11 And when they heard it, they were glad, and promised to give him money. And he sought how he might conveniently betray him.
12 And the first day of unleavened bread, when they killed the passover, his disciples said unto him, Where wilt thou that we go and prepare that thou mayest eat the passover?
13 And he sendeth forth two of his disciples, and saith unto them, Go ye into the city, and there shall meet you a man bearing a pitcher of water: follow him.
14 And wheresoever he shall go in, say ye to the goodman of the house, The Master saith, Where is the guestchamber, where I shall eat the passover with my disciples?

Mark 15:42 tells us it was this evening during which Jesus ate his dinner one day early. Mark further mentions that Jesus died on the Day of Preparation.

Mark 15:42-44
42 And now when the even was come, because it was the preparation, that is, the day before the sabbath,
43 Joseph of Arimathaea, an honourable counsellor, which also waited for the kingdom of God, came, and went in boldly unto Pilate, and craved the body of Jesus.
44 And Pilate marvelled if he were already dead: and calling unto him the centurion, he asked him whether he had been any while dead.
We are told that the Jewish rulers wanted to kill Jesus before the feast, because they feared the people would become upset at the brutality and work attributed to the death.

Mark 14:1-2
1 After two days was the feast of the passover, and of unleavened bread: and the chief priests and the scribes sought how they might take him by craft, and put him to death.
2 But they said, Not on the feast day, lest there be an uproar of the people.

This means it was the day before Nisan 15 when Jesus died. Thus, Jesus died in the afternoon of Nisan 14.
He was captured in the night (after the day started upon sundown.) The trial of Jesus lasted less than one day, with his crucifixion beginning on the cross around noon of Nisan 14 and his death occurring before sundown of the same day.
Now we are presented with a problem. Having established the pattern of 490 years, we should be able to track back to pinpoint the exact date of the birth of Jesus. However, that does not seem to work. What does jump out of the calendar is the exact length of time between the dedication to the Lord in the temple after his birth, as described in Leviticus 12, to the day of the resurrection.

Leviticus 12
1 And the LORD spake unto Moses, saying,
2 Speak unto the children of Israel, saying, If a woman have conceived seed, and born a man child: then she shall be unclean seven days; according to the days of the separation for her infirmity shall she be unclean.
3 And in the eighth day the flesh of his foreskin shall be circumcised.

4 And she shall then continue in the blood of her purifying three and thirty days; she shall touch no hallowed thing, nor come into the sanctuary, until the days of her purifying be fulfilled.

5 But if she bear a maid child, then she shall be unclean two weeks, as in her separation: and she shall continue in the blood of her purifying threescore and six days.

6 And when the days of her purifying are fulfilled, for a son, or for a daughter, she shall bring a lamb of the first year for a burnt offering, and a young pigeon, or a turtledove, for a sin offering, unto the door of the tabernacle of the congregation, unto the priest:

7 Who shall offer it before the LORD, and make an atonement for her; and she shall be cleansed from the issue of her blood. This is the law for her that hath born a male or a female.

8 And if she be not able to bring a lamb, then she shall bring two turtles, or two young pigeons; the one for the burnt offering, and the other for a sin offering: and the priest shall make an atonement for her, and she shall be clean.

An astonishing solution

The law of Moses required that the mother should present the son on the fortieth day after his birth, with an offering to the priest at the temple. The day of the birth was counted as day one, so the offering was made on his 39th day of life. That means that the day of presentation at the temple fell on Sunday, May 14, 1 B.C.. Because the Savior lived 33 years, that means the time from the presentation at the temple to his death was very close to 33 Enoch-fixed years. But, there is an exact match between his dedication and resurrection. It is exactly 33 years of 364 days from his presentation at the temple to his resurrection. That was an astounding amount of information, but it can be broken down and restated as follows:

The time period being looked at begins in 458 B.C. and ends in 33 A.D. There is no year zero, so we must subtract for that. 458 + 33 = 491. 491 – 1 = 490. Now we are down to the days within the proper year. The Enochian calendar is adjusted so that each year begins around the Equinox in March.

The month of Abib should always start in the spring. Spring begin at the equinox, when the sun (apparently) crosses the equator, between 3/19 and 3/22, as reckoned by the Roman Calendar. Scriptures indicate the first month should always start in the same season of the year, which is spring. Please compare the King James Version with the Revised Standard Version.

"It seems to have been understood all over the world, from ancient times until now, that the vernal equinox signals the arrival of spring and the autumnal equinox signals the arrival of fall. ... Wait until the sun signals the arrival of spring at the equinox, then select the first visible new crescent for the beginning of months: ... the first month of the year to you."

The Jewish calendar was changed to keep Passover at the beginning of spring by looking to the first new moon after the spring equinox and start the year. This will always keep Passover in spring and Tabernacles in fall. The Enochian calendar was set to being on the Sunday closest to the Equinox. In the years each are examining, these events were in sync.

Design or Coincidence?

The calendar of Enoch is the only calendar that fits the prophecy of Daniel without any manipulations. Now, we must decide if it is by design or by coincidence.

Bibliography

Laurence, The Book of Enoch (Oxford, 1821) Translations & Commentaries;
Dillmann, Das Buch Henoch (1853);
Schodde, The Book of Enoch (1882);
Charles, The Book of Enoch (1893);
Cyrus Gordon and Gary Rendsburg, The Bible And The Ancient Near East (1997)
Various articles and research

Conclusion of 1 Enoch:
Thoughts from the Author

Both men and angels were given the highest gift in the universe, that of free will. We have the power of choice. Evil resides within the problem of choice. It is free will that convicts us. We are guilty of being evil because we can choose good. Free will is the very foundation of love, and the cornerstone of evil.

It is free will which allows us to decide whether we will seek the glories of heaven or torment of hell. Whether one believes in a physical hell or not is beside the point. We, like Enoch, have the ability to transcend ourselves and become more than we now are. We, like the Grigori, can be trapped within our selfish choices and grieve the outcome for all eternity. Whether or not our judgment comes from the Lord, or from within, it is coming to each of us.

2 Peter 3:9-12 The Lord is not slack concerning his promise, as some men count slackness; but is longsuffering to us-ward, not willing that any should perish, but that all should come to repentance. 10 But the day of the Lord will come as a thief in the night; in which the heavens shall pass away with a great noise, and the elements shall melt with fervent heat, the earth also and the works that are therein shall be burned up. 11 Seeing then that all these things shall be dissolved, what manner of persons ought ye to be in all holy conversation and godliness, 12 Looking for and hasting unto the coming of the day of God, wherein the heavens being on fire shall be dissolved, and the elements shall melt with fervent heat?

1 Enoch- And wait until sin has passed away indeed, for their names shall be blotted out of the Book of Life and out of the holy books, and their (children) seed shall be destroyed forever, and their spirits shall be killed, and they shall cry and lament in a place that is a chaotic desert, and they shall be burned in the fire; for there is no earth there.

4 I saw something there like an invisible cloud; because it was so deep I could not look over it, and I saw a flame of fire blazing brightly, and things like shining mountains circling and sweeping back and forth.

The Book of Jubilees
The Little Genesis,
The Apocalypse of Moses

Joseph Lumpkin

INTRODUCTION

The *Book of Jubilees,* also known as *The Little Genesis* and *The Apocalypse of Moses,* opens with an extraordinary claim of authorship. It is attributed to the very hand of Moses; penned while he was on Mount Sinai, as an angel of God dictated to him regarding those events that transpired from the beginning of the world. The story is written from the viewpoint of the angel. The angelic monolog takes place after the exodus of the children of Israel out of Egypt. The setting is atop Mount Sinai, where Moses was summoned by God. The text then unfolds as the angel reveals heaven's viewpoint of history. We are led through the creation of man, Adam's fall from grace, the union of fallen angels and earthly women, the birth of demonic offspring, the cleansing of the earth by flood, and the astonishing claim that man's very nature was somehow changed, bringing about a man with less sinful qualities than his antediluvian counterpart. The story goes on to fill in many details in Israel's history, ending at the point in time when the narrative itself takes place, after the exodus.

Scholars believe Jubilees was composed in the second century B.C. The Hebrew fragments found at Qumran are part of a Jewish library that contained other supporting literature such as the Book of Enoch and others. An analysis of the chronological development in the shapes of letters in the manuscripts confirms that Jubilees is pre-Christian in date and seems to have been penned between 100 and 200 B.C.   Based on records of the High Priests at the time, we can further narrow the date of writing to between 140 and 100 B.C.

The book of Jubilees is also cited in the Qumran Damascus Document in pre-Christian texts.

The Book of Jubilees was originally written in Hebrew. The author was a Pharisee (a doctor of the law), or someone very familiar with scripture and religious law. Since the scrolls were found in what is assumed to be an Essene library, and were dated to the time the Essene community was active, the author was probably a member of that particular religious group. Jubilees represents a hyper-legalistic and midrashic tendency, which was part of the Essene culture at the time.

"Midrash" – refers to writings containing extra-legal material of anecdotal or allegorical nature, designed either to clarify historical material, or to teach a moral point.

Jubilees represents a midrash on Genesis 1:1 through Exodus 12:50 which depicts the episodes from creation with the observance of the Sabbath by the angels and men to Israel's escape from Egyptian bondage.

Although originally written in Hebrew, the Hebrew texts were completely lost until the find at Qumran. Fragments of Jubilees were discovered among the Dead Sea Scrolls. At least fourteen copies of the Book of Jubilees have been identified from caves 1, 2, 3 and 11 at Qumran. This makes it clear that the Book of Jubilees was a popular and probably authoritative text for the community whose library was concealed in the caves. These fragments are actually generations closer to the original copies than many books in our accepted Bible. Unfortunately, the fragments found at Qumran were only pieces of the texts and offered the briefest of glimpses of the entire book. The only complete versions of the Book of Jubilees are in Ethiopic, which in turn were translations of a Greek version.

Four Ethiopian manuscripts of Jubilees were found to be hundreds of years old. Of these, the fifteenth and sixteenth century texts are the truest and least corrupted when compared to the fragments found at Qumran. There are also citations of Jubilees in Syriac literature that may reflect a lost translation from Hebrew. Pieces of Latin translations have also been found.

Other fragments of a Greek version are quoted or referenced by Justin Martyr, Origen, Diodorus of Antioch, Isidore of Alexandria, Isidore of Seville, Eutychius, Patriarch of Alexandria, John of Malala, and Syncellus. This amount of various information and translations is enough to allow us to reconstruct the original to a great degree. The internal evidence of Jubilees shows very little tampering by Christians during its transmission and subsequent translations, thus allowing a clear view of certain Jewish beliefs being propagated at the time of its origin. By removing certain variances, we can isolate Christian alterations and mistakes in translations with a reasonable degree of confidence. Due to the poor condition of the fragments of Qumran, we may never be able to confirm certain key phrases in Hebrew. Thus, as with many texts, including those of our own Bible, in the end we must trust in the accuracy of the ancient translators.

It should be noted that the books of Jubilees, Enoch, and Jasher present stories of "The Watchers"; a group of angels sent to earth to record and teach, but who fell by their own lust and pride into a demonic state. Both Enoch and Jubilees refer to a solar-based calendar. This may show a conflict or transition at the time of their penning since Judaism now uses a lunar-based calendar.

Laws, rites, and functions are observed and noted in Jubilees. Circumcision is emphasized in both humans and angels. Angelic observance of Sabbath laws as well as parts of Jewish religious laws are said to have been observed in heaven before they were revealed to Moses.

To the Qumran community, complete obedience to the Laws of Moses entailed observing a series of holy days and festivals at a particular time according to a specific calendar. The calendar described in Jubilees is one of 364 days, divided into four seasons of three months each with thirteen weeks to a season. Each month had 30 days with one day added at certain times for each of the four seasons. With 52 weeks in a year, the festival and holy days recur at the same point each year. This calendar became a hallmark of an orthodox Qumran community.

The adherence to a specific calendar is one of many ways the Book of Jubilees shows the devotion to religious law. The law had been placed at the pinnacle of importance in the lives of the community at Qumran. All aspects of life were driven by a seemingly obsessive compliance to every jot and tittle of the law. The Book Of Jubilees confirms what can only be inferred from the books of Ezra, Nehemiah, and Zechariah, that the law and those who carried it out were supreme.

As the law took hold, by its nature, it crystallized the society. Free expression died, smothered under a mantle of hyperorthodoxy. Since free thought invited accusations of violations of the law or claims of heresy, prudence, a closed mind, and a silent voice prevailed. Free thought was limited to religious or apocryphal writings, which upheld the orthodox positions of the day. The silent period between Malachi and Mark may be a reflection of this stasis. Jubilees, Enoch, and other apocryphal books found in the Qumran caves are a triumph over the unimaginative mindset brought on by making religious law supreme and human expression contrary to law punishable by death. It may be an odd manifestation that such a burst of creativity was fueled by the very search for order that suppressed free thought in the first place.

The Book of Jubilees seems to be an attempt to answer and explain all questions left unanswered in the Book of Genesis as well as to bolster the position of the religious law. It attempts to trace the source of religious laws back to an ancient beginning thereby adding weight and sanction.

In the Book of Jubilees, we discover the origin of the wife of Cain. There is information offered about angels and the beginnings of the human race, how demons came into existence, and the place of Satan in the plans of God. Information is offered in an attempt to make perfect sense of the vagaries left in Genesis. For the defense of order and law and to maintain religious law as the center point of Jewish life, Jubilees was written as an answer to both pagan Greeks and liberal Jews. From the divine placement of law and order to its explanation of times and events, Jubilees is a panorama of legalism.

The name "Jubilees" comes from the division of time into eras known as Jubilees. One Jubilee occurs after the equivalent of forty-nine years, or seven Sabbaths or weeks of years has passed. It is the numerical perfection of seven sevens. In a balance and symmetry of years, the Jubilee occurs after seven cycles of seven or forty-nine years have been completed. Thus, the fiftieth year is a Jubilee year. Time is told by referencing the number of Jubilees that have transpired from the time the festival was first kept. For example, Israel entered Canaan at the close of the fiftieth jubilee, which is about 2450 BCE.

The obsession with time, dates, and the strict observance of festivals are all evidence of legalism taken to the highest level.

Based on the approximate time of writing, Jubilees was created in the time of the Maccabees, in the high priesthood of Hyrcanus. In this period of time the appearance of the Messiah and the rise of the Messianic kingdom were viewed as imminent. Followers were preparing themselves for the arrival of the Messiah and the establishment of His eternal kingdom.

Judaism was in contact with the Greek culture at the time. The Greeks were known to be philosophers and were developing processes of critical thinking. One objective of Jubilees was to defend Judaism against the attacks of the Hellenists and to prove that the law was logical, consistent, and valid. Attacks against paganism and non-believers are embedded in the text along with defense of the law and its consistency through proclamations of the law being observed by the angels in heaven from the beginning of creation.

Moral lessons are taught by use of the juxtaposition of the "satans" and their attempts to test and lead mankind into sin against the warning and advice of scriptural wisdom from Moses and his angels.

Mastema is mentioned only in The Book of Jubilees and in the Fragments of a Zadokite Work. Mastema is Satan. The name Mastema is derived from the Hebrew, "Mastim," meaning "adversary." The word occurs as singular and plural. The word is equivalent to Satan (adversary or accuser). This is similar to the chief Satan and his class of "satans" in 1 Enoch 40:7.

Mastema is subservient to God. His task is to tempt men to sin and if they do, he accuses them in the presence of the Throne of God. He and his minions lead men into sin but do not cause the sin. Once men have chosen to sin, they lead them from sin to destruction. Since man is given free will, sin is a choice, with Mastema simply encouraging and facilitating the decision. The choice, we can assume, is our own and the destruction that follows is "self-destruction."

Beliar is also mentioned. Beliar is the Greek name for Belial or Beliaal. The name in its Hebrew equivalent means "without value." This was a demon known by the Jews as the chief of all the devils. Belial is the leader of the Sons of Darkness. Belial is mentioned in the Fragments of a Zadokite fragment along with Mastema, which states that at the time of the Antichrist, Belial shall be let loose against Israel, as God spoke through Isaiah the prophet. Belial is sometimes presented as an agent of God's punishment although he is considered a "satan."

Although it is impossible to explore here in any detail the ramification of superhuman entities and their culpability in man's sin, it is important to mention that Judaism had no doctrine of original sin. The fall of Adam and Eve may have removed man from the perfect environment and the curses that followed may have shortened his lifespan, but propagation of sin through the bloodline was not considered. Sin seemed to affect only man and the animals he was given dominion over. Yet, man continued to sin, and to increase in his capacity and modes of sin. The explanation offered for man's inability to resist is the existence of fallen angels; spiritual, superhuman creations whose task it was to teach us but who now tempt and mislead men. In the end, the world declines and crumbles under the evil influence of the fallen angels turned demons called, "The Watchers."

With the establishment of the covenant between Abraham and God, we are told that God had appointed spirits to "mislead" all the nations but would not assign a spirit to lead or mislead the children of Isaac but God himself would be leading them.

Within the text are recurring numbers. Seven, being the number of perfection, is the most common. The number three is cited, being the number of completion. However, the number twenty-two occurs in the accounts of creation and lineage. It is worth noting that there are twenty-two letters in the Hebrew alphabet. The number twenty-two represents a type of Godly assignment or appointment. It is also the number of the perfect foundation and of the God-given language. It is presented within the text as a reminder that God established the ways of the Jews and gave the Hebrew language and writing first and only to the Jews.

The angels converse in Hebrew and it is the heavenly tongue. The law is written by God using this alphabet thus the law is also holy. All men spoke Hebrew until the time of Babel when it was lost. However, when Abraham dedicated himself to God, his ears were opened and his tongue was sanctified and Hebrew was again spoken and understood.

Finally, the entire text is based on the numbers of forty-nine and fifty. Forty-nine represents the pinnacle of perfection, being made up of seven times seven. The number fifty, which is the number of the Jubilee, is the number of grace. In this year slaves were to be set free, debts were forgiven, and grace filled the land and people.

Drawing from the theology and myths at the time, the book of Jubilees expands and embellishes on the creation story, the fall of Adam and Eve, and the fall of the angels. The expanded detail written into the text may have been one reason it was eventually rejected. However, the effects of the book can still be seen throughout the Judeo-Christian beliefs of today. The theology espoused in Jubilees can be seen in the angelology and demonology taught in the Christian churches of today and widely held by many Jews.

In an attempt to answer questions left unaddressed in Genesis the writer confronts the origin and identification of Cain's wife. According to The Book Of Jubilees, Cain married his sister, as did all of the sons of Adam and Eve, except Abel, who was murdered. This seemed offensive to some, since it flies in the face of the very law it was written to defend. Yet, this seemed to the writer to be the lesser of evils, given the problematic questions. Inbreeding is dismissed with the observation that the law was not fully given and understood then. The effects of the act were mute due to the purity of the newly created race.

The seeming discrepancy between divine command of Adam's death decree and the timing of his death is addressed. Seeing that Adam continued to live even after he ate the fruit, which was supposed to bring on his death, the writer set about to clarify God's actions. The problem is explained away in a single sentence. Since a day in heaven is as a thousand years on earth and Adam died having lived less than a thousand years this meant he died in the same heavenly day. Dying within the same day of the crime was acceptable.

In an astonishing parallel to the Book Of Enoch, written at about the same time as Jubilees, the Watchers, or sons of God mentioned in Genesis 6, fell from grace when they descended to earth and had sex with the daughters of men. In the Book of Enoch, the angels descended for the purpose of seducing the women of earth. However, in The Book Of Jubilee the angels were sent to teach men, but after living on earth for a while, were tempted by their own lust and fell. The offspring of this unholy union were bloodthirsty and cannibalistic giants. The Book of Jubilees indicates that the offspring were somehow different, yet they are divided into categories of the Naphidim (or Naphilim, depending or the transliteration), the Giants, and the Eljo. (Naphil are mentioned but this is the singular of Naphilim.)

As sin spread throughout the world and the minds of men were turned toward evil, God saw no altarnative but to cleanse the earth with a flood and establish a "new nature" in man that does not have to sin. It is this new nature that the messiah will meet in mankind when He comes. As far as this author is aware, the re-creation of man's nature is mentioned in no other book. This idea of human nature being altared as it exited before the flood is found nowhere else but in Jubilees.

The angelic narrator tells us there were times in Israel's history when no evil existed and all men lived in accord. We are also told when and where the satans were allowed to attack and confound Israel. In this narrative, God uses his satans to harden the hearts of the Egyptians compelling them to pursue Israel and be destroyed.

The Book of Jubilees had other names throughout its history and propagation. "The Little Genesis" is another name given to this text. The description of "Little" does not refer to the size of the book, but to its canonical disposition.

"The Apocalypse of Moses" is another name denoting the same work. This title seems to have been used for only a short period of time. It refers to the revelation given to Moses as the recipient of all the knowledge disclosed in the book. The term "Apocalypse" means to make known or to reveal. With the exception of minor differences picked up through translation and copying, the three titles represent the same text.

About the Translation

The translation presented herein is based in part on that of R.H. Charles and his works of 1902 through 1913. Although the translation seems to be a faithful one, his scholarly tone, pedantry, and quasi-Elizabethan language made the text less than accessible. The pleonasm of the text as well as the ancient writer's tendency to repeat phrases for the sake of emphasis added to the general lack of readability. Furthermore, many of the verse breaks occurred in mid-sentence and certainly in mid-thought, adding confusion when viewing the text. All of these difficulties were corrected.

To aid in comprehension, it was decided that the text would be put through three phases of change. First, all verse breaks would be aligned with sentence breaks and with complete streams of thought when possible. Next, all archaic words and phrases would be replaced with their modern equivalent. Lastly, convoluted sentence structure would be clarified and rewritten. Notes of explanation and clarification are added in parentheses.

Due to the vast differences in societal structure and rules, certain phrases remained in their archaic form, seeing that they had no direct equivalence in our western culture. One such phrase is "uncovered the skirt." This phrase indicates the person was seen naked. In most cases it carries a connotation of intercourse. If one were to "uncover his father's skirt" it indicates the father's wife or concubine has been seen naked, usually with the intent of having sex with her.

When possible, the poetic flow of the text would be kept, but not at the expense of understanding. Various translations of each verse were referenced in order to compare and contrast differing viewpoints. The best rendering of the text was chosen and written into a more modern and readable format.

Since the book of Jubilees is written from the viewpoint of the angel narrating or dictating the text, when the words "I," "we," and "us" appear and the words are not readily connected to anyone within the sentence, it can be assumed the angel is referring to himself or the angelic host to which he belongs. When the narrator uses the word "you" he is referring to Moses, to whom the angel is speaking and dictating.

For simplicity's sake, it was decided to keep the word "soul" in the translation as related to the blood of animal and man. The phrase, "The soul is in the blood," will occur several times in the texts. It should be noted that the soul is the "life force," which came from God and belongs to God. It was considered sacred. It did not belong to man and was to be offered to God alone. Since blood represented life itself, it must be the centerpiece of any animal sacrifice. Sin or transgression of the law was punishable by death. Life must be offered as payment. The life force of an animal was offered in place of the life of the sinner. The blood of the animal represents this life.

Now, let us delve into this fascinating and illuminating book.

THE BOOK OF JUBILEES
THE LITTLE GENESIS,
THE APOCALYPSE OF MOSES

This is the history of how the days were divided and of the days of the law and of the testimony, of the events of the years, and of the weeks of years, of their Jubilees throughout all the years of the world, as the Lord spoke to Moses on Mount Sinai when he went up to receive the tablets of the law and the commandment, according to the voice of God when he said to him, "Go up to the top of the Mount."

[Chapter 1]

1 It happened in the first year of the exodus of the children of Israel out of Egypt, in the third month, on the sixteenth day of the month, that God spoke to Moses, saying, "Come up to Me on the Mountain, and I will give you two tablets of stone of the law and the commandment, which I have written, that you may teach them."

2 Moses went up into the mountain of God, and the glory of the Lord rested on Mount Sinai, and a cloud overshadowed it six days.

3 He called to Moses on the seventh day out of the middle of the cloud, and the appearance of the glory of the Lord was like a flame on the top of the mountain.

4 Moses was on the mountain forty days and forty nights, and God taught him the earlier and the later history of the division of all the days of the law and of the testimony.

5 He said, "Open your heart to every word which I shall speak to you on this mountain, and write them in a book in order that their generations may see how I have not forsaken them for all the evil which they have committed when they transgressed the covenant which I establish between Me and you for their generations this day on Mount Sinai.

6 It will come to pass when all these things come on them, that they will recognize that I am more righteous than they in all their judgments and in all their actions, and they will recognize that I have truly been with them.

7 Write all these words for yourself which I speak to you today, for I know their rebellion and their stubbornness, before I brought them into the land of which I swore to their fathers, to Abraham and to Isaac and to Jacob, saying, " Unto your offspring will I give a land flowing with milk and honey.

8 They will eat and be satisfied, and they will turn to strange gods, to gods that cannot deliver them from any of their tribulation, and this witness shall be heard for a witness against them.

9 They will forget all My commandments, even all that I command them, and they will walk in the ways of the Gentiles, and after their uncleanness, and after their shame, and will serve their gods, and these will prove to them an offence and a tribulation and an sickness and a trap.

10 Many will perish and they will be taken captive, and will fall into the hands of the enemy, because they have forsaken My laws and My commandments, and the festivals of My covenant, and My sabbaths, and My holy place which I have made holy for Myself in their presence, and My tabernacle, and My sanctuary, which I have made holy for Myself in the midst of the land, that I should set My name on it, that it should reside there.

11 They will make themselves high places and places of worship and graven images. Each will worship graven images of his own making, Thus they will go astray. They will sacrifice their children to demons, and to all errors their hearts can work.

12 I will send witnesses to them that I may testify against them, but they will not hear. They will kill the witnesses. They will persecute those who seek the law, and they will abolish and change everything (in the Law) so as to work evil before My eyes.

13 I will hide My face from them. I will deliver them into the hand of the Gentiles. They will be captured like prey for their eating. I will remove them from the out of the land. I will scatter them among the Gentiles.

14 And they will forget My law and all My commandments and all My judgments. They will go astray regarding the observance of new moons, and sabbaths, and festivals, and jubilees, and laws.

15 After this they will turn to Me from among the Gentiles with all their heart and with all their soul and with all their strength, and I will gather them from among all the Gentiles, and they will seek me. I shall be found by them when they seek me with all their heart and with all their soul.

16 I will allow them to see abounding peace with righteousness. I will remove them, the plant of uprightness, with all My heart and with all My soul, and they shall be for a blessing and not for a curse, and they shall be the

head and not the tail.

17 I will build My sanctuary among them, and I will dwell with them, and I will be their God and they shall be My people in truth and righteousness.

18 I will not forsake them nor fail them; for I am the Lord their God."

19 Moses fell on his face and prayed and said, 'O Lord my God, do not forsake Your people and Your inheritance, so that they should wander in the error of their hearts, and do not deliver them into the hands of their enemies, the Gentiles, so that they should rule over them and cause them to sin against You.

20 Let your mercy, O Lord, be lifted up on Your people, and create in them an upright spirit, and let not the spirit of Beliar rule over them to accuse them before You, and to ensnare them from all the paths of righteousness, so that they may perish from before Your face.

21 But they are Your people and Your inheritance, which You have delivered with Your great power from the hands of the Egyptians, create in them a clean heart and a holy spirit, and let them not be ensnared in their sins from now on until eternity."

22 The Lord said to Moses, "I know their contrariness and their thoughts and their stubbornness, and they will not be obedient until they confess their own sin and the sin of their fathers.

23 After this they will turn to Me in all uprightness and with all their heart and with all their soul, and I will circumcise the foreskin of their heart and the foreskin of the heart of their offspring, and I will create in them a holy spirit, and I will cleanse them so that they shall not turn away from Me from that day to eternity.

24 And their souls will cling to Me and to all My commandments, and they will fulfill My commandments, and I will be their Father and they shall be My children.

25 They all shall be called children of the living God, and every angel and every spirit shall know, yes, they shall know that these are My children, and that I am their Father in uprightness and righteousness, and that I love them.

26 Write down for yourself all these words which I say to you on this mountain, from the first to the last, which shall come to pass in all the divisions of the days in the law and in the testimony and in the weeks and the jubilees to eternity, until I descend and dwell with them throughout eternity."

27 He said to the angel of the presence (of the Lord), "Write for Moses from the beginning of creation until My sanctuary has been built among them for all eternity.

28 The Lord will appear to the eyes of all, and all shall know that I am the God of Israel and the Father of all the children of Jacob, and King on Mount Zion for all eternity. And Zion and Jerusalem shall be holy."

29 The angel of the presence (of the Lord) who went before the camp of Israel took the tables of the divisions of the years, written from the time of the creation, concerning the law and the testimony of the weeks of the jubilees, according to the individual years, according to the numbering of all the jubilees, from the day of the new creation when the heavens and the earth shall be renewed and all their creation according to the powers of the heaven, and according to all the creation of the earth, until the sanctuary of the Lord shall be made in Jerusalem on Mount Zion, and all the stars and planets be renewed for healing, peace, and blessing for all the elect of Israel, and that this is the way it may be from that day and to all the days of the earth.

[Chapter 2]

1 The angel of the presence (of the Lord) spoke to Moses according to the word of the Lord, saying, "Write the complete history of the creation, how in six days the Lord God finished all His works and all that He created, and kept Sabbath on the seventh day and made it holy for all ages, and appointed it as a sign for all His works.

2 For on the first day He created the heavens which are above and the earth and the waters and all the spirits which serve before him which are the angels of the presence (of the Lord), and the angels of sanctification, and the angels of the spirit of fire, and the angels of the spirit of the winds, and the angels of the spirit of the clouds, and of darkness, and of snow and of hail and of white frost, and the angels of the voices and of the thunder and of the lightning, and the angels of the spirits of cold and of heat, and of winter and of spring and of autumn and of summer and of all the spirits of his creatures which are in the heavens and on the earth, He created the bottomless pit and the darkness, evening and night, and the light, dawn and day, which He has prepared in the knowledge of His heart.

3 When we saw His works, we praised Him, and worshiped before Him because of all His works; for seven great works did He create on the first day.

4 On the second day He created the sky between the waters (above and below), and the waters were divided on

that day. Half of them went up above the sky and half of them went down below the sky that was in the middle over the face of the whole earth. And this was the only work God created on the second day.

5 On the third day He commanded the waters to pass from off the face of the whole earth into one place, and the dry land to appear.

6 The waters did as He commanded them, and they receded from off the face of the earth into one place, and the dry land appeared.

7 On that day He created for them all the seas according to their separate gathering-places, and all the rivers, and the gatherings of the waters in the mountains and on all the earth, and all the lakes, and all the dew of the earth, and the seed which is sown, and all sprouting things, and fruit-bearing trees, and trees of the wood, and the garden of Eden, in Eden and throughout. These four great works God created on the third day.

8 On the fourth day He created the sun and the moon and the stars, and set them in the sky of the heaven, to give light on all the earth, and to rule over the day and the night, and divide the light from the darkness.

9 God appointed the sun to be a great sign on the earth for days and for sabbaths and for months and for feasts and for years and for sabbaths of years and for jubilees and for all seasons of the years.

10 And it divides the light from the darkness for prosperity that all things may prosper which sprout and grow on the earth. These three kinds He made on the fourth day.

11 On the fifth day He created great sea monsters in the depths of the waters, for these were the first things of flesh that were created by his hands, the fish and everything that moves in the waters, and everything that flies, the birds and all their kind.

12 And the sun rose above them to make them prosper, and the sun rose above everything that was on the earth, everything that sprouts out of the earth, and all fruit-bearing trees, and all flesh.

13 He created these three kinds on the fifth day. On the sixth day He created all the animals of the earth, and all cattle, and everything that moves on the earth.

14 After all this He created mankind. He created a man and a woman, and gave him dominion over all that is on the earth, and in the seas, and over everything that flies, and over beasts, and over cattle, and over everything that moves on the earth, and over the whole earth, and over all this He gave him dominion.

15 He created these four kinds on the sixth day. And there were altogether two and twenty kinds.

16 He finished all his work on the sixth day. That is all that is in the heavens and on the earth, and in the seas and in the abysses, and in the light and in the darkness, and in everything.

17 He gave us a great sign, the Sabbath day, that we should work six days, but keep Sabbath on the seventh day from all work.

18 All the angels of the presence (of the Lord), and all the angels of sanctification, these two great types of angels He has told to tell us to keep the Sabbath with Him in heaven and on earth.

19 And He said to us, "Look, I will separate to Myself a people from among all the peoples, and these shall keep the Sabbath day, and I will sanctify them to Myself as My people, and will bless them; as I have sanctified the Sabbath day and do sanctify it to Myself, even so will I bless them, and they shall be My people and I will be their God.

20 I have chosen the offspring of Jacob from among all that I have seen, and have written him down as My first-born son, and have sanctified him to Myself forever and ever; and I will teach them the Sabbath day, that they may keep Sabbath on it from all work."

21 He created in it a sign in accordance with which they should keep Sabbath with us on the seventh day, to eat and to drink, and to bless Him who has created all things as He has blessed and sanctified to Himself a particular, exclusive people above all peoples, and that they should keep Sabbath together with us.

22 He caused His commands to rise up as a sweet odor acceptable before Him all the days.

23 There were two and twenty heads (representatives) of mankind from Adam to Jacob, and two and twenty kinds of work (creation) were made until the seventh day; this is blessed and holy; and the former also is blessed and holy; and this one serves with that one for sanctification and blessing.

24 Jacob and his offspring were granted that they should always be the blessed and holy ones of the first testimony and law, even as He had sanctified and blessed the Sabbath day on the seventh day.

25 He created heaven and earth and everything that He created in six days, and God made the seventh day holy, for all His works; therefore He commanded on its behalf that, whoever does any work on it shall die, and that he who defiles it shall surely die.

26 Because of this, command the children of Israel to observe this day that they may keep it holy and not do on it any work, and not to defile it, as it is holier than all other days.

27 And whoever profanes it shall surely die, and whoever does any work on it shall surely die eternally, that the children of Israel may observe this day throughout their generations, and not be rooted out of the land; for it is a holy day and a blessed day.

28 Every one who observes it and keeps Sabbath on it from all his work will be holy and blessed throughout all days as we are blessed.

29 Declare and say to the children of Israel the law of this day that they should keep Sabbath on it, and that they should not forsake it in the error of their hearts; and that it is not lawful to do any work on it which is not suitable, to do their own pleasure on it, and that they should not prepare anything to be eaten or drunk on it, and that it is not lawful to draw water, or bring in or take out through their gates any burden which they had not prepared for themselves on the sixth day in their dwellings.

30 They shall not bring or take anything from house to house on that day; for that day is more holy and blessed than any jubilee day of the jubilees; on this we kept Sabbath in the heavens before it was made known to any flesh to keep Sabbath on the earth.

31 The Creator of all things blessed it, but He did not sanctify all peoples and nations to keep Sabbath, but Israel alone, them alone He permitted to eat and drink and to keep Sabbath on the earth.

32 And the Creator of all things blessed this day which He had created for blessing and holiness and glory above all days.

33 This law and

[Chapter 3]

1 On the sixth day of the second week, according to the word of God, we brought to Adam all the beasts, and all the cattle, and all the birds, and everything that moves on the earth, and everything that moves in the water, according to their kinds, and according to their types, the beasts on the first day; the cattle on the second day; the birds on the third day; and all that moves on the earth on the fourth day; and that moves in the water on the fifth day.

2 And Adam named them all by their respective names. As he called them, so was their name.

3 On these five days Adam saw all these, male and female, according to every kind that was on the earth, but he was alone and found no helpmate.

4 The Lord said to us, "It is not good that the man should be alone, let us make a helpmate for him."

5 And the Lord our God caused a deep sleep to fall on him, and he slept, and He took from Adam a rib from among his ribs for the woman, and this rib was the origin of the woman. And He built up the flesh in its place, and built the woman.

6 He awakened Adam out of his sleep and on awakening he rose on the sixth day, and He brought her to him, and he knew her, and said to her, "This is now bone of my bones and flesh of my flesh; she shall be called my wife; because she was taken from her husband."

7 Therefore shall man and wife become one and therefore shall a man leave his father and his mother, and cling to his wife, and they shall be one flesh.

8 In the first week Adam was created, and from his rib, his wife. In the second week God showed her to him, and for this reason the commandment was given to keep in their defilement. A male should be purified in seven days, and for a female twice seven days.

9 After Adam had completed forty days in the land where he had been created, we brought him into the garden of Eden to till and keep it, but his wife we brought in on the eightieth day, and after this she entered into the garden of Eden.

10 And for this reason the commandment is written on the heavenly tablets in regard to her that gives birth, "If she bears a male, she shall remain unclean for seven days according to the first week of days, and thirty-three days shall she remain in the blood of her purifying, and she shall not touch any holy thing, nor enter into the sanctuary, until she completes these days which are decreed in the case of a male child.

11 But in the case of a female child she shall remain unclean two weeks of days, according to the first two weeks, and sixty-six days in the blood of her purification, and they will be in all eighty days."

12 When she had completed these eighty days we brought her into the Garden of Eden, for it is holier than all the earth besides and every tree that is planted in it is holy.

13 Therefore, there was ordained regarding her who bears a male or a female child the statute of those days that she should touch no holy thing, nor enter into the sanctuary until these days for the male or female child are

completed.

14 This is the law and testimony that was written down for Israel, in order that they should observe it all the days.

15 In the first week of the first jubilee, Adam and his wife were in the garden of Eden for seven years tilling and keeping it, and we gave him work and we instructed him to do everything that is suitable for tillage.

16 And he tilled the garden, and was naked and did not realize it, and was not ashamed. He protected the garden from the birds and beasts and cattle. He gathered its fruit, and ate, and put aside that which was left over for himself and for his wife.

17 After the completion of exactly seven years there, and in the second month, on the seventeenth day of the month, the serpent came and approached the woman, and the serpent said to the woman, "Has God commanded you saying, you shall not eat of every tree of the garden?"

18 She said to it, God said to us, of all the fruit of the trees of the garden, eat; but of the fruit of the tree which is in the middle of the garden God said to us, you shall not eat of it, neither shall you touch it, or you shall die."

19 The serpent said to the woman, "You shall not surely die. God does know that on the day you shall eat of it, your eyes will be opened, and you will be as gods, and you will know good and evil.

20 And the woman saw the tree that it was beautiful and pleasant to the eye, and that its fruit was good for food, and she took of it and ate.

21 First, she covered her shame with fig leaves and then she gave the fruit to Adam and he ate, and his eyes were opened, and he saw that he was naked.

22 He took fig leaves and sewed them together, and made an apron for himself, and covered his shame.

23 God cursed the serpent, and was very angry at it forever.

24 And He was very angry with the woman, because she listened to the voice of the serpent, and ate; and He said to her, "I will vastly multiply your sorrow and your pains, in sorrow you will bring forth children, and your master shall be your husband, and he will rule over you."

25 To Adam also he said, " Because you have listened to the voice of your wife, and have eaten of the tree of which I commanded you not to eat, cursed be the ground for your sake, thorns and thistles shall it produce for you, and you will eat your bread in the sweat of your face, until you return to the earth from where you were taken; for earth you are, and to earth will you return."

26 And He made for them coats of skin, and clothed them, and sent them out from the Garden of Eden.

27 On that day on which Adam went out from the Garden, he offered as a sweet odor an offering, frankincense, incense, and sweet spice, and spices in the morning with the rising of the sun from the day when he covered his shame.

28 On that day was closed the mouth of all beasts, and of cattle, and of birds, and of whatever walks, and of whatever moves, so that they could no longer speak, for they had all spoken one with another with one dialect and with one language.

29 All flesh that was in the Garden of Eden He sent out of the Garden of Eden, and all flesh was scattered according to its kinds, and according to its types to the places that had been created for them.

30 Of all the beasts and cattle only to Adam alone He gave the ability to cover his shame.

31 Because of this, it is prescribed on the heavenly tablets as touching all those who know the judgment of the law, that they should cover their shame, and should not uncover themselves as the Gentiles uncover themselves.

32 On the new moon of the fourth month, Adam and his wife went out from the Garden of Eden, and they dwelt in the land of Elda in the land of their creation.

33 And Adam called the name of his wife Eve.

34 And they had no son until the first jubilee, and after this he knew her.

35 Now he tilled the land as he had been instructed in the Garden of Eden.

[Chapter 4]

1 In the third week in the second jubilee she gave birth to Cain, and in the fourth (week of the) jubilee she gave birth to Abel, and in the fifth (week of the) jubilee she gave birth to her daughter Awan. (A week is seven years.)

2 In the first year of the third jubilee, Cain killed Abel because God accepted the sacrifice of Abel, and did not accept the offering of Cain.

3 And he killed him in the field, and his blood cried from the ground to heaven, complaining because he had killed him.

4 The Lord blamed Cain, because he had killed Abel, and He made him a fugitive on the earth because of the blood of his brother, and He cursed him on the earth.

5 Because of this it is written on the heavenly tablets, "Cursed is he who kills his neighbor treacherously, and let all who have seen and heard say, 'So be it', and the man who has seen and not reported it, let him be accursed as the one committing it."

6 For this reason we announce when we come before the Lord our God all the sin that is committed in heaven and on earth, and in light and in darkness, and everywhere.

7 And Adam and his wife mourned for Abel four weeks of years, and in the fourth year of the fifth week they became joyful, and Adam knew his wife again, and she gave birth to a son, and he called his name Seth, for he said "God has raised up a second offspring to us on the earth instead of Abel; for Cain killed him."

8 In the sixth week he begat his daughter Azura.

9 And Cain took Awan his sister to be his wife and she gave birth to Enoch at the close of the fourth jubilee.

10 In the first year of the first week of the fifth jubilee, houses were built on the earth, and Cain built a city, and called its name after the name of his son Enoch.

11 Adam knew Eve his wife and she gave birth to a total of nine sons. In the fifth week of the fifth jubilee Seth took Azura his sister to be his wife, and in the fourth year of the sixth week she gave birth to Enos.

12 He began to call on the name of the Lord on the earth.

13 In the seventh jubilee in the third week Enos took Noam his sister to be his wife, and she gave birth to a son in the third year of the fifth week, and he called his name Kenan.

14 At the close of the eighth jubilee Kenan took Mualeleth his sister to be his wife, and she gave birth to a son in the ninth jubilee, in the first week in the third year of this week, and he called his name Mahalalel.

15 In the second week of the tenth jubilee Mahalalel took to him to wife Dinah, the daughter of Barakiel the daughter of his father's brother, and she gave birth to a son in the third week in the sixth year, and he called his name Jared, for in his days the angels of the Lord descended on the earth, those who are named the Watchers, that they should instruct the children of men, and that they should do judgment and uprightness on the earth.

16 In the eleventh jubilee Jared took to himself a wife, and her name was Baraka, the daughter of Rasujal, a daughter of his father's brother, in the fourth week of this jubilee, and she gave birth to a son in the fifth week, in the fourth year of the jubilee, and he called his name Enoch.

17 He was the first among men that are born on earth who learned writing and knowledge and wisdom and who wrote down the signs of heaven according to the order of their months in a book, that men might know the seasons of the years according to the order of their separate months.

18 He was the first to write a testimony and he testified to the sons of men among the generations of the earth, and recounted the weeks of the jubilees, and made known to them the days of the years, and set in order the months and recounted the Sabbaths of the years as we made them, known to him.

19 And what was and what will be he saw in a vision of his sleep, as it will happen to the children of men throughout their generations until the day of judgment; he saw and understood everything, and wrote his testimony, and placed the testimony on earth for all the children of men and for their generations.

20 In the twelfth jubilee, in the seventh week of it, he took to himself a wife, and her name was Edna, the daughter of Danel, the daughter of his father's brother, and in the sixth year in this week she gave birth to a son and he called his name Methuselah.

21 He was with the angels of God these six jubilees of years, and they showed him everything that is on earth and in the heavens, the rule of the sun, and he wrote down everything.

22 And he testified to the Watchers, who had sinned with the daughters of men; for these had begun to unite themselves, so as to be defiled with the daughters of men, and Enoch testified against them all.

23 And he was taken from among the children of men, and we conducted him into the Garden of Eden in majesty and honor, and there he wrote down the condemnation and judgment of the world, and all the wickedness of the children of men.

24 Because of it God brought the waters of the flood on all the land of Eden; for there he was set as a sign and that he should testify against all the children of men, that he should recount all the deeds of the generations until the day of condemnation.

25 He burnt the incense of the sanctuary, even sweet spices acceptable before the Lord on the Mount.

26 For the Lord has four places on the earth, the Garden of Eden, and the Mount of the East, and this mountain on which you are this day, Mount Sinai, and Mount Zion which will be sanctified in the new creation for a sanctification of the earth; through it will the earth be sanctified from all its guilt and its uncleanness throughout the generations of the world.

27 In the fourteenth jubilee Methuselah took to himself a wife, Edna the daughter of Azrial, the daughter of his

father's brother, in the third week, in the first year of this week, and he begat a son and called his name Lamech.

28 In the fifteenth jubilee in the third week Lamech took to himself a wife, and her name was Betenos the daughter of Baraki'il, the daughter of his father's brother, and in this week she gave birth to a son and he called his name Noah, saying, "This one will comfort me for my trouble and all my work, and for the ground which the Lord has cursed."

29 At the close of the nineteenth jubilee, in the seventh week in the sixth year of it, Adam died, and all his sons buried him in the land of his creation, and he was the first to be buried in the earth.

30 He lacked seventy years of one thousand years, because one thousand years are as one day in the testimony of the heavens. Therefore was it written concerning the tree of knowledge, "On the day that you eat of it you shall die." Because of this he did not complete the one thousand years but instead he died during it.

31 At the close of this jubilee Cain was killed after him in the same year; because his house fell on him and he died in the middle of his house, and he was killed by its stones. With a stone he had killed Abel, and by a stone he was killed in righteous judgment.

32 For this reason it was ordained on the heavenly tablets, with the instrument with which a man kills his neighbor with the same shall he be killed. In the same manner that he wounded him, in like manner shall they deal with him."

33 In the twenty-fifth jubilee Noah took to himself a wife, and her name was Emzara, the daughter of Rake'el, the daughter of his father's brother, in the first year in the fifth week, and in the third year of it she gave birth to Shem, in the fifth year of it she gave birth to Ham, and in the first year in the sixth week she gave birth to Japheth.

[Chapter 5]

1 When the children of men began to multiply on the face of the earth and daughters were born to them, and the angels of God saw them on a certain year of this jubilee, that they were beautiful, and they took themselves wives of all whom they chose, and they gave birth to their sons and they were giants.

2 Because of them lawlessness increased on the earth and all flesh corrupted its way. Men and cattle and beasts and birds and everything that walked on the earth were all corrupted in their ways and their orders, and they began to devour each other. Lawlessness increased on the earth and the imagination and thoughts of all men were continually, totally evil.

3 God looked on the earth, and saw it was corrupt, and all flesh had corrupted its orders, and all that were on the earth had committed all manner of evil before His eyes.

4 He said that He would destroy man and all flesh on the face of the earth that He had created.

5 But Noah found grace before the eyes of the Lord.

6 And against the angels whom He had sent on the earth, He had boiling anger, and He gave commandment to root them out of all their dominion, and He commanded us to bind them in the depths of the earth, and look, they are bound in the middle of the earth, and are kept separate.

7 And against their sons went out a command from His mouth that they should be killed with the sword, and be left under heaven.

8 He said, "My spirit shall not always abide on man; for they also are flesh and their days shall be one hundred and twenty years."

9 He sent His sword into their presence that each should kill his neighbor, and they began to kill each other until they all fell by the sword and were destroyed from the earth.

10 And their fathers were witnesses of their destruction, and after this they were bound in the depths of the earth forever, until the day of the great condemnation, when judgment is executed on all those who have corrupted their ways and their works before the Lord.

11 He destroyed all wherever they were, and there was not one left of them whom He judged according to all their wickedness.

12 Through His work He made a new and righteous nature, so that they should not sin in their whole nature forever, but should be all righteous each in his own way always.

13 The judgment of all is ordained and written on the heavenly tablets in righteousness, even the judgment of all who depart from the path that is ordained for them to walk; and if they do not walk it, judgment is written down for every creature and for every kind.

14 There is nothing in heaven or on earth, or in light or in darkness, or in the abode of the dead or in the depth, or in the place of darkness that is not judged. All their judgments are ordained and written and engraved.

15 He will judge all, the great according to his greatness, and the small according to his smallness, and each according to his way.

16 He is not one who will regard the position of any person, nor is He one who will receive gifts, if He says that He will execute judgment on each.

17 If one gave everything that is on the earth, He will not regard the gifts or the person of any, nor accept anything at his hands, for He is a righteous judge.

18 Of the children of Israel it has been written and ordained, if they turn to him in righteousness He will forgive all their transgressions and pardon all their sins. It is written and ordained that He will show mercy to all who turn from all their guilt once each year.

19 And as for all those who corrupted their ways and their thoughts before the flood, no person was acceptable to God except Noah. His sons were saved in deference to him, and these God kept from the waters of the flood on his account; for Noah's heart was righteous in all his ways. He upheld the laws and did as God commanded him and he had not departed from anything that was ordained for him.

20 The Lord said that he would destroy everything on the earth, both men and cattle, and beasts, and birds of the air, and that which moves on the earth.

21 And He commanded Noah to make an ark, so that he might save himself from the waters of the flood.

22 And Noah made the ark in all respects as He commanded him, in the twenty-seventh jubilee of years, in the fifth week in the fifth year on the new moon of the first month.

23 He entered in the sixth year of it, in the second month, on the new moon of the second month, until the sixteenth; and he entered, and all that we brought to him, into the ark, and the Lord closed it from the outside on the seventeenth evening.

24 And the Lord opened seven floodgates of heaven, and He opened the mouths of the fountains of the great deep, seven mouths in number.

25 And the floodgates began to pour down water from the heaven forty days and forty closets, And the fountains of the deep also sent up waters, until the whole world was full of water.

26 The waters increased on the earth, by fifteen cubits (a cubit is about 18 inches) the waters rose above all the high mountains. And the ark was lift up from the earth. And it moved on the face of the waters.

27 And the water covered the face of the earth five months, which is one hundred and fifty days.

28 And the ark went and rested on the top of Lubar, one of the mountains of Ararat.

29 On the new moon in the fourth month the fountains of the great deep were closed and the floodgates of heaven were restrained; and on the new moon of the seventh month all the mouths of the bottomless gulfs of the earth were opened, and the water began to flow down into the deep below.

30 On the new moon of the tenth month the tops of the mountains were seen, and on the new moon of the first month the earth became visible.

31 The waters disappeared from the earth in the fifth week in the seventh year of it, and on the seventeenth day in the second month the earth was dry.

32 On the twenty-seventh of it he opened the ark, and sent out beasts, and cattle, and birds, and every moving thing.

[Chapter 6]

1 On the new moon of the third month he went out of the ark, and built an altar on that mountain.

2 And he made atonement for the earth, and took a kid and made atonement by its blood for all the guilt of the earth; for every thing that had been on it had been destroyed, except those that were in the ark with Noah.

3 He placed the fat of it on the altar, and he took an ox, and a goat, and a sheep and kids, and salt, and a turtle-dove, and the young of a dove, and placed a burnt sacrifice on the altar, and poured on it an offering mingled with oil, and sprinkled wine and sprinkled frankincense over everything, and caused a good and pleasing odor to arise, acceptable before the Lord.

4 And the Lord smelled the good and pleasing odor, and He made a covenant with Noah that there should not be any more floods to destroy the earth; that all the days of the earth seed-time and harvest should never cease; cold and heat, and summer and winter, and day and night should not change their order, nor cease forever.

5 "Increase and multiply on the earth, and become many, and be a blessing on it. I will inspire the fear of you and the dread of you in everything that is on earth and in the sea.

6 Look, I have given you all beasts, and all winged things, and everything that moves on the earth, and the fish in

the waters, and all things for food; as the green herbs, I have given you all things to eat.

7 But you shall not eat anything live or with blood in it, for the life of all flesh is in the blood, or your blood of your lives will be required. At the hand of every man, at the hand of every beast will I require the blood of man.

8 Whoever sheds man's blood by man shall his blood be shed, for in the image of God He made man.

9 Increase, and multiply on the earth."

10 Noah and his sons swore that they would not eat any blood that was in any flesh, and he made a covenant before the Lord God forever throughout all the generations of the earth in this month.

11 Because of this He spoke to you that you should make a covenant with the children of Israel with an oath. In this month, on the mountain you should sprinkle blood on them because of all the words of the covenant, which the Lord made with them forever.

12 This testimony is written concerning you that you should observe it continually, so that you should not eat on any day any blood of beasts or birds or cattle during all the days of the earth, and the man who eats the blood of beast or of cattle or of birds during all the days of the earth, he and his offspring shall be rooted out of the land.

13 And you will command the children of Israel to eat no blood, so that their names and their offspring may be before the Lord our God continually.

14 There is no limit of days, for this law. It is forever. They shall observe it throughout their generations, so that they may continue supplicating on your behalf with blood before the altar; every day and at the time of morning and evening they shall seek forgiveness on your behalf perpetually before the Lord that they may keep it and not be rooted out.

15 And He gave to Noah and his sons a sign that there should not again be a flood on the earth.

16 He set His bow (a rainbow) in the cloud as a sign of the eternal covenant that there should never again be a flood on the earth to destroy it for all the days of the earth.

17 For this reason it is ordained and written on the heavenly tablets, that they should celebrate the feast of weeks in this month once a year, to renew the covenant every year.

18 This whole festival was celebrated in heaven from the day of creation until the days of Noah, which were twenty-six jubilees and five weeks of years. Noah and his sons observed it for seven jubilees and one week of years, until the day of Noah's death. From the day of Noah's death his sons did away with it until the days of Abraham, and they ate blood.

19 But Abraham observed it, and Isaac and Jacob and his children observed it up to your days, and in your days the children of Israel forgot it until you celebrated it anew on this mountain.

20 Command the children of Israel to observe this festival in all their generations for a commandment to them, one day in the year in this month they shall celebrate the festival.

21 For it is the feast of weeks and the feast of first-fruits, this feast is twofold and of a double nature, according to what is written and engraved concerning it, celebrate it.

22 For I have written in the book of the first law, in that which I have written for you, that you should celebrate it in its season, one day in the year, and I explained to you its sacrifices that the children of Israel should remember and should celebrate it throughout their generations in this month, the same day in every year.

23 On the new moon of the first month, and on the new moon of the fourth month, and on the new moon of the seventh month, and on the new moon of the tenth month are the days of remembrance, and the days of the seasons in the four divisions of the year. These are written and ordained as a testimony forever.

24 Noah ordained them for himself as feasts for the generations forever, so that they have become a memorial to him.

25 On the new moon of the first month he was told to make for himself an ark, and on that day the earth was dry and he saw from the opened ark, the earth. On the new moon of the fourth month the mouths of the depths of the bottomless pit beneath were closed.

26 On the new moon of the seventh month all the mouths of the abysses of the earth were opened, and the waters began to descend into them.

27 On the new moon of the tenth month the tops of the mountains were seen, and Noah was glad.

28 Because of this he ordained them for himself as feasts for a memorial forever, and thus are they ordained.

29 And they placed them on the heavenly tablets, each had thirteen weeks; from one to another passed their memorial, from the first to the second, and from the second to the third, and from the third to the fourth.

30 All the days of the commandment will be two and fifty weeks of days, and these will make the entire year complete. Thus it is engraved and ordained on the heavenly tablets.

31 And there is no neglecting this commandment for a single year or from year to year.

32 Command the children of Israel that they observe the years according to this counting, three hundred and sixty-four days, and these will constitute a complete year, and they will not disturb its time from its days and from its feasts; for every thing will fall out in them according to their testimony, and they will not leave out any day nor disturb any feasts.

33 But if they neglect and do not observe them according to His commandment, then they will disturb all their seasons and the years will be dislodged from this order, and they will neglect their established rules.

34 And all the children of Israel will forget and will not find the path of the years, and will forget the new moons, and seasons, and sabbaths and they will wrongly determine all the order of the years.

35 For I know and from now on will I declare it to you, and it is not of my own devising; for the book lies written in the presence of me, and on the heavenly tablets the division of days is ordained, or they forget the feasts of the covenant and walk according to the feasts of the Gentiles after their error and after their ignorance.

36 For there will be those who will assuredly make observations of the moon and how it disturbs the seasons and comes in from year to year ten days too soon.

37 For this reason the years will come upon them when they disturb (misinterpret) the order, and make an abominable day the day of testimony, and an unclean day a feast day, and they will confound all the days, the holy with the unclean, and the unclean day with the holy; for they will go wrong as to the months and sabbaths and feasts and jubilees.

38 For this reason I command and testify to you that you may testify to them; for after your death your children will disturb them, so that they will not make the year three hundred and sixty-four days only, and for this reason they will go wrong as to the new moons and seasons and sabbaths and festivals, and they will eat all kinds of blood with all kinds of flesh.

[Chapter 7]

1 In the seventh week in the first year of it, in this jubilee, Noah planted vines on the mountain on which the ark had rested, named Lubar, one of the Ararat Mountains, and they produced fruit in the fourth year, and he guarded their fruit, and gathered it in that year in the seventh month.

2 He made wine from it and put it into a vessel, and kept it until the fifth year, until the first day, on the new moon of the first month.

3 And he celebrated with joy the day of this feast, and he made a burnt sacrifice to the Lord, one young ox and one ram, and seven sheep, each a year old, and a kid of the goats, that he might make atonement thereby for himself and his sons.

4 He prepared the kid first, and placed some of its blood on the flesh that was on the altar that he had made, and all the fat he laid on the altar where he made the burnt sacrifice, and the ox and the ram and the sheep, and he laid all their flesh on the altar.

5 He placed all their offerings mingled with oil on it, and afterwards he sprinkled wine on the fire which had previously been made on the altar, and he placed incense on the altar and caused a sweet odor to rise up which was acceptable before the Lord his God.

6 And he rejoiced and he and his children drank the wine with joy.

7 It was evening, and he went into his tent, and being drunken he lay down and slept, and was uncovered in his tent as he slept.

8 And Ham saw Noah his father naked, and went out and told his two brothers (ridiculed his father to his two brothers) who were outside.

9 Shem took his garment and arose, he and Japheth, and they placed the garment on their shoulders and went backward and covered the shame of their father, and their faces were backward.

10 Noah awoke from sleep and knew all (abuse) that his younger son had done to him. He cursed him saying, "Cursed be Canaan; an enslaved servant shall he be to his brothers."

11 And he blessed Shem, and said, "Blessed be the Lord God of Shem, and Canaan shall be his servant.

12 God shall enlarge Japheth, and God shall dwell in the dwelling of Shem, and Canaan shall be his servant."

13 Ham knew that his father had cursed, him, his younger son, and he was displeased that he had cursed him, his son. And Ham parted from his father, he and his sons with him, Cush and Mizraim and Put and Canaan.

14 And he built for himself a city and called its name after the name of his wife Ne'elatama'uk.

15 Japheth saw it, and became envious of his brother, and he too built for himself a city, and he called its name after the name of his wife Adataneses.

16 Shem dwelt with his father Noah, and he built a city close to his father on the mountain, and he too called its name after the name of his wife Sedeqetelebab.

17 These three cities are near Mount Lubar; Sedeqetelebab in front of the mountain on its east; and Na'eltama'uk on the south; Adatan'eses towards the west.

18 These are the sons of Shem, Elam, and Asshur, and Arpachshad who was born two years after the flood, and Lud, and Aram.

19 The sons of Japheth, Gomer, Magog, Madai , Javan, Tubal and Meshech and Tiras, these are the descendants of Noah.

20 In the twenty-eighth jubilee Noah began to direct his sons in the ordinances and commandments, and all the judgments that he knew, and he exhorted his sons to observe righteousness, and to cover the shame of their flesh, and to bless their Creator, and honor father and mother, and love their neighbor, and guard their souls from fornication and uncleanness and all iniquity.

21 Because of these three things came the flood on the earth, namely, the fornication that the Watchers committed against the law of their ordinances when they went whoring after the daughters of men, and took themselves wives of all they chose, and they made the beginning of uncleanness.

22 And they begat sons, the Naphilim (Naphidim), and they were all dissimilar, and they devoured one another, and the Giants killed the Naphil, and the Naphil killed the Eljo, and the Eljo killed mankind, and one man killed one another.

23 Every one committed himself to crime and injustice and to shed much blood, and the earth was filled with sin.

24 After this they sinned against the beasts and birds, and all that moved and walked on the earth, and much blood was shed on the earth, and men continually desired only what was useless and evil.

25 And the Lord destroyed everything from the face of the earth. Because of the wickedness of their deeds, and because of the blood they had shed over all the earth, He destroyed everything. "

26 We were left, I and you, my sons, and everything that entered with us into the ark, and behold I see your works before me that you do not walk in righteousness, for in the path of destruction you have begun to walk, and you are turning one against another, and are envious one of another, and so it comes that you are not in harmony, my sons, each with his brother.

27 For I see the demons have begun their seductions against you and against your children and now I fear on your behalf, that after my death you will shed the blood of men on the earth, and that you, too, will be destroyed from the face of the earth.

28 For whoever sheds man's blood, and who ever eats the blood of any flesh, shall all be destroyed from the earth.

29 There shall be no man left that eats blood, or that sheds the blood of man on the earth, nor shall there be left to him any offspring or descendants living under heaven. Into the abode of the dead shall they go, and into the place of condemnation shall they descend, and into the darkness of the deep shall they all be removed by a violent death.

30 Do not smear blood on yourself or let it remain on you. Out of all the blood there shall be shed and out of all the days in which you have killed any beasts or cattle or whatever flies on the earth you must do a good work to your souls by covering that which has been shed on the face of the earth.

31 You shall not be like him who eats blood, but guard yourselves that none may eat blood before you, cover the blood, for thus have I been commanded to testify to you and your children, together with all flesh.

32 Do not permit the soul (life) to be eaten with the flesh, that your blood, which is your life, may not be required at the hand of any flesh that sheds it on the earth.

33 For the earth will not be clean from the blood that has been shed on it, for only through the blood of him that shed it will the earth be purified throughout all its generations.

34 Now, my children, listen, have judgment and righteousness that you maybe planted in righteousness over the face of the whole earth, and your glory lifted up in the presence of my God, who spared me from the waters of the flood.

35 Look, you will go and build for yourselves cities, and plant in them all the plants that are on the earth, and moreover all fruit-bearing trees.

36 For three years the fruit of everything that is eaten will not be gathered, and in the fourth year its fruit will be accounted holy, offered as first fruit, acceptable before the Most High God, who created heaven and earth and all things.

37 Let them offer in abundance the first of the wine and oil as first-fruits on the altar of the Lord, who receives it, and what is left let the servants of the house of the Lord eat before the altar which receives it.

38 In the fifth year make the release so that you release it in righteousness and uprightness, and you shall be

righteous, and all that you plant shall prosper. For this is how Enoch did it, the father of your father commanded Methuselah, his son, and Methuselah commanded his son Lamech, and Lamech commanded me all the things that his fathers commanded him.

39 I also will give you commandment, my sons, as Enoch commanded his son in the first jubilees, while still living, the seventh in his generation, he commanded and testified to his son and to his son's sons until the day of his death.

[Chapter 8]

1 In the twenty-ninth jubilee, in the beginning of first week, Arpachshad took to himself a wife and her name was Rasu'eja, the daughter of Susan, the daughter of Elam, and she gave birth to a son in the third year in this week, and he called his name Kainam.

2 The son grew, and his father taught him writing, and he went to seek for himself a place where he might seize a city for himself.

3 He found writing which former generations had carved on a rock, and he read what was on it, and he transcribed it and sinned because of it, for it contained the teaching of the Watchers, which they had used to observe the omens of the sun and moon and stars in all the signs of heaven.

4 He wrote it down and said nothing of it, for he was afraid to speak to Noah about it or he would be angry with him because of it.

5 In the thirtieth jubilee, in the second week, in the first year of it, he took to himself a wife, and her name was Melka, the daughter of Madai, the son of Japheth, and in the fourth year he begat a son, and called his name Shelah; for he said, "Truly I have been sent."

6 Shelah grew up and took to himself a wife, and her name was Mu'ak, the daughter of Kesed, his father's brother, in the one and thirtieth jubilee, in the fifth week, in the first year of it.

7 And she gave birth to a son in the fifth year of it, and he called his name Eber, and he took to himself a wife, and her name was Azurad, the daughter of Nebrod, in the thirty-second jubilee, in the seventh week, in the third year of it.

8 In the sixth year of it, she gave birth to a son, and he called his name Peleg, for in the days when he was born the children of Noah began to divide the earth among themselves, for this reason he called his name Peleg.

9 They divided it secretly among themselves, and told it to Noah.

10 In the beginning of the thirty-third jubilee they divided the earth into three parts, for Shem and Ham and Japheth, according to the inheritance of each, in the first year in the first week, when one of us (angels) who had been sent, was with them.

11 He called his sons, and they drew close to him, they and their children, and he divided the earth into the lots, which his three sons were to take in possession, and they reached out their hands, and took the writing out of the arms of Noah, their father.

12 There came out on the writing as Shem's lot the middle of the earth that he should take as an inheritance for himself and for his sons for the generations of eternity. From the middle of the mountain range of Rafa, from the mouth of the water from the river Tina, and his portion goes towards the west through the middle of this river, and it extends until it reaches the water of the abysses, out of which this river goes out and pours its waters into the sea Me'at, and this river flows into the great sea.

13 All that is towards the north is Japheth's, and all that is towards the south belongs to Shem. And it extends until it reaches Karaso, this is in the center of the tongue of land that looks towards the south.

14 His portion extends along the great sea, and it extends in a straight line until it reaches the west of the tongue that looks towards the south, for this sea is named the tongue of the Egyptian Sea.

15 And it turns from here towards the south towards the mouth of the great sea on the shore of its waters, and it extends to the west to Afra, and it extends until it reaches the waters of the river Gihon, and to the south of the waters of Gihon, to the banks of this river.

16 It extends towards the east, until it reaches the Garden of Eden, to the south of it and from the east of the whole land of Eden and of the whole east, it turns to the east and proceeds until it reaches the east of the mountain named Rafa, and it descends to the bank of the mouth of the river Tina.

17 This portion came out by lot for Shem and his sons, that they should possess it forever to his generations forever.

18 Noah rejoiced that this portion came out for Shem and for his sons, and he remembered all that he had spoken

with his mouth in prophecy; for he had said, "Blessed be the Lord God of Shem and may the Lord dwell in the dwelling of Shem."

19 He knew that the Garden of Eden is the holy of holies, and the dwelling of the Lord, and Mount Sinai the center of the desert, and Mount Zion which is the center of the navel of the earth, these three were created as holy places facing each other.

20 And he blessed the God of gods, who had put the word of the Lord into his mouth, and the Lord forever.

21 And he knew that a blessed portion and a blessing had come to Shem and his sons and to their generations forever which was the whole land of Eden and the whole land of the Red Sea, and the whole land of the east and India, and on the Red Sea and the mountains of it, and all the land of Bashan, and all the land of Lebanon and the islands of Kaftur, and all the mountains of Sanir and Amana, and the mountains of Asshur in the north, and all the land of Elam, Asshur, and Babel, and Susan and Ma'edai, and all the mountains of Ararat, and all the region beyond the sea, which is beyond the mountains of Asshur towards the north, a blessed and spacious land, and all that is in it is very good.

22 Ham received the second portion, beyond the Gihon towards the south to the right of the Garden, and it extends towards the south and it extends to all the mountains of fire, and it extends towards the west to the sea of 'atel and it extends towards the west until it reaches the sea of Ma'uk which was that sea into which everything that is not destroyed descends.

23 It goes out towards the north to the limits of Gadir, and it goes out to the coast of the waters of the sea to the waters of the great sea until it draws near to the river Gihon, and goes along the river Gihon until it reaches the right of the Garden of Eden.

24 This is the land that came out for Ham as the portion which he was to occupy forever for himself and his sons to their generations forever.

25 Japheth received the third portion beyond the river Tina to the north of the outflow of its waters, and it extends north-easterly to the whole region of Gog, and to all the country east of it.

26 It extends northerly, and it extends to the mountains of Qelt towards the north, and towards the sea of Ma'uk, and it goes out to the east of Gadir as far as the region of the waters of the sea.

27 It extends until it approaches the west of Fara and it returns towards Aferag, and it extends easterly to the waters of the sea of Me'at.

28 It extends to the region of the river Tina in a northeasterly direction until it approaches the boundary of its waters towards the mountain Rafa, and it turns round towards the north.

29 This is the land that came out for Japheth and his sons as the portion of his inheritance that he should possess five great islands, and a great land in the north, for himself and his sons, for their generations forever.

30 But it is cold, and the land of Ham is hot, and the land of Shem is neither hot nor cold, but it is of blended cold and heat.

[Chapter 9]

1 Ham divided among his sons, and the first portion came out for Cush towards the east, and to the west of him for Mizraim, and to the west of him for Put, and to the west of him on the sea for Canaan.

2 Shem also divided among his sons, and the first portion came out for Elam and his sons, to the east of the river Tigris until it approaches the east, the whole land of India, and on the Red Sea on its coast, and the waters of Dedan, and all the mountains of Mebri and Ela, and all the land of Susan and all that is on the side of Pharnak to the Red Sea and the river Tina.

3 Asshur received the second Portion, all the land of Asshur and Nineveh and Shinar and to the border of India, and it ascends and skirts the river.

4 Arpachshad received the third portion, all the land of the region of the Chaldees to the east of the Euphrates, bordering on the Red Sea, and all the waters of the desert close to the tongue of the sea which looks towards Egypt, all the land of Lebanon and Sanir and Amana to the border of the Euphrates.

5 Aram received the fourth portion, all the land of Mesopotamia between the Tigris and the Euphrates to the north of the Chaldees to the border of the mountains of Asshur and the land of Arara.

6 Lud got the fifth portion, the mountains of Asshur and all surrounding to them until it reaches the Great Sea, and until it reaches the east of Asshur his brother.

7 Japheth also divided the land of his inheritance among his sons.

8 The first portion came out for Gomer to the east from the north side to the river Tina, and in the north there

came out for Magog all the inner portions of the north until it reaches to the sea of Me'at.

9 Madai received as his portion that he should possess from the west of his two brothers to the islands, and to the coasts of the islands.

10 Javan got the fourth portion, every island and the islands that are towards the border of Lud.

11 For Tubal there came out the fifth portion in the middle of the tongue that approaches towards the border of the portion of Lud to the second tongue, to the region beyond the second tongue to the third tongue.

12 Meshech received the sixth portion, that is the entire region beyond the third tongue until it approaches the east of Gadir.

13 Tiras got the seventh portion, four great islands in the middle of the sea, which reach to the portion of Ham, and the islands of Kamaturi came out by lot for the sons of Arpachshad as his inheritance.

14 Thus the sons of Noah divided to their sons in the presence of Noah their father, and he bound them all by an oath, and invoked a curse on every one that sought to seize any portion which had not fallen to him by his lot.

15 They all said, "so be it; so be it " (amen and amen) for themselves and their sons forever throughout their generations until the day of judgment, on which the Lord God shall judge them with a sword and with fire for all the unclean wickedness of their errors, that they have filled the earth with, which are transgression, uncleanness and fornication and sin.

[Chapter 10]

1 In the third week of this jubilee the unclean demons began to lead astray the children of the sons of Noah, and to make them sin and to destroy them.

2 The sons of Noah came to Noah their father, and they told him about the demons that were leading astray and blinding and slaying his sons' sons.

3 And he prayed before the Lord his God, and said,

"God of the spirits of all flesh, who have shown mercy to me and have spared me and my sons from the waters of the flood,

and have not caused me to die as You did the sons of perdition; For Your grace has been great toward me,

and great has been Your mercy to my soul. Let Your grace be lifted up on my sons, and do not let the wicked spirits rule over them or they will destroy them from the earth.

4 But bless me and my sons, so that we may increase and multiply and replenish the earth.

5 You know how Your Watchers, the fathers of these spirits, acted in my day, and as for these spirits which are living, imprison them and hold them fast in the place of condemnation, and let them not bring destruction on the sons of your servant, my God; for these are like cancer and are created in order to destroy.

6 Let them not rule over the spirits of the living; for You alone can exercise dominion over them. And let them not have power over the sons of the righteous from now and forever."

7 And the Lord our God commanded us (angels) to bind all of them.

8 The chief of the spirits, Mastema, came and said, "Lord, Creator, let some of them remain before me, and let them listen to my voice, and do all that I shall say to them; for if some of them are not left to me, I shall not be able to execute the power of my will on the sons of men, for these are for corruption and leading astray before my judgment, for great is the wickedness of the sons of men."

9 He said, "Let one-tenth of them remain before him, and let nine-tenths of them descend into the place of condemnation."

10 He commanded one of us to teach Noah all their medicines, for He knew that they would not walk in uprightness, nor strive in righteousness.

11 We did according to all His words, all the malignant evil ones we bound in the place of condemnation and a tenth part of them we left that they might be subject in the presence of Satan on the earth.

12 We explained to Noah all the medicines of their diseases, together with their seductions, how he might heal them with herbs of the earth.

13 Noah wrote down all things in a book as we instructed him concerning every kind of medicine. Thus the evil spirits were precluded from hurting the sons of Noah.

14 He gave all that he had written to Shem, his eldest son, for he loved him greatly above all his sons.

15 And Noah slept with his fathers, and was buried on Mount Lubar in the land of Ararat.

16 Nine hundred and fifty years he completed in his life, nineteen jubilees and two weeks and five years.

17 In his life on earth he was greater than all the children of men except Enoch because of his righteousness he

was perfect. For Enoch's office was ordained for a testimony to the generations of the world, so that he should recount all the deeds of generation to generation, until the day of judgment.

18 In the three and thirtieth jubilee, in the first year in the second week, Peleg took to himself a wife, whose name was Lomna the daughter of Sina'ar, and she gave birth to a son for him in the fourth year of this week, and he called his name Reu, for he said, "Look the children of men have become evil because the building a city and a tower in the land of Shinar was for an evil purpose."

19 For they departed from the land of Ararat eastward to Shinar, for in his days they built the city and the tower, saying, "Come, let us rise up by the tower into heaven."

20 They began to build, and in the fourth week they made brick with fire, and the bricks served them for stone, and the clay with which they cemented them together was asphalt which comes out of the sea, and out of the fountains of water in the land of Shinar.

21 They built it, forty-three years were they building it. Its breadth was 203 bricks, and the height of a brick was the third of one; its height amounted to 5433 cubits and 2 palms, and the extent of one wall was thirteen times 600 feet and of the other thirty times 600 feet.

22 And the Lord our God said to us, "Look, they are one people, and they begin to do this, and now nothing will be withheld from them. Let us go down and confound their language, that they may not understand one another's speech, and they may be dispersed into cities and nations, and they will not be in agreement together with one purpose until the day of judgment."

23 And the Lord descended, and we descended with him to see the city and the tower that the children of men had built.

24 He confounded their language, and they no longer understood one another's speech, and they then ceased to build the city and the tower.

25 For this reason the whole land of Shinar is called Babel, because the Lord confounded all the language of the children of men there, and from that place they were dispersed into their cities, each according to his language and his nation.

26 Then, the Lord sent a mighty wind against the tower and it fell to the earth, and behold it was between Asshur and Babylon in the land of Shinar, and they called its name "Overthrow."

27 In the fourth week in the first year in the beginning of it in the four and thirtieth jubilee, were they dispersed from the land of Shinar.

28 Ham and his sons went into the land that he was to occupy, which he acquired as his portion in the land of the south.

29 Canaan saw the land of Lebanon to the river of Egypt was very good, and he did not go into the land of his inheritance to the west that is to the sea, and he dwelt in the land of Lebanon, eastward and westward from the border of Jordan and from the border of the sea.

30 Ham, his father, and Cush and Mizraim, his brothers, said to him, "You have settled in a land which is not yours, and which did not fall to us by lot, do not do so. If you do you and your sons will be conquered in the land and be accursed through a war. By war you have settled, and by war will your children fall, and you will be rooted out forever.

31 Do not live in the land of Shem, for to Shem and to his sons did it come by their lot.

32 Cursed are you, and cursed will you be beyond all the sons of Noah, by the curse by which we bound ourselves by an oath in the presence of the holy judge, and in the presence of Noah our father."

33 But he did not listen to them, and settled in the land of Lebanon from Hamath to the border of Egypt, he and his sons until this day. For this reason that land is named Canaan. And Japheth and his sons went towards the sea and settled in the land of their portion, and Madai saw the land of the sea and it did not please him, and he begged Ham and Asshur and Arpachshad, his wife's brother for a portion, and he dwelt in the land of Media, near to his wife's brother until this day.

34 And he called his and his son's dwelling-place, Media, after the name of their father Madai.

[Chapter 11]

1 In the thirty-fifth jubilee, in the third week, in the first year of it, Reu took to himself a wife, and her name was 'Ora, the daughter of 'Ur, the son of Kesed, and she gave birth to a son, and he called his name Seroh, in the

seventh year of this week in this jubilee.

2 The sons of Noah began to war with each other, to take captives and kill each other, and to shed the blood of men on the earth, and to eat blood, and to build strong cities, and walls, and towers, and individuals began to exalt themselves above the nation, and to establish kingdoms, and to go to war, people against people, and nation against nation, and city against city, and all began to do evil, and to acquire arms, and to teach their sons war, and they began to capture cities, and to sell male and female slaves.

3 Ur, the son of Kesed, built the city of Ara of the Chaldees, and called its name after his own name and the name of his father.

4 And they made themselves molten images, and they worshipped the idols and the molten image they had made for themselves, and they began to make graven images and unclean and shadowy presence, and malevolent and malicious spirits assisted and seduced them into committing transgression and uncleanness.

5 Prince Mastema exerted himself to do all this, and he sent out other spirits, which were put under his control, to do all manner of wrong and sin, and all manner of transgression, to corrupt and destroy, and to shed blood on the earth.

6 For this reason he called the name of Seroh, Serug, for every one turned to do all manner of sin and transgression.

7 He grew up, and dwelt in Ur of the Chaldees, near to the father of his wife's mother, and he worshipped idols, and he took to himself a wife in the thirty-sixth jubilee, in the fifth week, in the first year of it, and her name was Melka, the daughter of Kaber, the daughter of his father's brother.

8 She gave birth to Nahor, in the first year of this week, and he grew and dwelt in Ur of the Chaldees, and his father taught him the sciences of the Chaldees to divine and conjure, according to the signs of heaven.

9 In the thirty-seventh jubilee in the sixth week, in the first year of it, he took to himself a wife, and her name was 'Ijaska, the daughter of Nestag of the Chaldees.

10 And she gave birth to Terah in the seventh year of this week.

11 Prince Mastema sent ravens and birds to devour the seed that was sown in the land, in order to destroy the land, and rob the children of men of their labors. Before they could plow in the seed, the ravens picked it from the surface of the ground.

12 This is why he called his name Terah because the ravens and the birds reduced them to destitution and devoured their seed.

13 The years began to be barren, because of the birds, and they devoured all the fruit of the trees from the trees, it was only with great effort that they could harvest a little fruit from the earth in their days.

14 In this thirty-ninth jubilee, in the second week in the first year, Terah took to himself a wife, and her name was 'Edna, the daughter of Abram, the daughter of his father's sister.

15 In the seventh year of this week she gave birth to a son, and he called his name Abram, by the name of the father of his mother, for he had died before his daughter had conceived a son.

16 And the child began to understand the errors of the earth that all went astray after graven images and after uncleanness,
and his father taught him writing, and he was two weeks of years old, and he separated himself from his father, that he might not worship idols with him.

17 He began to pray to the Creator of all things that He might spare him from the errors of the children of men, and that his portion should not fall into error after uncleanness and vileness.

18 The time came for the sowing of seed in the land, and they all went out together to protect their seed against the ravens, and Abram went out with those that went, and the child was a lad of fourteen years.

19 A cloud of ravens came to devour the seed, and Abram ran to meet them before they settled on the ground, and cried to them before they settled on the ground to devour the seed, and said, "Descend not, return to the place from where you came," and they began to turn back.

20 And he caused the clouds of ravens to turn back that day seventy times, and of all the ravens throughout all the land where Abram was there settled not so much as one.

21 All who were with him throughout all the land saw him cry out, and all the ravens turn back, and his name became great in all the land of the Chaldees.

22 There came to him this year all those that wished to sow, and he went with them until the time of sowing ceased, and they sowed their land, and that year they brought enough grain home to eat and they were satisfied.

23 In the first year of the fifth week Abram taught those who made implements for oxen, the artificers in wood, and they made a vessel above the ground, facing the frame of the plow, in order to put the seed in it, and the seed

fell down from it on the share of the plow, and was hidden in the earth, and they no longer feared the ravens.
24 After this manner they made vessels above the ground on all the frames of the plows, and they sowed and tilled all the land, according as Abram commanded them, and they no longer feared the birds.

[Chapter 12]

1 In the sixth week, in the seventh year of it, that Abram said to Terah his father, saying, "Father!"
2 He said, "Look, here am I, my son." He said, "What help and profit have we from those idols which you worship, and in the presence of which you bow yourself?
3 For there is no spirit in them. They are dumb forms, and they mislead the heart.
4 Do not worship them, Worship the God of heaven, who causes the rain and the dew to fall on the earth and does everything on the earth, and has created everything by His word, and all life is from His presence.
5 Why do you worship things that have no spirit in them?
For they are the work of men's hands, and you bear them on your shoulders, and you have no help from them, but they are a great cause of shame to those who make them, and they mislead the heart of those who worship them. Do not worship them."
6 His father said to him, "I also know it, my son, but what shall I do with a people who have made me serve them?
7 If I tell them the truth, they will kill me, because their soul clings to them so they worship them and honor them.
8 Keep silent, my son, or they will kill you." And these words he spoke to his two brothers, and they were angry with him and he kept silent.
9 In the fortieth jubilee, in the second week, in the seventh year of it, Abram took to himself a wife, and her name was Sarai, the daughter of his father, and she became his wife.
10 Haran, his brother, took to himself a wife in the third year of the third week, and she gave birth to a son in the seventh year of this week, and he called his name Lot.
11 Nahor, his brother, took to himself a wife.
12 In the sixtieth year of the life of Abram, that is, in the fourth week, in the fourth year of it, Abram arose in the night and burned the house of the idols, and he burned all that was in the house and no man knew it.
13 And they arose and sought to save their gods from the fire.
14 Haran hasted to save them, but the fire flamed over him, and he was burnt in the fire, and he died in Ur of the Chaldees before Terah his father, and they buried him in Ur of the Chaldees.
15 Terah went out from Ur of the Chaldees, he and his sons, to go into the land of Lebanon and into the land of Canaan, and he dwelt in the land of Haran, and Abram dwelt with Terah his father in Haran two weeks of years.
16 In the sixth week, in the fifth year of it, Abram sat up all night on the new moon of the seventh month to observe the stars from the evening to the morning, in order to see what would be the character of the year with regard to the rains, and he was alone as he sat and observed.
17 And a word came into his heart and he said, "All the signs of the stars, and the signs of the moon and of the sun are all in the hand of the Lord. Why do I search them out?
18 If He desires, He causes it to rain, morning and evening, and if He desires, He withholds it, and all things are in his hand."
19 He prayed in the night and said, "My God, God Most High, You alone are my God, and You and Your dominion have I chosen. And You have created all things, and all things that are the work of Your hands.
20 Deliver me from the hands of evil spirits who have dominion over the thoughts of men's hearts, and let them not lead me astray from You, my God. And establish me and my offspring forever so that we do not go astray from now and forever."
21 He said, "Shall I return to Ur of the Chaldees who are trying to find me? Should I return to them? Am I to remain here in this place? The right path is before You. Make it prosper in the hands of your servant that he may fulfill it and that I may not walk in the deceitfulness of my heart, O my God."
22 He stopped speaking and stopped praying, and then the word of the Lord was sent to him through me, saying, "Get out of your country, and from your kindred and from the house of your father and go to a land which I will show you, and I shall make you a great and numerous nation.
23 And I will bless you and I will make your name great,
and you will be blessed in the earth, and in You shall all families of the earth be blessed, and I will bless them that bless you, and curse them that curse you.

24 I will be a God to you and your son, and to your son's son, and to all your offspring, fear not, from now on and to all generations of the earth I am your God."

25 The Lord God said, "Open his mouth and his ears, that he may hear and speak with his mouth, with the language which has been revealed," for it had ceased from the mouths of all the children of men from the day of the overthrow of Babel.

26 And I opened his mouth, and his ears and his lips, and I began to speak with him in Hebrew in the tongue of the creation.

27 He took the books of his fathers, and these were written in Hebrew, and he transcribed them, and he began from then on to study them, and I made known to him that which he could not understand, and he studied them during the six rainy months.

28 In the seventh year of the sixth week he spoke to his father and informed him, that he would leave Haran to go into the land of Canaan to see it and return to him.

29 Terah his father said to him; "Go in peace. May the eternal God make your path straight. And the Lord be with you, and protect you from all evil, and grant to you grace, mercy and favor before those who see you, and may none of the children of men have power over you to harm you. Go in peace.

30 If you see a land pleasant to your eyes to dwell in, then arise and take me with you and take Lot with you, the son of Haran your brother as your own son, the Lord be with you.

31 Nahor your brother leave with me until you return in peace, and we go with you all together."

[Chapter 13]

1 Abram journeyed from Haran, and he took Sarai, his wife, and Lot, his brother Haran's son and they went to the land of Canaan, and he came into Asshur, and proceeded to Shechem, and dwelt near a tall oak.

2 He saw the land was very pleasant from the border of Hamath to the tall oak.

3 The Lord said to him, "To you and to your offspring I will give this land."

4 He built an altar there, and he offered on it a burnt sacrifice to the Lord, who had appeared to him.

5 He left from that place and went to the mountain Bethel on the west and Ai on the east, and pitched his tent there.

6 He saw the land was very wide and good, and everything grew on it, vines, and figs, and pomegranates, oaks, and ilexes, and turpentine and oil trees, and cedars and cypresses, and date trees, and all trees of the field, and there was water on the mountains.

7 And he blessed the Lord who had led him out of Ur of the Chaldees, and had brought him to this land.

8 In the first year, in the seventh week, on the new moon of the first month, he built an altar on this mountain, and called on the name of the Lord and said, "You, the eternal God, are my God."

9 He offered on the altar a burnt sacrifice to the Lord that He should be with him and not forsake him all the days of his life.

10 He left that place and went toward the south, and he came to Hebron and Hebron was built at that time, and he lived there two years, and he went from that place into the land of the south, to Bealoth, and there was a famine in the land.

11 Abram went into Egypt in the third year of the week, and he dwelt in Egypt five years before his wife was torn away from him.

12 Now, Tanais in Egypt was built seven years after Hebron.

13 When Pharaoh seized Sarai, the wife of Abram the Lord plagued Pharaoh and his house with great plagues because of Sarai, Abram's wife.

14 Abram was celebrated and admired because of his great possessions of sheep, and cattle, and donkeys, and horses, and camels, and menservants, and maidservants, and in silver and gold. Lot and his brother's son were also wealthy.

15 Pharaoh gave back Sarai, the wife of Abram, and he sent him out of the land of Egypt, and he journeyed to the place where he had pitched his tent at the beginning, to the place of the altar, with Ai on the east, and Bethel on the west, and he blessed the Lord his God who had brought him back in peace.

16 In the forty-first jubilee in the third year of the first week, that he returned to this place and offered on it a burnt sacrifice, and called on the name of the Lord, and said, "You, the most high God, are my God forever and ever."

17 In the fourth year of this week Lot parted from him, and Lot lived in Sodom, and the men of Sodom sinned greatly.

18 It grieved him in his heart that his brother's son had parted from him because Abram had no children.

19 After Lot had parted from him, in the fourth year of this week. In that year when Lot was taken captive, the Lord said to Abram, "Lift up your eyes from the place where you are dwelling, northward and southward, and westward and eastward.

20 All the land that you see I will give to you and to your offspring forever, and I will make your offspring as the sand of the sea, though a man may number the dust of the earth, yet your offspring shall not be numbered.

21 Arise, walk through the land in the length of it and the breadth of it, and see it all. To your offspring will I give it." And Abram went to Hebron, and lived there.

22 And in this year came Chedorlaomer, king of Elam, and Amraphel, king of Shinar, and Arioch king of Sellasar, and Tergal, king of nations, and killed the king of Gomorrah, and the king of Sodom fled, and many fell through wounds in the valley of Siddim, by the Salt Sea.

23 They took captive Sodom and Adam and Zeboim, and they took Lot captive, the son of Abram's brother, and all his possessions, and they went to Dan.

24 One who had escaped came and told Abram that his brother's son had been taken captive.

25 And Abram equipped his household servants for Abram, and for his offspring, a tenth of the first-fruits to the Lord, and the Lord ordained it as a law forever that they should give it to the priests who served before Him, that they should possess it forever.

26 There is no limit of days to this law, for He has ordained it for the generations forever that they should give to the Lord the tenth of everything, of the seed and of the wine and of the oil and of the cattle and of the sheep.

27 He gave it to His priests to eat and to drink with joy before Him.

28 The king of Sodom came and bowed down to him, and said, "Our Lord Abram, give to us the souls which you have rescued, but let the booty be yours."

29 And Abram said to him, "I lift up my hands to the Most High God, that from a thread to a shoe-latchet I shall not take anything that is yours so that you could never say, I have made Abram rich, except only what the young men, Aner and Eschol, and Mamre have eaten, and the portion of the men who went with me. These shall take their portion."

[Chapter 14]

1 After these things, in the fourth year of this week, on the new moon of the third month, the word of the Lord came to Abram in a dream, saying, "Fear not, Abram, I am your defender, and your reward will be very great."

2 He said, "Lord, Lord, what will you give me, seeing I go from here childless, and the son of Maseq, the son of my handmaid, Eliezer of Damascus, he will be my heir, and to me you have given no offspring."

3 He said to him, "This man will not be your heir, but one that will come out of your own bowels. He will be your heir."

4 And He brought him out abroad, and said to him, "Look toward heaven and number the stars if you are able to number them."

5 He looked toward heaven, and beheld the stars. And He said to him, "so shall your offspring be."

6 And he believed in the Lord, and it was counted to him as righteousness.

7 God said to him, "I am the Lord that brought you out of Ur of the Chaldees, to give you the land of the Canaanites to possess it forever, and I will be God to you and to your offspring after you."

8 He said, "Lord, Lord, how shall I know that I shall inherit it?"

9 God said to him, "Take Me a heifer of three years, and a goat of three years, and a sheep of three years, and a turtle-dove, and a pigeon."

10 And he took all these in the middle of the month and he dwelt at the oak of Mamre, which is near Hebron.

11 He built an altar there, and sacrificed all these. He poured their blood on the altar, and divided them in half, and laid them over against each other, but the birds he did not divide.

12 Birds came down on the pieces, and Abram drove them away, and did not permit the birds to touch them.

13 It happened, when the sun had set, that an ecstasy fell on Abram, and such a horror of great darkness fell on him, and it was said to Abram, "Know of a surety that your offspring shall be a stranger in a land that is not theirs, and they shall be brought into bondage, and afflicted for four hundred years.

14 The nation also to whom they will be in bondage will I judge, and after that they shall come out from that place with many possessions.

15 You will go to your fathers in peace, and be buried in a good old age.

16 But in the fourth generation they shall return here, for the iniquity of the Amorites is not yet full."

17 And he awoke from his sleep, and he arose, and the sun had set; and there was a flame, and a furnace was smoking, and a flame of fire passed between the pieces.

18 On that day the Lord made a covenant with Abram, saying, "To your offspring will I give this land, from the river of Egypt to the great river, the river Euphrates, the Kenites, the Kenizzites, the Kadmonites, the Perizzites, and the Rephaim, the Phakorites, and the Hivites, and the Amorites, and the Canaanites, and the Girgashites, and the Jebusites.

19 The day passed, and Abram offered the pieces, and the birds, and their fruit offerings, and their drink offerings, and the fire devoured them.

20 On that day we made a covenant with Abram, in the same way we had covenanted with Noah in this month; and Abram renewed the festival and laws for himself forever.

21Abram rejoiced, and made all these things known to Sarai his wife. He believed that he would have offspring, but she did not bear.

22 Sarai advised her husband Abram, and said to him, "Go in to Hagar, my Egyptian maid, it may be that I shall build up offspring to you by her."

23Abram listened to the voice of Sarai his wife, and said to her, "Do so." And Sarai took Hagar, her maid, the Egyptian, and gave her to Abram, her husband, to be his wife.

24 He went in to her, and she conceived and gave birth to a son, and he called his name Ishmael, in the fifth year of this week; and this was the eighty-sixth year in the life of Abram.

[Chapter 15]

1 In the fifth year of the fourth week of this jubilee, in the third month, in the middle of the month, Abram celebrated the feast of the first-fruits of the grain harvest.

2 And he made new offerings on the altar, the first-fruits of the produce to the Lord, a heifer, and a goat, and a sheep on the altar as a burnt sacrifice to the Lord; their fruit offerings and their drink offerings he offered on the altar with frankincense.

3 The Lord appeared to Abram, and said to him, "I am God Almighty. Examine yourself and demonstrate yourself before me and be perfect.

4 I will make My covenant between Me and you, and I will multiply you greatly."

5 Abram fell on his face, and God talked with him, and said, "My law is with you, and you will be the father of many nations.

6 Neither shall your name any more be called Abram, but your name from now on, even forever, shall be Abraham.

7 For I have made you the father of many nations.

8 I will make you very great, and I will make you into nations, and kings shall come forth from you.

9 I shall establish My covenant between Me and you, and your offspring after you, throughout their generations, for an eternal covenant, so that I may be a God to you, and to your offspring after you.

10 You may possess the land where you have been a sojourner, the land of Canaan, and you will possess it forever, and I will be their God."

11 The Lord said to Abraham, "Keep my covenant, you and your offspring after you, and circumcise every male among you, and circumcise your foreskins, and it shall be a token of an eternal covenant between Me and you.

12 And the eighth day you shall circumcise the child, every male throughout your generations, him that is born in the house, or whom you have bought with money from any stranger, whom you have acquired who is not of your offspring.

13 He that is born in your house shall surely be circumcised, and those whom you have bought with money shall be circumcised, and My covenant shall be in your flesh for an eternal ordinance.

14 The uncircumcised male who is not circumcised in the flesh of his foreskin on the eighth day, that soul shall be cut off from his people, for he has broken My covenant."

15 God said to Abraham, "As for Sarai your wife, her name shall no more be called Sarai, but Sarah shall be her name.

16 I will bless her, and give you a son by her, and I will bless him, and he shall become a nation, and kings of

nations shall proceed from him."

17 Abraham fell on his face, and rejoiced, and said in his heart, "Shall a son be born to him that is a hundred years old, and shall Sarah, who is ninety years old, bring forth?"

18 Abraham said to God, "Oh, that Ishmael might live before you!"

19 God said, "Yea, and Sarah also shall bear you a son, and you will call his name Isaac, and I will establish My covenant with him, an everlasting covenant, and for his offspring after him.

20 And as for Ishmael also have I heard you, and behold I will bless him, and make him great, and multiply him greatly, and he shall beget twelve princes, and I will make him a great nation.

21 But My covenant will I establish with Isaac, whom Sarah shall bear to you this time next year."

22 God ceased speaking with him, and God went up from Abraham.

23 Abraham did according as God had said to him, and he took Ishmael his son, and all that were born in his house, and whom he had bought with his money, every male in his house, and circumcised the flesh of their foreskin.

24 On that same day was Abraham circumcised, and all the men of his house, and all those whom he had bought with money from the children of the stranger were circumcised with him.

25 This law is for all the generations forever, and there is no variance of days, and no omission of one day out of the eight days, for it is an eternal law, ordained and written on the heavenly tablets.

26 Every one that is born, the flesh of whose foreskin is not circumcised on the eighth day, does not belong to the children of the covenant which the Lord made with Abraham, but instead they belong to the children of destruction; nor is there any other sign on him that he is the Lord's, but he is destined to be destroyed and killed from the earth, and to be rooted out of the earth, for he has broken the covenant of the Lord our God.

27 All the angels of the presence (of the Lord) and all the angels of sanctification have been created already circumcised from the day of their creation, and before the angels of the presence (of the Lord) and the angels of sanctification He has sanctified Israel, that they should be with Him and with His holy angels.

28 Command the children of Israel and let them observe the sign of this covenant for their generations as an eternal law, and they will not be rooted out of the land.

29 For the command is ordained for a covenant, that they should observe it forever among all the children of Israel.

30 For Ishmael and his sons and his brothers, and Esau, the Lord did not cause them to come to Him, and he did not choose them. Although they are the children of Abraham, He knew them, but He chose Israel to be His people.

31 He sanctified them, and gathered them from among all the children of men; for there are many nations and many peoples, and all are His, and over all nations He has placed spirits in authority to lead them astray from Him.

32 But over Israel He did not appoint any angel or spirit, for He alone is their ruler, and He will preserve them and require them at the hand of His angels and His spirits, and at the hand of all His powers in order that He may preserve them and bless them, that they may be His and He may be theirs from now on forever.

33 I announce to you that the children of Israel will not keep true to this law, and they will not circumcise their sons according to all this law; for in the flesh of their circumcision they will omit this circumcision of their sons, and all of the sons of Beliar will leave their sons uncircumcised as they were born.

34 There will be great wrath from the Lord against the children of Israel because they have forsaken His covenant and turned aside from His word, and provoked (God) and blasphemed, because they do not observe the ordinance of this law; for they have treated their genitalia like the Gentiles, so that they may be removed and rooted out of the land. And there will no more be pardon or forgiveness to them for all the sin of this eternal error.

[Chapter 16]

1 On the new moon of the fourth month we appeared to Abraham, at the oak of Mamre, and we talked with him, and we announced to him that Sarah, his wife, would give him a son.

2 And Sarah laughed, for she heard that we had spoken these words to Abraham. We warned her, and she became afraid, and denied that she had laughed because of the words.

3 We told her the name of her son, as his name is ordained and written in the heavenly tablets and it is Isaac.

4 We told her that when we returned to her at a set time, she would have conceived a son.

5 In this month the Lord executed his judgments on Sodom, and Gomorrah, and Zeboim, and all the region of the Jordan, and He burned them with fire and brimstone, and destroyed them and they are destroyed until this day, because of all their works. They are wicked and vast sinners, and they defile themselves and commit fornication in their flesh, and work uncleanness on the earth as I have told you.

6 In like manner, God will execute judgment on the places where they have done similar to the uncleanness of the Sodomites, and they will suffer a judgment like that of Sodom.

7 But for Lot, we made an exception, for God remembered Abraham, and sent him out from the place of the overthrow.

8 And he and his daughters committed sin on the earth, such as had not been on the earth since the days of Adam until his time, for the man had sex with his daughters.

9 It was commanded and engraved concerning all his offspring, on the heavenly tablets, to remove them and root them out, and to execute judgment on them like the judgment of Sodom, and to leave no offspring of that man on earth on the day of condemnation.

10 In this month Abraham moved from Hebron, and departed and lived between Kadesh and Shur in the mountains of Gerar.

11 In the middle of the fifth month he moved from that place, and lived at the Well of the Oath.

12 In the middle of the sixth month the Lord visited Sarah and did to her as He had spoken and she conceived.

13 And she gave birth to a son in the third month. In the middle of the month, at the time of which the Lord had spoken to Abraham, on the festival of the first-fruits of the harvest, Isaac was born.

14 Abraham circumcised his son on the eighth day, he was the first that was circumcised according to the covenant that is ordained forever.

15 In the sixth year of the fourth week we came to Abraham at the Well of the Oath, and we appeared to him.

16 We returned in the seventh month, and found Sarah with child before us and we blessed him, and we announced to him all the things that had been decreed concerning him, so that he should not die until he should beget six more sons and saw them before he died.

17 But in Isaac should his name and offspring be called, and that all the offspring of his sons should be Gentiles, and be counted with the Gentiles; but from the sons of Isaac one should become a holy offspring, and should not be counted among the Gentiles.

18 For he should become the portion (dowry) of the Most High, and all his offspring had fallen into the possession of God, that they should be to the Lord a people for His possession above all nations and that they should become a kingdom and priests and a holy nation.

19 We went our way, and we announced to Sarah all that we had told him, and they both rejoiced with very great joy.

20 He built there an altar to the Lord who had delivered him, and who was causing him to rejoice in the land of his sojourning, and he celebrated a festival of joy in this month for seven days, near the altar which he had built at the Well of the Oath.

21 He built tents for himself and for his servants on this festival, and he was the first to celebrate the feast of tabernacles on the earth.

22 During these seven days he brought a burnt offering to the Lord each day to the altar consisting of two oxen, two rams, seven sheep, one male goat, for a sin offering that he might atone thereby for himself and for his offspring.

23 As an offering of thanks he brought, seven rams, seven kids, seven sheep, and seven male goats, and their fruit offerings and their drink offerings; and he burnt all the fat of it on the altar, a chosen offering to the Lord for a sweet smelling odor.

24 Morning and evening he burnt fragrant substances, frankincense and incense, and sweet spice, and nard, and myrrh, and spice, and aromatic plants; all these seven he offered, crushed, mixed together in equal parts and pure.

25 And he celebrated this feast during seven days, rejoicing with all his heart and with all his soul, he and all those who were in his house, and there was no stranger with him, nor any that was uncircumcised.

26 He blessed his Creator who had created him in his generation, for He had created him according to His good pleasure. God knew and perceived that from him would arise the plant of righteousness for the eternal generations, and from him a holy offspring, so that it should become like Him who had made all things.

27 He blessed and rejoiced, and he called the name of this festival the festival of the Lord, a joy acceptable to the

Most High God.

28 And we blessed him forever, and all his offspring after him throughout all the generations of the earth, because he celebrated this festival in its season, according to the testimony of the heavenly tablets.

29 For this reason it is ordained on the heavenly tablets concerning Israel, that they shall celebrate the feast of tabernacles seven days with joy, in the seventh month, acceptable before the Lord as a statute forever throughout their generations every year.

30 To this there is no limit of days; for it is ordained forever regarding Israel that they should celebrate it and dwell in tents, and set wreaths on their heads, and take leafy boughs, and willows from the brook.

31Abraham took branches of palm trees, and the fruit of good and pleasing trees, and every day going round the altar with the branches seven times a day in the morning, he praised and gave thanks to his God for all things in joy.

[Chapter 17]

1 In the first year of the fifth week Isaac was weaned in this jubilee, and Abraham made a great banquet in the third month, on the day his son Isaac was weaned.

2 Ishmael, the son of Hagar, the Egyptian, was in front of Abraham, his father, in his place, and Abraham rejoiced and blessed God because he had seen his sons and had not died childless.

3 He remembered the words which He had spoken to him on the day that Lot had departed from him, and he rejoiced because the Lord had given him offspring on the earth to inherit the earth, and he blessed with all his mouth the Creator of all things.

4 Sarah saw Ishmael playing and dancing, and Abraham rejoicing with great joy, and she became jealous of Ishmael and said to Abraham, "Throw out this bondwoman and her son. The son of this bondwoman will not be heir with my son, Isaac."

5 And the situation was troubling to Abraham, because of his maidservant and because of his son, because he did not want to drive them from him.

6 God said to Abraham "Let it not be troubling in your sight, because of the child and because of the bondwoman. Listen to Sarah and to all her words and do them, for in Isaac shall your name and offspring be called.

7 But as for the son of this bondwoman I will make him a great nation, because he is of your offspring."

8 Abraham got up early in the morning, and took bread and a bottle of water, and placed them on the shoulders of Hagar and the child, and sent her away.

9 And she departed and wandered in the wilderness of Beersheba, and the water in the bottle was spent, and the child was thirsty, and was not able to go on, and fell down.

10 His mother took him and laid him under an olive tree, and went and sat her down over away from him at the distance of a bow-shot; for she said, "Let me not see the death of my child," and she sat and wept.

11 An angel of God, one of the holy ones, said to her, "Why do you weep, Hagar? Stand. Take the child, and hold him in your hand, for God has heard your voice, and has seen the child."

12 She opened her eyes, and she saw a well of water, and she went and filled her bottle with water, and she gave her child a drink, and she arose and went towards the wilderness of Paran.

13 And the child grew and became an archer, and God was with him, and his mother took him a wife from among the daughters of Egypt.

14 She (the wife) gave birth to a son, and he called his name Nebaioth; for she said, "The Lord was close to me when I called on him."

15 In the seventh week, in the first year of it, in the first month in this jubilee, on the twelfth of this month, there were voices in heaven regarding Abraham, that he was faithful in all that He told him, and that he loved the Lord, and that in every affliction he was faithful.

16 Prince Mastema came and said before God, "Look, Abraham loves Isaac his son, and he delights in him above all things, tell him to offer him as a burnt-offering on the altar, and You will see if he will do this command, and You will know if he is faithful in everyway that You test him.

17 The Lord knew that Abraham was faithful throughout all his afflictions, for He had tried him through his country and with famine, and had tried him with the wealth of kings, and had tried him again through his wife,

when she was torn from him, and with circumcision; and had tried him through Ishmael and Hagar, his maid-servant, when he sent them away.

18 In everything that He had tried him, he was found faithful, and his soul was not impatient, and he was not slow to act, because he was faithful and a lover of the Lord.

[Chapter *18*]

1 God said to him, "Abraham. Abraham." and he said, "Look, here am I."

2 He said, "Take your beloved son, Isaac, whom you love, and go to the high country, and offer him on one of the mountains which I will point out to you."

3 He got early in the morning and saddled his donkey, and took two young men with him, and Isaac his son, and split the wood of the burnt offering, and he went to the place on the third day, and he saw the place afar off.

4 He came to a well of water (near Mount Moriah), and he said to his young men, "You stay here with the donkey, and I and the lad shall go yonder, and when we have worshipped we shall come back to you."

5 He took the wood of the burnt-offering and laid it on Isaac his son, and he took the fire and the knife, and they went both of them together to that place.

6 Isaac said to his father, "Father" and he said, "Here am I, my son." He said to him, "Look, we have the fire, and the knife, and the wood, but where is the sheep for the burnt-offering, father?"

7 He said, "God will provide for himself a sheep for a burnt-offering, my son." And he neared the place of the mountain of God.

8 He built an altar, and he placed the wood on the altar, and bound Isaac his son, and placed him on the wood that was on the altar, and stretched out his hand to take the knife to kill Isaac, his son.

9 I stood in the presence of him, and before prince Mastema, (and the holy angels stood and wept over the altar as prince Mastema and his angels rejoiced and said "Isaac will be destroyed and we will see if Abraham is faithful), and the Lord said, "Command him not to lay his hand on the lad, nor to do anything to him, for I have shown that he fears the Lord."

10 I called to him from heaven, and said to him, "Abraham, Abraham." and he was terrified and said, "Here am I."

11 I said to him, "Lay not your hand on the lad, neither do anything to him; for now I have shown that you fear the Lord, and have not withheld your son, your first-born son, from me."

12 Prince Mastema was put to shame (and was bound by the angels); and Abraham lifted up his eyes and looked and saw a ram caught by his horns, and Abraham went and took the ram and offered it as a burnt-offering in place of his son.

13 Abraham called that place "The Lord has seen," so that it is said the Lord has seen. This is Mount Zion.

14 The Lord called Abraham by his name a second time from heaven, as he caused us to appear to speak to him in the name of the Lord.

15 He said, "By Myself have I sworn," said the Lord, "Because you have done this thing, and have not withheld your son, your beloved son, from Me, that in blessing I will bless you, and in multiplying I will multiply your offspring as the stars of heaven, and as the sand which is on the seashore.

16 Your offspring shall inherit the cities of their enemies, and in your offspring shall all nations of the earth be blessed. Because you have obeyed My voice, and I have shown to all that you are faithful to Me in all that I have said to you, "Go in peace."

17 Abraham went back to his young men, and they stood and went back together to Beersheba, and Abraham lived by the Well of the Oath.

18 And he celebrated this festival every year, seven days with joy, and he called it the festival of the Lord according to the seven days during which he went and returned in peace.

19 Accordingly, it has been ordained and written on the heavenly tablets regarding Israel and its children that they should observe this festival seven days with the joy of festival.

[Chapter *19*]

1 In the first year of the first week in the forty-second jubilee, Abraham returned and lived across from Hebron, in Kirjath Arba for two weeks of years.

2 In the first year of the third week of this jubilee the days of the life of Sarah were completed, and she died in Hebron.

3 Abraham went to mourn over her and bury her, and we tested him to see if his spirit was patient and he had neither anger nor contempt in the words of his mouth, and he was found patient in this and was not disturbed.

4 In patience of spirit he discussed with the children of Heth that they should give him a place in which to bury his dead.

5 And the Lord gave him grace before all who saw him, and he asked the sons of Heth in gentleness, and they gave him the land of the double cave over beside Mamre, that is Hebron, for four hundred pieces of silver.

6 They said to him, "We shall give it to you for nothing," but he would not take it from them for nothing, for he gave the price of the place and paid the money in full. And he bowed down before them twice, and after this he buried his dead in the double cave.

7 All the days of the life of Sarah were one hundred and twenty-seven years, that is, two jubilees and four weeks and one year, these are the days of the years of the life of Sarah.

8 This is the tenth trial with which Abraham was tested, and he was found faithful and patient in spirit.

9 He did not say a single word regarding the rumor in the land of how God had said that He would give it to him and to his offspring after him, but instead he begged for a place there to bury his dead. Because he was found faithful, it was recorded on the heavenly tablets that he was the friend of God.

10 In the fourth year of it (this jubilee) he took a wife for his son Isaac and her name was Rebecca the daughter of Bethuel, the son of Nahor, the brother of Abraham the sister of Laban and daughter of Bethuel; and Bethuel was the son of Melca, who was the wife of Nahor, the brother of Abraham.

11 Abraham took to himself a third wife from among the daughters of his household servants, for Hagar had died before Sarah, and her name was Keturah,. And she gave birth to six sons, Zimram, and Jokshan, and Medan, and Midian, and Ishbak, and Shuah, in the two weeks of years.

12 In the sixth week, in the second year of it, Rebecca gave birth to two sons of Isaac, Jacob and Esau.

13 And Jacob had no beard and was a straight and tall man who dwelt in tents, and Esau was a powerful a man of the field, and was hairy.

14 The youths grew, and Jacob learned to write, but Esau did not learn, for he was a man of the field and a hunter, and he learned war, and all his deeds were fierce.

15 Abraham loved Jacob, but Isaac loved Esau.

16 And Abraham saw the deeds of Esau, and he knew that in Jacob should his name and offspring be called. He called Rebecca and gave commandment regarding Jacob, for he knew that she too loved Jacob much more than Esau.

17 He said to her, "My daughter, watch over my son Jacob, for he shall take my place on the earth. He shall be a blessing throughout the children of men and for the glory of all the offspring of Shem.

18 I know that the Lord will choose him to be a people (nation) and a possession to Himself, above all peoples that are on the face of the earth.

19 Isaac, my son, loves Esau more than Jacob, but I see that you truly love Jacob.

20 Add still further to your kindness to him, and regard him in love, for he shall be a blessing to us on the earth from now on to all generations of the earth.

21 Let your hands be strong and let your heart rejoice in your son Jacob, for I have loved him far beyond all my sons. He shall be blessed forever, and his offspring shall fill the whole earth.

22 If a man can number the sand of the earth, his offspring also shall be numbered.

23 And all the blessings with which the Lord has blessed me and my offspring shall belong to Jacob and his offspring always.

24 In his offspring shall my name be blessed, and the name of my fathers, Shem, Noah, Enoch, Mahalalel, Enos, Seth, and Adam. And these shall serve to lay the foundations of the heaven, and to strengthen the earth, and to renew all the stars and planets which are in the sky.

27 He called Jacob and kissed him in front of Rebecca, his mother, and blessed him, and said, "Jacob, my beloved son, whom my soul loves, may God bless you from above the sky, and may He give you all the blessings with which He blessed Adam, Enoch, Noah, and Shem; and all the things of which He told me, and all the things which He promised to give me, may He cause to be yours and your offspring forever, according to the days of heaven above the earth.

28 And the Spirits of Mastema shall not rule over you or over your offspring or turn you from the Lord, who is your God from now on forever.

29 May the Lord God be a father to you and may you be like His first-born son, and to the people always. Go in peace, my son."

30 And they both went out together from Abraham.

31 Rebecca loved Jacob, with all her heart and with all her soul, very much more than Esau, but Isaac loved Esau much more than Jacob.

[Chapter 20]

1 In the forty-second jubilee, in the first year of the seventh week, Abraham called Ishmael, and his twelve sons, and Isaac and his two sons, and the six sons of Keturah, and their sons.

2 And he commanded them that they should observe the way of the Lord, that they should work righteousness, and love each his neighbor, and act in this manner among all men, that they should each walk with regard to the ways of the Lord to do judgment and righteousness on the earth.

3 He also commanded them that they should circumcise their sons, according to the covenant, which God had made with them, and not deviate to the right or the left of all the paths which the Lord had commanded us, and that we should keep ourselves from all fornication and uncleanness.

4 He said, "If any woman or maid commits fornication among you, burn her with fire. And do not let them commit fornication with her with their eyes or their heart; and do not let them take to themselves wives from the daughters of Canaan, because the offspring of Canaan will be rooted out of the land."

5 He told them about the judgment on the giants, and the judgment on the Sodomites, how they had been judged because of their wickedness, and had died because of their fornication and uncleanness, and corruption through fornication together.

6 He said, "Guard yourselves from all fornication and uncleanness, and from all pollution of sin, or you will make our name a curse, and your whole life a shame, and all your sons to be destroyed by the sword, and you will become accursed like Sodom, and all that is left of you shall be as the sons of Gomorrah.

7 I implore you, my sons, love the God of heaven and cling to all His commandments.

8 Do not walk after their idols and after their ways of uncleanness, and do not make yourselves molten or graven gods. They are empty, and there is no spirit in them, for they are work of men's hands, and all who trust in them, trust in nothing.

9 Do not serve them, nor worship them, but serve the most high God, and worship Him continually, and hope for His presence always, and work uprightness and righteousness before Him, that He may have pleasure in you and grant you His mercy, and send rain on you morning and evening, and bless all your works which you have performed on the earth, and bless your bread and your water, and bless the fruit of your womb and the fruit of your land, and the herds of your cattle, and the flocks of your sheep.

10 You will be for a blessing on the earth, and all nations of the earth will desire you, and bless your sons in my name, that they may be blessed as I am."

11 He gave to Ishmael and to his sons, and to the sons of Keturah, gifts, and sent them away from Isaac his son, and he gave everything to Isaac his son.

12 Ishmael and his sons, and the sons of Keturah and their sons, went together and settled from Paran to the border of Babylon in all the land that is toward the East facing the desert.

13 These mingled (intermarried) with each other, and their names were called Arabs, and Ishmaelites.

[Chapter 21]

1 In the sixth year of the seventh week of this jubilee Abraham called Isaac his son, and commanded him, saying, "I have become old. I do not know the day of my death but I am full of my days.

2 I am one hundred and seventy-five years old, and throughout all the days of my life I have remembered the

Lord, and sought with all my heart to do His will, and to walk uprightly in all His ways.

3 My soul has hated idols. I have given my heart and spirit to the observance of the will of Him who created me.

4 For He is the living God, and He is holy and faithful, and He is righteous beyond all, and He is no respecter of men or of their gifts, for God is righteous, and executes judgment on all those who transgress His commandments and despise His covenant.

5 My son, observe His commandments and His law and His judgments, and do not walk after the abominations and after the graven images and after the molten images.

6 And eat no blood at all of animals or cattle, or of any bird that flies in the heaven.

7 If you kill a sacrificial animal as an acceptable peace offering, kill it, and pour out its blood on the altar. Place all the fat of the offering on the altar with fine flour and the meat offering mingled with oil with its drink offering. Place them all together on the altar of burnt offering. It is a sweet odor before the Lord.

8 You will offer the fat of the sacrifice of thanks offerings on the fire which is on the altar, and the fat which is on the belly, and all the fat on the inside, behind the two kidneys, and all the fat that is on them, and lobes of the liver you will remove, together with the kidneys.

9 Offer all these for a sweet odor acceptable before the Lord, with its meat-offering and with its drink-offering, and the bread of the offering to the Lord.

10 Eat its meat on that day and on the second day, but do not let the sun go down on it until it is eaten. Let nothing be left over for the third day, for it is not acceptable. Let it no longer be eaten, and all who eat of it will bring sin on themselves, for thus I have found it written in the books of my forefathers, and in the words of Enoch, and in the words of Noah.

11 On all your offerings you will scatter salt, and do not let the salt of the covenant be lacking in all your offerings before the Lord.

12 As regards the wood of the sacrifices, beware to bring only these and no other wood to the altar in addition to these, cypress, bay, almond, fir, pine, cedar, savin, fig, olive, myrrh, laurel, and aspalathus.

13 Of these kinds of wood lay on the altar under the sacrifice, such as have been tested as to their appearance, and do not lay on it any split or dark wood, but only hard and clean wood, without fault, a healthy, new growth. Do not lay old wood on it, because there is no longer fragrance in it as before.

14 Besides these kinds of wood there is none other that you will place on the altar, for the fragrance is dispersed, and the smell of its fragrance will not go up to heaven.

15 Observe this commandment and do it, my son, that you may be upright in all your deeds.

16 Be clean in your body at all times. Wash yourself with water before you approach to offer on the altar. Wash your hands and your feet before you draw near to the altar, and when you are done sacrificing, wash your hands and feet again.

17 Let no blood appear on you or on your clothes. Be on your guard against blood, my son. Be on your guard continually and cover it with dust.

18 Do not eat any blood for it is the soul. Eat no blood whatsoever.

19 Take no payment for shedding the blood of man, or it will cause it to be shed without fear of punishment, without judgment. It is the blood that is shed that causes the earth to sin, and the earth cannot be cleansed from the blood of man except by the blood of he who shed it.

20 Take no present or gift for the blood of man, blood for blood, that you may be accepted before the Lord, the Most High God. He is the defense of the good, so that you may be preserved from all evil, and that He may withhold you from every kind of death.

21 I see, my son, all the works of the children of men are sin and wickedness, and all their deeds are uncleanness and an abomination and a pollution, and there is no righteousness in them.

22 Beware, or you will walk in their ways and tread in their paths, and commit a sin worthy of death before the Most High God. He will hide His face from you and give you back into the hands of your transgression, and root you out of the land, and your offspring likewise from under heaven, and your name and your offspring shall perish from the whole earth.

23 Turn away from all their deeds and all their uncleanness, and observe the laws of the Most High God, and do His will and be upright in all things.

24 If you do this, He will bless you in all your deeds, and will raise up from you a plant of righteousness through all the earth, throughout all generations of the earth, and my name and your name shall not be forgotten under heaven forever.

25 Go, my son in peace. May the Most High God, my God and your God, strengthen you to do His will, and may

He bless all your offspring and the remainder of your offspring for the generations forever, with all righteous blessings, that you may be a blessing on all the earth."
26 And he went out from him rejoicing.

[Chapter 22]

1 In the first week in the forty-fourth jubilee, in the second year, that is, the year in which Abraham died, Isaac and Ishmael came from the Well of the Oath to celebrate the feast of weeks which is the feast of the first-fruits of the harvest to Abraham, their father, and Abraham rejoiced because his two sons had come.
2 Isaac had many possessions in Beersheba, and Isaac desired to go and see his possessions and to return to his father.
3 In those days Ishmael came to see his father, and they both came together, and Isaac offered a sacrifice for a burnt offering, and presented it on the altar of his father that he had made in Hebron.
4 He offered a thanks offering and made a feast of joy in the presence of Ishmael, his brother, and Rebecca made new cakes from the new grain, and gave them to Jacob, her son, to take them to Abraham, his father, from the first-fruits of the land, that he might eat and bless the Creator of all things before he died.
5 Isaac, also, sent Jacob to Abraham with an offering of his best for thanks so that he might eat and drink.
6 He ate and drank, and blessed the Most High God, who has created heaven and earth, who has made all the fat things of the earth, and given them to the children of men that they might eat and drink and bless their Creator.
7 "And now I give thanks to You, my God, because you have caused me to see this day, behold, I am one hundred three score and fifteen years, an old man and full of days, and all my days have been peace to me.
8 The sword of the adversary has not overcome me in all that You have given me and my children all the days of my life until this day.
9 My God, may Your mercy and Your peace be on Your servant, and on the offspring of his sons, that they may be to You a chosen nation and an inheritance from among all the nations of the earth from now on to all the days of the generations of the earth, to all the ages."
10 He called Jacob and said, "My son Jacob, may the God of all bless you and strengthen you to do righteousness, and His will before Him, and may He choose you and your offspring that you may become a people for His inheritance according to His will always.
11 My son, Jacob, draw near and kiss me." And he drew near and kissed him, and he said, "Blessed be my son Jacob and all the sons of God Most High, to all the ages. May God give to you an offspring of righteousness; and some of your sons may He sanctify throughout the whole earth. May nations serve you, and all the nations bow themselves before your offspring.
12 Be strong in the presence of men, and exercise authority over all the offspring of Seth. Then your ways and the ways of your sons will be justified, so that they shall become a holy nation.
13 May the Most High God give you all the blessings with which He has blessed me and He blessed Noah and Adam. May they rest on the sacred head of your offspring from generation to generation forever.
14 May He cleanse you from all unrighteousness and impurity so that you may be forgiven all the transgressions, which you have committed ignorantly. May He strengthen you, and bless you.
15 May you inherit the whole earth, and may He renew His covenant with you so that you may be to Him a nation for His inheritance for all the ages, and so that He may be to you and to your offspring a God in truth and righteousness throughout all the days of the earth.
16 My son Jacob, remember my words. Observe the commandments of Abraham, your father, separate yourself from the nations (gentiles), and do not eat with them. Do not emulate their works, and do not associate with them because their works are unclean, and all their ways are a pollution and an abomination and uncleanness.
17 They offer their sacrifices to the dead and they worship evil spirits, and they eat over the graves, and all their works are empty and nothingness.
18 They have no heart to understand and their eyes do not see what their works are, and how they go astray by saying to a piece of wood, "You are my God," and to a stone, "You are my Lord and you are my deliverer," because the stone and wood have no heart.
19 And as for you, my son Jacob, may the Most High God help you and the God of heaven bless you and remove you from their uncleanness and from all their error.

20 Jacob, be warned. Do not take a wife from any offspring of the daughters of Canaan, for all his offspring are to be rooted out of the earth.

21 Because of the transgression of Ham, Canaan erred, and all his offspring shall be destroyed from the earth including any remnant of it, and none springing from him shall exist except on the day of judgment.

22 And as for all the worshippers of idols and the profane, there shall be no hope for them in the land of the living, and no one on earth will remember them, for they shall descend into the abode of the dead, and they shall go into the place of condemnation. As the children of Sodom were taken away from the earth, so will all those who worship idols be taken away.

23 Fear not, my son Jacob. Be not dismayed, son of Abraham. May the Most High God preserve you from destruction, and may He deliver you from all the paths of error.

24 This house have I built for myself that I might put my name on it in the earth. It is given to you and to your offspring forever, and it will be named the house of Abraham. It is given to you and your offspring forever, for you will build my house and establish my name before God forever. Your offspring and your name will stand throughout all generations of the earth."

25 He ceased commanding him and blessing him.

26 The two lay together on one bed, and Jacob slept in the embracing arms of Abraham, his father's father, and he kissed him seven times, and his affection and his heart rejoiced over him.

27 He blessed him with all his heart and said, "The Most High God, the God of all, and Creator of all, who brought me out from Ur of the Chaldees that He might give me this land to inherit forever, that I might establish a holy offspring.

28 Blessed be the Most High forever."

29 And he blessed Jacob and said, "May Your grace and Your mercy be lift up on my son, over whom I rejoice with all my heart and my affection and on his offspring always.

30 Do not forsake him, nor diminish him from now to the days of eternity, and may Your eyes be opened on him and on his offspring, that You may preserve him, and bless him, and may sanctify him as a nation for Your inheritance. Bless him with all Your blessings from now to all the days of eternity, and renew Your covenant and Your grace with him and with his offspring according to all Your good pleasure to all the generations of the earth."

[Chapter 23]

1 He placed Jacob's two fingers on his eyes, and he blessed the God of gods, and he covered his face and stretched out his feet and slept the sleep of eternity, and was gathered to his fathers.

2 In spite of all this, Jacob was lying in his embracing arms, and knew not that Abraham, his father's father, was dead.

3 Jacob awoke from his sleep, and realized Abraham was cold as ice, and he said, "Father, father," but there was no answer, and he knew that he was dead.

4 He arose from his embracing arms and ran and told Rebecca, his mother, and Rebecca went to Isaac in the night, and told him and they went together, and Jacob with them, and a lamp was in his hand, and when they had gone in they found Abraham lying dead.

5 Isaac fell on the face of his father and wept and kissed him.

6 Ishmael, his son, heard the voices in the house of Abraham, and he arose, and went to Abraham his father, and wept over Abraham his father, he and all the house of Abraham, and they wept greatly.

7 His sons, Isaac and Ishmael, buried him in the double cave, near Sarah his wife, and all the men of his house, and Isaac and Ishmael, and all their sons, and all the sons of Keturah in their places wept for him forty days and then the days of weeping for Abraham were ended.

8 He lived three jubilees and four weeks of years, one hundred and seventy-five years, and completed the days of his life, being old and full of days.

9 For the days of the lives of their forefathers were nineteen jubilees; and after the Flood they began to grow less than nineteen jubilees, and to decrease in jubilees, and to grow old quickly, and to be full of their days because of the many types of hardships and the wickedness of their ways, with the exception of Abraham.

10 For Abraham was perfect in all his deeds with the Lord, and well-pleasing in righteousness all the days of his

life. Yet, he did not complete four jubilees in his life, when he had grown old because of the wickedness in the world, and was full of his days.

11 All the generations which shall arise from this time until the day of the great judgment shall grow old quickly, before they complete two jubilees, and their knowledge shall forsake them because of their old age and all their knowledge shall vanish away.

12 In those days, if a man lives a jubilee and a-half of years, they shall say regarding him, "He has lived long," and the greater part of his days are pain and sorrow and hardship, and there is no peace. For calamity follows on calamity, and wound on wound, and hardship on hardship, and evil deeds on evil deeds, and illness on illness, and all judgments of destruction such as these, piled one on another, illness and overthrow, and snow and frost and ice, and fever, and chills, and mental and physical incapacity, and famine, and death, and sword, and captivity, and all kinds of calamities and pains.

13 All of these shall come on an evil generation, which transgresses on the earth. Their works are uncleanness and fornication, and pollution and abominations.

14 Then they shall say, "The days of the forefathers were many, lasting a thousand years, and were good; but the days of our lives, if a man lives a long life are three score years and ten, and, if he is strong, four score years, and those evil, and there is no peace in the days of this evil generation."

15 In that generation the sons shall convict their fathers and their elders of sin and unrighteousness, and of the words of their mouths and the great wickedness which they perform, and concerning their forsaking the covenant which the Lord made between them and Him. They should observe and do all His commandments and His ordinances and all His laws, without departing either to the right hand or the left.

16 For all have done evil, and every mouth speaks sinfully and all their works are unclean and an abomination, and all their ways are pollution, uncleanness, and destruction.

17 The earth shall be destroyed because of all their works, and there shall be no fruit (seed) of the vine, and no oil; for their actions are altogether faithless, and they shall all perish together, beasts and cattle and birds, and all the fish of the sea, because of the children of men.

18 They shall quarrel with one another, the young with the old, and the old with the young, the poor with the rich, the lowly with the great, and the beggar with the prince, because of the law and the covenant; for they have forgotten the commandments, and covenant, and feasts, and months, and Sabbaths, and jubilees, and all judgments.

19 They shall use swords and war to turn them back to the way, but they shall not return until much blood has been shed on the earth, one by another.

20 Those who have escaped shall not return from their wickedness to the way of righteousness, but they shall all raise themselves to a high status through deceit and wealth, that they may each steal all that belongs of his neighbor, and they shall name the great name (of God), but not in truth and not in righteousness, and they shall defile the holy of holies with their uncleanness and the corruption of their pollution.

21 A great punishment shall come because of the deeds of this generation, and the Lord will give them over to the sword and to judgment and to slavery, and to be plundered and consumed.

22 And He will arouse the Gentile sinners against them, who have neither mercy nor compassion, and who shall respect no one, neither old nor young, nor any one, for they are more wicked, strong, and evil than all the children of men.

23 They shall use violence against Israel and shall violate Jacob, and much blood shall be shed on the earth, and there shall be none to gather the dead and none to bury them.

24 In those days they shall cry aloud, and call and pray that they may be saved from the hand of the sinners, the Gentiles. But none shall be excluded (none shall be saved).

25 The heads of the children shall be white with grey hair, and a child of three weeks shall appear old like a man of one hundred years, and their work and worth shall be destroyed by hardship and oppression.

26 In those days the children shall begin to study the laws, and to seek the commandments, and to return to the path of righteousness.

27 The days shall begin to grow many and increase among those children of men until their days draw close to one thousand years, and to a greater number of years than before age was recorded.

28 There shall be neither old man nor one who is aged, for all shall be as children and youths.

29 All their days shall be full and they shall live in peace and in joy, and there shall be neither Satan nor any evil destroyer because all their days shall be days of blessing and healing.

30 And at that time the Lord will heal His servants, and they shall rise up and see great peace, and drive out their

adversaries. The righteous shall understand and be thankful, and rejoice with joy forever and ever, and they shall see all their judgments and all their curses enacted on their enemies.

31 Their bones shall rest in the earth, and their spirits shall have much joy, and they shall know that it is the Lord who executes judgment, and shows mercy to hundreds and thousands and to all that love Him.

32 Moses, write down these words. Write them and record them on the heavenly tablets for a testimony for the generations forever.

[Chapter 24]

1 It happened after the death of Abraham, that the Lord blessed Isaac his son, who arose from Hebron and went and dwelt at the Well of the Vision in the first year of the third week of this jubilee, seven years.

2 In the first year of the fourth week a famine began in the land, besides the first famine, which had been in the days of Abraham.

3 Jacob made lentil soup, and Esau came from the field hungry. He said to Jacob his brother, "Give me some of this red soup."

4 Jacob said to him, "Sell to me your birthright and I will give you bread, and also some of this lentil soup." And Esau said in his heart, "If I shall die what good is my birthright to me?"

5 He said to Jacob, "I give it to you." And Jacob said, "Swear to me, this day," and he swore to him.

6 And Jacob gave his brother Esau bread and soup, and he ate until he was satisfied, and Esau despised his birthright. For this reason was Esau's name called Edom (red), because of the red soup which Jacob gave him for his birthright.

7 And Jacob became the elder, and Esau was brought down from his dignity.

8 The famine covered the land, and Isaac departed to go down into Egypt in the second year of this week, and went to the king of the Philistines to Gerar, into the presence of Abimelech.

9 The Lord appeared to him and said to him, "Do not go down into Egypt. Dwell in the land that I shall tell you of, and sojourn in this land, and I will be with you and bless you.

10 For to you and to your offspring will I give all this land, and I will establish My oath which I swore to Abraham your father, and I will multiply your offspring as the stars of heaven, and will give to your offspring all this land.

11 And in your offspring shall all the nations of the earth be blessed, because your father obeyed My voice, and kept My ways and My commandments, and My laws, and My ordinances, and My covenant; and now do as you are told and dwell in this land."

12 And he dwelt in Gelar three weeks of years. And Abimelech commanded concerning him, and concerning all that was his, saying, "Any man that shall touch him or anything that is his shall surely die."

13 Isaac grew strong among the Philistines, and he got many possessions, oxen and sheep and camels and donkeys and a great household.

14 He sowed in the land of the Philistines and brought in a hundred-fold, and Isaac became very great, and the Philistines envied him.

15 Now all the wells that the servants of Abraham had dug during the life of Abraham, the Philistines had stopped them after the death of Abraham, and filled them with dirt.

16 Abimelech said to Isaac, "Go from us, for you are much mightier than we." Isaac departed from that place in the first year of the seventh week, and sojourned in the valleys of Gerar.

17 And they dug the wells of water again which the servants of Abraham, his father, had dug, and which the Philistines had filled after the death of Abraham his father, and he called their names as Abraham his father had named them.

18 The servants of Isaac dug a well in the valley, and found fresh, flowing water, and the shepherds of Gerar bickered with the shepherds of Isaac, saying, "The water is ours." Isaac called the name of the well "Perversity," because they had been perverse with us.

19 And they dug a second well, and they fought for that also, and he called its name "Enmity."

20 He left that place and they dug another well, and for that they did not fight, and he called the name of it "Room," and Isaac said, "Now the Lord has made room for us, and we have increased in the land."

21 And he went up from that place to the Well of the Oath in the first year of the first week in the forty-fourth jubilee.

22 The Lord appeared to him in the night of the new moon of the first month, and said to him, "I am the God of

Abraham your father; fear not, for I am with you, and shall bless you and shall surely multiply your offspring as the sand of the earth, for the sake of Abraham my servant."

23 And he built an altar there, which Abraham his father had first built, and he called on the name of the Lord, and he offered sacrifice to the God of Abraham his father.

24 They dug a well and they found fresh, flowing water.

25 The servants of Isaac dug another well and did not find water, and they went and told Isaac that they had not found water, and Isaac said, "I have sworn this day to the Philistines and this thing has been announced to us."

26 And he called the name of that place the Well of the

Oath, because there he had sworn to Abimelech and Ahuzzath, his friend, and also to Phicol, who was the commander and his host.

27 Isaac knew that day that he had sworn to them under pressure to make peace with them.

28 On that day Isaac cursed the Philistines and said, "Cursed be the Philistines to the day of wrath and indignation from among all nations. May God make them a disdain and a curse and an object of anger and indignation in the hands of the Gentile sinners and in the hands of the Kittim.

29 Whoever escapes the sword of the enemy and the Kittim, may the righteous nation root them out in judgment from under heaven. They shall be the enemies and foes of my children throughout their generations on the earth.

30 No part of them will remain. Not even one shall be spared on the day of the wrath of judgment. The offspring of the Philistines will experience destruction, rooting out, and expulsion from the earth and this is all that is in store for them. There shall not be a name or an offspring left on the earth for these Caphtorim (the seat of the Philistine state).

31 For though he rises up to heaven, he shall be brought down, and though he makes himself strong on earth, from there shall he be dragged out, and though he hide himself among the nations, even from that place shall he be rooted out.

32 Though he descends into the abode of the dead, his condemnation shall be great, and he shall have no peace there.

33 If he goes into captivity by the hands of those that seek his life they shall kill him on the way (to his imprisonment), and neither his name nor offspring shall be left on all the earth. Into an eternal curse shall he depart."

34 It is written and engraved concerning him on the heavenly tablets, that on the day of judgment he will be rooted out of the earth.

[Chapter 25]

1 In the second year of this week in this jubilee, Rebecca called Jacob her son, and spoke to him, saying, "My son, do not take a wife from the daughters of Canaan as Esau, your brother, who took two wives of the daughters of Canaan, and they have made my soul bitter with all their unclean acts, for all their actions are fornication and lust, and there is no righteousness in them, because their deeds are evil.

2 I love you greatly, my son, and my heart and my affection bless you every hour of the day and in every night.

3 Now, my son, listen to my voice, and do the will of your mother, and do not take a wife of the daughters of this land, but only from the house of my father, and of those related to my father.

4 If you will take you a wife of the house of my father, the Most High God will bless you, and your children shall be a righteous generation and a holy offspring." And then spoke Jacob to Rebecca, his mother, and said to her, "Look, mother, I am nine weeks of years old, and I have neither been with nor have I touched any woman, nor have I engaged myself to any, nor I have even thought of taking me wife of the daughters of Canaan.

5 For I remember, mother, the words of Abraham, our father, for he commanded me not to take a wife of the daughters of Canaan, but to take me a wife from the offspring of my father's house and from my kind folks.

6 I have heard before that daughters have been born to Laban, your brother, and I have set my heart on them to take a wife from among them.

7 For this reason I have guarded myself in my spirit against sinning or being corrupted in any way throughout all the days of my life; for with regard to lust and fornication, Abraham, my father, gave me many commands.

8 Despite all that he has commanded me, these two and twenty years my brother has argued with me, and spoken frequently to me and said, "My brother, take a wife that is a sister of my two wives," but I refused to do as he has done.

9 I swear before you mother, that all the days of my life I will not take me a wife from the daughters of the

offspring of Canaan, and I will not act wickedly as my brother has done.

10 Do not be afraid mother, be assured that I shall do your will and walk in uprightness, and not corrupt my ways forever."

11 When she heard this, she lifted up her face to heaven and extended the fingers of her hands, and opened her mouth and blessed the Most High God, who had created the heaven and the earth, and she gave Him thanks and praise.

12 She said, "Blessed be the Lord God, and may His holy name be blessed forever and ever. He has given me Jacob as a pure son and a holy offspring; for he is Yours, and Yours shall his offspring be continually, throughout all the generations forever.

13 Bless him, O Lord, and place in my mouth the blessing of righteousness, that I may bless him."

14 At that hour, when the spirit of righteousness descended into her mouth, she placed both her hands on the head of Jacob, and said, "Blessed are You, Lord of righteousness and God of the ages, and may You bless him beyond all the generations of men.

15 My Son, may He give you the path of righteousness, and reveal righteousness to your offspring.

16 May He make your sons many during your life, and may they arise according to the number of the months of the year. And may their sons become many and great beyond the stars of heaven, and may their numbers be more than the sand of the sea.

17 May He give them this good and pleasing land, as He said He would give it to Abraham and to his offspring after him always, and may they hold it as a possession forever.

18 My son, may I see blessed children born to you during my life, and may all your offspring be blessed and holy.

19 And as you have refreshed your mother's spirit during her life, the womb of her that gave birth to you blesses you now. My affection and my heart (breasts) bless you and my mouth and my tongue greatly praise you.

20 Increase and spread over the earth. May your offspring be perfect in the joy of heaven and earth forever. May your offspring rejoice, and on the great day of peace may they have peace.

21 May your name and your offspring endure to all the ages, and may the Most High God be their God, and may the God of righteousness dwell with them, and may His sanctuary be built by you all the ages.

22 Blessed be he that blesses you, and all flesh that curses you falsely, may it be cursed."

23 And she kissed him, and said to him, "May the Lord of the world love you as the heart of your mother and her affection rejoice in you and bless you." And she ceased from blessing.

[Chapter 26]

1 In the seventh year of this week Isaac called Esau, his elder son, and said to him, " I am old, my son, and my sight is dim, and I do not know the day of my death.

2 Now, take your hunting weapons, your quiver, and your bow, and go out to the field, and hunt and catch me venison, my son, and make me flavorful meat, like my soul loves, and bring it to me that I may eat, and that my soul may bless you before I die."

3 But Rebecca heard Isaac speaking to Esau.

4 Esau went out early to the field to hunt and catch and bring home meat to his father.

5 Rebecca called Jacob, her son, and said to him, "Look, I heard Isaac, your father, speak to Esau, your brother, saying, "Hunt for me, and make me flavorful meat, and bring it to me that I may eat and bless you before the Lord before I die."

6 Now, my son, do as you are told and do as I command you. Go to your flock and fetch me two good kids of the goats, and I will make them good tasting meat for your father, like he loves, and you will bring it to your father that he may eat and bless you to the Lord before he dies."

7 Jacob said to Rebecca his mother, "Mother, I shall not withhold anything which my father would eat and which would please him, but I am afraid that he will recognize my voice and wish to touch me.

8 And you know that I am smooth, and Esau, my brother, is hairy, and I he will see me an evildoer because I am doing something that he has not told me to do and he will be very angry with me, and I shall bring on myself a curse, and not a blessing."

9 Rebecca, his mother, said to him, "Your curse be on me, my son, just do as you are told."

10 Jacob obeyed the voice of Rebecca, his mother, and went and brought back two good and fat goat kids, and brought them to his mother, and his mother made them tasty meat like he loved.

11 Rebecca took the good and pleasing clothes of Esau, her elder son, which was with her in the house, and she

clothed Jacob, her younger son, with them, and she put the skins of the kids on his hands and on the exposed parts of his neck.

12 And she gave the meat and the bread, which she had prepared, to her son Jacob.

13 Jacob went in to his father and said, "I am your son. I have done as you asked me. Arise and sit and eat of that which I have caught, father, that your soul may bless me."

14 Isaac said to his son, "How have you found game so quickly, my son?"

15 Jacob said, "Because the Lord your God caused me to find."

16 Isaac said to him, "Come closer, that I may feel you, my son, and know if you are my son Esau or not."

17 Jacob went near to Isaac, his father, and he felt him and said, "The voice is Jacob's voice, but the hands are the hands of Esau," and he did not recognize him, because it was a decision from heaven to remove his power of perception and Isaac discerned not, because his hands were hairy as his brother Esau's, so Isaac blessed him.

18 He said, "Are you my son Esau? " and Jacob said, "I am your son," and Isaac said, "Bring it to me that I may eat of that which you have caught, my son, that my soul may bless you."

19 And Jacob brought it to him, and he ate, and Jacob brought him wine and he drank.

20 Isaac, his father, said to him, "Come close and kiss me, my son."

21 He came close and kissed Isaac. And he smelled the smell of his raiment, and he blessed Jacob and said, "Look, the smell of my son is as the smell of a full field which the Lord has blessed.

22 May the Lord give you of the dew of heaven and of the dew of the earth, and plenty of corn and oil. Let nations serve you and peoples bow down to you.

23 Be ruler over your brothers, and let your mother's sons bow down to you; and may all the blessings that the Lord has blessed me and blessed Abraham, my father, be imparted to you and to your offspring forever. Cursed be he that curses you, and blessed be he that blesses you."

24 It happened as soon as Isaac had made an end of blessing his son Jacob, that Jacob had went away from Isaac his father and hid himself.

25 Esau, his brother, came in from his hunting. And he also made flavorful meat, and brought it to his father and Esau said to his father, "Let my father arise, and eat of my venison that your soul may bless me."

26 Isaac, his father, said to him, "Who are you?" Esau said to him, "I am your first born, your son Esau. I have done as you have commanded me."

27 Isaac was very greatly surprised, and said, "Who is he that has hunted and caught and brought it to me, and I have eaten of all before you came, and have blessed him, and he shall be blessed, and all his offspring forever."

28 It happened when Esau heard the words of his father Isaac that he cried with a very loud and bitter cry, and said to his father, "Bless me also, father!"

29 Isaac said to him, "Your brother came with trickery, and has taken away your blessing."

30 He said, "Now I know why his name is Jacob. Behold, he has supplanted me these two times, he took away my birth-right, and now he has taken away my blessing."

31 Esau said, "Have you not reserved a blessing for me, father?" and Isaac answered and said to Esau, "Look, I have made him your lord, and all his brothers have I given to him for servants. I have strengthened him with plenty of corn and wine and oil. Now what shall I do for you, my son?"

32 Esau said to Isaac, his father, "Have you only one blessing, father? Please. Bless me, also, father."

33 Esau lifted up his voice and wept. And Isaac answered and said to him, "Far from the dew of the earth shall be your dwelling, and far from the dew of heaven from above.

34 By your sword will you live, and you will serve your brother.

35 It shall happen that when you become great, and do shake his yoke from off your neck, you will sin completely and commit a sin worthy of death, and your offspring shall be rooted out from under heaven."

36 Esau kept threatening Jacob because of the blessing his father blessed him with, and he said in his heart, "May the days of mourning for my father come now, so that I may kill my brother Jacob."

[Chapter 27]

1 Rebecca was told Esau's words in a dream, and Rebecca sent for Jacob her younger son, and said to him, "Look, Esau, your brother, will take vengeance on you and kill you.

2 Now, therefore, my son, do as you are told, and get up and flee to Laban, my brother, to Haran, and stay with him a few days until your brother's anger fades away, and he removes his anger from you, and forgets all that you have done. Then I will send for you to come from that place."

3 Jacob said, "I am not afraid. If he wishes to kill me, I will kill him."

4 But she said to him, "Let me not be bereft of both my sons on one day."

5 Jacob said to Rebecca, his mother, "Look, you know that my father has become old, and does not see because his eyes are dull. If I leave him he will think it is wrong. If I leave him and go away from you, my father will be angry and will curse me.

6 I will not go. When he sends me, only then will I go."

7 Rebecca said to Jacob, "I will go in and speak to him, and he will send you away."

8 Rebecca went in and said to Isaac, "I hate my life because of the two daughters of Heth, whom Esau has taken as wives. If Jacob take a wife from among the daughters of the land such as these, I could not live with it, because the daughters of Canaan are evil."

9 Isaac called Jacob and blessed him, and warned him and said to him, "Do not take you a wife of any of the daughters of Canaan. Arise and go to Mesopotamia, to the house of Bethuel, your mother's father, and take a wife from that place of the daughters of Laban, your mother's brother.

10 And God Almighty bless you and increase and multiply you that you may become a company of nations, and give you the blessings of my father, Abraham, to you and to your offspring after you, that you may inherit the land that you travel in and all the land which God gave to Abraham. Go in peace, my son."

11 Isaac sent Jacob away, and he went to Mesopotamia, to Laban the son of Bethuel the Syrian, the brother of Rebecca, Jacob's mother.

12 It happened after Jacob had departed to Mesopotamia that the spirit of Rebecca was grieved for her son, and she wept.

13 Isaac said to Rebecca, "My sister, weep not because of Jacob, my son, for he goes in peace, and in peace will he return.

14 The Most High God will preserve him from all evil and will be with him. He will not forsake him all his days, for I know that his ways will be made to prosper in all things wherever he goes, until he return in peace to us, and we see him in peace. Fear not on his account, my sister, for he is on the upright path and he is a perfect man, and he is faithful and will not perish. Weep not."

15 Isaac comforted Rebecca because of her son Jacob, and blessed him.

16 Jacob went from the Well of the Oath to go to Haran on the first year of the second week in the forty-fourth jubilee, and he came to Luz on the mountains, that is, Bethel, on the new moon of the first month of this week, and he came to the place at dusk and turned from the way to the west of the road that is close, and that night he slept there, for the sun had set.

17 He took one of the stones of that place (as a pillow) and laid down under the tree, and he was journeying alone, and he slept.

18 Jacob dreamt that night, and saw a ladder set up on the earth, and the top of it reached to heaven, and he saw the angels of the Lord ascended and descended on it, and behold, the Lord stood on it.

19 And He spoke to Jacob and said, "I am the Lord God of Abraham, your father, and the God of Isaac. The land you are sleeping on I will give to you and to your offspring after you.

20 Your offspring shall be as the dust of the earth, and you will increase to the west and to the east, to the north and the south, and in you and in your offspring shall all the families of the nations be blessed.

21 Behold, I will be with you, and will keep you wherever you go. I will bring you into this land again in peace. I will not leave you until I do everything that I told you."

22 Jacob awoke from his sleep and said, "Truly this place is the house of the Lord, and I did not know it."

23 He was afraid and said, "I am afraid because this place is none other than the house of God, and this is the gate of heaven, and I did not know it."

24 Jacob got up early in the morning, and took the stone that he had placed under his head and set it up as a pillar for a sign. And he poured oil on the top of it. And he called the name of that place Bethel, but the name of the place was previously Luz.

25 And Jacob vowed a vow to the Lord, saying, "If the Lord will be with me, and will keep me in the way that I go, and give me bread to eat and clothes to put on, so that I come again to my father's house in peace, then the Lord shall be my God, and this stone which I have set up as a pillar for a sign in this place shall be the Lord's house, and of all that you gave me, I shall give the tenth to you, my God."

[Chapter 28]

1 He went on his journey, and came to the land of the east, to Laban, the brother of Rebecca, and he was with him, and Jacob served Laban for Rachel his daughter one week of years. In the first year of the third week of years he said to him, "Give me my wife, for whom I have served you seven years ," and Laban said to Jacob, "I will give you your wife."

2 Laban made a feast, and took Leah his elder daughter, and gave her to Jacob as a wife, and gave Leah Zilpah for a handmaid; and Jacob did not know, for he thought that she was Rachel.

3 He went in to her, and saw she was Leah; and Jacob was angry with Laban, and said to him, "Why have you done this to me?

4 Did I not serve you for Rachel and not for Leah? Why have you wronged me?

5 Take your daughter, and I will go. You have done evil to me." For Jacob loved Rachel more than Leah because Leah's eyes were weak, but her form was very beautiful. Rachel had beautiful eyes and a beautiful and very voluptuous form.

6 Laban said to Jacob, "It is not done that way in our country, we do not to give the younger before the elder." And it is not right to do this; for thus it is ordained and written in the heavenly tablets, that no one should give his younger daughter before the elder; but the elder one is given first and after her the younger. The man who does so will have guilt placed against him in heaven, and none is righteous that does this thing, for this deed is evil before the Lord.

7 Command the children of Israel that they not do this thing. Let them neither take nor give the younger before they have given the elder, for it is very wicked."

8 And Laban said to Jacob, "Let the seven days of the feast pass by, and I shall give you Rachel, that you may serve me another seven years, that you may pasture my sheep as you did in the former week (of years)."

9 On the day when the seven days of the feast of Leah had passed, Laban gave Rachel to Jacob, that he might serve him another seven years, and he gave Rachel, Bilhah, the sister of Zilpah, as a handmaid.

10 He served yet other seven years for Rachel, for Leah had been given to him for nothing, since it was Rachel he wanted.

11 And the Lord opened the womb of Leah, and she conceived and gave birth to a son for Jacob, and he called his name Reuben, on the fourteenth day of the ninth month, in the first year of the third week.

12 But the womb of Rachel was closed, for the Lord saw that Leah was hated and Rachel loved.

13 Again Jacob went in to Leah, and she conceived, and gave birth to a second son for Jacob, and he called his name Simeon, on the twenty-first of the tenth month, and in the third year of this week.

14 Again Jacob went in to Leah, and she conceived, and gave birth to a third son, and he called his name Levi, in the new moon of the first month in the sixth year of this week.

15 Again Jacob went in to her, and she conceived, and gave birth to a fourth son, and he called his name Judah, on the fifteenth of the third month, in the first year of the fourth week.

16 Because of all this Rachel envied Leah, for she did not bear a child, and she said to Jacob, "Give me children;" and Jacob said, "Have I withheld from you the fruits of your womb? Have I left you?"

17 And when Rachel saw that Leah had given birth to four sons for Jacob: Reuben and Simeon and Levi and Judah, she said to him, "Go in to Bilhah my handmaid, and she will conceive, and bear a son for me."

18 She gave him Bilhah, her handmaid, to wife. And he went in to her, and she conceived, and gave birth to a son, and he called his name Dan, on the ninth of the sixth month, in the sixth year of the third week.

19 Jacob went in again to Bilhah a second time, and she conceived, and gave birth to another son for Jacob, and Rachel called his name Napthali, on the fifth of the seventh month, in the second year of the fourth week.

20 When Leah saw that she had become sterile and could no longer have children, she envied Rachel, and she also gave her handmaid Zilpah to Jacob to wife, and she conceived, and gave birth to a son, and Leah called his name Gad, on the twelfth of the eighth month, in the third year of the fourth week.

21 He went in to her again, and she conceived and gave birth to a second son, and Leah called his name Asher, on the second of the eleventh month, in the fifth year of the fourth week.

22 Jacob went in to Leah, and she conceived, and gave birth to a son, and she called his name Issachar, on the fourth of the fifth month, in the fourth year of the fourth week, and she gave him to a nurse.

23 Jacob went in again to her, and she conceived, and gave birth to two children, a son and a daughter, and she called the name of the son Zabulon, and the name of the daughter Dinah, in the seventh day of the seventh month, in the sixth year of the fourth week.

24 The Lord was gracious to Rachel, and opened her womb, and she conceived, and gave birth to a son, and she called his name Joseph, on the new moon of the fourth month, in the sixth year in this fourth week.

25 In the days when Joseph was born, Jacob said to Laban, "Give me my wives and sons, and let me go to my father Isaac, and let me make a household for myself; for I have completed the years in which I have served you for your two daughters, and I will go to the house of my father."
26 Laban said to Jacob, "Stay with me and I will pay you wages, and pasture my flock for me again, and take your wages."
27 They agreed with one another that he should give him as his wages those of the lambs and kids which were born spotted black and white, these were to be his wages.
28 All the sheep brought out spotted and speckled and black, variously marked, and they brought out again lambs like themselves, and all that were spotted were Jacob's and those which were not spotted were Laban's.
29 Jacob's possessions multiplied greatly, and he possessed oxen and sheep and donkeys and camels, and men-servants and maid-servants.
30 Laban and his sons envied Jacob, and Laban took back his sheep from him, and he envied him and watched him for an opportunity to do evil.

[Chapter 29]

1 It happened when Rachel had given birth to Joseph, that Laban went to shear his sheep; for they were distant from him, a three-day journey.
2 Jacob saw that Laban was going to shear his sheep, and Jacob called Leah and Rachel, and spoke sweetly to them in order to convince them to come with him to the land of Canaan.
3 For he told them how he had seen everything in a dream. All that God had spoken to him that he should return to his father's house, and they said, "To every place where you go we will go with you."
4 Jacob blessed the God of Isaac his father, and the God of Abraham his father's father, and he arose and placed his wives and his children on donkeys, and took all his possessions and crossed the river, and came to the land of Gilead, and Jacob hid his intention from Laban and did not tell him.
5 In the seventh year of the fourth week Jacob turned his face toward Gilead in the first month, on the twenty-first of it.
6 Laban pursued and overtook Jacob in the mountain of Gilead in the third month, on the thirteenth of it. And the Lord did not permit him to injure Jacob for he appeared to him in a dream by night.
7 Laban spoke to Jacob. On the fifteenth of those days Jacob made a feast for Laban, and for all who came with him, and Jacob swore to Laban that day, and Laban also swore to Jacob, that neither should cross the mountain of Gilead to do evil to the other.
8 He made a heap (of stones) for a witness there; wherefore the name of that place is called, "The Heap of Witness," after this heap.
9 But before they used to call the land of Gilead the land of the Rephaim. The Rephaim were born giants whose height was ten, nine, eight, down to seven cubits.
10 Their dwelling place was from the land of the children of Ammon to Mount Hermon, and the seats of their kingdom were Karnaim and Ashtaroth, and Edrei, and Misur, and Beon.
11 The Lord destroyed them because of the evil of their deeds, for they were malevolent, and the Amorites were wicked and sinful. There is no people today which has committed the full range of their sins, and their life on the earth was shortened.
12 Jacob sent Laban away, and he departed into Mesopotamia, the land of the East, and Jacob returned to the land of Gilead.
13 He passed over the Jabbok in the ninth month, on the eleventh of it. On that day Esau, his brother, came to him, and he was reconciled to him, and departed from him to the land of Seir, but Jacob dwelt in tents.
14 In the first year of the fifth week in this jubilee he crossed the Jordan, and dwelt beyond the Jordan. He pastured his sheep from the sea of the heap to Bethshan, and to Dothan and to the forest of Akrabbim.
15 He sent his father Isaac all of his possessions such as clothing, and food, and meat, and drink, and milk, and butter, and cheese, and some dates of the valley.
16 Four times a year, he sent gifts to his mother Rebecca who was living at the tower of Abraham. He sent the gifts between the times of the months between plowing and reaping, and between autumn and the rain season, and between winter and spring.
17 For Isaac had returned from the Well of the Oath and gone up to the tower of his father Abraham, and he dwelt there apart from his son Esau.

18 For in the days when Jacob went to Mesopotamia, Esau took to himself a wife Mahalath, the daughter of Ishmael,

and he gathered together all the flocks of his father and his wives, and went up and dwelt on Mount Seir, and left Isaac his father at the Well of the Oath alone.

19 And Isaac went up from the Well of the Oath and dwelt in the tower of Abraham his father on the mountains of Hebron, and that is where Jacob sent all that he did send to his father and his mother from time to time, all they needed, and they blessed Jacob with all their heart and with all their soul.

[Chapter *30*]

1 In the first year of the sixth week he went up to Salem, to the east of Shechem, in the fourth month, and he went in peace. Shechem, the son of Hamor, the Hivite, the prince of the land carried off Dinah, the daughter of Jacob, into the house, and he had sex with her and defiled her. She was a little girl, a child of twelve years.

2 He begged his father and her brothers that she might be given to him as a wife.

3 Jacob and his sons were very angry because of the men of Shechem, for they had defiled Dinah, their sister. They spoke to them while planning evil acts and they dealt deceitfully with them and tricked them.

4 Simeon and Levi came unexpectedly to Shechem and executed judgment on all the men of Shechem, and killed all the men whom they found in it. They did not leave a single one remaining in it. They killed all in hand to hand battle because they had dishonored their sister Dinah.

5 Let it not again be done from now on that a daughter of Israel be defiled. Judgment is ordained in heaven against them that they should destroy all the men of the Shechemites with the sword because they had committed shame in Israel.

6 The Lord delivered them into the hands of the sons of Jacob that they might exterminate them with the sword and execute judgment on them. That it might not again be done in Israel that a virgin of Israel should be defiled.

7 If there is any man in Israel who wishes to give his daughter or his sister to any man who is of the offspring of the Gentiles he shall surely die. They shall stone him, for he has committed shame in Israel. They shall burn the woman with fire, because she has dishonored the name of the house of her father, and she shall be rooted out of Israel.

8 Do not let an adulteress and let no uncleanness be found in Israel throughout all the days of the generations of the earth. For Israel is holy to the Lord, and every man who has defiled it shall surely die. They shall stone him.

9 For it has been ordained and written in the heavenly tablets regarding all the offspring of Israel. He who defiles it shall surely die. He shall be killed by stoning. There is no limit of days for this law. There is no remission, and no atonement.

10 The man who has defiled his daughter shall be rooted out from every corner of all Israel, because he has given of his offspring to Moloch (a pagan God, the worship of which involved burning the child alive), and committed impurity and defiled his child.

11 Moses, command the children of Israel and exhort them not to give their daughters to the Gentiles, and not to take for their sons any of the daughters of the Gentiles, for this is abominable before the Lord.

12 It is because of this that I have written all the deeds of the Shechemites, which they committed against Dinah, and placed them in the words of the Law for you. I have also written how the sons of Jacob spoke, saying, "We will not give our daughter to a man who is uncircumcised, for that is a reproach to us."

13 It is a reproach to Israel that anyone take the daughters of the Gentiles, for this is unclean and abominable to Israel.

14 Israel will not be free from this uncleanness if it has a wife of the daughters of the Gentiles, or has given any of its daughters to a man who is of any of the Gentiles.

15 There will be plague upon plague, and curse upon curse, and every judgment and plague and curse will come if he does this thing, or if they ignore those who commit uncleanness, or defile the sanctuary of the Lord, or those who profane His holy name. If any of these happen the whole nation together will be judged for all the uncleanness and profanation of this man.

16 There will be no judging people by their position and no receiving fruits, or offerings, or burnt-offerings, or fat, or the fragrance of sweet odor from his hands. It will be unacceptable and so warn every man and woman in Israel who defiles the sanctuary.

17 For this reason I have commanded you, saying, "Give this testimony to Israel, see how the Shechemites and their sons fared? See how they were delivered into the hands of two sons of Jacob, and they killed them under torture? It was counted to them for righteousness, and it is written down to them for righteousness.

18 The offspring of Levi were chosen for the priesthood, and to be Levites, that they might minister before the Lord, as we do, continually. Levi and his sons will be blessed forever, for he was zealous to execute righteousness and judgment and vengeance on all those who arose against Israel.

19 So they wrote a testimony in his favor of blessing and righteousness on the heavenly tablets in the presence of the God of all.

20 We remember the righteousness that the man fulfilled during his life, throughout the years, until a thousand generations they will record it. It will come to him and to his descendants after him, and he has been recorded on the heavenly tablets as a friend and a righteous man.

21 All this account I have written for you, and have commanded you to tell the children of Israel, so that they will not commit sin nor transgress the laws nor break the covenant which has been ordained for them. They should fulfill it and be recorded as friends (of God).

22 But if they transgress and work uncleanness in any way, they will be recorded on the heavenly tablets as adversaries (of God), and they will be blotted out of the book of life. Instead, they will be recorded in the book of those who will be destroyed and with those who will be rooted out of the earth.

23 On the day when the sons of Jacob killed Shechem it was written in the record in their favor in heaven that they had executed righteousness and uprightness and vengeance on the sinners, and it was written for a blessing.

24 They brought Dinah, their sister, out of the house of Shechem. They took everything that was in Shechem captive. They took their sheep and their oxen and their donkeys, and all their wealth, and all their flocks, and brought them all to Jacob their father.

25 He reproached them because they had put the city to the sword for he feared those who dwelt in the land, the Canaanites and the Perizzites.

26 The dread of the Lord was on all the cities that are near Shechem. They did not fight or chase after the sons of Jacob, for terror had fallen on them.

[Chapter 31]

1 On the new moon of the month, Jacob spoke to all the people of his house, saying, "Purify yourselves and change your clothes, and let us get up and go to Bethel where I vowed a vow to Him on the day when I fled from Esau my brother. Let us do this because God has been with me and brought me into this land in peace. You must put away the strange gods that you raise among you."

2 They gave up the strange gods and that which was in their ears and which was on their necks and the idols which Rachel stole from Laban her father she gave wholly to Jacob. And he burnt and broke them to pieces and destroyed them, and hid them under an oak, which is in the land of Shechem.

3 He went up on the new moon of the seventh month to Bethel. And he built an altar at the place where he had slept, and he set up a pillar there, and he sent word to his father, Isaac, and his mother, Rebecca. He asked to come to Isaac. There, Jacob wished to offer his sacrifice.

4 Isaac said, "Let my son, Jacob, come, and let me see him before I die."

5 Jacob went to his father, Isaac, and his mother, Rebecca, to the house of his father Abraham, and he took two of his sons with him, Levi and Judah.

6 Rebecca came out from the tower to the front of it to kiss Jacob and embrace him, for her spirit had revived when she heard, "Look Jacob your son has come," and she kissed him.

7 She saw his two sons and she recognized them. She said to him, "Are these your sons, my son?" and she embraced them and kissed them, and blessed them, saying, "In you shall the offspring of Abraham become illustrious, and you shall prove a blessing on the earth."

8 Jacob went in to Isaac his father, to the room where he lay, and his two sons were with him. He took his father's hand, stooped down, he kissed him. Isaac held on to the neck of Jacob his son, and wept on his neck.

9 The darkness left the eyes of Isaac, and he saw the two sons of Jacob, Levi, and Judah. And he said, "Are these your sons, my son? Because they look like you."

10 He said to Isaac, "They were truly my sons, and you have clearly seen that they are truly my sons."

11 They came near to him, and he turned and kissed them and embraced them both together.

12 The spirit of prophecy came down into his mouth, and he took Levi by his right hand and Judah by his left.

13 He turned to Levi first, and began to bless him first, and said to him, "May the God of all, the very Lord of all the ages, bless you and your children throughout all the ages.

14 May the Lord give to you and your offspring greatness and great glory from among all flesh. May the Lord cause you and your offspring to draw near to Him to serve in His sanctuary like the angels of the presence (of the Lord) and as the holy ones. The offspring of your sons shall be for the glory and greatness and holiness of God. May He make them great throughout all the ages. They shall be judges and princes, and chiefs of all the offspring of the sons of Jacob. They shall speak the word of the Lord in righteousness, and they shall judge all His judgments in righteousness.

15 They shall declare My ways to Jacob and My paths to Israel. The blessing of the Lord shall be given in their mouths to bless all the offspring of the beloved.

16 Your mother has called your name Levi, and rightly has she called your name. You will be joined to the Lord and be the companion of all the sons of Jacob. Let His table be your table, and let your sons eat from it. May your table be full throughout all generations, and let your food not fail in all the ages.

17 Let all who hate you fall down before you, and let all your adversaries be rooted out and perish. Blessed be he that blesses you, and cursed be every nation that curses you."

18 To Judah he said, "May the Lord give you strength and power to put all that hate you under your feet. You and one of your sons will be a prince over the sons of Jacob. May your name and the name of your sons go out across every land and region.

19 Then shall the Gentiles fear you, and all the nations and people shall shake (with fear of you). In you will be the help of Jacob, and in you will be found the salvation of Israel.

20 When you sit on the throne, which honors of your righteousness, there shall be great peace for all the offspring of the sons of the beloved. Blessed be he that blesses you, and cursed be all that hate you, afflict you, or curse you. They shall be rooted out and destroyed from the earth."

21 He turned, kissed him again, and embraced him, and rejoiced greatly because he had seen the sons of his son, Jacob, clearly and truly.

22 He stepped out from between his feet and fell down. He bowed down to him, and blessed them. He rested there with Isaac, his father, that night, and they ate and drank with joy.

23 He made the two sons of Jacob sleep, the one on his right hand and the other on his left. It was counted to him for righteousness.

24 Jacob told his father everything during the night about how the Lord had shown him great mercy, and how he had caused him to prosper in all his ways, and how he protected him from all evil.

25 Isaac blessed the God of his father Abraham, who had not withdrawn his mercy and his righteousness from the sons of his servant Isaac.

26 In the morning, Jacob told his father, Isaac, the vow, which he had vowed to the Lord. He told him of the vision which he had seen, and that he had built an altar. He told him that everything was ready for the sacrifice to be made before the Lord as he had vowed. He had come to set him on a donkey.

27 Isaac said to Jacob his son, "I am not able to go with you, for I am old and not able to endure the way. Go in peace, my son. I am one hundred and sixty-five years this day. I am no longer able to journey. Set your mother on a donkey and let her go with you.

28 I know that you have come on my account, my son. May this day be blessed on which you have seen me alive, and I also have seen you, my son.

29 May you prosper and fulfill the vow that you have vowed. Do not put off your vow, for you will be called to account for the vow. Now hurry to perform it, and may He who has made all things be pleased. It is to Him you have vowed the vow."

30 He said to Rebecca, "Go with Jacob your son," and Rebecca went with Jacob her son, and Deborah with her, and they came to Bethel.

31 Jacob remembered the prayer with which his father had blessed him and his two sons, Levi and Judah. He rejoiced and blessed the God of his fathers, Abraham and Isaac.

32 He said, "Now I know that my sons and I have an eternal hope in the God of all." Thus is it ordained concerning the two. They recorded it as an eternal testimony to them on the heavenly tablets how Isaac blessed his sons.

[Chapter 32]

1 That night he stayed at Bethel, and Levi dreamed that they had ordained and made his sons and him the priests of the Most High God forever. Then he awoke from his sleep and blessed the Lord.

2 Jacob rose early in the morning, on the fourteenth of this month, and he gave a tithe for all that came with him, both of men and cattle, both of gold and every vessel and garment. Yes, he gave tithes of all.

3 In those days Rachel became pregnant with her son Benjamin. Jacob counted his sons starting from him and going to the oldest and Levi fell to the portion of the Lord. (Levi was the third son – three is the number of spiritual completeness.) His father clothed him in the garments of the priesthood and filled his hands.

4 On the fifteenth of this month, he brought fourteen oxen from among the cattle, and twenty-eight rams, and forty-nine sheep, and seven lambs, and twenty-one kids of the goats to the altar as a burnt-offering on the altar of sacrifice. The offering was well pleasing and a sweet odor before God.

5 This was his offering, done in acknowledgement of the vow in which he had promised that he would give a tenth, with their fruit-offerings and their drink- offerings.

6 When the fire had consumed it, he burnt incense over the fire, and for a thank-offering he sacrificed two oxen and four rams and four sheep, four male goats, and two sheep of a year old, and two kids of the goats. This he did daily for seven days.

7 He, his men, and all his sons were eating this with joy during seven days and blessing and thanking the Lord, who had delivered him out of all his tribulation and had given him His promise.

8 He tithed all the clean animals, and made a burnt sacrifice, but he did not give the unclean animals to Levi his son. He gave him (responsibility for) all the souls of the men. Levi acted in the priestly office at Bethel in the presence of Jacob his father, in preference to his ten brothers. He was a priest there, and Jacob gave his vow, and he gave a tithe to the Lord again and sanctified it, and it became holy to Him.

9 For this reason it is ordained on the heavenly tablets as a law for the offering of the tithe should be eaten in the presence of the Lord every year, in the place where it is chosen that His name should live and reside. This law has no limit of days forever.

10 This law is written so that it may be fulfilled every year. The second tithe should be eaten in the presence of the Lord, in the place where it has been chosen, and nothing shall be left over from it from this year to the following year.

11 In its year shall the seed be eaten until the days of the gathering of the seed of the year. The wine shall be consumed until the days of the wine, and the oil until the days of its season.

12 All that is left of it and all that becomes old will be regarded as spoiled, let it be burnt with fire, for it is unclean.

13 Let them eat it together in the sanctuary, and let them not permit it to become old.

14 All the tithes of the oxen and sheep shall be holy to the Lord, and shall belong to His priests. They will eat before Him from year to year, for thus is it ordained and written on the heavenly tablets regarding the tithe.

15 On the following night, on the twenty-second day of this month, Jacob resolved to build that place and to surround the court with a wall, and to sanctify it and make it holy forever, for himself and his children after him.

16 The Lord appeared to him by night and blessed him and said to him, "Your name shall not be called Jacob, but they will call your name Israel."

17 And He said to him again, "I am the Lord who created the heaven and the earth, and I will increase you and multiply you greatly, and kings shall come forth from you, and they shall be judges everywhere the foot of the sons of men have walked.

18 I will give to your offspring all the earth that is under heaven. They shall judge all the nations, as they desire. After that they shall possess the entire earth and inherit it forever."

19 And He finished speaking with him, and He went up from him.

20 Jacob watched until He had ascended into heaven.

21 In a vision at night he saw an angel descend from heaven with seven tablets in his hands, and he gave them to Jacob, and he read them and knew all that was written on it that would happen to him and his sons throughout all the ages.

22 He showed him all that was written on the tablets, and said to him, "Do not build on this place, and do not make it an eternal sanctuary, and do not live here. This is not the place. Go to the house of Abraham your father and live with Isaac, your father, until the day he dies.

23 For in Egypt you will die in peace, and in this land you will be buried with honor in the sepulcher of your fathers, with Abraham and Isaac.

24 Do not fear. As you have seen and read it shall all be. Write down everything that you have seen and read."

25 Jacob said, "Lord, how can I remember all that I have read and seen?" He said to him, "I will bring all things to your remembrance."

26 He ascended from Jacob, and Jacob awoke from his sleep. He remembered everything that he had read and seen, and he wrote down all the words.

27 He celebrated there yet another day, and he sacrificed on that day as he had sacrificed on all the former days. He called its name "Addition," because this day was added, and the former days he called "The Feast."

28 It was made known and revealed to him and it is written on the heavenly tablets that he should celebrate the day, and add it to the seven days of the feast.

29 Its name was called "Addition," because that it was recorded among the days of the feast days, according to the number of the days of the year.

30 In the night, on the twenty-third of this month, Deborah, Rebecca's nurse died, and they buried her beneath the city under the oak of the river. He called the name of this place, "The river of Deborah," and he called the oak, "The oak of the mourning of Deborah."

31 Rebecca departed and returned to her house, to his father Isaac. Jacob sent rams and sheep and male goats by her so that she should prepare a meal for his father such as he desired.

32 He followed his mother until he came to the land of Kabratan, and he lived there.

33 Rachel gave birth to a son in the night, and called his name "son of my sorrow", for she broke down while giving birth to him, but his father called his name Benjamin. This happened on the eleventh day of the eighth month in the first of the sixth week of this jubilee.

34 Rachel died there and she was buried in the land of Ephrath, the same is Bethlehem, and Jacob built a pillar on the grave of Rachel, on the road above her grave.

[Chapter 33]

1 Jacob went and lived to the south of Magdaladra'ef. He and Leah, his wife, went to his father, Isaac, on the new moon of the tenth month.

2 Reuben saw Bilhah, Rachel's maid, the concubine of his father, bathing in water in a secret place, and he loved her.

3 He hid himself at night, and he entered the house of Bilhah at night. He found her sleeping alone on a bed in her house.

4 He had sex with her. She awoke and saw that is was Reuben lying with her in the bed. She uncovered the border of her covering and grabbed him and cried out when she discovered that it was Reuben.

5 She was ashamed because of him and released her hand from him, and he fled.

6 Because of this, she mourned greatly and did not tell it to any one.

7 When Jacob returned and sought her, she said to him, "I am not clean for you. I have been defiled in regard to you. Reuben has defiled me, and has had sex with me in the night. I was asleep and did not realize he was there until he uncovered my skirt and had sex with me."

8 Jacob was very angry with Reuben because he had sex with Bilhah, because he had uncovered his father's skirt.

9 Jacob did not approach her again because Reuben had defiled her. And as for any man who uncovers his father's skirt his deed is greatly wicked, for he is disgusting to the Lord.

10 For this reason it is written and ordained on the heavenly tablets that a man should not lie with his father's wife, and should not uncover his father's skirt. This is unclean and they shall surely die together, the man who lies with his father's wife and the woman also, for they have committed uncleanness on the earth.

11 There shall be nothing unclean before our God in the nation that He has chosen for Himself as a possession.

12 Again, it is written a second time, "Cursed be he who lies with the wife of his father, for he has uncovered his father's shame." All the holy ones of the Lord said, "So be it. So be it."

13 "Moses, command the children of Israel so that they observe this word. It entails a punishment of death. It is unclean, and there is no atonement forever for the man who has committed this. He is to be put to death. Kill him by stoning. Root him out from among the people of our God.

14 No man who does so in Israel will be permitted to remain alive a single day on the earth. He is abominable and unclean.

15 Do not let them say, "Reuben was granted life and forgiveness after he had sex with his father's concubine, although she had a husband, and her husband, Jacob, his father, was still alive."

16 Until that time the ordinance and judgment and law had not been revealed in its completeness for all. In your days it has been revealed as a law of seasons and of days. It is an everlasting law for all generations forever. For this law has no limit of days, and no atonement for it.

17 They must both be rooted out of the entire nation. On the day they committed it they shall be killed.

18 Moses, write it down for Israel that they may observe it, and do according to these words, and not commit a sin punishable by death. The Lord our God is judge, who does not respect persons (position) and accepts no gifts.

19 Tell them these words of the covenant, that they may hear and observe, and be on their guard with respect to them, and not be destroyed and rooted out of the land; for an uncleanness, and an abomination, and a contamination, and a pollution are all they who commit it on the earth before our God.

20 There is no greater sin on earth than fornication that they commit. Israel is a holy nation to the Lord its God, and a nation of inheritance. It is a priestly and royal nation and for His own possession. There shall appear no such uncleanness among the holy nation.

21 In the third year of this sixth week, Jacob and all his sons went and lived in the house of Abraham, near Isaac his father and Rebecca his mother.

22 These were the names of the sons of Jacob, the first-born

Reuben, Simeon, Levi, Judah, Issachar, Zebulon, which are the sons of Leah. The sons of Rachel are Joseph and Benjamin. The sons of Bilhah are Dan and Naphtali; and the sons of Zilpah, Gad and Asher. Dinah is the daughter of Leah, the only daughter of Jacob.

23 They came and bowed themselves to Isaac and Rebecca. When they saw them they blessed Jacob and all his sons, and Isaac rejoiced greatly, for he saw the sons of Jacob, his younger son and he blessed them.

[Chapter 34]

1 In the sixth year of this week of the forty-fourth jubilee Jacob sent his sons and his servants to pasture their sheep in the pastures of Shechem.

2 The seven kings of the Amorites assembled themselves together (to fight) against them and kill them. They hid themselves under the trees, to take their cattle as booty.

3 Jacob, Levi, Judah and Joseph were in the house with Isaac their father, for his spirit was sorrowful, and they could not leave him. Benjamin was the youngest, and for this reason he remained with his father.

4 The king of Taphu, the king of Aresa, the king of Seragan, the king of Selo, the king of Ga'as, the king of Bethoron, the king of Ma'anisakir, and all those who dwell in these mountains and who dwell in the woods in the land of Canaan came.

5 They announced to Jacob saying, "Look, the kings of the Amorites have surrounded your sons, and plundered their herds."

6 And he left his house, he and his three sons and all the servants of his father, and his own servants, and he went against them with six thousand men, who carried swords.

7 He killed them in the pastures of Shechem, and pursued those who fled, and he killed them with the edge of the sword, and he killed Aresa and Taphu and Saregan and Selo and Amani sakir and Gaga'as, and he recovered his herds.

8 He conquered them, and imposed tribute on them that they should pay him five fruit products of their land. He built (the cities of) Robel and Tamnatares.

9 He returned in peace, and made peace with them, and they became his servants until the day that he and his sons went down into Egypt.

10 In the seventh year of this week he sent Joseph from his house to the land of Shechem to learn about the welfare of his brothers. He found them in the land of Dothan.

11 They dealt treacherously with him, and formed a plot against him to kill him, but they changed their minds and sold him to Ishmaelite merchants. They brought him down into Egypt, and they sold him to Potiphar, the eunuch of Pharaoh, the chief of the cooks and priest of the city of Elew."

12 The sons of Jacob slaughtered a kid, and dipped Joseph's coat in the blood and sent it to Jacob their father on the tenth of the seventh month.

13 They brought it to him in the evening and he mourned all that night. He became feverish with mourning for Joseph's death, and he said, "An evil beast has devoured Joseph". All the members of his house mourned and grieved with him that day.

14 His sons and his daughter got up to comfort him, but he refused to be comforted for his son.

15 On that day Bilhah heard that Joseph had perished, and she died mourning him. She was living in Qafratef, and Dinah, his daughter, died after Joseph had perished.

16 There were now three reasons for Israel to mourn in one month. They buried Bilhah next to the tomb of Rachel, and Dinah, his daughter. They were (all) buried there.

17 He mourned for Joseph one year, and did not cease, for he said, "Let me go down to my grave mourning for my son."

18 For this reason it is ordained for the children of Israel that they should remember and mourn on the tenth of the seventh month. On that day the news came which made Jacob weep for Joseph. On this day they should make atonement for their sins for themselves with a young goat on the tenth of the seventh month, once a year, for they had grieved the sorrow of their father regarding Joseph his son.

19 This day, once a year, has been ordained that they should grieve on it for their sins, and for all their transgressions and for all their errors, so that they might cleanse themselves.

20 After Joseph perished, the sons of Jacob took to themselves wives. The name of Reuben's wife is Ada; and the name of Simeon's wife is Adlba'a, a Canaanite. The name of Levi's wife is Melka, of the daughters of Aram, of the offspring of the sons of Terah. The name of Judah's wife is Betasu'el, a Canaanite. The name of Issachar's wife is Hezaqa, and the name of Zabulon's wife is Ni'iman. The name of Dan's wife is Egla. The name of Naphtali's wife is Rasu'u, of Mesopotamia. The name of Gad's wife is Maka. The name of Asher's wife is Ijona. The name of Joseph's wife is Asenath, the Egyptian. The name of Benjamin's wife is Ijasaka.

21 And Simeon repented, and took a second wife from Mesopotamia as his brothers had done.

[Chapter 35]

1 In the first year of the first week of the forty-fifth jubilee Rebecca called Jacob, her son, and commanded him regarding his father and regarding his brother, that he should honor them all the days of his life.

2 Jacob said, "I will do everything you have commanded. I will honor them. This will be honor and greatness to me, and righteousness before the Lord.

3 Mother, you know from the time I was born until this day, all my deeds and all that is in my heart. I always think good concerning all.

4 Why should I not do this thing which you have commanded me, that I should honor my father and my brother?

5 Tell me, mother, what perversity have you seen in me and I shall turn away from it, and mercy will be on me."

6 She said to him, "My son, in all my days I have not seen any perverseness in you, but only upright deeds. Yet, I will tell you the truth, my son, I shall die this year. I shall not survive this year in my life. I have seen the day of my death in a dream. I should not live beyond a hundred and fifty-five years. I have completed all the days that I am to live my life."

7 Jacob laughed at the words of his mother because his mother had said she should die. She was sitting across from him in possession of her strength, and she was still strong. She came and went (as she wished). She could see well, and her teeth were strong. No sickness had touched her all the days of her life.

8 Jacob said to her, "If my days of life are close to yours and my strength remains with me as your strength has, I would be blessed, mother. You will not die. You are simply joking with me regarding your death."

9 She went in to Isaac and said to him, " I make one request of you. Make Esau swear that he will not injure Jacob, nor pursue him with intent to harm him. You know Esau's thoughts have been perverse from his youth, and there is no goodness in him. He desires to kill him after you die.

10 You know all that he has done since the day Jacob, his brother, went to Haran until this day. He has forsaken us with his whole heart, and has done evil to us. He has stolen your flocks and carried off all your possessions while you watched.

11 When we asked him and begged him for what was our own, he did as a man (stranger) who was taking pity on us (giving a token like one giving alms to a beggar).

12 He is bitter against you because you blessed Jacob, your perfect and upright son. There is no evil but only goodness in Jacob. Since he came from Haran to this day he has not robbed us of anything. He always brings us everything in its season. He rejoices and blesses us with all his heart when we take his hands. He has not parted from us since he came from Haran until this day, and he remains with us continually at home honoring us."

13 Isaac said to her, "I also know and see the deeds of Jacob who is with us, how he honors us with all his heart. Before, I loved Esau more than Jacob because he was the first-born, but now I love Jacob more than Esau, for Esau has done many evil deeds, and there is no righteousness in him. All his ways are unrighteousness and violence.

14 My heart is troubled because of all his deeds. Neither he nor his offspring will be exempt because they are

those who will be destroyed from the earth and who will be rooted out from under heaven. He and his children have forsaken the God of Abraham and gone after his wives (wives' gods) and after their uncleanness and after their error.

15 You told me to make him swear that he will not kill Jacob his brother, but even if he swears, he will not abide by his oath. He will not do good but evil only.

16 If he desires to kill Jacob, his brother, then into Jacob's hands he will be given. He will not escape from Jacob's hands.

17 Do not be afraid for Jacob, for the guardian of Jacob is great, powerful, honored, and praised more than the guardian of Esau."

18 Rebecca called for Esau and he came to her, and she said to him, "I have a request of you, my son. Promise to do it, my son."

19 He said, "I will do everything that you say to me, and I will not refuse your request."

20 She said to him, "I ask you that the day I die, you will take me in and bury me near Sarah, your father's mother, and that you and Jacob will love each other and that neither will desire evil against the other, but (have) mutual love only. Do this so you will prosper, my son, and be honored in the all of the land, and no enemy will rejoice over you. You will be a blessing and a mercy in the eyes of all those that love you."

21 He said, "I will do all that you have told me. I shall bury you on the day you die near Sarah, my father's mother, as you have desired that her bones may be near your bones.

22 Jacob, my brother, I shall love above all flesh. I have only one brother in all the earth but him. It is only what is expected of me. It is no great thing if I love him, for he is my brother, and we were sown together in your body, and together came we out from your womb. If I do not love my brother, whom shall I love?

23 I beg you to exhort Jacob concerning me and concerning my sons, for I know that he will assuredly be king over me and my sons, for on the day my father blessed him he made him the higher and me the lower.

24 I swear to you that I shall love him, and not desire evil against him all the days of my life but good only."

25 And he swore to her regarding all this matter. While Esau was there, she called Jacob and gave him her orders according to the words that she had spoken to Esau.

26 He said, "I shall do your pleasure, believe me that no evil will proceed from me or from my sons against Esau. I shall be first in nothing except in love only."

27 She and her sons ate and drank that night, and she died, three jubilees and one week and one year old on that night. Her two sons, Esau and Jacob, buried her in the double cave near Sarah, their father's mother.

[Chapter 36]

1 In the sixth year of this week Isaac called his two sons Esau and Jacob, and they came to him, and he said to them, "My sons, I am going the way of my fathers, to the eternal house where my fathers are.

2 Bury me near Abraham my father, in the double cave in the field of Ephron the Hittite, where Abraham purchased a sepulcher to bury in. Bury me in the sepulcher I dug for myself.

3 I command you, my sons, to practice righteousness and uprightness on the earth, so that the Lord may do to you what he said he would do to Abraham and to his offspring.

4 Love one another. Love your brothers as a man who loves his own soul. Let each seek how he may benefit his brother, and act together on the earth. Let them love each other as their own souls.

5 I command and warn you to reject idols. Hate them, and do not love them. They are fully deceptive to those that worship them and for those that bow down to them.

6 Remember the Lord God of Abraham, your father, and how I worshipped Him and served Him in righteousness and in joy, that God might multiply you and increase your offspring as the multitude of stars in heaven, and establish you on the earth as the plant of righteousness, which will not be rooted out to all the generations forever.

7 And now I shall make you swear a great oath, for there is no oath which is greater than that which is by the name glorious, honored, great, splendid, wonderful and mighty, which created the heavens and the earth and all things together, that you will fear Him and worship Him.

8 Each will love his brother with affection and righteousness. Neither will desire to do evil against his brother from now on forever all the days of your life so that you may prosper in all your deeds and not be destroyed.

9 If either of you plans evil against his brother, know that he that plans evil shall fall into his brother's hand, and shall be rooted out of the land of the living, and his offspring shall be destroyed from under heaven.

10 But on that day there will be turbulence, curses, wrath, anger, and will He burn his land and his city and all that is his with a devouring fire like the fire He sent to burn Sodom and he shall be blotted out of the book of the discipline of the children of men, and he will not be recorded in the book of life. He shall be added in the book of destruction. He shall depart into eternal curses. Their condemnation may be always renewed in hate and in curses and in wrath and in torment and in anger and in plagues and in disease forever.

11 My sons, this, I say and testify to you, will be the result according to the judgment which shall come on the man who wishes to injure his brother."

12 Then he divided all his possessions between the two on that day, and he gave the larger portion to him that was the first-born, and the tower and all that was around it, and all that Abraham possessed at the Well of the Oath.

13 He said, "This larger portion I will give to the first-born."

14 Esau said, "I have sold and relinquished my birthright to Jacob. Let it be given to him. I have nothing to say regarding it, for it is his."

15 Isaac said, "May a blessing rest on you, my sons, and on your offspring this day. You have given me rest, and my heart is not pained concerning the birthright, or that you should work wickedness because of it.

16 May the Most High God bless the man and his offspring forever that does righteousness."

17 He stopped commanding them and blessing them, and they ate and drank together in front of him, and he rejoiced because there was one mind between them, and they went out from him and rested that day and slept.

18 Isaac slept on his bed that day rejoicing. He slept the eternal sleep, and died one hundred and eighty years old. He lived twenty-five weeks and five years; and his two sons, Esau and Jacob, buried him.

19 After that Esau went to the land of Edom, to the mountains of Seir, and lived there.

20 Jacob lived in the mountains of Hebron, in the high place of the land in which his father Abraham had journeyed. He worshipped the Lord with all his heart. He had divided the days of his generations according to the commands he had seen.

21 Leah, his wife, died in the fourth year of the second week of the forty-fifth jubilee, and he buried her in the double cave near Rebecca his mother to the left of the grave of Sarah, his father's mother. All her sons and his sons came to mourn over Leah, his wife, with him and to comfort him regarding her. He was lamenting her for he loved her greatly after Rachel, her sister, died. She was perfect and upright in all her ways and she honored Jacob. All the days that she lived with him he did not hear from her mouth a harsh word, for she was gentle, peaceable, upright and honorable.

22 And he remembered all the deeds she had done during her life and he lamented her greatly. He loved her with all his heart and with all his soul.

[Chapter 37]

1 On the day that Isaac, the father of Jacob and Esau died, the sons of Esau heard that Isaac had given the elder's portion to his younger son, Jacob, and they were very angry.

2 They argued with their father, saying, "Why has your father given Jacob the portion of the elder and passed you over even though you are the elder and Jacob the younger?"

3 He said to them, "Because I sold my birthright to Jacob for a small portion of lentils (lentil soup), and on the day my father sent me to hunt, catch, and bring him something that he should eat and bless me, Jacob came with deceit and brought my father food and drink. My father blessed him and put me under his hand.

4 Now our father has caused Jacob and me to swear that we shall not devise evil plans against his brother (each other), and that we shall continue in love and in peace each with his brother and not make our ways corrupt."

5 They said to him, "We shall not listen to you to make peace with him. We are stronger than him and we are more powerful than he is. We shall depose him and kill him, and destroy him and his sons. If you will not go with us, we shall hurt you also.

6 Listen! Let us send to Aram, Philistia, Moab, and Ammon. Let us take chosen men who are trained in battle, and let us go against him and do battle with him. Let us exterminate him from the earth before he grows strong."

7 Their father said to them, "Do not go and do not make war with him or you shall fall before him."

8 They said to him, "This is how you have acted from your youth until this day. You have continued to put your neck under his yoke. We shall not listen to these words."

9 Then they sent to Aram, and to Aduram to the friend of their father, and they also hired one thousand chosen men of war.

10 And there came to them from Moab and from the children of Ammon, those who were hired, one thousand chosen men, and from Philistia, one thousand chosen warriors, and from Edom and from the Horites one thousand chosen warriors, and from the Kittim mighty warriors.

11 They said to their father, "Go out with them and lead them or else we shall kill you."

12 And he was filled with boiling anger on seeing that his sons were forcing him to go before them to lead them against Jacob, his brother.

13 But afterward he remembered all the evil that lay hidden in his heart against Jacob his brother, and he did not remember the oath he had sworn to his father and to his mother that he would plan no evil against Jacob, his brother, all his days.

14 Because Jacob was in mourning for his wife Leah, he did not know they were coming to battle against him until they approached the tower with four thousand soldiers and chosen warriors. The men of Hebron sent to him saying, "Look your brother has come against you to fight. He has with him four thousand men carrying swords, shields, and weapons." They told him this because they loved Jacob more than Esau.

15 So they told him, for Jacob was a more gracious and merciful man than Esau.

16 But Jacob would not believe until they came very near to the tower.

17 He closed the gates of the tower; and he stood on the battlements and spoke to his brother Esau and said, "Noble is the comfort you have come to give me concerning the death of my wife. Is this the oath that you swore to your father and again to your mother before they died? You have broken the oath, and on the moment that you swore to your father you were condemned."

18 Then Esau answered and said to him, "Neither the children of men nor the beasts of the earth have sworn an oath of righteousness and kept it forever. Every day they lay evil plans one against another regarding how they might kill their adversary or foe.

19 You will hate my children and me forever, so there is no observing the tie of brotherhood with you.

20 Hear these words that I declare to you. If the boar can change its skin and make its bristles as soft as wool, or if it can cause horns to sprout out on its head like the horns of a stag or of a sheep, then will I observe the tie of brotherhood with you. Like breasts separate themselves from their mother (and fight), you and I have never been brothers.

21 If the wolves make peace with the lambs and not devour or do them violence, and if their hearts are towards them for good, then there shall be peace in my heart towards you. If the lion becomes the friend of the ox and makes peace with him and if he is bound under one yoke with him and plows with him, then will I make peace with you.

22 When the raven becomes white as the raza (a white bird?), then know that I have loved you and shall make peace with you. You will be rooted out, and your sons shall be rooted out, and there shall be no peace for you."

23 Jacob saw that Esau had decided in his heart to do evil toward him, and that he desired with all his soul to kill him. Jacob saw that Esau had come pouncing like the wild boar which charges the spear that is set to pierce and kill it, and yet does not even slow down. Then he spoke to his own people and to his servants and told them that Esau and his men were going to attack him and all his companions.

[Chapter 38]

1 After that Judah spoke to Jacob, his father, and said to him, "Bend your bow, father, and send forth your arrows and bring down the adversary and kill the enemy. You have the power to do it. We will not kill your brother because he is your kin and he is like you, so we will honor his life."

2 Then Jacob bent his bow and sent forth the arrow and struck Esau, his brother, on the right side of his chest and killed him.

3 And again he sent forth an arrow and struck Adoran the Aramaean, on the left side of his chest, and it drove him backward and killed him. Then the sons of Jacob and their servants went out, dividing themselves into companies on the four sides of the tower.

4 Judah went out in front. Naphtali and Gad along with fifty servants went to the south side of the tower, and they killed all they found before them. Not one individual escaped.

5 Levi, Dan, and Asher went out on the east side of the tower along with fifty men, and they killed the warriors of Moab and Ammon.

6 Reuben, Issachar, and Zebulon went out on the north side of the tower along with fifty men and they killed the warriors of the Philistines.

7 Reuben's son, Simeon, Benjamin, and Enoch went out on the west side of the tower along with fifty men and they killed four hundred men, stout warriors of Edom and of the Horites. Six hundred fled, and four of the sons of Esau fled with them, and left their father lying killed, as he had fallen on the hill that is in Aduram.

8 And the sons of Jacob pursued them to the mountains of Seir. And Jacob buried his brother on the hill that is in Aduram, and he returned to his house.

9 The sons of Jacob crushed the sons of Esau in the mountains of Seir, and made them bow their necks so that they became servants of the sons of Jacob.

10 They sent a message to their father to inquire whether they should make peace with them or kill them.

11 Jacob sent word to his sons that they should make peace. They made peace with them but also placed the yoke of servitude on them, so that they paid tribute to Jacob and to his sons always.

12 And they continued to pay tribute to Jacob until the day that he went down to Egypt.

13 The sons of Edom have not escaped the yoke of servitude imposed by the twelve sons of Jacob until this day.

14 These are the kings that reigned in Edom before there was any king over the children of Israel (until this day) in the land of Edom.

15 And Balaq, the son of Beor, reigned in Edom, and the name of his city was Danaba. Balaq died, and Jobab, the son of Zara of Boser, ruled in his place.

16 Jobab died, and Asam, of the land of Teman, ruled in his place.

17 Asam died, and Adath, the son of Barad, who killed Midian in the field of Moab, ruled in his place, and the name of his city was Avith.

18 Adath died, and Salman, from Amaseqa, ruled in his place.

19 Salman died, and Saul of Ra'aboth by the river, ruled in his place. Saul died, and Ba'elunan, the son of Achbor, ruled in his place.

20 Ba'elunan, the son of Achbor died, and Adath ruled in his place, and the name of his wife was Maitabith, the daughter of Matarat, the daughter of Metabedza'ab. These are the kings who reigned in the land of Edom.

[Chapter 39]

1 Jacob lived in the land that his father journeyed in, which is the land of Canaan.

2 These are the generations of Jacob. Joseph was seventeen years old when they took him down into the land of Egypt, and Potiphar, a eunuch of Pharaoh, the chief cook, bought him.

3 He made Joseph the manager over Potiphar's entire house and the blessing of the Lord came on the house of the Egyptian because of Joseph. And the Lord caused him to prosper in all that he did.

4 The Egyptian turned everything over to the hands of Joseph because he saw that the Lord was with him, and that the Lord caused him to prosper him in all that he did.

5 Joseph's appearance was beautiful, and his master's wife watched Joseph, and she loved him and wanted him to have sex with her.

6 But he did not surrender his soul because he remembered the Lord and the words which Jacob, his father, used to read to him from the writings of Abraham, that no man should commit fornication with a woman who has a husband. For him the punishment of death has been ordained in the heavens before the Most High God, and the sin will be recorded against him in the eternal books, which are always in the presence of the Lord.

7 Joseph remembered these words and refused to have sex with her.

8 And she begged him for a year, but he refused and would not listen.

9 But while he was in the house she embraced him and held him tightly in order to force him to sleep with her. She closed the doors of the house and held on to him, but he left his garment in her hands and broke through the door and ran out from her presence.

10 The woman saw that he would not sleep with her, and she slandered him in the presence of his master, saying "Your Hebrew servant, whom you love, sought to force me to have sex with him. When I shouted for help he fled and left his garment in my hands. I tried to stop him but he broke through the door."

11 When the Egyptian saw Joseph's garment and the broken door, and heard the words of his wife, he threw Joseph into prison and put him in the place where the prisoners of the king were kept.

12 He was there in the prison, and the Lord gave Joseph favor in the sight of the chief of the prison guards and caused him to have compassion for Joseph, because he saw that the Lord was with him, and that the Lord made all that he did to prosper.

13 He turned over all things into his hands, and the chief of the prison guards knew of nothing that was going on

in the prison, because Joseph did everything for him, and the Lord perfected it. He remained there two years.

14 In those days Pharaoh, king of Egypt, was very angry at his two eunuchs, the chief butler, and the chief baker. He put them in the prison facility of the house of the chief cook, where Joseph was kept.

15 The chief of the prison guards appointed Joseph to serve them, and he served them.

16 They both dreamed a dream, the chief butler and the chief baker, and they told it to Joseph.

17 As he interpreted to them so it happened to them, and Pharaoh restored the chief butler to his office and he killed the chief baker as Joseph had interpreted to them.

18 But the chief butler forgot Joseph was in the prison, although he had informed him of what would happen to him. He did not remember to inform Pharaoh of how Joseph had told him (about his dream), because he forgot.

[Chapter 40]

1 In those days Pharaoh dreamed two dreams in one night concerning a famine that was to be in all the land, and he awoke from his sleep and called all the magicians and interpreters of dreams that were in Egypt. He told them his two dreams but they were not able to tell him what they meant.

2 Then the chief butler remembered Joseph and told the king of him, and he brought him out from the prison, and the king told his two dreams to him.

3 He said before Pharaoh that his two dreams were one, and he said to him, "Seven years shall come in which there shall be plenty in all the land of Egypt, but after that, seven years of famine. Such a famine as has not been in all the land.

4 Now, let Pharaoh appoint administrators in all the land of Egypt, and let them store up food in every city throughout all the years of plenty, and there will be food for the seven years of famine, and those of the land will not perish through the famine, even though it will be very severe."

5 The Lord gave Joseph favor and mercy in the eyes of Pharaoh. Pharaoh said to his servants, "We shall not find such a wise and prudent man like this man, because the spirit of the Lord is with him."

6 And he appointed Joseph the second in command in his entire kingdom and gave him authority over all Egypt, and placed him on the second chariot of Pharaoh to ride.

7 And he clothed him with fine linen clothes, and he put a gold chain around his neck, and a crier proclaimed before him "El" "El wa Abirer," and he placed a ring on his hand and made him ruler over all his house, and lifted him up before the people, and said to him, "Only on the throne shall I be greater than you."

8 Joseph ruled over all the land of Egypt, and all the governors of Pharaoh, and all his servants, and all those who did the king's business loved him because he walked in uprightness, because he was without pride and arrogance. He did not judge people by their position, and did not accept gifts, but he judged all the people of the land in uprightness.

9 The land of Egypt was at peace before Pharaoh because of Joseph, because the Lord was with him, and the Lord gave him favor and mercy for all his generations before all those who knew him and those who heard of him, and Pharaoh's kingdom was run efficiently, and there was no Satan (adversary) and no evil person in it.

10 And the king called Joseph's name Sephantiphans, and gave Joseph the daughter of Potiphar, the daughter of the priest of Heliopolis, the chief cook to marry.

11 On the day that Joseph stood before Pharaoh he was thirty years old.

12 In that year Isaac died. Things transpired as Joseph had said in the interpretation of Pharaoh's dream and there were seven years of plenty over all the land of Egypt, and the land of Egypt abundantly produced, one measure producing eighteen hundred measures.

13 Joseph gathered food into every city until they were full of grain and they could no longer count or measure it because of its multitude.

[Chapter 41]

1 In the forty-fifth jubilee, in the second week, and in the second year, Judah took his first-born Er, a wife from the daughters of Aram, named Tamar.

2 But he hated her, and did not have sex with her, because her mother was of the daughters of Canaan, and he wished to take him a wife of the lineage of his mother, but Judah, his father, would not permit him to do that.

3 Er, the first-born of Judah, was wicked, and the Lord killed him.

4 And Judah said to Onan, his brother, "Go in to your brother's wife and perform the duty of a husband's brother

to her, and raise up offspring to your brother."

5 Onan knew that the offspring would not be his, but his brother's only, and he went into the house of his brother's wife, and spilt his seed (ejaculates) on the ground, and he was wicked in the eyes of the Lord, and He killed him.

6 Judah said to Tamar, his daughter-in-law, "Remain in your father's house as a widow until Shelah, my son has grown up, and I shall give you to him to wife."

7 He grew up, but Bedsu'el, the wife of Judah, did not permit her son Shelah to marry. Bedsu'el, Judah's wife, died in the fifth year of this week.

8 In the sixth year Judah went up to shear his sheep at Timnah.

9 And they told Tamar, "Look, your father-in-law is going up to Timnah to shear his sheep." And she took off her widow's clothes, and put on a veil, and adorned herself, and sat in the gate connecting the road to Timnah.

10 As Judah was going along he saw her, and thought she was a prostitute, and he said to her, "Let me come in to you," and she said to him, "Come in," and he went in.

11 She said to him, "Give me my pay," and he said to her, "I have nothing with me except my ring that is on my finger, my necklace, and my staff which is in my hand."

12 She said to him, "Give them to me until you send me my pay." And he said to her, "I will send to you a kid of the goats", and he gave her his ring, necklace, and staff, and she conceived by him.

13 Judah went to his sheep, and she went to her father's house.

14 Judah sent a kid of the goats by the hand of his shepherd, an Adullamite, but he could not find her, so he asked the people of the place, saying, "Where is the prostitute who was here?"

15 They said to him, "There is no prostitute here with us." And he returned and informed Judah that he had not found her, "I asked the people of the place, and they said to me, "There is no prostitute here." "

16 He said, "If you see her give the kids to her or we become a cause of ridicule." And when she had completed three months, it was revealed that she was with child, and they told Judah, saying, "Look Tamar, your daughter-in-law, is with child by whoredom."

17 And Judah went to the house of her father, and said to her father and her brothers, "Bring her out, and let them burn her, for she has committed uncleanness in Israel."

18 It happened when they brought her out to burn her that she sent to her father-in-law the ring and the necklace, and the staff, saying, "Tell us whose are these, because by him am I with child."

19 Judah acknowledged, and said, "Tamar is more righteous than I am.

20 Do not let them burn her." For that reason she was not given to Shelah, and he did not again approach her and after that she gave birth to two sons, Perez and Zerah, in the seventh year of this second week.

21 At this time the seven years of fruitfulness were completed, of which Joseph spoke to Pharaoh.

22 Judah acknowledged the evil deed that he had done because he had sex with his daughter-in-law, and he hated himself for it.

23 He acknowledged that he had transgressed and gone astray, because he had uncovered the skirt of his son, and he began to lament and to supplicate before the Lord because of his transgression.

24 We told him in a dream that it was forgiven him because he supplicated earnestly, and lamented, and did not commit the act again.

25 And he received forgiveness because he turned from his sin and from his ignorance, because he transgressed greatly before our God. Every one that acts like this, every one who has sex with his mother-in-law, let them burn him alive with fire. Because there is uncleanness and pollution on them, let them burn them alive.

26 Command the children of Israel that there should be no uncleanness among them, because every one who has sex with his daughter-in-law or with his mother-in-law has committed

uncleanness. Let them burn the man who has had sex with her with fire, and likewise burn the woman, so that God will turn away wrath and punishment from Israel.

27 We told Judah that his two sons had not had sex with her, and for this reason his offspring was established for a second generation, and would not be rooted out.

28 For in single-mindedness he had gone and sought for punishment, namely, according to the judgment of Abraham, which he had commanded his sons. Judah had sought to burn her alive.

[Chapter 42]

1 In the first year of the third week of the forty-fifth jubilee the famine began to come into the land, and the rain refused to be given to the earth. None whatsoever fell.

2 The earth became barren, but in the land of Egypt there was food, because Joseph had gathered the seed of the land in the seven years of plenty and had preserved it.

3 The Egyptians came to Joseph that he might give them food, and he opened the storehouses where the grain of the first year was stored, and he sold it to the people of the land for gold.

4 Jacob heard there was food in Egypt, and he sent his ten sons that they should procure food for him in Egypt, and they arrived among those that went there, but Benjamin he did not send.

5 Joseph recognized them, but they did not recognize him. He spoke to them and questioned them, and he said to them, "Are you not spies and have you not come to explore ways to enter this land?"

6 And he put them in custody.

7 After that, he set them free again, and detained Simeon alone and sent his nine brothers away.

8 He filled their sacks with corn, and he put their gold back in their sacks, and they did not know it. Joseph then commanded them to bring their younger brother, because they had told him their father was living and also their younger brother.

9 They went up from the land of Egypt and they came to the land of Canaan. There they told their father all that had happened to them, and how the ruler of the country had spoken rudely to them, and had seized Simeon until they should bring Benjamin.

10 Jacob said, "You have taken my children from me! Joseph is gone and Simeon also is gone, and now you will take Benjamin away. I am the victim of your wickedness."

11 He said, "My son will not go down with you because fate may have it that he would fall sick. Their mother gave birth to two sons, and one has died, and this one also you will take from me. If, by fate, he took a fever on the road, you would turn my old age to sorrow and death."

12 He saw that every man's money had been returned to him in his sack, and for this reason he feared to send him.

13 The famine increased and became grievous in the land of Canaan, and in all lands except in the land of Egypt. Egypt had food because many of the children of the Egyptians had stored up their seed for food from the time when they saw Joseph gathering seed together and putting it in storehouses and preserving it for the years of famine.

14 The people of Egypt fed themselves on it during the first year of their famine but when Israel saw that the famine was very serious in the land, and that there was no deliverance, he said to his sons, "Go again, and procure food for us so that we will not die."

15 They said, "We shall not go unless our youngest brother go with us!"

16 Israel saw that if he did not send Benjamin with them, they would all perish because of the famine.

17 Reuben said, "Give him to me, and if I do not bring him back to you, kill my two sons in payment for his soul." Israel said to Reuben, "He shall not go with you."

18 Judah came near and said, "Send him with me, and if I do not bring him back to you, let me bear your blame all the days of my life."

19 He sent him with them in the second year of this week on the first day of the month.

20 They all came to the land of Egypt, and they had presents in their hands of sweet spice, almonds, turpentine nuts, and pure honey.

21 And they went and stood before Joseph, and he saw Benjamin his brother, and he knew him, and said to them, "Is this your youngest brother?" They said to him, "It is he."

22 He said, "The Lord be gracious to you, my son!" And he sent Benjamin into his house and he brought out Simeon to them. Joseph made a feast for them, and they presented to him the gifts that they had brought in their hands.

23 They ate before Joseph and he gave them all a portion of food, but the portion of food given to Benjamin was seven times larger than any of theirs.

24 And they ate and drank and got up and remained with their donkeys.

25 Joseph devised a plan whereby he might learn their thoughts as to whether they desired peace or not. He said to the steward who was over his house, "Fill all their sacks with food. Place their money back in their vessels. Put my cup, the silver cup out of which I drink, in the sack of the youngest and send them away."

[Chapter 43]

1 He did as Joseph had told him, and filled all their sacks with food for them and put their money back into their sacks, and put the cup in Benjamin's sack.

2 Early in the morning they departed, and it happened that when they had gone from that place, Joseph said to the steward of his house, "Pursue them, run and seize them, and say, 'You have repaid my kindness with evil. You have stolen from me the silver cup out of which my lord drinks.'

3 Bring me back their youngest brother. Go! Get him quickly before I go to my seat of judgment (judge you guilt of disobeying an order). "

4 He ran after them and said the words as he was told. They said to him, "God forbid that your servants should do this thing, and steal any utensil or money from the house of your lord, like the things we found in our sacks the first time we, your servants, came back from the land of Canaan.

5 We have not stolen any utensil. How could we? Look here in our sacks and search, and wherever you find the cup in the sack of any man among us, let him be killed, and we and our donkeys will serve your lord."

6 He said to them, "Not so. If I find it, the man whose sack I find it in I shall take as a servant, and the rest of you shall return in peace to your house."

7 He was searching in their vessels, beginning with the eldest and ending with the youngest, when it was found in Benjamin's sack.

8 They ripped their garments in frustration, and placed their belongings back on their donkeys, and returned to the city and came to the house of Joseph. They all bowed themselves with their faces to the ground in front of him.

9 Joseph said to them, "You have done evil." They said, "What shall we say and how shall we defend ourselves? Our lord has discovered the transgression of his servants; and now we and our donkeys are the servants of our lord."

10 Joseph said to them, "I too fear the Lord. As for you, go to your homes and let your brother be my servant, because you have done evil. I delight in this cup as no one else delights in his cup and yet you have stolen it from me."

11 Judah said, "O my lord, I pray you to let your servant speak a word in my lord's ear. Your servant's mother had two sons for our father. One went away and was lost, and has not been found since. This one alone is left of his mother, and your servant our father loves him. He would die if the lad were lost to him.

12 When we go to your servant our father, and the lad is not with us, it will happen that he will die. We will have brought so much sorrow on our father it will bring his death.

13 Now rather let me, your servant, stay here as a bondsman to my lord instead of the boy. Let the lad go with his brothers, because I will stand in for him at the hand of your servant our father. If I do not bring him back, your servant will bear the blame of our father forever."

14 Joseph saw that they were all in accord in doing good to one another. Then, he could not refrain himself, and he told them that he was Joseph.

15 And he conversed with them in the Hebrew tongue and hugged their necks and wept.

16 At first they did not recognize him and then they began to weep. He said to them, "Do not weep for me, but hurry and bring my father to me. See, it is my mouth that speaks and the eyes of my brother Benjamin see me.

17 Pay attention. This is the second year of the famine, and there are still five years to come without harvest or fruit of trees or plowing.

18 You and your households come down quickly, so that you won't die because of the famine. Do not be grieved for your possessions, because the Lord sent me before you to set things in order that many people might live.

19 Tell my father that I am still alive. You see that the Lord has made me as a father to Pharaoh, and ruler over his house and over all the land of Egypt.

20 Tell my father of all my glory, and all the riches and glory that the Lord has given me."

21 By the command of Pharaoh's mouth, he gave them chariots and provisions for the way, and he gave them all multi-colored raiment and silver.

22 He sent corn, raiment, silver, and ten donkeys that carried all of this to his father, and he sent them away.

23 They went up and told their father that Joseph was alive, and was measuring out corn to all the nations of the earth, and that he was ruler over all the land of Egypt.

24 But their father did not believe it, because he was not in his right mind. But when he saw the wagons, which

Joseph had sent, the life of his spirit revived, and he said, "It is enough for me if Joseph lives. I will go down and see him before I die."

[Chapter 44]

1 Israel took his journey from Haran's house on the new moon of the third month, and he stopped at the Well of the Oath on the way and he offered a sacrifice to the God of his father Isaac on the seventh of this month.
2 Jacob remembered the dream that he had at Bethel, and he feared to go down into Egypt.
3 He was thinking of sending word to Joseph to come to him because he did not want to go down. He remained there seven days, hoping fate would permit him to see a vision as to whether he should remain or go down.
4 He celebrated the harvest festival of the first-fruits with old grain, because in all the land of Canaan there was not a handful of seed in the ground because the famine was affecting all the beasts, and cattle, and birds, and all men.
5 On the sixteenth the Lord appeared to him, and said to him, "Jacob, Jacob," and he said, "Here I am."
6 And He said to him, "I am the God of your fathers, the God of Abraham and Isaac. Do not be afraid to go down into Egypt, because I will be there to make you a great nation. I will go down with you, and I will bring you up again. You will be buried in this land and Joseph will put his hands on your eyes (to close them in death). Do not be afraid. Go down into Egypt."
7 And his sons got up and placed their father and their possessions on wagons.
8 Israel got up from the Well of the Oath on the sixteenth of this third month, and he went to the land of Egypt.
9 Israel sent Judah before him to his son Joseph to examine the Land of Goshen, because Joseph had told his brothers that they should come and live there so they could be near him.
10 This was the best land in Egypt. It was near to him and suitable for all of the cattle they had.
11 These are the names of the sons of Jacob who went into Egypt with Jacob their father; Reuben, the First-born of Israel and his sons Enoch, and Pallu, and Hezron and Carmi, making five.
12 Simeon and his sons Jemuel, and Jamin, and Ohad, and Jachin, and Zohar, and Shaul, the son of the Zephathite woman, making seven.
13 Levi and his sons Gershon, and Kohath, and Merari, making four.
14 Judah and his sons Shela, and Perez, and Zerah, making four.
15 Issachar and his sons Tola, and Phua, and Jasub, and Shimron, making five.
16 Zebulon and his sons Sered, and Elon, and Jahleel, making four.
17 These are the sons of Jacob and their sons whom Leah bore to Jacob in Mesopotamia, six, and their one sister, Dinah and all the souls of the sons of Leah, and their sons, who went with Jacob their father into Egypt. Twenty-nine souls, and Jacob, making thirty, were the number of people that went into Egypt.
18 And the sons of Zilpah, Leah's handmaid, the wife of Jacob, who bore to Jacob Gad and Ashur and their sons who went with him into Egypt.
19 The sons of Gad are Ziphion, and Haggi, and Shuni, and Ezbon, and Eri, and Areli, and Arodi, which make eight souls in total. The sons of Asher are Imnah, and Ishvah, and Ishvi, and Beriah, and Serah, and their one sister, which makes six in total.
20 All the souls were fourteen, and all those of Leah were forty-four.
21 The sons of Rachel, the wife of Jacob are Joseph and Benjamin.
22 There were born to Joseph in Egypt before his father came into Egypt, those whom Asenath, daughter of Potiphar, priest of Heliopolis gave birth to him, Manasseh, and Ephraim. The wife and children of Joseph totaled three.
23 The sons of Benjamin, Bela and Becher and Ashbel, Gera, and Naaman, and Ehi, and Rosh, and Muppim, and Huppim, and Ard with Benjamin totaled eleven.
24 And all the souls of Rachel were fourteen.
25 And the sons of Bilhah, the handmaid of Rachel, the wife of Jacob, whom she gave birth to Jacob, were Dan and Naphtali. These are the names of their sons who went with them into Egypt.
26 The sons of Dan were Hushim, and Samon, and Asudi. and "Ijaka, and Salomon, all totaling six.
27 All but one died the year in which they entered into Egypt, and there was left to Dan only Hushim.
28 These are the names of the sons of Naphtali: Jahziel, and Guni and Jezer, and Shallum, and 'Iv.
29 And 'Iv, who was born after the years of famine, died in Egypt.
30 All the souls (offspring) of Rachel were twenty-six.

31 All the souls (offspring) of Jacob, which went into Egypt, were seventy souls.

32 These are his children and his children's children, in all seventy, but five died in Egypt in the time of Joseph's rule and they had no children.

33 In the land of Canaan two sons of Judah died, Er and Onan, and they had no children, and the children of Israel buried those who died, and they were counted among the seventy Gentile nations.

[Chapter 45]

1 On the new moon of the fourth month, in the second year of the third week of the forty-fifth jubilee, Israel went into the country of Egypt, to the land of Goshen.

2 Joseph went to meet his father, Jacob, in the land of Goshen, and he hugged his father's neck and wept.

3 Israel said to Joseph, "Now that I have seen you let me die and may the Lord God of Israel, the God of Abraham, and the God of Isaac, who has not withheld His mercy and His grace from His servant Jacob, be blessed.

4 It is enough for me to have seen your face while I am yet alive. Yes, this is the true vision which I saw at Bethel.

5 Blessed be the Lord my God forever and ever, and blessed be His name."

6 Joseph and his brothers ate bread in the presence of their father and drank wine, and Jacob rejoiced with very great joy because he saw Joseph eating with his brothers and drinking in the presence of him, and he blessed the Creator of all things who had preserved him, and had preserved for him his twelve sons.

7 Joseph had given his father and his brothers as a gift the right of dwelling in the land of Goshen and in Rameses and the entire region around it, which he ruled over in the presence of Pharaoh.

8 Israel and his sons dwelt in the land of Goshen, the best part of the land of Egypt, and Israel was one hundred and thirty years old when he came into Egypt. Joseph nourished his father and his brothers and also their possessions (servants) with bread as much as they needed for the seven years of the famine.

9 The land of Egypt became available for purchase because of the famine, and Joseph acquired all the land of Egypt for Pharaoh in return for food, and he got possession of the people and their cattle and everything for Pharaoh.

10 The years of the famine were completed, and Joseph gave the people in the land seed and food that they might sow the land in the eighth year, because the river had overflowed all the land of Egypt.

11 For in the seven years of the famine it had not overflowed and had irrigated only a few places on the banks of the river, but now it overflowed and the Egyptians sowed the land, and it produced much corn that year.

12 This was the first year of the fourth week of the forty-fifth jubilee. Joseph took one-fifth of the corn of the harvest for the king and left four parts for them for food and for seed, and Joseph made it a law for Egypt until this day.

13 Israel lived in the land of Egypt seventeen years, and all the days which he lived were three jubilees, one hundred and forty-seven years, and he died in the fourth year of the fifth week of the forty-fifth jubilee.

14 Israel blessed his sons before he died and told them everything that they would go through in the land of Egypt. He revealed to them what they would live through in the last days, and he blessed them and gave Joseph two portions of the land.

15 He slept with his fathers, and he was buried in the double cave in the land of Canaan, near Abraham his father, in the grave which he dug for himself in the land of Hebron.

16 And he gave all his books and the books of his fathers to Levi, his son so that he might preserve them and replicate them for his children until this day.

[Chapter 46]

1 It happened that after the death of Jacob the children of Israel continued to multiply in the land of Egypt, and they became a great nation, and they were in one accord of heart, so that brother loved brother and every man helped his brother. They increased abundantly and multiplied greatly, ten weeks of years, all the days of the life of Joseph.

2 There was neither Satan nor any evil in all the days of the life of Joseph after his father, Jacob (had died),

because all the Egyptians respected the children of Israel all the days of the life of Joseph.

3 Joseph died, being a hundred and ten years old. He lived seventeen years in the land of Canaan, and ten years he was a servant, and three years in prison, and eighty years he was under the king, ruling all the land of Egypt.

4 He died and so did all his brothers and all of that generation. But, he commanded the children of Israel before he died that they should carry his bones with them when they went out from the land of Egypt.

5 And he made them swear regarding his bones, because he knew that the Egyptians would not bring his bones out of Egypt or bury him in the land of Canaan, because while dwelling in the land of Assyria, king Makamaron, the king of Canaan, fought against Egypt in the valley and killed the king of Egypt there, and pursued the Egyptians to the gates of "Ermon.

6 But he was not able to enter, because another king, a new king, had become king of Egypt, and he was stronger than he (Makamaron), and he returned to the land of Canaan, and the gates of Egypt were closed so that none came or went from Egypt.

7 Joseph died in the forty-sixth jubilee, in the sixth week, in the second year, and they buried him in the land of Egypt, and all his brothers died after him.

8 The king of Egypt went to war against the king of Canaan in the forty-seventh jubilee, in the second week in the second year, and the children of Israel brought out all the bones of the children of Jacob except the bones of Joseph, and they buried them in the field in the double cave in the mountain.

9 Then, most of them returned to Egypt, but a few of them remained in the mountains of Hebron, and Amram your father remained with them.

10 The king of Canaan was victorious over the king of Egypt, and he closed the gates of Egypt.

11 He devised an evil plan against the children of Israel to afflict them. He said to the people of Egypt, "Look, the people of the children of Israel have increased and multiplied more than we.

12 Let us use wisdom and deal with them before they become too many. Let us make them our slaves before we go to war and they rise up against us on the side of our enemies. Before they leave and fight against us let us do this because their hearts and faces (allegiances) are towards the land of Canaan."

13 He set over them taskmasters to enforce slavery, and they built strong cities for Pharaoh, Pithom, and Raamses and they built all the walls and all the fortifications, which had fallen in the cities of Egypt.

14 They enslaved them with harshness, and the more they were evil toward them, the more they increased and multiplied.

15 And the people of Egypt despised the children of Israel.

[Chapter 47]

1 In the seventh week, in the seventh year, in the forty-seventh jubilee, your father went out from the land of Canaan, and you (Moses) were born in the fourth week, in the sixth year of it, in the forty-eighth jubilee; this was the time of tribulation for the children of Israel.

2 Pharaoh, the king of Egypt, issued a command ordering them to throw all their newborn male children into the river.

3 And they threw them into the river for seven months until the day that you were born. It is said that your mother hid you for three months.

4 She made an ark for you, and covered it with pitch and tar, and placed it in the reeds on the bank of the river. She placed you in it seven days. Your mother came by night and nursed you. By day Miriam, your sister, guarded you from the birds.

5 In those days Tharmuth, the daughter of Pharaoh, came to bathe in the river, and she heard you crying. She told her maids to bring you out, and they brought you to her.

6 She took you out of the ark, and she had compassion on you.

7 Your sister said to her, "Shall I go and call to you one of the Hebrew women to nurse this baby for you?" And she said to her, "Go."

8 Your sister went and called your mother, Jochebed, and Pharaoh's daughter gave her wages (employed her), and she nursed you.

9 Afterwards, when you grew up, they brought you to the daughter of Pharaoh, and you became her son. Amram, your father, taught you writing. After you had completed three weeks (twenty-seven years) they brought you into the royal court.

10 You were three weeks of years at court until the time when you went out from the royal court and saw an

Egyptian beating your friend who was of the children of Israel, and you killed him and hid him in the sand.

11 On the second day you came across two children of Israel quarreling together, and you asked the one who was doing wrong, "Why did you hit your brother?"

12 He was angry and indignant, and said, "Who made you a prince and a judge over us?

13 Do you want to kill me like you killed the Egyptian yesterday?" You were afraid and you fled on because of these words.

[Chapter 48]

1 In the sixth year of the third week of the forty-ninth jubilee you fled and went to live in the land of Midian for five weeks and one year. You returned to Egypt in the second week in the second year in the fiftieth jubilee.

2 You know what He said to you on Mount Sinai, and what prince Mastema desired to do with you when you returned to Egypt.

3 Did he (Mastema) not seek to kill you with all his power and to deliver the Egyptians from your hand when he saw that you were sent to execute judgment and to take revenge on the Egyptians?

4 But I delivered you out of his hand, and you performed the signs and wonders which you were sent to perform in Egypt against Pharaoh, and against all of his household, and against his servants and his people.

5 The Lord exacted a great vengeance on them for Israel's sake, and struck them through the plagues of blood, frogs, lice, dog-flies, malignant boils, breaking out in pustules, the death of their cattle, and the plague of hailstones. He destroyed everything that grew from them by plagues of locusts, which devoured the remainder left by the hail, and by darkness, and by the death of the first-born of men and animals. The Lord took vengeance on all of their idols and burned them with fire.

6 Everything was sent through your hand, that you should declare these things before they were done. You spoke with the king of Egypt in the presence of all his servants and in the presence of his people and everything took place according to your words. Ten great and terrible judgments came on the land of Egypt so that you might execute vengeance on Egypt for Israel.

7 And the Lord did everything for Israel's sake according to His covenant, which he had ordained with Abraham. He took vengeance on them because they had brought them by force into bondage.

8 Prince Mastema stood against you, and sought to deliver you into the hands of Pharaoh. He helped the Egyptian sorcerers when they stood up and committed the evil acts they did in your presence. Indeed, we permitted them to work, but the remedies we did not allow to be worked by their hands.

9 The Lord struck them with malignant ulcers (hemorrhoids?), and they were not able to stand. They could not perform a single sign because we destroyed them.

10 Even after all of these signs and wonders, prince Mastema was not put to shame because he took courage and cried to the Egyptians to pursue you with all the power the Egyptians had, with their chariots, and with their horses, and with all the hosts of the peoples of Egypt.

11 But I stood between the Egyptians and Israel, and we delivered Israel out of his hand, and out of the hand of his people. The Lord brought them through the middle of the sea as if it were dry land.

12 The Lord our God threw all the people whom he (Mastema) brought to pursue Israel into the middle of the sea, into the depths of the bottomless pit, beneath the children of Israel, even as the people of Egypt had thrown their (Israel's) children into the river. He took vengeance on one million of them. In addition to one thousand strong and energetic men were destroyed because of the death of the suckling children of your people, which they had thrown into the river.

13 On the fourteenth day and on the fifteenth and on the sixteenth and on the seventeenth and on the eighteenth days, prince Mastema was bound and imprisoned and placed behind the children of Israel so that he might not accuse them.

14 On the nineteenth day we let them (Mastema and his demons) loose so that they might help the Egyptians pursue the children of Israel.

15 He hardened their hearts and made them stubborn, and the plan was devised by the Lord our God that He might strike the Egyptians and throw them into the sea.

16 On the fourteenth day we bound him that he might not accuse the children of Israel on the day when they asked the Egyptians for vessels and garments, vessels of silver, and vessels of gold, and vessels of bronze, in order to exact from the Egyptians a price in return for the bondage they had been forced to serve.

17 We did not lead the children of Israel from Egypt empty handed.

[Chapter 49]

1 Remember the commandment which the Lord commanded you concerning the Passover. You should celebrate it in its season on the fourteenth day of the first month. You should kill the sacrifice before evening. They should eat it by night on the evening of the fifteenth from the time of the setting of the sun.

2 Because on this night, at the beginning of the festival and the beginning of the joy, you were eating the Passover (lamb) in Egypt, when all the powers of Mastema had been let loose to kill all the first-born in the land of Egypt, from the first-born of Pharaoh to the first-born of the captive maid-servant in the mill, and even the first-born of the cattle.

3 This is the sign that the Lord gave them, in every house on the door post on which they saw the blood of a lamb of the first year they should not enter to kill, but should pass by it, that all those should be exempt that were in the house because the sign of the blood was on its door posts.

4 And the powers of the Lord did everything as the Lord commanded them, and they passed by all the children of Israel, and the plague did not come on them to destroy them, cattle, man, or dog.

5 The plague was oppressive in Egypt, and there was no house in Egypt where there was not one dead, and weeping, and lamentation.

6 All Israel was eating the flesh of the paschal lamb, and drinking the wine, and was praising, and blessing, and giving thanks to the Lord God of their fathers, and they were ready to get out from under the yoke of Egypt and the evil bondage.

7 Remember this day all the days of your life. Observe it from year to year all the days of your life, once a year, on its day, according to all the law of it. Do not forsake it from day to day, or from month to month.

8 It is an eternal law, and engraved on the heavenly tablets regarding all the children of Israel that they should observe it on its day once a year, every year, throughout all their generations. There is no limit of days, for this is a law forever.

9 The man who is free from uncleanness, and does not come to observe Passover on the occasion of its day and does not bring an acceptable offering before the Lord to eat and to drink before the Lord on the day of its festival will be guilty. If he is clean and close at hand (near the temple) and does not come, he shall be cut off because he did not offer the offering of the Lord in its appointed season. He shall take the guilt on himself.

10 Let the children of Israel come and observe the passover on the day of its fixed time, on the fourteenth day of the first month, between the evenings, from the third part of the day to the third part of the night, for two portions of the day are given to the light, and a third part to the evening.

11 The Lord commanded you to observe it between the evenings.

12 And it is not permissible to kill the sacrifice during any period of light, but only during the period bordering on the evening, and let them eat it at the time of the evening, until the third part of the night. Whatever is left over of all its flesh from the third part of the night and onwards is to be burned with fire.

13 They shall not cook it with water (boil or seethe it), nor shall they eat it raw, but roast it on the fire. They shall eat it with care, making sure its head with the inwards and its feet are roasted with fire, and they shall not break any bone of it, for of the children of Israel no bone shall be crushed.

14 For this reason the Lord commanded the children of Israel to observe the passover on the day of its fixed time, and they shall not break a bone of it, because it is a festival day He commanded. There was no passing over from any other day or any other month, but on the exact day let the festival be observed.

15 Command the children of Israel to observe the passover throughout their days, every year, once a year on the day of its fixed time, and it shall be a memorial well pleasing in the presence of the Lord, and no plague shall come on them to kill or to strike in that year in which they celebrate the passover in its season in every respect according to His command.

16 And they shall not eat it outside the sanctuary of the Lord, but before the sanctuary of the Lord, and all the people of the congregation of Israel shall celebrate it in its appointed season.

17 Every man twenty years of age and upward, who has come on the day of the Passover shall eat it in the sanctuary of your God before the Lord. This is how it is written and ordained. They should eat it in the sanctuary of the Lord.

18 When the children of Israel come into the land of Canaan that they are to possess, set up the tabernacle (tent) of the Lord within the land occupied by one of their tribes until the sanctuary of the Lord has been built in the land. There, let them come and celebrate the passover at tabernacle of the Lord, and let them kill it before the Lord from

year to year.

19 When the house of the Lord has been built in the land of their inheritance, they shall go there and kill the Passover (lamb) in the evening, at sunset, at the third part of the day.

20 They shall offer its blood on the threshold of the altar, and shall place its fat on the fire, which is on the altar, and they shall eat its flesh roasted with fire in the yard of the house, which has been sanctified in the name of the Lord.

21 They may not celebrate the passover in their cities, nor in any place except at the tabernacle of the Lord, or before His house where His name has dwelt. They shall not stray from the Lord.

22 Moses, command the children of Israel to observe the ordinances of the passover, as it was commanded to you. Declare to them every year the purpose and time of the festival of unleavened bread. They should eat unleavened bread seven days. They should observe its festival and bring an offering every day during those seven days of joy before the Lord on the altar of your God.

23 Celebrate this festival with haste as when you went out from Egypt and you entered into the wilderness of Shur, because on the shore of the sea you completed it (the exodus).

[Chapter 50]

1 I made this law known to you the days of the Sabbaths in the desert of Sinai, between Elim and Sinai.

2 I told you of the Sabbaths of the land on Mount Sinai, and I told you of the jubilee years in the sabbaths of years, but have I not told you the year of it until you enter the land which you are to possess.

3 Keep the sabbaths of the land while they live on it, and they shall know the jubilee year.

4 I have ordained for you the year of weeks and the years and the jubilees. There are forty-nine jubilees from the days of Adam until this day, and one week and two years, and there are forty years yet to come for learning the commandments of the Lord, until they pass over into the land of Canaan, crossing the Jordan to the west.

5 The jubilees shall pass by until Israel is cleansed from all guilt of fornication, and uncleanness, and pollution, and sin, and error, and it dwells with confidence in all the land. There shall be no more Satan or any evil one, and the land shall be clean from that time forever.

6 I have written down the commandment for them regarding the Sabbaths and all the judgments of its laws for you.

7 Six days will you labor, but the seventh day is the Sabbath of the Lord your God.

8 You shall do no manner of work in it, you and your sons, and your menservants and your maidservants, and all your cattle and travelers also who lodge with you. The man that does any work on it shall die. Whoever desecrates that day, whoever has sex with his wife, whoever says he will do something on it, or he that will set out on a journey on it in regard to any buying or selling, or whoever draws water on it which he had not prepared for himself on the sixth day, and whoever takes up any burden to carry it out of his tent or out of his house shall die.

9 You shall do no work whatsoever on the Sabbath day except what you have prepared for yourselves on the sixth day, so as to eat, and drink, and rest. Keep Sabbath free from all work on that day. It is to bless the Lord your God, who has given you a day of festival and a holy day, and a day of the holy kingdom. This is a day for Israel among all their days forever.

10 Great is the honor which the Lord has given to Israel that they should eat, drink, and be satisfied on this festival day. Rest on it from all labor, which belongs to the labor of the children of men, except burning frankincense and bringing offerings and sacrifices before the Lord for days and for Sabbaths.

11 Only this work shall be done on the Sabbath days in the sanctuary of the Lord your God so that they may atone for Israel with sacrifice continually from day to day for a memorial pleasing before the Lord, so that He may always receive them from day to day according to what you have been commanded.

12 Every man who does any work on it, or takes a trip, or tills his farm, whether in his house or any other place, and whoever lights a fire, or rides a beast, or travels by ship on the sea shall die. And whoever strikes or kills anything, or slaughters a beast or a bird, or whoever catches an animal or a bird or a fish, or whoever fasts or makes war on the Sabbaths, the man who does any of these things on the Sabbath shall die. This is done so that the children of Israel will observe the Sabbaths according to the commandments regarding the Sabbaths of the land. It is written in the tablets, which He gave into my hands that I should write out for you the laws of the seasons, and the seasons according to the division of their days.

This completes the account of the division of the days.

Bibliography

The Book of Jubilees
R.H. Charles, London, 1902

"The Apocrypha and Pseudepigrapha of the Old Testament"
R.H. Charles Oxford, Clarendon Press, 1913

"Jubilees," The Old Testament Pseudepigrapha
O. S. Wintermute, 1983

J. VanderKam, The Book of Jubilees (2001)

Beyond the Essene Hypothesis
By Gabriele Boccancci
Wm. B. Eerdmans Publishing 1998

The Book of Jasher

The J. H. Parry Text In Modern English

Edited by Joseph Lumpkin

The History Of The Book Of Jasher

The Book Of Jasher, or Sefer Ha Yashar, is referred to in the books of Joshua and Second Samuel of the Holy Bible.

"Behold it is written in the Book of Jasher."--II Samuel, i. 18
"Is not this written in the Book of Jasher?"--Joshua, x. 13.

Jasher (Yashar) is a Hebrew word meaning "upright". Jasher is not the name of the author or any prophet or judge of Israel, as scholars had previously thought. The name refers to the fact that the record, facts, and history are upright, correct, and thus, trustworthy.

The value of The Book of Jasher is seen in the large quantity of additional detail revealed in the period between divine creation and the time of Joshua's leadership over Israel when the Israelites enter into the land of Canaan.

The Book of Jasher includes details about the antediluvian patriarchs, angels, watchers, the flood, the tower of Babel, and many other events mentioned in the Bible. The tales are expanded and infused with detail not previously available.

This means we receive insight into the lives of Abraham, Noah, Enoch, Joseph, and many other biblical figures. We come to understand how they became great and why they acted as they did. We are also given hitherto unknown knowledge of historical events. We are shown how God's hand shaped history through his love and anger. We see how his disappointment with men and angels ended in earth's near total destruction.

We learn how the power of Nimrod, the great hunter, arose. We are told how all animals were guided to the ark of Noah, and why the tower of Babel was attacked by God and angels. Such detailed accounts bring the Old Testament into an understandable focus.

According to the Encyclopedia Judaica, Volume 14, p. 1099, Jasher was "probably written in the 13th century A.D." However, some scholars have proposed various dates between the 9th century and 16th century A.D.

There are three separate and different books named Jasher, however the Mormon Church, otherwise known as The Church of Jesus Christ of Latter-day Saints, considers this rendition of Jasher to be the book referenced in the Old Testament. The belief of the church leadership is bolstered by the preface in the 1625 version, which claims its original source came from the ruins of Jerusalem in 70 A.D.

Jasher is held in high repute by many Mormons but is not officially endorsed by the Mormon Church. The official stance of the Mormon Church falls short of making Jasher part of their Holy Scriptures but does endorse the book as being valid and authentic. The Mormon Church places the book of Jasher on the same level as other apocryphal writings and states in the church magazine, The Ensign, After reviewing the standard scholarly analysis of how the book appears to have been composed of old Jewish legends, the book of Jasher is considered to be of great benefit to the reader. The article concluded with an injunction to treat it according to the Lord's advice on how to study the Apocrypha. The article goes on to quote the church stance on the Apocrypha.

"Verily, thus saith the Lord unto you concerning the Apocrypha — There are many things contained therein that are true, and it is mostly translated correctly; There are many things contained therein that are not true, which are interpolations by the hands of men. Verily, I say unto you, that it is not needful that the Apocrypha should be translated. Therefore, whoso readeth it, let him understand, for the Spirit manifesteth truth; And whoso is enlightened by the Spirit shall obtain benefit And whoso receiveth not by the Spirit, cannot be benefitted. Therefore it is not needful that it should be translated. Amen." (D.&C. 91:1-6)

In the early 1800s, Moses Samuel of Liverpool, England, was given a copy of the 1625 A.D. Hebrew work. Jasher, he found, was written in a theological or Rabbinical type of Hebrew, which is a more classical Hebrew. Samuel translated the text into English and in 1839 sold it to Mordecai Manuel Noah, a Jewish New York publisher, who published it in 1840.

Copyright of the translation was obtained by J. H. Parry & Company in Salt Lake City, who published it in 1887.

Samuel's translation was written in "Elizabethan or King James" English and contained archaic words, phrases, and idioms.

The translation offered here is taken from the J. H. Parry translation with all archaic language and idioms edited and restated in modern English.

According to Bernard Wasserstein, in the Transactions of the Jewish Historical Society of England Vol. XXXV, Samuel translated into English the pseudo-biblical Book of Jasher, a supposedly ancient Hebrew text which Samuel convinced himself was authentic. After failing to persuade the Royal Asiatic Society to publish it, he sold his translation for £150 in 1839 to the American Jewish newspaper-owner and philanthropist Mordecai M. Noah. It appeared in New York the following year but with Noah's name and not Samuel's on the title page. "I did not put my name to it as my Patron and myself differed about its authenticity", Samuel later explained. This was odd since Noah seems to have had a lower opinion of the work's authenticity than Samuel. The translation was accepted as accurate, but the publication provoked criticism by scholars who rejected the claims made on behalf of the text. It won acceptance, however, by the Mormon prophet Joseph Smith. (p. 2)

The prophet, Joseph Smith's attraction to the book was due in part to the history contained in the preface of the book.

According to the history documented in the preface of the Book of Jasher, Titus destroyed Jerusalem in 70 A.D. but the book was miraculously rescued at that time. During the destruction of the Jewish temple a Roman officer named Sidrus discovered a Hebrew scholar hiding in a library. The officer took the scholar and all the books safely back to his estates in Seville, Spain. The manuscript was transferred to the Jewish college in Cordova, Spain. The book was kept there until its printings in Venice in 1625.

There is no evidence to substantiate these claims, but there is nothing to conclusively dismiss the claims either.

In reality, it is possible that a Jew living in Spain or Italy may have penned the book, but we have no way to be definite regarding the date of writing of the original book. Part of the confusion arises from the fact that Jasher seems to be a compilation of several stories gathered by priests over many generations. Most of the stories and history contain reliable, authentic Jewish terms and traditions. It is the weight of these correct facts and references that lend credence to the authenticity of the seed literature that formed Jasher.

Scholars view Jasher with much skepticism due to the absence of any evidence or mention of the book prior to 1625. The basis of the stories contained in Jasher are mythically old, but the book itself has not been found in its present form prior to the printing in the 1600s. However, it is the opinion of the editor that Jasher will offer some insight into the murky and sometimes sparse historical landscape of Genesis. At the least, we may state that the book reflects what the priestly scholars who wrote the book believed.

The texts presented here represents an accurate version of the Book of Jasher rendered in modern English. Although the book was translated in the 1800s, the translator chose to use the more stilted and less accessible Elizabethan or King James style of English in order to add weight and religious authority to the text. This made the book less than pleasant to read for the modern audience. In the translation before you archaic words and expressions were replaced with their modern counterparts. A word for word replacement was not attempted. When an archaic word needed to be replaced with a phrase for the purpose of clarity this technique was embraced so as to render the text readily understandable. It is our sincere hope our goal was accomplished and the reader will find this version interesting and easy to read.

The Book of Jasher

THIS IS THE BOOK OF THE GENERATIONS OF MAN WHOM GOD CREATED ON THE EARTH ON THE DAY WHEN THE LORD GOD MADE HEAVEN AND EARTH.

CHAPTER 1

1 God said, Let us make man in our image, in our likeness, and God created man in his own image.

2 God formed man from the dirt, and he blew into his nostrils the breath of life, and man became a living soul with the capacity of speech.

3 And the Lord said, It is not good for man to be alone; I will make him a helper and a mate.

4 The Lord caused a deep sleep to come on Adam, and he slept. God took away one of his ribs, and he fashioned flesh on it, and formed it and brought it to Adam. Adam awoke from his sleep, and saw a woman was standing in front of him.

5 He said, This is bone of my bones and it shall be called woman, because it has been taken from man. Adam named her Eve, because she was the mother of all living (mankind).

6 God blessed them and on the day he created them he called their names Adam and Eve. The Lord God said, Be prolific and reproduce and fill the earth.

7 The Lord God took Adam and his wife, and he placed them in the garden of Eden to farm it and to keep it. He commanded them and said, "You may eat from every tree of the garden, but you may never eat from the tree of the knowledge of good and evil. On the day that you eat thereof you will certainly die.

8 When God had blessed and commanded them, he departed from them. Adam and his wife lived in the garden according to the command which the Lord had commanded them.

9 The serpent, which God had created with them in the earth, came to them to incite them to go contrary to the command of God which he had commanded them.

10 And the serpent enticed and persuaded the woman to eat from the tree of knowledge, and the woman listened to the voice of the serpent, and she went contrary to the word of God, and took from the tree of the knowledge of good and evil, and she ate, and she took from it and gave also to her husband and he ate.

11 And Adam and his wife went contrary to the command of God which he commanded them, and God knew it, and his anger was set ablaze against them and he cursed them.

12 And the Lord God drove them that day from the garden of Eden, to till the ground from which they were taken, and they went and lived at the east of the garden of Eden; and Adam had sex with his wife Eve and she bore two sons and three daughters.

13 She called the name of the first born Cain, saying, I have obtained a man from the Lord, and the name of the other she called Abel, for she said, Empty we came into the earth, and empty we shall be taken from it.

14 And the boys grew up and their father gave them a possession in the land; and Cain was a farmer of the ground, and Abel a keeper of sheep.

15 And it was at the expiration of a few years, that they brought a first-fruit offering to the Lord, and Cain brought from the fruit of the ground, and Abel brought from the firstlings of his flock from the fat thereof, and God turned and inclined to Abel and his offering, and a fire came down from the Lord from heaven and consumed it.

16 And to Cain and his offering the Lord did not turn, and he did not incline to it, for he had brought from the inferior fruit of the ground before the Lord, and Cain was jealous against his brother Abel on account of this, and he sought an opportunity to kill him.

17 Some time after, Cain and Abel his brother went one day into the field to do their work; and they were both in the field, Cain farming and plowing his ground, and Abel feeding his flock; and the flock passed that part which Cain had plowed in the ground, and it sorely grieved Cain on this account.

18 And Cain approached his brother Abel in anger, and he said to him, What gives you the right to come and live here and bring your flock to feed in my land?

19 And Abel answered his brother Cain and said to him, What gives you the right to eat the flesh of my flock and clothe yourself with their wool?

20 Take off the wool of my sheep with which you have clothed yourself, and pay me for their resources you have

used and flesh which you have eaten, and when you shall have done this, I will then go from your land as you have said.

21 Cain said to his brother Abel, Certainly if I kill you this day, who will require your blood from me?

22 And Abel answered Cain, saying, Certainly God who has made us in the earth, he will avenge my cause, and he will require my blood from you should you kill me, for the Lord is the judge and arbiter, and it is he who will repay man according to his evil, and the wicked man according to the wickedness that he may do on earth.

23 And now, if you should kill me here, certainly God knows your secret views, and will judge you for the evil which you did declare to do to me this day.

24 When Cain heard the words which Abel his brother had spoken, the anger of Cain was set ablaze against his brother Abel for declaring this thing.

25 Cain hurried and rose up, and took the iron part of his plowing instrument, with which he suddenly struck his brother and he killed him, and Cain spilt the blood of his brother Abel on the earth, and the blood of Abel streamed on the earth before the flock.

26 And after this Cain repented having slain his brother, and he was sadly grieved, and he wept over him and it troubled him greatly.

27 Cain rose up and dug a hole in the field, wherein he put his brother's body, and he turned the dust over it.

28 And the Lord knew what Cain had done to his brother, and the Lord appeared to Cain and said to him, Where is Abel your brother that was with you?

29 And Cain lied, and said, I do not know. Am I my brother's keeper? And the Lord said to him, What have you done? The voice of your brother's blood cries to me from the ground where you have slain him.

30 For you have slain your brother and have lied before me, and imagined in your heart that I saw you not, nor knew all your actions.

31 But you did this thing and did kill your brother for naught and because he spoke rightly to you, and now, therefore, cursed be you from the ground which opened its mouth to receive your brother's blood from your hand, and wherein you did bury him.

32 It shall be when you shall till it, the land will no longer give you its strength as in the beginning, for thorns and thistles shall the ground produce, and you shall be moving and wandering in the earth until the day of your death.

33 And at that time Cain went out from the presence of the Lord, from the place where he was, and he went moving and wandering in the land toward the east of Eden, he and all those belonging to him.

34 Cain had sex with his wife in those days, and she conceived and gave birth to a son, and he called his name Enoch, saying, In that time the Lord began to give him rest and quiet in the earth.

35 At that time Cain also began to build a city: and he built the city and he called the name of the city Enoch, according to the name of his son; for in those days the Lord had given him rest on the earth, and he did not move about and wander as in the beginning.

36 And Irad was born to Enoch, and Irad had Mechuyael and Mechuyael had Methusael.

CHAPTER 2

1 It was in the hundred and thirtieth year of the life of Adam on the earth, that he again had sex with Eve his wife, and she conceived and gave birth to a son and he looked like Adam, and she called his name Seth, saying, Because God has appointed me another offspring in the place of Abel, for Cain has slain him.

2 And Seth lived one hundred and five years, and he had a son; and Seth called the name of his son Enosh, saying, Because in that time the sons of men began to reproduce, and to afflict their souls and hearts by disobeying and rebelling against God.

3 It was in the days of Enosh that the sons of men continued to rebel and go contrary to God, to increase the anger of the Lord against the sons of men.

4 And the sons of men went and they served other gods, and they forgot the Lord who had created them in the earth: and in those days the sons of men made images of brass and iron, wood and stone, and they bowed down and served them.

5 Every man made his god and they bowed down to them, and the sons of men turned away from the Lord all the days of Enosh and his children; and the anger of the Lord was set ablaze on account of their works and abominations which they did in the earth.

6 The Lord caused the waters of the river Gihon to overwhelm them, and he destroyed and consumed them, and

he destroyed the third part of the earth. Notwithstanding this, the sons of men did not turn from their evil ways, and their hands were yet extended to do evil in the sight of the Lord.

7 In those days there was neither sowing nor reaping in the earth; and there was no food for the sons of men and the famine was very great in those days.

8 And the seed which they sowed in those days in the ground became thorns, thistles and briers; for from the days of Adam was this declaration concerning the earth, of the curse of God, which he cursed the earth, on account of the sin which Adam sinned before the Lord.

9 And it was when men continued to rebel and go contrary to God, and to corrupt their ways, that the earth also became corrupt.

10 And Enosh lived ninety years and he had Cainan.

11 Cainan grew up and he was forty years old, and he became wise and had knowledge and skill in all wisdom, and he reigned over all the sons of men, and he led the sons of men to wisdom and knowledge; for Cainan was a very wise man and had understanding in all wisdom, and with his wisdom he ruled over spirits and demons.

12 Cainan knew by his wisdom that God would destroy the sons of men for having sinned on earth, and that the Lord would in the latter days bring on them the waters of the flood.

13 And in those days Cainan wrote on tablets of stone what was to take place in time to come, and he put them in his treasure troves.

14 Cainan reigned over the whole earth, and he turned some of the sons of men to the service of God.

15 When Cainan was seventy years old, he had three sons and two daughters.

16 These are the names of the children of Cainan; the name of the first born was Mahlallel, the second was Enan, and the third was Mered, and their sisters were Adah and Zillah; these are the five children of Cainan that were born to him.

17 Lamech, the son of Methusael, became related to Cainan by marriage, and he took his two daughters for his wives, and Adah conceived and gave birth to a son to Lamech, and she called his name Jabal.

18 And she again conceived and gave birth to a son, and called his name Jubal; and Zillah, her sister, was unable to conceive in those days and had no offspring.

19 For in those days the sons of men began to trespass against God, and to go contrary to the commandments which he had given Adam, to be prolific and reproduce in the earth.

20 Some of the sons of men caused their wives to drink a mixture that would render them unable to conceive, in order that they might retain their figures and their beautiful appearance might not fade.

21 And when the sons of men caused some of their wives to drink, Zillah drank with them.

22 The child-bearing women appeared abominable in the sight of their husbands and they treated them as widows, while their husbands lived with those unable to conceive and to those women they were attached.

23 And in the end of days and years, when Zillah became old, the Lord opened her womb.

24 She conceived and gave birth to a son and she called his name Tubal Cain, saying, After I had withered away have I obtained him from the Almighty God.

25 And she conceived again and gave birth to a daughter, and she called her name Naamah, for she said, After I had withered away have I obtained pleasure and delight.

26 Lamech was old and advanced in years, and his eyes were dim that he could not see, and Tubal Cain, his son, was leading him and it was one day that Lamech went into the field and Tubal Cain his son was with him, and while they were walking in the field, Cain the son of Adam advanced towards them; for Lamech was very old and could not see much, and Tubal Cain his son was very young.

27 Tubal Cain told his father to draw his bow, and with the arrows he struck Cain, who was yet far off, and he killed him, because he appeared be an animal to them.

28 And the arrows entered Cain's body although he was at a distance from them, and he fell to the ground and died.

29 The Lord rewarded Cain's evil according to his wickedness, which he had done to his brother Abel, according to the word of the Lord which he had spoken.

30 And it came to pass when Cain had died, that Lamech and Tubal went to see the animal which they had slain, and they saw, and behold Cain their grandfather was fallen dead on the earth.

31 Lamech was very much grieved at having done this, and in clapping his hands together (in grief) he struck his son and caused his death.

32 And the wives of Lamech heard what Lamech had done, and they sought to kill him.

33 The wives of Lamech hated him from that day, because he killed Cain and Tubal Cain, and the wives of

Lamech separated from him, and would not listen to him in those days.

34 And Lamech came to his wives, and he begged them to listen to him about this matter.

35 He said to his wives Adah and Zillah, Hear my voice O wives of Lamech, attend to my words, for now you have imagined and said that I killed a man with my wounds, and a child with my stripes for they did no violence, but certainly know that I am old and grey-headed, and that my eyes are heavy through age, and I did this thing unknowingly.

36 And the wives of Lamech listened to him in this matter, and they returned to him with the advice of their father Adam, but they bore no children to him from that time, knowing that God's anger was increasing in those days against the sons of men, to destroy them with the waters of the flood for their evil acts.

37 Mahlallel the son of Cainan lived sixty-five years and he had Jared; and Jared lived sixty-two years and he had Enoch.

CHAPTER 3

1 Enoch lived sixty-five years and he had Methuselah; and Enoch walked with God after having a son, Methuselah, and he served the Lord, and despised the evil ways of men.

2 And the soul of Enoch was wrapped up in the instruction of the Lord, in knowledge and in understanding; and he wisely retired from the sons of men, and cloistered himself from them for many days.

3 It was at the expiration of many years, while he was serving the Lord, and praying before him in his house, that an angel of the Lord called to him from Heaven, and he said, Here am I.

4 And he said, Rise, go forth from your house and from the place where you hide yourself, and appear to the sons of men, in order that you may teach them the way in which they should go and the work which they must accomplish in order to enter into the ways of God.

5 Enoch rose up according to the word of the Lord, and went forth from his house, from his place and from the chamber in which he was concealed; and he went to the sons of men and taught them the ways of the Lord, and at that time assembled the sons of men and acquainted them with the instruction of the Lord.

6 He ordered it to be proclaimed in all places where the sons of men lived, saying, Where is the man who wishes to know the ways of the Lord and good works? Let him come to Enoch.

7 And all the sons of men then assembled to him, for all who desired this thing went to Enoch, and Enoch reigned over the sons of men according to the word of the Lord, and they came and bowed to him and they heard his word.

8 The spirit of God was on Enoch, and he taught all his men the wisdom of God and his ways, and the sons of men served the Lord all the days of Enoch, and they came to hear his wisdom.

9 And all the kings of the sons of men, both greatest and least, together with their princes and judges, came to Enoch when they heard of his wisdom, and they bowed down to him, and they also required of Enoch to reign over them, to which he consented.

10 They assembled in all, one hundred and thirty kings and princes, and they made Enoch king over them and they were all under his power and command.

11 And Enoch taught them wisdom, knowledge, and the ways of the Lord; and he made peace among them, and peace was throughout the earth during the life of Enoch.

12 Enoch reigned over the sons of men two hundred and forty-three years, and he did justice and righteousness with all his people, and he led them in the ways of the Lord.

13 These are the generations of Enoch, Methuselah, Elisha, and Elimelech, three sons; and their sisters were Melca and Nahmah, and Methuselah lived eighty-seven years and he had Lamech.

14 It was in the fifty-sixth year of the life of Lamech when Adam died. Nine hundred and thirty years old was he at his death. His two sons, with Enoch and Methuselah his son, buried him with great grandeur, as at the burial of kings, in the cave which God had told him.

15 And in that place all the sons of men mourned and wept greatly on account of Adam; it has therefore become a custom among the sons of men to this day.

16 Adam died because he ate of the tree of knowledge; he and his children after him, as the Lord God had spoken.

17 And it was in the year of Adam's death which was the two hundred and forty-third year of the reign of Enoch, in that time Enoch resolved to separate himself from the sons of men and to cloister himself as at first in order to

serve the Lord.

18 Enoch did so, but did not entirely cloister himself from them, but kept away from the sons of men three days and then went to them for one day.

19 During the three days that he was in his chamber, he prayed to, and praised the Lord his God, and the day on which he went and appeared to his subjects he taught them the ways of the Lord, and all they asked him about the Lord he told them.

20 And he did in this manner for many years, and he afterward concealed himself for six days, and appeared to his people one day in seven; and after that once in a month, and then once in a year, until all the kings, princes and sons of men sought for him, and desired again to see the face of Enoch, and to hear his word; but they could not, as all the sons of men were greatly afraid of Enoch, and they feared to approach him on account of the Godlike awe that was seated on his countenance; therefore no man could look at him, fearing he might be punished and die.

21 All the kings and princes resolved to assemble the sons of men, and to come to Enoch, thinking that they might all speak to him at the time when he should come forth among them, and they did so.

22 The day came when Enoch went forth and they all assembled and came to him, and Enoch spoke to them the words of the Lord and he taught them wisdom and knowledge, and they bowed down before him and they said, May the king live! May the king live!

23 Some time after, when the kings and princes and the sons of men were speaking to Enoch, and Enoch was teaching them the ways of God, an angel of the Lord then called to Enoch from heaven, and wished to bring him up to heaven to make him reign there over the sons of God, as he had reigned over the sons of men on earth.

24 When at that time Enoch heard this he went and assembled all the inhabitants of the earth, and taught them wisdom and knowledge and gave them divine instructions, and he said to them, I have been required to ascend into heaven; but I do not know the day of my going.

25 And now therefore I will teach you wisdom and knowledge and will give you instruction before I leave you, how to act on earth so that you may live (as you should); and he did so.

26 He taught them wisdom and knowledge, and gave them instruction, and he rebuked them, and he placed before them statutes and judgments to do on earth, and he made peace among them, and he taught them everlasting life, and lived with them some time teaching them all these things.

27 At that time the sons of men were with Enoch, and Enoch was speaking to them, and they lifted up their eyes and the likeness of a great horse descended from heaven, and the horse paced in the air.

28 And they told Enoch what they had seen, and Enoch said to them, On my account does this horse descend on earth; the time is come when I must go from you and I shall no more be seen by you.

29 The horse descended at that time and stood before Enoch, and all the sons of men that were with Enoch saw him.

30 Enoch then again ordered a voice to be proclaimed, saying, Where is the man who delights to know the ways of the Lord his God, let him come this day to Enoch before he is taken from us.

31 All the sons of men assembled and came to Enoch that day; and all the kings of the earth with their princes and counselors remained with him that day; and Enoch then taught the sons of men wisdom and knowledge, and gave them divine instruction; and he bade them serve the Lord and walk in his ways all the days of their lives, and he continued to make peace among them.

32 It was after this that he rose up and rode on the horse; and he went forth and all the sons of men went after him, about eight hundred thousand men; and they went with him one day's journey.

33 And the second day he said to them, Return home to your tents, why will you go? Perhaps you may die; and some of them went from him, and those that remained went with him six day's journey; and Enoch said to them every day, Return to your tents, that you may die; but they were not willing to return, and they went with him.

34 And on the sixth day some of the men remained and clung to him, and they said to him, We will go with you to the place where you go; as the Lord lives, only death shall separate us.

35 They urged so much to go with him that he ceased speaking to them; and they went after him and would not return.

36 When the kings returned they caused a census to be taken, in order to know the number of remaining men that went with Enoch; and it was on the seventh day that Enoch ascended into heaven in a whirlwind, with horses and chariots of fire.

37 And on the eighth day all the kings that had been with Enoch sent to bring back the number of men that were with Enoch, in that place from which he ascended into heaven.

38 All those kings went to the place and they found the earth there filled with snow, and on the snow were large stones of snow, and one said to the other, Come, let us break through the snow and see, perhaps the men that remained with Enoch are dead, and are now under the stones of snow, and they searched but could not find Enoch, for he had ascended into heaven.

CHAPTER 4

1 All the days that Enoch lived on earth, were three hundred and sixty-five years.

2 And when Enoch had ascended into heaven, all the kings of the earth rose and took Methuselah his son and anointed him, and they caused him to reign over them in the place of his father.

3 Methuselah acted uprightly in the sight of God, as his father Enoch had taught him, and he likewise during the whole of his life taught the sons of men wisdom, knowledge and the fear of God, and he did not turn from the good way either to the right or to the left.

4 But in the latter days of Methuselah, the sons of men turned from the Lord; they corrupted the earth, they robbed and plundered each other, and they rebelled against God; they went contrary to, they corrupted their ways, and would not listen to the voice of Methuselah, but rebelled against him.

5 And the Lord was greatly wroth against them, and the Lord continued to destroy the offspring in those days, so that there was neither sowing nor reaping in the earth.

6 For when they sowed the ground in order that they might obtain food for their support, behold, thorns and thistles were produced which they did not sow.

7 And still the sons of men did not turn from their evil ways, and their hands were still extended to do evil in the sight of God, and they provoked the Lord with their evil ways, and the Lord was very wroth, and repented that he had made man.

8 He thought to destroy and annihilate them and he did so.

9 In those days when Lamech the son of Methuselah was one hundred and sixty years old, Seth the son of Adam died.

10 And all the days that Seth lived were nine hundred and twelve years, and he died.

11 Lamech was one hundred and eighty years old when he took Ashmua, the daughter of Elishaa the son of Enoch his uncle, and she conceived.

12 And at that time the sons of men sowed the ground, and a little food was produced, yet the sons of men did not turn from their evil ways, and they trespassed and rebelled against God.

13 The wife of Lamech conceived and gave birth to a son at that time, at the revolution of the year.

14 And Methuselah called his name Noah, saying, The earth was in his days at rest and free from corruption, and Lamech his father called his name Menachem, saying, This one shall comfort us in our works and miserable toil in the earth, which God had cursed.

15 The child grew up and was weaned, and he went in the ways of his father Methuselah, perfect and upright with God.

16 And all the sons of men departed from the ways of the Lord in those days as they multiplied on the face of the earth with sons and daughters, and they taught one another their evil practices and they continued sinning against the Lord.

17 Every man made to himself a god, and they robbed and plundered every man his neighbor as well as his relative, and they corrupted the earth, and the earth was filled with violence.

18 And their judges and rulers went to the daughters of men and took their wives by force from their husbands according to their choice, and the sons of men in those days took from the cattle of the earth, the beasts of the field and the fowls of the air, and taught the mixture of animals of one species with the other, in order therewith to provoke the Lord; and God saw the whole earth and it was corrupt, for all flesh had corrupted its ways on earth, all men and all animals.

19 And the Lord said, I will blot out man that I created from the face of the earth, yea from man to the birds of the air together with cattle and beasts that are in the field, for I repent that I made them.

20 All men who walked in the ways of the Lord died in those days, before the Lord brought the evil on man which he had declared, for this was from the Lord that they should not see the evil which the Lord spoke of concerning the sons of men.

21 And Noah found grace in the sight of the Lord, and the Lord chose him and his children to raise up offspring

on the face of the whole earth.

CHAPTER 5

1 It was in the eighty-fourth year of the life of Noah that Enoch the son of Seth died; he was nine hundred and five years old at his death.

2 In the one hundred and seventy ninth year of the life of Noah, Cainan the son of Enosh died, and the age of Cainan was nine hundred and ten years, and he died.

3 And in the two hundred and thirty fourth year of the life of Noah, Mahlallel the son of Cainan died, and the days of Mahlallel were eight hundred and ninety-five years, and he died.

4 Jared the son of Mahlallel died in those days, in the three hundred and thirty-sixth year of the life of Noah; and all the days of Jared were nine hundred and sixty-two years, and he died.

5 And all who followed the Lord died in those days, before they saw the evil which God declared to do on earth.

6 After the lapse of many years, in the four hundred and eightieth year of the life of Noah, when all those men who followed the Lord had died away from among the sons of men, and only Methuselah was then left, God said to Noah and Methuselah,

7 Speak ye, and proclaim to the sons of men, saying, Thus says the Lord, return from your evil ways and turn away from your works, and the Lord will repent of the evil that he declared to do to you, so that it shall not come to pass.

8 For thus says the Lord, Behold I give you a period of one hundred and twenty years; if you will turn to me and turn away from your evil ways, then will I also turn away from the evil which I told you, and it shall not exist, says the Lord.

9 And Noah and Methuselah spoke all the words of the Lord to the sons of men, day after day, constantly speaking to them.

10 But the sons of men would not listen to them, nor incline their ears to their words, and they were stubborn.

11 And the Lord granted them a period of one hundred and twenty years, saying, If they will return, then will God repent of the evil, so as not to destroy the earth.

12 Noah the son of Lamech refrained from taking a wife in those days to beget children, for he said, Certainly now God will destroy the earth, wherefore then shall I beget children?

13 Noah was a just man, he was perfect in his generation, and the Lord chose him to raise up offspring from his offspring on the face of the earth.

14 And the Lord said to Noah, Take to you a wife, and beget children, for I have seen you righteous before me in this generation.

15 You shall raise up offspring, and your children with you, in the midst of the earth; and Noah went and took a wife, and he chose Naamah the daughter of Enoch, and she was five hundred and eighty years old.

16 And Noah was four hundred and ninety-eight years old, when he took Naamah for a wife.

17 Naamah conceived and gave birth to a son, and he called his name Japheth, saying, God has enlarged me in the earth; and she conceived again and gave birth to a son, and he called his name Shem, saying, God has made me a remnant, to raise up descendants the midst of the earth.

18 And Noah was five hundred and two years old when Naamah gave birth to Shem, and the boys grew up and went in the ways of the Lord, in all that Methuselah and Noah their father taught them.

19 Lamech the father of Noah, died in those days; yet verily he did not go with all his heart in the ways of his father, and he died in the hundred and ninety-fifth year of the life of Noah.

20 And all the days of Lamech were seven hundred and seventy years, and he died.

21 All the sons of men who knew the Lord, died in that year before the Lord brought evil on them; for the Lord willed them to die, so as not to behold the evil that God would bring on their brothers and relatives, as he had so declared to do.

22 In that time, the Lord said to Noah and Methuselah, Stand forth and proclaim to the sons of men all the words that I spoke to you in those days, perchance they may turn from their evil ways, and I will then repent of the evil and will not bring it.

23 And Noah and Methuselah stood forth, and said in the ears of the sons of men, all that God had spoken concerning them.

24 But the sons of men would not listen, neither would they incline their ears to all their declarations.

25 It was after this that the Lord said to Noah, The end of all flesh is come before me on account of their evil

deeds, and behold I will destroy the earth.

26 And take with you gopher wood, and go to a certain place and make a large ark, and place it in that spot.

27 Thus shall you make it; three hundred cubits in length, fifty cubits broad and thirty cubits high.

28 And you shall make a door, open at its side, and to a cubit you shall finish above, and cover it within and without with pitch.

29 And behold I will bring the flood of waters on the earth, and all flesh will be destroyed; from under the heavens all that is on earth shall perish.

30 You and your household shall go and gather two couple of all living things, male and female, and shall bring them to the ark, to raise up offspring from them on earth.

31 Gather to you all food that is eaten by all the animals, that there may be food for you and for them.

32 You shall choose for your sons three maidens from the daughters of men, and they shall be wives to your sons.

33 And Noah rose up, and he made the ark, in the place where God had commanded him, and Noah did as God had ordered him.

34 In his five hundred and ninety-fifth year Noah commenced to make the ark, and he made the ark in five years, as the Lord had commanded.

35 Then Noah took the three daughters of Eliakim, son of Methuselah, for wives for his sons, as the Lord had commanded Noah.

36 It was at that time Methuselah the son of Enoch died; he was nine hundred and sixty years old at his death.

CHAPTER 6

1 At that time, after the death of Methuselah, the Lord said to Noah, Go with your household into the ark; behold I will gather to you all the animals of the earth, the beasts of the field and the fowls of the air, and they shall all come and surround the ark.

2 You shall go and seat yourself by the doors of the ark, and all the beasts, the animals, and the fowls, shall assemble and place themselves before you, and such of them as will come and crouch before you, you shall take and deliver into the hands of your sons, who will bring them to the ark, and all that will stand before you you shall leave.

3 And the Lord brought this about on the next day, and animals, beasts and fowls came in great multitudes and surrounded the ark.

4 Noah went and seated himself by the door of the ark, and of all flesh that crouched before him he brought into the ark, and all that stood before him he left on earth.

5 A lioness came with her two whelps, male and female, and the three crouched before Noah; the two whelps rose up against the lioness and struck her, and made her flee from her place, and she went away, and they returned to their places and crouched on the earth before Noah.

6 And the lioness ran away, and stood in the place of the lions.

7 And Noah saw this and wondered greatly, and he rose and took the two whelps and brought them into the ark.

8 Noah brought into the ark from all living creatures that were on earth, so that there was none left but those which Noah brought into the ark.

9 Two and two came to Noah into the ark, but from the clean animals and clean fowls, he brought seven couples as God had commanded him.

10 And all the animals, and beasts, and fowls were still there, and they surrounded the ark at every place, and the rain had not descended till seven days after.

11 On that day the Lord caused the whole earth to shake, and the sun darkened, and the foundations of the world raged, and the whole earth was moved violently, and the lightning flashed, and the thunder roared, and all the fountains in the earth were broken up, such as was not known to the inhabitants before; and God did this mighty act in order to terrify the sons of men, that there might be no more evil on earth.

12 And still the sons of men would not return from their evil ways, and they increased the anger of the Lord at that time, and did not even direct their hearts to all this.

13 At the end of seven days, in the six hundredth year of the life of Noah, the waters of the flood were on the earth.

14 All the fountains of the deep were broken up, and the windows of heaven were opened, and the rain was on

the earth forty days and forty nights.

15 And Noah and his household, and all the living creatures that were with him, came into the ark on account of the waters of the flood, and the Lord shut him| in.

16 All the sons of men that were left on the earth became exhausted through evil on account of the rain, for the waters were coming more violently on the earth, and the animals and beasts were still surrounding the ark.

17 And the sons of men assembled together, about seven hundred thousand men and women, and they came to Noah to the ark.

18 They called to Noah, saying, Open for us that we may come to you in the ark--and wherefore| shall we die?

19 And Noah, with a loud voice answered them from the ark, saying, Have you not all rebelled against the Lord, and said that he does not exist? Therefore the Lord brought on you this evil, to destroy and cut you off from the face of the earth.

20 Is not this the thing that I spoke to you of one hundred and twenty years back, and you would not listen to the voice of the Lord, and now do you desire to live on earth?

21 They said to Noah, We are ready to return to the Lord; only open for us that we may live and not die.

22 And Noah answered them, saying, Behold now that you see the trouble of your souls, you wish to return to the Lord; why did you not return during these hundred and twenty years, which the Lord granted you as the determined period?

23 But now you come and tell me this on account of the troubles of your souls, now also the Lord will not listen to you, neither will he give ear| to you on this day, so that you will not now succeed in your wishes.

24 The sons of men approached in order to break into the ark, to come in on account of the rain, for they could not bear the rain on them.

25 And the Lord sent all the beasts and animals that stood around the ark. And the beasts overpowered them and drove them from that place, and every man went his way and they again scattered themselves on the face of the earth.

26 The rain was still descending on the earth, and it descended forty days and forty nights, and the waters prevailed greatly on the earth; all flesh that was on the earth or in the waters died, whether men, animals, beasts, creeping things or birds of the air, and there only remained Noah and those that were with him in the ark.

27 The waters prevailed and they greatly increased on the earth, and they lifted up the ark and it was raised from the earth.

28 And the ark floated on the face of the waters; it was tossed on the waters so that all the living creatures within were turned about like pottage in a cauldron.

29 Great anxiety seized all the living creatures that were in the ark, and the ark was like to be broken.

30 And all the living creatures that were in the ark were terrified: the lions roared, and the oxen lowed, and the wolves howled, and every living creature in the ark spoke and lamented in its own language, so that their voices reached to a great distance, and Noah and his sons cried and wept in their troubles; they were greatly afraid that they had reached the gates of death.

31 And Noah prayed to the Lord, and cried to him on account of this, and he said, O Lord help us, for we have no strength to bear this evil that has encompassed us, for the waves of the waters have surrounded us, mischievous torrents have terrified us, the snares of death have come before us; answer us, O Lord, answer us, light up your countenance toward us and be gracious to us, redeem us and deliver us.

32 The Lord listened to the voice of Noah, and the Lord remembered him.

33 And a wind passed over the earth; the waters were still and the ark rested.

34 The fountains of the deep and the windows of heaven were stopped, and the rain from heaven was restrained.

35 And the waters decreased in those days, and the ark rested on the mountains of Ararat.

36 Noah then opened the windows of the ark, and Noah still called out to the Lord at that time and he said, O Lord, who did form the earth and the heavens and all that are therein, bring forth our souls from this confinement, and from the prison wherein you have placed us, for I am much wearied with sighing.

37 And the Lord listened to the voice of Noah, and said to him, When you have completed a full year you shall then go forth.

38 And at the revolution of the year, when a full year was completed to Noah's dwelling in the ark, the waters were dried from off the earth, and Noah put off the covering of the ark.

39 At that time, on the twenty-seventh day of the second month, the earth was dry, but Noah and his sons and those that were with him did not go out from the ark until the Lord told them.

40 And the day came that the Lord told them to go out, and they all went out from the ark.

41 They went and returned every one to his way and to his place, and Noah and his sons lived in the land that God had told them; they served the Lord all their days, and the Lord blessed Noah and his sons on their going out from the ark.

42 And he said to them, Be prolific and fill all the earth; become strong and increase abundantly in the earth and reproduce therein.

CHAPTER 7

1 And these are the names of the sons of Noah: Japheth, Ham and Shem; and children were born to them after the flood, for they had taken wives before the flood.

2 These are the sons of Japheth: Gomer, Magog, Madai, Javan, Tubal, Meshech, and Tiras, seven sons.

3 And the sons of Gomer were Askinaz, Rephath and Tegarmah.

4 And the sons of Magog were Elichanaf and Lubal.

5 And the children of Madai were Achon, Zeelo, Chazoni and Lot.

6 And the sons of Javan were Elisha, Tarshish, Chittim and Dudonim.

7 And the sons of Tubal were Ariphi, Kesed and Taari.

8 And the sons of Meshech were Dedon, Zaron and Shebashni.

9 And the sons of Tiras were Benib, Gera, Lupirion and Gilak; these are the sons of Japheth according to their families, and their numbers in those days were about four hundred and sixty men.

10 And these are the sons of Ham: Cush, Mitzraim, Phut and Canaan, four sons; and the sons of Cush were Seba, Havilah, Sabta, Raama and Satecha, and the sons of Raama were Sheba and Dedan.

11 And the sons of Mitzraim were Lud, Anom and Pathros, Chasloth and Chaphtor.

12 And the sons of Phut were Gebul, Hadan, Benah and Adan.

13 And the sons of Canaan were Zidon, Heth, Amori, Gergashi, Hivi, Arkee, Seni, Arodi, Zimodi and Chamothi.

14 These are the sons of Ham, according to their families, and their numbers in those days were about seven hundred and thirty men.

15 And these are the sons of Shem: Elam, Ashur, Arpachshad, Lud and Aram, five sons; and the sons of Elam were Shushan, Machul and Harmon.

16 And the sons of Ashar were Mirus and Mokil, and the sons of Arpachshad were Shelach, Anar and Ashcol.

17 And the sons of Lud were Pethor and Bizayon, and the sons of Aram were Uz, Chul, Gather and Mash.

18 These are the sons of Shem, according to their families; and their numbers in those days were about three hundred men.

19 These are the generations of Shem: Shem had Arpachshad and Arpachshad had Shelach, and Shelach had Eber and to Eber were born two children, the name of one was Peleg, for in his days the sons of men were divided, and in the latter days the earth was divided.

20 And the name of the second was Yoktan, meaning that in his day the lives of the sons of men were diminished and lessened.

21 These are the sons of Yoktan: Almodad, Shelaf, Chazarmoveth, Yerach, Hadurom, Ozel, Diklah, Obal, Abimael, Sheba, Ophir, Havilah and Jobab; all these are the sons of Yoktan.

22 And Peleg his brother had Yen, and Yen had Serug, and Serug had Nahor and Nahor had Terah, and Terah was thirty-eight years old, and he had Haran and Nahor.

23 And Cush the son of Ham, the son of Noah, took a wife in those days in his old age, and she gave birth to a son, and they called his name Nimrod, saying, At that time the sons of men again began to rebel and go contrary to God; the child grew up, and his father loved him greatly, for he was the son of his old age.

24 The garments of skin which God made for Adam and his wife, when they went out of the garden, were given to Cush.

25 For after the death of Adam and his wife, the garments were given to Enoch, the son of Jared, and when Enoch was taken up to God, he gave them to Methuselah, his son.

26 At the death of Methuselah, Noah took them and brought them to the ark, and they were with him until he went out of the ark.

27 And in their going out, Ham stole those garments from Noah his father; he took them and hid them from his brothers.

28 When Ham had his first born Cush, he gave him the garments in secret, and they were with Cush many days.

29 Cush also concealed them from his sons and brothers, and when Cush had begotten Nimrod, he gave him those garments through his love for him, and Nimrod grew up, and when he was twenty years old he put on those garments.

30 Nimrod became strong when he put on the garments, and God gave him might and strength, and he was a mighty hunter in the earth. He was a mighty hunter in the field, and he hunted the animals and he built altars, and he offered on them the animals before the Lord.

31 Nimrod strengthened himself, and he rose up from among his brothers, and he fought the battles of his brothers against all their enemies round about.

32 The Lord delivered all the enemies of his brothers in his hands, and God prospered him from time to time in his battles, and he reigned on earth.

33 Therefore it became current in those days, when a man ushered forth those that he had trained up for battle, he would say to them, like God did to Nimrod who was a mighty hunter in the earth and who succeeded in the battles that prevailed against his brothers, that he delivered them from the hands of their enemies: so may God strengthen us and deliver us this day.

34 And when Nimrod was forty years old, there was a war between his brothers and the children of Japheth, so that they were in the power of their enemies.

35 Nimrod went forth at that time, and he assembled all the sons of Cush and their families, about four hundred and sixty men; he hired also from some of his friends and acquaintances about eighty men, and he gave them their hire; he went with them to battle, and when he was on the road, Nimrod strengthened the hearts of the people that went with him.

36 And he said to them, Do not fear, neither be alarmed, for all our enemies will be delivered into our hands, and you may do with them as you please.

37 All the men that went were about five hundred, and they fought against their enemies; they destroyed them, and subdued them, and Nimrod placed standing officers over them in their respective places.

38 He took some of their children as security, and they were all servants to Nimrod and to his brothers, and Nimrod and all the people that were with him turned homeward.

39 When Nimrod had joyfully returned from battle, after having conquered his enemies, all his brothers, together with those who knew him before, assembled to make him king over them and they placed the regal crown on his head.

40 He set over his subjects and people, princes, judges, and rulers, as is the custom among kings.

41 He placed Terah the son of Nahor the prince of his host, and he dignified him and elevated him above all his princes.

42 And while he was reigning according to his heart's desire, after having conquered all his enemies around, he advised with his counselors to build a city for his palace, and they did so.

43 They found a large valley opposite to the east, and they built him a large and extensive city, and Nimrod called the name of the city that he built Shinar, for the Lord had vehemently shaken his enemies and destroyed them.

44 Nimrod lived in Shinar, and he reigned securely, and he fought with his enemies and he subdued them; he prospered in all his battles, and his kingdom became very great.

45 All nations and tongues heard of his fame, and they gathered themselves to him, and they bowed down to the earth; they brought him offerings, and he became their lord and king, and they all lived with him in the city at Shinar; Nimrod reigned in the earth over all the sons of Noah, and they were all under his power and counsel.

46 And all the earth was of one tongue and words of union, but Nimrod did not go in the ways of the Lord; he was more wicked than all the men that were before him, from the days of the flood until those days.

47 He made gods of wood and stone, he bowed down to them, he rebelled against the Lord, and taught all his subjects and the people of the earth his wicked ways; Mardon his son was more wicked than his father.

48 And every one that heard of the acts of Mardon the son of Nimrod would say, concerning him, From the wicked goes forth wickedness. Therefore it became a proverb in the whole earth, saying, From the wicked goes forth wickedness, and it was current in the words of men from that time to this.

49 Terah the son of Nahor, prince of Nimrod's host, was in those days very great in the sight of the king and his subjects, and the king and princes loved him, and they elevated him very high.

50 And Terah took a wife and her name was Amthelo the daughter of Cornebo; the wife of Terah conceived and gave birth to a son in those days.

51 Terah was seventy years old when he had him, and Terah called the name of his son Abram, because the king

had raised him in those days, and dignified him above all his princes that were with him.

CHAPTER 8

1 It was in the night that Abram was born, that all the servants of Terah, and all the wise men of Nimrod and his conjurors came and ate and drank in the house of Terah, and they rejoiced with him on that night.

2 When all the wise men and conjurors went out from the house of Terah, they lifted up their eyes toward heaven that night to look at the stars; they saw, and behold, one very large star came from the east and ran in the heavens; he swallowed up the four stars from the four sides of the heavens.

3 And all the wise men of the king and his conjurors were astonished at the sight, and the sages understood this matter, and they knew its import.

4 They said to each other, This only betokens the child that has been born to Terah this night, who will grow up and be prolific, and reproduce, and possess all the earth, he and his children for ever, and he and his descendants will kill great kings, and inherit their lands.

5 The wise men and conjurors went home that night; in the morning all these wise men and conjurors rose up early, and assembled in an appointed house.

6 And they spoke and said to each other, Behold the sight that we saw last night is hidden from the king; it has not been made known to him.

7 And should this thing get known to the king in the latter days, he will say to us, Why have you concealed this matter from me, and then we shall all suffer death; therefore, now let us go and tell the king the sight which we saw, and the interpretation thereof, and we shall then remain clear.

8 And they did so; they all went to the king and bowed down to him to the ground, and they said, May the king live, may the king live.

9 We heard that a son was born to Terah the son of Nahor, the prince of your host, and we last night came to his house, and we ate and drank and rejoiced with him that night.

10 And when your servants went out from the house of Terah, to go to our respective homes to abide there for the night, we lifted up our eyes to heaven and we saw a great star coming from the east, and the same star ran with great speed and swallowed up four great stars, from the four sides of the heavens.

11 And your servants were astonished at the sight which we saw, and were greatly terrified; we made our judgment on the sight and knew by our wisdom the proper interpretation thereof, that this thing applies to the child that is born to Terah, who will grow up and reproduce greatly, and become powerful and kill all the kings of the earth, and inherit all their lands, he and his offspring forever.

12 Now our lord and king, behold we have truly acquainted you with what we have seen concerning this child.

13 If it seems good to the king to give his father value for this child, we will kill him before he shall grow up and increase in the land, and his evil increase against us, that we and our children perish through his evil.

14 And the king heard their words and they seemed good in his sight, and he sent and called for Terah, and Terah came before the king.

15 And the king said to Terah, I have been told that a son was last night born to you, and after this manner was observed in the heavens at his birth.

16 And now therefore give me the child, that we may kill him before his evil springs up against us, and I will give you for his value, your house full of silver and gold.

17 Terah answered the king and said to him: My Lord and king, I have heard your words, and your servant shall do all that his king desires.

18 But my lord and king, I will tell you what happened to me last night, that I may see what advice the king will give his servant, and then I will answer the king on what he has just spoken. The king said, Speak.

19 And Terah said to the king, Ayon, son of Mored, came to me last night, saying,

20 Give to me the great and beautiful horse that the king gave you, and I will give you silver and gold, and straw and provender for its value; and I said to him, Wait till I see the king concerning your words, and behold whatever the king says, that will I do.

21 And now my lord and king, behold I have made this thing known to you, and the advice which my king will give to his servant, that will I follow.

22 The king heard the words of Terah, and his anger was set ablaze and he considered him in the light of a fool.

23 And the king answered Terah and said to him, Are you so silly, ignorant, or deficient in understanding to do

this thing, to give your beautiful horse for silver and gold or even for straw and provender?

24 Are you so short of silver and gold that you should do this thing, because you cannot obtain straw and provender to feed your horse? And what is silver and gold to you, or straw and provender, that you should give away that fine horse which I gave you, like which there is none to be had on the whole earth?

25 The king left off speaking, and Terah answered the king, saying, Like to this has the king spoken to his servant;

26 I beseech you, my lord and king, what is this which you did say to me, Give your son that we may kill him, and I will give you silver and gold for his value; what shall I do with silver and gold after the death of my son? Who shall inherit me? Certainly then at my death, the silver and gold will return to my king who gave it.

27 And when the king heard the words of Terah, and the parable which he brought concerning the king, it grieved him greatly and he was troubled at this thing, and his anger burned within him.

28 And Terah saw that the anger of the king was set ablaze against him, and he answered the king, saying, All that I have is in the king's power; whatever the king desires to do to his servant, that let him do, yea, even my son, he is in the king's power, without value in exchange, he and his two brothers that are older than he.

29 And the king said to Terah, No, but I will purchase your younger son for a price.

30 Terah answered the king, saying, I beseech you my lord and king to let your servant speak a word before you, and let the king hear the word of his servant, and Terah said, Let my king give me three days' time till I consider this matter within myself, and consult with my family concerning the words of my king; and he pressed the king greatly to agree to this.

31 The king listened to Terah, and he did so and he gave him three days' time. Terah went out from the king's presence, and he came home to his family and spoke to them all the words of the king; and the people were greatly afraid.

32 And it was in the third day that the king sent to Terah, saying, Send me your son for a price as I spoke to you; and should you not do this, I will send and kill all you have in your house, so that you shall not even have a dog remaining.

33 And Terah hurried (as the thing was urgent from the king), and he took a child from one of his servants, which his handmaid had born to him that day, and Terah brought the child to the king and received value for him.

34 And the Lord was with Terah in this matter, that Nimrod might not cause Abram's death. The king took the child from Terah and with all his might dashed his head to the ground, for he thought it had been Abram; this was concealed from him from that day, and it was forgotten by the king, as it was the will of Providence not to suffer Abram's death.

35 And Terah took Abram his son secretly, together with his mother and nurse, and he concealed them in a cave, and he brought them their provisions monthly.

36 The Lord was with Abram in the cave and he grew up, and Abram was in the cave ten years, and the king and his princes, soothsayers and sages, thought that the king had killed Abram.

CHAPTER 9

1 And Haran, the son of Terah, Abram's oldest brother, took a wife in those days.

2 Haran was thirty-nine years old when he took her; and the wife of Haran conceived and gave birth to a son, and he called his name Lot.

3 She conceived again and gave birth to a daughter, and called her name Milca; and she again conceived and gave birth to a daughter and called her name Sarai.

4 Haran was forty-two years old when he had Sarai, which was in the tenth year of the life of Abram; and in those days Abram and his mother and nurse went out from the cave, as the king and his subjects had forgotten the affair of Abram.

5 When Abram came out from the cave, he went to Noah and his son Shem, and he remained with them to learn the instruction of the Lord and his ways; no man knew where Abram was, and Abram served Noah and Shem his son for a long time.

6 Abram was in Noah's house thirty-nine years, and Abram knew the Lord from three years old; he went in the ways of the Lord until the day of his death, as Noah and his son Shem had taught him, and all the sons of the earth in those days greatly went contrary to the Lord, and they rebelled against him and they served other gods. They forgot the Lord who had created them in the earth; and the inhabitants of the earth made to themselves, at that time, every man his god; gods of wood and stone which could neither speak, hear, nor deliver, and the sons

of men served them and they became their gods.

7 The king and all his servants, and Terah with all his household were then the first of those that served gods of wood and stone.

8 And Terah had twelve gods of large size, made of wood and stone, after the twelve months of the year, and he served each one monthly, and every month Terah would bring his meat offering and drink offering to his gods; thus did Terah all the days.

9 All that generation were wicked in the sight of the Lord, and they thus made every man his god, but they turned away from the Lord who had created them.

10 And there was not a man found in those days in the whole earth who knew the Lord (for they served each man his own god) except Noah and his household; and all those who were under his counsel knew the Lord in those days.

11 Abram the son of Terah was becoming great in those days in the house of Noah, and no man knew it, and the Lord was with him.

12 The Lord gave Abram an understanding heart, and he knew all the works of that generation were vain, and that all their gods were vain and were of no avail.

13 And Abram saw the sun shining on the earth, and Abram said to himself, Certainly now this sun that shines on the earth is God, and him will I serve.

14 And Abram served the sun in that day and he prayed to him, and when evening came the sun set as usual, and Abram said within himself, Certainly this cannot be God?

15 And Abram still continued to speak within himself, Who is he who made the heavens and the earth? Who created on earth? Where is he?

16 And night darkened over him; he lifted up his eyes toward the west, north, south, and east, and he saw that the sun had vanished from the earth, and the day became dark.

17 And Abram saw the stars and moon before him, and he said, Certainly this is the God who created the whole earth as well as man, and behold these his servants are gods around him: and Abram served the moon and prayed to it all that night.

18 And in the morning when it was light and the sun shone on the earth as usual, Abram saw all the things that the Lord God had made on earth.

19 And Abram said to himself, Certainly these are not gods that made the earth and all mankind, but these are the servants of God. And Abram remained in the house of Noah and there knew the Lord and his ways. He served the Lord all the days of his life, and all that generation forgot the Lord, and served other gods of wood and stone, and rebelled all their days.

20 And king Nimrod reigned securely, and all the earth was under his control, and all the earth was of one tongue and words of union.

21 And all the princes of Nimrod and his great men took counsel together: Phut, Mitzraim, Cush and Canaan with their families, and they said to each other, Come let us build ourselves a city and in it a strong tower and its top reaching heaven, and we will make ourselves famed so that we may reign on the whole world, in order that the evil of our enemies may cease from us; that we may reign mightily over them, and that we may not become scattered over the earth on account of their wars.

22 They all went before the king, and they told the king these words, and the king agreed with them in this affair, and he did so.

23 All the families assembled consisting of about six hundred thousand men, and they went to seek an extensive piece of ground to build the city and the tower, and they sought in the whole earth and they found none like one valley at the east of the land of Shinar, about two days' walk, and they journeyed there and they lived there.

24 And they began to make bricks and burn fires to build the city and the tower that they had imagined to complete.

25 And the building of the tower was to them a transgression and a sin, and they began to build it While they were building against the Lord God of heaven, they imagined in their hearts to war against him and to ascend into heaven.

26 And all these people and all the families divided themselves in three parts; the first said, We will ascend into heaven and fight against him; the second said, We will ascend to heaven and place our own gods there and serve them; and the third part said, We will ascend to heaven and strike him with bows and spears. And God knew all their works and all their evil thoughts, and he saw the city and the tower which they were building.

27 They built themselves a great city and a very high and strong tower; on account of its height, the mortar and

bricks did not reach the builders in their ascent to it until those who went up had completed a full year, and after that, they reached the builders and gave them the mortar and the bricks; thus was it done daily.

28 And behold these ascended and others descended the whole day; and if a brick should fall from their hands and get broken, they would all weep over it; if a man fell and died, none of them would look at him.

29 The Lord knew their thoughts, and it came to pass when they were building they cast the arrows toward the heavens, and all the arrows fell on them filled with blood; when they saw them they said to each other, Certainly we have slain all those that are in heaven.

30 For this was from the Lord in order to cause them to err, and in order to destroy them from off the face of the ground.

31 They built the tower and the city, and they did this thing daily until many days and years were elapsed.

32 And God said to the seventy angels who stood foremost before him, to those who were near to him, saying, Come let us descend and confuse their tongues, that one man shall not understand the language of his neighbor, and they did so to them.

33 From that day following, they forgot each man his neighbor's tongue, and they could not understand to speak in one tongue; when the builder took from the hands of his neighbor lime or stone which he did not order, the builder would cast it away and throw it on his neighbor, that he would die.

34 And they did so many days, and they killed many of them in this manner.

35 The Lord struck the three divisions that were there, and he punished them according to their works and designs; those who said, We will ascend to heaven and serve our gods, became like apes and elephants; those who said, We will strike the heaven with arrows, the Lord killed them, one man through the hand of his neighbor; and the third division of those who said, We will ascend to heaven and fight against him, the Lord scattered them throughout the earth.

36 Those who were left among them, when they knew and understood the evil which was coming on them, turned away from the building, and they also became scattered on the face of the whole earth.

37 And they ceased building the city and the tower; therefore he called that place Babel, for there the Lord confounded the Language of the whole earth; behold it was at the east of the land of Shinar.

38 As to the tower which the sons of men built, the earth opened its mouth and swallowed up one third part thereof, and a fire also descended from heaven and burned another third, and the other third is left to this day; it is of that part which was aloft, and its circumference is three days' walk.

39 Many of the sons of men died in that tower, a people without number.

CHAPTER 10

1 Peleg the son of Eber died in those days, in the forty-eighth year of the life of Abram son of Terah, and all the days of Peleg were two hundred and thirty-nine years.

2 When the Lord had scattered the sons of men on account of their sin at the tower, behold they spread forth into many divisions, and all the sons of men were dispersed into the four corners of the earth.

3 And all the families became each according to its language, its land, or its city.

4 And the sons of men built many cities according to their families, in all the places where they went, and throughout the earth where the Lord had scattered them.

5 Some of them built cities in places from which they later abandoned, and they called these cities after their own names, or the names of their children, or after their particular occurrences.

6 The sons of Japheth, the son of Noah went and built themselves cities in the places where they were scattered; they called all their cities after their names, and the sons of Japheth were divided on the face of the earth into many divisions and languages.

7 And these are the sons of Japheth according to their families: Gomer, Magog, Medai, Javan, Tubal, Meshech and Tiras; these are the children of Japheth according to their generations.

8 Tthe children of Gomer, according to their cities, were the Francum, who dwell in the land of Franza, by the river Franza, by the river Senah.

9 And the children of Rephath are the Bartonim, who dwell in the land of Bartonia by the river Ledah, which empties its waters in the great sea Gihon, that is, Oceanus.

10 The children of Tugarma are ten families, and these are their names: Buzar, Parzunac, Balgar, Elicanum, Ragbib, Tarki, Bid, Zebuc, Ongal and Tilmaz; all these spread and rested in the north and built themselves cities.

11 And they called their cities after their own names; those are they who abide by the rivers Hithlah and Italac to

this day.

12 But the families of Angoli, Balgar and Parzunac, they dwelll by the great river Dubnee; and the names of their cities are also according to their own names.

13 The children of Javan are the Javanim who dwell in the land of Makdonia, and the children of Medaiare are the Orelum that dwell in the land of Curson, and the children of Tubal are those that dwell in the land of Tuskanah by the river Pashiah.

14 The children of Meshech are the Shibashni and the children of Tiras are Rushash, Cushni, and Ongolis; all these went and built themselves cities; those are the cities that are situated by the sea Jabus by the river Cura, which empties itself into the river Tragan.

15 And the children of Elishah are the Almanim, and they also went and built themselves cities; those are the cities situated between the mountains of Job and Shibathmo; and of them were the people of Lumbardi who dwell opposite the mountains of Job and Shibathmo, and they conquered the land of Italia and remained there to this day.

16 The children of Chittim are the Romim who dwell in the valley of Canopia by the river Tibreu.

17 The children of Dudonim are those who dwell in the cities of the sea Gihon, in the land of Bordna.

18 These are the families of the children of Japheth according to their cities and languages when they were scattered after the tower; they called their cities after their names and occurrences; and these are the names of all their cities according to their families which they built in those days after the tower.

19 And the children of Ham were Cush, Mitzraim, Phut and Canaan according to their generation and cities.

20 All these went and built themselves cities as they found fit places for them, and they called their cities after the names of their fathers Cush, Mitzraim, Phut and Canaan.

21 The children of Mitzraim are the Ludim, Anamim, Lehabim, Naphtuchim, Pathrusim, Casluchim and Caphturim, seven families.

22 All these dwell by the river Sihor, that is the brook of Egypt, and they built themselves cities and called them after their own names.

23 The children of Pathros and Casloch intermarried together, and from them went forth the Pelishtim, the Azathim, and the Gerarim, the Githim and the Ekronim, in all five families; these also built themselves cities, and they called their cities after the names of their fathers to this day.

24 The children of Canaan also built themselves cities, and they called their cities after their names, eleven cities and others without number.

25 Four men from the family of Ham went to the land of the plain; these are the names of the four men: Sodom, Gomorrah, Admah and Zeboyim.

26 And these men built themselves four cities in the land of the plain, and they called the names of their cities after their own names.

27 They and their children and all belonging to them lived in those cities, and they were prolific and multiplied greatly and lived peaceably.

28 Seir the son of Hur, son of Hivi, son of Canaan, went and found a valley opposite to Mount Paran, and he built a city there; he and his seven sons and his household lived there, and he called the city which he built Seir, according to his name; that is the land of Seir to this day.

29 These are the families of the children of Ham, according to their languages and cities, when they were scattered to their countries after the tower.

30 Some of the children of Shem, son of Noah, father of all the children of Eber, also went and built themselves cities in the places wherein they were scattered, and they called their cities after their names.

31 The sons of Shem were Elam, Ashur, Arpachshad, Lud and Aram, and they built themselves cities and called the names of all their cities after their names.

32 Ashur, son of Shem, and his children and household went forth at that time, a very large body of them, and they went to a distant land that they found; they met with a very extensive valley in the land that they went to, and they built themselves four cities, and they called them after their own names and occurrences.

33 And these are the names of the cities which the children of Ashur built: Ninevah, Resen, Calach and Rehobother; the children of Ashur dwell there to this day.

34 The children of Aram also went and built themselves a city, and they called the name of the city Uz after their eldest brother; they dwell therein. That is the land of Uz to this day.

35 And in the second year after the tower a man from the house of Ashur, whose name was Bela, went from the land of Ninevah to sojourn with his household wherever he could find a place; they came until opposite the cities

of the plain against Sodom, and they lived there.

36 And the man rose up and built there a small city, and called its name Bela, after his name; that is the land of Zoar to this day.

37 These are the families of the children of Shem according to their language and cities, after they were scattered on the earth after the tower.

38 And every kingdom, city, and family of the families of the children of Noah built themselves many cities after this.

39 And they established governments in all their cities in order to be regulated by their orders; so did all the families of the children of Noah forever.

CHAPTER 11

1 Nimrod son of Cush was still in the land of Shinar, and he reigned over it and lived there, and he built cities in the land of Shinar.

2 These are the names of the four cities which he built, and he called their names after the occurrences that happened to them in the building of the tower:

3 He called the first Babel, saying, Because the Lord there confounded the language of the whole earth.   The name of the second he called Erech, because from there God dispersed them.

4 And the third he called Eched, saying there was a great battle at that place; the fourth he called Calnah, because his princes and mighty men were consumed there, and they troubled the Lord; they rebelled and went contrary to him.

5 When Nimrod had built these cities in the land of Shinar, he placed in them the remainder of his people, his princes and his mighty men that were left in his kingdom.

6 Nimrod lived in Babel, and there he renewed his reign over the rest of his subjects, and he reigned securely, and the subjects and princes of Nimrod called his name Amraphel, saying that at the tower his princes and men fell through his means.

7 Notwithstanding this, Nimrod did not return to the Lord, and he continued in wickedness and teaching wickedness to the sons of men; and Mardon, his son, was worse than his father and continued to add to the abominations of his father.

8 And he caused the sons of men to sin; therefore it is said, From the wicked goes forth wickedness.

9 At that time there was war between the families of the children of Ham, as they were dwelling in the cities which they had built.

10 And Chedorlaomer, king of Elam, went away from the families of the children of Ham; he fought with them and he subdued them, and he went to the five cities of the plain; he fought against them and he subdued them, and they were under his control.

11 And they served him twelve years and gave him a yearly tax.

12 At that time Nahor, son of Serug died, in the forty-ninth year of the life of Abram, son of Terah.

13 In the fiftieth year of the life of Abram, son of Terah, Abram came forth from the house of Noah, and went to his father's house.

14 And Abram knew the Lord, and he followed in his ways and instructions, and the Lord his God was with him.

15 Terah his father was in those days still captain of the host of king Nimrod, and he still followed strange gods.

16 And Abram came to his father's house and saw twelve gods standing there in their temples, and the anger of Abram was set ablaze when he saw these images in his father's house.

17 And Abram said, As the Lord lives these images shall not remain in my father's house; so shall the Lord who created me do to me if in three days' time I do not break them all.

18 Abram went from them, and his anger burned within him. And Abram hurried and went from the chamber to his father's outer court, and he found his father sitting in the court, and all his servants with him, and Abram came and sat before him.

19 Abram asked his father, saying, Father, tell me where is God who created heaven and earth, and all the sons of men on earth, and who created you and me. And Terah answered his son Abram and said, Behold those who created us are all with us in the house.

20 And Abram said to his father, My lord, show them to me I pray you. And Terah brought Abram into the chamber of the inner court, and Abram saw, and behold the whole room was full of gods of wood and stone, twelve great images and others less than they without number.

21 And Terah said to his son, Behold these are they which made all you see on earth, and which created me and

you, and all mankind.

22 Terah bowed down to his gods, and he then went away from them, and Abram, his son, went away with him.

23 When Abram had gone from them he went to his mother and sat before her, and he said to his mother, Behold, my father has shown me those who made heaven and earth, and all the sons of men.

24 Now, therefore, hurry and fetch a kid from the flock, and make of it savory meat, that I may bring it to my father's gods as an offering for them to eat; perhaps I may thereby become acceptable to them.

25 And his mother did so; she fetched a kid, and made savory meat thereof, and brought it to Abram, and Abram took the savory meat from his mother and brought it before his father's gods, and he drew nigh to them that they might eat; and Terah his father, did not know of it.

26 Abram saw on the day when he was sitting among them, that they had no voice, no hearing, no motion, and not one of them could stretch forth his hand to eat.

27 And Abram mocked them, and said, Certainly the savory meat that I prepared has not pleased them, or perhaps it was too little for them, and for that reason they would not eat; therefore tomorrow I will prepare fresh savory meat, better and more plentiful than this, in order that I may see the result.

28 It was on the next day that Abram directed his mother concerning the savory meat, and his mother rose and fetched three fine kids from the flock; she made of them some excellent savory meat, such as her son was fond of, and she gave it to her son Abram, and Terah his father did not know of it.

29 Abram took the savory meat from his mother and brought it before his father's gods into the chamber; he came nigh to them that they might eat, and he placed it before them, and Abram sat before them all day thinking perhaps they might eat.

30 Abram viewed them, and behold they had neither voice nor hearing, nor did one of them stretch forth his hand to the meat to eat.

31 And in the evening of that day in that house Abram was clothed with the spirit of God.

32 He called out and said, Woe to my father and this wicked generation, whose hearts are all inclined to vanity, who serve these idols of wood and stone which can neither eat, smell, hear nor speak, who have mouths without speech, eyes without sight, ears without hearing, hands without feeling, and legs which cannot move; like them are those that made them and that trust in them.

33 When Abram saw all these things his anger was set ablaze against his father, and he hurried and took a hatchet in his hand, and came to the chamber of the gods; he broke all his father's gods.

34 And when he was done breaking the images, he placed the hatchet in the hand of the great god which was there before them, and he went out; and Terah his father came home, for he had heard at the door the sound of the striking of the hatchet; so Terah came into the house to know what this was about.

35 Terah, having heard the noise of the hatchet in the room of images, ran to the room to the images, and he met Abram going out.

36 And Terah entered the room and found all the idols fallen down and broken, and the hatchet in the hand of the largest, which was not broken, and the savory meat which Abram his son had made was still before them.

37 When Terah saw this his anger was greatly set ablaze, and he hurried and went from the room to Abram.

38 And he found Abram his son still sitting in the house; and he said to him, What is this work you have done to my gods?

39 Abram answered Terah his father and he said, Not so my lord, for I brought savory meat before them, and when I came near to them with the meat that they might eat, they all at once stretched forth their hands to eat before the great one had put forth his hand to eat.

40 And the large one saw their works that they did before him, and his anger was violently set ablaze against them, and he went and took the hatchet that was in the house and came to them and broke them all, and behold the hatchet is yet in his hand as you see.

41 And Terah's anger was set ablaze against his son Abram, when he spoke this; and Terah said to Abram his son in his anger, What is this tale that you have told? You speak lies to me.

42 Is there in these gods spirit, soul or power to do all you have told me? Are they not wood and stone, and have I not myself made them, and can you speak such lies, saying that the large god that was with them struck them? It is you that did place the hatchet in his hands, and then said he struck them all.

43 Abram answered his father and said to him, And how can you then serve these idols in whom there is no power to do any thing? Can those idols in which you trust deliver you? Can they hear your prayers when you call on them? Can they deliver you from the hands of your enemies, or will they fight your battles for you against your enemies, that you should serve wood and stone which can neither speak nor hear?

44 And now certainly it is not good for you nor for the sons of men that are connected with you, to do these things; are you so silly, so foolish or so short of understanding that you will serve wood and stone, and do after this manner?

45 And forget the Lord God who made heaven and earth, and who created you in the earth, and thereby bring a great evil on your souls in this matter by serving stone and wood?

46 Did not our fathers in days of old sin in this manner, and the Lord God of the universe brought the waters of the flood on them and destroyed the whole earth?

47 And how can you continue to do this and serve gods of wood and stone, who cannot hear, or speak, or deliver you from oppression, thereby bringing down the anger of the God of the universe on you?

48 Now therefore my father refrain from this, and bring not evil on your soul and the souls of your household.

49 And Abram hurried and sprang from before his father, and took the hatchet from his father's largest idol, with which Abram broke it and ran away.

50 Terah, seeing all that Abram had done, hurried to go from his house; he went to the king and he came before Nimrod and stood before him, and he bowed down to the king and the king said, What do you want?

51 And he said, I beseech you my lord, to hear me--Now fifty years back a child was born to me, and thus has he done to my gods and thus has he spoken; and now therefore, my lord and king, send for him that he may come before you, and judge him according to the law, that we may be delivered from his evil.

52 The king sent three men of his servants, and they went and brought Abram before the king. And Nimrod and all his princes and servants were that day sitting before him, and Terah also sat before them.

53 And the king said to Abram, What is this that you have done to your father and to his gods? And Abram answered the king in the words that he spoke to his father, and he said, The large god that was with them in the house did to them what you have heard.

54 And the king said to Abram, Had they power to speak and eat and do as you have said? And Abram answered the king, saying, And if there be no power in them why do you serve them and cause the sons of men to err through your follies?

55 Do you imagine that they can deliver you or do anything small or great, that you should serve them? And why will you not sense the God of the whole universe, who created you and in whose power it is to kill and keep alive?

56 0 foolish, simple, and ignorant king, woe to you forever.

57 I thought you would teach your servants the upright way, but you have not done this; you have filled the whole earth with your sins and the sins of your people who have followed your ways.

58 Do you not know, or have you not heard, that this evil which you do, our ancestors sinned therein in days of old, and the eternal God brought the waters of the flood on them and destroyed them all, and also destroyed the whole earth on their account? And will you and your people rise up now and do like this work, in order to bring down the anger of the Lord God of the universe, and to bring evil on you and the whole earth?

59 Now therefore put away this evil deed which you did, and serve the God of the universe, as your soul is in his hands, and then it will be well with you.

60 And if your wicked heart will not listen to my words to cause you to turn away from your evil ways, and to serve the eternal God, then you will die in shame in the latter days, you, your people and all who are connected with you, hearing your words or walking in your evil ways.

61 When Abram had ceased speaking before the king and princes, Abram lifted up his eyes to the heavens, and he said, The Lord sees all the wicked, and he will judge them.

CHAPTER 12

1 When the king heard the words of Abram he ordered him to be put into prison; and Abram was ten days in prison.

2 At the end of those days the king ordered that all the kings, princes and governors of different provinces and the sages should come before him, and they sat before him, and Abram was still in the house of confinement.

3 The king said to the princes and sages, Have you heard what Abram, the son of Terah, has done to his father? Thus has he done to him, and I ordered him to be brought before me, and thus has he spoken; his heart did not misgive him, neither did he stir in my presence, and behold now he is confined in the prison.

4 Therefore decide what judgment is due to this man who reviled the king; who spoke and did all the things that

you heard.

5 And they all answered the king saying, The man who reviles the king should be hanged on a tree; but having done all the things that he said and having despised our gods, he must therefore be burned to death, for this is the law in this matter.

6 If it pleases the king to do this, let him order his servants to kindle a fire both night and day in your brick furnace, and then we will cast this man into it. And the king did so, and he commanded his servants that they should prepare a fire for three days and three nights in the king's furnace, that is in Casdim; and the king ordered them to take Abram from prison and bring him out to be burned.

7 And all the king's servants, princes, lords, governors, and judges, and all the inhabitants of the land, about nine hundred thousand men, stood opposite the furnace to see Abram.

8 And all the women and little ones crowded on the roofs and towers to see what was going on with Abram, and they all stood together at a distance; and there was not a man left that did not come that day to behold the scene.

9 When Abram was come, the conjurors of the king and the sages saw Abram, and they cried out to the king, saying, Our sovereign lord, certainly this is the man whom we know to have been the child at whose birth the great star swallowed the four stars, which we declared to the king fifty years ago.

10 And behold now his father has also gone contrary to your commands, and mocked you by bringing you another child, which you did kill.

11 And when the king heard their words, he was greatly angered, and he ordered Terah to be brought before him.

12 And the king said, Have you heard what the conjurors have spoken? Now tell me truly, how did you? If you shall speak truth you shall be acquitted.

13 Seeing that the king's anger was so much set ablaze, Terah said to the king, My lord and king, you have heard the truth, and what the sages have spoken is right. And the king said, How could you do this thing, to go contrary to my orders and to give me a child that you did not beget, and to take value for him?

14 Terah answered the king, Because my tender feelings were excited for my son, at that time, I took a son of my handmaid, and I brought him to the king.

15 And the king said, Who advised you to do this? Tell me, do not hide anything from me, and then you shall not die.

16 And Terah was greatly terrified in the king's presence, and he said to the king, It was Haran my eldest son who advised me to do this. Haran was in those days that Abram was born, two and thirty years old.

17 But Haran did not advise his father to do anything, for Terah said this to the king in order to deliver his soul from the king, for he feared greatly. The king said to Terah, Haran your son who advised you to do this shall die through fire with Abram; for the sentence of death is on him for having rebelled against the king's desire in doing this thing.

18 Haran at that time felt inclined to follow the ways of Abram, but he kept it within himself.

19 And Haran said in his heart, Behold now the king has seized Abram on account of these things which Abram did, and it shall come to pass, that if Abram prevail over the king I will follow him, but if the king prevail I will go after the king.

20 When Terah had spoken this to the king concerning Haran his son, the king ordered Haran to be seized with Abram.

21 And they brought them both, Abram and Haran his brother, to cast them into the fire; and all the inhabitants of the land and the king's servants and princes and all the women and little ones were there standing over them that day.

22 And the king's servants took Abram and his brother, and they stripped them of all their clothes excepting their lower garments which were on them.

23 And they bound their hands and feet with linen cords, and the servants of the king lifted them up and cast them both into the furnace.

24 The Lord loved Abram and he had compassion over him, and the Lord came down and delivered Abram from the fire and he was not burned.

25 But all the cords with which they bound him were burned, while Abram remained and walked about in the fire.

26 Haran died when they had cast him into the fire, and he was burned to ashes, for his heart was not perfect with the Lord; and those men who cast him into the fire, the flame of the fire spread over them, and they were burned, and twelve of them died.

27 Abram walked in the midst of the fire three days and three nights, and all the servants of the king saw him

walking in the fire, and they came and told the king, saying, Behold we have seen Abram walking about in the midst of the fire, and even the lower garments which are on him are not burned, but the cord with which he was bound is burned.

28 When the king heard their words his heart fainted and he would not believe them; so he sent other faithful princes to see this matter, and they went and saw it and told it to the king. And the king rose to go and see it, and he saw Abram walking to and fro in the midst of the fire, and he saw Haran's body burned, and the king wondered greatly.

29 The king ordered Abram to be taken out from the fire; and his servants approached to take him out and they could not, for the fire was round about and the flame ascending toward them from the furnace.

30 The king's servants fled from it, and the king rebuked them, saying, Make haste and bring Abram out of the fire that you shall not die.

31 The servants of the king again approached to bring Abram out, and the flames came on them and burned their faces so that eight of them died.

32 When the king saw that his servants could not approach the fire that would burn them,, the king called to Abram, O servant of the God who is in heaven, go forth from amidst the fire and come here before me. And Abram listened to the voice of the king, and he went forth from the fire and came and stood before the king.

33 When Abram came out, the king and all his servants saw Abram coming before the king with his lower garments on him that were not burned, but the cord with which he was bound was burned.

34 And the king said to Abram, How is it that you were not burned in the fire?

35 Abram said to the king, The God of heaven and earth in whom I trust and who has all in his power, he delivered me from the fire into which you did cast me.

36 Haran the brother of Abram was burned to ashes, and they sought for his body; they found it consumed.

37 Haran was eighty-two years old when he died in the fire of Casdim. And the king, princes, and inhabitants of the land, seeing that Abram was delivered from the fire, came and bowed down to Abram.

38 And Abram said to them, Do not bow down to me, but bow down to the God of the world who made you, and serve him, and go in his ways for it is he who delivered me from out of this fire; it is he who created the souls and spirits of all men, and formed man in his mother's womb, and brought him forth into the world; it is he who will deliver those who trust in him from all pain.

39 This thing seemed very wonderful in the eyes of the king and princes, that Abram was saved from the fire and that Haran was burned. And the king gave Abram many presents and he gave him his two head servants from the king's house; the name of one was Oni and the name of the other was Eliezer.

40 All the kings, princes and servants gave Abram many gifts of silver and gold and pearl, and the king and his princes sent him away, and he went in peace.

41 Abram went forth from the king in peace, and many of the king's servants followed him, and about three hundred men joined him.

42 And Abram returned on that day and went to his father's house, he and the men that followed him, and Abram served the Lord his God all the days of his life; he walked in his ways and followed his law.

43 From that day forward Abram inclined the hearts of the sons of men to serve the Lord.

44 At that time Nahor and Abram took to themselves wives, the daughters of their brother Haran; the wife of Nahor was Milca and the name of Abram's wife was Sarai. And Sarai, wife of Abram, was unable to conceive; she had no children in those days.

45 At the expiration of two years from Abram's going out of the fire, that is in the fifty-second year of his life, behold king Nimrod sat in Babel on the throne, and the king fell asleep and dreamed that he was standing with his troops and hosts in a valley opposite the king's furnace.

46 And he lifted up his eyes and saw a man in the likeness of Abram coming forth from the furnace; he came and stood before the king with his drawn sword, and then sprang to the king with his sword, when the king fled from the man, for he was afraid; while he was running, the man threw an egg on the king's head, and the egg became a great river.

47 And the king dreamed that all his troops sank in that river and died, and the king took flight with three men who were before him and he escaped.

48 The king looked at these men and they were clothed in princely dresses as the garments of kings, and had the appearance and majesty of kings.

49 And while they were running, the river again turned to an egg before the king; there came forth from the egg a young bird which came before the king, and flew at his head and plucked out the king's eye.

50 The king was grieved at the sight, and he awoke out of his sleep and his spirit was agitated; he felt a great terror.

51 In the morning the king rose from his couch in fear, and he ordered all the wise men and magicians to come before him, when the king related his dream to them.

52 And a wise servant of the king, whose name was Anuki, answered the king, saying, This is nothing else but the evil of Abram and his offspring which will spring up against my Lord and king in the latter days.

53 And behold the day will come when Abram and his offspring and the children of his household will war with my king, and they will strike all the king's hosts and his troops.

54 And as to what you have said concerning three men which you did see like yourself, and which did escape, this means that only you will escape with three kings from the kings of the earth who will be with you in battle.

55 And that which you saw of the river which turned to an egg as at first, and the young bird plucking out your eye, this means nothing else but the offspring of Abram which will kill the king in latter days.

56 This is my king's dream, and this is its interpretation, and the dream is true, and the interpretation which your servant has given you is right.

57 Now therefore my king, certainly you know that it is now fifty-two years since your sages saw this at the birth of Abram, and if my king will suffer Abram to live in the earth it will be to the injury of my lord and king, for all the days that Abram lives neither you nor your kingdom will be established, for this was known formerly at his birth; and why will not my king kill him, that his evil may be kept from you in latter days?

58 And Nimrod listened to the voice of Anuki; he sent some of his servants in secret to go and seize Abram and bring him before the king to suffer death.

59 Eliezer, Abram's servant whom the king had given him, was at that time in the presence of the king, and he heard what Anuki had advised the king, and what the king had said to cause Abram's death.

60 Eliezer said to Abram, Hasten, rise up and save your soul, that you may not die through the hands of the king, for thus did he see in a dream concerning you, and thus did Anuki interpret it, and thus also did Anuki advise the king concerning you.

61 Abram listened to the voice of Eliezer, and Abram hurried and ran for safety to the house of Noah and his son Shem, and he concealed himself there and found a place of safety; and the king's servants came to Abram's house to seek him, but they could not find him, and they searched throughout the country and he was not to be found; they went and searched in every direction and he was not to be met with.

62 And when the king's servants could not find Abram they returned to the king, but the king's anger against Abram was stilled, as they did not find him, and the king drove from his mind this matter concerning Abram.

63 Abram was concealed in Noah's house for one month, until the king had forgotten this matter, but Abram was still afraid of the king; and Terah came to see Abram his son secretly in the house of Noah, and Terah was very great in the eyes of the king.

64 Abram said to his father, Do you not know that the king thinks to kill me, and to annihilate my name from the earth by the advice of his wicked counselors?

65 Now whom have you here and what have you in this land? Arise, let us go together to the land of Canaan, that we may be delivered from his hand, that you not perish also through him in the latter days.

66 Do you not know or have you not heard, that it is not through love that Nimrod gives you all this honor, but it is only for his benefit that he bestows all this good on you?

67 And if he does to you greater good than this, certainly these are only vanities of the world, for wealth and riches cannot avail in the day of wrath and anger.

68 Now therefore listen to my voice, and let us arise and go to the land of Canaan, out of the reach of injury from Nimrod; and serve the Lord who created you in the earth and it will be well with you; and cast away all the vain things which you pursue.

69 And Abram ceased to speak when Noah and his son Shem answered Terah, saying, True is the word which Abram hath said to you.

70 And Terah listened to the voice of his son Abram, and Terah did all that Abram said, for this was from the Lord that the king should not cause Abram's death.

CHAPTER 13

1 Terah took his son Abram and his grandson Lot, the son of Haran, and Sarai his daughter-in-law, the wife of his son Abram, and all the souls of his household and went with them from Ur Casdim to go to the land of Canaan.

And when they came as far as the land of Haran they remained there, for it was very good land for pasture, and of sufficient territory for those who accompanied them.

2 And the people of the land of Haran saw that Abram was good and upright with God and men, and that the Lord his God was with him. Some of the people of the land of Haran came and joined Abram, and he taught them the instruction of the Lord and his ways; these men remained with Abram in his house and they adhered to him.

3 Abram remained in the land three years, and at the expiration of three years the Lord appeared to Abram and said to him; I am the Lord who brought you forth from Ur Casdim, and delivered you from the hands of all your enemies.

4 Now therefore if you will listen to my voice and keep my commandments, my statutes and my laws, I will cause your enemies to fall before you. I will reproduce your descendants like the stars of heaven, and I will send my blessing on all the works of your hands, and you shall lack nothing.

5 Arise now, take your wife and all belonging to you and go to the land of Canaan and remain there. And I, God, will be there for you and I will bless you. And Abram rose and took his wife and all belonging to him, and he went to the land of Canaan as the Lord had told him; and Abram was fifty years old when he went from Haran.

6 Abram came to the land of Canaan and lived in the midst of the city, and there he pitched his tent among the children of Canaan, inhabitants of the land.

7 The Lord appeared to Abram when he came to the land of Canaan, and said to him, This is the land which I gave to you and to your descendants after you forever, and I will make them like the stars of heaven, and I will give to your descendants all the lands which you see for an inheritance.

8 And Abram built an altar in the place where God had spoken to him, and there Abram called on the name of the Lord.

9 At that time, at the end of three years of Abram's dwelling in the land of Canaan, in that year Noah died, which was the fifty-eighth year of the life of Abram; all the days that Noah lived were nine hundred and fifty years and he died.

10 Abram lived in the land of Canaan, he, his wife, and all belonging to him, and all those that accompanied him, together with those that joined him from the people of the land; but Nahor, Abram's brother, and Terah his father, and Lot the son of Haran and all belonging to them lived in Haran.

11 In the fifth year of Abram's dwelling in the land of Canaan the people of Sodom and Gomorrah and all the cities of the plain revolted from the power of Chedorlaomer, king of Elam; for all the kings of the cities of the plain had served Chedorlaomer for twelve years, and given him a yearly tax, but in those days in the thirteenth year, they rebelled against him.

12 In the tenth year of Abram's dwelling in the land of Canaan there was war between Nimrod king of Shinar and Chedorlaomer king of Elam, and Nimrod came to fight with Chedorlaomer and to subdue him.

13 For Chedorlaomer was at that time one of the princes of the hosts of Nimrod, and when all the people at the tower were dispersed and those that remained were also scattered on the face of the earth, Chedorlaomer went to the land of Elam and reigned over it and rebelled against his lord.

14 In those days when Nimrod saw that the cities of the plain had rebelled, he came with pride and anger to war with Chedorlaomer, and Nimrod assembled all his princes and subjects, about seven hundred thousand men, and went against Chedorlaomer, and Chedorlaomer went out to meet him with five thousand men, and they prepared for battle in the valley of Babel which is between Elam and Shinar.

15 All those kings fought there, and Nimrod and his people were smitten before the people of Chedorlaomer, and there fell from Nimrod's men about six hundred thousand, and Mardon the king's son fell among them.

16 And Nimrod fled and returned in shame and disgrace to his land, and he was under subjection to Chedorlaomer for a long time, and Chedorlaomer returned to his land and sent princes of his host to the kings that lived around him, to Arioch king of Elasar, and to Tidal king of Goyim, and made a covenant with them, and they were all obedient to his commands.

17 It was in the fifteenth year of Abram's dwelling in the land of Canaan, which is the seventieth year of the life of Abram, the Lord appeared to Abram in that year and said to him, I am the Lord who brought you out from Ur Casdim to give you this land for an inheritance.

18 Now therefore walk before me and be perfect and keep my commands, for to you and to your descendants I will give this land for an inheritance, from the river Mitzraim to the great river Euphrates.

19 And you shall come to your fathers in peace and in good age, and the fourth generation shall return here in this land and shall inherit it forever. And Abram built an altar, and he called on the name of the Lord who appeared to him, and he brought up sacrifices on the altar to the Lord.

20 At that time Abram returned and went to Haran to see his father and mother, and his father's household, and Abram and his wife and all belonging to him returned to Haran; Abram lived in Haran five years.

21 And many of the people of Haran, about seventy-two men, followed Abram and Abram taught them the instruction of the Lord and his ways, and he taught them to know the Lord.

22 In those days the Lord appeared to Abram in Haran, and he said to him, Behold, I spoke to you twenty years ago saying,

23 Go forth from your land, from your birth-place and from your father's house, to the land which I have shown you to give it to you and to your children, for there in that land I will bless you, and make you a great nation, and make your name great, and in you shall the families of the earth be blessed.

24 Now therefore arise, go forth from this place, you, your wife, and all belonging to you, also every one born in your house and all the souls you have made in Haran, and bring them out with you from here, and rise to return to the land of Canaan.

25 And Abram arose and took his wife Sarai and all belonging to him and all that were born to him in his house and the souls which they had made in Haran, and they came out to go to the land of Canaan.

26 Abram went and returned to the land of Canaan, according to the word of the Lord. And Lot the son of his brother Haran went with him; Abram was seventy-five years old when he went forth from Haran to return to the land of Canaan.

27 And he came to the land of Canaan according to the word of the Lord to Abram, and he pitched his tent and he lived in the plain of Mamre, and with him was Lot his brother's son, and all belonging to him.

28 And the Lord again appeared to Abram and said, To your offspring I will give this land; there he built an altar to the Lord who appeared to him, which is still to this day in the plains of Mamre.

CHAPTER 14

1 In those days there was in the land of Shinar a wise man who had understanding in all wisdom, and of a beautiful appearance, but he was poor and indigent; his name was Rikayon and he was hard set to support himself.

2 And he resolved to go to Egypt, to Oswiris the son of Anom king of Egypt, to show the king his wisdom; for perhaps he might find grace in his sight, to raise him up and give him maintenance; and Rikayon did so.

3 When Rikayon came to Egypt he asked the inhabitants of Egypt concerning the king, and the inhabitants of Egypt told him the custom of the king of Egypt, for it was then the custom of the king of Egypt that he went from his royal palace and was seen abroad only one day in the year, and after that the king would return to his palace to remain there.

4 On the day when the king went forth he passed judgment in the land, and every one having a suit came before the king that day to obtain his request.

5 When Rikayon heard of the custom in Egypt and that he could not come into the presence of the king, he grieved greatly and was very sorrowful.

6 In the evening Rikayon went out and found a house in ruins, formerly a bake house in Egypt, and he abode there all night in bitterness of soul and pinched with hunger, and sleep was removed from his eyes.

7 And Rikayon considered within himself what he should do in the town until the king made his appearance, and how he might maintain himself there.

8 And he rose in the morning and walked about, and met in his way those who sold vegetables and various sorts of offspring with which they supplied the inhabitants.

9 Rikayon wished to do the same in order to get a maintenance in the city, but he was unacquainted with the custom of the people, and he was like a blind man among them.

10 And he went and obtained vegetables to sell for his support, and the crowd assembled about him and ridiculed him, and took his vegetables from him and left him nothing.

11 He rose up from there in bitterness of soul, and went sighing to the bake house in which he had remained all the night before, and he slept there the second night.

12 On that night again he reasoned within himself how he could save himself from starvation, and he devised a scheme how to act.

13 And he rose up in the morning and acted ingeniously, and went and hired thirty strong men of the crowd, carrying their war instruments in their hands, and he led them to the top of the Egyptian sepulchre, and he placed

them there.

14 He commanded them, saying, Thus says the king, Strengthen yourselves and be valiant men, and let no man be buried here until two hundred pieces of silver be given, and then he may be buried; and those men did according to the order of Rikayon to the people of Egypt the whole of that year.

15 In eight months time Rikayon and his men gathered great riches of silver and gold, and Rikayon took a great quantity of horses and other animals, and he hired more men, and he gave them horses and they remained with him.

16 When the year came round, at the time the king went forth into the town, all the inhabitants of Egypt assembled together to speak to him concerning the work of Rikayon and his men.

17 The king went forth on the appointed day, and all the Egyptians came before him and cried to him, saying,

18 May the king live forever. What is this thing you do in the town to your servants, not to allow a dead body buried until so much silver and gold be given? Was there ever the like to this done in the whole earth, from the days of former kings, yes even from the days of Adam, to this day, that the dead should be buried only for a set price?

19 We know it to be the custom of kings to take a yearly tax from the living, but you do not only do this, but from the dead also you exact a tax day by day.

20 Now, O king, we can no more bear this, for the whole city is ruined on this account, and do you not know it?

21 When the king heard all that they had spoken he was very angry, and his anger burned within him at this affair, for he had known nothing of it.

22 And the king said, Who and where is he that dares to do this wicked thing in my land without my command? Certainly you will tell me.

23 They told him all the works of Rikayon and his men, and the king's anger was aroused, and he ordered Rikayon and his men to be brought before him.

24 And Rikayon took about a thousand children, sons and daughters, and clothed them in silk and embroidery, and he set them on horses and sent them to the king by means of his men, and he also took a great quantity of silver and gold and precious stones, and a strong and beautiful horse, as a present for the king, with which he came before the king and bowed down to the earth before him; the king, his servants and all the inhabitants of Egypt wondered at the work of Rikayon; they saw his riches and the presents that he had brought to the king.

25 It greatly pleased the king and he wondered at it; and when Rikayon sat before him the king asked him concerning all his works, and Rikayon spoke all his words wisely before the king, his servants and all the inhabitants of Egypt.

26 When the king heard the words of Rikayon and his wisdom, Rikayon found grace in his sight, and he met with grace and kindness from all the servants of the king and from all the inhabitants of Egypt, on account of his wisdom and excellent speeches, and from that time they loved him greatly.

27 And the king answered and said to Rikayon, Thy name shall no more be called Rikayon but Pharaoh shall be your name, since you did exact a tax from the dead; and he called his name Pharaoh.

28 The king and his subjects loved Rikayon for his wisdom, and they consulted with all the inhabitants of Egypt to make him prefect under the king.

29 All the inhabitants of Egypt and its wise men did so, and it was made a law in Egypt.

30 They made Rikayon Pharaoh prefect under Oswiris king of Egypt, and Rikayon Pharaoh governed over Egypt, daily administering justice to the whole city, but Oswiris the king would judge the people of the land one day in the year, when he went out to make his appearance.

31 And Rikayon Pharaoh cunningly usurped the government of Egypt, and he exacted a tax from all the inhabitants of Egypt.

32 And all the inhabitants of Egypt greatly loved Rikayon Pharaoh, and they made a decree to call every king that should reign over them and their descendants in Egypt, Pharaoh.

33 Therefore all the kings that reigned in Egypt from that time forward were called Pharaoh to this day.

CHAPTER 15

1 In that year there was a heavy famine throughout the land of Canaan, and the inhabitants of the land could not remain on account of the famine for it was very severe.

2 Abram and all belonging to him rose and went down to Egypt on account of the famine, and when they were at

the brook Mitzraim they remained there some time to rest from the fatigue of the road.

3 Abram and Sarai were walking at the border of the brook Mitzraim, and Abram beheld his wife Sarai that she was very beautiful.

4 And Abram said to his wife Sarai, Since God has created you with such a beautiful countenance, I am afraid of the Egyptians that they will kill me and take you away, for the fear of God is not in these places.

5 Certainly then you shall do this, Say you are my sister to all that may ask you, in order that it may be well with me, and that we may live and not be put to death.

6 And Abram commanded the same to all those that came with him to Egypt on account of the famine; also his nephew Lot he commanded, saying, If the Egyptians ask you concerning Sarai say she is the sister of Abram.

7 And yet with all these orders Abram did not put confidence in them, but he took Sarai and placed her in a chest and concealed it among their vessels, for Abram was greatly concerned about Sarai on account of the wickedness of the Egyptians.

8 Abram and all belonging to him rose up from the brook Mitzraim and came to Egypt; and they had scarcely entered the gates of the city when the guards stood up to them saying, Give tithe to the king from what you have, and then you may come into the town; Abram and those that were with him did so.

9 Abram and the people that were with him came to Egypt and they brought the chest in which Sarai was concealed, and the Egyptians saw the chest.

10 And the king's servants approached Abram, saying, What have you here in this chest which we have not seen? Now open the chest and give tithe to the king of all that it contains.

11 Abram said, This chest I will not open, but all you demand on it I will give. And Pharaoh's officers answered Abram, saying, It is a chest of precious stones, give us the tenth of its value.

12 Abram said, All that you desire I will give, but you must not open the chest.

13 And the king's officers pressed Abram; they reached the chest and opened it with force, and they saw a beautiful woman was in the chest.

14 When the officers of the king saw Sarai they were struck with admiration at her beauty, and all the princes and servants of Pharaoh assembled to see Sarai, for she was very beautiful. The king's officers ran and told Pharaoh all that they had seen, and they praised Sarai to the king; Pharaoh ordered her to be brought, and the woman came before the king.

15 Pharaoh observed Sarai and she pleased him greatly, and he was struck with her beauty; the king rejoiced greatly on her account, and made presents to those who brought him the news concerning her.

16 The woman was then brought to Pharaoh's house, and Abram grieved on account of his wife; he prayed to the Lord to deliver her from the hands of Pharaoh.

17 And Sarai also prayed at that time and said, O Lord God you did tell my Lord Abram to go from his land and from his father's house to the land of Canaan, and you did promise to do well with him if he would perform your commands; now behold we have done that which you commanded us; we left our land and our families, and we went to a strange land and to a people whom we have not known before.

18 We came to this land to avoid the famine, and this evil accident has befallen me; now therefore, O Lord God, deliver us and save us from the hand of this oppressor, and do well with me for the sake of your mercy.

19 The Lord listened to the voice of Sarai, and the Lord sent an angel to deliver Sarai from the power of Pharaoh.

20 The king came and sat before Sarai and behold an angel of the Lord was standing over them, and he appeared to Sarai and said to her, Do not fear, for the Lord has heard your prayer.

21 The king approached Sarai and said to her, What is that man to you who brought you here? and she said, He is my brother.

22 The king said, It is incumbent on us to make him great, to elevate him and to do to him all the good which you shall command us. At that time the king sent to Abram silver and gold and precious stones in abundance, together with cattle, men servants and maid servants; and the king ordered Abram to be brought and he sat in the court of the king's house, and the king greatly exalted Abram on that night.

23 The king approached to speak to Sarai and he reached out his hand to touch her when the angel struck him heavily; he was terrified and he refrained from reaching to her.

24 And when the king came near to Sarai, the angel struck him to the ground, and acted thus to him the whole night, and the king was terrified.

25 The angel on that night struck heavily all the servants of the king, and his whole household, on account of Sarai, and there was a great lamentation that night among the people of Pharaoh's house.

26 And Pharaoh, seeing the evil that befell him, said, Certainly on account of this woman has this thing happened

to me, and he removed himself at some distance from her and spoke pleasing words to her.

27 The king said to Sarai, Tell me I pray you concerning the man with whom you came here; and Sarai said, This man is my husband, and I said to you that he was my brother for I was afraid that you would put him to death through wickedness.

28 And the king kept away from Sarai, and the plagues of the angel of the Lord ceased from him and his household; Pharaoh knew that he was smitten on account of Sarai, and the king was greatly astonished at this.

29 In the morning the king called for Abram and said to him, What is this you have done to me? Why did you say, She is my sister, since I wanted to take her as a wife, and this heavy plague has therefore come on me and my household.

30 Now therefore here is your wife, take her and go from our land so we don't all die on her account. And Pharaoh took more cattle, men servants and maid servants, and silver and gold, to give to Abram, and he returned to him Sarai his wife.

31 And the king took a maiden whom he had by his concubines, and he gave her to Sarai for a handmaid.

32 The king said to his daughter, It is better for you my daughter to be a handmaid in this man's house than to be mistress in my house, after we have seen the evil that came upon us on account of this woman.

33 Abram arose, and he and all belonging to him went away from Egypt; and Pharaoh ordered some of his men to accompany him and all that went with him.

34 And Abram returned to the land of Canaan, to the place where he had made the altar, where he at first had pitched his tent.

35 Lot the son of Haran, Abram's brother, had a heavy stock of cattle, flocks and herds and tents, for the Lord was bountiful to them on account of Abram.

36 When Abram was dwelling in the land the herdsmen of Lot quarrelled with the herdsmen of Abram, for their property was too great for them to remain together in the land, and the land could not bear them on account of their cattle.

37 When Abram's herdsmen went to feed their flock they would not go into the fields of the people of the land, but the cattle of Lot's herdsmen did otherwise, for they were allowed to feed in the fields of the people of the land.

38 And the people of the land saw this occurrence daily, and they came to Abram and quarrelled with him on account of Lot's herdsmen.

39 And Abram said to Lot, What is this you are doing to me, to make me despicable to the inhabitants of the land, that you ordered your herdsman to feed your cattle in the fields of other people? Do you not know that I am a stranger in this land among the children of Canaan, and why will you do this to me?

40 Abram quarrelled daily with Lot on account of this, but Lot would not listen to Abram; he continued to do the same and the inhabitants of the land came and told Abram.

41 And Abram said to Lot, How long will you be to me a stumbling block with the inhabitants of the land? Now I petition you let there be no more quarrelling between us, for we are kinsmen.

42 I request you to separate from me, go and choose a place where you may dwell with your cattle and all belonging to you, but keep yourself at a distance from me, you and your household.

43 And don't be afraid in going from me, for if any one does an injury to you, let me know and I will avenge your cause from him, only remove from me.

44 When Abram had spoken all these words to Lot, then Lot arose and lifted up his eyes toward the plain of Jordan.

45 And he saw that all of this place was well watered, and good for man as well as affording pasture for the cattle.

46 Lot went from Abram to that place, and he there pitched his tent and he lived in Sodom, and they were separated from each other.

47 And Abram lived in the plain of Mamre, which is in Hebron, and he pitched his tent there, and Abram remained in that place many years.

CHAPTER 16

1 At that time Chedorlaomer king of Elam sent to all the neighboring kings, to Nimrod, king of Shinar who was then under his power, and to Tidal, king of Goyim, and to Arioch, king of Elasar, with whom he made a covenant, saying, Come up to me and assist me, that we may strike all the towns of Sodom and its inhabitants, for

they have rebelled against me these thirteen years.

2 These four kings went up with all their camps, about eight hundred thousand men, and they went as they were, and struck every man they found in their road.

3 And the five kings of Sodom and Gomorrah, Shinab king of Admah, Shemeber king of Zeboyim, Bera king of Sodom, Bersha king of Gomorrah, and Bela king of Zoar, went out to meet them, and they all joined together in the valley of Siddim.

4 These nine kings made war in the valley of Siddim; and the kings of Sodom and Gomorrah were smitten before the kings of Elam.

5 The valley of Siddim was full of lime pits and the kings of Elam pursued the kings of Sodom, and the kings of Sodom with their camps fled and fell into the lime pits; all that remained went to the mountain for safety. The five kings of Elam came after them and pursued them to the gates of Sodom, and they took all that there was in Sodom.

6 They plundered all the cities of Sodom and Gomorrah, and they also took Lot, Abram's brother's son, and his property; they seized all the goods of the cities of Sodom, and they went away. Unic, Abram's servant, who was in the battle, saw this, and told Abram all that the kings had done to the cities of Sodom, and that Lot was taken captive by them.

7 Abram heard this, and he rose up with about three hundred and eighteen men that were with him, and that night he pursued these kings and struck them; they all fell before Abram and his men, and there was none remaining but the four kings who fled, and they each went his own road.

8 Abram recovered all the property of Sodom, and he also recovered Lot and his property, his wives and little ones and all belonging to him, so that Lot lacked nothing.

9 And when he returned from smiting these kings, he and his men passed the valley of Siddim where the kings had made war together.

10 Bera king of Sodom, and the rest of his men that were with him, went out from the lime pits into which they had fallen, to meet Abram and his men.

11 And Adonizedek king of Jerusalem, the same was Shem, went out with his men to meet Abram and his people, with bread and wine, and they remained together in the valley of Melech.

12 Adonizedek blessed Abram, and Abram gave him a tenth from all that he had brought from the spoil of his enemies, for Adonizedek was a priest before God.

13 And all the kings of Sodom and Gomorrah who were there, with their servants, approached Abram and begged him to return their servants whom he had made captive, and to take to himself all the property.

14 Abram answered the kings of Sodom, saying, As the Lord lives who created heaven and earth, and who redeemed my soul from all affliction, and who delivered me this day from my enemies and gave them into my hand, I will not take anything belonging to you, that you may not boast tomorrow, saying, Abram became rich from our property that he saved.

15 For the Lord my God in whom I trust said to me, You shall lack nothing, for I will bless you in all the works of your hands.

16 Now here is all belonging to you, take it and go; as the Lord lives I will not take from a living soul down to a shoetie or thread, excepting the expense of the food of those who went out with me to battle, as also the portions of the men who went with me, Anar, Ashcol, and Mamre, they and their men, as well as those also who had remained to watch the baggage, they shall take their portion of the spoil.

17 And the kings of Sodom gave Abram according to all that he had said; they pressed him to take of whatever he chose, but he would not.

18 He sent away the kings of Sodom and the remainder of their men, and he gave them orders about Lot, and they went to their respective places.

19 And Lot, his brother's son, he also sent away with his property, and he went with them, and Lot returned to his home, to Sodom, and Abram and his people returned to their home to the plains of Mamre, which is in Hebron.

20 At that time the Lord again appeared to Abram in Hebron, and he said to him, Do not fear, your reward is very great before me, for I will not leave you until I shall have multiplied you and blessed you and made your offspring like the stars in heaven, which cannot be measured nor numbered.

21 And I will give to your descendants all these lands that you see with your eyes, I will give them for an inheritance forever, only be strong and do not fear, walk before me and be perfect.

22 In the seventy-eighth year of the life of Abram, in that year Reu died, the son of Peleg, and all the days of Reu

were two hundred and thirty-nine years, and he died.

23 And Sarai, the daughter of Haran, Abram's wife, was still unable to conceive in those days; she did not bear to Abram either son or daughter.

24 When she saw that she gave birth to no children she took her handmaid Hagar, whom Pharaoh had given her, and she gave her to Abram her husband for a wife.

25 For Hagar learned all the ways of Sarai as Sarai taught her; she was not in any way deficient in following her good ways.

26 Sarai said to Abram, Behold here is my handmaid Hagar, go to her that she may bring forth on my knees, that I may also obtain children through her.

27 At the end of ten years of Abram's dwelling in the land of Canaan, which is the eighty-fifth year of Abram's life, Sarai gave Hagar to him.

28 And Abram listened to the voice of his wife Sarai; he took his handmaid Hagar and Abram came to her and she conceived.

29 When Hagar saw that she had conceived she rejoiced greatly, and her mistress was despised in her eyes; she said within herself, This can only be that I am better before God than Sarai my mistress, for all the days that my mistress has been with my lord, she did not conceive, but me the Lord has caused in so short a time to conceive by him.

30 And when Sarai saw that Hagar had conceived by Abram, Sarai was jealous of her handmaid, and Sarai said within herself, This is certainly nothing else but that she must be better than I am.

31 Sarai said to Abram, My wrong be on you, for at the time when you prayed before the Lord for children why did you not pray on my account, that the Lord should give me offspring from you?

32 When I speak to Hagar in your presence she hates my word because she has conceived so you will say nothing to her; may the Lord judge between me and you for what you have done to me.

33 And Abram said to Sarai, Behold your handmaid is in your hand, do to her as it may seem good in your eyes; and Sarai afflicted her, and Hagar fled from her to the wilderness.

34 An angel of the Lord found her in the place where she had fled, by a well, and he said to her, Do not fear, for I will reproduce your offspring, for you shall bear a son and you shall call his name Ishmael; now then return to Sarai your mistress, and submit yourself under her hands.

35 And Hagar called the place of that well Beer-lahai-roi; it is between Kadesh and the wilderness of Bered.

36 And Hagar at that time returned to her master's house, and at the end of days Hagar gave birth to a son to Abram, and Abram called his name Ishmael; and Abram was eighty-six years old when he had him.

CHAPTER 17

1 In those days, in the ninety-first year of the life of Abram, the children of Chittim made war with the children of Tubal, for when the Lord had scattered the sons of men on the face of the earth, the children of Chittim went and settled in the plain of Canopia, and they built themselves cities there and lived by the river Tibreu.

2 The children of Tubal lived in Tuscanah, and their boundaries reached the river Tibreu, and the children of Tubal built a city in Tuscanan, and they called the name Sabinah, after the name of Sabinah son of Tubal their father, and they lived there to this day.

3 It was at that time the children of Chittim made war with the children of Tubal, and the children of Tubal were smitten before the children of Chittim; the children of Chittim caused three hundred and seventy men to fall from the children of Tubal.

4 At that time the children of Tubal swore to the children of Chittim, saying, You shall not intermarry among us, and no man shall give his daughter to any of the sons of Chittim.

5 For all the daughters of Tubal were in those days fair, for no women were then found in the whole earth so fair as the daughters of Tubal.

6 And all who delighted in the beauty of women went to the daughters of Tubal and took wives from them, and the sons of men, kings and princes, who greatly delighted in the beauty of women, took wives in those days from the daughters of Tubal.

7 At the end of three years after the children of Tubal had sworn to the children of Chittim not to give them their daughters for wives, about twenty men of the children of Chittim went to take some of the daughters of Tubal, but they found none.

8 For the children of Tubal kept their oaths not to intermarry with them, and they would not break their oaths.

9 In the days of harvest the children of Tubal went into their fields to get in their harvest, when the young men of Chittim assembled and went to the city of Sabinah, and each man took a young woman from the daughters of Tubal, and they came to their cities.

10 And the children of Tubal heard of it and they went to make war with them; they could not prevail over them, for the mountain was very high; when they saw they could not prevail over them they returned to their land.

11 And at the revolution of the year the children of Tubal went and hired about ten thousand men from those cities that were near them, and they went to war with the children of Chittim.

12 And the children of Tubal went to war with the children of Chittim, to destroy their land and to distress them. In this engagement the children of Tubal prevailed over the children of Chittim, and the children of Chittim, seeing that they were greatly distressed, lifted up the children which they had had by the daughters of Tubal, on the wall which had been built, to be before the eyes of the children of Tubal.

13 And the children of Chittim said to them, Have you come to make war with your own sons and daughters, and have we not been considered your flesh and bones from that time till now?

14 When the children of Tubal heard this they ceased to make war with the children of Chittim, and they went away.

15 They returned to their cities and the children of Chittim at that time assembled and built two cities by the sea; they called one Purtu and the other Ariza.

16 And Abram the son of Terah was then ninety-nine years old.

17 At that time the Lord appeared to him and said, I will make my covenant between me and you, and I will greatly reproduce your offspring, and this is the covenant which I make between me and you, that every male child be circumcised, you and your descendants after you.

18 At eight days old shall it be circumcised, and this covenant shall be in your flesh for an everlasting covenant.

19 And now therefore your name shall no more be called Abram but Abraham, and your wife shall no more be called Sarai but Sarah.

20 For I will bless you both, and I will reproduce your descendants, that you shall become a great nation, and kings shall come forth from you.

CHAPTER 18

1 Abraham rose and did all that God had ordered him; he took the men of his household and those bought with his money, and he circumcised them as the Lord had commanded him.

2 There was not one left whom he did not circumcise, and Abraham and his son Ishmael were circumcised in the flesh of their foreskin; Ishmael was thirteen years old when he was circumcised in the flesh of his foreskin.

3 And in the third day Abraham went out of his tent and sat at the door to enjoy the heat of the sun, during the pain of his flesh.

4 The Lord appeared to him in the plain of Mamre and sent three of his ministering angels to visit him, and he was sitting at the door of the tent. He lifted his eyes and saw three men were coming from a distance; he rose up and ran to meet them, and he bowed down to them and brought them into his house.

5 And he said to them, If now I have found favor in your sight, turn in and eat a morsel of bread. He urged them, they turned in and he gave them water and they washed their feet, and he placed them under a tree at the door of the tent.

6 Abraham ran and took a calf, tender and good, and he hurried to kill it, and gave it to his servant Eliezer to dress.

7 And Abraham came to Sarah into the tent, and said to her, Make ready quickly three measures of fine meal, knead it and make cakes to cover the pot containing the meat, and she did so.

8 Abraham hurried and brought before them butter and milk, beef and mutton, and put it before them to eat, before the flesh of the calf was sufficiently done, and they ate.

9 When they were done eating one of them said to him, I will return to you according to the time of life, and Sarah your wife shall have a son.

10 And the men afterward departed and went their ways, to the places to which they were sent.

11 In those days all the people of Sodom and Gomorrah, and of the whole five cities, were greatly wicked and sinful against the Lord. They provoked the Lord with their abominations, and they grew worse as they aged abominably and scornfully before the Lord, and their wickedness and crimes were in those days great before the

Lord.

12 They had in their land a very extensive valley, about half a day's walk, and in it there were fountains of water and a great deal of herbage surrounding the water.

13 All the people of Sodom and Gomorrah went there four times a year, with their wives and children and all belonging to them, and they rejoiced there with timbrels and dances.

14 In the time of rejoicing they would all rise and lay hold of their neighbor's wives, and some, the virgin daughters of their neighbors, and they enjoyed them; each man saw his wife and daughter in the hands of his neighbor and did not say a word.

15 And they did so from morning to night; afterward they returned home each man to his house and each woman to her tent; so they always did four times in the year.

16 Also when a stranger came into their cities and brought goods which he had purchased with a view to dispose of there, the people of these cities would assemble, men, women and children, young and old, and go to the man and take his goods by force, giving a little to each man until there was an end to all the goods of the owner which he had brought into the land.

17 And if the owner of the goods quarreled with them, saying, What is this work which you have done to me, then they would approach him one by one, and each would show him the little which he took and taunt him, saying, I only took that little which you did give me; when he heard this from them all, he would arise and go from them in sorrow and bitterness of soul. Then they would all arise and go after him, and drive him out of the city with great noise and tumult.

18 There was a man from the country of Elam who was leisurely going on the road, seated on his ass, which carried a fine mantle of varied colors, and the mantle was bound with a cord on the ass.

19 The man was on his journey passing through the street of Sodom when the sun set in the evening; he remained there in order to abide during the night, but no one would let him into his house. At that time there was in Sodom a wicked and mischievous man, one skillful to do evil, and his name was Hedad.

20 And he lifted up his eyes and saw the traveler in the street of the city, and he came to him and said, Whence come you and where do you go?

21 The man said to him, I am traveling from Hebron to Elam where I belong, and as I passed the sun set and no one would invite me to enter his house; you have bread and water and also straw and feed for my ass, and I am short of nothing.

22 And Hedad answered and said to him, All that you shall want shall be supplied by me, but in the street you shall not abide all night.

23 Hedad brought him to his house, and he took off the mantle from the ass with the cord, and brought them to his house. He gave the ass straw and feed while the traveler ate and drank in Hedad's house, and he abode there that night.

24 And in the morning the traveler rose up early to continue his journey, when Hedad said to him, Wait, comfort your heart with a morsel of bread and then go, and the man did so; and he remained with him, and they both ate and drank together during the day, then the man rose up to go.

25 And Hedad said to him, Behold now the day is declining, you had better remain all night that your heart may be comforted; and he pressed him so that he tarried there all night, and on the second day he rose up early to go away, when Hedad pressed him, saying, Comfort your heart with a morsel of bread and then go, and he remained and ate with him also the second day. Then the man rose up to continue his journey.

26 And Hedad said to him, Behold now the day is declining, remain with me to comfort your heart and in the morning rise up early and go your way.

27 The man would not remain, but rose and saddled his ass, and while he was saddling his ass the wife of Hedad said to her husband, Behold this man has remained with us for two days eating and drinking and he has given us nothing, and now shall he go away from us without giving anything? Hedad said to her, Be silent.

28 And the man saddled his ass to go, and he asked Hedad to give him the cord and mantle to tie it on the ass.

29 And Hedad said to him, What do you say? And he said to him, That you my lord shall give me the cord and the mantle made with varied colors which you concealed in your house to take care of it.

30 And Hedad answered the man, saying, This is the interpretation of your dream, the cord which you did see means that your life will be lengthened out like a cord, and having seen the mantle colored with all sorts of colors, means that you shall have a vineyard in which you will plant trees of all fruits.

31 And the traveler answered, saying, Not so my lord, for I was awake when I gave you the cord and also a mantle woven with different colors, which you took off the ass to put by for me; and Hedad answered and said,

Certainly I have told you the interpretation of your dream and it is a good dream, and this is the interpretation of it.

32 Now the sons of men give me four pieces of silver, which is my charge for interpreting dreams, and of you only I require three pieces of silver.

33 And the man was provoked at the words of Hedad, and he cried bitterly, and he brought Hedad to Serak judge of Sodom.

34 And the man laid his cause before Serak the judge, when Hedad replied, saying, It is not so, but thus the matter stands. And the judge said to the traveler, This man Hedad tells you truth, for he is famed in the cities for the accurate interpretation of dreams.

35 And the man cried at the word of the judge, and he said, Not so my Lord, for it was in the day that I gave him the cord and mantle which was on the ass, in order to put them by in his house; they both disputed before the judge, the one saying, Thus the matter was, and the other declaring otherwise.

36 Hedad said to the man, Give me four pieces of silver that I charge for my interpretations of dreams; I will not make any allowance; give me the expense of the four meals that you ate in my house.

37 And the man said to Hedad, Truly I will pay you for what I ate in your house, only give me the cord and mantle which you did conceal in your house.

38 Hedad replied before the judge and said to the man, Did I not tell you the interpretation of your dream? The cord means that your days shall be prolonged like a cord, and the mantle, that you will have a vineyard in which you will plant all kinds of fruit trees.

39 This is the proper interpretation of your dream, now give me the four pieces of silver that I require as a compensation, for I will make you no allowance.

40 And the man cried at the words of Hedad and they both quarreled before the judge; the judge gave orders to his servants, who drove them rashly from the house.

41 And they went away quarreling from the judge. When the people of Sodom heard them, they gathered about them and spoke harshly against the stranger, and they drove him rashly from the city.

42 And the man continued his journey on his ass with bitterness of soul, lamenting and weeping.

43 And while he was on his way he wept at what had happened to him in the corrupt city of Sodom.

CHAPTER 19

1 The cities of Sodom had four judges to four cities, and these were their names, Serak in the city of Sodom, Sharkad in Gomorrah, Zabnac in Admah, and Menon in Zeboyim.

2 Eliezer Abraham's servant applied to them different names, and he converted Serak to Shakra, Sharkad to Shakrura, Zebnac to Kezobim, and Menon to Matzlodin.

3 By desire of their four judges the people of Sodom and Gomorrah had beds erected in the streets of the cities and if a man came to these places, they laid hold of him and brought him to one of their beds and by force made him to lie in them.

4 As he lay down, three men would stand at his head and three at his feet, and measure him by the length of the bed; if the man was less than the bed, these six men would stretch him at each end, and when he cried out to them they would not answer him.

5 If he was longer than the bed, they would draw together the two sides of the bed at each end, until the man had reached the gates of death.

6 And if he continued to cry out to them, they would answer him, saying, Thus it shall be done to a man that comes into our land.

7 When men heard all these things that the people of the cities of Sodom did, they refrained from coming there.

8 And when a poor man came to their land they would give him silver and gold, and cause a proclamation in the whole city not to give him a morsel of bread to eat. If the stranger should remain there some days and die from hunger, not having been able to obtain a morsel of bread, then at his death all the people of the city would come and take their silver and gold which they had given to him.

9 Those that could recognize the silver or gold which they had given him took it back, and at his death they also stripped him of his garments, and they would fight about them; he that prevailed over his neighbor took them.

10 After that they would carry him and bury him under some of the shrubs in the desert; so they did all the days to any one that came to them and died in their land.

11 And in the course of time Sarah sent Eliezer to Sodom, to see Lot and inquire after his welfare.

12 Eliezer went to Sodom, and he met a man of Sodom fighting with a stranger, and the man of Sodom stripped the poor man of all his clothes and went away.

13 And this poor man cried to Eliezer and begged his favor on account of what the man of Sodom had done to him.

14 He said to him, Why do you act thus to the poor man who came to your land?

15 The man of Sodom answered Eliezer, saying, Is this man your brother, or have the people of Sodom made you a judge this day, that you speak about this man?

16 Eliezer strove with the man of Sodom on account of the poor man, and when Eliezer approached to recover the poor man's clothes from the man of Sodom, he hurried and with a stone struck Eliezer in the forehead.

17 The blood flowed copiously from Eliezer's forehead, and when the man saw the blood he caught hold of Eliezer, saying, Give me my wage for having rid you of this bad blood that was in your forehead, for such is the custom and the law in our land.

18 And Eliezer said to him, You have wounded me and require me to pay you your wage? Eliezer would not listen to the words of the man of Sodom.

19 And the man laid hold of Eliezer and brought him to Shakra the judge of Sodom for judgment.

20 The man spoke to the judge, saying, I beseech you my lord, thus has this man done, for I struck him with a stone that the blood flowed from his forehead, and he is unwilling to give me my wage.

21 And the judge said to Eliezer, This man speaks truth to you, give him his wage, for this is the custom in our land. Eliezer heard the words of the judge, and he lifted up a stone and struck the judge; the stone struck on his forehead, and the blood flowed copiously from the forehead of the judge, and Eliezer said, If this then is the custom in your land give to this man what I should have given him, for this has been your decision; you did decree it.

22 And Eliezer left the man of Sodom with the judge, and he went away.

23 When the kings of Elam had made war with the kings of Sodom, the kings of Elam captured all the property of Sodom and they took Lot captive with his property, and when it was told to Abraham he went and made war with the kings of Elam. He recovered from their hands all the property of Lot as well as the property of Sodom.

24 At that time the wife of Lot gave birth to a daughter, and he called her name Paltith, saying, Because God had delivered him and his whole household from the kings of Elam. Paltith daughter of Lot grew up, and one of the men of Sodom took her for a wife.

25 And a poor man came into the city to seek a maintenance, and he remained in the city some days, and all the people of Sodom caused a proclamation of their custom not to give this man a morsel of bread to eat until he dropped dead on the earth, and they did so.

26 And Paltith the daughter of Lot saw this man lying in the streets starved with hunger and no one would give him any thing to keep him alive; he was just on the point of death.

27 And her soul was filled with pity on account of the man and she fed him secretly with bread for many days, and the soul of this man was revived.

28 For when she went forth to fetch water she would put the bread in the water pitcher, and when she came to the place where the poor man was, she took the bread from the pitcher and gave it him to eat; so she did many days.

29 And all the people of Sodom and Gomorrah wondered how this man could bear starvation for so many days.

30 And they said to each other, This can only be because he eats and drinks, for no man can bear starvation for so many days or live as this man has, without even his countenance changing. Three men concealed themselves in a place where the poor man was stationed to know who it was that brought him bread to eat.

31 Paltith daughter of Lot went forth that day to fetch water and she put bread into her pitcher of water; she went to draw water by the poor man's place and took out the bread from the pitcher and gave it to the poor man and he ate it.

32 And the three men saw what Paltith did to the poor man, and they said to her, It is you then who have supported him, and therefore he has not starved, nor changed in appearance nor died like the rest.

33 The three men went out of the place in which they were concealed, and they seized Paltith and the bread which was in the poor man's hand.

34 They took Paltith and brought her before their judges, and they said to them, Thus did she do, and it is she who supplied the poor man with bread, therefore he did not die all this time; now therefore declare to us the punishment due to this woman for having gone contrary to our law.

35 And the people of Sodom and Gomorrah assembled and set ablaze a fire in the street of the city, and they took

the woman and cast her into the fire and she was burned to ashes.

36 In the city of Admah there was a woman to whom they did the same.

37 For a traveler came into the city of Admah to stay there all night, with the intention of going home in the morning. He sat opposite the door of the house of the young woman's father, to remain there, as the sun had set when he had reached that place; the young woman saw him sitting by the door of the house.

38 He asked her for a drink of water and she said to him, Who art you? And he said to her, I was this day going on the road, and reached here when the sun set, so I will stay here all night, and in the morning I will arise early and continue my journey.

39 And the young woman went into the house and fetched the man bread and water to eat and drink.

40 This affair became known to the people of Admah, and they assembled and brought the young woman before the judges, that they should judge her for this act.

41 And the judge said, The judgment of death must pass on this woman because she went contrary to our law, and this therefore is the decision concerning her.

42 The people of those cities assembled and brought out the young woman, and anointed her with honey from head to foot, as the judge had decreed, and they placed her before a swarm of bees which were then in their hives, and the bees flew on her and stung her that her whole body was swelled.

43 The young woman cried out on account of the bees, but no one took notice of her or pitied her, and her cries ascended to heaven.

44 And the Lord was provoked at this and at all the works of the cities of Sodom, for they had abundance of food, and had tranquility among them, and still would not sustain the poor and the needy. In those days their evil doings and sins became great before the Lord.

45 The Lord sent for two of the angels that had come to Abraham's house, to destroy Sodom and its cities.

46 And the angels rose up from the door of Abraham's tent, after they had eaten and drunk, and they reached Sodom in the evening, and Lot was then sitting in the gate of Sodom. When he saw them he rose to meet them, and he bowed down to the ground.

47 He welcomed them greatly and brought them into his house, and he gave them food which they ate, and they stayed all night in his house.

48 And the angels said to Lot, Arise, go forth from this place, you and all belonging to you, that you not be consumed in the iniquity of this city, for the Lord will destroy this place.

49 The angels laid hold on the hand of Lot and on the hand of his wife, and on the hands of his children, and all belonging to him, and they brought him forth and set him outside of the cities.

50 And they said to Lot, Escape for your life. He fled and all belonging to him.

51 Then the Lord rained on Sodom and on Gomorrah and on all these cities brimstone and fire from the Lord out of heaven.

52 And he overthrew these cities, all the plain and all the inhabitants of the cities, and that which grew on the ground; Ado the wife of Lot looked back to see the destruction of the cities, for her compassion was moved on account of her daughters who remained in Sodom, for they did not go with her.

53 And when she looked back she became a pillar of salt, and it is yet in that place to this day.

54 The oxen which stood in that place daily licked up the salt to the extremities of their feet, and in the morning it would spring forth afresh, and they again licked it up to this day.

55 Lot and two of his daughters that remained with him fled and escaped to the cave of Adullam, and they remained there for some time.

56 And Abraham rose up early in the morning to see what had been done to the cities of Sodom; and he looked and beheld the smoke of the cities going up like the smoke of a furnace.

57 Lot and his two daughters remained in the cave, and they made their father drink wine, and they lay with him, for they said there was no man on earth that could produce descendants from them, for they thought that the whole earth was destroyed.

58 They both lay with their father and conceived and gave birth to sons. The first born called the name of her son Moab, saying, From my father did I conceive him; he is the father of the Moabites to this day.

59 And the younger also called her son Benami; he is the father of the children of Ammon to this day.

60 After this Lot and his two daughters went away from there, and he lived on the other side of the Jordan with his two daughters and their sons, and the sons of Lot grew up, and they went and took themselves wives from the land of Canaan, and they had children and they were prolific and multiplied.

CHAPTER 20

1 At that time Abraham journeyed from the plain of Mamre and he went to the land of the Philistines, and he lived in Gerar; it was in the twenty-fifth year of Abraham's being in the land of Canaan, and the hundredth year of the life of Abraham, that he came to Gerar in the land of the Philistines.

2 And when they entered the land he said to Sarah his wife, Say you are my sister, to any one that shall ask you, in order that we may escape the evil of the inhabitants of the land.

3 As Abraham was dwelling in the land of the Philistines, the servants of Abimelech, king of the Philistines, saw that Sarah was greatly beautiful, and they asked Abraham concerning her, and he said, She is my sister.

4 And the servants of Abimelech went to Abimelech, saying, A man from the land of Canaan is come to dwell in the land, and he has a sister that is exceeding fair.

5 Abimelech heard the words of his servants who praised Sarah to him, and Abimelech sent his officers, and they brought Sarah to the king.

6 And Sarah came to the house of Abimelech; the king saw that Sarah was beautiful, and she pleased him greatly.

7 And he approached her and said to her, What is that man to you with whom you did come to our land? And Sarah answered and said, He is my brother, and we came from the land of Canaan to dwell wherever we could find a place.

8 Abimelech said to Sarah, Behold my land is before you, place your brother in any part of this land that pleases you, and it will be our duty to exalt and elevate him above all the people of the land since he is your brother.

9 And Abimelech sent for Abraham, and Abraham came to Abimelech.

10 Abimelech said to Abraham, Behold I have given orders that you shall be honored as you desire on account of your sister Sarah.

11 And Abraham went forth from the king, and the king's present followed him.

12 As at evening time, before men laid down to rest, the king was sitting on his throne, and a deep sleep fell on him, and he lay on the throne and slept till morning.

13 He dreamed that an angel of the Lord came to him with a drawn sword in his hand, and the angel stood over Abimelech and wished to kill him with the sword; the king was terrified in his dream and said to the angel, In what have I sinned against you that you come to kill me with your sword?

14 And the angel answered and said to Abimelech, Behold you die on account of the woman which last night you brought to your house, for she is a married woman, the wife of Abraham who came to your house; now therefore return that man his wife, for she is his wife; should you not return her, know that you will certainly die, you and all belonging to you.

15 On that night there was a great outcry in the land of the Philistines, and the inhabitants of the land saw the figure of a man standing with a drawn sword in his hand, and he struck the inhabitants of the land with the sword, yes, he continued to strike them.

16 And the angel of the Lord struck the whole land of the Philistines on that night, and there was a great confusion on that night and on the following morning.

17 Every womb was closed, and all their issues, and the hand of the Lord was on them on account of Sarah, wife of Abraham, whom Abimelech had taken.

18 And in the morning Abimelech rose with terror and confusion and with a great dread; he sent and had his servants called in; he related his dream to them, and the people were greatly afraid.

19 One man standing among the servants of the king answered the king, saying, O sovereign king, restore this woman to her husband, for he is her husband, for the same happened to the king of Egypt when this man came to Egypt.

20 He said concerning his wife, She is my sister, for such is his manner of doing when he comes to dwell in the land in which he is a stranger.

21 Pharaoh sent and took this woman for a wife and the Lord brought on him grievous plagues until he returned the woman to her husband.

22 Now therefore, O sovereign king, know what happened last night to the whole land, for there was a very great consternation and great pain and lamentation, and we know that it was on account of the woman which you did take.

23 Now, therefore, restore this woman to her husband, that it should not happen to us as it did to Pharaoh king of Egypt and his subjects, and that we may not die. Abimelech hurried and had Sarah called for, and she came before him, and he had Abraham called for, and he came before him.

24 Abimelech said to them, What is this work you have been doing in saying you are brother and sister, and I took this woman for a wife?

25 And Abraham said, Because I thought I would suffer death on account of my wife; and Abimelech took flocks and herds, and men servants and maid servants, and a thousand pieces of silver, and he gave them to Abraham, and he returned Sarah to him.

26 Abimelech said to Abraham, Behold the whole land is before you, dwell in it wherever you shall choose.

27 And Abraham and Sarah, his wife, went forth from the king's presence with honor and respect, and they lived in the land, even in Gerar.

28 All the inhabitants of the land of the Philistines and the king's servants were still in pain through the plague which the angel had inflicted on them the whole night on account of Sarah.

29 Abimelech sent for Abraham, saying, Pray now for your servants to the Lord your God, that he may put away this mortality from among us.

30 And Abraham prayed on account of Abimelech and his subjects, and the Lord heard the prayer of Abraham, and he healed Abimelech and all his subjects.

CHAPTER 21

1 It was at that time the end of a year and four months of Abraham's dwelling in the land of the Philistines in Gerar, that God visited Sarah, and the Lord remembered her and she conceived and gave birth to a son to Abraham.

2 Abraham called the name of the son which Sarah gave birth to him, Isaac.

3 And Abraham circumcised his son Isaac at eight days old, as God had commanded Abraham to do to his descendants after him; Abraham was one hundred and Sarah ninety years old when Isaac was born to them.

4 The child grew up and was weaned, and Abraham made a great feast on the day that Isaac was weaned.

5 Shem and Eber and all the great people of the land, and Abimelech king of the Philistines and his servants, and Phicol, the captain of his host, came to eat and drink and rejoice at the feast which Abraham made on the day of his son Isaac's being weaned.

6 Also Terah, the father of Abraham, and Nahor his brother, came from Haran, they and all belonging to them, for they greatly rejoiced on hearing that a son had been born to Sarah.

7 They came to Abraham, and they ate and drank at the feast which Abraham made on the day of Isaac's being weaned.

8 Terah and Nahor rejoiced with Abraham, and they remained with him many days in the land of the Philistines.

9 At that time Serug the son of Reu died, in the first year of the birth of Isaac son of Abraham.

10 And all the days of Serug were two hundred and thirty-nine years, and he died.

11 Ishmael the son of Abraham was grown up in those days; he was fourteen years old when Sarah gave birth to Isaac to Abraham.

12 And God was with Ishmael the son of Abraham, and he grew up, and he learned to use the bow and became an archer.

13 When Isaac was five years old he was sitting with Ishmael at the door of the tent.

14 Ishmael came to Isaac and seated himself opposite to him, and he took the bow and drew it and put the arrow in it, and intended to kill Isaac.

15 Sarah saw the act which Ishmael desired to do to her son Isaac, and it grieved her greatly on account of her son; she sent for Abraham, and said to him, Cast out this bondwoman and her son, for her son shall not be heir with my son, for thus did he seek to do to him this day.

16 Abraham listened to the voice of Sarah, and he rose up early in the morning. He took twelve loaves and a bottle of water which he gave to Hagar, and sent her away with her son, and Hagar went with her son to the wilderness. They lived in the wilderness of Paran with the inhabitants of the wilderness; Ishmael was an archer, and he lived in the wilderness a long time.

17 He and his mother afterward went to the land of Egypt, and they lived there; Hagar took a wife for her son from Egypt, and her name was Meribah.

18 And the wife of Ishmael conceived and gave birth to four sons and two daughters. Ishmael and his mother and his wife and children afterward went and returned to the wilderness.

19 They made themselves tents in the wilderness, in which they lived, and they continued to travel and then to

rest monthly and yearly.

20 And God gave Ishmael flocks and herds and tents on account of Abraham his father, and the man increased in cattle.

21 Ishmael lived in deserts and in tents, traveling and resting for a long time, and he did not see the face of his father.

22 Some time later, Abraham said to Sarah his wife, I will go and see my son Ishmael, for I have a desire to see him, for I have not seen him for a long time.

23 Abraham rode on one of his camels to the wilderness to seek his son Ishmael, for he heard that he was dwelling in a tent in the wilderness with all belonging to him.

24 Abraham went to the wilderness and reached the tent of Ishmael about noon, and he asked after Ishmael; he found the wife of Ishmael sitting in the tent with her children, and Ishmael her husband and his mother were not with them.

25 Abraham asked the wife of Ishmael, saying, Where has Ishmael gone? And she said, He has gone to the field to hunt. Abraham was still mounted on the camel, for he would not get off to the ground as he had sworn to his wife Sarah that he would not get off from the camel.

26 And Abraham said to Ishmael's wife, My daughter, give me a little water that I may drink, for I am fatigued from the journey.

27 And Ishmael's wife answered and said to Abraham, We have neither water nor bread. She continued sitting in the tent and did not notice Abraham, neither did she ask him who he was.

28 But she was beating her children in the tent, and she was cursing them, and she also cursed her husband Ishmael and reproached him. Abraham heard the words of Ishmael's wife to her children, and he was very angry and displeased.

29 Abraham called to the woman to come out to him from the tent, and the woman came and stood opposite to Abraham, for Abraham was still mounted on the camel.

30 And Abraham said to Ishmael's wife, When your husband Ishmael returns home say these words to him,

31 A very old man from the land of the Philistines came here to seek you, and thus was his appearance and figure; I did not ask him who he was, and seeing you were not here he spoke to me and said, When Ishmael your husband returns tell him thus did this man say, When you come home put away this nail of the tent which you have placed here, and place another nail in its stead.

32 Abraham finished his instructions to the woman, and he turned and went off on the camel homeward.

33 After that Ishmael came from the hunt by him and his mother, and returned to the tent, and his wife spoke these words to him,

34 A very old man from the land of the Philistines came to seek you, and thus was his appearance and figure; I did not ask him who he was, and seeing you were not at home he said to me, When your husband comes home tell him, thus says the old man, Put away the nail of the tent which you have placed here and place another nail in its stead.

35 Ishmael heard the words of his wife, and he knew that it was his father, and that his wife did not honor him.

36 And Ishmael understood his father's words that he had spoken to his wife, and Ishmael listened to the voice of his father; Ishmael cast off that woman and she went away.

37 Ishmael afterward went to the land of Canaan, and he took another wife and he brought her to his tent to the place where he then lived.

38 And at the end of three years Abraham said, I will go again and see Ishmael my son, for I have not seen him for a long time.

39 He rode on his camel and went to the wilderness, and he reached the tent of Ishmael about noon.

40 He asked after Ishmael, and his wife came out of the tent and said, He is not here my lord, for he has gone to hunt in the fields, and to feed the camels. And the woman said to Abraham, Turn in my lord into the tent, and eat a morsel of bread, for your soul must be wearied on account of the journey.

41 And Abraham said to her, I will not stop for I am in haste to continue my journey, but give me a little water to drink, for I have thirst; the woman hurried and ran into the tent and she brought out water and bread to Abraham, which she placed before him and she urged him to eat; he ate and drank and his heart was comforted and he blessed his son Ishmael.

42 He finished his meal and he blessed the Lord, and he said to Ishmael's wife, When Ishmael comes home say these words to him,

43 A very old man from the land of the Philistines came here and asked after you, and you were not here; and I

brought out bread and water and he ate and drank and his heart was comforted.

44 And he spoke these words to me: When Ishmael your husband comes home, say to him, The nail of the tent which you have is very good, do not put it away from the tent.

45 Abraham finished commanding the woman, and he rode off to his home to the land of the Philistines; and when Ishmael came to his tent his wife went forth to meet him with joy and a cheerful heart.

46 And she said to him, An old man came here from the land of the Philistines and thus was his appearance, and he asked after you and you were not here, so I brought out bread and water, and he ate and drank and his heart was comforted.

47 And he spoke these words to me, When Ishmael your husband comes home say to him, The nail of the tent which you have is very good, do not put it away from the tent.

48 Ishmael knew that it was his father, and that his wife had honored him, and the Lord blessed Ishmael.

CHAPTER 22

1 Ishmael then rose up and took his wife and his children and his cattle and all belonging to him, and he journeyed from there and he went to his father in the land of the Philistines.

2 Abraham related to Ishmael his son the transaction with the first wife that Ishmael took, according to what she did.

3 Ishmael and his children lived with Abraham many days in that land, and Abraham lived in the land of the Philistines a long time.

4 And the days increased and reached twenty six years; after that Abraham with his servants and all belonging to him went from the land of the Philistines and removed to a great distance, and they came near to Hebron and remained there. The servants of Abraham dug wells of water, and Abraham and all belonging to him lived by the water. The servants of Abimelech king of the Philistines heard the report that Abraham's servants had dug wells of water in borders of the land.

5 They came and quarreled with the servants of Abraham and robbed them of the great well which they had dug.

6 Abimelech king of the Philistines heard of this affair; he with Phicol the captain of his host and twenty of his men came to Abraham, and Abimelech spoke to Abraham concerning his servants; Abraham rebuked Abimelech concerning the well of which his servants had robbed him.

7 Abimelech said to Abraham, As the Lord lives who created the whole earth, I did not hear of the act which my servants did to your servants until this day.

8 And Abraham took seven ewe lambs and gave them to Abimelech, saying, Take these, I pray you, from my hands that it may be a testimony for me that I dug this well.

9 Abimelech took the seven ewe lambs which Abraham had given to him, for he had also given him cattle and herds in abundance; Abimelech swore to Abraham concerning the well, therefore he called that well Beersheba, for there they both swore concerning it.

10 And they both made a covenant in Beersheba, and Abimelech rose up with Phicol the captain of his host and all his men; they returned to the land of the Philistines, and Abraham and all belonging to him lived in Beersheba and he was in that land a long time.

11 Abraham planted a large grove in Beersheba, and he made to it four gates facing the four sides of the earth; he planted a vineyard in it, so that if a traveler came to Abraham he entered any gate which was in his road, and remained there and ate and drank and satisfied himself and then departed.

12 For the house of Abraham was always open to the sons of men that passed and returned, who came daily to eat and drink in the house of Abraham.

13 Any man who had hunger and came to Abraham's house, Abraham would give him bread that he might eat and drink and be satisfied; any one that came naked to his house he would clothe with garments as he might choose and give him silver and gold, and make known to him the Lord who had created him in the earth; this did Abraham all his life.

14 Abraham and his children and all belonging to him lived in Beersheba, and he pitched his tent as far as Hebron.

15 And Abraham's brother Nahor and his father and all belonging to them lived in Haran, for they did not come with Abraham to the land of Canaan.

16 And children were born to Nahor which Milca the daughter of Haran, and sister to Sarah, Abraham's wife,

gave birth to, to him.

17 These are the names of those that were born to him: Uz, Buz, Kemuel, Kesed, Chazo, Pildash, Tidlaf, and Bethuel, being eight sons; these are the children of Milca which she gave birth to, to Nahor, Abraham's brother.

18 And Nahor had a concubine and her name was Reumah, and she also gave birth to, to Nahor: Zebach, Gachash, Tachash and Maacha, being four sons.

19 The children that were born to Nahor were twelve sons besides his daughters, and they also had children born to them in Haran.

20 And the children of Uz the first born of Nahor were Abi, Cheref, Gadin, Melus, and Deborah their sister.

21 And the sons of Buz were Berachel, Naamath, Sheva, and Madonu.

22 And the sons of Kemuel were Aram and Rechob.

23 And the sons of Kesed were Anamlech, Meshai, Benon and Yifi; the sons of Chazo were Pildash, Mechi and Opher.

24 And the sons of Pildash were Arud, Chamum, Mered and Moloch.

25 And the sons of Tidlaf were Mushan, Cushan and Mutzi.

26 And the children of Bethuel were Sechar, Laban and their sister Rebecca.

27 These are the families of the children of Nahor, that were born to them in Haran; and Aram the son of Kemuel and Rechob his brother went away from Haran, and they found a valley in the land by the river Euphrates.

28 And they built a city there, and they called the name of the city after the name of Pethor the son of Aram, that is Aram Naherayim to this day.

29 The children of Kesed also went to dwell where they could find a place, and they found a valley opposite to the land of Shinar, and they lived there.

30 There they built themselves a city, and they called the name of the city Kesed after the name of their father; that is the land Kasdim to this day, and the Kasdim lived in that land and they were prolific and multiplied greatly.

31 Terah, father of Nahor and Abraham, went and took another wife in his old age, and her name was Pelilah, and she conceived and gave birth to him a son and he called his name Zoba.

32 Terah lived twenty-five years after he had Zoba.

33 And Terah died in that year, that is in the thirty-fifth year of the birth of Isaac son of Abraham.

34 The days of Terah were two hundred and five years, and he was buried in Haran.

35 Zoba the son of Terah lived thirty years and he had Aram, Achlis and Merik.

36 Aram, son of Zoba son of Terah, had three wives and he had twelve sons and three daughters; the Lord gave to Aram the son of Zoba, riches and possessions, and abundance of cattle, and flocks and herds, and the man increased greatly.

37 Aram the son of Zoba and his brother and all his household journeyed from Haran, and they went to dwell where they should find a place, for their property was too great to remain in Haran; for they could not stop in Haran together with their brothers the children of Nahor.

38 Aram the son of Zoba went with his brothers, and they found a valley at a distance toward the eastern country and they lived there.

39 They also built a city there, and they called the name thereof Aram, after the name of their eldest brother; that is Aram Zoba to this day.

40 Isaac the son of Abraham was growing up in those days, and Abraham his father taught him the way of the Lord to know the Lord, and the Lord was with him.

41 When Isaac was thirty-seven years old, Ishmael his brother was going about with him in the tent.

42 And Ishmael boasted of himself to Isaac, saying, I was thirteen years old when the Lord spoke to my father to circumcise us, and I did according to the word of the Lord which he spoke to my father, and I gave my soul to the Lord, and I did not go contrary to his word which he commanded my father.

43 Isaac answered Ishmael, saying, Why do you boast to me about this, about a little bit of your flesh which you did take from your body, concerning which the Lord commanded you?

44 As the Lord lives, the God of my father Abraham, if the Lord should say to my father, Take now your son Isaac and bring him up an offering before me, I would not refrain but I would joyfully accede to it.

45 And the Lord heard the word that Isaac spoke to Ishmael, and it seemed good in the sight of the Lord, and he thought to try Abraham in this matter.

46 The day arrived when the sons of God came and placed themselves before the Lord, and Satan also came with the sons of God before the Lord.

47 And the Lord said to Satan, Wherefore do you come? Satan answered the Lord and said, From going to and fro in the earth, and from walking up and down in it.

48 And the Lord said to Satan, What is your word to me concerning all the children of the earth? Satan answered the Lord and said, I have seen all the children of the earth who serve you and remember you when they require anything from you.

49 When you give them the thing which they require from you, they sit at their ease and turn away from you, and they remember you no more.

50 Have you seen Abraham the son of Terah, who at first had no children? He served you and erected altars to you wherever he came, and he brought up offerings on them, and he proclaimed your name continually to all the children of the earth.

51 And now that his son Isaac is born to him, he has forsaken you, he has made a great feast for all the inhabitants of the land, and the Lord he has forgotten.

52 For amidst all that he has done he brought you no offering; neither burnt offering nor peace offering, neither ox, lamb nor goat of all that he killed on the day that his son was weaned.

53 Even from the time of his son's birth till now, being thirty-seven years, he built no altar before you, nor brought any offering to you, for he saw that you did give what he requested before you, and he therefore turned away from you.

54 And the Lord said to Satan, Have you thus considered my servant Abraham? for there is none like him on earth, a perfect and an upright man before me, one that fears God and avoids evil; as I live, were I to say to him, Bring up Isaac your son before me, he would not withhold him from me, much more if I told him to bring up a burnt offering before me from his flock or herds.

55 Satan answered the Lord and said, Speak then now to Abraham as you have said, and you will see whether he will not this day go contrary to and cast aside your words.

CHAPTER 23

1 At that time the word of the Lord came to Abraham, and said to him, Abraham. And Abraham said, Here I am.

2 He said to him, Take now your son, your only son whom you love, even Isaac, and go to the land of Moriah, and offer him there for a burnt offering on one of the mountains which shall be shown to you, for there you will see a cloud and the glory of the Lord.

3 And Abraham said within himself, How shall I separate my son Isaac from Sarah his mother, in order to bring him up for a burnt offering before the Lord?

4 Abraham came into the tent, and he sat before Sarah his wife, and he spoke these words to her,

5 My son Isaac is grown up and he has not for some time studied the service of his God; tomorrow I will go and bring him to Shem, and Eber his son, and there he will learn the ways of the Lord. For they will teach him to know the Lord as well as to know that when he prays continually before the Lord, he will answer him; there he will know the way of serving the Lord his God.

6 And Sarah said, You have spoken well, go my lord and do to him as you have said, but remove him not at a great distance from me, neither let him remain there too long, for my soul is bound within his soul.

7 Abraham said to Sarah, My daughter, let us pray to the Lord our God that he may do good with us.

8 And Sarah took her son Isaac and he abode all that night with her, and she kissed and embraced him, and gave him instructions till morning.

9 She said to him, O my son, how can my soul separate itself from you? And she still kissed him and embraced him, and she gave Abraham instructions concerning him.

10 Sarah said to Abraham, O my lord, I pray you take care of your son, and watch over him, for I have no other son or daughter but him.

11 Turn not away from him. If he is hungry give him bread, and if he is thirsty give him water to drink; do not let him go on foot, neither let him sit in the sun.

12 Neither let him go by himself in the road, neither force him from whatever he may desire, but do to him as he may say to you.

13 Sarah wept bitterly the whole night on account of Isaac, and she gave him instructions till morning.

14 In the morning Sarah selected a very fine and beautiful garment from those garments which she had in the house, that Abimelech had given to her.

15 She dressed Isaac her son with them, and she put a turban on his head; she enclosed a precious stone in the top of the turban, and gave them provision for the road. They went forth, and Isaac went with his father Abraham, and some of their servants accompanied them to see them on their way.

16 Sarah went out with them, and she accompanied them on the road to see them off; they said to her, Return to the tent.

17 When Sarah heard the words of her son Isaac she wept bitterly, and Abraham her husband wept with her, and their son wept with them a great weeping; also those who went with them wept greatly.

18 And Sarah caught hold of her son Isaac, and she held him in her arms, and she embraced him and continued to weep with him. And Sarah said, Who knows if after this day I shall ever see you again?

19 They still wept together, Abraham, Sarah and Isaac, and all those that accompanied them on the road wept with them, and Sarah afterward turned away from her son, weeping bitterly; then all her men servants and maid servants returned with her to the tent.

20 And Abraham went with Isaac his son to bring him up as an offering before the Lord, as He had commanded him.

21 Abraham took two of his young men with him, Ishmael the son of Hagar and Eliezer his servant, and they went together with them. While they were walking in the road the young men spoke these words to themselves,

22 Ishmael said to Eliezer, Now my father Abraham is going with Isaac to bring him up for a burnt offering to the Lord, as He commanded him.

23 When he returns he will give to me all he possesses, to inherit after him, for I am his firstborn.

24 And Eliezer answered Ishmael and said, Certainly Abraham did cast you away with your mother, and swear that you should not inherit any thing of all he possesses. To whom will he give all that he has, with all his treasures, but to me his servant, who has been faithful in his house, who has served him night and day, and has done all he desired me? To me he will bequeath at his death all he possesses.

25 While Abraham was proceeding with his son Isaac along the road, Satan came and appeared to Abraham in the figure of a very aged man, humble and of contrite spirit; he approached Abraham and said to him, Are you silly or brutish, that you go to do this thing today to your only son?

26 For God gave you a son in your latter days, in your old age, and will you go and slaughter him today because he committed no violence, and will you cause the soul of your only son to perish from the earth?

27 Do you not know and understand that this thing cannot be from the Lord? For the Lord cannot do to man such evil on earth to say to him, Go slaughter your child.

28 Abraham heard this and knew that it was the word of Satan who endeavored to draw him aside from the way of the Lord, but Abraham would not listen to the voice of Satan, and Abraham rebuked him so that he went away.

29 Satan returned and came to Isaac; he appeared to Isaac in the figure of a young man comely and well favored.

30 He approached Isaac and said to him, Do you not know and understand that your old silly father brings you to the slaughter today for nothing?

31 Now therefore, my son, do not listen or attend to him, for he is a silly old man; let not your precious soul and beautiful figure be lost from the earth.

32 And Isaac heard this, and said to Abraham, Have you heard, my father, that which this man has spoken? Even thus has he spoken.

33 And Abraham answered his son Isaac and said to him, Take heed of him and do not listen to his words, nor attend to him, for he is Satan, endeavoring to draw us aside this day from the commands of God.

34 Abraham still rebuked Satan, and Satan went from them; seeing he could not prevail over them he hid himself from them, and he went and passed before them in the road; he transformed himself to a large brook of water in the road. Abraham and Isaac and his two young men reached that place, and they saw a brook large and powerful as the mighty waters.

35 They entered the brook and passed through it, and the waters at first reached their legs.

36 And they went deeper in the brook and the waters reached up to their necks. They were all terrified on account of the water and while they were going over the brook Abraham recognized that place, and he knew that there was no water there before.

37 Abraham said to his son Isaac, I know this place in which there was no brook or water, now therefore it is Satan who does all this to us, to draw us aside on this day from the commands of God.

38 And Abraham rebuked him and said to him, The Lord rebuke you, O Satan, begone from us for we go by the commands of God.

39 And Satan was terrified at the voice of Abraham, and he went away from them; the place again became dry land as it was at first.

40 Abraham went with Isaac toward the place that God had told him.

41 And on the third day Abraham lifted up his eyes and saw the place at a distance which God had told him of.

42 A pillar of fire appeared to him that reached from the earth to heaven, and a cloud of glory on the mountain, and the glory of the Lord was seen in the cloud.

43 And Abraham said to Isaac, My son, do you see in that mountain, which we perceive at a distance, that which I see on it?

44 And Isaac answered and said to his father, I see and there is a pillar of fire and a cloud, and the glory of the Lord is seen on the cloud.

45 And Abraham knew that his son Isaac was accepted before the Lord for a burnt offering.

46 Abraham said to Eliezer and to Ishmael his son, Do you also see that which we see on the mountain which is at a distance?

47 And they answered and said, We see nothing more than like the other mountains of the earth. Abraham knew that they were not accepted before the Lord to go with them, and Abraham said to them, Stay here with the ass while I and Isaac my son will go to yonder mount and worship there before the Lord and then return to you.

48 Eliezer and Ishmael remained in that place, as Abraham had commanded.

49 And Abraham took wood for a burnt offering and placed it on his son Isaac, and he took the fire and the knife, and they both went to that place.

50 When they were on the way Isaac said to his father, Behold, I see here the fire and wood, and where then is the lamb that is to be the burnt offering before the Lord?

51 And Abraham answered his son Isaac, saying, The Lord has made choice of you my son, to be a perfect burnt offering instead of the lamb.

52 And Isaac said to his father, I will do all that the Lord spoke to you with joy and cheerfulness of heart.

53 Abraham again said to Isaac his son, Is there in your heart any thought or counsel concerning this, which is not proper? Tell me my son, I pray you, O my son conceal it not from me.

54 And Isaac answered his father Abraham and said to him, O my father, as the Lord lives and as your soul lives, there is nothing in my heart to cause me to deviate either to the right or to the left from the word that he has spoken to you.

55 Neither limb nor muscle has moved or stirred at this, nor is there in my heart any thought or evil counsel concerning this.

56 But I am of joyful and cheerful heart in this matter, and I say, Blessed is the Lord who has this day chosen me to be a burnt offering before Him.

57 Abraham greatly rejoiced at the words of Isaac, and they went on and came together to that place that the Lord had spoken of.

58 Abraham approached to build the altar in that place, and Abraham was weeping. Isaac took stones and mortar until they had finished building the altar.

59 And Abraham took the wood and placed it in order on the altar which he had built.

60 He took his son Isaac and bound him in order to place him on the wood which was on the altar, to kill him for a burnt offering before the Lord.

61 Isaac said to his father, Bind me securely and then place me on the altar that I should not turn and move, and break loose from the force of the knife on my flesh and thereof profane the burnt offering; and Abraham did so.

62 Isaac still said to his father, O my father, when you have slain me and burnt me for an offering, take with you that which remains of my ashes to bring to Sarah my mother, and say to her, This is the sweet smelling savor of Isaac. But do not tell her this if she should sit near a well or on any high place, that she would cast her soul after me and die.

63 And Abraham heard the words of Isaac, and he lifted up his voice and wept when Isaac spake these words. Abraham's tears gushed down on Isaac his son, and Isaac wept bitterly; he said to his father, Hasten, O my father, and do with me the will of the Lord our God as He has commanded you.

64 The hearts of Abraham and Isaac rejoiced at this thing which the Lord had commanded them; but the eye wept bitterly while the heart rejoiced.

65 And Abraham bound his son Isaac and placed him on the altar on the wood, and Isaac stretched forth his neck on the altar before his father. Abraham stretched forth his hand to take the knife to kill his son as a burnt offering before the Lord.

66 At that time the angels of mercy came before the Lord and spoke to him concerning Isaac, saying,

67 0 Lord, you are a merciful and compassionate King over all that you have created in heaven and in earth, and you support them all; give therefore ransom and redemption instead of your servant Isaac, and pity and have compassion on Abraham and Isaac his son who are this day performing your commands.

68 Have you seen, O Lord, how Isaac the son of Abraham your servant is bound down to the slaughter like an animal? Now therefore let your pity be roused for them, O Lord.

69 At that time the Lord appeared to Abraham and called to him from heaven, and said to him, Lay not your hand on the lad, neither do anything to him, for now I know that you fear God in performing this act, and in not withholding your son, your only son, from me.

70 And Abraham lifted up his eyes and looked, and behold, a ram was caught in a thicket by his horns; that was the ram which the Lord God had created in the earth in the day that he made earth and heaven.

71 For the Lord had prepared this ram from that day, to be a burnt offering instead of Isaac.

72 This ram was advancing to Abraham when Satan caught hold of him and entangled his horns in the thicket, so that he might not advance to Abraham, in order that Abraham might kill his son.

73 And Abraham, seeing the ram advancing to him and Satan withholding him, fetched him and brought him before the altar; he loosened his son Isaac from his binding, and he put the ram in his stead. Abraham killed the ram on the altar, and brought it up as an offering in the place of his son Isaac.

74 Abraham sprinkled some of the blood of the ram on the altar, and he exclaimed and said, This is in the place of my son, and may it be considered this day as the blood of my son before the Lord.

75 And all that Abraham did on this occasion by the altar, he would exclaim and say, This is in place of my son, and may it this day be considered before the Lord in the place of my son; and Abraham finished the whole service by the altar, and the service was accepted before the Lord, and was accounted as if it had been Isaac; and the Lord blessed Abraham and his descendants on that day.

76 Satan went to Sarah, and he appeared to her in the figure of an old man very humble and meek, and Abraham was yet engaged in the burnt offering before the Lord.

77 And he said to her, Do you not know all the work that Abraham has made with your only son this day? For he took Isaac and built an altar, and killed him, and brought him up as a sacrifice on the altar; Isaac cried and wept before his father, but he looked not at him, neither did he have compassion over him.

78 Satan repeated these words, and he went away from her. Sarah heard all the words of Satan, and she imagined him to be an old man from among the sons of men who had been with her son, and had come and told her these things.

79 And Sarah lifted up her voice and wept and cried out bitterly on account of her son; she threw herself on the ground and she cast dust on her head, and she said, O my son, Isaac my son, O that I had this day died instead of you. And she continued to weep and said, It grieves me for you, O my son, my son Isaac, O that I had died this day in your stead.

80 She still continued to weep, and said, It grieves me for you after I have reared you and have brought you up; now my joy is turned into mourning over you; I who had a longing for you, and cried and prayed to God till I gave birth to you at ninety years old. And now you have served this day for the knife and the fire, to be made an offering.

81 But I console myself with you, my son, in its being the word of the Lord, for you did perform the command of your God. Who can go contrary to the word of our God, in whose hands is the soul of every living creature?

82 You are just, O Lord our God, for all your works are good and righteous; for I also am rejoiced with your word which you did command; while my eye weeps bitterly my heart rejoices.

83 Sarah laid her head on the bosom of one of her handmaids, and she became as still as a stone.

84 Afterward she rose up and went about making inquiries till she came to Hebron; she inquired of all those whom she met walking in the road and no one could tell her what had happened to her son.

85 She came with her maid servants and men servants to Kireath-arba, which is Hebron, and she asked concerning her son; she remained there while she sent some of her servants to seek where Abraham had gone with Isaac. They went to seek him in the house of Shem and Eber, and they could not find him, and they sought throughout the land and he was not there.

86 And then Satan came to Sarah in the shape of an old man; he came and stood before her, and said to her, I spoke falsely to you, for Abraham did not kill his son and he is not dead. When she heard the word her joy was so greatly violent on account of her son, that her soul went out through joy; she died and was gathered to her people.

87 When Abraham had finished his service he returned with his son Isaac to his young men, and they rose up and went together to Beersheba, and they came home.

88 And Abraham sought for Sarah, and could not find her, and he made inquiries concerning her. They said to him, She went as far as Hebron to seek you both where you had gone, for thus was she informed.

89 Abraham and Isaac went to her to Hebron, and when they found that she was dead they lifted up their voices and wept bitterly over her; Isaac fell on his mother's face and wept over her, and he said, O my mother, my mother, how have you left me, and where have you gone? O how, how have you left me!

90 And Abraham and Isaac wept greatly and all their servants wept with them on account of Sarah, and they mourned over her a great and heavy mourning.

CHAPTER 24

1 The life of Sarah was one hundred and twenty-seven years, and Sarah died; and Abraham rose up from before his dead to seek a burial place to bury his wife Sarah. He went and spoke to the children of Heth, the inhabitants of the land, saying,

2 I am a stranger and a sojourner with you in your land; give me possession of a burial place in your land, that I may bury my dead from before me.

3 And the children of Heth said to Abraham, Behold the land is before you, in the choice of our sepulchers bury your dead, for no man shall withhold you from burying your dead.

4 Abraham said to them, If you are agreeable to this, go and entreat Ephron the son of Zochar for me, requesting that he may give me the cave of Machpelah which is in the end of his field, and I will purchase it of him for whatever he desires for it.

5 And Ephron lived among the children of Heth, and they went and called for him, and he came before Abraham. Ephron said to Abraham, Behold all you require your servant will do; Abraham said, No, but I will buy the cave and the field which you have for value, in order that it may be for possession of a burial place forever.

6 And Ephron answered and said, Behold the field and the cave are before you, give whatever you desire. Abraham said, Only at full value will I buy it from your hand, and from the hands of those that go in at the gate of your city, and from the hand of your descendants forever.

7 Ephron and all his brothers heard this, and Abraham weighed to Ephron four hundred shekels of silver in the hands of Ephron and in the hands of all his brothers. Abraham wrote this transaction; he wrote it and testified it with four witnesses.

8 And these are the names of the witnesses: Amigal son of Abishna the Hittite, Adichorom son of Ashunach the Hivite, Abdon son of Achiram the Gomerite, Bakdil the son of Abudish the Zidonite.

9 Abraham took the book of the purchase and placed it in his treasures, and these are the words that Abraham wrote in the book, namely:

10 That the cave and the field Abraham bought from Ephron the Hittite and from his descendants, and from those that go out of his city, and from their descendants forever, are to be a purchase to Abraham and to his descendants and to those that go forth from his loins, for a possession of a burial place forever. And he put a signet to it and testified it with witnesses.

11 The field and the cave that was in it and all that place were made sure to belong to Abraham and to his descendants after him, from the children of Heth; behold it is before Mamre in Hebron which is in the land of Canaan.

12 After this Abraham buried his wife Sarah there, and that place and all its boundary became to Abraham and to his descendants for a possession of a burial place.

13 And Abraham buried Sarah with pomp as observed at the interment of kings, and she was buried in very fine and beautiful garments.

14 At her bier was Shem, his sons Eber and Abimelech, together with Anar, Ashcol and Mamre, and all the grandees of the land followed her bier.

15 The days of Sarah were one hundred and twenty-seven years and she died, and Abraham made a great and heavy mourning, and he performed the rites of mourning for seven days.

16 And all the inhabitants of the land comforted Abraham and Isaac his son on account of Sarah.

17 When the days of their mourning passed by Abraham sent away his son Isaac. He went to the house of Shem

and Eber, to learn the ways of the Lord and his instructions, and Abraham remained there three years.

18 At that time Abraham rose up with all his servants, and they went and returned homeward to Beersheba, and Abraham and all his servants remained in Beersheba.

19 At the revolution of the year Abimelech king of the Philistines died in that year; he was one hundred and ninety-three years old at his death. Abraham went with his people to the land of the Philistines, and they comforted the whole household and all his servants, and then he turned and went home.

20 It was after the death of Abimelech that the people of Gerar took Benmalich his son, and he was only twelve years old, and they made him lay the place of his father.

21 And they called his name Abimelech after the name of his father, for thus it was their custom to do in Gerar. Abimelech reigned instead of Abimelech his father, and he sat on his throne.

22 And Lot the son of Haran also died in those days, in the thirty-ninth year of the life of Isaac; all the days that Lot lived were one hundred and forty years and he died.

23 And these are the children of Lot, that were born to him by his daughters; the name of the first born was Moab, and the name of the second was Benami.

24 The two sons of Lot went and took themselves wives from the land of Canaan, and they gave birth to children to them. The children of Moab were Ed, Mayon, Tarsus, and Kanvil, four sons; these are fathers to the children of Moab to this day.

25 And all the families of the children of Lot went to dwell wherever they should light on, for they were prolific and increased abundantly.

26 And they went and built themselves cities in the land where they lived, and they called the names of the cities which they built after their own names.

27 Nahor the son of Terah, brother to Abraham, died in those days in the fortieth year of the life of Isaac. All the days of Nahor were one hundred and seventy-two years; he died and was buried in Haran.

28 And when Abraham heard that his brother was dead he grieved sadly, and he mourned over his brother many days.

29 Abraham called for Eliezer his head servant to give him orders concerning his house, and he came and stood before him.

30 And Abraham said to him, Behold I am old, I do not know the day of my death; for I am advanced in days; now therefore rise up, go forth and do not take a wife for my son from this place and from this land, from the daughters of the Canaanites among whom we dwell.

31 But go to my land and to my birthplace, and take from there a wife for my son. The Lord God of Heaven and earth who took me from my father's house and brought me to this place, and said to me, To your offspring will I give this land for an inheritance forever, he will send his angel before you and prosper your way, that you may obtain a wife for my son from my family and from my father's house.

32 The servant answered his master Abraham and said, Behold I go to your birthplace and to your father's house, and take a wife for your son from there; but if the woman be not willing to follow me to this land, shall I take your son back to the land of your birthplace?

33 And Abraham said to him, See that you do not bring my son here again, for the Lord before whom I have walked will send his angel before you and prosper your way.

34 Eliezer did as Abraham ordered him, and Eliezer swore to Abraham his master on this matter; and Eliezer rose up and took ten camels of the camels of his master, and ten men from his master's servants with him, and they rose up and went to Haran, the city of Abraham and Nahor, in order to fetch a wife for Isaac the son of Abraham. While they were gone Abraham sent to the house of Shem and Eber, and they brought from there his son Isaac.

35 Isaac came home to his father's house to Beersheba, while Eliezer and his men came to Haran; and they stopped in the city by the watering place, and he made his camels to kneel down by the water and they remained there.

36 Eliezer, Abraham's servant, prayed and said, O God of Abraham my master; send me I pray you good speed this day and show kindness to my master, that you shall appoint this day a wife for my master's son from his family.

37 And the Lord listened to the voice of Eliezer, for the sake of his servant Abraham, and he happened to meet with the daughter of Bethuel, the son of Milcah, the wife of Nahor, brother to Abraham, and Eliezer came to her house.

38 Eliezer related to them all his concerns, and that he was Abraham's servant; they greatly rejoiced at him.

39 And they all blessed the Lord who brought this thing about; they gave him Rebecca, the daughter of Bethuel,

for a wife for Isaac.

40 The young woman was of a beautiful appearance; she was a virgin, and Rebecca was ten years old in those days.

41 And Bethuel and Laban and his children made a feast on that night, and Eliezer and his men came and ate and drank and rejoiced there on that night.

42 Eliezer rose up in the morning, he and the men that were with him, and he called to the whole household of Bethuel, saying, Send me away that I may go to my master; they rose up and sent away Rebecca and her nurse Deborah, the daughter of Uz, and they gave her silver and gold, men servants and maid servants, and they blessed her.

43 And they sent Eliezer away with his men and the servants took Rebecca; he went and returned to his master to the land of Canaan.

44 Isaac took Rebecca and she became his wife, and he brought her into the tent.

45 And Isaac was forty years old when he took Rebecca, the daughter of his uncle Bethuel, for a wife.

CHAPTER 25

1 It was at that time that Abraham again took a wife in his old age, and her name was Keturah, from the land of Canaan.

2 She gave birth to, to him: Zimran, Jokshan, Medan, Midian, Ishbak and Shuach, being six sons. And the children of Zimran were Abihen, Molich and Narim.

3 The sons of Jokshan were Sheba and Dedan, and the sons of Medan were Amida, Joab, Gochi, Elisha and Nothach; and the sons of Midian were Ephah, Epher, Chanoch, Abida and Eldaah.

4 The sons of Ishbak were Makiro, Beyodua and Tator.

5 The sons of Shuach were Bildad, Mamdad, Munan and Meban; all these are the families of the children of Keturah the Canaanitish woman which she gave birth to, to Abraham the Hebrew.

6 And Abraham sent all these away, and he gave them gifts; they went away from his son Isaac to dwell wherever they would find a place.

7 And all these went to the mountain at the east, and they built themselves six cities in which they lived to this day.

8 But the children of Sheba and Dedan, children of Jokshan, with their children, did not dwell with their brothers in their cities; they journeyed and encamped in the countries and wildernesses to this day.

9 And the children of Midian, son of Abraham, went to the east of the land of Cush. There they found a large valley in the eastern country, and remained there and built a city. They lived therein; that is the land of Midian to this day.

10 Midian lived in the city which he built, he and his five sons and all belonging to him.

11 And these are the names of the sons of Midian according to their names in their cities: Ephah, Epher, Chanoch, Abida and Eldaah.

12 And the sons of Ephah were Methach, Meshar, Avi and Tzanua, and the sons of Epher were Ephron, Zur, Alirun and Medin; the sons of Chanoch were Reuel, Rekem, Azi, Alyoshub and Alad.

13 The sons of Abida were Chur, Melud, Kerury, Molchi; and the sons of Eldaah were Miker, and Reba, and Malchiyah and Gabol. These are the names of the Midianites according to their families, and afterward the families of Midian spread throughout the land of Midian.

14 These are the generations of Ishmael the son of Abraham, whom Hagar, Sarah's handmaid, gave birth to, to Abraham.

15 And Ishmael took a wife from the land of Egypt, and her name was Ribah, the same is Meribah.

16 And Ribah gave birth to, to Ishmael: Nebayoth, Kedar, Adbeel, Mibsam and their sister Bosmath.

17 And Ishmael cast away his wife Ribah, and she went from him and returned to Egypt to the house of her father. She lived there, for she had been very bad in the sight of Ishmael, and in the sight of his father Abraham.

18 And Ishmael afterward took a wife from the land of Canaan, and her name was Malchuth, and she gave birth to, to him: Nishma, Dumah, Masa, Chadad, Tema, Yetur, Naphish and Kedma.

19 These are the sons of Ishmael, and these are their names, being twelve princes according to their nations. And the families of Ishmael afterward spread forth, and Ishmael took his children and all the property that he had gained, together with the souls of his household and all belonging to him, and they went to dwell where they

should find a place.

20 They went and lived near the wilderness of Paran, and their dwelling was from Havilah to Shur, that is before Egypt as you come toward Assyria.

21 Ishmael and his sons lived in the land, and they had children born to them, and they were prolific and increased abundantly.

22 These are the names of the sons of Nebayoth the first born of Ishmael: Mend, Send, Mayon; and the sons of Kedar were Alyon, Kezem, Chamad and Eli.

23 The sons of Adbeel were Chamad and Jabin; and the sons of Mibsam were Obadiah, Ebedmelech and Yeush; these are the families of the children of Ribah the wife of Ishmael.

24 The sons of Mishma the son of Ishmael were Shamua, Zecaryon and Obed; and the sons of Dumah were Kezed, Eli, Machmad and Amed.

25 The sons of Masa were Melon, Mula and Ebidadon; and the sons of Chadad were Azur, Minzar and Ebedmelech; and the sons of Tema were Seir, Sadon and Yakol.

26 The sons of Yetur were Merith, Yaish, Alyo, and Pachoth; and the sons of Naphish were Ebed-Tamed, Abiyasaph and Mir; and the sons of Kedma were Calip, Tachti, and Omir; these were the children of Malchuth the wife of Ishmael according to their families.

27 All these are the families of Ishmael according to their generations, and they lived in those lands wherein they had built themselves cities to this day.

28 Rebecca the daughter of Bethuel, the wife of Abraham's son Isaac, was unable to conceive in those days, she had no children. Isaac lived with his father in the land of Canaan, and the Lord was with Isaac. Arpachshad the son of Shem the son of Noah died in those days, in the forty-eighth year of the life of Isaac, and all the days that Arpachshad lived were four hundred and thirty-eight years, and he died.

CHAPTER 26

1 In the fifty-ninth year of the life of Isaac the son of Abraham, Rebecca his wife was still unable to conceive in those days.

2 And Rebecca said to Isaac, Truly I have heard, my lord, that your mother Sarah was unable to conceive in her days until my Lord Abraham, your father, prayed for her and she conceived by him.

3 Now therefore stand up, you also pray to God and he will hear your prayer and remember us through his mercies.

4 And Isaac answered his wife Rebecca, saying, Abraham has already prayed for me to God to reproduce his descendants, now therefore this barrenness must proceed to us from you.

5 And Rebecca said to him, But arise now you also and pray, that the Lord may hear your prayer and grant me children. Isaac listened to the words of his wife, and Isaac and his wife rose up and went to the land of Moriah to pray there and to seek the Lord, and when they had reached that place Isaac stood up and prayed to the Lord on account of his wife because she was unable to conceive.

6 And Isaac said, O Lord God of heaven and earth, whose goodness and mercies fill the earth, you who did take my father from his father's house and from his birthplace, and brought him to this land, and did say to him, To your descendants I will give the land, and you did promise him and did declare to him, I will reproduce your descendants as the stars of heaven and as the sand of the sea, now may your words be verified which you did speak to my father.

7 For you are the Lord our God, our eyes are toward you to give us descendants of men, as you did promise us, for you are the Lord our God and our eyes are directed toward you only.

8 And the Lord heard the prayer of Isaac the son of Abraham; the Lord was entreated of him and Rebecca his wife conceived.

9 And in about seven months after the children struggled together within her, it pained her greatly and she was wearied on account of them. She said to all the women who were then in the land, Did such a thing happen to you as it has to me? And they said to her, No.

10 And she said to them, Why am I alone in this among all the women that were on earth? And she went to the

land of Moriah to seek the Lord on account of this; she went to Shem and Eber his son to make inquiries of them in this matter, that they should seek the Lord in this thing respecting her.

11 She also asked Abraham to seek and inquire of the Lord about all that had befallen her.

12 They all inquired of the Lord concerning this matter, and they brought her word from the Lord and told her, Two children are in your womb, and two nations shall rise from them; one nation shall be stronger than the other, and the greater shall serve the younger.

13 When her days to be delivered were completed, she knelt down, and behold there were twins in her womb, as the Lord had spoken to her.

14 The first came out red all over like a hairy garment, and all the people of the land called his name Esau, saying, This one was made complete from the womb.

15 And after that came his brother, and his hand took hold of Esau's heel, therefore they called his name Jacob.

16 Isaac, the son of Abraham, was sixty years old when he had them.

17 The boys grew up to their fifteenth year, and they came among the society of men. Esau was a designing and deceitful man, and an expert hunter in the field; Jacob was a man perfect and wise, dwelling in tents, feeding flocks and learning the instructions of the Lord and the commands of his father and mother.

18 Isaac and the children of his household lived with his father Abraham in the land of Canaan, as God had commanded them.

19 Ishmael the son of Abraham went with his children and all belonging to them; they returned there to the land of Havilah, and they lived there.

20 And all the children of Abraham's concubines went to dwell in the land of the east, for Abraham had sent them away from his son and had given them presents, and they went away.

21 Abraham gave all that he had to his son Isaac, and he also gave him all his treasures.

22 And he commanded him saying, Do you not know and understand the Lord is God in heaven and in earth, and there is no other beside him?

23 It was he who took me from my father's house, and from my birthplace, and gave me all the delights on earth; who delivered me from the counsel of the wicked, for in him I did trust.

24 He brought me to this place, and delivered me from Ur Casdim, and said to me, To your descendants I will give all these land and they shall inherit them when they keep my commandments, my statutes and my judgments that I have commanded you, and which I shall command them.

25 Now therefore my son, listen to my voice, and keep the commandments of the Lord your God, which I commanded you. Do not turn from the right way either to the right or to the left, in order that it may be well with you and your children after you forever.

26 And remember the wonderful works of the Lord and his kindness that he has shown toward us, in having delivered us from the hands of our enemies; the Lord our God caused them to fall into our hands; now therefore keep all that I have commanded you and turn not away from the commandments of your God; serve none beside him, in order that it may be well with you and your descendants after you.

27 Teach your children and your descendants the instructions of the Lord and his commandments, and teach them the upright way in which they should go, in order that it may be well with them forever.

28 Isaac answered his father and said to him, That which my Lord has commanded thatI will do, and I will not depart from the commands of the Lord my God; I will keep all that he commanded me. And Abraham blessed his son Isaac, and also his children, and Abraham taught Jacob the instruction of the Lord and his ways.

29 It was at that time that Abraham died, in the fifteenth year of the life of Jacob and Esau, the sons of Isaac, and all the days of Abraham were one hundred and seventy-five years. He died and was gathered to his people in good old age, old and satisfied with days, and Isaac and Ishmael his sons buried him.

30 When the inhabitants of Canaan heard that Abraham was dead, they all came with their kings and princes and all their men to bury Abraham.

31 All the inhabitants of the land of Haran, all the families of the house of Abraham, all the princes and grandees, and the sons of Abraham by the concubines, all came when they heard of Abraham's death. They rewarded Abraham's kindness, and comforted Isaac his son, and they buried Abraham in the cave which he bought from Ephron the Hittite and his children, for the possession of a burial place.

32 All the inhabitants of Canaan, and all those who had known Abraham, wept for Abraham a whole year; men and women mourned over him.

33 Alll the little children, and all the inhabitants of the land wept on account of Abraham, for Abraham had been good to them all, because he had been upright with God and men.

34 There arose not a man who feared God like Abraham, for he had feared his God from his youth, and had served the Lord, and had gone in all his ways during his life from his childhood to the day of his death.

35 And the Lord was with him and delivered him from the counsel of Nimrod and his people; when he made war with the four kings of Elam he conquered them.

36 He brought all the children of the earth to the service of God and he taught them the ways of the Lord, and caused them to know the Lord.

37 He formed a grove and planted a vineyard therein, and he had always prepared in his tent meat and drink to those that passed through the land, that they might satisfy themselves in his house.

38 The Lord God delivered the whole earth on account of Abraham.

39 It was after the death of Abraham that God blessed his son Isaac and his children, and the Lord was with Isaac as he had been with his father Abraham, for Isaac kept all the commandments of the Lord as Abraham his father had commanded him; he did not turn to the right or to the left from the right path which his father had commanded him.

CHAPTER 27

1 Esau at that time, after the death of Abraham, frequently went in the field to hunt.

2 Nimrod king of Babel, the same was Amraphel, also frequently went with his mighty men to hunt in the field, and to walk about with his men in the cool of the day.

3 Nimrod was observing Esau all those days, for jealousy was formed in the heart of Nimrod against Esau.

4 On a certain day Esau went in the field to hunt, and he found Nimrod walking in the wilderness with his two men.

5 All his mighty men and his people were with him in the wilderness, but they kept at a distance; they went from him in different directions to hunt, and Esau concealed himself from Nimrod, and he lurked for him in the wilderness.

6 And Nimrod and his men that were with him did not know him. Nimrod and his men frequently walked about in the field at the cool of the day, and to know where his men were hunting in the field.

7 Nimrod and two of his men that were with him came to the place where they were, when Esau appeared suddenly from his lurking place, drew his sword, and hurriedly ran to Nimrod and cut off his head.

8 Esau fought a desperate fight with the two men that were with Nimrod, and when they called out to him, Esau turned to them and struck them to death with his sword.

9 All the mighty men of Nimrod, who had left him to go to the wilderness, heard the cry at a distance, and they knew the voices of those two men; they ran to know the cause of it and they found their king and the two men that were with him lying dead in the wilderness.

10 When Esau saw the mighty men of Nimrod coming at a distance, he fled, and thereby escaped. Esau took the valuable garments of Nimrod which Nimrod's father had bequeathed to Nimrod, with which Nimrod prevailed over the whole land; he ran and concealed them in his house.

11 Esau took those garments and ran into the city on account of Nimrod's men, and he came to his father's house wearied and exhausted from fight, and he was ready to die through grief when he approached his brother Jacob and sat before him.

12 And he said to his brother Jacob, Behold I shall die this day; wherefore then do I want the birthright? And Jacob acted wisely with Esau in this matter, and Esau sold his birthright to Jacob, for it was so brought about by the Lord.

13 Esau's portion in the cave of the field of Machpelah, which Abraham had bought from the children of Heth for the possession of a burial ground, Esau also sold to Jacob, and Jacob bought all this from his brother Esau for value given.

14 Jacob wrote all of this in a book and he testified the same with witnesses, and sealed it, and the book remained in the hands of Jacob.

15 When Nimrod the son of Cush died, his men lifted him up and brought him in consternation, and buried him in his city, and all the days that Nimrod lived were two hundred and fifteen years and he died.

16 The days that Nimrod reigned on the people of the land were one hundred and eighty-five years; and Nimrod

died by the sword of Esau in shame and contempt, and the descendants of Abraham caused his death as he had seen in his dream.

17 At the death of Nimrod his kingdom became divided into many divisions, and all those parts that Nimrod reigned over were restored to the respective kings of the land, who recovered them after the death of Nimrod. All the people of the house of Nimrod were for a long time enslaved to all the other kings of the land.

CHAPTER 28

1 In those days, after the death of Abraham, in that year the Lord brought a heavy famine in the land. While the famine was raging in the land of Canaan, Isaac rose up to go down to Egypt on account of the famine, as his father Abraham had done.

2 And the Lord appeared that night to Isaac and said to him, Do not go down to Egypt but rise and go to Gerar, to Abimelech king of the Philistines, and remain there till the famine shall cease.

3 Isaac rose up and went to Gerar, as the Lord commanded him, and he remained there a full year.

4 And when Isaac came to Gerar, the people of the land saw that Rebecca his wife was of a beautiful appearance, and the people of Gerar asked Isaac concerning his wife, and he said, She is my sister, for he was afraid to say she was his wife that the people of the land should kill him on account of her.

5 The princes of Abimelech went and praised the woman to the king, but he answered them not, neither did he give attention to their words.

6 But he heard them say that Isaac declared her to be his sister, so the king reserved this within himself.

7 And when Isaac had remained three months in the land, Abimelech looked out the window, and he saw Isaac was sporting with Rebecca his wife, for Isaac lived in the outer house belonging to the king, so that the house of Isaac was opposite the house of the king.

8 And the king said to Isaac, What is this you have done to us in saying of your wife, She is my sister? How easily might one of the great men of the people have lain with her, and you would then have brought guilt on us.

9 And Isaac said to Abimelech, Because I was afraid that I die on account of my wife, therefore I said, She is my sister.

10 At that time Abimelech gave orders to all his princes and great men, and they took Isaac and Rebecca his wife and brought them before the king.

11 The king commanded that they should dress them in princely garments, and make them ride through the streets of the city, and proclaim before them throughout the land, saying, This is the man and this is his wife; whoever touches this man or his wife shall certainly die. And Isaac returned with his wife to the king's house, and the Lord was with Isaac and he continued to become great and lacked nothing.

12 And the Lord caused Isaac to find favor in the sight of Abimelech, and in the sight of all his subjects, and Abimelech acted well with Isaac, for Abimelech remembered the oath and the covenant that existed between his father and Abraham.

13 Abimelech said to Isaac, Behold the whole earth is before you; dwell wherever it may seem good in your sight until you shall return to your land. Abimelech gave Isaac fields and vineyards and the best part of the land of Gerar, to sow and reap and eat the fruits of the ground until the days of the famine would have passed by.

14 And Isaac sowed in that land, and received a hundred-fold in the same year, and the Lord blessed him.

15 The man became great, and he had possession of flocks and possession of herds and a great store of servants.

16 When the days of the famine had passed away the Lord appeared to Isaac and said to him, Rise up, go forth from this place and return to your land, to the land of Canaan; Isaac rose up and returned to Hebron which is in the land of Canaan, he and all belonging to him as the Lord commanded him.

17 Ater this Shelach the son at Arpachshad died in that year, which is the eighteenth year of the lives of Jacob and Esau; all the days that Shelach lived were four hundred and thirty-three years and he died.

18 At that time Isaac sent his younger son Jacob to the house of Shem and Eber, and he learned the instructions of the Lord; Jacob remained in the house of Shem and Eber for thirty-two years; Esau his brother did not go for he was not willing to go, and he remained in his father's house in the land of Canaan.

19 Esau was continually hunting in the fields to bring home what he could get, so did Esau all the days.

20 Esau was a designing and deceitful man, one who hunted after the hearts of men and inveigled them, and Esau was a valiant man in the field; in the course of time he went as usual to hunt and came as far as the field of Seir, the same is Edom.

21 And he remained in the land of Seir hunting in the field a year and four months.

22 Esau there saw in the land of Seir the daughter of a man of Canaan, and her name was Jehudith, the daughter of Beeri, son of Epher, from the families of Heth the son of Canaan.

23 Esau took her for a wife, and he came to her; forty years old was Esau when he took her, and he brought her to Hebron, the land of his father's dwelling place, and he lived there.

24 It came to pass in those days, in the hundred and tenth year of the life of Isaac, that is in the fiftieth year of the life of Jacob, in that year Shem the son of Noah died; Shem was six hundred years old at his death.

25 And when Shem died Jacob returned to his father to Hebron which is in the land of Canaan.

26 And in the fifty-sixth year of the life of Jacob, people came from Haran, and Rebecca was told concerning her brother Laban the son of Bethuel.

27 The wife of Laban was unable to conceive in those days, and gave birth to no children, and also all his handmaids gave birth to none, to him.

28 And the Lord afterward remembered Adinah the wife of Laban, and she conceived and gave birth to twin daughters, and Laban named his daughters: the name of the elder Leah, and the name of the younger Rachel.

29 And those people came and told these things to Rebecca, and Rebecca rejoiced greatly that the Lord had visited her brother and that he had gotten children.

CHAPTER 29

1 Isaac the son of Abraham became old and advanced in days, and his eyes became heavy through age; they were dim and could not see.

2 At that time Isaac called to Esau his son, saying, Get I pray you your weapons, your quiver and your bow; rise up and go forth into the field and get me some venison, make me savory meat and bring it to me that I may eat in order that I may bless you before my death, as I have now become old and gray-headed.

3 And Esau did so; he took his weapon and went forth into the field to hunt for venison, as usual, to bring to his father as he had ordered him, so that he might bless him.

4 And Rebecca heard all the words that Isaac had spoken to Esau, and she hurried and called her son Jacob, saying, Thus did your father speak to your brother Esau, and thus did I hear, now therefore hurry and make that which I shall tell you.

5 Rise up and go, I pray you, to the flock and fetch me two fine kids of the goats; I will get the savory meat for your father and you shall bring the savory meat that he may eat before your brother will have come from the hunt, in order that your father may bless you.

6 And Jacob hurried and did as his mother had commanded him, and he made the savory meat and brought it before his father before Esau had come from his hunt.

7 And Isaac said to Jacob, Who are you, my son? And he said, I am your first born Esau. I have done as you did order me, now therefore rise up I pray you and eat of my hunt, in order that your soul may bless me as you did speak to me.

8 And Isaac rose up and he ate and drank, and his heart was comforted; he blessed Jacob and Jacob went away from his father. As soon as Isaac had blessed Jacob and had gone away from him, behold Esau came from his hunt in the field, and he also made savory meat and brought it to his father to eat thereof and to bless him.

9 And Isaac said to Esau, And who was he that has taken venison and brought it me before you came and whom I did bless? And Esau knew that his brother Jacob had done this, and the anger of Esau was set ablaze against his brother Jacob that he had acted thus toward him.

10 And Esau said, Is he not rightly called Jacob? For he has supplanted me twice, he took away my birthright and now he has taken away my blessing. And Esau wept greatly. When Isaac heard the voice of his son Esau weeping, Isaac said to Esau, What can I do, my son, your brother came with subtlety and took away your blessing? Esau hated his brother Jacob on account of the blessing that his father had given him, and his anger was greatly roused against him.

11 And Jacob was very much afraid of his brother Esau; he rose up and fled to the house of Eber the son of Shem, and he concealed himself there on account of his brother. Jacob was sixty-three years old when he went forth from the land of Canaan from Hebron, and Jacob was concealed in Eber's house fourteen years on account of his brother Esau, and he continued there to learn the ways of the Lord and his commandments.

12 When Esau saw that Jacob had fled and escaped from him, and that Jacob had cunningly obtained the blessing, then Esau grieved greatly. He was also troubled at his father and mother; he rose up and took his wife and went

away from his father and mother to the land of Seir, and he lived there. Esau saw there a woman from among the daughters of Heth whose name was Bosmath, the daughter of Elon the Hittite, and he took her for a wife in addition to his first wife, and Esau called her name Adah, saying the blessing had in that time passed from him.

13 And Esau lived in the land of Seir six months without seeing his father and mother, and afterward Esau took his wives and rose up and returned to the land of Canaan. And Esau placed his two wives in his father's house in Hebron.

14 The wives of Esau troubled and provoked Isaac and Rebecca with their works, for they walked not in the ways of the Lord, but served their father's gods of wood and stone as their father had taught them; they were more wicked than their father.

15 They went according to the evil desires of their hearts, and they sacrificed and burnt incense to the Baalim, and Isaac and Rebecca became weary of them.

16 And Rebecca said, I am weary of my life because of the daughters of Heth; if Jacob took a wife of the daughters of Heth, such as these which are of the daughters of the land, what good then is life to me?

17 In those days Adah the wife of Esau conceived and gave birth to him a son, and Esau called the name of the son that was born to him Eliphaz, and Esau was sixty-five years old when she gave birth to him.

18 Ishmael the son of Abraham died in those days, in the sixty-fourth year of the life of Jacob, and all the days that Ishmael lived were one hundred and thirty-seven years and he died.

19 And when Isaac heard that Ishmael was dead he mourned for him, and Isaac lamented over him many days.

20 At the end of fourteen years of Jacob's residing in the house of Eber, Jacob desired to see his father and mother, and Jacob came to the house of his father and mother to Hebron, and Esau had in those days forgotten what Jacob had done to him in having taken the blessing from him.

21 And when Esau saw Jacob coming to his father and mother he remembered what Jacob had done to him, and he was greatly incensed against him and he sought to kill him.

22 And Isaac the son of Abraham was old and advanced in days, and Esau said, Now my father's time is drawing nigh that he must die, and when he shall die I will kill my brother Jacob.

23 This was told to Rebecca, and she hurried and sent and called for Jacob her son, and she said to him, Arise, go and flee to Haran to my brother Laban and remain there for some time, until your brother's anger be turned from you and then shall you come back.

24 And Isaac called to Jacob and said to him, Take not a wife from the daughters of Canaan, for thus did our father Abraham command us according to the word of the Lord which he had commanded him, saying, Unto your offspring will I give this land; if your children keep my covenant that I have made with you, then I will also perform to your children that which I have spoken to you and I will not turn away from them.

25 Now therefore my son listen to my voice, to all that I shall command you, and refrain from taking a wife from among the daughters of Canaan; arise, go to Haran to the house of Bethuel your mother's father, and take to you a wife from there from the daughters of Laban your mother's brother.

26 Therefore be careful that you should not forget the Lord your God and all his ways in the land to which you go, and should get connected with the people of the land and pursue vanity and turn away from the Lord your God.

27 But when you come to the land there serve the Lord, do not turn to the right or to the left from the way which I commanded you and which you did learn.

28 And may the Almighty God grant you favor in the sight of the people of the earth, that you may take there a wife according to your choice; one who is good and upright in the ways of the Lord.

29 May God give to you and your descendants the blessing of your father Abraham, and make you prolific and reproduce, and may you become a multitude of people in the land where you go; may God cause you to return to this land, the land of your father's dwelling, with children and with great riches, with joy and with pleasure.

30 And Isaac finished commanding Jacob and blessing him, and he gave him many gifts, together with silver and gold, and he sent him away. Jacob listened to his father and mother; he kissed them and arose and went to Padan-aram, and Jacob was seventy-seven years old when he went out from the land of Canaan from Beersheba.

31 When Jacob went away to go to Haran Esau called to his son Eliphaz, and secretly spoke to him, saying, Now hurry, take your sword in your hand and pursue Jacob and pass before him in the road, and lurk for him; kill him with your sword in one of the mountains, and take all belonging to him and come back.

32 Eliphaz the son of Esau was an active man and expert with the bow as his father had taught him, and he was a noted hunter in the field and a valiant man.

33 Eliphaz did as his father had commanded him, and Eliphaz was at that time thirteen years old; Eliphaz rose up

and went and took ten of his mother's brothers with him and pursued Jacob.

34 He closely followed Jacob, and he lurked for him in the border of the land of Canaan opposite to the city of Shechem.

35 And Jacob saw Eliphaz and his men pursuing him; Jacob stood still in the place in which he was going, in order to know what this was, for he did not know the thing. Eliphaz drew his sword and he went on advancing, he and his men, toward Jacob. And Jacob said to them, Why have you come here, and what does it mean that you pursue with your swords?

36 And Eliphaz came near to Jacob and he answered and said to him, Thus did my father command me, and now therefore I will not deviate from the orders which my father gave me. When Jacob saw that Esau had spoken to Eliphaz to employ force, Jacob then approached and supplicated Eliphaz and his men, saying to him,

37 Behold all that I have and which my father and mother gave to me, that you should take and go from me, and do not kill me; may this thing be accounted to you a righteousness.

38 And the Lord caused Jacob to find favor in the sight of Eliphaz the son of Esau, and his men, and they listened to the voice of Jacob, and they did not put him to death; Eliphaz and his men took all belonging to Jacob together with the silver and gold that he had brought with him from Beersheba; they left him nothing.

39 Eliphaz and his men went away from him and they returned to Esau to Beersheba, and they told him all that had occurred to them with Jacob, and they gave him all that they had taken from Jacob.

40 Esau was indignant at Eliphaz his son, and at his men that were with him, because they had not put Jacob to death.

41 And they answered and said to Esau, Because Jacob supplicated us in this matter not to kill him, our pity was increased toward him, and we took all belonging to him and brought it to you. Esau took all the silver and gold which Eliphaz had taken from Jacob and he put them by in his house.

42 At that time when Esau saw that Isaac had blessed Jacob, and had commanded him, saying, You shall not take a wife from among the daughters of Canaan, and that the daughters of Canaan were bad in the sight of Isaac and Rebecca,

43 Then he went to the house of Ishmael his uncle, and in addition to his older wives he took Machlath the daughter of Ishmael, the sister of Nebayoth, for a wife.

CHAPTER 30

1 Jacob went forth continuing his road to Haran, and he came as far as mount Moriah, and he stayed there all night near the city of Luz. The Lord appeared there to Jacob on that night and said to him, I am the Lord God of Abraham and the God of Isaac your father; the land on which you dwell I will give to you and your descendants.

2 Behold I am with you and will keep you wherever you go, and I will reproduce your descendants as the stars of Heaven, and I will cause all your enemies to fall before you; when they make war with you they shall not prevail over you, and I will bring you again to this land with joy, with children, and with great riches.

3 Jacob awoke from his sleep and he rejoiced greatly at the vision which he had seen, and he called the name of that place Bethel.

4 Jacob rose up from that place quite jubilant, and when he walked his feet felt light to him for joy, and he went from there to the land of the children of the East, and returned to Haran and sat by the shepherd's well.

5 There he found some men going from Haran to feed their flocks, and Jacob made inquiries of them, and they said, We are from Haran.

6 And he said to them, Do you know Laban, the son of Nahor? And they said, We know him and look, his daughter Rachel is coming along to feed her father's flock.

7 While he was yet speaking with them, Rachel the daughter of Laban came to feed her father's sheep, for she was a shepherdess.

8 When Jacob saw Rachel, the daughter of Laban, his mother's brother, he ran and kissed her and lifted up his voice and wept.

9 Jacob told Rachel that he was the son of Rebecca, her father's sister, and Rachel ran and told her father; Jacob continued to cry because he had nothing with him to bring to the house of Laban.

10 When Laban heard that his sister's son Jacob had come, he ran, kissed him and embraced him, brought him

into the house and gave him bread, and he ate.

11 And Jacob related to Laban what his brother Esau had done to him, and what his son Eliphaz had done to him in the road.

12 Jacob resided in Laban's house for one month, and Jacob ate and drank in the house of Laban, and afterward Laban said to Jacob, Tell me what shall be your wages, for how can you serve me for nothing?

13 Laban had no sons but only daughters; his other wives and handmaids were still unable to conceive in those days. These are the names of Laban's daughters which his wife Adinah had borne to him: the name of the elder was Leah and the name of the younger was Rachel. Leah was tender-eyed, but Rachel was beautiful and well favored, and Jacob loved her.

14 And Jacob said to Laban, I will serve you seven years for Rachel your younger daughter; and Laban consented to this and Jacob served Laban seven years for his daughter Rachel.

15 In the second year of Jacob's dwelling in Haran, that is in the seventy ninth year of the life of Jacob, Eber the son of Shem died; he was four hundred and sixty-four years old at his death.

16 And when Jacob heard that Eber was dead he grieved greatly; he lamented and mourned over him many days.

17 In the third year of Jacob's dwelling in Haran, Bosmath, the daughter of Ishmael, the wife of Esau, gave birth to him a son, and Esau called his name Reuel.

18 And in the fourth year of Jacob's residence in the house of Laban, the Lord visited Laban and remembered him on account of Jacob, and sons were born to him: his first born was Beor, his second was Alib, and the third was Chorash.

19 The Lord gave Laban riches and honor, sons and daughters, and the man increased greatly on account of Jacob.

20 In those days Jacob served Laban in all manner of work, in the house and in the field, and the blessing of the Lord was in all that belonged to Laban in the house and in the field.

21 In the fifth year Jehudith died, the daughter of Beeri, the wife of Esau, in the land of Canaan, and she had no sons but daughters only.

22 These are the names of her daughters which she gave birth to, to Esau: the name of the elder was Marzith, and the name of the younger was Puith.

23 And when Jehudith died, Esau rose up and went to Seir to hunt in the field, as usual, and Esau lived in the land of Seir for a long time.

24 In the sixth year Esau took for a wife, in addition to his other wives, Ahlibamah, the daughter of Zebeon the Hivite, and Esau brought her to the land of Canaan.

25 And Ahlibamah conceived and gave birth to, to Esau, three sons: Yeush, Yaalan, and Korah.

26 In those days, in the land of Canaan, there was a quarrel between the herdsmen of Esau and the herdsmen of the inhabitants of the land of Canaan, for Esau's cattle and goods were too abundant for him to remain in the land of Canaan, in his father's house; the land of Canaan could not bear him on account of his cattle.

27 And when Esau saw that his quarreling increased with the inhabitants of the land of Canaan, he rose up and took his wives and his sons and his daughters, and all belonging to him, and the cattle which he possessed, and all his property that he had acquired in the land of Canaan; he went away from the inhabitants of the land to the land of Seir, and Esau and all belonging to him lived in the land of Seir.

28 But from time to time Esau would go and see his father and mother in the land of Canaan, and Esau intermarried with the Horites, and he gave his daughters to the sons of Seir, the Horite.

29 He gave his elder daughter Marzith to Anah, the son of Zebeon, his wife's brother, and Puith he gave to Azar, the son of Bilhan the Horite; Esau lived in the mountain, he and his children, and they were prolific and multiplied.

CHAPTER 31

1 In the seventh year, Jacob's service to Laban was completed, and Jacob said to Laban, Give me my wife, for the days of my service are fulfilled; Laban did so, and Laban and Jacob assembled all the people of that place and they made a feast.

2 In the evening Laban came to the house, and afterward Jacob came there with the people of the feast, and Laban extinguished all the lights that were there in the house.

3 Jacob said to Laban, Why do you do this thing to us? And Laban answered, Such is our custom to act in this

land.

4 Afterward Laban took his daughter Leah, and he brought her to Jacob, and he came to her and Jacob did not know that she was Leah.

5 And Laban gave his daughter Leah his maid Zilpah for a handmaid.

6 All the people at the feast knew what Laban had done to Jacob, but they didn't tell a thing to Jacob.

7 All the neighbors came that night to Jacob's house, and they ate and drank and rejoiced, and played before Leah on timbrels, and with dances, and they responded before Jacob, Heleah, Heleah.

8 Jacob heard their words but did not understand their meaning, but he thought such might be their custom in this land.

9 And the neighbors spoke these words before Jacob during the night, and all the lights that were in the house Laban had that night been extinguished.

10 In the morning, when daylight appeared, Jacob turned to his wife and he saw it was Leah that had been lying in his bosom, and Jacob said, So now I know what the neighbors said last night, Heleah, they said, and I knew it not.

11 Jacob called to Laban, and said to him, What is this that you did to me? Certainly I served you for Rachel; why did you deceive me and give me Leah?

12 Laban answered Jacob, saying, Not so is it done in our place to give the younger before the elder; therefore if you desire to take her sister likewise, take her to you for the service which you will serve me for another seven years.

13 Jacob did so, and he also took Rachel for a wife; he served Laban seven years more, and Jacob also came to Rachel, and he loved Rachel more than Leah; Laban gave her his maid Bilhah for a handmaid.

14 When the Lord saw that Leah was hated, the Lord opened her womb and she conceived and gave birth to Jacob four sons in those days.

15 And these are their names: Reuben, Simeon, Levi, and Judah, and afterward she ceased bearing.

16 At that time Rachel was unable to conceive and had no children, and Rachel envied her sister Leah. When Rachel saw that she gave birth to no children to Jacob, she took her handmaid Bilhah, and she gave birth to Jacob two sons, Dan and Naphtali.

17 When Leah saw that she had ceased bearing, she also took her handmaid Zilpah, and she gave her to Jacob for a wife. Jacob also came to Zilpah, and she gave birth to Jacob two sons, Gad and Asher.

18 Leah again conceived and gave birth to Jacob in those days two sons and one daughter, and these are their names: Issachar, Zebulon, and their sister Dinah.

19 Rachel was still unable to conceive in those days and Rachel prayed to the Lord at that time, and she said, O Lord God remember me and visit me, I beg you, for now my husband will cast me off, for I have borne him no children.

20 Now O Lord God, hear my supplication before you, and see my affliction, and give me children like one of the handmaids, that I may no more bear my reproach.

21 God heard her and opened her womb, and Rachel conceived and gave birth to a son, and she said, The Lord has taken away my reproach. She called his name Joseph, saying, May the Lord add to me another son; Jacob was ninety-one years old when she gave birth to him.

22 At that time Jacob's mother, Rebecca, sent her nurse Deborah the daughter of Uz, and two of Isaac's servants to Jacob.

23 They came to Jacob to Haran and said to him, Rebecca has sent us to you that you shall return to your father's house to the land of Canaan; Jacob listened to them of this which his mother had spoken.

24 At that time, the other seven years which Jacob served Laban for Rachel were completed, and it was at the end of fourteen years that he had lived in Haran, Jacob said to Laban, Give me my wives and send me away that I may go to my land, for behold my mother did send to me from the land at Canaan that I should return to my father's house.

25 And Laban said to him, Not so I pray you; if I have found favor in your sight do not leave me; tell me your wages and I will give them, and remain with me.

26 Jacob said to him, This is what you shall give me for wages, that I shall this day pass through all your flock and take away from them every lamb that is speckled and spotted and such as are brown among the sheep, and among the goats, and if you will do this thing for me I will return and feed your flock and keep them as at first.

27 Laban did so, and Laban removed from his flock all that Jacob had said and gave them to him.

28 And Jacob placed all that he had removed from Laban's flock in the hands of his sons, and Jacob was feeding

the remainder of Laban's flock.

29 When the servants of Isaac which he had sent to Jacob saw that Jacob would not return with them to the land of Canaan to his father, they went away from him and returned home to the land of Canaan.

30 And Deborah remained with Jacob in Haran; she did not return with the servants of Isaac to the land of Canaan, and Deborah resided with Jacob's wives and children in Haran.

31 Jacob served Laban six years longer, and when the sheep brought forth, Jacob removed from them such as were speckled and spotted, as he had determined with Laban; Jacob did so at Laban's for six years, and the man increased abundantly. He had cattle and maid servants and men servants, camels, and asses.

32 Jacob had two hundred drove of cattle, and his cattle were of large size and of beautiful appearance and were very productive; all the families of the sons of men desired to get some of the cattle of Jacob, for they were greatly prosperous.

33 Many of the sons of men came to procure some of Jacob's flock, and Jacob gave them a sheep for a man servant or a maid servant or for an ass or a camel, or whatever Jacob desired from them they gave him.

34 Jacob obtained riches and honor and possessions by means of these transactions with the sons of men, and the children of Laban envied him of this honor.

35 In the course of time he heard the words of Laban's sons, saying, Jacob has taken away all that was our father's, and of that which was our father's has he acquired all this glory.

36 And Jacob observed the countenance of Laban and of his children, and it was not toward him in those days as it had been before.

37 The Lord appeared to Jacob at the expiration of the six years, and said to him, Arise, go forth out of this land, and return to the land of your birthplace and I will be with you.

38 And Jacob rose up at that time and he mounted his children and wives and all belonging to him on camels, and he went forth to go to the land of Canaan to his father Isaac.

39 Laban did not know that Jacob had gone from him, for Laban had been sheep-shearing that day.

40 Rachel stole her father's images, and she took them and concealed them on the camel on which she sat, and she went on.

41 And this is the manner of the images: in taking a man who is the firstborn and slaying him and taking the hair off his head; taking salt and salting the head and anointing it in oil, then taking a small tablet of copper or a tablet of gold and writing the name on it and placing the tablet under his tongue; taking the head with the tablet under the tongue and putting it in the house and lighting up lights before it and bowing down to it.

42 And at the time when they bow down to it, it speaks to them in all matters that they ask of it, through the power of the name which is written in it.

43 And some make them in the figures of men, of gold and silver, and go to them in times known to them, and the figures receive the influence of the stars, and tell them future things; in this manner were the images which Rachel stole from her father.

44 Rachel stole these images which were her father's in order that Laban might not know through them where Jacob had gone.

45 Laban came home and he asked concerning Jacob and his household, and he was not to be found; Laban sought his images to know where Jacob had gone, and could not find them. He went to some other images, and he inquired of them and they told him that Jacob had fled from him to his father's, to the land of Canaan.

46 Laban then rose up and took his brothers and all his servants, and he went forth and pursued Jacob, and he overtook him in mount Gilead.

47 And Laban said to Jacob, What is this you have done to me to flee and deceive me, and lead my daughters and their children as captives taken by the sword?

48 You did not suffer me to kiss them and send them away with joy, and you did steal my gods and did go away.

49 And Jacob answered Laban, saying, Because I was afraid that you would take your daughters by force from me; and now with whomsoever you find your gods he shall die.

50 And Laban searched for the images and he examined in all Jacob's tents and furniture, but could not find them.

51 And Laban said to Jacob, We will make a covenant together and it shall be a testimony between me and you; if you shall afflict my daughters, or shall take other wives besides my daughters, even God shall be a witness between me and you in this matter.

52 And they took stones and made a heap, and Laban said, This heap is a witness between me and you. He called the name thereof Gilead.

53 Jacob and Laban offered sacrifice on the mount, and they ate there by the heap, and they stayed in the mount

all night.   Laban rose up early in the morning; he wept with his daughters and he kissed them, and he returned to his place.

54 He hurried and sent off his son Beor, who was seventeen years old, with Abichorof the son of Uz, the son of Nahor, and with them were ten men.

55 They hurried and went and passed on the road before Jacob, and they came by another road to the land of Seir.

56 They came to Esau and said to him, Thus says your brother and relative, your mother's brother Laban, the son of Bethuel, saying,

57 Have you heard what Jacob your brother has done to me, who first came to me naked and gave birth to? I went to meet him and brought him to my house with honor; I made him great, and I gave him my two daughters for wives and also two of my maids.

58 And God blessed him on my account; he increased abundantly, and had sons, daughters and maid servants.

59 He has also an immense stock of flocks and herds, camels and asses, also silver and gold in abundance; when he saw that his wealth increased, he left me while I went to shear my sheep, and he rose up and fled in secrecy.

60 He lifted his wives and children on camels, and he led away all his cattle and property which he acquired in my land, and he lifted up his countenance to go to his father Isaac, to the land of Canaan.

61 He did not let me kiss my daughters and their children; he led my daughters as captives taken by the sword, and he also stole my gods and he fled.

62 And now I have left him in the mountain of the brook of Jabuk, him and all belonging to him; he lacks nothing.

63 If it be your wish to go to him, go then and there you will find him, and you can do to him as your soul desires; and Laban's messengers came and told Esau all these things.

64 Esau heard all the words of Laban's messengers, and his anger was greatly set ablaze against Jacob, and he remembered his hatred, and his anger burned within him.

65 Esau hurried and took his children and servants and the souls of his household, being sixty men; he went and assembled all the children of Seir the Horite and their people, being three hundred and forty men. He took all this number of four hundred men with drawn swords, and he went to Jacob to strike him.

66 Esau divided this number into several parts, and he took the sixty men of his children and servants and the souls of his household as one head, and gave them in care of Eliphaz his eldest son.

67 The remaining heads he gave to the care of the six sons of Seir the Horite, and he placed every man over his generations and children.

68 The whole of this camp went as it was, and Esau went among them toward Jacob, and he conducted them with speed.

69 And Laban's messengers departed from Esau and went to the land of Canaan, and they came to the house of Rebecca the mother of Jacob and Esau.

70 They told her saying, Behold your son Esau has gone against his brother Jacob with four hundred men, for he heard that he was coming, and he is gone to make war with him, and to strike him and to take all that he has.

71 Rebecca hurried and sent seventy two men from the servants of Isaac to meet Jacob on the road; for she said, Perhaps Esau may make war in the road when he meets him.

72 These messengers went on the road to meet Jacob, and they met him in the road of the brook on the opposite side of the brook Jabuk. Jacob said when he saw them, This camp is destined to me from God. And Jacob called the name of that place Machnayim.

73 And Jacob knew all his father's people, and he kissed them and embraced them and came with them.   Jacob asked them concerning his father and mother, and they said, They were well.

74 These messengers said to Jacob, Rebecca your mother has sent us to you, saying, I have heard, my son, that your brother Esau has gone forth against you on the road with men from the children of Seir the Horite.

75 Therefore, my son, listen to my voice and see with your counsel what you will do; when he comes up to you, supplicate him, and do not speak rashly to him, and give him a present from what you possess, and from what God has favored you with.

76 And when he asks you concerning your affairs, conceal nothing from him, perhaps he may turn from his anger against you and you will thereby save your soul, you and all belonging to you, for it is your duty to honor him, for he is your elder brother.

77 When Jacob heard the words of his mother which the messengers had spoken to him, Jacob lifted up his voice and wept bitterly, and did as his mother then commanded him.

CHAPTER 32

1 At that time Jacob sent messengers to his brother Esau toward the land of Seir, and he spoke to him words of supplication.

2 He commanded them, saying, Thus shall you say to my lord, to Esau, Thus says your servant Jacob, Let not my lord imagine that my father's blessing with which he did bless me has proved beneficial to me.

3 For I have been these twenty years with Laban, and he deceived me and changed my wages ten times, as it has all been already told to my lord.

4 And I served him in his house very laboriously, and God afterward saw my affliction, my labor and the work of my hands, and he caused me to find grace and favor in his sight.

5 And afterward through God's great mercy and kindness I acquired oxen and asses and cattle, and men servants and maid servants.

6 And now I am coming to my land and my home to my father and mother, who are in the land of Canaan; I have sent to let my lord know all this in order to find favor in the sight of my lord, so that he may not imagine that I have of myself obtained wealth, or that the blessing with which my father blessed me has benefited me.

7 Those messengers went to Esau, and found him on the borders of the land of Edom going toward Jacob, and four hundred men of the children of Seir the Horite were standing with drawn swords.

8 And the messengers of Jacob told Esau all the words that Jacob had spoken to them concerning Esau.

9 Esau answered them with pride and contempt and said to them, Certainly I have heard and truly it has been told to me what Jacob has done to Laban, who exalted him in his house and gave him his daughters for wives, and he had sons and daughters, and abundantly increased in wealth and riches in Laban's house through his means.

10 When he saw that his wealth was abundant and his riches great he fled with all belonging to him, from Laban's house, and he led Laban's daughters away from the face of their father, as captives taken by the sword without telling him of it.

11 And not only to Laban has Jacob done thus but also to me has he done so and has twice supplanted me, and shall I be silent?

12 Now therefore I have this day come with my camps to meet him, and I will do to him according to the desire of my heart.

13 And the messengers returned and came to Jacob and said to him, We came to your brother, to Esau, and we told him all your words, and thus has he answered us; behold he comes to meet you with four hundred men.

14 Now then know and see what you shall do, and pray before God to deliver you from him.

15 And when he heard the words of his brother which he had spoken to the messengers of Jacob, Jacob was greatly afraid and he was distressed.

16 And Jacob prayed to the Lord his God, and he said, O Lord God of my fathers, Abraham and Isaac, you did say to me when I went away from my father's house, saying,

17 I am the Lord God of your father Abraham and the God of Isaac, to you do I give this land and your descendants after you, and I will make your descendants as the stars of heaven, and you shall spread forth to the four sides of heaven, and in you and in your offspring shall all the families of the earth be blessed.

18 You did establish your words, and did give to me riches and children and cattle, as the utmost wishes of my heart did you give to your servant; you gave to me all that I asked from you, so that I lacked nothing.

19 Afterward you said to me, Return to your parents and to your birth place and I will still do well with you.

20 And now that I have come, and you did deliver me from Laban, I shall fall in the hands of Esau who will kill me, yea, together with the mothers of my children.

21 Now therefore, O Lord God, deliver me, I pray you, also from the hands of my brother Esau, for I am greatly afraid of him.

22 And if there is no righteousness in me, do it for the sake of Abraham and my father Isaac.

23 For I know that through kindness and mercy I have acquired this wealth; now therefore I beseech you to deliver me this day with your kindness and to answer me.

24 And Jacob ceased praying to the Lord; he divided the people that were with him with the flocks and cattle into two camps, and he gave the half to the care of Damesek, the son of Eliezer, Abraham's servant, for a camp, with his children; the other half he gave to the care of his brother Elianus the son of Eliezer, to be for a camp with his children.

25 And he commanded them, saying, Keep yourselves at a distance with your camps, and do not come too near

each other, and if Esau comes to one camp and kills it, the other camp at a distance from it will escape him.

26 Jacob tarried there that night, and during the whole night he gave his servants instructions concerning the forces and his children.

27 The Lord heard the prayer of Jacob on that day, and the Lord then delivered Jacob from the hands of his brother Esau.

28 The Lord sent three angels of the angels of heaven, and they went before Esau and came to him.

29 And these angels appeared to Esau and his people as two thousand men, riding on horses furnished with all sorts of war instruments, and they appeared in the sight of Esau and all his men to be divided into four camps, with four chiefs to them.

30 And one camp went on and they found Esau coming with four hundred men toward his brother Jacob, and this camp ran toward Esau and his people and terrified them. Esau fell off the horse in alarm, and all his men separated from him in that place, for they were greatly afraid.

31 And the whole camp shouted after them when they fled from Esau, and all the warlike men answered, saying,

32 Certainly we are the servants of Jacob, who is the servant of God, and who then can stand against us? And Esau said to them, O then, my lord and brother Jacob is your lord, whom I have not seen for these twenty years, and now that I have this day come to see him, do you treat me in this manner?

33 And the angels answered him saying, As the Lord lives, were not Jacob of whom you speak your brother, we would not let one remain from you and your people, but only on account of Jacob we will do nothing to them.

34 And this camp passed from Esau and his men and it went away, and Esau and his men had gone from them about a league when the second camp came toward him with all sorts of weapons, and they also did to Esau and his men as the first camp had done to them.

35 And when they had left it to go on, behold the third camp came toward him and they were all terrified, and Esau fell off the horse, and the whole camp cried out, and said, Certainly we are the servants of Jacob, who is the servant of God, and who can stand against us?

36 Esau again answered them saying, O then, Jacob my lord and your lord is my brother, and for twenty years I have not seen his countenance and hearing this day that he was coming, I went this day to meet him, and do you treat me in this manner?

37 They answered him, and said to him, As the Lord lives, were not Jacob your brother as you did say, we would not leave a remnant from you and your men, but on account of Jacob of whom you speak being your brother, we will not meddle with you or your men.

38 And the third camp also passed from them, and he still continued his road with his men toward Jacob, when the fourth camp came toward him, and they also did to him and his men as the others had done.

39 When Esau beheld the evil which the four angels had done to him and to his men, he became greatly afraid of his brother Jacob, and he went to meet him in peace.

40 And Esau concealed his hatred against Jacob, because he was afraid for his life on account of his brother Jacob, and because he imagined that the four camps that he had lighted on were Jacob's servants.

41 And Jacob tarried that night with his servants in their camps, and he resolved with his servants to give to Esau a present from all that he had with him, and from all his property; Jacob rose up in the morning, he and his men, and they chose from among the cattle a present for Esau.

42 And this is the amount of the present which Jacob chose from his flock to give to his brother Esau: he selected two hundred and forty head from the flocks, and he selected from the camels and asses thirty each, and of the herds he chose fifty kine.

43 He put them all in ten droves, and he placed each sort by itself; he delivered them into the hands of ten of his servants, each drove by itself.

44 He commanded them, and said to them, Keep yourselves at a distance from each other, and put a space between the droves, and when Esau and those who are with him shall meet you and ask you, saying, Whose are you, and where do you go, and to whom belongs all this before you, you shall say to them, We are the servants of Jacob, and we come to meet Esau in peace, and behold Jacob comes behind us.

45 And that which is before us is a present sent from Jacob to his brother Esau.

46 And if they shall say to you, Why does he delay behind you, from coming to meet his brother and to see his face, then you shall say to them, Certainly he comes joyfully behind us to meet his brother, for he said, I will appease him with the present that goes to him, and after this I will see his face; per chance he will accept me.

47 So the whole present passed on in the hands of his servants, and went before him on that day, and he lodged that night with his camps by the border of the brook of Jabuk. He rose up in the middle of the night and took his

wives and his maid servants and all belonging to him, and that night he passed them over the ford Jabuk.

48 When he passed all belonging to him over the brook, Jacob was left by himself; a man met him, and he wrestled with him that night until the breaking of the day, and the hollow of Jacob's thigh was out of joint through wrestling with him.

49 At the break of day the man left Jacob there, and he blessed him and went away; Jacob passed the brook at the break of day, and he rested on his thigh.

50 And the sun rose on him when he had passed the brook, and he came up to the place of his cattle and children.

51 They went on till midday, and while they were going the present was passing on before them.

52 And Jacob lifted up his eyes and looked, and behold Esau was at a distance, coming along with many men, about four hundred, and Jacob was greatly afraid of his brother.

53 Jacob hurried and divided his children to his wives and his handmaids, and his daughter Dinah he put in a chest, and delivered her into the hands of his servants.

54 He passed before his children and wives to meet his brother, and he bowed down to the ground, yes, he bowed down seven times until he approached his brother. And God caused Jacob to find grace and favor in the sight of Esau and his men, for God had heard the prayer of Jacob.

55 The fear of Jacob and his terror fell on his brother Esau, for Esau was greatly afraid of Jacob for what the angels of God had done to Esau, and Esau's anger against Jacob was turned into kindness.

56 And when Esau saw Jacob running toward him, he also ran toward him and he embraced him, and he fell on his neck, and they kissed and they wept.

57 And God put fear and kindness toward Jacob in the hearts of the men that came with Esau, and they also kissed Jacob and embraced him.

58 Also Eliphaz, the son of Esau, with his four brothers, sons of Esau, wept with Jacob, and they kissed him and embraced him, for the fear of Jacob had fallen on them all.

59 And Esau lifted up his eyes and saw the women with their children, the children of Jacob, walking behind Jacob and bowing along the road to Esau.

60 And Esau said to Jacob, Who are these with you, my brother? Are they your children or your servants? And Jacob answered Esau and said, They are my children which God hath graciously given to your servant.

61 While Jacob was speaking to Esau and his men, Esau beheld the whole camp, and he said to Jacob, How did you get the whole camp that I met last night? And Jacob said, To find favor in the sight of my lord, it is that which God graciously gave to your servant.

62 The present came before Esau, and Jacob pressed Esau, saying, Take I pray you the present that I have brought to my lord. And Esau said, Why should I? Keep that which you have to yourself.

63 And Jacob said, It is incumbent on me to give all this, since I have seen your face, that you still live in peace.

64 Esau refused to take the present, and Jacob said to him, I beseech you my lord, if now I have found favor in your sight, then receive my present at my hand, for I have therefore seen your face, as you I had seen a god-like face, because you were pleased with me.

65 And Esau took the present, and Jacob also gave to Esau silver and gold and bdellium, for he pressed him so much that he took them.

66 Esau divided the cattle that were in the camp, and he gave half to the men who had come with him, for they had come on hire, and the other half he delivered to the hands of his children.

67 The silver and gold and bdellium he gave in the hands of Eliphaz his eldest son, and Esau said to Jacob, Let us remain with you, and we will go slowly along with you until you come to my place with me, that we may dwell there together.

68 And Jacob answered his brother and said, I would do as my lord speaks to me, but my lord knows that the children are tender, and the flocks and herds with their young who are with me go but slowly, for if they went swiftly they would all die, for you know their burdens and their fatigue.

69 Therefore let my lord pass on before his servant, and I will go on slowly for the sake of the children and the flock until I come to my lord's place to Seir.

70 And Esau said to Jacob, I will place with you some of the people that are with me to take care of you in the road, and to bear your fatigue and burden, and he said, I will do so, my lord, if I may find grace in your sight?

71 Behold I will come to you to Seir to dwell there together as you have spoken, go then with your people for I will follow you.

72 Jacob said this to Esau in order to remove Esau and his men from him, so that Jacob might afterward go to his father's house to the land of Canaan.

73 Esau listened to the voice of Jacob, and Esau returned with the four hundred men that were with him on their road to Seir, and Jacob and all belonging to him went that day as far as the extremity of the land of Canaan in its borders, and he remained there some time.

CHAPTER 33

1 Some time after Jacob went away from the borders of the land, he came to the land of Shalem, that is the city of Shechem, which is in the land of Canaan, and he rested in front of the city.

2 And he bought a parcel of the field which was there from the children of Hamor, the people of the land, for five shekels.

3 Jacob there built himself a house and pitched his tent there, and he made booths for his cattle; therefore he called the name of that place Succoth.

4 And Jacob remained in Succoth a year and six months.

5 At that time some of the women of the inhabitants of the land went to the city of Shechem to dance and rejoice with the daughters of the people of the city, and when they went forth then Rachel and Leah the wives of Jacob with their families also went to behold the rejoicing of the daughters of the city.

6 And Dinah the daughter of Jacob also went along with them and saw the daughters of the city, and they remained there before these daughters while all the people of the city were standing by them to behold their rejoicings, and all the great people of the city were there.

7 Shechem the son of Hamor, the prince of the land was also standing there to see them.

8 Shechem saw Dinah the daughter of Jacob sitting with her mother before the daughters of the city, and the damsel pleased him greatly, and he asked his friends and his people, saying, Whose daughter is that sitting among the women whom I do not know in this city?

9 And they said to him, Certainly this is the daughter of Jacob the son of Isaac the Hebrew, who has lived in this city for some time, and when it was reported that the daughters of the land were going forth to rejoice she went with her mother and maid servants to sit among them as you see.

10 Shechem saw Dinah the daughter of Jacob, and when he looked at her his soul became fixed on Dinah.

11 And he sent and had her taken by force, and Dinah came to the house of Shechem; he seized her forcibly and lay with her and humbled her, and he loved her greatly and placed her in his house.

12 And they came and told the thing to Jacob, and when Jacob heard that Shechem had defiled his daughter Dinah, Jacob sent twelve of his servants to fetch Dinah from the house of Shechem, and they went and came to the house of Shechem to take away Dinah from there.

13 When they came Shechem went out to them with his men and drove them from his house, and he would not let them come before Dinah, but Shechem was sitting with Dinah kissing and embracing her before their eyes.

14 The servants of Jacob came back and told him, saying, When we came, he and his men drove us away, and thus did Shechem do to Dinah before our eyes.

15 Jacob knew moreover that Shechem had defiled his daughter, but he said nothing; his sons were feeding his cattle in the field, and Jacob remained silent till their return.

16 Before his sons came home Jacob sent two maidens from his servants' daughters to take care of Dinah in the house of Shechem, and to remain with her, and Shechem sent three of his friends to his father Hamor the son of Chiddekem, the son of Pered, saying, Get me this damsel for a wife.

17 Hamor the son of Chiddekem the Hivite came to the house of Shechem his son, and he sat before him, and Hamor said to his son, Shechem, Is there not a woman among the daughters of your people, that you will take an Hebrew woman who is not of your people?

18 And Shechem said to him, Her only must you get for me, for she is delightful in my sight. Hamor did according to the word of his son, for he was greatly beloved by him.

19 And Hamor went forth to Jacob to commune with him concerning this matter, and when he had gone from the house of his son Shechem, before he came to Jacob to speak to him, the sons of Jacob had come from the field as soon as they heard the thing that Shechem the son of Hamor had done.

20 And the men were very much grieved concerning their sister, and they all came home fired with anger, before the time of gathering in their cattle.

21 They came and sat before their father and they spoke to him set ablaze with wrath, saying, Certainly death is due to this man and to his household, because the Lord God of the whole earth commanded Noah and his children that man shall never rob, nor commit adultery; now behold Shechem has both ravaged and committed fornication with our sister, and not one of all the people of the city spoke a word to him.

22 Certainly you know and understand that the judgment of death is due to Shechem, and to his father, and to the whole city on account of the thing which he has done.

23 And while they were speaking before their father in this matter, Hamor the father of Shechem came to speak to Jacob the words of his son concerning Dinah, and he sat before Jacob and before his sons.

24 And Hamor spoke to them, saying, The soul of my son Shechem longs for your daughter; I pray you give her to him for a wife and intermarry with us; give us your daughters and we will give you our daughters, and you shall dwell with us in our land and we will be as one people in the land.

25 For our land is very extensive, so dwell and trade therein and get possessions in it, and do therein as you desire, and no one shall prevent you by saying a word to you.

26 And Hamor ceased speaking to Jacob and his sons, and behold Shechem his son had come after him, and he sat before them.

27 And Shechem spoke before Jacob and his sons, saying, May I find favor in your sight that you will give me your daughter, and whatever you say to me that will I do for her.

28 Ask me for abundance of dowry and gift, and I will give it, and whatever you say to me that will I do, and whoever he be that will rebel against your orders, he shall die; only give me the damsel for a wife.

29 And Simeon and Levi answered Hamor and Shechem his son deceitfully, saying, All you have spoken to us we will do for you.

30 And behold our sister is in your house, but keep away from her until we send to our father Isaac concerning this matter, for we can do nothing without his consent.

31 For he knows the ways of our father Abraham, and whatever he says to us we will tell you; we will conceal nothing from you.

32 And Simeon and Levi spoke this to Shechem and his father in order to find a pretext, and to seek counsel what was to be done to Shechem and to his city in this matter.

33 And when Shechem and his father heard the words of Simeon and Levi, it seemed good in their sight, and Shechem and his father rose to go home.

34 And when they had gone, the sons of Jacob said to their father, Behold, we know that death is due to these wicked ones and to their city, because they went contrary to that which God had commanded to Noah and his children and his descendants after them.

35 And also because Shechem did this thing to our sister Dinah in defiling her, for such vileness shall never be done among us.

36 Now therefore know and see what you will do, and seek counsel and pretext what is to be done to them, in order to kill all the inhabitants of this city.

37 Simeon said to them, Here is a proper advice for you: tell them to circumcise every male among them as we are circumcised, and if they do not wish to do this, we shall take our daughter from them and go away.

38 And if they consent to do this and will do it, then when they are sunk down with pain, we will attack them with our swords, as on one who is quiet and peaceable, and we will kill every male person among them.

39 Simeon's advice pleased them, and Simeon and Levi resolved to do to them as it was proposed.

40 And on the next morning Shechem and Hamor his father came again to Jacob and his sons, to speak concerning Dinah, and to hear what answer the sons of Jacob would give to their words.

41 And the sons of Jacob spoke deceitfully to them, saying, We told our father Isaac all your words, and your words pleased him.

42 But he spoke to us, saying, Thus did Abraham his father command him from God the Lord of the whole earth, that any man who is not of his descendants that should wish to take one of his daughters, shall cause every male belonging to him to be circumcised, as we are circumcised, and then we may give him our daughter for a wife.

43 Now we have made known to you all our ways that our father spoke to us, for we cannot do this of which you spoke to us, to give our daughter to an uncircumcised man, for it is a disgrace to us.

44 But herein we will consent to you, to give you our daughter, and we will also take to ourselves your daughters, and will dwell among you and be one people as you have spoken, if you will listen to us and consent to be like us, to circumcise every male belonging to you as we are circumcised.

45 And if you will not listen to us, to have every male circumcised as we are circumcised, as we have commanded, then we will come to you, and take our daughter from you and go away.

46 Shechem and his father Hamor heard the words of the sons of Jacob, and the thing pleased them greatly, and Shechem and his father Hamor hurried to do the wishes of the sons of Jacob, for Shechem was very fond of Dinah, and his soul was riveted to her.

47 Shechem and his father Hamor hurried to the gate of the city, and they assembled all the men of their city and spoke to them the words of the sons of Jacob, saying,

48 We came to these men, the sons of Jacob, and we spoke to them concerning their daughter, and these men will consent to do according to our wishes, and behold our land is of great extent for them, and they will dwell in it, and trade in it, and we shall be one people; we will take their daughters, and our daughters we will give to them for wives.

49 But only on this condition will these men consent to do this thing, that every male among us be circumcised as they are circumcised, as their God commanded them, and when we shall have done according to their instructions to be circumcised, then they will dwell among us, together with their cattle and possessions, and we shall be as one people with them.

50 When all the men of the city heard the words of Shechem and his father Hamor, then all the men of their city were agreeable to this proposal, and they obeyed to be circumcised; for Shechem and his father Hamor were greatly esteemed by them, being the princes of the land.

51 On the next day, Shechem and Hamor his father rose up early in the morning, and they assembled all the men of their city into the middle of the city, and they called for the sons of Jacob, who circumcised every male belonging to them on that day and the next.

52 And they circumcised Shechem and Hamor his father, and the five brothers of Shechem, and then every one rose up and went home; for this thing was from the Lord against the city of Shechem, and from the Lord was Simeon's counsel in this matter, in order that the Lord might deliver the city of Shechem into the hands of Jacob's two sons.

CHAPTER 34

1 The number of all the males that were circumcised were six hundred and forty-five men, and two hundred and forty-six children.

2 But Chiddekem, son of Pered, the father of Hamor, and his six brothers, would not listen to Shechem and his father Hamor; they would not be circumcised, for the proposal of the sons of Jacob was loathsome in their sight, and their anger was greatly roused at this, that the people of the city had not listened to them.

3 In the evening of the second day, they found eight small children who had not been circumcised, for their mothers had concealed them from Shechem and his father Hamor, and from the men of the city.

4 And Shechem and his father Hamor sent to have them brought before them to be circumcised, when Chiddekem and his six brothers sprang at them with their swords, and sought to kill them.

5 And they sought to kill also Shechem and his father Hamor and they sought to kill Dinah with them on account of this matter.

6 They said to them, What is this thing that you have done? Are there no women among the daughters of your brothers the Canaanites, that you wish to take to yourselves daughters of the Hebrews, whom ye knew not before, and will do this act which your fathers never commanded you?

7 Do you imagine that you will succeed through this act which you have done? And what will you answer in this affair to your brothers the Canaanites who will come tomorrow and ask you concerning this thing?

8 If your act shall not appear just and good in their sight, what will you do for your lives, and me for our lives, in your not having listened to our voices?

9 And if the inhabitants of the land and all your brothers the children of Ham, shall hear of your act, saying,

10 On account of a Hebrew woman did Shechem and Hamor his father, and all the inhabitants of their city, do that with which they had been unacquainted and which their ancestors never commanded them, where then will you fly or where conceal your shame all your days before your brothers, the inhabitants of the land of Canaan?

11 Now therefore we cannot bear up against this thing which you have done, neither can we be burdened with this yoke on us which our ancestors did not command us.

12 Behold tomorrow we will go and assemble all our brothers, the Canaanitish brothers who dwell in the land, and we will all come and strike you and all those who trust in you, that there shall not be a remnant left from you or them.

13 And when Hamor and his son Shechem and all the people of the city heard the words of Chiddekem and his brothers, they were terribly afraid of their lives at their words, and they repented of what they had done.

14 And Shechem and his father Hamor answered their father Chiddekem and his brothers, and they said to them,

All the words which you spoke to us are true.

15 Now do not say, nor imagine in your hearts that on account of the love of the Hebrews we did this thing that our ancestors did not command us.

16 But because we saw that it was not their intention and desire to accede to our wishes concerning their daughter as to our taking her, except on this condition, so we listened to their voices and did this act which you saw in order to obtain our desire from them.

17 And when we shall have obtained our request from them, we will then return to them and do to them that which you say to us.

18 We petition you then to wait and tarry until our flesh will be healed and we again become strong, and we will then go together against them, and do to them that which is in your hearts and in ours.

19 And Dinah the daughter of Jacob heard all these words which Chiddekem and his brothers had spoken, and what Hamor and his son Shechem and the people of their city had answered them.

20 She hurried and sent one of her maidens, that her father had sent to take care of her in the house of Shechem, to Jacob her father and to her brothers, saying:

21 Thus did Chiddekem and his brothers advise concerning you, and thus did Hamor and Shechem and the people of the city answer them.

22 And when Jacob heard these words he was filled with wrath, and he was indignant at them, and his anger was set ablaze against them.

23 And Simeon and Levi swore and said, As the Lord lives, the God of the whole earth, by this time tomorrow, there shall not be a remnant left in the whole city.

24 Twenty young men had concealed themselves who were not circumcised, and these young men fought against Simeon and Levi, and Simeon and Levi killed eighteen of them, and two fled from them and escaped to some lime pits that were in the city, and Simeon and Levi sought for them, but could not find them.

25 And Simeon and Levi continued to go about in the city, and they killed all the people of the city at the edge of the sword, and they left none remaining.

26 There was a great consternation in the midst of the city, and the cry of the people of the city ascended to heaven, and all the women and children cried aloud.

27 And Simeon and Levi killed all the city; they left not a male remaining in the whole city.

28 And they killed Hamor and Shechem his son at the edge of the sword, and they brought away Dinah from the house of Shechem and they went from there.

29 The sons of Jacob went and returned, and came on the slain, and spoiled all their property which was in the city and the field.

30 And while they were taking the spoil, three hundred men stood up and threw dust at them and struck them with stones. Then Simeon turned to them and he killed them all with the edge of the sword, and Simeon turned before Levi and came into the city.

31 They took away their sheep and their oxen and their cattle, and also the remainder of the women and little ones, and they led all these away; they opened a gate and went out and came to their father Jacob with vigor.

32 When Jacob saw all that they had done to the city, and saw the spoil that they took from them, Jacob was very angry at them, and Jacob said to them, What is this that you have done to me? I had obtained rest among the Canaanitish inhabitants of the land; none of them meddled with me.

33 And now you have done this to make me obnoxious to the inhabitants of the land, among the Canaanites and the Perizzites, and I am but of a small number; they will all assemble against me and kill me when they hear of your work with their brothers, and I and my household will be destroyed.

34 Simeon and Levi and all their brothers with them answered their father Jacob and said to him, Behold we live in the land, and shall Shechem do this to our sister? Why are you silent at all that Shechem has done? And shall he deal with our sister as with a harlot in the streets?

35 The number of women whom Simeon and Levi took captives from the city of Shechem, whom they did not kill, was eighty-five who had not known man.

36 And among them was a young damsel of beautiful appearance and well favored, whose name was Bunah, and Simeon took her for a wife, and the number of the males which they took captives and did not kill was forty-seven men, and the rest they killed.

37 All the young men and women that Simeon and Levi had taken captives from the city of Shechem were servants to the sons of Jacob and to their children after them, until the day of the sons of Jacob going forth from the land of Egypt.

38 And when Simeon and Levi had gone forth from the city, the two young men that were left, who had concealed themselves in the city and did not die among the people of the city, rose up; these young men went into the city and walked about in it, and found the city desolate without man, and only women weeping, and these young men cried out and said, Behold, this is the evil which the sons of Jacob the Hebrew did to this city in their having this day destroyed one of the Canaanitish cities, and were not afraid of their lives of all the land of Canaan.

39 These men left the city and went to the city of Tapnach, and they came there and told the inhabitants of Tapnach all that had befallen them, and all that the sons of Jacob had done to the city of Shechem.

40 The information reached Jashub king of Tapnach, and he sent men to the city of Shechem to see those young men, for the king did not believe them in this account, saying, How could two men lay waste such a large town as Shechem?

41 The messengers of Jashub came back and told him, saying, We came to the city, and it is destroyed, there is not a man there; only weeping women; neither is any flock or cattle there, for all that was in the city the sons of Jacob took away.

42 Jashub wondered at this, saying, How could two men do this thing to destroy so large a city, and not one man able to stand against them?

43 For the like has not been from the days of Nimrod, and not even from the remotest time, has the like taken place; and Jashub, king of Tapnach, said to his people, Be courageous and we will go and fight against these Hebrews, and do to them as they did to the city; we will avenge the cause of the people of the city.

44 Jashub, king of Tapnach, consulted with his counselors about this matter, and his advisers said to him, Alone you will not prevail over the Hebrews, for they must be powerful to do this work to the whole city.

45 If two of them laid waste the whole city, and no one stood against them, certainly if you will go against them, they will all rise against us and destroy us likewise.

46 But if you will send to all the kings that surround us, and let them come together, then we will go with them and fight against the sons of Jacob; then you will prevail against them.

47 Jashub heard the words of his counselors, and their words pleased him and his people, and he did so; Jashub king of Tapnach sent to all the kings of the Amorites that surrounded Shechem and Tapnach, saying,

48 Go up with me and assist me, and we will strike Jacob the Hebrew and all his sons, and destroy them from the earth, for thus did he do to the city of Shechem, and do you not know of it?

49 And all the kings of the Amorites heard the evil that the sons of Jacob had done to the city of Shechem, and they were greatly astonished at them.

50 The seven kings of the Amorites assembled with all their armies about ten thousand men with drawn swords, and they came to fight against the sons of Jacob; Jacob heard that the kings of the Amorites had assembled to fight against his sons, and Jacob was greatly afraid; it distressed him.

51 And Jacob exclaimed against Simeon and Levi, saying, What is this act that you did? Why have you injured me, to bring against me all the children of Canaan to destroy me and my household? For I was at rest, even I and my household, and you have done this thing to me and provoked the inhabitants of the land against me by your proceedings.

52 Judah answered his father, saying, Was it for naught my brothers Simeon and Levi killed all the inhabitants of Shechem? Certainly it was because Shechem had humbled our sister, and went contrary to the command of our God to Noah and his children, for Shechem took our sister away by force, and committed fornication with her.

53 Shechem did all this evil and not one of the inhabitants of his city interfered with him, to say, Why will you do this? Certainly for this my brothers went and struck the city, and the Lord delivered it into their hands, because its inhabitants had gone contrary to the commands of our God. Is it then for naught that they have done all this?

54 Now why are you afraid or distressed, and why are you displeased at my brothers, and why is your anger set ablaze against them?

55 Certainly our God who delivered into their hand the city of Shechem and its people, he will also deliver into our hands all the Canaanitish kings who are coming against us, and we will do to them as my brothers did to Shechem.

56 Now be tranquil about them and cast away your fears, but trust in the Lord our God, and pray to him to assist us and deliver us, and deliver our enemies into our hands.

57 Judah called to one of his father's servants, Go now and see where those kings who are coming against us are situated with their armies.

58 And the servant went and looked far off, and went up opposite Mount Sihon, and saw all the camps of the

kings standing in the fields, and he returned to Judah and said, Behold the kings are situated in the field with all their camps, a people greatly numerous like the sand on the seashore.

59 And Judah said to Simeon and Levi, and to all his brothers, Strengthen yourselves and be sons of valor, for the Lord our God is with us, do not fear them.

60 Stand forth each man, equipped with his weapons of war, his bow and his sword, and we will go and fight against these uncircumcised men; the Lord is our God, He will save us.

61 They rose up, and each put on his weapons of war, great and small, eleven sons of Jacob, and all the servants of Jacob with them.

62 All the servants of Isaac who were with Isaac in Hebron, all came to them equipped in all sorts of war instruments, and the sons of Jacob and their servants, being one hundred and twelve men, went towards these kings, and Jacob also went with them.

63 And the sons of Jacob sent to their father Isaac the son of Abraham to Hebron, the same is Kireath-arba, saying,

64 Pray we beseech you for us to the Lord our God, to protect us from the hands of the Canaanites who are coming against us, and to deliver them into our hands.

65 Isaac the son of Abraham prayed to the Lord for his sons, and he said, O Lord God, you did promise my father, saying, I will reproduce your descendants as the stars of heaven, and you did also promise me, and establish you your word, now that the kings of Canaan are coming together, to make war with my children because they committed no violence.

66 Now therefore, O Lord God, God of the whole earth, pervert, I pray you, the counsel of these kings that they may not fight against my sons.

67 And impress the hearts of these kings and their people with the terror of my sons and bring down their pride, that they may turn away from my sons.

68 With your strong hand and outstretched arm deliver my sons and their servants from them, for power and might are in your hands to do all this.

69 And the sons of Jacob and their servants went toward these kings, and they trusted in the Lord their God, and while they were going, Jacob their father also prayed to the Lord and said, O Lord God, powerful and exalted God, who has reigned from days of old, from thence till now and forever;

70 You are He who stirs up wars and causes them to cease, in your hand are power and might to exalt and to bring down; O may my prayer be acceptable before you that you may turn to me with your mercies, to impress the hearts of these kings and their people with the terror of my sons, and terrify them and their camps, and with your great kindness deliver all those that trust in you, for it is you who can bring people under us and reduce nations under our power.

CHAPTER 35

1 All the kings of the Amorites came and took their stand in the field to consult with their counselors what was to be done with the sons of Jacob, for they were still afraid of them, saying, Take notice that two of them killed the whole city of Shechem.

2 And the Lord heard the prayers of Isaac and Jacob, and he filled the hearts of all these kings' advisers with great fear and terror that they unanimously exclaimed,

3 Are you silly or is there no understanding in you, that you will fight with the Hebrews; why will you take delight in your own destruction this day?

4 See, two of them came to the city of Shechem without fear or terror, and they killed all the inhabitants of the city, that no man stood up against them, and how will you be able to fight with them all?

5 Certainly you know that their God is greatly fond of them and has done mighty things for them, such as have not been done from days of old and among all the gods of nations; there is none can do like his mighty deeds.

6 Certainly he delivered their father Abraham, the Hebrew, from the hand of Nimrod, and from the hand of all his people who had many times sought to kill him.

7 He delivered him also from the fire in which king Nimrod had cast him, and his God delivered him from it.

8 And who else can do like this? Certainly it was Abraham who killed the five kings of Elam when they had touched his brother's son who in those days lived in Sodom.

9 And took his servant that was faithful in his house and a few of his men, and they pursued the kings of Elam in one night and killed them; then restored to his brother's son all his property which they had taken from him.

10 Certainly you know the God of these Hebrews is much delighted with them, and they are also delighted with him, for they know that he delivered them from all their enemies.

11 And consider this, through his love toward his God, Abraham took his only and precious son and intended to bring him up as a burnt offering to his God; had it not been for God who prevented him from doing this, he would then have done it through his love to his God.

12 God saw all his works and swore to him, and promised him that he would deliver his sons and all his descendants from every trouble that would befall them, because he had done this thing and through his love to his God stifled his compassion for his child.

13 And have you not heard what their God did to Pharaoh king of Egypt and to Abimelech king of Gerar through taking Abraham's wife, who said of her, She is my sister; that they might kill him on account of her and think of taking her for a wife? And God did to them and their people all that you heard of.

14 And then, we ourselves saw with our own eyes that Esau, the brother of Jacob, came to him with four hundred men with the intention of slaying him, for he remembered that he had taken away from him his father's blessing.

15 And he went to meet him when he came from Syria to strike the mother with the children, and who delivered him from his hands but his God in whom he trusted? He delivered him from the hand of his brother and also from the hands of his enemies, and certainly he again will protect them.

16 Who does not know that it was their God who inspired them with strength to do to the town of Shechem the evil which you heard of?

17 Could it then be with their own strength that two men could destroy such a large city as Shechem had it not been for their God in whom they trusted? He spoke and did to them all this to kill the inhabitants of the city in their city.

18 And can you then prevail over them who have come forth together from your city to fight with all of them, even if a thousand times as many more should come to your assistance?

19 Certainly you know and understand that you do not come to fight with them, but you come to war with their God who chose them, and you have therefore all come this day to be destroyed.

20 So refrain from this evil which you are endeavoring to bring on yourselves, and it will be better for you not to go to battle with them, although they are but few in numbers, because their God is with them.

21 When the kings of the Amorites heard all the words of their advisers, their hearts were filled with terror; they were afraid of the sons of Jacob and would not fight against them.

22 They inclined to believe the words of their advisers and they listened to all their words. The words of the counselors greatly pleased the kings, and they did so.

23 And the kings turned and refrained from the sons of Jacob, for they dared not approach them to make war with them; they were greatly afraid of them, and their hearts melted within them from their fear.

24 For this proceeded from the Lord to them; he heard the prayers of his servants Isaac and Jacob, for they trusted in him. And all these kings returned with their camps on that day, each to his own city, and they did not at that time fight with the sons of Jacob.

25 The sons of Jacob kept their station that day till evening opposite mount Sihon, and seeing that these kings did not come to fight against them, the sons of Jacob returned home.

CHAPTER 36

1 At that time the Lord appeared to Jacob saying, Arise, go to Bethel and remain there; make there an altar to the Lord who appears to you, who delivered you and your sons from affliction.

2 And Jacob rose up with his sons and all belonging to him; they went and came to Bethel according to the word of the Lord.

3 Jacob was ninety-nine years old when he went up to Bethel, and Jacob and his sons and all the people that were with him remained in Bethel in Luz; he built an altar there to the Lord who appeared to him, and Jacob and his sons remained in Bethel six months.

4 At that time Deborah the daughter of Uz, the nurse of Rebecca, who had been with Jacob died and Jacob buried her beneath Bethel under an oak that was there.

5 And Rebecca the daughter of Bethuel, the mother of Jacob, also died at that time in Hebron, the same is Kireath-arba. She was buried in the cave of Machpelah which Abraham had bought from the children of Heth.

6 And the life of Rebecca was one hundred and thirty-three years, and she died. When Jacob heard that his mother Rebecca was dead he wept bitterly for his mother, and made a great mourning for her and for Deborah her nurse beneath the oak. He called the name of that place Allon-bachuth.

7 Laban the Syrian died in those days, for God struck him because he went contrary to the covenant that existed between him and Jacob.

8 Jacob was a hundred years old when the Lord appeared to him and blessed him and called his name Israel, and Rachel the wife of Jacob conceived in those days.

9 At that time Jacob and all belonging to him journeyed from Bethel to go to his father's house, to Hebron.

10 And while they were going on the road, and there was yet but a little way to come to Ephrath, Rachel gave birth to a son; she had hard labor and died.

11 Jacob buried her on the way to Ephrath, which is Bethlehem, and he set a pillar on her grave which is there to this day; the days of Rachel were forty-five years when she died.

12 Jacob called the name of his son that was born to him, which Rachel gave birth to, Benjamin, for he was born to him in the land on the right hand.

13 It was after the death of Rachel that Jacob pitched his tent in the tent of her handmaid Bilhah.

14 And Reuben was jealous for his mother Leah on account of this; he was filled with anger, and he rose up in his anger and went and entered the tent of Bilhah and then removed his father's bed.

15 At that time the portion of birthright, together with the kingly and priestly offices, was removed from the sons of Reuben for he had profaned his father's bed; the birthright was given to Joseph, the kingly office to Judah, and the priesthood to Levi, because Reuben had defiled his father's bed.

16 These are the generations of Jacob who were born to him in Padan-aram, and the sons of Jacob were twelve:

17 The sons of Leah were Reuben the first born, and Simeon, Levi, Judah, Issachar, Zebulun, and their sister Dinah; and the sons of Rachel were Joseph and Benjamin.

18 The sons of Zilpah, Leah's handmaid, were Gad and Asher, and the sons of Bilhah, Rachel's handmaid, were Dan and Naphtali; these are the sons of Jacob which were born to him in Padan-aram.

19 Jacob and his sons and all belonging to him journeyed and came to Mamre, which is Kireath-arba, that is in Hebron, where Abraham and Isaac sojourned; Jacob with his sons and all belonging to him lived with his father in Hebron.

20 His brother Esau, his sons and all belonging to him went to the land of Seir and lived there and had possessions in the land of Seir, and the children of Esau were prolific and multiplied greatly in the land of Seir.

21 These are the generations of Esau that were born to him in the land of Canaan, and the sons of Esau were five:

22 And Adah gave birth to, to Esau, his first born Eliphaz, and she also gave birth to, to him, Reuel, and Ahlibamah gave birth to, to him, Jeush, Yaalam and Korah.

23 These are the children of Esau who were born to him in the land of Canaan; the sons of Eliphaz the son of Esau were: Teman, Omar, Zepho, Gatam, Kenaz and Amalex; the sons of Reuel were Nachath, Zerach, Shamah and Mizzah.

24 The sons of Jeush were Timnah, Alvah, Jetheth; the sons of Yaalam were Alah, Phinor and Kenaz.

25 And the sons of Korah were Teman, Mibzar, Magdiel and Eram; these are the families of the sons of Esau according to their territories in the land of Seir.

26 These are the names of the sons of Seir the Horite, inhabitants of the land of Seir: Lotan, Shobal, Zibeon, Anah, Dishan, Ezer and Dishon, being seven sons.

27 The children of Lotan were Hori, Heman and their sister Timna, that is Timna who came to Jacob and his sons; they would not give ear to her and she became a concubine to Eliphaz the son of Esau; she gave birth to, to him, Amalek.

28 And the sons of Shobal were Alvan, Manahath, Ebal, Shepho, and Onam, and the sons of Zibeon were Ajah, and Anah; this was that Anah who found the Yemim in the wilderness when he fed the asses of Zibeon his father.

29 And while he was feeding his father's asses he led them to the wilderness at different times to feed them.

30 There was a day that he brought them to one of the deserts on the seashore, opposite the wilderness of the people, and while he was feeding them, suddenly a very heavy storm came from the other side of the sea and rested on the asses that were feeding there, and they all stood still.

31 Afterward about one hundred and twenty great and terrible animals came out from the wilderness at the other side of the sea; they all came to the place where the asses were, and they placed themselves there.

32 And those animals, from their middle downward, were in the shape of the children of men; from their middle

upward, some had the likeness of bears, and some the likeness of the keephas, with tails behind them from between their shoulders reaching down to the earth, like the tails of the ducheephath. These animals came and mounted and rode on these asses, and led them away, and they went away to this day.

33 One of these animals approached Anah, struck him with his tail, and then fled from that place.

34 And when he saw this work he was greatly afraid of his life, and he fled and escaped to the city.

35 He related to his sons and brothers all that had happened to him, and many men went to seek the asses but could not find them. Anah and his brothers went no more to that place from that day on for they were greatly afraid for their lives.

36 The children of Anah the son of Seir, were Dishon and his sister Ahlibamah; the children of Dishon were Hemdan, Eshban, Ithran and Cheran; the children of Ezer were Bilhan, Zaavan and Akan, and the children of Dishon were Uz and Aran.

37 These are the families of the children of Seir the Horite, according to their dukedoms in the land of Seir.

38 Esau and his children lived in the land of Seir the Horite, the inhabitant of the land, and they had possessions in it and were prolific and multiplied greatly. Jacob and his children and all belonging to them lived with their father Isaac in the land of Canaan, as the Lord had commanded Abraham their father.

CHAPTER 37

1 In the one hundred and fifth year of the life of Jacob, that is the ninth year of Jacob's dwelling with his children in the land of Canaan, he came from Padan-aram.

2 And in those days Jacob journeyed with his children from Hebron; they went and returned to the city of Shechem, they and all belonging to them and they lived there, for the children of Jacob obtained good and fattening pasture land for their cattle in the city of Shechem, the city of Shechem having then been rebuilt; there were in it about three hundred men and women.

3 Jacob and his children and all belonging to him lived in the part of the field which Jacob had bought from Hamor the father of Shechem, when he came from Padan-aram before Simeon and Levi had smitten the city.

4 And all those kings of the Canaanites and Amorites that surrounded the city of Shechem heard that the sons of Jacob had again come to Shechem and lived there.

5 They said, Shall the sons of Jacob the Hebrew again come to the city and dwell therein, after that they have smitten its inhabitants and driven them out? Shall they now return and also drive out those who are dwelling in the city or kill them?

6 And all the kings of Canaan again assembled, and they came together to make war with Jacob and his sons.

7 Jashub king of Tapnach sent also to all his neighboring kings, to Elan king of Gaash, and to Ihuri king of Shiloh, and to Parathon king of Chazar, and to Susi king of Sarton, and to Laban king of Bethchoran, and to Shabir king of Othnay-mah, saying,

8 Come up to me and assist me, and let us strike Jacob the Hebrew and his sons and all belonging to him, for they are again come to Shechem to possess it and to kill its inhabitants as before.

9 And all these kings assembled together and came with all their camps, a people greatly plentiful like the sand on the seashore, and they were all opposite to Tapnach.

10 Jashub king of Tapnach went forth to them with all his army, and he encamped with them opposite to Tapnach outside the city; all these kings they divided into seven divisions, being seven camps against the sons of Jacob.

11 And they sent a declaration to Jacob and his son, saying, All of you come forth to us that we may have an interview together in the plain, and revenge the cause of the men of Shechem whom you killed in their city; you will now again return to the city of Shechem and dwell therein, and kill its inhabitants as before.

12 The sons of Jacob heard this and their anger was set ablaze greatly at the words of the kings of Canaan, and ten of the sons of Jacob hurried and rose up, and each of them put on his weapons of war; and there were one hundred and two of their servants with them equipped in battle array.

13 And all these men, the sons of Jacob with their servants, went toward these kings and Jacob their father was with them; they all stood on the heap of Shechem.

14 Jacob prayed to the Lord for his sons, and he spread forth his hands to the Lord, and said, O God, you are an Almighty God, you are our father; you did form us and we are the works of your hands; I pray you deliver my sons through your mercy from the hand of their enemies who are this day coming to fight with them and save them from their hand, for in your hand is power and might to save the few from the many.

15 And give to my sons, your servants, strength of heart and might to fight with their enemies, to subdue them, and to make their enemies fall before them. Let not my sons and their servants die through the hands of the children of Canaan.

16 But if it seems good in your eyes to take away the lives of my sons and their servants, take them in your great mercy through the hands of your ministers, that they may not perish this day by the hands of the kings of the Amorites.

17 When Jacob ceased praying to the Lord the earth shook from its place, and the sun darkened, and all these kings were terrified and a great consternation seized them.

18 The Lord listened to the prayer of Jacob, and the Lord impressed the hearts of all the kings and their hosts with the terror and awe of the sons of Jacob.

19 For the Lord caused them to hear the voice of chariots, and the voice of mighty horses from the sons of Jacob, and the voice of a great army accompanying them.

20 And these kings were seized with great terror at the sons of Jacob; while they were standing in their quarters, behold the sons of Jacob advanced on them with one hundred and twelve men, with a great and tremendous shouting.

21 And when the kings saw the sons of Jacob advancing toward them, they were still more panic stricken; they were inclined to retreat from before the sons of Jacob as at first and not to fight with them.

22 But they did not retreat, saying, It would be a disgrace to us to retreat twice from before the Hebrews.

23 The sons of Jacob came near and advanced against all these kings and their armies, and what they saw was a very mighty people, numerous as the sand of the sea.

24 And the sons of Jacob called to the Lord and said, Help us O Lord, help us and answer us, for we trust in you, and let us not die by the hands of these uncircumcised men who this day have come against us.

25 The sons of Jacob put on their weapons of war and they took in their hands each man his shield and his javelin, and they approached to do battle.

26 And Judah, the son of Jacob, ran first before his brothers and ten of his servants with him, and he went toward these kings.

27 Jashub, king of Tapnach, also came forth first with his army before Judah, and Judah saw Jashub and his army coming toward him, and Judah's wrath was set ablaze; his anger burned within him, and he approached to the fight in which Judah ventured his life.

28 Jashub and all his army were advancing toward Judah and he was riding on a very strong and powerful horse; Jashub was a very valiant man, and covered with iron and brass from head to foot.

29 And while he was on the horse, he shot arrows with both hands from before and behind, as was his manner in all his battles; he never missed the place to which he aimed his arrows.

30 When Jashub came to fight with Judah and was darting many arrows against Judah, the Lord bound the hand of Jashub and all the arrows that he shot rebounded on his own men.

31 And in spite of this Jashub kept advancing toward Judah, to challenge him with the arrows, but the distance between them was about thirty cubits. When Judah saw Jashub darting forth his arrows against him, he ran to him with his wrath-excited strength.

32 Judah took up a large stone from the ground, its weight was sixty shekels, and Judah ran toward Jashub and with the stone struck him on his shield, so that Jashub was stunned with the blow and fell off his horse to the ground.

33 The shield burst asunder out of the hand of Jashub, and through the force of the blow sprang to the distance of about fifteen cubits, and the shield fell before the second camp.

34 The kings that came with Jashub saw at a distance the strength of Judah, the son of Jacob, and what he had done to Jashub; they were terribly afraid of Judah.

35 And they assembled near Jashub's camp, seeing his confusion, and Judah drew his sword and struck forty-two men of the camp of Jashub, and the whole of Jashub's camp fled before Judah. No man stood against him and they left Jashub and fled from him, and Jashub was still prostrate on the ground.

36 Jashub, seeing that all the men of his camp had fled from him, hurried and rose up with terror against Judah and stood on his legs opposite Judah.

37 And Jashub had a single combat with Judah, placing shield toward shield, and Jashub's men all fled for they were greatly afraid of Judah.

38 Jashub took his spear in his hand to strike Judah on his head, but Judah had quickly placed his shield to his head against Jashub's spear so that the shield of Judah received the blow from Jashub's spear, and the shield was

split in two.

39 And when Judah saw that his shield was split, he hastily drew his sword and struck Jashub at his ankles and cut off his feet, so that Jashub fell on the ground and the spear fell from his hand.

40 Judah hastily picked up Jashub's spear with which he severed his head and cast it next to his feet.

41 When the sons of Jacob saw what Judah had done to Jashub, they all ran into the ranks of the other kings and the sons of Jacob fought with the army of Jashub and the armies of all the kings that were there.

42 The sons of Jacob caused fifteen thousand of their men to fall, and they struck them as if smiting at gourds, and the rest fled for their lives.

43 Judah was still standing by the body of Jashub and stripped Jashub of his coat of mail.

44 Judah also took off the iron and brass that were around Jashub, and then nine men of the captains of Jashub came along to fight against Judah.

45 Judah hurried and took up a stone from the ground, and with it struck one of them on the head; his skull was fractured and the body also fell from the horse to the ground.

46 And the eight captains that remained, seeing the strength of Judah, were greatly afraid and they fled; Judah with his ten men pursued them and they overtook them and killed them.

47 The sons of Jacob were still smiting the armies of the kings, and they killed many of them, but those kings daringly kept their stand with their captains and did not retreat from their places; they shouted against those of their armies that fled from before the sons of Jacob, but none would listen to them, for they were afraid for their lives that they should die.

48 And all the sons of Jacob, after having smitten the armies of the kings, returned and came before Judah; Judah was still slaying the eight captains of Jashub and stripping off their garments.

49 And Levi saw Elon, king of Gaash, advancing toward him with his fourteen captains to strike him, but Levi did not know it for certain.

50 Elon with his captains approached nearer, and Levi looked back and saw that battle was coming to him from the rear. Levi ran with twelve of his servants, and they went and killed Elon and his captains with the edge of the sword.

CHAPTER 38

1 Ihuri king of Shiloh came up to assist Elon and he approached Jacob, when Jacob drew his bow that was in his hand and with an arrow struck Ihuri, which caused his death.

2 And when Ihuri king of Shiloh was dead, the four remaining kings fled from their station with the rest of the captains; they endeavored to retreat, saying, We have no more strength with the Hebrews after their having killed the three kings and their captains who were more powerful than we are.

3 When the sons of Jacob saw that the remaining kings had left their station, they pursued them and Jacob also came from the heap of Shechem from the place where he was standing; they went after the kings and they approached them with their servants.

4 And the kings and the captains with the rest of their armies, seeing that the sons of Jacob approached them, were afraid for their lives and fled till they reached the city of Chazar.

5 The sons of Jacob pursued them to the gate of the city of Chazar, and they struck a great smiting among the kings and their armies, about four thousand men. While they were smiting the army of the kings, Jacob was occupied with his bow, confining himself to smiting the kings and killed them all.

6 And he killed Parathon king of Chazar at the gate of the city of Chazar and afterward struck Susi king of Sarton, and Laban king of Bethchorin, and Shabir king of Machnaymah; he killed them all with arrows, an arrow to each of them, and they died.

7 The sons of Jacob, seeing that all the kings were dead and that they were broken up and retreating, continued to carry on the battle with the armies of the kings opposite the gate of Chazar, and they still struck about four hundred of their men.

8 Three men of the servants of Jacob fell in that battle and when Judah saw that three of his servants had died, it grieved him greatly and his anger burned within him against the Amorites.

9 And all the men that remained of the armies of the kings were greatly afraid for their lives, and they ran and broke the gate of the walls of the city of Chazar; they all entered the city for safety.

10 They concealed themselves in the midst of the city of Chazar, for the city of Chazar was very large and

extensive, and when all these armies had entered the city, the sons of Jacob ran after them to the city.

11 Four mighty men, experienced in battle, went forth from the city and stood against the entrance of the city with drawn swords and spears in their hands; they placed themselves opposite the sons of Jacob and would not let them enter the city.

12 Naphtali ran and came between them and with his sword struck two of them, and cut off their heads at one stroke.

13 He turned to the other two and saw that they had fled; he pursued them, overtook them, struck them and killed them.

14 When the sons of Jacob came to the city and saw there was another wall to the city, they sought for the gate of the wall and could not find it; Judah sprang on the top of the wall and Simeon and Levi followed him, and they all three descended from the wall into the city.

15 Simeon and Levi killed all the men who ran for safety into the city and also the inhabitants of the city with their wives and little ones they killed with the edge of the sword, and the cries of the city ascended up to heaven.

16 And Dan and Naphtali sprang on the wall to see what caused the noise of the wailing, for the sons of Jacob felt anxious about their brothers; they heard the inhabitants of the city speaking with weeping and pleas, saying, Take all that we possess in the city and go away, only do not put us to death.

17 When Judah, Simeon, and Levi had ceased smiting the inhabitants of the city, they ascended the wall and called to Dan and Naphtali, who were on the wall, and to the rest of their brothers; Simeon and Levi informed them of the entrance into the city, and all the sons of Jacob came to gather the spoil.

18 And the sons of Jacob took the spoil of the city of Chazar, the flocks and herds, and the property, and they took all that could be captured, and went away that day from the city.

19 On the next day the sons of Jacob went to Sarton, for they heard that the men of Sarton who had remained in the city were assembling to fight with them for having slain their king. Sarton was a very high and fortified city, and it had a deep rampart surrounding the city.

20 And the pillar of the rampart was about fifty cubits and its breadth forty cubits; there was no place for a man to enter the city on account of the rampart. The sons of Jacob saw the rampart of the city, and they sought an entrance in it but could not find it.

21 For the entrance to the city was at the rear, and every man that wished to come into the city came by that road and went around the whole city, and afterwards entered the city.

22 The sons of Jacob seeing they could not find the way into the city, their anger was set ablaze greatly, and the inhabitants of the city seeing that the sons of Jacob were coming to them were greatly afraid of them, for they had heard of their strength and what they had done to Chazar.

23 And the inhabitants of the city of Sarton could not go out toward the sons of Jacob after having assembled in the city to fight against them, that they might thereby not get into the city. But when they saw that they were coming toward them, they were greatly afraid of them, for they had heard of their strength and what they had done to Chazar.

24 So the inhabitants of Sarton speedily took away the bridge of the road of the city from its place, before the sons of Jacob came, and they brought it into the city.

25 The sons of Jacob came and sought the way into the city, and could not find it and the inhabitants of the city went up to the top of the wall, and saw that the sons of Jacob were seeking an entrance into the city.

26 The inhabitants of the city reproached the sons of Jacob from the top of the wall and they cursed them, and the sons of Jacob heard the reproaches and they were greatly incensed; their anger burned within them.

27 The sons of Jacob were provoked at them, and they all rose and sprang over the rampart with the force of their strength, and through their might passed the forty cubits' breadth of the rampart.

28 And when they had passed the rampart they stood under the wall of the city, and they found all the gates of the city enclosed with iron doors.

29 The sons of Jacob came near to break open the doors of the gates of the city, and the inhabitants did not let them, for from the top of the wall they were casting stones and arrows on them.

30 And the number of the people that were on the wall was about four hundred men, and when the sons of Jacob saw that the men of the city would not let them open the gates of the city, they sprang and ascended the top of the wall, and Judah went up first to the east part of the city.

31 And Gad and Asher went up after him to the west corner of the city, and Simeon and Levi to the north, and Dan and Reuben to the south.

32 The men who were on the top of the wall, the inhabitants of the city, seeing that the sons of Jacob were coming

up to them, all fled from the wall, descended into the city and concealed themselves in the middle of the city.

33 Issachar and Naphtali that remained under the wall approached and broke the gates of the city, and set ablaze a fire at the gates of the city that the iron melted, and all the sons of Jacob came into the city, they and all their men; they fought with the inhabitants of the city of Sarton and struck them with the edge of the sword, and no man stood up before them.

34 About two hundred men fled from the city and they all went and hid themselves in a certain tower in the city; Judah pursued them to the tower and broke down the tower which fell on the men, and they all died.

35 The sons of Jacob went up the road of the roof of that tower, and they looked and there was another strong and high tower at a distance in the city, and the top of it reached to heaven. The sons of Jacob hurried and descended and went with all their men to that tower, and found it filled with about three hundred men, women and little ones.

36 The sons of Jacob struck a great smiting among those men in the tower and they ran away and fled from them.

37 And Simeon and Levi pursued them when twelve mighty and valiant men came out to them from the place where they had concealed themselves.

38 And those twelve men maintained a strong battle against Simeon and Levi, and Simeon and Levi could not prevail over them; those valiant men broke the shields of Simeon and Levi, and one of them struck at Levi's head with his sword when Levi hastily placed his hand to his head, for he was afraid of the sword. The sword struck Levi's hand, and the hand of Levi was nearly cut off.

39 Levi seized the sword of the valiant man in his hand and took it forcibly from the man; with it he struck at the head of the powerful man and he severed his head.

40 Eleven men approached to fight with Levi, for they saw that one of them was killed; the sons of Jacob fought but the sons of Jacob could not defeat them, for those men were very powerful.

41 And the sons of Jacob seeing that they could not win over them, Simeon gave a loud and tremendous shriek, and the eleven powerful men were stunned at the voice of Simeon's shrieking.

42 Judah at a distance knew the voice of Simeon's shouting, and Naphtali and Judah ran with their shields to Simeon and Levi and found them fighting with those powerful men, unable to defeat them as their shields were broken.

43 Naphtali saw that the shields of Simeon and Levi were broken and he took two shields from his servants and brought them to Simeon and Levi.

44 And Simeon, Levi and Judah on that day fought all three against the eleven mighty men until the time of sunset, but they could not win over them.

45 This was told to Jacob, and he was very grieved; he prayed to the Lord, and he and Naphtali his son went against these mighty men.

46 Jacob approached, drew his bow, and came near to the mighty men, and killed three of their men with the bow; the remaining eight turned back and then the war waged against them in the front and rear. They were greatly afraid for their lives and could not stand before the sons of Jacob, and they fled from before them.

47 In their flight they met Dan and Asher coming toward them, and they suddenly fell on them and fought with them, and killed two of them; Judah and his brothers pursued them and struck the remainder of them, and killed them.

48 All the sons of Jacob returned and walked through the city searching if they could find any men; they found about twenty young men in a cave in the city; Gad and Asher struck them all and Dan and Naphtali lighted on the rest of the men who had fled and escaped from the second tower, and they struck them all.

49 The sons of Jacob struck all the inhabitants of the city of Sarton, but the women and little ones they left in the city and did not kill them.

50 And all the inhabitants of the city of Sarton were powerful men; one of them would pursue a thousand, and two of them would not flee from ten thousand of the rest of men.

51 The sons of Jacob killed all the inhabitants of the city of Sarton with the edge of the sword; no man stood up against them, and they left the women in the city.

52 The sons of Jacob took all the spoil of the city and captured what they desired, and they took flocks and herds and property from the city; the sons of Jacob did to Sarton and its inhabitants as they had done to Chazar and its inhabitants, and they turned and went away.

CHAPTER 39

1 When the sons of Jacob went from the city of Sarton, they had gone about two hundred cubits when they met the inhabitants of Tapnach coming toward them, for they went out to fight with them because they had smitten the king of Tapnach and all his men.

2 So all that remained in the city of Tapnach came out to fight with the sons of Jacob and they thought to retake from them the booty and the spoil which they had captured from Chazar and Sarton.

3 The rest of the men of Tapnach fought with the sons of Jacob in that place, and the sons of Jacob struck them and they fled before them. They pursued them to the city of Arbelan and they all fell before the sons of Jacob.

4 The sons of Jacob returned and came to Tapnach to take away the spoil of Tapnach; when they came to Tapnach they heard that the people of Arbelan had gone out to meet them to save the spoil of their brothers. The sons of Jacob left ten of their men in Tapnach to plunder the city, and they went out toward the people of Arbelan.

5 The men of Arbelan went out with their wives to fight with the sons of Jacob, for their wives were experienced in battle; they went out, about four hundred men and women.

6 And all the sons of Jacob shouted with a loud voice; they all ran toward the inhabitants of Arbelan with a great and tremendous voice.

7 The inhabitants of Arbelan heard the noise of the shouting of the sons of Jacob and their roaring like the noise of lions and like the roaring of the sea and its waves.

8 And fear and terror possessed their hearts on account of the sons of Jacob; they were terribly afraid of them and they retreated and fled before them into the city. The sons of Jacob pursued them to the gate of the city and they came on them in the city.

9 The sons of Jacob fought with them in the city, and all their women were engaged in slinging against the sons of Jacob; the combat was very severe among them all of that day till evening.

10 And the sons of Jacob could not prevail over them; the sons of Jacob had almost perished in that battle. The sons of Jacob cried to the Lord and greatly gained strength toward evening; the sons of Jacob struck all the inhabitants of Arbelan by the edge of the sword, men, women and little ones.

11 Also the remainder of the people who had fled from Sarton, the sons of Jacob struck them in Arbelan, and the sons of Jacob did to Arbelan and Tapnach as they had done to Chazar and Sarton. When the women saw that all the men were dead, they went on the roofs of the city and struck the sons of Jacob by showering down stones like rain.

12 And the sons of Jacob hurried and came into the city and seized all the women and struck them with the edge of the sword. The sons of Jacob captured all the spoil and booty, flocks and herds and cattle.

13 The sons of Jacob did to Machnaymah as they had done to Tapnach, to Chazar and to Shiloh, and they turned from there and went away.

14 On the fifth day the sons of Jacob heard that the people of Gaash had gathered against them to battle, because they had slain their king and their captains, for there had been fourteen captains in the city of Gaash, and the sons of Jacob had slain them all in the first battle.

15 And the sons of Jacob that day put on their weapons of war, and they marched to battle against the inhabitants of Gaash. In Gaash there was a strong and mighty people of the people of the Amorites; Gaash was the strongest and best fortified city of all the cities of the Amorites, and it had three walls.

16 The sons of Jacob came to Gaash and they found the gates of the city locked and about five hundred men standing at the top of the outer-most wall; a people numerous as the sand on the sea shore were in ambush for the sons of Jacob from outside the city at the rear.

17 And the sons of Jacob approached to open the gates of the city, and while they were drawing near to it, those who were in ambush at the rear of the city came forth from their places and surrounded the sons of Jacob.

18 The sons of Jacob were enclosed between the people of Gaash, and the battle was both to their front and rear; all the men that were on the wall were casting from the wall on them, arrows and stones.

19 And Judah, seeing that the men of Gaash were getting too strong for them, gave a most piercing and tremendous shriek and all the men of Gaash were terrified at the voice of Judah's cry; men fell from the wall at his powerful shriek and all those that were from without and within the city were greatly afraid of their lives.

20 And the sons of Jacob still came closer to break the doors of the city when the men of Gaash threw stones and arrows on them from the top of the wall, and made them flee from the gate.

21 The sons of Jacob returned against the men of Gaash who were with them from outside the city and they

struck them terribly, as striking against gourds, and they could not stand against the sons of Jacob for fright and terror had seized them at the shriek of Judah.

22 The sons of Jacob killed all those men who were outside the city, and the sons of Jacob still drew nearer to make an entrance into the city and to fight under the city walls, but they could not for all the inhabitants of Gaash who remained in the city had surrounded the walls of Gaash in every direction; the sons of Jacob were unable to approach the city to fight with them.

23 The sons of Jacob came near to one corner to fight under the wall; the inhabitants of Gaash threw arrows and stones on them like showers of rain, and they fled from under the wall.

24 And the people of Gaash who were on the wall, seeing that the sons of Jacob could not prevail over them from under the wall, reproached the sons of Jacob in these words, saying,

25 What is the matter with you in the battle that you cannot prevail? Can you then do to the mighty city of Gaash and its inhabitants as you did to the cities of the Amorites that were not so powerful? Certainly to those weak ones among us you did those things and killed them in the entrance of the city, for they had no strength when they were terrified at the sound of your shouting.

26 And will you now then be able to fight in this place? Certainly here you will all die, and we will avenge the cause of those cities that you have laid waste.

27 And the inhabitants of Gaash greatly reproached the sons of Jacob and reviled them with their gods, and continued to cast arrows and stones on them from the wall.

28 Judah and his brothers heard the words of the inhabitants of Gaash and their anger was greatly roused, and Judah was zealous of his God in this matter, and he called out and said, O Lord, help, send help to us and our brothers.

29 And he ran at a distance with all his might with his drawn sword in his hand, and he sprang from the earth and by dint of his strength mounted the wall, and his sword fell from his hand.

30 And Judah shouted on the wall, and all the men that were on the wall were terrified; some of them fell from the wall into the city and died, and those who were yet on the wall, when they saw Judah's strength were greatly afraid and fled for their lives into the city for safety.

31 And some were emboldened to fight with Judah on the wall; they came close to kill him when they saw there was no sword in Judah's hand and they thought of casting him from the wall to his brothers; twenty men of the city came up to assist them, they surrounded Judah and all shouted over him, and approached him with drawn swords; they terrified Judah, and Judah cried out to his brothers from the wall.

32 And Jacob and his sons drew the bow from under the wall, and struck three of the men that were on the top of the wall, and Judah continued to cry and he exclaimed, O Lord help us, O Lord deliver us, and he cried out with a loud voice on the wall, and the cry was heard at a great distance.

33 After this cry he again repeated a shout, and all the men who surrounded Judah on the top of the wall were terrified; they each threw his sword from his hand at the sound of Judah's shouting and his tremor and fled.

34 Judah took the swords which had fallen from their hands and he fought with them and killed twenty of their men on the wall.

35 About eighty men and women still ascended the wall from the city and they all surrounded Judah, and the Lord impressed the fear of Judah in their hearts so that they were unable to approach him.

36 And Jacob and all who were with him drew the bow from under the wall, and they killed ten men on the wall; they fell below the wall in front of Jacob and his sons.

37 And the people on the wall seeing that twenty of their men had fallen still ran toward Judah with drawn swords, but they could not approach him for they were greatly terrified at Judah's strength.

38 And one of their mighty men whose name was Arud approached to strike Judah on the head with his sword, when Judah hastily put his shield to his head; the sword hit the shield and it was split in two.

39 This mighty man after he had struck Judah ran for his life at the fear of Judah, and his feet slipped on the wall and he fell among the sons of Jacob who were below the wall, and the sons of Jacob struck him and killed him.

40 And Judah's head pained him from the blow of the powerful man; Judah had nearly died from it.

41 And Judah cried out on the wall owing to the pain produced by the blow, when Dan heard him, and his anger burned within him; he also rose up and went a distance and ran and sprang from the earth and mounted the wall with his wrath-excited strength.

42 And when Dan came on the wall near to Judah, all the men on the wall fled who had stood against Judah; they went up to the second wall and they threw arrows and stones on Dan and Judah from the second wall and endeavored to drive them from the wall.

43 And the arrows and stones struck Dan and Judah and they had nearly been killed on the wall; wherever Dan and Judah fled from the wall they were attacked with arrows and stones from the second wall.

44 Jacob and his sons were still at the entrance of the city below the first wall, and they were not able to draw their bow against the inhabitants of the city as they could not be seen by them, being on the second wall.

45 Dan and Judah, when they could no longer bear the stones and arrows that fell on them from the second wall, both sprang onto the second wall near the people of the city; when the people of the city who were on the second wall saw that Dan and Judah had come to them on the second wall, they all cried out and descended below between the walls.

46 Jacob and his sons heard the noise of the shouting from the people of the city and they were still at the entrance of the city; they were anxious about Dan and Judah who were not seen by them, they being on the second wall.

47 Naphtali went up with his wrath-excited might and sprang on the first wall to see what caused the noise of shouting which they had heard in the city; Issachar and Zebulun came near to break the doors of the city, and they opened the gates of the city and came into the city.

48 Naphtali leaped from the first wall to the second and came to assist his brothers; the inhabitants of Gaash who were on the wall, seeing that Naphtali was the third who had come up to assist his brothers, all fled and descended into the city, and Jacob and all his sons and all their young men came into the city to them.

49 Judah and Dan and Naphtali descended from the wall into the city and pursued the inhabitants of the city, and Simeon and Levi were from outside the city and didn't know that the gate was opened; they went up from there to the wall and came down to their brothers into the city.

50 The inhabitants of the city had all descended into the city and the sons of Jacob came to them from different directions; the battle waged against them from the front and the rear, and the sons of Jacob struck them terribly and killed about twenty thousand of them men and women; not one of them could stand up against the sons of Jacob.

51 And the blood flowed plentifully in the city, and it was like a brook of water; the blood flowed like a brook to the outer part of the city, and reached the desert of Bethchorin.

52 And the people of Bethchorin saw at a distance the blood flowing from the city of Gaash and about seventy men from among them ran to see the blood, and they came to the place where the blood was.

53 They followed the track of the blood and came to the wall of the city of Gaash, and they saw the blood issue from the city. They heard the voice of crying from the inhabitants of Gaash, for it ascended to heaven, and the blood was continuing to flow abundantly like a brook of water.

54 And all the sons of Jacob were still smiting the inhabitants of Gaash, and were engaged in slaying them till evening, about twenty thousand men and women. And the people of Chorin said, Certainly this is the work of the Hebrews, for they are still carrying on war in all the cities of the Amorites.

55 And those people hurried and ran to Bethchorin, and each took his weapons of war; they cried out to all the inhabitants of Bethchorin, who also put on their weapons of war to go and fight with the sons of Jacob.

56 When the sons of Jacob had done smiting the inhabitants of Gaash, they walked about the city to strip all the slain. Coming into the innermost part of the city and farther on they met three very powerful men, and there was no sword in their hand.

57 The sons of Jacob came up to the place where they were and the powerful men ran away; one of them had taken Zebulun, who he saw was a young lad and of short stature, and with his might dashed him to the ground.

58 And Jacob ran to him with his sword and Jacob struck him below his loins with the sword and cut him in two, and the body fell on Zebulun.

59 The second one approached and seized Jacob to fell him to the ground; Jacob turned to him and shouted to him, while Simeon and Levi ran and struck him on the hips with the sword and felled him to the ground.

60 And the powerful man rose up from the ground with wrath-excited might; Judah came to him before he had gained his footing and struck him on the head with the sword, and his head was split and he died.

61 The third powerful man, seeing that his companions were killed, ran from before the sons of Jacob and the sons of Jacob pursued him into the city; while the powerful man was fleeing he found one of the swords of the inhabitants of the city, he picked it up and turned to the sons of Jacob and fought them with that sword.

62 The powerful man ran to Judah to strike him on the head with the sword, and there was no shield in the hand of Judah; while he was aiming to strike him, Naphtali hastily took his shield and put it to Judah's head and the sword of the powerful man hit the shield of Naphtali, and Judah escaped the sword.

63 Simeon and Levi ran onto the powerful man with their swords and struck at him forcibly with their swords,

and the two swords entered the body of the powerful man and divided it in two, length-wise.

64 And the sons of Jacob struck the three mighty men at that time, together with all the inhabitants of Gaash, and the day was about to decline.

65 And the sons of Jacob walked about Gaash and took all the spoil of the city, even the little ones and women they did not allow to live, and the sons of Jacob did to Gaash as they had done to Sarton and Shiloh.

CHAPTER 40

1 And the sons of Jacob led away all the spoil of Gaash, and went out of the city by night.

2 They were going out marching toward the castle of Bethchorin, and the inhabitants of Bethchorin were going to the castle to meet them; on that night the sons of Jacob fought with the inhabitants of Bethchorin, in the castle of Bethchorin.

3 And all the inhabitants of Bethchorin were mighty men; one of them would not flee from before a thousand men, and they fought on that night on the castle; their shouts were heard on that night from afar and the earth quaked at their shouting.

4 And all the sons of Jacob were afraid of those men as they were not accustomed to fight in the dark, and they were greatly perplexed. The sons of Jacob cried to the Lord, saying, Give help to us O Lord, deliver us that we may not die by the hands of these uncircumcised men.

5 And the Lord listened to the voice of the sons of Jacob, and the Lord caused great terror and confusion to seize the people of Bethchorin; they fought among themselves with one another in the darkness of night, and struck each other in great numbers.

6 The sons of Jacob, knowing that the Lord had brought a spirit of perverseness among those men, and that they fought each man with his neighbor, went forth from among the bands of the people of Bethchorin and went as far as the descent of the castle of Bethchorin, and farther. They stayed there securely with their young men on that night.

7 And the people of Bethchorin fought the whole night, one man with his brother, and the other with his neighbor; they cried out in every direction on the castle and their cry was heard at a distance, and the whole earth shook at their voice for they were powerful above all the people of the earth.

8 And all the inhabitants of the cities of the Canaanites, the Hittites, the Amorites, the Hivites and all the kings of Canaan, and also those who were on the other side of the Jordan heard the noise of the shouting that night.

9 They said, Certainly these are the battles of the Hebrews who are fighting against the seven cities, who came near to them; who can stand against those Hebrews?

10 All the inhabitants of the cities of the Canaanites and all those who were on the other side of the Jordan were greatly afraid of the sons of Jacob, for they said, Behold the same will be done to us as was done to those cities, for who can stand against their mighty strength?

11 And the cries of the Chorinites were very great on that night and continued to increase; they struck each other till morning, and numbers of them were killed.

12 And the morning appeared; all the sons of Jacob rose up at daybreak and went up to the castle, and they struck those who remained of the Chorinites in a terrible manner and they were all killed in the castle.

13 And the sixth day appeared, and all the inhabitants of Canaan saw at a distance all the people of Bethchorin lying dead in the castle of Bethchorin, and scattered about as the carcasses of lambs and goats.

14 And the sons of Jacob led all the spoil which they had captured from Gaash and went to Bethchorin; they found the city full of people like the sand of the sea, and they fought with them, and the sons of Jacob struck them there till evening time.

15 And the sons of Jacob did to Bethchorin as they had done to Gaash and Tapnach, and as they had done to Chazar, to Sarton and to Shiloh.

16 The sons of Jacob took with them the spoil of Bethchorin and all the spoil of the cities, and on that day they went home to Shechem.

17 And the sons of Jacob came home to the city of Shechem and they remained outside the city, and then rested there from the war, and stayed there all night.

18 And all their servants together with all the spoil that they had taken from the cities, were left outside the city, and they did not enter the city, for they said, Perhaps there may yet be more fighting against us, and they may come to besiege us in Shechem.

19 Jacob and his sons and their servants remained that night and the next day in the portion of the field which Jacob had purchased from Hamor for five shekels, and all that they had captured was with them.

20 All the booty which the sons of Jacob had captured was in the portion of the field, immense as the sand on the seashore.

21 The inhabitants of the land observed them from afar, and they all were afraid of the sons of Jacob who had done this thing, for no king from the days of old had ever done the like.

22 The seven kings of the Canaanites resolved to make peace with the sons of Jacob, for they were greatly afraid for their lives on account of the sons of Jacob.

23 And on that day, being the seventh day, Japhia king of Hebron sent secretly to the king of Ai, and to the king of Gibeon, and to the king of Shalem, and to the king of Adulam, and to the king of Lachish, and to the king of Chazar, and to all the Canaanitish kings who were under their subjection, saying,

24 Go up with me, and come to me that we may go to the sons of Jacob, and I will make peace with them and form a treaty with them, that all your lands not be destroyed by the swords of the sons of Jacob as they did to Shechem and the cities around it, as you have heard and seen.

25 And when you come to me, do not come with many men, but let every king bring his three head captains and every captain bring three of his officers.

26 And come all of you to Hebron; we will go together to the sons of Jacob and request them to form a treaty of peace with us.

27 And all those kings did as the king of Hebron had sent to them, for they were all under his counsel and command, and all the kings of Canaan assembled to go to the sons of Jacob to make peace with them; the sons of Jacob returned and went to the portion of the field that was in Shechem, for they did not put confidence in the kings of the land.

28 And the sons of Jacob returned and remained in the portion of the field ten days, and no one came to make war with them.

29 When the sons of Jacob saw that there was no appearance of war, they all assembled and went to the city of Shechem, and the sons of Jacob remained in Shechem.

30 And at the expiration of forty days, all the kings of the Amorites assembled from all their places and came to Hebron, to Japhia, king of Hebron.

31 The number of kings that came to Hebron to make peace with the sons of Jacob was twenty-one kings, and the number of captains that came with them was sixty-nine, and their men were one hundred and eighty-nine; all these kings and their men rested by Mount Hebron.

32 And the king of Hebron went out with his three captains and nine men, and these kings resolved to go to the sons of Jacob to make peace.

33 They said to the king of Hebron, Go before us with your men, speak for us to the sons of Jacob, and we will come after you and confirm your words, and the king of Hebron did so.

34 The sons of Jacob heard that all the kings of Canaan had gathered together and rested in Hebron, and the sons of Jacob sent four of their servants as spies, saying, Go and spy these kings, and search and examine their men whether they are few or many, and if they are but few in number, count them all and come back.

35 And the servants of Jacob went secretly to these kings, and did as the sons of Jacob had commanded them. On that day they came back to the sons of Jacob, and said to them, We came to those kings, and they are few in number; we counted them all, and surely there were two hundred and eighty-eight, kings and men.

36 The sons of Jacob said, They are but few in number, therefore we will not all go out to them. In the morning the sons of Jacob rose up and chose sixty-two of their men, and ten of the sons of Jacob went with them; and they put on their weapons of war, for they said, They are coming to make war with us. For they didn't know that they were coming to make peace with them.

37 And the sons of Jacob went with their servants to the gate of Shechem, toward those kings, and their father Jacob was with them.

38 And when they had come forth, there the king of Hebron and his three captains and nine men with him were coming along the road toward the sons of Jacob; the sons of Jacob lifted up their eyes, and saw at a distance Japhia, king of Hebron, with his captains, coming toward them, And the sons of Jacob took their stand at the place of the gate of Shechem, and did not proceed.

39 The king of Hebron continued to advance, he and his captains, until he came near to the sons of Jacob; he and his captains bowed down to them to the ground, and the king of Hebron sat with his captains in front of Jacob and his sons.

40 The sons of Jacob said to him, What has happened to you, O king of Hebron? Why have you come to us this day? What do you require from us? And the king of Hebron said to Jacob, I petition you my lord, all the kings of the Canaanites have this day come to make peace with you.

41 And the sons of Jacob heard the words of the king of Hebron; they would not consent to his proposals; the sons of Jacob had no faith in him, for they imagined that the king of Hebron had spoken deceitfully to them.

42 The king of Hebron knew from the words of the sons of Jacob that they did not believe his words, and the king of Hebron approached nearer to Jacob, and said to him, I beg you, my lord, to be assured that all these kings have come to you on peaceable terms, for they have not come with all their men, neither did they bring their weapons of war with them, for they have come to seek peace from my lord and his sons.

43 The sons of Jacob answered the king of Hebron, saying, Go to all these kings and if you speak truth to us, let them each come singly before us; if they come to us unarmed, we shall then know that they seek peace from us.

44 And Japhia, king of Hebron, sent one of his men to the kings and they all came before the sons of Jacob, and bowed down to them to the ground; these kings sat before Jacob and his sons and spoke to them, saying,

45 We have heard all that you did to the kings of the Amorites with your sword and greatly mighty arm, so that no man could stand up before you; we were afraid of you for the sake of our lives, that it would happen to us as it did to them.

46 So we have come to you to form a treaty of peace between us, and now therefore contract with us a covenant of peace and truth, that you will not meddle with us, inasmuch as we have not meddled with you.

47 And the sons of Jacob knew that they had really come to seek peace from them. And the sons of Jacob listened to them, and formed a covenant with them.

48 The sons of Jacob swore to them that they would not meddle with them, and all the kings of the Canaanites swore also to them, and the sons of Jacob made them pay tribute from that day forward.

49 And after this all the captains of these kings came with their men before Jacob, with presents in their hands for Jacob and his sons, and they bowed down to him to the ground.

50 These kings then urged the sons of Jacob and begged of them to return all the spoil they had captured from the seven cities of the Amorites, and the sons of Jacob did so; they returned all that they had captured, the women, the little ones, the cattle and all the spoil which they had taken, and they sent them off; they went away each to his city.

51 And all these kings again bowed down to the sons of Jacob, and they sent or brought them many gifts in those days; the sons of Jacob sent off these kings and their men, and they went peaceably away from them to their cities, and the sons of Jacob also returned to their home, to Shechem.

52 And there was peace from that day forward between the sons of Jacob and the kings of the Canaanites, until the children of Israel came to inherit the land of Canaan.

CHAPTER 41

1 At the revolution of the year the sons of Jacob journeyed from Shechem, and they came to Hebron, to their father Isaac; they lived there, but their flocks and herds they fed daily in Shechem, for there was there in those days good and fattening pasture. Jacob and his sons and all their household lived in the valley of Hebron.

2 It was in those days, in that year, being the hundred and sixth year of the life of Jacob, in the tenth year of Jacob's coming from Padan-aram, that Leah the wife of Jacob died; she was fifty-one years old when she died in Hebron.

3 Jacob and his sons buried her in the cave of the field of Machpelah, which is in Hebron, which Abraham had bought from the children of Heth for the possession of a burial place.

4 The sons of Jacob lived with their father in the valley of Hebron; all the inhabitants of the land knew their strength and their fame went throughout the land.

5 Joseph the son of Jacob and his brother Benjamin, the sons of Rachel, the wife of Jacob, were yet young in those days, and did not go out with their brothers during their battles in all the cities of the Amorites.

6 And when Joseph saw the strength of his brothers and their greatness, he praised them and extolled them, but he ranked himself greater than them and extolled himself above them; Jacob, his father, also loved him more than any of his sons for he was a son of his old age, and through his love toward him he made him a coat of many

colors.

7 And when Joseph saw that his father loved him more than his brothers, he continued to elevate himself above his brothers, and he brought to his father evil reports concerning them.

8 The sons of Jacob seeing all of Joseph's conduct toward them, and that their father loved him more than any of them, hated him and could not ever speak peaceably to him.

9 Joseph was seventeen years old, and he was still magnifying himself above his brothers, and thought of raising himself above them.

10 At that time he dreamed a dream, and he came to his brothers and told them his dream, and he said to them, I dreamed a dream, and behold we were all binding sheaves in the field, and my sheaf rose and placed itself on the ground and your sheaves surrounded it and bowed down to it.

11 And his brothers answered him and said to him, What means this dream that you did dream? Do you imagine in your heart to reign or rule over us?

12 And he still came and told the thing to his father Jacob, and Jacob kissed Joseph when he heard these words from his mouth, and Jacob blessed Joseph.

13 When the sons of Jacob saw that their father had blessed Joseph and had kissed him, and that he loved him greatly, they became jealous of him and hated him all the more.

14 After this Joseph dreamed another dream and related the dream to his father in the presence of his brothers, and Joseph said to his father and brothers, Behold I have again dreamed a dream, and behold the sun and the moon and the eleven stars bowed down to me.

15 And his father heard the words of Joseph and his dream, and seeing that his brothers hated Joseph on account of this matter, Jacob therefore rebuked Joseph before his brothers on account of this thing, saying, What does this dream mean which you have dreamed, and this magnifying yourself before your brothers who are older than you are?

16 Do you imagine in your heart that I and your mother and your eleven brothers will come and bow down to you, that you speak these things?

17 And his brothers were jealous of him on account of his words and dreams; they continued to hate him, and Jacob reserved the dreams in his heart.

18 The sons of Jacob went one day to feed their father's flock in Shechem, for they were still herdsmen in those days; while the sons of Jacob were that day feeding in Shechem they delayed, and the time of gathering in the cattle was passed, and they had not arrived.

19 And Jacob saw that his sons were delayed in Shechem, and Jacob said within himself, Perhhaps the people of Shechem have risen up to fight against them, therefore they have delayed coming today.

20 And Jacob called Joseph his son and commanded him, saying, Behold your brothers are feeding in Shechem this day and look, they have not yet come back; therefore go and see where they are, and bring back word to me concerning the welfare of your brothers and the welfare of the flock.

21 And Jacob sent his son Joseph to the valley of Hebron; Joseph came for his brothers to Shechem, and could not find them, and Joseph went toward the field which was near Shechem to see where his brothers had turned. But he missed his road in the wilderness and didn't know which way he should go.

22 And an angel of the Lord found him wandering in the road toward the field, and Joseph said to the angel of the Lord, I seek my brothers; have you not heard where they are feeding? And the angel of the Lord said to Joseph, I saw your brothers feeding here, and I heard them say they would go to feed in Dothan.

23 Joseph listened to the voice of the angel of the Lord, and he went to his brothers in Dothan and he found them in Dothan feeding the flock.

24 Joseph advanced to his brothers but before he had come near them, they had resolved to kill him.

25 Simeon said to his brothers, Behold the man of dreams is coming to us this day, so now come and let us kill him and cast him into one of the pits that are in the wilderness; when his father shall seek him from us, we will say an evil beast has devoured him.

26 Reuben heard the words of his brothers concerning Joseph and said to them, You should not do this thing, for how can we look up to our father Jacob? Cast him into this pit to die there, but do not put forth a hand on him to spill his blood. Reuben said this in order to deliver him from their hand, to bring him back to his father.

27 When Joseph came to his brothers he sat before them, and they rose upon him and seized him and struck him to the earth, and stripped the coat of many colors which he had on.

28 They took him and cast him into a pit and in the pit there was no water, but serpents and scorpions. And Joseph was afraid of the serpents and scorpions that were in the pit. Joseph cried out with a loud voice and the

Lord hid the serpents and scorpions in the sides of the pit, and they did no harm to Joseph.

29 And Joseph called out from the pit to his brothers, and said to them, What have I done to you, and in what have I sinned? Why do you not fear the Lord concerning me? Am I not of your bones and flesh, and is not Jacob your father, my father? Why do you do this thing to me this day, and how will you be able to look up to our father Jacob?

30 And he continued to cry out and call to his brothers from the pit, and he said, O Judah, Simeon, and Levi, my brothers, lift me up from the place of darkness in which you have placed me, and come this day to have compassion on me, you children of the Lord and sons of Jacob my father. And if I have sinned to you, are you not the sons of Abraham, Isaac, and Jacob? If they saw an orphan they had compassion over him, or one that was hungry, they gave him bread to eat, or one that was thirsty, they gave him water to drink, or one that was naked, they covered him with garments!

31 And how then can you withhold your pity from your brother, for I am of your flesh and bones, and if I have sinned to you, certainly you will do this on account of my father!

32 Joseph spoke these words from the pit, and his brothers could not listen to him, nor incline their ears to the words of Joseph, and Joseph was crying and weeping in the pit.

33 And Joseph said, O that my father knew this day, the act which my brothers have done to me and the words which they have this day spoken to me.

34 All his brothers heard his cries and weeping in the pit, and his brothers went and removed themselves from the pit, so that they might not hear the cries of Joseph and his weeping in the pit.

CHAPTER 42

1 They went and sat on the opposite side, about the distance of a bow-shot, and they sat there to eat bread; while they were eating they held counsel together what was to be done with him, whether to kill him or to bring him back to his father.

2 They were holding the counsel when they lifted up their eyes, and saw at once there was a company of Ishmaelites coming at a distance by the road of Gilead, going down to Egypt.

3 And Judah said to them, What gain will it be to us if we kill our brother? Perhaps God will require him from us; this then is the counsel proposed concerning him, which you shall do to him: Look at this company of Ishmaelites going down to Egypt,

4 So now let us dispose of him to them and let not our hand be on him; they will lead him along with them and he will be lost among the people of the land and we will not put him to death with our own hands. And the proposal pleased his brothers and they did according to the word of Judah.

5 While they were discussing this matter and before the company of Ishmaelites had come up to them, seven trading men of Midian passed by them; as they passed they were thirsty and they lifted up their eyes and saw the same pit in which Joseph was held, and they looked and saw every species of bird was on him.

6 These Midianites ran to the pit to drink water for they thought that it contained water, and on coming to the pit they heard the voice of Joseph crying and weeping in there, and they looked down into the pit, and they saw there was a youth of good-looking appearance and well-favored.

7 They called to him and said, Who are you and who brought you here, and who placed you in this pit in the wilderness? And they all assisted to raise up Joseph and they drew him out and brought him up from the pit, and took him and went away on their journey and passed by his brothers.

8 And these said to them, Why do you do this, to take our servant from us and to go away? Certainly we placed this youth in the pit because he rebelled against us, and you come and bring him up and lead him away; now then give us back our servant.

9 And the Midianites answered and said to the sons of Jacob, Is this your servant, or does this man attend you? Perhaps you are all his servants, for he is more handsome and well-favored than any of you, and why do you all speak falsely to us?

10 So we will not listen to your words nor give you our attention, for we found the youth in the pit in the wilderness and we took him; we will therefore go on.

11 And all the sons of Jacob approached them and rose up to them and said to them, Give us back our servant, and why will you all die by the edge of the sword? And the Midianites cried out against them and they drew their swords and approached to fight with the sons of Jacob.

12 Then Simeon rose up from his seat against them, and sprang on the ground and drew his sword and approached the Midianites and he gave a terrible shout before them, so that his shouting was heard at a distance, and the earth shook at Simeon's shouting.

13 The Midianites were terrified on account of Simeon and the noise of his shouting, and they fell on their faces and were excessively alarmed.

14 Simeon said to them, Surely I am Simeon, the son of Jacob the Hebrew, who have only with my brothers destroyed the city of Shechem and the cities of the Amorites; so shall God moreover do to me if all your brothers, the people of Midian, and also the kings of Canaan, were to come with you; they could not fight against me.

15 Now therefore give us back the youth whom you have taken, or I'll give your flesh to the birds of the skies and the beasts of the earth.

16 The Midianites were more afraid of Simeon, and they approached the sons of Jacob with terror and fright, and with pathetic words, saying,

17 Certainly you have said that the young man is your servant and that he rebelled against you, and therefore you placed him in the pit; what then will you do with a servant who rebels against his master? So now sell him to us, and we will give you all that you require for him. The Lord was pleased to do this in order that the sons of Jacob should not kill their brother.

18 And the Midianites saw that Joseph was of a good-looking appearance and well-favored; they desired him in their hearts and were urgent to purchase him from his brothers.

19 The sons of Jacob listened to the Midianites and they sold their brother Joseph to them for twenty pieces of silver. Reuben their brother was not with them, and the Midianites took Joseph and continued their journey to Gilead.

20 They were going along the road, and the Midianites repented of what they had done, in having purchased the young man, and one said to the other, What is this thing that we have done, in taking this youth from the Hebrews who is of good-looking appearance and well-favored?

21 Perhaps this youth is stolen from the land of the Hebrews, and why then have we done this thing? If he should be sought for and found in our hands we shall die through him.

22 Now certainly hardy and powerful men have sold him to us, the strength of one of whom you saw this day; perhaps they stole him from his land with their might and with their powerful arm, and have therefore sold him to us for the small value which we gave to them.

23 While they were thus discussing together, they looked and saw the company of Ishmaelites which was coming at first, and which the sons of Jacob saw, was advancing toward the Midianites; the Midianites said to each other, Come let us sell this youth to the company of Ishmaelites who are coming toward us. We will take for him the little that we gave for him, and we will be delivered from his evil.

24 And they did so, and they reached the Ishmaelites, and the Midianites sold Joseph to the Ishmaelites for twenty pieces of silver which they had given for him to his brothers.

25 And the Midianites went on their road to Gilead, and the Ishmaelites took Joseph and they let him ride on one of the camels, and they were leading him to Egypt.

26 When Joseph heard that the Ishmaelites were proceeding to Egypt, Joseph lamented and wept at this thing that he was to be so far removed from the land of Canaan, from his father, and he wept bitterly while he was riding on the camel. One of their men observed him, and made him go down from the camel and walk on foot, and still Joseph continued to cry and weep, and he said, O my father, my father.

27 One of the Ishmaelites rose up and struck Joseph on the cheek, and still he continued to weep; and Joseph was fatigued in the road, and was unable to proceed on account of the bitterness of his soul; they all struck him and afflicted him in the road, and they terrified him in order that he might cease from weeping.

28 And the Lord saw the condition of Joseph and his trouble, and the Lord brought down on those men darkness and confusion, and the hand of everyone that struck him became withered.

29 And they said to each other, What is this thing that God has done to us in the road? And they knew not that this befell them on account of Joseph. And the men proceeded on the road, and they passed along the road of Ephrath where Rachel was buried.

30 Joseph reached his mother's grave, and Joseph hurried and ran to his mother's grave, and fell on the grave and wept.

31 Joseph cried aloud on his mother's grave and said, O my mother, my mother, O you who did give me birth, awake now, and rise and see your son, how he has been sold for a slave, and no one to pity him.

32 O rise and see your son, weep with me on account of my troubles, and see the heart of my brothers.

33 Arouse my mother, arouse, awake from your sleep for me, and direct your battles against my brothers. O how have they stripped me of my coat and sold me already twice for a slave, and separated me from my father, and there is no one to pity me.

34 Arouse and lay your cause against them before God, and see whom God will justify in the judgment, and whom he will condemn.

35 Rise, O my mother, rise, awake from your sleep and see my father how his soul is with me this day, and comfort him and ease his heart.

36 And Joseph continued to speak these words, and Joseph cried aloud and wept bitterly on his mother's grave; and he ceased speaking, and from bitterness of heart he became still as a stone on the grave.

37 And Joseph heard a voice speaking to him from beneath the ground, which answered him with bitterness of heart, and with a voice of weeping and praying in these words:

38 My son, my son Joseph, I have heard the voice of your weeping and the voice of your lamentation; I have seen your tears; I know your troubles, my son, and it grieves me for your sake, and abundant grief is added to my grief.

39 Now therefore my son, Joseph my son, hope in the Lord, and wait for him and do not fear, for the Lord is with you, he will deliver you from all trouble.

40 Rise my son, go down to Egypt with your masters and do not fear, for the Lord is with you, my son. And she continued to speak like these words to Joseph, and she was still.

41 And Joseph heard this, and he wondered greatly at this, and he continued to weep. After this one of the Ishmaelites observed him crying and weeping on the grave, and his anger was set ablaze against him, and he drove him from there, and he struck him and cursed him.

42 And Joseph said to the men, May I find grace in your sight to take me back to my father's house, and he will give you abundance of riches.

43 And they answered him, saying, Are you not a slave, and where is your father? And if you had a father you would not already twice have been sold for a slave for so little value; their anger was still roused against him, and they continued to strike him and to chastise him, and Joseph wept bitterly.

44 The Lord saw Joseph's affliction, and the Lord again struck these men, and chastised them, and the Lord caused darkness to envelope them on the earth, and the lightning flashed and the thunder roared, and the earth shook at the voice of the thunder and of the mighty wind; the men were terrified and knew not where they should go.

45 The beasts and camels stood still, and they led them, but they would not go, they struck them, and they crouched on the ground; the men said to each other, What is this that God has done to us? What are our transgressions and what are our sins that this thing has thus befallen us?

46 One of them answered and said to them, Perhaps on account of the sin of afflicting this slave has this thing happened this day to us; now we should implore him strongly to forgive us and then we shall know on whose account this evil befalls us; if God willl have compassion over us, then we shall know that all this comes to us on account of the sin of afflicting this slave.

47 And the men did so, and they supplicated Joseph and pressed him to forgive them; and they said, We have sinned to the Lord and to you, now therefore vouchsafe to request of your God that he shall put away this death from among us, for we have sinned to him.

48 Joseph did according to their words and the Lord listened to Joseph, and the Lord put away the plague which he had inflicted on those men on account of Joseph; the beasts rose up from the ground and they conducted them, and they went on; the raging storm abated and the earth became tranquilized and the men proceeded on their journey to go down to Egypt. The men knew that this evil had befallen them on account of Joseph.

49 And they said to each other, We now know that it was on account of his affliction that this evil befell us; now why shall we bring this death on our souls? Let us hold counsel what to do to this slave.

50 And one answered and said, Certainly he told us to bring him back to his father; so come, let us take him back and we will go to the place that he will tell us, and take from his family the price that we gave for him and we will then go away.

51 One answered again and said, Behold this counsel is very good, but we cannot do so for the way is very far from us, and we cannot leave our road.

52 One more answered and said to them, This is the counsel to be adopted, we will not swerve from it; behold we are this day going to Egypt and when we shall have come to Egypt, we will sell him there at a high price, and we will be delivered from his evil.

53 And this thing pleased the men and they did so; they continued their journey to Egypt with Joseph.

CHAPTER 43

1 When the sons of Jacob had sold their brother Joseph to the Midianites, their hearts were smitten on account of him and they repented of their acts, and they sought for him to bring him back but could not find him.

2 Reuben returned to the pit in which Joseph had been put in order to lift him out and restore him to his father; Reuben stood by the pit and heard not a word. He called out Joseph! Joseph! and no one answered or uttered a word.

3 And Reuben said, Joseph has died through fright, or some serpent has caused his death. Reuben descended into the pit, searched for Joseph and could not find him in the pit, and he came out again.

4 And Reuben tore his garments and he said, The child is not there, and how shall I reconcile my father about him if he is dead? He went to his brothers and found them grieving on account of Joseph, and counseling together how to appease their father about him. Reuben said to his brothers, I came to the pit and behold Joseph was not there, what then shall we say to our father, for my father will only seek the lad from me.

5 His brothers answered him saying, Thus and thus we did, and our hearts afterward struck us on account of this act, and we now sit to seek a pretext how we shall appease our father to it.

6 And Reuben said to them, What is this you have done to bring down the grey hairs of our father in sorrow to the grave? This thing is not good that you have done.

7 And Reuben sat with them, and they all rose up and swore to each other not to tell this thing to Jacob. They all said, The man who will tell this to our father or his household, or who will report this to any of the children of the land, we will all rise up against him and kill him with the sword.

8 And the sons of Jacob feared each other in this matter, from the youngest to the oldest; no one spoke a word, and they concealed the thing in their hearts.

9 Afterward they sat down to determine and invent something to say to their father Jacob concerning all these things.

10 Issachar said to them, Here is advice for you if it seems good in your eyes to do this thing. Take the coat which belongs to Joseph and tear it, and kill a kid of the goats and dip it in its blood.

11 And send it to our father and when he sees it he will say an evil beast has devoured him, therefore tear his coat and behold his blood will be on his coat, and by your doing this we shall be free of our father's murmurings.

12 Issachar's advice pleased them and they listened to him, and they did according to the word of Issachar which he had counselled them.

13 They hurried and took Joseph's coat and tore it, and they killed a kid of the goats and dipped the coat in the blood of the kid, and then trampled it into the dust. They sent the coat to their father Jacob by the hand of Naphtali, and they commanded him to say these words:

14 We had gathered in the cattle and had come as far as the road to Shechem and farther, when we found this coat on the road in the wilderness dipped in blood and in dust; now therefore know whether it is your son's coat or not.

15 And Naphtali went and he came to his father and he gave him the coat, and he spoke to him all the words which his brothers had commanded him.

16 Jacob saw Joseph's coat and he knew it and he fell on his face to the ground, and became as still as a stone Afterward he rose up and cried out with a loud and weeping voice and said, It is the coat of my son Joseph!

17 Jacob hurried and sent one of his servants to his sons, who went to them and found them coming along the road with the flock.

18 The sons of Jacob came to their father about evening, and behold their garments were torn and dust was on their heads, and they found their father crying out and weeping with a loud voice.

19 Jacob said to his sons, Tell me truly what evil have you this day suddenly brought on me? They answered their father Jacob, saying, We were coming along this day after the flock had been gathered in, and we came as far as the city of Shechem by the road in the wilderness; we found this coat filled with blood on the ground, and we knew it and we sent it to you so you could know it.

20 Jacob heard the words of his sons and he cried out with a loud voice, and he said, It is the coat of my son; an

evil beast has devoured him. Joseph is rent in pieces, for I sent him this day to see whether it was well with you and well with the flocks and to bring me word again from you; he went as I commanded him, and this has happened to him today while I thought my son was with you.

21 And the sons of Jacob answered and said, He did not come to us, neither have we seen him from the time of our going out from you until now.

22 When Jacob heard their words he again cried out aloud, and he rose up and tore his garments; he put sackcloth on his loins and he wept bitterly; he mourned and lifted up his voice in weeping and exclaimed and said these words,

23 Joseph my son, O my son Joseph, I sent you this day after the welfare of your brothers, and behold you have been torn in pieces; through my hand has this happened to my son.

24 It grieves me for you Joseph my son, it grieves me for you; how sweet you were to me during life, and now how greatly bitter is your death to me.

25 0 that I had died in your stead Joseph my son, for it grieves me sadly for you my son, O my son, my son. Joseph my son, where are you, and where have you been drawn? Arouse, arouse from your place, and come and see my grief for you, O my son Joseph.

26 Come now and number the tears gushing from my eyes down my cheeks, and bring them up before the Lord, that his anger may turn from me.

27 0 Joseph my son, how did you fall, by the hand of one by whom no one had fallen from the beginning of the world to this day; for you have been put to death by the smiting of an enemy, inflicted with cruelty, but certainly I know that this has happened to you on account of the multitude of my sins.

28 Arise now and see how bitter is my trouble for you my son, although I did not rear you nor fashion you nor give you breath and soul, but it was God who formed you and built your bones and covered them with flesh and breathed in your nostrils the breath of life, and then he gave you to me.

29 Now truly God who gave you to me, he has taken you from me; such then has happened to you.

30 And Jacob continued to speak like these words concerning Joseph, and he wept bitterly; he fell to the ground and became still.

31 All the sons of Jacob seeing their father's trouble repented of what they had done, and they also wept bitterly.

32 And Judah rose up and lifted his father's head from the ground, and placed it on his lap; he wiped his father's tears from his cheeks, and Judah wept a very great weeping while his father's head was reclining on his lap, still as a stone.

33 The sons of Jacob saw their father's trouble, and they lifted up their voices and continued to weep; Jacob was yet lying on the ground still as a stone.

34 And all his sons and his servants and his servant's children rose up and stood round him to comfort him, and he refused to be comforted.

35 The whole household of Jacob rose up and mourned a great mourning on account of Joseph and their father's trouble, and the sad news reached Isaac, the son of Abraham, the father of Jacob, and he wept bitterly on account of Joseph, he and all his household. He went from the place where he lived in Hebron, and his men with him, and he comforted Jacob his son but he refused to be comforted.

36 And after this, Jacob rose up from the ground, and his tears were running down his cheeks, and he said to his sons, Rise up and take your swords and your bows, and go forth into the field, and seek whether you can find my son's body and bring it to me that I may bury it.

37 Seek also, I pray you, among the beasts and hunt them, and that which shall come the first before you seize and bring it to me; perhaps the Lord will this day pity my affliction, and prepare before you that which tore my son in pieces; bring it to me, and I will avenge the cause of my son.

38 And his sons did as their father had commanded them, and they rose up early in the morning, and each took his sword and his bow in his hand, and they went forth into the field to hunt the beasts.

39 And Jacob was still crying aloud and weeping and walking to and fro in the house, and smiting his hands together, saying, Joseph my son, Joseph my son.

40 The sons of Jacob went into the wilderness to seize the beasts, and there a wolf came toward them; they seized him and brought him to their father and said to him, This is the first we have found, and we have brought him to you as you did command us, and your son's body we could not find.

41 And Jacob took the beast from the hands of his sons, and he cried out with a loud and weeping voice, holding the beast in his hand, and he spoke with a bitter heart to the beast, Why did you devour my son Joseph, and how did you have no fear of the God of the earth, or of my trouble for my son Joseph?

42 You did devour my son for nothing. He committed no violence. I was responsible for him. God will require him that is persecuted.

43 And the Lord opened the mouth of the beast in order to comfort Jacob with its words, and it answered Jacob and spoke these words to him,

44 As God lives who created us in the earth, and as your soul lives, my lord, I did not see your son, neither did I tear him to pieces, but from a distant land I also came to seek my son who went from me this day, and I know not whether he is living or dead.

45 And I came this day into the field to seek my son, and your sons found me, and seized me and increased my grief, and have this day brought me before you, and I have now spoken all my words to you.

46 Now therefore, O son of man, I am in your hands, and do to me this day as it may seem good in your sight, but by the life of God who created me, I did not see your son nor did I tear him to pieces, neither has the flesh of man entered my mouth all the days of my life.

47 When Jacob heard the words of the beast he was greatly astonished, and sent forth the beast from his hand, and she went her way.

48 And Jacob was still crying aloud and weeping for Joseph day after day, and he mourned for his son many days.

CHAPTER 44

1 The sons of Ishmael who had bought Joseph from the Midianites, who had bought him from his brothers, went to Egypt with Joseph. They came on the borders of Egypt and when they came near to Egypt, they met four men of the sons of Medan the son of Abraham, who had gone forth from the land of Egypt on their journey.

2 The Ishmaelites said to them, Do you desire to purchase this slave from us? And they said, Deliver him over to us, and they delivered Joseph over to them; they observed him that he was a very good-looking youth and they purchased him for twenty shekels.

3 The Ishmaelites continued their journey to Egypt and the Medanim also returned that day to Egypt. The Medanim said to each other, Look, we have heard that Potiphar, an officer of Pharaoh, captain of the guard, seeks a good servant who willl stand before him to attend him, and to make him overseer over his house and all belonging to him.

4 So let us sell him for what we may desire, if he is able to give us that which we shall require for him.

5 And these Medanim came to the house of Potiphar, and said to him, We have heard that you seek a good servant to attend you; here we have a servant that will please you, if you can give to us that which we may desire and we will sell him to you.

6 And Potiphar said, Bring him before me, and I will see him; if he please me I will give to you that which you may require for him.

7 And the Medanim went and brought Joseph and placed him before Potiphar, and he observed him, and he pleased him greatly and Potiphar said to them, Tell me what you require for this youth.

8 And they said, Four hundred pieces of silver we desire for him. Potiphar said, I will give it if you bring me the record of his sale to you and will tell me his history for perhaps he may be stolen, for this youth is neither a slave nor the son of a slave, but I observe in him the appearance of a goodly and handsome person.

9 And the Medanim went and brought to him the Ishmaelites who had sold him to them, and they told him, saying, He is a slave and we sold him to them.

10 And Potiphar heard the words of the Ishmaelites in his giving the silver to the Medanim, and the Medanim took the silver and went on their journey; the Ishmaelites also returned home.

11 Potiphar took Joseph and brought him to his house that he might serve him, and Joseph found favor in the sight of Potiphar; he placed confidence in him and made him overseer over his house, and all that belonged to him he delivered over into his hand.

12 And the Lord was with Joseph and he became a prosperous man; the Lord blessed the house of Potiphar for the sake of Joseph.

13 And Potiphar left all that he had in the hands of Joseph; Joseph was one that caused things to come in and go out, and everything was regulated by his wish in the house of Potiphar.

14 And Joseph was eighteen years old, a youth with beautiful eyes and of very good appearance, and no one was like him in all the land of Egypt.

15 At that time while he was in his master's house, going in and out of the house and attending his master, Zelicah, his master's wife lifted up her eyes toward Joseph and she looked at him, and behold he was a youth handsome and well-favored.

16 And she coveted his beauty in her heart, and her soul was fixed on Joseph, and she enticed him day after day, and Zelicah persuaded Joseph daily, but Joseph did not lift up his eyes to give attention to his master's wife.

17 And Zelicah said to him, How goodly are your appearance and form, truly I have looked at all the slaves and have not seen so beautiful a slave as you are. Joseph said to her, Certainly he who created me in my mother's womb created all mankind.

18 She said to him, How beautiful are your eyes, with which you have dazzled all the inhabitants of Egypt, men and women. He said to her, How beautiful they are while we are alive, but should you behold them in the grave, certainly you would move away from them.

19 And she said to him, How beautiful and pleasing are all your words; take now, I pray you, the harp which is in the house, and play with your hands and let us hear your words.

20 And he said to her, How beautiful and pleasing are my words when I speak the praise of my God and his glory. She said to him, How very beautiful is the hair of your head, find the golden comb which is in the house, take it I pray you, and curl the hair of your head.

21 And he said to her, How long will you speak these words? Stop uttering these words to me, and rise and attend to your domestic affairs.

22 And she said to him, There is no one in my house, and there is nothing to attend to but to your words and to your wish. Yet in spite of all this, she could not bring Joseph to her, neither did he place his eyes on her, but directed his eyes below to the ground.

23 Zelicah desired Joseph in her heart that he should lie with her; at the time that Joseph was sitting in the house doing his work, Zelicah came and sat before him, and she enticed him daily with her discourse to lie with her, or even to look at her, but Joseph would not listen to her.

24 And she said to him, If you will not do according to my words, I will treat you with the punishment of death, and put an iron yoke on you.

25 And Joseph said to her, Certainly God who created man loosens the fetters of prisoners, and it is he who will deliver me from your prison and from your judgment.

26 When she could not persuade him and her soul being still fixed on him, her desire threw her into a grave sickness.

27 All the women of Egypt came to visit her and said to her, Why are you in this declining state? You lack nothing; certainly your husband is a great and esteemed prince in the sight of the king, should you lack anything of what your heart desires?

28 Zelicah answered them, saying, This day it shall be made known to you from where this disorder comes which you see in me, and she commanded her maid servants to prepare food for all the women; she made a banquet for them, and all the women ate in the house of Zelicah.

29 And she gave them knives to peel the citrons to eat them, and she commanded that they should dress Joseph in costly garments, that he should appear before them, and Joseph came before their eyes and all the women looked on Joseph and could not take their eyes from off him; they all cut their hands with the knives that they had in their hands, and all the citrons that were in their hands were filled with blood.

30 And they knew not what they had done but they continued to look at the beauty of Joseph, and did not turn their eyelids from him.

31 Zelicah saw what they had done, and she said to them, What is this work that you have done? Look, I gave you citrons to eat and you have all cut your hands.

32 And all the women saw their hands, and truly they were full of blood, and their blood flowed down on their garments. They said to her, This slave in your house has overcome us, and we could not turn our eyelids from him on account of his beauty.

33 She said to them, Certainly this happened to you in the moment that you looked at him, and you could not contain yourselves from him; how then can I refrain when he is constantly in my house, and I see him day after day going in and out of my house? How then can I keep from declining or even from perishing on account of this?

34 And they said to her, The words are true, for who can see this beautiful form in the house and refrain from him, and is he not your slave and attendant in your house, and why do you not tell him that which is in your heart, but allow your soul to perish through this matter?

35 And she said to them, I am daily endeavoring to persuade him, and he will not consent to my wishes; I promised him everything that is good, and yet I could meet with no return from him; I am therefore in a declining state as you see.

36 Zelicah became very ill on account of her desire toward Joseph, and she was desperately lovesick on account of him; but all the people of the house of Zelicah and her husband knew nothing of this matter, that Zelicah was ill on account of her love to Joseph.

37 All the people of her house asked her, saying, Why are you ill and declining, and lack nothing? And she said to them, I know not this thing which daily is increasing on me.

38 All the women and her friends came daily to see her, and they spoke with her, and she said to them, This can only be through the love of Joseph. They said to her, Entice him and seize him secretly; perhaps he may listen to you and put off this death from you.

39 And Zelicah became worse from her love to Joseph, and she continued to decline, till she scarcely had strength to stand.

40 On a certain day Joseph was doing his master's work in the house, and Zelicah came secretly and fell suddenly on him; Joseph rose up against her, he was more powerful than she, and he brought her down to the ground.

41 And Zelicah wept on account of the desire of her heart toward him, and she begged him with weeping, and her tears flowed down her cheeks; she spoke to him in a voice of pleading and in bitterness of soul, saying,

42 Have you ever heard, seen or known of so beautiful a woman as I am, or better than myself, who speaks daily to you, falls into a decline through love for you, confers all this honor on you, and still you will not listen to my voice?

43 If it be through fear of your master that he punish you, as the king lives no harm shall come to you from your master through this thing; now, therefore do listen to me, and consent for the sake of the honor which I have conferred on you, and put off this death from me, for why should I die for your sake? And she ceased to speak.

44 And Joseph answered her, saying, Keep away from me, and leave this matter to my master; behold my master knows not what there is with me in the house, for all that belongs to him he has delivered into my hands, and how shall I do these things in my master's house?

45 For he has also greatly honored me in his house, and he has also made me overseer over his house, and he has exalted me, and there is no one greater in this house than I am, and my master has refrained nothing from me, excepting you who are his wife. How then can you speak these words to me, and how can I do this great evil and sin to God and to your husband?

46 Now therefore keep away from me, and speak no more such words as these, for I will not listen to your words. But Zelicah would not listen to Joseph when he spoke these words to her; she daily enticed him to listen to her.

47 It was after this that the brook of Egypt was filled above all its sides, and all the inhabitants of Egypt went forth, and also the king and princes went forth with timbrels and dances, for it was a great rejoicing in Egypt and a holiday at the time of the overflow of the sea Sihor, and they went there to rejoice all the day.

48 And when the Egyptians went out to the river to rejoice, as was their custom, all the people of the house of Potiphar went with them. But Zelicah would not go with them for she said, I am unable to. She remained alone in the house, and no other person was with her in the house.

49 And she rose up and ascended to her temple in the house, and dressed herself in princely garments, and she placed on her head precious stones of onyx stones, inlaid with silver and gold, and she beautified her face and skin with all sorts of women's purifying liquids, and she perfumed the temple and the house with cassia and frankincense, and she spread myrrh and aloes. Afterward she sat in the entrance of the temple, in the passage of the house, through which Joseph passed to do his work, and then Joseph came from the field and entered the house to do his master's work.

50 He came to the place through which he had to pass and saw all the work of Zelicah, and he turned back.

51 Zelicah saw Joseph turning back from her; she called out to him, saying What ails you Joseph? Come to your work, and look, I will make room for you until you will have passed to your seat.

52 And Joseph returned and came to the house, and passed from there to the place of his seat, and he sat down to do his master's work as usual and behold Zelicah came to him and stood before him in princely garments, and the scent from her clothes was spread some distance.

53 She hurried and caught hold of Joseph and his garments, and said to him, As the king lives if you will not perform my request you shall die this day. And she hurried and stretched forth her other hand and drew a sword from beneath her garments, and she placed it on Joseph's neck; she said, Rise and perform my request, and if not you will die this day.

54 Joseph was afraid of her doing this thing, and he rose up to flee from her; she seized the front of his garments, and in the terror of his flight the garment which Zelicah seized was torn; Joseph left the garment in the hand of Zelicah and he fled and got out, for he was afraid.

55 When Zelicah saw that Joseph's garment was torn and that he had left it in her hand, and had fled, she was afraid for her life, that the report should spread concerning her. She rose up and acted with cunning and put off the garments in which she was dressed, and she put on her other garments.

56 She took Joseph's garment and laid it beside her, and she went and seated herself in the place where she had sat in her illness, before the people of her house had gone out to the river. She called a young lad who was then in the house, and she ordered him to call the people of the house to her.

57 And when she saw them she said to them with a loud voice and lamentation, See what a Hebrew your master has brought to me in the house, for he came this day to lie with me.

58 For when you had gone out he came to the house, and seeing that there was no person in the house, he came to me and caught hold of me with intent to lie with me.

59 And I seized his garments and tore them and called out against him with a loud voice, and when I had lifted up my voice he was afraid for his life and left his garment before me, and fled.

60 The people of her house spoke nothing, but their wrath was very much set ablaze against Joseph, and they went to his master and told him the words of his wife.

61 Potiphar came home enraged, and his wife cried out to him, saying, What is this thing that you have done to me in bringing a Hebrew servant into my house, for he came to me this day to sport with me; thus did he do to me this day.

62 Potiphar heard the words of his wife and ordered Joseph to be punished with severe stripes, and they did so to him.

63 While they were smiting him, Joseph called out with a loud voice, and he lifted up his eyes to heaven, and he said, O Lord God, you know that I am innocent of all these things, and why shall I die this day through falsehood, by the hand of these uncircumcised wicked men whom you know?

64 And while Potiphar's men were beating Joseph, he continued to cry out and weep, and there was a child there eleven months old, and the Lord opened the mouth of the child, and he spake these words before Potiphar's men, who were smiting Joseph, saying,

65 What do you want of this man, and why do you do this evil to him? My mother speaks falsely and utters lies; thus was the transaction.

66 And the child told them accurately all that happened, and all the words of Zelicah to Joseph day after day did he relate to them.

67 And all the men heard the words of the child and they wondered greatly at the child's words, and the child ceased to speak and became still.

68 Potiphar was very much ashamed at the words of his son, and he commanded his men not to beat Joseph anymore, and the men ceased beating Joseph.

69 Potiphar took Joseph and ordered him to be brought to justice before the priests, who were judges belonging to the king, in order to judge him concerning this affair.

70 Potiphar and Joseph came before the priests who were the king's judges, and he said to them, Decide I beg you, what judgment is due to a servant, for thus has he done.

71 And the priests said to Joseph, Why did you do this thing to your master? and Joseph answered them, saying, Not so my lords, thus was the matter; and Potiphar said to Joseph, Certainly I entrusted in your hands all that belonged to me, and I withheld nothing from you but my wife, and how could you do this evil?

72 And Joseph answered saying, Not so my lord, as the Lord lives, and as your soul lives, my lord, the word which you did hear from your wife is untrue, for thus was the affair this day.

73 A year has elapsed to me since I have come to your house; have you seen any iniquity in me, or any thing which might cause you to demand my life?

74 The priests said to Potiphar, Send, we pray you, and let them bring before us Joseph's torn garment, and let us see the tear in it, and if it shall be that the tear is in front of the garment, then his face must have been opposite to her and she must have caught hold of him to come to her, and with deceit did your wife do all that she has spoken.

75 They brought Joseph's garment before the priests who were judges, and they saw and behold the tear was in front of Joseph, and all the judging priests knew that she had pressed him, and they said, The judgment of death is not due to this slave for he has done nothing, but his judgment is that he be placed in the prison house on

account of the report, which through him has gone forth against your wife.

76 Potiphar heard their words and he placed him in the prison house, the place where the king's prisoners are confined, and Joseph was in the house of confinement twelve years.

77 And in spite of this, his master's wife did not turn from him, and she did not cease from speaking to him day after day to listen to her, and at the end of three months Zelicah continued going to Joseph to the house of confinement day by day, and she enticed him to listen to her, and Zelicah said to Joseph, How long will you remain in this house? But listen now to my voice, and I will bring you out of this house.

78 And Joseph answered her, saying, It is better for me to remain in this house than to listen to your words, to sin against God; she said to him, If you will not perform my wish, I will pluck out your eyes, add fetters to your feet, and will deliver you into the hands of them whom you did not know before.

79 Joseph answered her and said, Behold the God of the whole earth is able to deliver me from all that you can do to me, for he opens the eyes of the blind, and loosens those that are bound, and preserves all strangers who are unacquainted with the land.

80 And when Zelicah was unable to persuade Joseph to listen to her, she ceased going to entice him; Joseph was still confined in the house of confinement. And Jacob the father of Joseph, and all his brothers who were in the land of Canaan still mourned and wept in those days on account of Joseph, for Jacob refused to be comforted for his son Joseph, and Jacob cried aloud and wept and mourned all those days.

CHAPTER 45

1 It was in that year, which is the year of Joseph's going down to Egypt after his brothers had sold him, that Reuben the son of Jacob went to Timnah and took a wife Eliuram, the daughter of Avi the Canaanite, and he came to her.

2 And Eliuram the wife of Reuben conceived and gave birth, to him: Hanoch, Palu, Chetzron and Carmi, four sons; and Simeon his brother took his sister Dinah for a wife, and she gave birth to, to him: Memuel, Yamin, Ohad, Jachin and Zochar, five sons.

3 Afterward he came to Bunah the Canaanitish woman, the same is Bunah whom Simeon took captive from the city of Shechem, and Bunah was before Dinah and attended to her; Simeon came to her, and she gave birth to him, Saul.

4 And Judah went at that time to Adulam, and he came to a man of Adulam, and his name was Hirah; Judah saw there the daughter of a man from Canaan, and her name was Aliyath, the daughter of Shua. He took her and came to her, and Aliyath gave birth to, to Judah: Er, Onan and Shiloh, three sons.

5 Levi and Issachar went to the land of the east, and they took to themselves for wives the daughters of Jobab the son of Yoktan, the son of Eber; Jobab the son of Yoktan had two daughters; the name of the elder was Adinah, and the name of the younger was Aridah.

6 And Levi took Adinah, and Issachar took Aridah, and they came to the land of Canaan, to their father's house; Adinah gave birth to, to Levi: Gershon, Kehath and Merari, three sons.

7 And Aridah gave birth to, to Issachar: Tola, Puvah, Job and Shomron, four sons; Dan went to the land of Moab and took for a wife Aphlaleth, the daughter of Chamudan the Moabite, and he brought her to the land of Canaan.

8 Aphlaleth was unable to conceive, she had no children, and God afterward remembered Aphlaleth the wife of Dan, and she conceived and gave birth to a son; she called his name Chushim.

9 And Gad and Naphtali went to Haran and took from there the daughters of Amuram the son of Uz, the son of Nahor, for wives.

10 And these are the names of the daughters of Amuram: the name of the elder was Merimah, and the name of the younger Uzith; Naphtali took Merimah, and Gad took Uzith and brought them to the land of Canaan, to their father's house.

11 And Merimah gave birth to, to Naphtali: Yachzeel, Guni, Jazer and Shalem, four sons; and Uzith gave birth to, to Gad: Zephion, Chagi, Shuni, Ezbon, Eri, Arodi and Arali, seven sons.

12 Asher went forth and took Adon the daughter of Aphlal, the son of Hadad, the son of Ishmael, for a wife and he brought her to the land of Canaan.

13 And Adon the wife of Asher died in those days, she had no children; it was after the death of Adon that Asher went to the other side of the river and took for a wife Hadurah the daughter of Abimael, the son of Eber, the son

of Shem.

14 The young woman was of a beautiful appearance and a woman of sense, and she had been the wife of Malkiel the son of Elam, the son of Shem.

15 Hadurah gave birth to a daughter to Malkiel, and he called her name Serach, and Malkiel died after this and Hadurah went and remained in her father's house.

16 After the death of the wife at Asher he went and took Hadurah for a wife, and brought her to the land of Canaan, and Serach her daughter he also brought with them; she was three years old and the child was brought up in Jacob's house.

17 And the girl was of a beautiful appearance and she went in the holy ways of the children of Jacob; she lacked nothing, and the Lord gave her wisdom and understanding.

18 Hadurah the wife of Asher conceived and gave birth to, to him: Yimnah, Yishvah, Yishvi and Beriah, four sons.

19 Zebulun went to Midian and took for a wife Merishah the daughter of Molad, the son of Abida, the son of Midian, and brought her to the land of Canaan.

20 And Merushah gave birth to, to Zebulun: Sered, Elon and Yachleel, three sons.

21 Jacob sent to Aram, the son of Zoba, the son of Terah, and he took for his son Benjamin Mechalia the daughter of Aram, and she came to the land of Canaan to the house of Jacob; Benjamin was ten years old when he took Mechalia the daughter of Aram for a wife.

22 And Mechalia conceived and gave birth to, to Benjamin: Bela, Becher, Ashbel, Gera and Naaman, five sons; Benjamin afterward went and took for a wife Aribath, the daughter of Shomron, the son of Abraham, in addition to his first wife, and he was eighteen years old; Aribath gave birth to, to Benjamin: Achi, Vosh, Mupim, Chupim, and Ord, five sons.

23 In those days Judah went to the house of Shem and took Tamar the daughter of Elam, the son of Shem, for a wife for his first born Er.

24 And Er came to his wife Tamar, and she became his wife; when he came to her he outwardly destroyed his offspring, and his work was evil in the sight of the Lord, and the Lord killed him.

25 It was after the death of Er, Judah's first born, that Judah said to Onan, Go to your brother's wife and marry her as the next of kin and raise up children to your brother.

26 And Onan took Tamar for a wife and he came to her; Onan also did like the work of his brother, and his work was evil in the sight of the Lord, and he killed him also.

27 When Onan died, Judah said to Tamar, Remain in your father's house until my son Shiloh will have grown up; Judah had no more delight in Tamar, to give her to Shiloh, for he said, Perhaps he will also die like his brothers.

28 And Tamar rose up and went and remained in her father's house, and Tamar was in her father's house for some time.

29 At the revolution of the year, Aliyath the wife of Judah died; Judah was comforted for his wife, and after the death of Aliyath, Judah went up with his friend Hirah to Timnah to shear their sheep.

30 Tamar heard that Judah had gone up to Timnah to shear the sheep, and that Shiloh was grown up, and Judah did not delight in her.

31 And Tamar rose up and put off the garments of her widowhood; she put on a veil and entirely covered herself; she went and sat in the public thoroughfare which is on the road to Timnah.

32 Judah passed and saw her and took her and he came to her, and she conceived by him; at the time of being delivered there were twins in her womb, and he called the name of the first Perez and the name of the second Zarah.

CHAPTER 46

1 In those days Joseph was still confined in the prison house in the land of Egypt.

2 At that time the attendants of Pharaoh were standing before him, the chief of the butlers and the chief of the bakers which belonged to the king of Egypt.

3 And the butler took wine and placed it before the king to drink, and the baker placed bread before the king to eat, and the king drank of the wine and ate of the bread; he and his servants and ministers that ate at the king's table.

4 And while they were eating and drinking, the butler and the baker remained there, and Pharaoh's ministers found many flies in the wine which the butler had brought, and stones of nitre were found in the baker's bread.

5 And the captain of the guard placed Joseph as an attendant on Pharaoh's officers, and Pharaoh's officers were in confinement one year.

6 At the end of the year, they both dreamed dreams in one night, in the place of confinement where they were, and in the morning Joseph came to them to attend on them as usual. He saw them and their countenances were dejected and sad.

7 And Joseph asked them, Why are your countenances sad? They said, we dreamed a dream and there was no one here to interpret it. Joseph said to them, Relate, I pray you, your dream to me, and God shall give you an answer of peace as you desire.

8 The butler related his dream to Joseph and said, I saw in my dream there was a large vine before me and on that vine I saw three branches; the vine speedily blossomed and reached a great height, and its clusters were ripened and became grapes.

9 And I took the grapes and pressed them in a cup, and placed it in Pharaoh's hand and he drank; and Joseph said to him, The three branches that were on the vine are three days.

10 Yet within three days, the king will order you to be brought out and he will restore you to your office; you shall give the king his wine to drink as at first when you were his butler; but let me find favor in your sight, so that you shall remember me to Pharaoh when it will be well with you; do this kindness to me and get me brought forth from this prison, for I was stolen away from the land of Canaan and was sold for a slave in this place.

11 Also that which was told you concerning my master's wife is false, for they placed me in this dungeon for nothing. The butler answered Joseph, saying, If the king deals well with me as at first, as you last interpreted to me, I will do all that you desire and get you brought out of this dungeon.

12 And the baker, seeing that Joseph had accurately interpreted the butler's dream, also approached and related the whole of his dream to Joseph.

13 He said to him, In my dream I looked and there were three white baskets on my head; I looked again and then there were in the upper-most basket all manner of baked meats for Pharaoh; there the birds were eating them from off my head.

14 And Joseph said to him, The three baskets which you saw are three days, yet within three days Pharaoh will take off your head and hang you on a tree, and the birds will eat your flesh from off you, as you saw in your dream.

15 In those days the queen was about to be delivered, and on that day she gave birth to a son to the king of Egypt; they announced that the king had gotten his firstborn son and all the people of Egypt together with the officers and servants of Pharaoh rejoiced greatly.

16 On the third day of his birth Pharaoh made a feast for his officers and servants, for the hosts of the land of Zoar and of the land of Egypt.

17 And all the people of Egypt and the servants of Pharaoh came to eat and drink with the king at the feast of his son, and to rejoice at the king's rejoicing.

18 All the officers of the king and his servants were rejoicing at that time for eight days at the feast, and they made merry with all sorts of musical instruments, with timbrels and with dances in the king's house for eight days.

19 And the butler, to whom Joseph had interpreted his dream, forgot Joseph and did not mention him to the king as he had promised, for this thing was from the Lord in order to punish Joseph because he had trusted in man.

20 And Joseph remained after this in the prison house two years, until he had completed twelve years.

CHAPTER 47

1 Isaac the son of Abraham was still living in those days in the land of Canaan; he was very aged, one hundred and eighty years old, and Esau his son, the brother of Jacob, was in the land of Edom; he and his sons had possessions in it among the children of Seir.

2 And Esau heard that his father's time was drawing near to die, and he and his sons and household came to the land of Canaan to his father's house. Jacob and his sons went forth from the place where they lived in Hebron and they all came to their father Isaac, and they found Esau and his sons in the tent.

3 And Jacob and his sons sat before his father Isaac, and Jacob was still mourning for his son Joseph.

4 And Isaac said to Jacob, Bring your sons here to me and I will bless them; and Jacob brought his eleven children

before his father Isaac.

5 And Isaac placed his hands on all the sons of Jacob, and he took hold of them and embraced them, and kissed them one by one. Isaac blessed them on that day and he said to them, May the God of your fathers bless you and increase your offspring like the stars of heaven for number.

6 Isaac also blessed the sons of Esau, saying, May God cause you to be a dread and a terror to all that will behold you, and to all your enemies.

7 Isaac called Jacob and his sons and they all came and sat before Isaac, and Isaac said to Jacob, The Lord God of the whole earth said to me, Unto your offspring I will give this land for an inheritance if your children keep my statutes and my ways, and I will perform to them the oath which I swore to your father Abraham.

8 Now therefore my son, teach your children and your children's children to fear the Lord, and to go in the good way which will please the Lord your God, for if you keep the ways of the Lord and his statutes the Lord will also keep to you his covenant with Abraham, and will do well with you and your descendants always.

9 When Isaac had finished commanding Jacob and his children, he gave up the ghost and died, and was gathered to his people.

10 And Jacob and Esau fell on the face of their father Isaac, and they wept, and Isaac was one hundred and eighty years old when he died in the land of Canaan, in Hebron. His sons carried him to the cave of Machpelah, which Abraham had bought from the children of Heth for a possession of a burial place.

11 And all the kings of the land of Canaan went with Jacob and Esau to bury Isaac, and all the kings of Canaan showed Isaac great honor at his death.

12 The sons of Jacob and the sons of Esau went barefooted round about, walking and lamenting until they reached Kireath-arba.

13 And Jacob and Esau buried their father Isaac in the cave of Machpelah, which is in Kireath-arba in Hebron; they buried him with very great honor, as at the funeral of kings.

14 Jacob and his sons, and Esau and his sons, and all the kings of Canaan made a great and heavy mourning, and they buried him and mourned for him many days.

15 At the death of Isaac, he left his cattle and his possessions and all belonging to him to his sons; and Esau said to Jacob, Behold I pray you, all that our father has left we will divide into two parts, and I will have the choice; Jacob said, We will do so.

16 Jacob took all that Isaac had left in the land of Canaan, the cattle and the property, and he placed them in two parts before Esau and his sons, and he said to Esau, Behold all this is before you, choose to yourself the half which you will take.

17 And Jacob said to Esau, Hear I pray you what I will speak to you, saying, The Lord God of heaven and earth spoke to our fathers Abraham and Isaac, saying, Unto your descendants will I give this land for an inheritance forever.

18 Now therefore all that our father has left is before you, and behold all the land is before you; choose from them what you desire.

19 If you desire the whole land take it for you and your children forever, and I will take these riches, and if you desire the riches take them with you, and I will take this land for me and for my children to inherit forever.

20 Nebayoth, the son of Ishmael, was then in the land with his children, and Esau went on that day and consulted with him, saying,

21 Thus has Jacob spoken to me; thus has he answered me, now give your advice and we will listen.

22 And Nebayoth said, What is this that Jacob hath spoken to you? Behold all the children of Canaan are dwelling securely in their land, and Jacob says he will inherit it with his descendants all the days.

23 Go now therefore and take all your father's riches and leave Jacob your brother in the land, as he has spoken.

24 And Esau rose up and returned to Jacob, and did all that Nebayoth the son of Ishmael had advised; and Esau took all the riches that Isaac had left, the souls, the beasts, the cattle and the property, and all the riches; he gave nothing to his brother Jacob, and Jacob took all the land of Canaan, from the brook of Egypt to the river Euphrates, and he took it for an everlasting| possession, and for his children and for his descendants after him forever.

25 Jacob also took from his brother Esau the cave of Machpelah, which is in Hebron, which Abraham had bought from Ephron for a possession of a burial place for him and his descendants forever.

26 And Jacob wrote all these things in the book of purchase, and he signed it, and testified all this with four faithful witnesses.

27 These are the words which Jacob wrote in the book, saying: The land of Canaan and all the cities of the Hittites,

the Hivites, the Jebusites, the Amorites, the Perizzites, and the Gergashites, all the seven nations from the river of Egypt to the river Euphrates.

28 And the city of Hebron Kireath-arba, and the cave which is in it, the whole did Jacob buy from his brother Esau for value, for a possession and for an inheritance for his descendants after him forever.

29 And Jacob took the book of purchase and the signature, the command and the statutes and the revealed book, and he placed them in an earthen vessel in order that they should remain for a long time, and he delivered them into the hands of his children.

30 Esau took all that his father had left him after his death from his brother Jacob, and he took all the property, from man and beast, camel and ass, ox and lamb, silver and gold, stones and bdellium, and all the riches which had belonged to Isaac the son of Abraham; there was nothing left which Esau did not take to himself from all that Isaac had left after his death.

31 Esau took all this and he and his children went home to the land of Seir the Horite, away from his brother Jacob and his children.

32 And Esau had possessions among the children of Seir, and Esau returned not to the land of Canaan from that day forward.

33 The whole land of Canaan became an inheritance to the children of Israel for an everlasting inheritance, and Esau with all his children inherited the mountain of Seir.

CHAPTER 48

1 In those days, after the death of Isaac, the Lord commanded and caused a famine on the whole earth.

2 At that time Pharaoh, king of Egypt, was sitting on his throne in the land of Egypt; he lay in his bed and dreamed dreams and Pharaoh saw in his dream that he was standing by the side of the river of Egypt.

3 While he was standing he saw seven fat fleshed and well favored cattle come up out of the river.

4 And seven other cattle, lean fleshed and ill favored, came up after them, and the seven ill favored ones swallowed up the well favored ones, and still their appearance was ill as at first.

5 And he awoke; he slept again and he dreamed a second time, and he saw seven ears of corn come up on one stalk, full and good, and seven thin ears blasted with the east wind sprang up after them, and the thin ears swallowed up the full ones, then Pharaoh awoke out of his dream.

6 In the morning the king remembered his dreams and his spirit was sadly troubled on account of his dreams, and the king hurried, sent and called for all the magicians of Egypt and the wise men, and they came and stood before Pharaoh.

7 And the king said to them, I have dreamed dreams, and there is none to interpret them; they said to the king, relate your dreams to your servants and let us hear them.

8 And the king related his dreams to them, and they all answered and said with one voice to the king, May the king live forever; this is the interpretation of your dreams.

9 The seven good cattle which you saw denotes seven daughters that will be born to you in the latter days, and the seven cattle which you saw come up after them and swallowed them up, are for a sign that the daughters which will be born to you will all die in the lifetime of the king.

10 And that which you saw in the second dream of seven full good ears of corn coming up on one stalk, this is their interpretation: that you will build to yourself in the latter days seven cities throughout the land of Egypt; that which you saw of the seven poor ears of corn springing up after them and swallowing them up while you saw them with your eyes, is for a sign that the cities which you will build will all be destroyed in the latter days, in the lifetime of the king.

11 And when they spoken these words the king did not incline his ear to their words, neither did he fix his heart on them, for the king knew in his wisdom that they did not give a proper interpretation of the dreams; when they had finished speaking before the king, he answered them, saying, What is this thing that you have spoken to me? Certainly you have uttered falsely and spoken lies; therefore now give the proper interpretation of my dreams, that you may not die.

12 The king commanded after this, and he sent and called again for other wise men, and they came and stood before the king. The king related his dreams to them, and they all answered him according to the first interpretation; the king's anger was set ablaze and he was very upset. A nd the king said to them, Certainly you speak lies and utter falsehood in what you have said.

13 The king commanded that a proclamation should be issued throughout the land of Egypt, saying, It is determined by the king and his great men, that any wise man who knows and understands the interpretation of dreams, and will not come this day before the king, shall die.

14 The man that will declare to the king the proper interpretation of his dreams, there shall be given to him all that he will require from the king. And all the wise men of the land of Egypt came before the king, together with all the magicians and sorcerers that were in Egypt and in Goshen, in Rameses, in Tachpanches, in Zoar, and in all the places on the borders of Egypt; they all stood before the king.

15 And all the nobles and the princes, and the attendants belonging to the king, came together from all the cities of Egypt and they all sat before the king, and the king related his dreams before the wise men and the princes; all that sat before the king were astonished at the vision.

16 And all the wise men who were before the king were greatly divided in their interpretation of his dreams; some of them interpreted them to the king, saying, The seven good cattle are seven kings, who from the king's lineage will be raised over Egypt.

17 And the seven bad cattle are seven princes who will stand up against them in the latter days and destroy them; the seven ears of corn are the seven great princes belonging to Egypt, who will fall in the hands of the seven less powerful princes of their enemies, in the wars of our lord the king.

18 And some of them interpreted to the king in this manner, saying, The seven good cattle are the strong cities of Egypt, and the seven bad cattle are the seven nations of the land of Canaan, who will come against the seven cities of Egypt in the latter days and destroy them.

19 And that which you saw in the second dream, of seven good and bad ears of corn, is a sign that the government of Egypt will again return to your descendants as at first.

20 And in this reign the people of the cities of Egypt will turn against the seven cities of Canaan who are stronger than they are and will destroy them, and the government of Egypt will return to your descendants.

21 Some of them said to the king, This is the interpretation of your dreams; the seven good cattle are seven queens, whom you will take for wives in the latter days, and the seven bad cattle denote that those women will all die in the lifetime of the king.

22 And the seven good and bad ears of corn which you did see in the second dream are fourteen children, and it will be in the latter days that they will stand up and fight among themselves, and seven of them will strike the seven that are more powerful.

23 Some of them said these words to the king, The seven good cattle denote that seven children will be born to you, and they will kill seven of your children's children in the latter days; and the seven good ears of corn which you saw in the second dream are those princes against whom seven other less powerful princes will fight and destroy them in the latter days, and avenge your children's cause, and the government will again return to your offspring.

24 The king heard all the words of the wise men of Egypt and their interpretation of his dreams, and none of them pleased the king.

25 And the king knew in his wisdom that they did not altogether speak correctly in all these words, for this was from the Lord to frustrate the words of the wise men of Egypt in order that Joseph might go forth from the house of confinement, and in order that he should become great in Egypt.

26 The king saw that none among all the wise men and magicians of Egypt spoke correctly to him, and the king's wrath was set ablaze, and his anger burned within him.

27 And the king commanded that all the wise men and magicians should go out from before him, and they all went out from before the king with shame and disgrace.

28 Then the king commanded that a proclamation be sent throughout Egypt to kill all the magicians that were in Egypt, and not one of them should be allowed to live.

29 And the captains of the guards belonging to the king rose up, and each man drew his sword; they began to strike the magicians of Egypt and the wise men.

30 After this Merod, chief butler to the king, came and bowed down before the king and sat before him.

31 The butler said to the king, May the king live forever, and his government be honored in the land.

32 You were angry with your servant in those days now two years past and did place me in the ward, and I was for some time in the ward, I and the chief of the bakers.

33 And there was with us a Hebrew servant belonging to the captain of the guard, his name was Joseph, for his master had been angry with him and placed him in the house of confinement, and he attended us there.

34 Some time after when we were in the ward, we dreamed dreams in one night, I and the chief of the bakers; we

dreamed, each man according to the interpretation of his dream.

35 And we came in the morning and told them to that servant, and he interpreted to us our dreams, to each man according to his dream he correctly interpreted.

36 And it came to pass as he interpreted to us, so was the event; there fell not to the ground any of his words.

37 Now therefore my lord and king do not kill the people of Egypt for nothing; consider that the slave is still confined in the house by the captain of the guard his master, in the house of confinement.

38 If it pleases the king let him send for him that he may come before you and he will make known to you the correct interpretation of the dream which you did dream.

39 The king heard the words of the chief butler, and the king ordered that the wise men of Egypt should not be slain.

40 And the king ordered his servants to bring Joseph before him, and the king said to them, Go to him and do not terrify him that he be confused and will not know to speak properly.

41 The servants of the king went to Joseph, and they brought him hastily out of the dungeon; the king's servants shaved him, and he changed his prison garment and came before the king.

42 The king was sitting on his royal throne in a princely dress surrounded with a golden ephod, and the fine gold which was on it sparkled, and the gem and the ruby and the emerald, together with all the precious stones that were on the king's head dazzled the eye, and Joseph wondered greatly at the king.

43 And the throne on which the king sat was covered with gold and silver and with onyx stones, and it had seventy steps.

44 It was their custom throughout the land of Egypt that every man who came to speak to the king, if he was a prince or one that was respected in the sight of the king, he ascended to the king's throne as far as the thirty-first step, and the king would descend to the thirty-sixth step and speak with him.

45 If he was one of the common people, he ascended to the third step, and the king would descend to the fourth and speak to him, as their custom was. Also any man who understood to speak in all the seventy languages, he ascended the seventy steps, and went up and spoke till he reached the king.

46 And any man who could not complete the seventy, he ascended as many steps as the languages which he knew to speak in.

47 It was customary in those days in Egypt that no one should reign over them, but one who understood to speak in the seventy languages.

48 When Joseph came before the king he bowed down to the ground before the king, and he ascended to the third step, and the king sat on the fourth step and spoke with Joseph.

49 The king said to Joseph, I dreamed a dream, and there is no interpreter to interpret it properly, and I commanded that all the magicians of Egypt and the wise men thereof should come before me; I related my dreams to them, and no one has properly interpreted them to me.

50 After this I heard about you, that you are a wise man, and can correctly interpret every dream that you hear.

51 And Joseph answered Pharaoh, saying, Let Pharaoh relate his dreams that he dreamed; certainly the interpretations belong to God. And Pharaoh related his dreams to Joseph, the dream of the cattle, and the dream of the ears of corn, and the king ceased speaking.

52 Joseph was then clothed with the spirit of God before the king, and he knew all the things that would befall the king from that day forward; he knew the proper interpretation of the king's dream, and he spoke before the king.

53 Joseph found favor in the sight of the king, and the king listened carefully and with his heart, and he heard all the words of Joseph. And Joseph said to the king, Do not imagine that they are two dreams, for it is only one dream, for that which God has chosen to do throughout the land he has shown to the king in his dream, and this is the proper interpretation of your dream:

54 The seven good cattle and ears of corn are seven years, and the seven bad cattle and ears of corn are also seven years; it is one dream.

55 Know this, the seven years that are coming there will be a great plenty throughout the land, and after that the seven years of famine will follow them, a very severe famine; all the plenty will be forgotten from the land, and the famine will consume the inhabitants of the land.

56 The king dreamed one dream, and the dream was therefore repeated to Pharaoh because the thing is established by God, and God will shortly bring it to pass.

57 Now therefore I will give you counsel and deliver your soul and the souls of the inhabitants of the land from the evil of the famine, that you search throughout your kingdom for a man very discreet and wise, who knows all the affairs of government, and appoint him to superintend over the land of Egypt.

58 And let the man whom you place over Egypt appoint officers under him, that they gather in all the food of the good years that are coming, and let them lay up corn and deposit it in your appointed stores.

59 And let them keep that food for the seven years of famine, that it may be available for you and your people and your whole land, and that you and your land be not cut off by the famine.

60 Let all the inhabitants of the land also be ordered that they gather in, every man the produce of his field, of all sorts of food, during the seven good years, and that they place it in their stores; that it may be available for them in the days of the famine and that they may live on it.

61 This is the proper interpretation of your dream, and this is the counsel given to save your soul and the souls of all your subjects.

62 The king answered and said to Joseph, Who says and who knows that your words are correct? And he said to the king, This shall be a sign for you respecting all my words, that they are true and that my advice is good for you.

63 Behold your wife sits this day on the stool of delivery, and she will bear you a son and you will rejoice with him; when your child shall have gone forth from his mother's womb, your firstborn son that has been born two years ago shall die, and you will be comforted in the child that will be born to you this day.

64 Joseph finished speaking these words to the king, and he bowed down to the king and he went out, and when Joseph had gone out from the king's presence, those signs which Joseph had spoken to the king came to pass on that day.

65 The queen gave birth to a son on that day and the king heard the glad tidings about his son, and he rejoiced, and when the reporter had gone forth from the king's presence, the king's servants found the firstborn son of the king fallen dead on the ground.

66 There was great lamentation and noise in the king's house, and the king heard it and said, What is the noise and lamentation that I have heard in the house? They told the king that his firstborn son had died, then the king knew that all Joseph's words that he had spoken were correct; the king was consoled for his son by the child that was born to him on that day as Joseph had said.

CHAPTER 49

1 After these things the king sent and assembled all his officers and servants, and all the princes and nobles belonging to the king, and they all came before the king.

2 And the king said to them, Behold you have seen and heard all the words of this Hebrew man, and all the signs which he declared would come to pass, and not any of his words have fallen to the ground.

3 You know that he has given a proper interpretation of the dream, and it will certainly come to pass; now therefore take counsel, and know what you will do and how the land will be delivered from the famine.

4 Search now and see whether the likes of him can be found, in whose heart there is wisdom and knowledge, and I will appoint him over the land.

5 For you have heard what the Hebrew man has advised concerning this to save the land from the famine, and I know that the land will not be delivered from the famine but with the advice of the Hebrew man, him that advised me.

6 And they all answered the king and said, The counsel which the Hebrew has given concerning this is good; now therefore, our lord and king, behold the whole land is in your hand, do that which seems good in your sight.

7 Him whom you choose, and whom you in your wisdom know to be wise and capable of delivering the land with his wisdom, him shall the king appoint to be under him over the land.

8 And the king said to all the officers: I have thought that since God has made known to the Hebrew man all that he has spoken, there is none so discreet and wise in the whole land as he is; if it seems good in your sight I will place him over the land, for he will save the land with his wisdom.

9 All the officers answered the king and said, But certainly it is written in the laws of Egypt, and it should not be violated, that no man shall reign over Egypt, nor be the second to the king, but one who has knowledge in all the languages of the sons of men.

10 Now therefore our lord and king, behold this Hebrew man can only speak the Hebrew language; how then can he be over us as the second under government, a man who not even knows our language?

11 Now we pray you send for him, and let him come before you, and prove him in all things, and do as you see fit.

12 And the king said, It shall be done tomorrow, and the thing that you have spoken is good. All the officers came on that day before the king.

13 But that night the Lord sent one of his ministering angels and he came into the land of Egypt to Joseph, and the angel of the Lord stood over Joseph; there Joseph was lying in the bed at night in his master's house in the dungeon, for his master had put him back into the dungeon on account of his wife.

14 The angel roused him from his sleep, and Joseph rose up and stood on his legs, and there the angel of the Lord was standing opposite to him; the angel of the Lord spoke with Joseph and he taught him all the languages of man in that night, and he called his name Jehoseph.

15 The angel of the Lord went from him and Joseph returned and lay on his bed, and Joseph was astonished at the vision which he saw.

16 It came to pass in the morning that the king sent for all his officers and servants and they all came and sat before the king, and the king ordered Joseph to be brought; the king's servants went and brought Joseph before Pharaoh.

17 And the king came forth and ascended the steps of the throne and Joseph spoke to the king in all languages; Joseph went up to him and spoke to the king until he arrived before the king in the seventieth step, and he sat before the king.

18 And the king greatly rejoiced on account of Joseph, and all the king's officers rejoiced greatly with the king when they heard all the words of Joseph.

19 That thing seemed good in the sight of the king and the officers, to appoint Joseph to be second to the king over the whole land of Egypt, and the king spoke to Joseph, saying,

20 Now you did give me counsel to appoint a wise man over the land of Egypt, in order with his wisdom to save the land from the famine. Now therefore, since God has made all this known to you, and all the words which you have spoken, there is not throughout the land a discreet and wise man like to you.

21 And your name no more shall be called Joseph, but Zaphnath Paaneah shall be your name; you shall be second to me, and according to your word shall be all the affairs of my government; at your word shall my people go out and come in.

22 Also from under your hand shall my servants and officers receive their salary which is given to them monthly, and to you shall all the people of the land bow down; only in my throne will I be greater than you.

23 And the king took off his ring from his hand and put it on the hand of Joseph, and the king dressed Joseph in a princely garment; he put a golden crown on his head, and he put a golden chain on his neck.

24 The king commanded his servants and they made him ride in the second chariot belonging to the king, that went opposite to the king's chariot. He caused him to ride on a great and strong horse from the king's horses, and to be conducted through the streets of the land of Egypt.

25 And the king commanded that all those that played on timbrels, harps and other musical instruments should go forth with Joseph; one thousand timbrels, one thousand mecholoth, and one thousand nebalim went after him.

26 And five thousand men, with drawn swords glittering in their hands, went marching and playing before Joseph; twenty thousand of the great men of the king, with girdles of skin covered with gold, marched at the right hand of Joseph, and twenty thousand at his left. All the women and girls went on the roofs or stood in the streets playing and rejoicing at Joseph, and gazed at the appearance of Joseph and at his beauty.

27 And the king's people went before him and behind him, perfuming the road with frankincense and with cassia and with all sorts of fine perfume, and scattered myrrh and aloes along the road. Twenty men proclaimed these words before him throughout the land in a loud voice:

28 Do you see this man whom the king has chosen to be his second? All the affairs of government shall be regulated by him, and he that disobeys his orders, or that does not bow down before him to the ground, shall die, for he would be rebelling against the king and his second person in command.

29 And when the heralds had ceased announcing, all the people of Egypt bowed down to the ground before Joseph and said, May the king live, also may his second one live; all the inhabitants of Egypt bowed down along the road, and when the heralds approached them, they bowed down; they rejoiced with all sorts of timbrels, pipes and harps before Joseph.

30 And Joseph on his horse lifted up his eyes to heaven, and called out and said, He raises the poor man from the dust. He lifts up the needy from the dunghill. O Lord of Hosts, happy is the man who trusts in you.

31 And Joseph passed throughout the land of Egypt with Pharaoh's servants and officers, and they showed him the whole land of Egypt and all the king's treasures.

32 Joseph returned and came that day before Pharaoh, and the king gave to Joseph a possession in the land of

Egypt, a possession of fields and vineyards. And the king gave to Joseph three thousand talents of silver and one thousand talents of gold, and onyx stones and bdellium and many gifts.

33 On the next day the king commanded all the people of Egypt to bring to Joseph offerings and gifts, and said that he that violated the command of the king should die; they made a high place in the street of the city and spread out garments there, and whoever brought anything to Joseph put it into the high place.

34 And all the people of Egypt cast something into the high place, one man a golden earring, and the other rings and earrings, and different vessels of gold and silver work, and onyx stones and bdellium he put on the high place; every one gave something of what he possessed.

35 And Joseph took all these and placed them in his treasuries, and all the officers and nobles belonging to the king exalted Joseph. They gave him many gifts, seeing that the king had chosen him to be his second in leadership.

36 The king sent to Potiphera, the son of Ahiram priest of On, and he took his young daughter Osnath and gave her to Joseph for a wife.

37 And the girl was very beautiful, a virgin, one whom man had not known, and Joseph took her for a wife; the king said to Joseph, I am Pharaoh, and beside you none shall dare to lift up his hand or his foot to regulate my people throughout the land of Egypt.

38 Joseph was thirty years old when he stood before Pharaoh, and Joseph went out from before the king and became the king's second in command in Egypt.

39 The king gave Joseph a hundred servants to attend him in his house, and Joseph also sent and purchased many servants and they remained in the house of Joseph.

40 Joseph then built for himself a very magnificent house like to the houses of kings, before the court of the king's palace, and he made in the house a large temple, very elegant in appearance and convenient for his residence; three years Joseph spent in erecting his house.

41 And Joseph made for himself a very elegant throne of an abundance of gold and silver, and he covered it with onyx stones and bdellium; he made on it the likeness of the whole land of Egypt, and the likeness of the river of Egypt that waters the whole land of Egypt. Joseph sat securely on his throne in his house and the Lord increased Joseph's wisdom.

42 And all the inhabitants of Egypt and Pharaoh's servants and his princes loved Joseph greatly, for this thing was from the Lord to Joseph.

43 And Joseph had an army that made war, going out in hosts and troops to the number of forty thousand six hundred men, capable of bearing arms to assist the king and Joseph against the enemy, besides the king's officers and his servants and inhabitants of Egypt without number.

44 And Joseph gave to his mighty men, and to all his army, shields and javelins, and caps and coats of mail and stones for slinging.

CHAPTER 50

1 At that time the children of Tarshish came against the sons of Ishmael, and made war with them, and the children of Tarshish fought the Ishmaelites for a long time.

2 The children of Ishmael were small in number in those days, and they could not succeed over the children of Tarshish, and they were extremely oppressed.

3 And the old men of the Ishmaelites sent a record to the king of Egypt, saying, Send I pray you to your servants: officers and army to help us to fight against the children of Tarshish, for we have been diminishing away for a long time.

4 And Pharaoh sent Joseph with the mighty men and army which were with him, and also his mighty men from the king's house.

5 They went to the land of Havilah to the children of Ishmael to assist them against the children of Tarshish, and the children of Ishmael fought with the children of Tarshish. Joseph struck the Tarshishites and he subdued all their land, and the children of Ishmael lived there to this day.

6 And when the land of Tarshish was subdued, all the Tarshishites ran away, and came to the border of their brothers the children of Javan; Joseph with all his mighty men and army returned to Egypt, not one man of them missing.

7 At the revolution of the year, in the second year of Joseph's reigning over Egypt, the Lord gave great plenty

throughout the land for seven years as Joseph had spoken, for the Lord blessed all the produce of the earth in those days for seven years; they ate and were greatly satisfied.

8 And Joseph at that time had officers under him, and they collected all the food of the good years, and heaped corn year by year, and they placed it in the treasuries of Joseph.

9 At any time when they gathered the food, Joseph commanded that they should bring the corn in the ears, and also bring with it some of the soil of the field, so that it would not spoil.

10 And Joseph did according to this year by year, and he heaped up corn like the sand of the sea for abundance, for his stores were immense and could not be numbered for abundance.

11 Also all the inhabitants of Egypt gathered all sorts of food in their stores in great abundance during the seven good years, but they did not do to it as Joseph did.

12 All the food which Joseph and the Egyptians had gathered during the seven years of plenty was secured for the land in stores for the seven years of famine, for the support of the whole land.

13 And the inhabitants of Egypt filled each man his store and his concealed place with corn, to be for support during the famine.

14 And Joseph placed all the food that he had gathered in all the cities of Egypt, and he closed all the stores and placed sentinels over them.

15 Joseph's wife Osnath the daughter of Potiphera gave birth to him two sons, Manasseh and Ephraim, and Joseph was thirty-four years old when he had them.

16 And the lads grew up and they followed in his ways and in his instructions; they did not deviate from the way which their father taught them, either to the right or left.

17 And the Lord was with the lads, and they grew up and had understanding and skill in all wisdom and in all the affairs of government. All the king's officers and his great men of the inhabitants of Egypt honored the lads, and they were brought up among the king's children.

18 The seven years of plenty that were throughout the land were at an end; the seven years of famine came after them as Joseph had spoken, and the famine spread throughout the land.

19 All the people of Egypt saw that the famine had begun in the land of Egypt, and all the people of Egypt opened their stores of corn for the famine hung over them.

20 And they found all the food that was in their stores full of vermin and not fit to eat, and the famine stayed throughout the land; all the inhabitants of Egypt came and cried before Pharaoh, for the famine was heavy on them.

21 And they said to Pharaoh, Give food to your servants; why shall we die through hunger before your eyes, even we and our little ones?

22 And Pharaoh answered them, saying, And why do you cry to me? Did not Joseph command that the corn should be laid up during the seven years of plenty for the years of famine? Why did you not listen to his voice?

23 And the people of Egypt answered the king, saying, As your soul lives, our lord, your servants have done all that Joseph ordered, for your servants also gathered in all the produce of their fields during the seven years of plenty and laid it in the stores to this day.

24 And when the famine prevailed over your servants we opened our stores, and behold all our produce was filled with vermin and was not fit for food.

25 When the king heard all that had befallen the inhabitants of Egypt, the king was greatly afraid on account of the famine, and he was much terrified; the king answered the people of Egypt, saying, Since all this has happened to you, go to Joseph, do whatever he shall say to you; do not go contrary to his commands.

26 And all the people of Egypt went forth and came to Joseph, and said to him, Give to us food, for why shall we die before you through hunger? We gathered in our produce during the seven years as you did command, and we put it in store, and thus has it happened to us.

27 And when Joseph heard all the words of the people of Egypt and what had happened to them, Joseph opened all his stores of the produce and he sold it to the people of Egypt.

28 And the famine stayed throughout the land, and the famine was in all countries, but in the land of Egypt there was produce for sale.

29 All the inhabitants of Egypt came to Joseph to buy corn, for the famine hung over them, and all their corn was spoiled, and Joseph daily sold it to all the people of Egypt.

30 And all the inhabitants of the land of Canaan and the Philistines, and those beyond the Jordan, and the children of the east and all the cities of the lands far and near heard that there was corn in Egypt, and they all came to Egypt to buy corn, for the famine hung over them.

31 Joseph opened the stores of corn and placed officers over them, and they daily stood and sold to all that came.

32 Joseph knew that his brothers also would come to Egypt to buy corn, for the famine spread throughout the earth. And Joseph commanded all his people that they should cause it to be announced throughout the land of Egypt, saying,

33 It is the pleasure of the king, of his second and of their great men, that any person who wishes to buy corn in Egypt shall not send his servants to Egypt to purchase, but his sons; also any Egyptian or Canaanite who shall come from any of the stores from buying corn in Egypt, if he goes and sells it throughout the land, he shall die, for no one shall buy but for the support of his household.

34 And any man leading two or three beasts shall die, for a man shall only lead his own beast.

35 Joseph placed sentinels at the gates of Egypt, and commanded them, saying, Any person who may come to buy corn, permit him not to enter until his name and the name of his father, and the name of his father's father be written down; whatever is written by day, send their names to me in the evening that I may know their names.

36 And Joseph placed officers throughout the land of Egypt; he commanded them to do all these things.

37 Joseph did all these things, and made these standards in order that he might know when his brothers would come to Egypt to buy corn; Joseph's people caused it daily to be announced in Egypt according to these words and standards which Joseph had commanded.

38 And all the inhabitants of the east and west country, and of all the earth, heard of the rules and regulations which Joseph had enacted in Egypt, and the inhabitants of the extreme parts of the earth came and they bought corn in Egypt day after day, and then went away.

39 All the officers of Egypt did as Joseph had commanded, and all that came to Egypt to buy corn, the gate keepers would write their names, and their fathers' names, and daily bring them in the evening to Joseph.

CHAPTER 51

1 Jacob afterward heard that there was corn in Egypt, and he called to his sons to go to Egypt to buy corn, for on them also did the famine occur, and he called to his sons, saying,

2 Behold I hear that there is corn in Egypt, and all the people of the earth go there to purchase; now therefore why will you show yourselves (pretend to be) satisfied before the whole earth? You go also down to Egypt and buy us a little corn among those that come there, that we may not die.

3 And the sons of Jacob listened to the voice of their father, and they rose up to go down to Egypt in order to buy corn among the rest that came there.

4 And Jacob their father commanded them, saying, When you come into the city do not enter together in one gate, on account of the inhabitants of the land.

5 And the sons of Jacob went forth and they went to Egypt, and the sons of Jacob did all as their father had commanded them; Jacob did not send Benjamin, for he said, Lest an accident might happen to him on the road like his brother. Ten of Jacob's sons went forth.

6 While the sons of Jacob were going on the road, they repented of what they had done to Joseph, and they spoke to each other, saying, We know that our brother Joseph went down to Egypt, and now we will seek him where we go, and if we find him we will take him from his master for a ransom, and if not, by force, and we will die for him.

7 And the sons of Jacob agreed to this thing and strengthened themselves on account of Joseph, to deliver him from the hand of his master, and the sons of Jacob went to Egypt; when they came near to Egypt they separated from each other, and they came through ten gates of Egypt, and the gate keepers wrote their names that day, and brought them to Joseph in the evening.

8 And Joseph read the names from the hand of the gatekeepers of the city, and he found that his brothers had entered at the ten gates of the city, and Joseph at once commanded that it should be proclaimed throughout the land of Egypt, saying,

9 Go forth all you store guards, close all the corn stores and let only one remain open, that those who come may purchase from it.

10 And all the officers of Joseph did so at that time, and they closed all the stores and left only one open.

11 Joseph gave the written names of his brothers to him that was set over the open store, and he said to him, Whosoever shall come to you to buy corn, ask his name, and when men of these names shall come before you, seize them and send them, and they did so.

12 And when the sons of Jacob came into the city, they joined together in the city to search for Joseph before they bought themselves corn.

13 And they went to the walls of the harlots and they sought Joseph there for three days, for they thought that Joseph would come in the walls of the harlots, for Joseph was very handsome and well favored; the sons of Jacob sought Joseph for three days and they could not find him.

14 The man who was set over the open store sought for those names which Joseph had given him, and he did not find them.

15 And he sent to Joseph, saying, These three days have passed, and those men whose names you gave to me have not come, so Joseph sent servants to search for the men in all Egypt, and to bring them before Joseph.

16 Joseph's servants went and came into Egypt and could not find them, and went to Goshen and they were not there, and then went to the city of Rameses and could not find them.

17 Joseph continued to send sixteen servants to seek his brothers, and they went and spread themselves in the four corners of the city; four of the servants went into the house of the harlots, and they found the ten men there searching for their brother.

18 Those four men took them and brought them before Joseph, and they bowed down to him to the ground. Joseph was sitting on his throne in his temple, clothed with princely garments, and on his head was a large crown of gold, and all the mighty men were sitting around him.

19 And the sons of Jacob saw Joseph, and his figure and good-looks and dignity of countenance seemed wonderful in their eyes, and they again bowed down to him to the ground.

20 Joseph saw his brothers and he knew them, but they knew him not, for Joseph was very great in their eyes, therefore they knew him not.

21 And Joseph spoke to them, saying, From where did you come? And they all answered and said, Thy servants have come from the land of Canaan to buy corn, for the famine prevails throughout the earth, and your servants heard that there was corn in Egypt, so they have come among the other comers to buy corn for their support.

22 And Joseph answered them, saying, If you have come to purchase as you say, why do you come through ten gates of the city? It can only be that you have come to spy through the land.

23 And they all together answered Joseph, and said, Not so my lord, we are right, your servants are not spies, but we have come to buy corn, for your servants are all brothers, the sons of one man in the land of Canaan, and our father commanded us, saying, When you come to the city do not enter together at one gate on account of the inhabitants of the land.

24 And Joseph again answered them and said, That is the thing which I spoke to you, you have come to spy through the land, therefore you all came through ten gates of the city; you have come to see how barren the land has become.

25 Certainly every one that comes to buy corn goes his way, and you are already three days in the land; what do you do in the walls of harlots in which you have been for these three days? Certainly spies do these things.

26 And they said to Joseph, Far be it from our lord to speak thus, for we are twelve brothers, the sons of our father Jacob, in the land of Canaan, the son of Isaac, the son of Abraham, the Hebrew; behold the youngest is with our father this day in the land of Canaan, and one is not, for he was lost from us, and we thought perhaps he might be in this land, so we are seeking him throughout the land, and have come even to the houses of harlots to seek him there.

27 And Joseph said to them, And have you then sought him throughout the earth, that there only remained Egypt for you to seek him in? And what also should your brother do in the houses of harlots, if he were in Egypt? Have you not said, that you are from the sons of Isaac, the son of Abraham, and what shall the sons of Jacob do then in the houses of harlots?

28 And they said to him, Because we heard that Ishmaelites stole him from us, and it was told to us that they sold him in Egypt, and your servant, our brother, is very handsome and well favored, so we thought he would certainly be in the houses of harlots, therefore your servants went there to seek him and give ransom for him.

29 Joseph still answered them, saying, Certainly you speak falsely and utter lies, to say of yourselves that you are the sons of Abraham; as Pharaoh lives you are spies, therefore you have come to the houses of harlots that you should not be known.

30 Joseph said to them, And now if you find him, and his master requires of you a great price, will you give it for him? And they said, It shall be given.

31 And he said to them, And if his master will not consent to part with him for a great price, what will you do to him on his account? And they answered him, saying, If he will not give him to us we will kill him, and take our

brother and go away.

32 And Joseph said to them, That is the thing which I have spoken to you; you are spies, for you are come to kill the inhabitants of the land, for we heard that two of your brothers struck all the inhabitants of Shechem, in the land of Canaan, on account of your sister, and you now come to do the same in Egypt on account of your brother.

33 Only hereby shall I know that you are true men; if you will send home one from among you to fetch your youngest brother from your father, and bring him here to me, and by doing this thing I will know that you are right.

34 And Joseph called to seventy of his mighty men, and he said to them, Take these men and bring them into the ward.

35 And the mighty men took the ten men, they laid hold of them and put them into the ward, and they were in the ward three days.

36 And on the third day Joseph had them brought out of the ward, and he said to them, Do this for yourselves if you be true men, so that you may live: one of your brothers shall be confined in the ward while you go and take home the corn for your household to the land of Canaan, and get your youngest brother, and bring him here to me, that I may know that you are true men when you do this thing.

37 And Joseph went out from them and came into the chamber, and wept a great weeping, for his pity was enlarged for them; he washed his face, and returned to them again, and he took Simeon from them and ordered him to be bound, but Simeon was not willing to be done so, for he was a very powerful man and they could not bind him.

38 And Joseph called to his mighty men and seventy valiant men came before him with drawn swords in their hands, and the sons of Jacob were terrified at them.

39 Joseph said to them, Seize this man and confine him in prison until his brothers come to him, and Joseph's valiant men hurried and they all laid hold of Simeon to bind him, and Simeon gave a loud and terrible shriek and the cry was heard at a distance.

40 All the valiant men of Joseph were so terrified at the sound of the shriek that they fell on their faces, and they were greatly afraid and fled.

41 And all the men that were with Joseph fled, for they were greatly afraid for their lives, and only Joseph and Manasseh his son remained there; Manassah the son of Joseph saw the strength of Simeon, and he was greatly angered.

42 And Manassah the son of Joseph rose up to Simeon, and Manassah struck Simeon a heavy blow with his fist against the back of his neck, and Simeon was stilled of his rage.

43 Manassah laid hold of Simeon and he seized him violently and he bound him and brought him into the house of confinement, and all the sons of Jacob were astonished at the act of the youth.

44 And Simeon said to his brothers, None of you must say that this is the smiting of an Egyptian, but it is the smiting of the house of my father.

45 After this Joseph ordered him to be called who was in charge of the storehouse, to fill their sacks with corn as much as they could carry, and to restore every man's money into his sack, and to give them provision for the road, and thus he did to them.

46 And Joseph commanded them, saying, Take care that you not go contrary to my orders to bring your brother as I have told you, and it shall be when you bring your brother here to me, then will I know that you are true men, and you shall traffic in the land, and I will restore to you your brother, and you shall return in peace to your father.

47 And they all answered and said, According as our lord speaks so will we do, and they bowed down to him to the ground.

48 Every man lifted his corn on his ass, and they went out to go to the land of Canaan to their father; and they came to the inn and Levi spread his sack to give feed to his ass, when he saw and there his money in full weight was still in his sack.

49 And the man was greatly afraid, and he said to his brothers, My money is returned, and look, it is even in my sack; the men were greatly afraid, and they said, What is this that God has done to us?

50 And they all said, And where is the Lord's kindness with our fathers, with Abraham, Isaac, and Jacob, that the Lord has this day delivered us into the hands of the king of Egypt to contrive against us?

51 Judah said to them, Certainly we are guilty sinners before the Lord our God in having sold our brother, our own flesh, and wherefore do you say, Where is the Lord's kindness with our fathers?

52 Reuben said to them, Said I not to you, do not sin against the lad, and you would not listen to me? Now God

requires him from us, and how dare you say, Where is the Lord's kindness with our fathers, while you have sinned to the Lord?

53 They stayed overnight in that place, and they rose up early in the morning and loaded their asses with their corn; they led them and went on and came to their father's house in the land of Canaan.

54 And Jacob and his household went out to meet his sons, and Jacob saw and behold their brother Simeon was not with them; Jacob said to his sons, Where is your brother Simeon, whom I do not see? And his sons told him all that had befallen them in Egypt.

CHAPTER 52

1 They entered their house, and every man opened his sack and they looked and there every man's bundle of money was there, at which they and their father were greatly terrified.

2 And Jacob said to them, What is this that you have done to me? I sent your brother Joseph to inquire after your welfare and you said to me: A wild beast did devour him.

3 And Simeon went with you to buy food and you say the king of Egypt hath confined him in prison, and you wish to take Benjamin to cause his death also, and bring down my grey hairs with sorrow to the grave on account of Benjamin and his brother Joseph.

4 Now therefore my son shall not go down with you, for his brother is dead and he is left alone, and mischief may befall him by the way in which you go, as it befell his brother.

5 Reuben said to his father, You shall kill my two sons if I do not bring your son and place him before you. Jacob said to his sons, Abide ye here and do not go down to Egypt, for my son shall not go down with you to Egypt, nor die like his brother.

6 And Judah said to them, Refrain from him until the corn is finished, and he will then say, Take down your brother, when he finds his own life and the life of his household in danger from the famine.

7 In those days the famine was severe throughout the land, and all the people of the earth went and came to Egypt to buy food, for the famine continued greatly among them, and the sons of Jacob remained in Canaan a year and two months until their corn was finished.

8 And it came to pass after their corn was finished, the whole household of Jacob was pinched with hunger, and all the infants of the sons of Jacob came together and they approached Jacob; they all surrounded him, and said to him, Give to us bread, for why shall we all perish through hunger in your presence?

9 Jacob heard the words of his son's children, and he wept a great weeping, and his pity was roused for them. Jacob called to his sons and they all came and sat before him.

10 And Jacob said to them, Have you not seen how your children have been weeping over me this day, saying, Give to us bread, and there is none? Now therefore return and buy for us a little food.

11 And Judah answered and said to his father, If you will send our brother with us we will go down and buy corn for you, and if you will not send him then we will not go down, for certainly the king of Egypt particularly requested us, saying, You shall not see my face unless your brother is with you. The king of Egypt is a strong and mighty king, and behold if we shall go to him without our brother we shall all be put to death.

12 Do you not know and have you not heard that this king is very powerful and wise, and there is no one like him in all the earth? Behold we have seen all the kings of the earth and we have not seen one like that king, the king of Egypt; certainly among all the kings of the earth there is none greater than Abimelech king of the Philistines, yet the king of Egypt is greater and mightier than he, and Abimelech can only be compared to one of his officers.

13 Father, you have not seen his palace and his throne, and all his servants standing before him; you have not seen that king on his throne in his pomp and royal appearance, dressed in his kingly robes with a large golden crown on his head; you have not seen the honor and glory which God has given to him, for there is no one like him in all the earth.

14 Father, you have not seen the wisdom, the understanding and the knowledge which God has given in his heart, nor heard his sweet voice when he spoke to us.

15 We know not, father, who made him acquainted with our names and all that happened to us, yet he asked also after you, saying, Is your father still living, and is it well with him?

16 You have not seen the affairs of the government of Egypt regulated by him, without inquiring of Pharaoh his lord; you have not seen the awe and fear which he impressed on all the Egyptians.

17 And also when we went from him, we were threatened of doing to Egypt like to the rest of the cities of the Amorites, and we were greatly angered against all his words which he spoke concerning us as spies; now when we shall again come before him his terror will fall on us all, and not one of us will be able to speak to him either a little or a great thing.

18 Now therefore father, send we pray you the lad with us, and we will go down and buy you food for our support, and not die through hunger. And Jacob said, Why have you dealt so ill with me to tell the king you had a brother? What is this thing that you have done to me?

19 And Judah said to Jacob his father, Give the lad into my care and we will rise up and go down to Egypt and buy corn, and then return, and it shall be when we return if the lad is not with us, then let me bear your blame forever.

20 Have you seen all our infants weeping over you through hunger and there is no power in your hand to satisfy them? Now let your pity be roused for them and send our brother with us and we will go.

21 For how will the Lord's kindness to our ancestors be manifested to you when you say that the king of Egypt will take away your son? As the Lord lives I will not leave him until I bring him and place him before you; but pray for us to the Lord, that he may deal kindly with us, to cause us to be received favorably and kindly before the king of Egypt and his men, for had we not delayed certainly by now we had returned a second time with your son.

22 And Jacob said to his sons, I trust in the Lord God that he may deliver you and give you favor in the sight of the king of Egypt, and in the sight of all his men.

23 Now therefore rise up and go to the man, and take for him in your hands a present from what can be obtained in the land and bring it before him, and may the Almighty God give you mercy before him that he may send Benjamin and Simeon your brothers with you.

24 And all the men rose up, and they took their brother Benjamin, and they took in their hands a large present of the best of the land, and they also took a double portion of silver.

25 And Jacob strictly commanded his sons concerning Benjamin, saying, Take care of him in the way in which you are going, and do not separate yourselves from him in the road, neither in Egypt.

26 And Jacob rose up from his sons and spread forth his hands and he prayed to the Lord on account of his sons, saying, O Lord God of heaven and earth, remember your covenant with our father Abraham, remember it with my father Isaac and deal kindly with my sons and deliver them not into the hands of the king of Egypt; do it I pray you O God for the sake of your mercies and redeem all my children and rescue them from Egyptian power, and send them their two brothers.

27 And all the wives of the sons of Jacob and their children lifted up their eyes to heaven and they all wept before the Lord, and cried to him to deliver their fathers from the hand of the king of Egypt.

28 Jacob wrote a record to the king of Egypt and gave it into the hand of Judah and into the hands of his sons for the king of Egypt, saying,

29 From your servant Jacob, son of Isaac, son of Abraham the Hebrew, the prince of God, to the powerful and wise king, the revealer of secrets, king of Egypt, greeting.

30 Be it known to my lord the king of Egypt, the famine was heavy on us in the land of Canaan, and I sent my sons to you to buy us a little food from you for our support.

31 For my sons surrounded me and I being very old cannot see with my eyes, for my eyes have become very dim through age, as well as with daily weeping for my son, for Joseph who was lost from before me; I commanded my sons that they should not enter the gates of the city when they came to Egypt, on account of the inhabitants of the land.

32 And I also commanded them to go about Egypt to seek for my son Joseph, perhaps they might find him there, and they did so, and you did consider them as spies of the land.

33 Have we not heard concerning you that you did interpret Pharaoh's dream and did speak truly to him? How then do you not know in your wisdom whether my sons are spies or not?

34 Now therefore, my lord and king, behold I have sent my son before you, as you did speak to my sons; I beg you to put your eyes on him until he is returned to me in peace with his brothers.

35 For do you not know, or have you not heard that which our God did to Pharaoh when he took my mother Sarah, and what he did to Abimelech king of the Philistines on account of her, and also what our father Abraham did to the nine kings of Elam, how he struck them all with a few men that were with him?

36 And also what my two sons Simeon and Levi did to the eight cities of the Amorites, how they destroyed them on account of their sister Dinah?

37 And also on account of their brother Benjamin they consoled themselves for the loss of his brother Joseph; what will they then do for him when they see the hand of any people prevailing over them, for his sake?

38 Do you not know, O king of Egypt, that the power of God is with us, and that also God ever hears our prayers and forsakes us not all the days?

39 And when my sons told me of your dealings with them, I called not to the Lord on account of you, for then you would have perished with your men before my son Benjamin came before you, but I thought that as Simeon my son was in your house, perhaps you might deal kindly with him, therefore I did not do this thing to you.

40 Now therefore behold Benjamin my son comes to you with my sons, take care of him and put your eyes on him, and then will God place his eyes over you and throughout your kingdom.

41 Now I have told you all that is in my heart, and behold my sons are coming to you with their brother; examine the face of the whole earth for their sake and send them back in peace with their brothers.

42 And Jacob gave the record to his sons into the care of Judah to give it to the king of Egypt.

CHAPTER 53

1 The sons of Jacob rose up and took Benjamin and all of the presents; they went and came to Egypt and they stood before Joseph.

2 And Joseph beheld his brother Benjamin with them and he saluted them, and these men came to Joseph's house.

3 Joseph commanded the superintendent of his house to give food to his brothers to eat, and he did so to them.

4 At noon time Joseph sent for the men to come before him with Benjamin, and the men told the superintendent of Joseph's house concerning the silver that was returned in their sacks; he said to them, It will be well with you, fear not. And he brought their brother Simeon to them.

5 And Simeon said to his brothers, The lord of the Egyptians has acted very kindly to me; he did not keep me bound, as you saw with your eyes, for when you went out from the city he let me free and dealt kindly with me in his house.

6 And Judah took Benjamin by the hand, and they came before Joseph, and they bowed down to him to the ground.

7 The men gave the present to Joseph and they all sat before him, and Joseph said to them, Is it well with you, is it well with your children, is it well with your aged father? And they said, It is well. And Judah took the record which Jacob had sent and gave it into the hand of Joseph.

8 Joseph read the letter and knew his father's writing, and he wished to weep; he went into an inner room and he wept a great weeping, and he came out.

9 He lifted up his eyes and observed his brother Benjamin and said, Is this your brother of whom you spoke to me? Benjamin approached Joseph, and Joseph placed his hand on his head and he said to him, May God be gracious to you my son.

10 And when Joseph saw his brother, the son of his mother, he again wished to weep, and he entered the chamber, and he wept there; he washed his face and came out and refrained from weeping; he said, Prepare food.

11 Joseph had a cup from which he drank; it was of silver beautifully inlaid with onyx stones and bdellium, and Joseph struck the cup in the sight of his brothers while they were sitting to eat with him.

12 Joseph said to the men, I know by this cup that Reuben the first born, Simeon and Levi and Judah, Issachar and Zebulun are children from one mother; seat yourselves to eat according to your births.

13 He also placed the others according to their births and said, I know that this your youngest brother has no brother; I, like him, have no brother; he shall therefore sit down to eat with me.

14 Benjamin went up before Joseph and sat on the throne and the men beheld the acts of Joseph, and they were astonished at them; the men ate and drank at that time with Joseph, and he then gave presents to them. Joseph gave one gift to Benjamin, and Manasseh and Ephraim saw the acts of their father, and they also gave presents to him, and Osnath gave him one present, and there were five presents in the hands of Benjamin.

15 Joseph brought out wine to drink, and they would not drink; they said, From the day in which Joseph was lost we have not drunk wine, nor eaten any delicacies.

16 And Joseph swore to them, and he pressed them hard; they drank plentifully with him on that day, and Joseph afterward turned to his brother Benjamin to speak with him, and Benjamin was still sitting on the throne before Joseph.

17 Joseph said to him, Have you had any children? And he said, Your servant has ten sons, and these are their

names: Bela, Becher, Ashbal, Gera, Naaman, Achi, Rosh, Mupim, Chupim, and Ord, and I called their names after my brother whom I have not seen.

18 He ordered them to bring before him his map of the stars, whereby Joseph knew all the times, and Joseph said to Benjamin, I have heard that the Hebrews are acquainted with all wisdom, do you know anything of this?

19 And Benjamin said, Thy servant knows all the wisdom which my father taught me. Joseph said to Benjamin, Look now at this instrument and understand where your brother Joseph is in Egypt, who you said went down to Egypt.

20 And Benjamin observed that instrument with the map of the stars of heaven, and he was wise and looked therein to know where his brother was. Benjamin divided the whole land of Egypt into four divisions, and he found that he who was sitting on the throne before him was his brother Joseph; Benjamin wondered greatly, and when Joseph saw that his brother Benjamin was so much astonished, he said to Benjamin, What have you seen, and why are you astonished?

21 Benjamin said to Joseph, I can see by this that Joseph my brother sits here with me on the throne, and Joseph said to him, I am Joseph your brother; reveal not this thing to your brothers. I will send you with them when they go away and I will command them to be brought back again into the city, and I will take you away from them.

22 And if they risk their lives and fight for you, then shall I know that they have repented of what they did to me; I will make myself known to them and if they turn away from you when I take you, then shall you remain with me, and I will fight with them, and they shall go away. I will not become known to them.

23 At that time Joseph commanded his officer to fill their sacks with food and to put each man's money into his sack, and to put the cup in the sack of Benjamin and give them provision for the road, and they did so to them.

24 On the next day the men rose up early in the morning and loaded their asses with their corn; they went forth with Benjamin, and went to the land of Canaan with their brother Benjamin.

25 They had not gone far from Egypt when Joseph commanded him that was set over his house, saying, Rise, pursue these men before they get too far from Egypt, and say to them, Why have you stolen my master's cup?

26 Joseph's officer rose up and he reached them, and he spoke to them all the words of Joseph; when they heard this thing they became greatly angry, and they said, He with whom your master's cup shall be found shall die, and we will also become slaves.

27 They hurried and each man brought down his sack from his ass, and they looked in their bags and the cup was found in Benjamin's bag; they all tore their garments and they returned to the city, and they struck Benjamin in the road, continually smiting him until he came into the city, and they stood before Joseph.

28 Judah's anger was set ablaze, and he said, This man has only brought me back to destroy Egypt this day.

29 The men came to Joseph's house, and they found Joseph sitting on his throne, and all the mighty men standing at his right and left.

30 And Joseph said to them, What is this act that you have done, that you took away my silver cup and went away? But I know that you took my cup in order to know thereby in what part of the land your brother was.

31 Judah said, What shall we say to our lord, what shall we speak and how shall we justify ourselves; God has this day found the iniquity of all your servants, therefore has he done this thing to us this day.

32 Joseph rose up and caught hold of Benjamin and took him from his brothers with violence, and he came to the house and locked the door at them; Joseph commanded him that was set over his house that he should say to them, Thus says the king, Go in peace to your father, behold I have taken the man in whose hand my cup was found.

CHAPTER 54

1 When Judah saw the dealings of Joseph with them, Judah approached him and broke open the door, and came with his brothers before Joseph.

2 And Judah said to Joseph, Let it not seem bothersome in the sight of my lord, may your servant I pray you speak a word before you? And Joseph said to him, Speak.

3 Judah spoke before Joseph and his brothers were there standing before them; Judah said to Joseph, Certainly when we first came to our lord to buy food, you did consider us as spies of the land, and we brought Benjamin before you, and you still make sport of us this day.

4 Now therefore let the king hear my words and send I pray you our brother that he may go along with us to our father, that your son not perish this day with all the souls of the inhabitants of Egypt.

5 Do you not know what two of my brothers, Simeon and Levi, did to the city of Shechem and to seven cities of the Amorites on account of our sister Dinah, and also what they would do for the sake of their brother Benjamin?

6 I with my strength, who am greater and mightier than both of them, come this day on you and your land if you are unwilling to send our brother.

7 Have you not heard what our God who made choice of us did to Pharaoh on account of Sarah our mother, whom he took away from our father, that he struck him and his household with heavy plagues; even to this day the Egyptians relate this wonder to each other? So will our God do to you on account of Benjamin whom you have this day taken from his father, and on account of the evils which you this day heap over us in your land; for our God will remember his covenant with our father Abraham and bring evil on you because you have grieved the soul of our father this day.

8 Now hear my words that I have this day spoken to you, and send our brother that he may go away that you and the people of your land not die by the sword, for you cannot all prevail over me.

9 Joseph answered Judah, saying, Why have you opened wide your mouth and why do you boast over us, saying, Strength is with you? As Pharaoh lives, if I command all my valiant men to fight with you, certainly you and these your brothers would sink into the mud.

10 Judah said to Joseph, Certainly it becomes you and your people to fear me; as the Lord lives if I once draw my sword I shall not sheathe it again until I shall this day have slain all Egypt, and I will begin with you and finish with Pharaoh your master.

11 And Joseph answered and said to him, Certainly strength belongs not alone to you; I am stronger and mightier than you; certainly if you draw your sword I will put it to your neck and the necks of all your brothers.

12 Judah said to him, Certainly if I this day open my mouth against you I would swallow you up that you be destroyed from off the earth and perish this day from your kingdom. And Joseph said, Certainly if you open your mouth I have power and might to close your mouth with a stone until you shall not be able to utter a word; see how many stones are before us, truly I can take a stone and force it into your mouth and break your jaws.

13 And Judah said, God is witness between us, that we have not hereto desired to battle with you, only give us our brother and we will go from you. Joseph answered and said, As Pharaoh lives, if all the kings of Canaan came together with you, you should not take him from my hand.

14 Now therefore go your way to your father, and your brother shall be to me a slave, for he has robbed the king's house. And Judah said, What is it to you or to the character of the king, certainly the king sends forth from his house, throughout the land, silver and gold either in gifts or expenses, and you still talk about your cup which you did place in our brother's bag and say that he has stolen it from you?

15 God forbid that our brother Benjamin or any of the offspring of Abraham should do this thing to steal from you, or from any one else, whether king, prince, or any man.

16 Now therefore cease this accusation that the whole earth not hear your words, saying, For a little silver the king of Egypt argued with the men, and he accused them and took their brother for a slave.

17 And Joseph answered and said, Take this cup and go from me and leave your brother for a slave, for it is the judgment of a thief to be a slave.

18 And Judah said, Why are you not ashamed of your words, to leave our brother and to take your cup? Certainly if you give us your cup, or a thousand times as much, we will not leave our brother for the silver which is found in the hand of any man, that we will not die over him.

19 Joseph answered, And why did you turn away from your brother and sell him for twenty pieces of silver to this day; why then will you not do the same to this your brother?

20 And Judah said, The Lord is witness between me and you that we desire not your battles; now therefore give us our brother and we will go from you without quarreling.

21 And Joseph answered and said, If all the kings of the land should assemble they will not be able to take your brother from my hand. Judah said, What shall we say to our father, when he sees that our brother comes not with us, and will grieve over him?

22 Joseph answered and said, This is the thing which you shall tell to your father, saying, The rope has gone after the bucket.

23 Judah said, Certainly you are a king, and why speak you these things, giving a false judgment? Woe to the king who is like you.

24 Joseph answered and said, There is no false judgment in the word that I spoke on account of your brother Joseph, for all of you sold him to the Midianites for twenty pieces of silver. And you all denied it to your father and said to him, An evil beast has devoured him; Joseph has been torn to pieces.

25 And Judah said, Behold the fire of Shem burns in my heart, now I will burn all your land with fire; Joseph answered and said, Certainly your sister-in-law Tamar, who killed your sons, extinguished the fire of Shechem.

26 Judah said, If I pluck out a single hair from my flesh, I will fill all Egypt with its blood.

27 Joseph answered and said, Such is your custom to do as you did to your brother whom you sold, and you dipped his coat in blood and brought it to your father in order that he might say an evil beast devoured him and here is his blood.

28 When Judah heard this thing he was greatly enraged and his anger burned within him, and there was before him in that place a stone, the weight of which was about four hundred shekels; Judah's anger was set ablaze and he took the stone in one hand and cast it to the heavens and caught it with his left hand.

29 He placed it afterward under his legs, and he sat on it with all his strength and the stone was turned into dust from the force of Judah.

30 Joseph saw the act of Judah and he was very much afraid, but he commanded Manassah his son and he also did with another stone like to the act of Judah, and Judah said to his brothers, Let not any of you say this man is an Egyptian, but by his doing this thing he is of our father's family.

31 And Joseph said, Not to you only is strength given, for we are also powerful men, and why will you boast over us all? Judah said to Joseph, Send I pray you our brother and ruin not your country this day.

32 And Joseph answered and said to them, Go and tell your father an evil beast has devoured him as you said concerning your brother Joseph.

33 Judah spoke to his brother Naphtali, and said to him, Hurry, go now and number all the streets of Egypt and come and tell me; Simeon said to him, Let not this thing be a trouble to you; now I will go to the mount and take up one large stone from the mount and level it at every one in Egypt, and kill all that are in it.

34 Joseph heard all these words that his brothers spoke before him, and they did not know that Joseph understood them for they imagined that he knew not to speak Hebrew.

35 Joseph was greatly afraid at the words of his brothers that they should destroy Egypt, and he commanded his son Manasseh, saying, Go now, hurry and gather to me all the inhabitants of Egypt, and all the valiant men together, and let them come to me now on horseback and on foot and with all sorts of musical instruments, and Manasseh went and did so.

36 Naphtali went as Judah had commanded him, for Naphtali was lightfooted as one of the swift stags, and he could walk on the ears of corn and they would not break under him.

37 He went and numbered all the streets of Egypt and found them to be twelve, and he came quickly and told Judah, and Judah said to his brothers, Hurry and put on every man his sword on his loins and we will come over Egypt and strike them all, and let not a remnant remain.

38 Judah said, Behold, I will destroy three of the streets with my strength, and you shall each destroy one street; when Judah was speaking this thing, then the inhabitants of Egypt and all the mighty men came toward them with all sorts of musical instruments and with loud shouting.

39 And their number was five hundred cavalry and ten thousand infantry, and four hundred men who could fight without sword or spear, only with their hands and strength.

40 And all the mighty men came with great storming and shouting, and they all surrounded the sons of Jacob and terrified them, and the ground quaked at the sound of their shouting.

41 When the sons of Jacob saw these troops they were greatly afraid of their lives, and Joseph did so in order to terrify the sons of Jacob to become tranquilized.

42 Judah, seeing some of his brothers terrified, said to them, Why are you afraid while the grace of God is with us? Judah saw all the people of Egypt surrounding them at the command of Joseph to terrify them, only Joseph commanded them, saying, Do not touch any of them.

43 Then Judah hurried and drew his sword and uttered a loud and bitter scream, and he struck with his sword, and he stomped on the ground and he still continued to shout against all the people.

44 When he did this thing the Lord caused the terror of Judah and his brothers to fall on the valiant men and all the people that surrounded them.

45 They all fled at the sound of the shouting, and they were terrified and fell one on the other, and many of them died as they fell, and they all fled from before Judah and his brothers and from before Joseph.

46 While they were fleeing, Judah and his brothers pursued them to the house of Pharaoh and they all escaped; Judah again sat before Joseph and roared at him like a lion, and gave a great and tremendous shriek at him.

47 The shriek was heard at a distance, and all the inhabitants of Succoth heard it, and all Egypt quaked at the sound of the shriek; also the walls of Egypt and of the land of Goshen fell in from the shaking of the earth, and

Pharaoh also fell from his throne on the ground; also all the pregnant women of Egypt and Goshen miscarried when they heard the noise of the shaking, for they were terribly afraid.

48 And Pharaoh sent word, saying, What is this thing that has this day happened in the land of Egypt? They came and told him all the things from beginning to end, and Pharaoh was alarmed and he wondered and was greatly afraid.

49 His fright increased when he heard all these things, and he sent to Joseph, saying, You have brought to me the Hebrews to destroy all Egypt; what will you do with that thievish slave? Send him away and let him go with his brothers, and let us not perish through their evil, even we, you and all Egypt.

50 And if you desire not to do this thing, cast off from you all my valuable things, and go with them to their land if you delightest in it, for they will this day destroy my whole country and kill all my people; even all the women of Egypt have miscarried through their scream. See what they have done merely by their shouting and speaking? And if they fight with the sword, they will destroy the land; now therefore choose that which you desire, whether me or the Hebrews, whether Egypt or the land of the Hebrews.

51 They came and told Joseph all the words of Pharaoh that he had said concerning him, and Joseph was greatly afraid at the words of Pharaoh and Judah and his brothers were still standing before Joseph indignant and enraged, and all the sons of Jacob roared at Joseph, like the roaring of the sea and its waves.

52 Joseph was greatly afraid of his brothers and on account of Pharaoh, and Joseph sought a way to make himself known to his brothers, that they should not destroy all Egypt.

53 Joseph commanded his son Manasseh, and Manasseh went and approached Judah and placed his hand on his shoulder, and the anger of Judah was stilled.

54 And Judah said to his brothers, Let no one of you say that this is the act of an Egyptian youth for this is the work of my father's house.

55 Joseph seeing and knowing that Judah's anger was stilled, he approached to speak to Judah in the language of mildness.

56 And Joseph said to Judah, Certainly you speak truth and have this day verified your assertions concerning your strength, and may your God who delights in you, increase your welfare; but tell me truly why from among all your brothers do you argue with me on account of the lad, as none of them have spoken one word to me concerning him.

57 And Judah answered Joseph, saying, Certainly you must know that I was security for the lad to his father, saying, If I brought him not to him I should bear his blame forever.

58 So I have approached you from among all my brothers, for I saw that you were unwilling to allow him to go from you; now therefore may I find grace in your sight that you shall send him to go with us and then I will remain as a substitute for him, to serve you in whatever you desire, for whereever you shall send me I will go to serve you with great energy.

59 Send me now to a mighty king who has rebelled against you, and you shall know what I will do to him and to his land; although he may have cavalry and infantry or an exceeding mighty people, I will kill them all and bring the king's head before you.

60 Do you not know or have you not heard that our father Abraham with his servant Eliezer struck all the kings of Elam with their hosts in one night, they left not one remaining? And ever since that day our father's strength was given to us for an inheritance, for us and our descendants forever.

61 Joseph answered and said, You speak truth, and falsehood is not in your mouth, for it was also told to us that the Hebrews have power and that the Lord their God delights much in them, and who then can stand before them?

62 However, on this condition will I send your brother, if you will bring before me his brother the son of his mother, of whom you said that he had gone from you down to Egypt; it shall come to pass when you bring to me his brother I will take him in his stead, because not one of you was security for him to your father. When he shall come to me, I will then send with you his brother for whom you have been security.

63 And Judah's anger was set ablaze against Joseph when he spoke this thing, and his eyes dropped blood with anger, and he said to his brothers, How does this man this day seek his own destruction and that of all Egypt!

64 And Simeon answered Joseph, saying, Did we not tell you at first that we knew not the particular spot to which he went, and whether he be dead or alive, and why does my lord speak these things?

65 Joseph, observing the countenance of Judah discerned that his anger began to kindle when he spoke to him, saying, Bring to me your other brother instead of this brother.

66 And Joseph said to his brothers, Certainly you said that your brother was either dead or lost, now if I should

call him this day and he should come before you, would you give him to me instead of his brother?

67 And Joseph began to speak and call out, Joseph, Joseph, come this day before me, and appear to your brothers and sit before them.

68 When Joseph spoke this thing before them, they looked each a different way to see from where Joseph would come before them.

69 And Joseph observed all their acts, and said to them, Why do you look here and there? I am Joseph whom you sold to Egypt, now therefore let it not grieve you that you sold me, for as a support during the famine did God send me from you.

70 And his brothers were terrified at him when they heard the words of Joseph, and Judah was greatly terrified at him.

71 When Benjamin heard the words of Joseph he was before them in the inner part of the house, and Benjamin ran to Joseph his brother and embraced him and fell on his neck, and they wept.

72 When Joseph's brothers saw that Benjamin had fallen on his brother's neck and wept with him, they also fell on Joseph and embraced him, and they wept a great weeping with Joseph.

73 And the voice was heard in the house of Joseph that they were Joseph's brothers, and it pleased Pharaoh greatly, for he was afraid of them that they should destroy Egypt.

74 Pharaoh sent his servants to Joseph to congratulate him concerning his brothers who had come to him, and all the captains of the armies and troops that were in Egypt came to rejoice with Joseph, and all Egypt rejoiced greatly about Joseph's brothers.

75 And Pharaoh sent his servants to Joseph, saying, Tell your brothers to fetch all belonging to them and let them come to me, and I will place them in the best part of the land of Egypt, and they did so.

76 Joseph commanded him that was set over his house to bring out to his brothers gifts and garments, and he brought out to them many garments being robes of royalty and many gifts, and Joseph divided them among his brothers.

77 And he gave to each of his brothers a change of garments of gold and silver, and three hundred pieces of silver, and Joseph commanded them all to be dressed in these garments, and to be brought before Pharaoh.

78 And Pharaoh, seeing that all Joseph's brothers were valiant men, and of beautiful appearance, greatly rejoiced.

79 And afterward they went out from the presence of Pharaoh to go to the land of Canaan, to their father, and their brother Benjamin was with them.

80 Joseph rose up and gave to them eleven chariots from Pharaoh, and Joseph gave to them his chariot on which he rode on the day of his being crowned in Egypt, to fetch his father to Egypt; Joseph sent to all his brothers' children, garments according to their numbers, and a hundred pieces of silver to each of them, and he also sent garments to the wives of his brothers from the garments of the king's wives, and he sent them.

81 He gave to each of his brothers ten men to go with them to the land of Canaan to serve them, to serve their children and all belonging to them in coming to Egypt.

82 Joseph sent by the hand of his brother Benjamin ten suits of garments for his ten sons, a portion above the rest of the children of the sons of Jacob.

83 And he sent to each fifty pieces of silver, and ten chariots on the account of Pharaoh; he sent to his father ten asses laden with all the luxuries of Egypt, and ten female asses laden with corn and bread and nourishment for his father and to all that were with him as provisions for the road.

84 And he sent to his sister Dinah garments of silver and gold, and frankincense and myrrh, and aloes and women's ornaments in great plenty; he sent the same from the wives of Pharaoh to the wives of Benjamin.

85 He gave to all his brothers, also to their wives, all sorts of onyx stones and bdellium, and from all the valuable things among the great people of Egypt, nothing of all the costly things was left but what Joseph sent of to his father's household.

86 He sent his brothers away, and they went, and he sent his brother Benjamin with them.

87 And Joseph went out with them to accompany them on the road to the borders of Egypt, and he commanded them concerning his father and his household to come to Egypt.

88 And he said to them, Do not quarrel on the road, for this thing was from the Lord to keep a great people from starvation, for there will be yet five years of famine in the land.

89 And he commanded them, saying, When you come to the land of Canaan, do not come suddenly before my father about this affair, but act in your wisdom.

90 And Joseph ceased to command them, and he turned and went back to Egypt, and the sons of Jacob went to the land of Canaan with joy and cheerfulness to their father Jacob.

91 Tthey came to the borders of the land, and they said to each other, What shall we do in this matter before our father, for if we come suddenly to him and tell him the matter, he will be greatly alarmed at our words and will not believe us.

92 They went along until they came near to their houses and they found Serach, the daughter of Asher, going forth to meet them; the damsel was very good and subtle, and knew how to play on the harp.

93 They called to her and she came before them and kissed them, and they took her and gave her a harp, saying, Go now before our father and sit before him; strike on the harp and speak these words.

94 And they commanded her to go to their house, and she took the harp and hurried before them, and she came and sat near Jacob.

95 She played well and sang, and uttered in the sweetness of her words: Joseph my uncle is living and he rules throughout the land of Egypt, and is not dead.

96 She continued to repeat and utter these words, and Jacob heard her words and they were agreeable to him.

97 He listened while she repeated them twice and three times, and joy entered the heart of Jacob at the sweetness of her words, and the spirit of God was on him and he knew all her words to be true.

98 Jacob blessed Serach when she spoke these words before him, and he said to her, My daughter, may death never prevail over you, for you have revived my spirit; only speak again before me as you have spoken, for you have uplifted me with all your words.

99 And she continued to sing these words and Jacob listened and it pleased him, and he rejoiced, and the spirit of God was on him.

100 While he was yet speaking with her, he saw his sons come to him with horses and chariots and royal garments and servants running before them.

101 Jacob rose up to meet them and saw his sons dressed in royal garments and he saw all the treasures that Joseph had sent to them.

102 They said to him, Be informed that our brother Joseph is living, and it is he who rules throughout the land of Egypt, and it is he who spoke to us as we told you.

103 Jacob heard all the words of his sons, and his heart palpitated at their words, for he could not believe them until he saw all that Joseph had given them and what he had sent him, and all the signs which Joseph had spoken to them.

104 They opened all before him, and showed him all that Joseph had sent; they gave to each what Joseph had sent him and he knew that they had spoken the truth, and he rejoiced greatly an account of his son.

105 Jacob said, It is enough for me that my son Joseph is still living; I will go and see him before I die.

106 And his sons told him all that had happened to them, and Jacob said, I will go down to Egypt to see my son and his children.

107 Jacob rose up and put on the garments which Joseph had sent him, and after he had washed and shaved his hair, he put on his head the turban which Joseph had sent him.

108 All the people of Jacob's house and their wives put on the garments which Joseph had sent to them, and they greatly rejoiced at Joseph that he was still living and that he was ruling in Egypt.

109 And all the inhabitants of Canaan heard of this thing, and they came and rejoiced much with Jacob that he was still living.

110 Jacob made a feast for them for three days, and all the kings of Canaan and nobles of the land ate and drank and rejoiced in the house of Jacob.

CHAPTER 55

1 It came to pass after this that Jacob said, I will go and see my son in Egypt and then come back to the land of Canaan of which God had spoken to Abraham, for I cannot leave the land of my birth-place.

2 Then the word of the Lord came to him, saying, Go down to Egypt with all your household and remain there; fear not to go down to Egypt for I will there make you a great nation.

3 Jacob said within himself, I will go and see my son whether the fear of his God is yet in his heart among all the inhabitants of Egypt.

4 And the Lord said to Jacob, Fear not about Joseph, for he still retains his integrity to serve me, as will seem good in your sight. Jacob rejoiced greatly concerning his son.

5 At that time Jacob commanded his sons and household to go to Egypt according to the word of the Lord to him,

and Jacob rose up with his sons and all his household, and he went out from the land of Canaan from Beersheba with joy and gladness of heart; they went to the land of Egypt.

6 It came to pass when they came near Egypt, Jacob sent Judah before him to Joseph that he might show him a situation in Egypt, and Judah did according to the word of his father; he hurried and ran and came to Joseph and they assigned for them a place in the land of Goshen for all his household, and Judah returned and came along the road to his father.

7 Joseph harnessed the chariot and assembled all his mighty men and his servants and all the officers of Egypt in order to go and meet his father Jacob, and Joseph's mandate was proclaimed in Egypt, saying, All that do not go to meet Jacob shall die.

8 On the next day Joseph went forth with all Egypt a great and mighty host, all dressed in garments of fine linen and purple and with instruments of silver and gold and with their instruments of war with them.

9 And they all went to meet Jacob with all sorts of musical instruments, with drums and timbrels, strewing myrrh and aloes all along the road; they all went after this fashion and the earth shook at their shouting.

10 All the women of Egypt went on the roofs of Egypt and on the walls to meet Jacob, and on the head of Joseph was Pharaoh's regal crown, for Pharaoh had sent it to him to put on at the time of his going to meet his father.

11 When Joseph came within fifty cubits of his father, he alighted from the chariot and he walked toward his father; when all the officers of Egypt and her nobles saw that Joseph had gone on foot toward his father, they also alighted and walked on foot toward Jacob.

12 And when Jacob approached the camp of Joseph, Jacob observed the camp that was coming toward him with Joseph and it gratified him, and Jacob was astonished at it.

13 Jacob said to Judah, Who is that man whom I see in the camp of Egypt dressed in kingly robes with a very red garment on him and a royal crown on his head, who has alighted from his chariot and is coming toward us? And Judah answered his father, saying, He is your son Joseph the king; and Jacob rejoiced in seeing the glory of his son.

14 Joseph came near to his father and he bowed to his father, and all the men of the camp bowed to the ground with him before Jacob.

15 And behold Jacob ran and hurried to his son Joseph and fell on his neck and kissed him, and they wept; Joseph also embraced his father and kissed him and they wept, and all the people of Egypt wept with them.

16 Jacob said to Joseph, Now I will die cheerfully after I have seen your face, that you are still living and with glory.

17 The sons of Jacob and their wives and their children and their servants, and all the household of Jacob wept greatly with Joseph and they kissed him and wept greatly with him.

18 Joseph and all his people returned home afterward to Egypt, and Jacob and his sons and all the children of his household came with Joseph to Egypt; Joseph placed them in the best part of Egypt, in the land of Goshen.

19 Joseph said to his father and his brothers, I will go up and tell Pharaoh, saying, My brothers and my father's household and all belonging to them have come to me, and now they are in the land of Goshen.

20 And Joseph did so and took from his brothers Reuben, Issachar, Zebulun and his brother Benjamin and he placed them before Pharaoh.

21 And Joseph spoke to Pharaoh, saying, My brothers and my father's household and all belonging to them, together with their flocks and cattle have come to me from the land of Canaan, to sojourn in Egypt; for the famine was severely on them.

22 And Pharaoh said to Joseph, Place your father and brothers in the best part of the land; withhold not from them all that is good, and cause them to eat of the best of the land.

23 And Joseph answered, saying, Yes, I have stationed them in the land of Goshen for they are shepherds, therefore let them remain in Goshen to feed their flocks, apart from the Egyptians.

24 And Pharaoh said to Joseph, Do with your brothers all that they shall say to you. And the sons of Jacob bowed down to Pharaoh, and they went forth from him in peace, and Joseph afterward brought his father before Pharaoh.

25 And Jacob came and bowed down to Pharaoh, and Jacob blessed Pharaoh, and he then went out; Jacob and all his sons and all his household lived in the land of Goshen.

26 In the second year, that is in the hundred and thirtieth year of the life of Jacob, Joseph maintained his father and his brothers and all his father's household with bread according to their little ones; all the days of the famine they lacked nothing.

27 And Joseph gave to them the best part of the whole land; the best of Egypt they had, all the days of Joseph, and

Joseph also gave to them and to all his father's household, clothes and garments year by year; the sons of Jacob remained securely in Egypt all the days of their brother.

28 And Jacob always ate at Joseph's table, Jacob and his sons did not leave Joseph's table day or night, besides what Jacob's children consumed in their houses.

29 And all Egypt ate bread during the days of the famine from the house of Joseph, for all the Egyptians sold all belonging to them on account of the famine.

30 Joseph purchased all the lands and fields of Egypt for bread on the account of Pharaoh, and Joseph supplied all Egypt with bread all the days of the famine; Joseph collected all the silver and gold that came to him for the corn which they bought throughout the land, and he accumulated much gold and silver, besides an immense quantity of onyx stones, bdellium and valuable garments which they brought to Joseph from every part of the land when their money was gone.

31 And Joseph took all the silver and gold that came into his hand, about seventy two talents of gold and silver, and also onyx stones and bdellium in great abundance, and Joseph went and concealed them in four parts; he concealed one part in the wilderness near the Red sea, and one part by the river Perath, and the third and fourth parts he concealed in the desert opposite to the wilderness of Persia and Media.

32 He took part of the gold and silver that was left and gave it to all his brothers, to all his father's household, and to all the women of his father's household; the rest he brought to the house of Pharaoh, about twenty talents of gold and silver.

33 Joseph gave all the gold and silver that was left to Pharaoh, and Pharaoh placed it in the treasury, and the days of the famine ceased after that in the land. They sowed and reaped in the whole land, and they obtained their usual quantity year by year; they lacked nothing.

34 And Joseph lived securely in Egypt and the whole land was under his advice, and his father and all his brothers lived in the land of Goshen and took possession of it.

35 Joseph was very aged, advanced in days, and his two sons Ephraim and Manasseh remained constantly in the house of Jacob, together with the children of the sons of Jacob their brothers, to learn the ways of the Lord and his law.

36 And Jacob and his sons lived in the land of Egypt in the land of Goshen, and they took possession of it, and they were prolific and multiplied in it.

CHAPTER 56

1 Jacob lived in the land of Egypt seventeen years, and the days of Jacob, and the years of his life were a hundred and forty seven years.

2 At that time Jacob was attacked with that illness of which he died and he sent and called for his son Joseph from Egypt, and Joseph his son came from Egypt and came to his father.

3 Jacob said to Joseph and to his sons, Behold I die, and the God of your ancestors will visit you and bring you back to the land which the Lord swore to give to you and to your children after you; now therefore when I am dead, bury me in the cave which is in Machpelah in Hebron in the land of Canaan, near my ancestors.

4 Jacob made his sons swear to bury him in Machpelah, in Hebron, and his sons swore to him concerning this thing.

5 And he commanded them, saying, Serve the Lord your God, for he who delivered your fathers will also deliver you from all trouble.

6 And Jacob said, Call all your children to me, and all the children of Jacob's sons came and sat before him, and Jacob blessed them, and he said to them, The Lord God of your fathers shall grant you a thousand times as much and bless you, and may he give you the blessing of your father Abraham. And all the children of Jacob's sons went forth on that day after he had blessed them.

7 On the next day Jacob again called for his sons and they all assembled and came to him and sat before him, and Jacob on that day blessed his sons before his death; each man did he bless according to his blessing. So it is written in the book of the law of the Lord pertaining to Israel.

8 And Jacob said to Judah, I know my son that you are a mighty man for your brothers; reign over them, and your sons shall reign over their sons forever.

9 Only teach your sons the bow and all the weapons of war, in order that they may fight the battles of their brother who will rule over his enemies.

10 And Jacob again commanded his sons on that day, saying, Behold I shall this day be gathered to my people; carry me up from Egypt and bury me in the cave of Machpelah as I have commanded you.

11 But take care I pray you that none of your sons carry me, only yourselves, and this is the manner you shall do to me, when you carry my body to go with it to the land of Canaan to bury me:

12 Judah, Issachar and Zebulun shall carry my bier at the eastern side; Reuben, Simeon and Gad at the south; Ephraim, Manasseh and Benjamin at the west; Dan, Asher and Naphtali at the north.

13 Let not Levi carry with you, for he and his sons will carry the ark of the covenant of the Lord with the Israelites in the camp, neither let Joseph my son carry, for as a king so let his glory be; but Ephraim and Manasseh shall be in their stead.

14 Thus shall you do to me when you carry me away; do not neglect anything of all that I command you and it shall come to pass when you do this to me, that the Lord will remember you favorably and your children after you forever.

15 And you my sons, honor each his brother and his relative, and command your children and your children's children after you to serve the Lord God of your ancestors always,

16 In order that you may prolong your days in the land, you and your children and your children's children forever, when you do what is good and upright in the sight of the Lord your God, to follow in all his ways.

17 And you, Joseph my son, forgive I pray you the prongs of your brothers and all their wrongdoings in the injury that they heaped on you, for God intended it for you and your children's benefit.

18 And O my son leave not your brothers to the inhabitants of Egypt, neither hurt their feelings, for behold I consign them to the hand of God and in your hand to guard them from the Egyptians; the sons of Jacob answered their father saying, O, our father, all that you have commanded us, so will we do; may God only be with us.

19 Jacob said to his sons, So may God be with you when you keep all his ways; turn not from his ways either to the right or the left in performing what is good and upright in his sight.

20 For I know that many and severe troubles will befall you in the latter days in the land, yes, your children and children's children; only serve the Lord and he will save you from all trouble.

21 It shall come to pass when you shall go after God to serve him and will teach your children after you, and your children's children, to know the Lord, then will the Lord raise up to you and your children a servant from among your children; the Lord will deliver you through his hand from all affliction, and bring you out of Egypt and bring you back to the land of your fathers to inherit it securely.

22 Jacob ceased commanding his sons, and he drew his feet into the bed. He died and was gathered to his people.

23 And Joseph fell on his father and he cried out and wept over him and he kissed him, and he called out in a bitter voice, and he said, O my father, my father.

24 His son's wives and all his household came and fell on Jacob, and they wept over him and cried in a very loud voice concerning Jacob.

25 All the sons of Jacob rose up together, and they tore their garments, and they all put sackcloth on their loins; they fell on their faces, and they cast dust on their heads toward the heavens.

26 And the thing was told to Osnath Joseph's wife; she rose up and put on a sack and she with all the Egyptian women came and mourned and wept for Jacob.

27 Also all the people of Egypt who knew Jacob came all on that day when they heard this thing, and all Egypt wept for many days.

28 Also from the land of Canaan the women came to Egypt when they heard that Jacob was dead, and they wept for him in Egypt for seventy days.

29 It came to pass after this that Joseph commanded his servants the doctors to embalm his father with myrrh and frankincense and all manner of incense and perfume, and the doctors embalmed Jacob as Joseph had commanded them.

30 And all the people of Egypt and the elders and all the inhabitants of the land of Goshen wept and mourned over Jacob, and all his sons and the children of his household lamented and mourned over their father Jacob many days.

31 After the days of his weeping had passed away, at the end of seventy days, Joseph said to Pharaoh, I will go up and bury my father in the land of Canaan as he made me swear, and then I will return.

32 Pharaoh sent Joseph, saying, Go up and bury your father as he said, and as he made you swear; Joseph rose up with all his brothers to go to the land of Canaan to bury their father Jacob as he had commanded them.

33 And Pharaoh commanded that it should be announced throughout Egypt, saying, Whoever goes not up with Joseph and his brothers to the land of Canaan to bury Jacob, shall die.

34 And all Egypt heard of Pharaoh's proclamation, and they all rose up together, and all the servants of Pharaoh, and the elders of his house, and all the elders of the land of Egypt went up with Joseph, and all the officers and nobles of Pharaoh went up as the servants of Joseph; they went to bury Jacob in the land of Canaan.

35 And the sons of Jacob carried the bier on which he lay; according to all that their father commanded them, so did his sons to him.

36 The bier was of pure gold, and it was inlaid round about with onyx stones and bdellium; and the covering of the bier was gold woven work, joined with threads, and over them were hooks of onyx stones and bdellium.

37 And Joseph placed on the head of his father Jacob a large golden crown, and he put a golden rod in his hand, and they surrounded the bier as was the custom of kings during their lives.

38 And all the troops of Egypt went before him in this array; at first all the mighty men of Pharaoh and the mighty men of Joseph, and after them the rest of the inhabitants of Egypt; they were all girded with swords and equipped with coats of mail, and the trappings of war were on them.

39 All the weepers and mourners went at a distance opposite to the bier, going and weeping and lamenting, and the rest of the people went after the bier.

40 Joseph and his household went together near the bier barefooted and weeping, and the rest of Joseph's servants went around him; each man had his ornaments on him and they were all armed with their weapons of war.

41 Fifty of Jacob's servants went in front of the bier and they scattered along the road myrrh and aloes, and all manner of perfume, and all the sons of Jacob that carried the bier walked on the perfumery; the servants of Jacob went before them spreading the perfume along the road.

42 And Joseph went up with a heavy camp, and they did after this manner every day until they reached the land of Canaan. They came to the threshing floor of Atad, which was on the other side of Jordan, and they mourned an extremely great and heavy mourning in that place.

43 And all the kings of Canaan heard of this thing and they all went forth, each man from his house, thirty-one kings of Canaan; they all came with their men to mourn and weep over Jacob.

44 All these kings observed Jacob's bier, and there Joseph's crown was on it; they also put their crowns on the bier and encircled it with crowns.

45 All these kings made in that place a great and heavy mourning with the sons of Jacob and Egypt over Jacob, for all the kings of Canaan knew the valor of Jacob and his sons.

46 And the report reached Esau, saying, Jacob died in Egypt, and his sons and all Egypt are conveying him to the land of Canaan to bury him.

47 Esau heard this thing, and he was dwelling in mount Seir; he rose up with his sons and all his people and all his household, a people greatly great, and they came to mourn and weep over Jacob.

48 And it came to pass, when Esau came he mourned for his brother Jacob, and all Egypt and all Canaan again rose up and mourned a great mourning with Esau over Jacob in that place

49 Joseph and his brothers brought their father Jacob from that place, and they went to Hebron to bury Jacob in the cave by his fathers.

50 They came to Kireath-arba, to the cave, and as they came Esau stood with his sons against Joseph and his brothers as a hindrance in the cave, saying, Jacob shall not be buried in here, for it belongs to us and to our father.

51 Joseph and his brothers heard the words of Esau's sons, and they were greatly angered, and Joseph approached Esau, saying, What is this thing which they have spoken? Certainly my father Jacob bought it from you for great riches after the death of Isaac, now five and twenty years ago, and also all the land of Canaan he bought from you and from your sons, and your descendants after you.

52 Jacob bought it for his sons and his descendants after him for an inheritance for ever, and why do you speak these things this day?

53 And Esau answered, saying, You speak falsely and utter lies, for I sold not anything belonging to me in all this land, as you say, neither did my brother Jacob buy what belonged to me in this land.

54 Esau spoke these things in order to deceive Joseph with his words, for Esau knew that Joseph was not present in those days when Esau sold all belonging to him in the land of Canaan to Jacob.

55 Joseph said to Esau, Certainly my father inserted these things with you in the record of purchase, and testified the record with witnesses, and behold it is with us in Egypt.

56 Esau answered, saying to him, Bring the record; all that you will find in the record, so we will do.

57 Joseph called to Naphtali his brother and said, Hurry quickly, stay not, and run I pray you to Egypt and bring all the records; the record of the purchase, the sealed record and the open record, and also all the first records in

which all the transactions of the birthright are written, bring with you.

58 You shall bring them to us here, that we may know from them all the words of Esau and his sons which they spoke this day.

59 And Naphtali listened to the voice of Joseph and he hurried and ran to go down to Egypt, and Naphtali was lighter on foot than any of the stags that were on the wilderness, for he could go on ears of corn without crushing them.

60 When Esau saw that Naphtali had gone to fetch the records, he and his sons increased their resistance against the cave, and Esau and all his people rose up against Joseph and his brothers to battle.

61 All the sons of Jacob and the people of Egypt fought with Esau and his men, and the sons of Esau and his people were smitten before the sons of Jacob, and the sons of Jacob killed of Esau's people forty men.

62 Chushim the son of Dan, the son of Jacob, was at that time with Jacob's sons, but he was about a hundred cubits distant from the place of battle, for he remained with the children of Jacob's sons by Jacob's bier to guard it.

63 And Chushim was dumb and deaf, still he understood the voice of consternation among men.

64 And he asked, saying, Why do you not bury the dead, and what is this great consternation? They answered him the words of Esau and his sons and he ran to Esau in the midst of the battle; he killed Esau with a sword; he cut off his head and it sprang to a distance, and Esau fell among the people of the battle.

65 When Chushim did this thing the sons of Jacob prevailed over the sons of Esau, and the sons of Jacob buried their father Jacob by force in the cave, and the sons of Esau watched it.

66 Jacob was buried in Hebron, in the cave of Machpelah which Abraham had bought from the sons of Heth for the possession of a burial place, and he was buried in very costly garments.

67 No king had such honor paid him as Joseph paid to his father at his death, for he buried him with great honor like the burial of kings.

68 And Joseph and his brothers made a mourning of seven days for their father.

CHAPTER 57

1 It was after this that the sons of Esau waged war with the sons of Jacob, and the sons of Esau fought with the sons of Jacob in Hebron, and Esau was still lying dead and not buried.

2 The battle was heavy between them, and the sons of Esau were smitten before the sons of Jacob, and the sons of Jacob killed of the sons of Esau eighty men, and not one died of the people of the sons of Jacob; the hand of Joseph prevailed over all the people of the sons of Esau, and he took Zepho, the son of Eliphaz, the son of Esau, and fifty of his men captive; he bound them with chains of iron, and gave them into the hands of his servants to bring them to Egypt.

3 It came to pass when the sons of Jacob had taken Zepho and his people captive, all those that remained were greatly afraid for their lives from the house of Esau, that they should also be taken captive; they all fled with Eliphaz the son of Esau and his people, with Esau's body, and they went on their road to Mount Seir.

4 They came to Mount Seir and they buried Esau in Seir, but they had not brought his head with them to Seir, for it was buried in that place where the battle had been in Hebron.

5 And it came to pass when the sons of Esau had fled from before the sons of Jacob, the sons of Jacob pursued them to the borders of Seir, but they did not kill a single man from among them when they pursued them, for Esau's body which they carried with them increased their confusion. So they fled and the sons of Jacob turned back from them and came up to the place where their brothers were in Hebron, and they remained there on that day, and on the next day until they rested from the battle.

6 It came to pass on the third day they assembled all the sons of Seir the Horite, and they assembled all the children of the east, a multitude of people like the sand of the sea, and they went and came down to Egypt to fight with Joseph and his brothers in order to deliver their brothers.

7 Joseph and all the sons of Jacob heard that the sons of Esau and the children of the east had come on them to do battle in order to deliver their brothers.

8 Joseph and his brothers and the strong men of Egypt went forth and fought in the city of Rameses, and Joseph and his brothers dealt out a tremendous blow among the sons of Esau and the children of the east.

9 They killed of them six hundred thousand men, and they killed among them all the mighty men of the children of Seir the Horite; there were only a few of them left, and they killed also a great many of the children of the east, and of the children of Esau; Eliphaz the son of Esau, and the children of the east all fled before Joseph and his

brothers.

10 Joseph and his brothers pursued them until they came to Succoth, and they yet killed of them in Succoth thirty men, and the rest escaped and they fled each to his city.

11 And Joseph and his brothers and the mighty men of Egypt turned back from them with joy and cheerfulness of heart, for they had smitten all their enemies.

12 Zepho the son of Eliphaz and his men were still slaves in Egypt to the sons of Jacob, and their pains increased.

13 When the sons of Esau and the sons of Seir returned to their land, the sons of Seir saw that they had all fallen into the hands of the sons of Jacob and the people of Egypt, on account of the battle of the sons of Esau.

14 And the sons of Seir said to the sons of Esau, You have seen and therefore you know that this camp was on your account, and not one mighty man or an adept one in war remaineth.

15 So now go forth from our land, go from us to the land of Canaan to the land of the dwelling of your fathers; wherefore shall your children inherit the effects of our children in latter days?

16 And the children of Esau would not listen to the children of Seir, and the children of Seir considered to make war with them.

17 The children of Esau sent secretly to Angeas king of Africa, the same is Dinhabah, saying,

18 Send to us some of your men and let them come to us, and we will fight together with the children of Seir the Horite, for they have resolved to fight with us to drive us away from the land.

19 And Angeas king of Dinhabah did so, for he was in those days friendly to the children of Esau, and Angeas sent five hundred valiant infantry to the children of Esau, and eight hundred cavalry.

20 The children of Seir sent to the children of the east and to the children of Midian, saying, You have seen what the children of Esau have done to us, on whose account we are almost all destroyed in their battle with the sons of Jacob.

21 So now come to us and assist us, and we will fight them together; we will drive them from the land and be avenged of the cause of our brothers who died for their sakes in their battle with their brothers the sons of Jacob.

22 And all the children of the east listened to the children of Seir, and they came to them about eight hundred men with drawn swords, and the children of Esau fought with the children of Seir at that time in the wilderness of Paran.

23 The children of Seir won over the sons of Esau, and the children of Seir killed on that day of the children of Esau in that battle about two hundred men of the people of Angeas king of Dinhabah.

24 And on the second day the children of Esau came again to fight a second time with the children of Seir, and the battle was severe on the children of Esau this second time, and it troubled them greatly on account of the children of Seir.

25 And when the children of Esau saw that the children of Seir were more powerful than they were, some men of the children of Esau turned and assisted the children of Seir their enemies.

26 And there fell yet of the people of the children of Esau in the second battle fifty-eight men of the people at Angeas king of Dinhabah.

27 And on the third day the children of Esau heard that some of their brothers had turned from them to fight against them in the second battle; and the children of Esau mourned when they heard this thing.

28 They said, What shall we do to our brothers who turned from us to assist the children of Seir our enemies? And the children of Esau again sent to Angeas king of Dinhabah, saying,

29 Send to us again other men that with them we may fight with the children of Seir, for they have already twice been stronger than we were.

30 And Angeas again sent to the children of Esau about six hundred valiant men, and they came to assist the children of Esau.

31 In ten days' time the children of Esau again waged war with the children of Seir in the wilderness of Paran, and the battle was very severe on the children of Seir; the children of Esau won this time over the children of Seir, and the children of Seir were smitten before the children of Esau; the children of Esau killed from them about two thousand men.

32 And all the mighty men of the children of Seir died in this battle, and there only remained their young children that were left in their cities.

33 All Midian and the children of the east went themselves in flight from the battle, and they left the children of Seir and fled when they saw that the battle was severe on them; the children of Esau pursued all the children of the east until they reached their land.

34 And the children of Esau killed yet of them about two hundred and fifty men and from the people of the

children of Esau there fell in that battle about thirty men, but this evil came on them through their brothers turning from them to assist the children of Seir the Horite; the children of Esau again heard of the evil doings of their brothers, and they again mourned on account of this thing.

35 It came to pass after the battle, the children of Esau turned back and came home to Seir, and the children of Esau killed those who had remained in the land of the children of Seir; they killed also their wives and little ones, they left not a soul alive except fifty young boys and girls whom they allowed to live; the children of Esau did not put them to death, and the boys became their slaves, and the girls they took for wives.

36 The children of Esau lived in Seir in the place of the children of Seir, and they inherited their land and took possession of it.

37 And the children of Esau took all belonging in the land to the children of Seir, also their flocks, their bullocks and their goods, and all belonging to the children of Seir did the children of Esau take. And the children of Esau lived in Seir in the place of the children of Seir to this day, and the children of Esau divided the land into divisions to the five sons of Esau, according to their families.

38 It came to pass in those days that the children of Esau resolved to crown a king over them in the land of which they possessed. And they said to each other, Not so, for he shall reign over us in our land; we shall be under his counsel and he shall fight our battles against our enemies, and they did so.

39 And all the children of Esau swore, saying, that none of their brothers should ever reign over them, but a strange man who is not of their brothers; for the souls of all the children of Esau were embittered every man against his son, brother and friend, on account of the evil they sustained from their brothers when they fought with the children of Seir.

40 So then the sons of Esau swore, saying, from that day forward they would not choose a king from their brothers, but one from a strange land to this day.

41 There was a man there from the people of Angeas king of Dinhabah; his name was Bela the son of Beor, who was a very valiant man, beautiful and admired and wise in all wisdom, and a man of sense and counsel; and there was none of the people of Angeas like him.

42 And all the children of Esau took him and anointed him and they crowned him for a king; they bowed down to him, and said, May the king live, may the king live.

43 They spread out the sheet, and they brought him each man earrings of gold and silver or rings or bracelets, and they made him very rich in silver and in gold, in onyx stones and bdellium, and they made him a royal throne; they placed a regal crown on his head and they built a palace for him and he lived therein, and he became king over all the children of Esau.

44 And the people of Angeas took their wages for their battle from the children of Esau, and they went and returned at that time to their master in Dinhabah.

45 And Bela reigned over the children of Esau thirty years, and the children of Esau lived in the land instead of the children of Seir, and they lived securely in their stead to this day.

CHAPTER 58

1 It came to pass in the thirty-second year of the Israelites going down to Egypt, that is in the seventy-first year of the life of Joseph, in that year died Pharaoh king of Egypt, and Magron his son reigned in his stead.

2 And Pharaoh commanded Joseph before his death to be a father to his son, Magron, and that Magron should be under the care of Joseph and under his counsel.

3 All Egypt consented to this thing that Joseph should be king over them, for all the Egyptians loved Joseph as before, only Magron the son of Pharaoh sat on his father's throne, and he became king in those days in his father's stead.

4 Magron was forty-one years old when he began to reign, and forty years he reigned in Egypt, and all Egypt called his name Pharaoh after the name of his father, as it was their custom to do in Egypt to every king that reigned over them.

5 And it came to pass when Pharaoh reigned in his father's stead, he placed the laws of Egypt and all the affairs of government in the hand of Joseph, as his father had commanded him.

6 Joseph became king over Egypt, for he superintended over all Egypt, and all Egypt was under his care and under his counsel, for all Egypt inclined to Joseph after the death of Pharaoh; they loved him greatly to reign over them.

7 But there were some people among them who did not like him, saying, No stranger shall reign over us. Still the whole government of Egypt was passed in those days onto Joseph, after the death of Pharaoh, he being the regulator, doing as he liked throughout the land without anyone interfering.

8 And all Egypt was under the care of Joseph, and Joseph made war with all his surrounding enemies, and he subdued them; also all the land and all the Philistines, to the borders of Canaan, did Joseph subdue; they were all under his power and they gave a yearly tax to Joseph.

9 Pharaoh king of Egypt sat on his throne in his father's stead, but he was under the control and counsel of Joseph, as he was at first under the control of his father.

10 Neither did he reign but in the land of Egypt only, under the counsel of Joseph, but Joseph reigned over the whole country at that time, from Egypt to the great river Perath.

11 And Joseph was successful in all his ways and the Lord was with him, and the Lord gave Joseph additional wisdom, and honor, and glory, and love toward him in the hearts of the Egyptians and throughout the land; Joseph reigned over the whole country forty years.

12 And all the countries of the Philistines and Canaan and Zidon, and on the other side of Jordan, brought presents to Joseph all his days, and the whole country was in the hands of Joseph, and they brought to him a yearly tribute as it was regulated, for Joseph had fought against all his surrounding enemies and subdued them; the whole country was in the hands of Joseph, and Joseph sat securely on his throne in Egypt.

13 Also all his brothers the sons of Jacob lived securely in the land, all the days of Joseph, and they were prolific and multiplied greatly in the land; they served the Lord all their days as their father Jacob had commanded them.

14 It came to pass at the end of many days and years, when the children of Esau were dwelling quietly in their land with Bela their king, that the children of Esau were prolific and multiplied in the land; they resolved to go and fight with the sons of Jacob and all Egypt, and to deliver their brother Zepho, the son of Eliphaz, and his men, for they were yet in those days slaves to Joseph.

15 The children of Esau sent to all the children of the east and they made peace with them, and all the children of the east came to them to go with the children of Esau to Egypt to battle.

16 There came also to them of the people of Angeas, king of Dinhabah; they also sent to the children of Ishmael and they also came to them.

17 And all this people assembled and came to Seir to assist the children of Esau in their battle, and this camp was very large and strong with people, numerous as the sand of the sea, about eight hundred thousand men, infantry and cavalry, and all these troops went down to Egypt to fight with the sons of Jacob; they encamped by Rameses.

18 And Joseph went forth with his brothers with the mighty men of Egypt, about six hundred men, and they fought with them in the land of Rameses; the sons of Jacob at that time again fought with the children of Esau, in the fiftieth year of the sons of Jacob going down to Egypt, that is the thirtieth year of the reign of Bela over the children of Esau in Seir.

19 And the Lord gave all the mighty men of Esau and the children of the east into the hand of Joseph and his brothers, and the people of the children of Esau and the children of the east were smitten before Joseph.

20 Of the people of Esau and the children of the east that were slain, there fell before the sons of Jacob about two hundred thousand men, and their king Bela the son of Beor fell with them in the battle. When the children of Esau saw that their king had fallen in battle and was dead, their hands became weak in the combat.

21 Joseph and his brothers and all Egypt were still smiting the people of the house of Esau, and all Esau's people were afraid of the sons of Jacob and fled from before them.

22 Joseph and his brothers and all Egypt pursued them a day's journey, and they killed yet from them about three hundred men, continuing to strike them in the road; they afterward turned back from them.

23 Joseph and all his brothers returned to Egypt, not one man was missing from them, but of the Egyptians there fell twelve men.

24 And when Joseph returned to Egypt he ordered Zepho and his men to be additionally bound, and they bound them in irons and they increased their grief.

25 All the people of the children of Esau, and the children of the east, returned in shame each to his city, for all the mighty men that were with them had fallen in battle.

26 When the children of Esau saw that their king had died in battle they hurried and took a man from the people of the children of the east; his name was Jobab the son of Zarach, from the land of Botzrah, and they caused him to reign over them instead of Bela their king.

27 Jobab sat on the throne of Bela as king in his stead, and Jobab reigned in Edom over all the children of Esau ten years; the children of Esau went no more to fight with the sons of Jacob from that day forward, for the sons of

Esau knew the courage of the sons of Jacob, and they were greatly afraid of them.

28 But from that day forward the children of Esau hated the sons of Jacob, and the hatred and enmity were very strong between them all the days, to this day.

29 And it came to pass after this, at the end of ten years, Jobab, the son of Zarach, from Botzrah, died, and the children of Esau took a man whose name was Chusham, from the land of Teman, and they made him king over them instead of Jobab; Chusham reigned in Edom over all the children of Esau for twenty years.

30 And Joseph, king of Egypt, and his brothers, and all the children of Israel lived securely in Egypt in those days, together with all the children of Joseph and his brothers, having no hindrance or evil accident and the land of Egypt was at that time at rest from war in the days of Joseph and his brothers.

CHAPTER 59

1 These are the names of the sons of Israel who lived in Egypt, who had come with Jacob; all the sons of Jacob came to Egypt, every man with his household.

2 The children of Leah were Reuben, Simeon, Levi, Judah, Issachar and Zebulun, and their sister Dinah.

3 And the sons of Rachel were Joseph and Benjamin.

4 And the sons of Zilpah, the handmaid of Leah, were Gad and Asher.

5 And the sons of Bilhah, the handmaid of Rachel, were Dan and Naphtali.

6 And these were their descendants that were born to them in the land of Canaan, before they came to Egypt with their father Jacob:

7 The sons of Reuben were Chanoch, Pallu, Chetzron and Carmi.

8 And the sons of Simeon were Jemuel, Jamin, Ohad, Jachin, Zochar and Saul, the son of the Canaanitish woman.

9 And the children of Levi were Gershon, Kehath and Merari, and their sister Jochebed, who was born to them in their going down to Egypt.

10 And the sons of Judah were Er, Onan, Shelah, Perez and Zarach.

11 And Er and Onan died in the land of Canaan; and the sons of Perez were Chezron and Chamul.

12 And the sons of Issachar were Tola, Puvah, Job and Shomron.

13 And the sons of Zebulun were Sered, Elon and Jachleel, and the son of Dan was Chushim.

14 And the sons of Naphtali were Jachzeel, Guni, Jetzer and Shilam.

15 And the sons of Gad were Ziphion, Chaggi, Shuni, Ezbon, Eri, Arodi and Areli.

16 And the children of Asher were Jimnah, Jishvah, Jishvi, Beriah and their sister Serach; and the sons of Beriah were Cheber and Malchiel.

17 And the sons of Benjamin were Bela, Becher, Ashbel, Gera, Naaman, Achi, Rosh, Mupim, Chupim and Ord.

18 And the sons of Joseph that were born to him in Egypt were Manasseh and Ephraim.

19 All the souls that went forth from the loins of Jacob were seventy souls; these are they who came with Jacob their father to Egypt to dwell there: and Joseph and all his brothers lived securely in Egypt, and they ate of the best of Egypt all the days of the life of Joseph.

20 And Joseph lived in the land of Egypt ninety-three years, and Joseph reigned over all Egypt eighty years.

21 When the days of Joseph drew near that he should die, he sent and called for his brothers and all his father's household, and they all came together and sat before him.

22 Joseph said to his brothers and all of his father's household, Behold I die, and God will certainly visit you and bring you up from this land to the land which he swore to your fathers to give to them.

23 And it shall be when God shall visit you to bring you up from here to the land of your fathers, then bring up my bones with you from here.

24 Joseph made the sons of Israel to swear for their descendants after them, saying, God will certainly visit you and you shall bring up my bones with you from here.

25 And it came to pass after this that Joseph died in that year, the seventy-first year of the Israelites going down to Egypt.

26 And Joseph was one hundred and ten years old when he died in the land of Egypt, and all his brothers and all his servants rose up and they embalmed Joseph, as was their custom, and his brothers and all Egypt mourned over him for seventy days.

27 And they put Joseph in a coffin filled with spices and all sorts of perfume; they buried him by the side of the river, that is Sihor, and his sons and all his brothers, and the whole of his father's household made a seven day's

mourning for him.

28 It came to pass after the death of Joseph, all the Egyptians began in those days to rule over the children of Israel; Pharaoh, king of Egypt, who reigned in his father's stead, took all the laws of Egypt and conducted the whole government of Egypt under his counsel, and he reigned securely over his people.

CHAPTER 60

1 And when the year came round, being the seventy-second year from the Israelites going down to Egypt, after the death of Joseph, Zepho the son of Eliphaz, the son of Esau, fled from Egypt, he and his men, and they went away.

2 And he came to Africa, which is Dinhabah, to Angeas king of Africa; Angeas received them with great honor, and he made Zepho the captain of his host.

3 And Zepho found favor in the sight of Angeas and in the sight of his people, and Zepho was captain of the host to Angeas king of Africa for many days.

4 Zepho enticed Angeas king of Africa to collect all his army to go and fight with the Egyptians, and with the sons of Jacob, and to avenge of them the cause of his brothers.

5 But Angeas would not listen to Zepho to do this thing, for Angeas knew the strength of the sons of Jacob, and what they had done to his army in their warfare with the children of Esau.

6 And Zepho was in those days very great in the sight of Angeas and in the sight of all his people, and he continually enticed them to make war against Egypt, but they would not.

7 It came to pass in those days there was in the land of Chittim a man in the city of Puzimna, whose name was Uzu, and he became degenerately deified by the children of Chittim; the man died and had no son, only one daughter whose name was Jania.

8 And the girl was greatly beautiful, admired and intelligent, there was none seen like her for beauty and wisdom throughout the land.

9 And the people of Angeas king of Africa saw her and they came and praised her to him; Angeas sent to the children of Chittim, and he requested to take her to himself for a wife, and the people of Chittim consented to give her to him for a wife.

10 When the messengers of Angeas were going forth from the land of Chittim to take their journey, behold the messengers of Turnus king of Bibentu came to Chittim, for Turnus king of Bibentu also sent his messengers to request Jania for him, to take to himself for a wife, for all his men had also praised her to him, therefore he sent all his servants to her.

11 The servants of Turnus came to Chittim, and they asked for Jania, to be taken to Turnus their king for a wife.

12 The people of Chittim said to them, We cannot give her, because Angeas king of Africa desired her to take her to him for a wife before you came, and that we should give her to him; now therefore we cannot do this thing to deprive Angeas of the girl in order to give her to Turnus.

13 For we are greatly afraid of Angeas that he come in battle against us and destroy us, and Turnus your master will not be able to deliver us from his hands.

14 When the messengers of Turnus heard all the words of the children of Chittim, they turned back to their master and told him all the words of the children of Chittim.

15 And the children of Chittim sent a memorial to Angeas, saying, Behold Turnus has sent for Jania to take her to him for a wife, and thus have we answered him; we heard that he has collected his whole army to go to war against you, and he intends to pass by the road of Sardunia to fight against your brother Lucus, and after that he will come to fight against you.

16 Angeas heard the words of the children of Chittim which they sent to him in the record, and his anger was set ablaze and he rose up and assembled his whole army and came through the islands of the sea, the road to Sardunia, to his brother Lucus king of Sardunia.

17 Niblos, the son of Lucus, heard that his uncle Angeas was coming, and he went out to meet him with a heavy army, and he kissed him and embraced him, and Niblos said to Angeas, When you ask my father after his welfare, when I shall go with you to fight with Turnus, ask of him to make me captain of his host. Angeas did so, and he came to his brother and his brother came to meet him, and he asked him after his welfare.

18 And Angeas asked his brother Lucus after his welfare, and to make his son Niblos captain of his host, and Lucus did so; Angeas and his brother Lucus rose up and they went toward Turnus to battle, and there was with

them a great army and a strong people.

19 And he came in ships, and they came into the province of Ashtorash, and behold Turnus came toward them, for he went forth to Sardunia, and intended to destroy it and afterward to pass on from there to Angeas to fight with him.

20 Angeas and Lucus his brother met Turnus in the valley of Canopia, and the battle was strong and mighty between them in that place.

21 And the battle was severe on Lucus king of Sardunia, and all his army fell, and Niblos his son fell also in that battle.

22 And his uncle Angeas commanded his servants and they made a golden coffin for Niblos and they put him into it, and Angeas again waged battle toward Turnus; Angeas was stronger than he, and he killed him, and he struck all his people with the edge of the sword, and Angeas avenged the cause of Niblos his brother's son and the cause of the army of his brother Lucus.

23 And when Turnus died, the hands of those that survived the battle became weak, and they fled from before Angeas and Lucus his brother.

24 Angeas and his brother Lucus pursued them to the highroad, which is between Alphanu and Romah, and they killed the whole army of Turnus with the edge of the sword.

25 Lucus king of Sardunia commanded his servants that they should make a coffin of brass, and that they should place therein the body of his son Niblos, and they buried him in that place.

26 And they built on it a high tower there on the highroad, and they called its name after the name of Niblos to this day; they also buried Turnus king of Bibentu there in that place with Niblos.

27 And so on the highroad between Alphanu and Romah the grave of Niblos is on one side and the grave of Turnus on the other, and a pavement is between them to this day.

28 When Niblos was buried, Lucus his father returned with his army to his land Sardunia, and Angeas his brother king of Africa went with his people to the city of Bibentu, that is the city of Turnus.

29 And the inhabitants of Bibentu heard of his fame and they were greatly afraid of him; they went forth to meet him with weeping and supplication, and the inhabitants of Bibentu entreated of Angeas not to kill them nor destroy their city; he did so, for Bibentu was in those days reckoned as one of the cities of the children of Chittim; so he did not destroy the city.

30 But from that day forward the troops of the king of Africa would go to Chittim to wreck and rob it, and whenever they went, Zepho the captain of the host of Angeas would go with them.

31 It was after this that Angeas turned with his army and they came to the city of Puzimna, and Angeas then took Jania the daughter of Uzu for a wife and brought her to his city to Africa.

CHAPTER 61

1 It came to pass at that time Pharaoh king of Egypt commanded all his people to make for him a strong palace in Egypt.

2 And he also commanded the sons of Jacob to assist the Egyptians in the building, and the Egyptians made a beautiful and elegant palace for a royal habitation; he lived there and he renewed his government and he reigned securely.

3 And Zebulun the son of Jacob died in that year, that is the seventy-second year of the going down of the Israelites to Egypt; Zebulun died a hundred and fourteen years old and was put into a coffin and given into the hands of his children.

4 And in the seventy-fifth year his brother Simeon died; he was a hundred and twenty years old at his death, and he was also put into a coffin and given into the hands of his children.

5 Zepho the son of Eliphaz the son of Esau, captain of the host to Angeas king of Dinhabah, was still daily enticing Angeas to prepare for battle to fight with the sons of Jacob in Egypt; Angeas was unwilling to do this thing, for his servants had related to him all the might of the sons of Jacob, what they had done to them in their battle with the children of Esau.

6 And Zepho was in those days daily enticing Angeas to fight with the sons of Jacob.

7 After some time Angeas listened to the words of Zepho and consented to him to fight with the sons of Jacob in

Egypt, and Angeas got all his people in order, a people numerous as the sand which is on the seashore, and he formed his resolution to go to Egypt to battle.

8 Among the servants of Angeas was a youth fifteen years old, Balaam the son of Beor was his name and the youth was very wise and understood the art of witchcraft.

9 And Angeas said to Balaam, Summon for us, I pray you, with the witchcraft, that we may know who will succeed in this battle to which we are now proceeding.

10 And Balaam ordered that they should bring him wax, and he made thereof the likeness of chariots and horsemen representing the army of Angeas and the army of Egypt; he put them in the cunningly prepared waters that he had for that purpose, and he took in his hand the boughs of myrtle trees, and he exercised his cunning; he joined them over the water, and there appeared to him in the water the resembling images of the hosts of Angeas falling before the resembling images of the Egyptians and the sons of Jacob.

11 Balaam told this thing to Angeas, and Angeas despaired and did not arm himself to go down to Egypt to battle, and he remained in his city.

12 And when Zepho the son of Eliphaz saw that Angeas despaired of going forth to battle with the Egyptians, Zepho fled from Angeas from Africa, and he went and came to Chittim.

13 And all the people of Chittim received him with great honor, and they hired him to fight their battles all the days; Zepho became greatly rich in those days, and the troops of the king of Africa still spread themselves in those days; the children of Chittim assembled and went to Mount Cuptizia on account of the troops of Angeas king of Africa who were advancing on them.

14 It was one day that Zepho lost a young heifer and he went to seek it, and he heard it lowing round about the mountain.

15 Zepho went and he saw that there was a large cave at the bottom of the mountain, and there was a great stone there at the entrance of the cave; Zepho split the stone and he came into the cave and he looked and there a large animal was devouring the ox; from the middle upward it resembled a man, and from the middle downward it resembled an animal, and Zepho rose up against the animal and killed it with his swords.

16 The inhabitants of Chittim heard of this thing, and they rejoiced greatly, and said, What shall we do to this man who has slain this animal that devoured our cattle?

17 And they all assembled to consecrate one day in the year to him, and they called the name thereof Zepho after his name; they brought to him drink offerings year after year on that day, and they brought to him gifts.

18 At that time Jania the daughter of Uzu wife of king Angeas became ill, and her illness was heavily felt by Angeas and his officers, and Angeas said to his wise men, What shall I do to Jania and how shall I heal her from her illness? And his wise men said to him, Because the air of our country is not like the air of the land of Chittim, and our water is not like their water, therefore from this has the queen become ill.

19 For through the change of air and water she became ill, and also because in her country she drank only the water which came from Purmah, which her ancestors had brought up with bridges.

20 And Angeas commanded his servants, and they brought to him in vessels of the waters of Purmah belonging to Chittim, and they weighed those waters with all the waters of the land of Africa, and they found those waters lighter than the waters of Africa.

21 Angeas saw this thing, and he commanded all his officers to assemble the hewers of stone in thousands and tens of thousands, and they hewed stone without number; the builders came and they built a greatly strong bridge and they conveyed the spring of water from the land of Chittim to Africa, and those waters were for Jania the queen and for all her concerns, to drink from and to bake, wash and bathe with, and also to water all offspring from which food can be obtained, and all fruit of the ground.

22 And the king commanded that they should bring of the soil of Chittim in large ships, and they also brought stones to build there; the builders built palaces for Jania the queen, and the queen became healed of her illness.

23 And at the revolution of the year the troops of Africa continued coming to the land of Chittim to rob as usual, and Zepho son of Eliphaz heard their report; he gave orders concerning them and he fought with them and they fled before him, and he delivered the land of Chittim from them.

24 And the children of Chittim saw the bravery of Zepho, and the children of Chittim resolved and made Zepho king over them; he became king over them and while he reigned they went to subdue the children of Tubal, and all the surrounding islands.

25 Their king Zepho led them and they made war with Tubal and the islands, and they subdued them; when they returned from the battle they renewed his government for him, and they built for him a very large palace for his royal habitation and seat, and they made a large throne for him; Zepho reigned over the whole land of Chittim

and over the land of Italia fifty years.

CHAPTER 62

1 In that year, being the seventy-ninth year of the Israelites going down to Egypt, Reuben the son of Jacob died, in the land of Egypt; Reuben was a hundred and twenty-five years old when he died and they put him into a coffin, and he was given into the hands of his children.
2 In the eightieth year his brother Dan died; he was a hundred and twenty years at his death, and he was also put into a coffin and given into the hands of his children.
3 In that year Chusham king of Edom died, and after him reigned Hadad the son of Bedad, for thirty-five years; in the eighty-first year Issachar the son of Jacob died in Egypt, and Issachar was a hundred and twenty-two years old at his death; he was put into a coffin in Egypt, and given into the hands of his children.
4 In the eighty-second year Asher his brother died, he was a hundred and twenty-three years old at his death, and he was placed in a coffin in Egypt and given into the hands of his children.
5 In the eighty-third year Gad died; he was a hundred and twenty-five years old at his death, and he was put into a coffin in Egypt and given into the hands of his children.
6 And it came to pass in the eighty-fourth year, that is the fiftieth year of the reign of Hadad, son of Bedad, king of Edom, that Hadad assembled all the children of Esau; he got his whole army in readiness, about four hundred thousand men, and he directed his way to the land of Moab; he went to fight with Moab and to make them subordinate to him.
7 The children of Moab heard this thing, and they were very much afraid; they sent to the children of Midian to assist them in fighting with Hadad, son of Bedad, king of Edom.
8 And Hadad came to the land of Moab, and Moab and the children of Midian went out to meet him; they placed themselves in battle array against him in the field of Moab.
9 Hadad fought with Moab, and there fell of the children of Moab and the children of Midian many slain ones, about two hundred thousand men.
10 The battle was very severe on Moab, and when the children of Moab saw that the battle was so severe, they weakened their hands and turned their backs, and left the children of Midian to carry on the battle.
11 And the children of Midian knew not the intentions of Moab, but they strengthened themselves in battle and fought with Hadad and all his army, and all Midian fell before him.
12 Hadad struck all Midian with a heavy smiting, and he killed them with the edge of the sword, he left none remaining of those who came to assist Moab.
13 When all the children of Midian had perished in battle, and the children at Moab had escaped, Hadad made all Moab at that time subservient to him, and they became under his hand; they gave a yearly tax as it was ordered, and Hadad turned and went back to his land.
14 At the revolution of the year, when the rest of the people of Midian that were in the land heard that all their brothers had fallen in battle with Hadad for the sake of Moab, because the children of Moab had turned their backs in battle and left Midian to fight, then five of the princes of Midian resolved with the rest of their brothers who remained in their land to fight with Moab to avenge the cause of their brothers.
15 The children of Midian sent to all their brothers the children of the east, and all their brothers, all the children of Keturah came to assist Midian to fight with Moab.
16 The children of Moab heard this thing, and they were greatly afraid that all the children of the east had assembled together against them for battle, and they the children of Moab sent a memorial to the land of Edom to Hadad the son of Bedad, saying,
17 Come now to us and assist us and we will strike Midian, for they all assembled together and have come against us with all their brothers the children of the east to battle, to avenge the cause of Midian that fell in battle.
18 Hadad, son of Bedad, king of Edom, went forth with his whole army and went to the land of Moab to fight with Midian, and Midian and the children of the east fought with Moab in the field of Moab, and the battle was very fierce between them.
19 Hadad struck all the children of Midian and the children of the east with the edge of the sword, and Hadad at that time delivered Moab from the hand of Midian; those that remained of Midian and of the children of the east fled before Hadad and his army, and Hadad pursued them to their land and struck them with a very heavy slaughter, and the slain fell in the road.

20 Hadad delivered Moab from the hand of Midian, for all the children of Midian had fallen by the edge of the sword, and Hadad turned and went back to his land.

21 And from that day forth, the children of Midian hated the children of Moab because they had fallen in battle for their sake, and there was a great and mighty enmity between them all the days.

22 And all that were found of Midian in the road of the land of Moab perished by the sword of Moab, and all that were found of Moab in the road of the land of Midian, perished by the sword of Midian; thus did Midian to Moab and Moab to Midian for many days.

23 It came to pass at that time that Judah the son of Jacob died in Egypt, in the eighty-sixth year of Jacob's going down to Egypt, and Judah was a hundred and twenty-nine years old at his death, and they embalmed him and put him into a coffin, and he was given into the hands of his children.

24 And in the eighty-ninth year Naphtali died; he was a hundred and thirty-two years old, and he was put into a coffin and given into the hands of his children.

25 It came to pass in the ninety-first year of the Israelites going down to Egypt, that is in the thirtieth year of the reign of Zepho the son of Eliphaz, the son of Esau, over the children of Chittim, the children of Africa came upon the children of Chittim to rob them as usual, but they had not come on them for these thirteen years.

26 They came to them in that year, and Zepho the son of Eliphaz went out to them with some of his men and struck them desperately, and the troops of Africa fled from before Zepho and the slain fell before him, and Zepho and his men pursued them, going on and smiting them until they were near to Africa.

27 And Angeas king of Africa heard the thing which Zepho had done, and it troubled him greatly, and Angeas was afraid of Zepho all the days.

CHAPTER 63

1 In the ninety-third year Levi, the son of Jacob, died in Egypt, and Levi was a hundred and thirty-seven years old when he died; they put him into a coffin and he was given into the hands of his children.

2 It came to pass after the death of Levi, when all Egypt saw that the sons of Jacob the brothers of Joseph were dead, all the Egyptians began to afflict the children of Jacob, and to embitter their lives from that day to the day of their going forth from Egypt. They took from their hands all the vineyards and fields which Joseph had given to them, and all the elegant houses in which the people of Israel lived, and all the valuables of Egypt, the Egyptians took all from the sons of Jacob in those days.

3 And the hand of all Egypt became more heavy in those days against the children of Israel, and the Egyptians injured the Israelites until the children of Israel were wearied of their lives on account of the Egyptians.

4 It came to pass in those days, in the hundred and second year of Israel's going down to Egypt, that Pharaoh king of Egypt died, and Melol his son reigned in his stead; all the mighty men of Egypt and all that generation which knew Joseph and his brothers died in those days.

5 And another generation rose up in their stead, which had not known the sons of Jacob and all the good which they had done to them, and all their might in Egypt.

6 And so all Egypt began from that day on to embitter the lives of the sons of Jacob, and to afflict them with all manner of hard labor, because they had not known their ancestors who had delivered them in the days of the famine.

7 This was also from the Lord for the children of Israel, to benefit them in their latter days in order that all the children of Israel might know the Lord their God.

8 And in order to know the signs and mighty wonders which the Lord would do in Egypt on account of his people Israel, in order that the children of Israel might fear the Lord God of their ancestors, and walk in all his ways, they and their descendants after them all the days.

9 Melol was twenty years old when he began to reign, and he reigned ninety-four years, and all Egypt called his name Pharaoh after the name of his father, as it was their custom to do to every king who reigned over them in Egypt.

10 At that time all the troops of Angeas king of Africa went forth to scatter along the land of Chittim as usual for robbery.

11 Zepho the son of Eliphaz the son of Esau heard their report, and he went forth to meet them with his army, and he fought them there in the road.

12 Zepho struck the troops of the king of Africa with the edge of the sword, and left none remaining of them, and

not even one returned to his master in Africa.

13 Angeas heard of this which Zepho the son of Eliphaz had done to all his troops, that he had destroyed them, and Angeas assembled all his troops, all the men of the land of Africa, a people numerous like the sand by the seashore.

14 And Angeas sent to Lucus his brother, saying, Come to me with all your men and help me to strike Zepho and all the children of Chittim who have destroyed my men; Lucus came with his whole army, a very great force, to assist Angeas his brother to fight with Zepho and the children of Chittim.

15 Zepho and the children of Chittim heard this thing, and they were greatly afraid and a great terror fell on their hearts.

16 Zepho also sent a letter to the land of Edom to Hadad the son of Bedad king of Edom and to all the children of Esau, saying,

17 I have heard that Angeas king of Africa is coming to us with his brother for battle against us, and we are greatly afraid of him, for his army is very great, particularly as he comes against us with his brother and his army likewise.

18 Now therefore come up also with me and help me, and we will fight together against Angeas and his brother Lucus, and you will save us out of their hands, but if not, know that we shall all die.

19 And the children of Esau sent a letter to the children of Chittim and to Zepho their king, saying, We cannot fight against Angeas and his people for a covenant of peace has been between us these many years, from the days of Bela the first king, and from the days of Joseph the son of Jacob king of Egypt with whom we fought on the other side of Jordan when he buried his father.

20 When Zepho heard the words of his brothers the children of Esau, he refrained from them, and Zepho was greatly afraid of Angeas.

21 And Angeas and Lucus his brother arrayed all their forces, about eight hundred thousand men, against the children of Chittim.

22 And all the children of Chittim said to Zepho, Pray for us to the God of your ancestors, perhaps he may deliver us from the hand of Angeas and his army, for we have heard that he is a great God and that he delivers all who trust in him.

23 Zepho heard their words, and Zepho sought the Lord and he said,

24 0 Lord God of Abraham and Isaac my ancestors, this day I know that you are a true God, and all the gods of the nations are vain and useless.

25 Remember now this day to me your covenant with Abraham our father, which our ancestors related to us, and do graciously with me this day for the sake of Abraham and Isaac our fathers; save me and the children of Chittim from the hand of the king of Africa who comes against us for battle.

26 And the Lord listened to the voice of Zepho, and he had regard for him on account of Abraham and Isaac, and the Lord delivered Zepho and the children of Chittim from the hand of Angeas and his people.

27 Zepho fought Angeas king of Africa and all his people on that day, and the Lord gave all the people of Angeas into the hands of the children of Chittim.

28 The battle was severe on Angeas, and Zepho struck all the men of Angeas and Lucus his brother with the edge of the sword, and there fell from them to the evening of that day about four hundred thousand men.

29 When Angeas saw that all his men perished, he sent a letter to all the inhabitants of Africa to come to him, to assist him in the battle, and he wrote in the letter, saying, All who are found in Africa let them come to me from ten years old and upward; let them all come to me, and behold if he comes not he shall die; all that he has, with his whole household, the king will take.

30 All the rest of the inhabitants of Africa were terrified at the words of Angeas, and there went out of the city about three hundred thousand men and boys, from ten years upward, and they came to Angeas.

31 And at the end of ten days Angeas renewed the battle against Zepho and the children of Chittim, and the battle was very great and strong between them.

32 And from the army of Angeas and Lucus, Zepho sent many of the wounded to him about two thousand men, and Sosiphtar the captain of the host of Angeas fell in that battle.

33 And when Sosiphtar had fallen, the African troops turned their backs to flee; they fled, and Angeas and Lucus his brother were with them.

34 Zepho and the children of Chittim pursued them, and they struck them still heavily on the road, about two hundred men; they pursued Azrubal the son of Angeas who had fled with his father, and they struck twenty of his men in the road, and Azrubal escaped from the children of Chittim, and they did not kill him.

35 Angeas and Lucus his brother fled with the rest of their men, and they escaped and came into Africa with terror and consternation, and Angeas feared all the days that Zepho the son of Eliphaz would go to war with him.

CHAPTER 64

1 Balaam the son of Beor was at that time with Angeas in the battle, and when he saw that Zepho conquered over Angeas, he fled from there and came to Chittim.

2 And Zepho and the children of Chittim received him with great honor, for Zepho knew Balaam's wisdom, and Zepho gave to Balaam many gifts and he remained with him.

3 When Zepho had returned from the war, he commanded all the children of Chittim to be numbered who had gone into battle with him, and there not one was missing.

4 Zepho rejoiced at this thing, and he renewed his kingdom, and he made a feast to all his subjects.

5 But Zepho remembered not the Lord and considered not that the Lord had helped him in battle, and that he had delivered him and his people from the hand of the king of Africa; he still walked in the ways of the children of Chittim and the wicked children of Esau to serve other gods which his brothers the children of Esau had taught him; it is therefore said, From the wicked goes forth wickedness.

6 Zepho reigned over all the children of Chittim securely, but knew not the Lord who had delivered him and all his people from the hand of the king of Africa; the troops of Africa came no more to Chittim to rob as usual, for they knew the power of Zepho who had smitten them all at the edge of the sword, so Angeas was afraid of Zepho the son of Eliphaz and the children of Chittim all the days.

7 At that time when Zepho had returned from the war, and when Zepho had seen how he conquered over all the people of Africa and had smitten them in battle at the edge of the sword, then Zepho advised with the children of Chittim to go to Egypt to fight with the sons of Jacob and with Pharaoh king of Egypt.

8 For Zepho heard that the mighty men of Egypt were dead and that Joseph and his brothers the sons of Jacob were dead, and that all their children, the children of Israel, remained in Egypt.

9 Zepho considered to go to fight against them and all Egypt to avenge the cause of his brothers the children of Esau, whom Joseph with his brothers and all Egypt had smitten in the land of Canaan, when they went up to bury Jacob in Hebron.

10 And Zepho sent messengers to Hadad, son of Bedad, king of Edom, and to all his brothers the children of Esau, saying,

11 Did you say that you would not fight against the king of Africa for he is a member of your covenant? Consider that I fought with him and struck him and all his people.

12 Now therefore I have resolved to fight against Egypt and the children of Jacob who are there, and I will be revenged of them for what Joseph, his brothers and ancestors did to us in the land of Canaan when they went up to bury their father in Hebron.

13 Now then if you are willing to come to me to assist me in fighting against them and Egypt, we shall avenge the cause of our brothers.

14 And the children of Esau listened to the words of Zepho, and the children of Esau gathered themselves together, a very great people; they went to assist Zepho and the children of Chittim in battle.

15 Zepho sent to all the children of the east and to all the children of Ishmael with words like these, and they gathered themselves and came to the assistance of Zepho and the children of Chittim in the war on Egypt.

16 And all these kings, the king of Edom and the children of the east, and all the children of Ishmael, and Zepho the king of Chittim went forth and arrayed all their hosts in Hebron.

17 The camp was very large, extending in length a distance of three days' journey, a people numerous as the sand on the seashore which cannot be counted.

18 And all these kings and their hosts went down and came against all Egypt in battle, and encamped together in the valley of Pathros.

19 All Egypt heard their report and they also gathered themselves together, all the people of the land of Egypt, and of all the cities belonging to Egypt about three hundred thousand men.

20 The men of Egypt sent also to the children of Israel who were in those days in the land of Goshen, to come to them in order to go and fight with these kings.

21 The men of Israel assembled and were about one hundred and fifty men, and they went into battle to assist the Egyptians.

22 The men of Israel and of Egypt went forth, about three hundred thousand men and one hundred and fifty men, and they went toward these kings to battle; they placed themselves outside the land of Goshen opposite Pathros.

23 The Egyptians believed not in Israel to go with them in their camps together for battle, for all the Egyptians said, Perhaps the children of Israel will deliver us into the hand of the children of Esau and Ishmael, for they are their brothers.

24 And all the Egyptians said to the children of Israel, Remain here together in your stand and we will go and fight against the children of Esau and Ishmael; if these kings should gain over us, then you all come together on them and assist us, and the children of Israel did so.

25 Zepho the son of Eliphaz the son of Esau king of Chittim and Hadad the son of Bedad king of Edom and all their camps, and all the children of the east, and children of Ishmael, a people numerous as sand, encamped together in the valley of Pathros opposite Tachpanches.

26 Balaam the son of Beor the Syrian was there in the camp of Zepho, for he came with the children of Chittim to the battle, and Balaam was a man highly honored in the eyes of Zepho and his men.

27 Zepho said to Balaam, Try by divination for us that we may know who will win the battle, we or the Egyptians.

28 And Balaam rose up and tried the art of divination, and he was skillful in the knowledge of it, but he was confused and the work was destroyed in his hand.

29 And he tried it again but it did not succeed; Balaam despaired of it and left it and did not complete it, for this was from the Lord in order to cause Zepho and his people to fall into the hand of the children of Israel, who had trusted in the Lord, the God of their ancestors, in their war.

30 Zepho and Hadad put their forces in battle array, and all the Egyptians went alone against them, about three hundred thousand men, and not one man of Israel was with them.

31 All the Egyptians fought with these kings opposite Pathros and Tachpanches, and the battle was severe against the Egyptians.

32 The kings were stronger than the Egyptians in that battle, and about one hundred and eighty men of Egypt fell on that day, and about thirty men of the forces of the kings, and all the men of Egypt fled from before the king; so the children of Esau and Ishmael pursued the Egyptians, continuing to strike them to the place where the camp of the children of Israel was.

33 And all the Egyptians cried to the children of Israel, saying, Hurry to us and assist us and save us from the hand of Esau, Ishmael and the children of Chittim.

34 The hundred and fifty men of the children of Israel ran from their station to the camps of these kings, and the children of Israel cried to the Lord their God to deliver them.

35 And the Lord listened to Israel, and the Lord gave all the men of the kings into their hands, and the children of Israel fought against these kings; the children of Israel struck about four thousand of the kings' men.

36 The Lord threw a great consternation into the camp of the kings, so that the fear of the children of Israel fell on them.

37 And all the hosts of the kings fled from before the children of Israel and the children of Israel pursued them continuing to strike them to the borders of the land of Cush.

38 The children of Israel killed of them in the road two thousand men, and of the children of Israel not one fell.

39 When the Egyptians saw that the children of Israel had fought with such few men with the kings, and that the battle was so very severe against them,

40 All the Egyptians were greatly afraid of their lives on account of the strong battle, and all Egypt fled, every man hiding himself from the arrayed forces; they hid themselves in the road, and they left the Israelites to fight alone.

41 And the children of Israel inflicted a terrible blow on the kings' men, and they returned from them after they had driven them to the border of the land of Cush.

42 All Israel knew the thing which the men of Egypt had done to them, that they had fled from them in battle, and had left them to fight alone.

43 So the children of Israel also acted with cunning, and as the children of Israel returned from battle, they found some of the Egyptians in the road and struck them there.

44 And while they killed them, they said to them these words:

45 Why did you go from us and leave us, being a few people to fight against these kings who had many people to strike us, that you might thereby save your own souls?

46 And of some which the Israelites met on the road, the children of Israel spoke to each other, saying, Smite, strike, for he is an Ishmaelite, or an Edomite, or from the children of Chittim; they stood over him and killed him, and they knew that he was an Egyptian.

47 The children of Israel did these things cunningly against the Egyptians because they had deserted in battle and had fled from them.

48 And the children of Israel killed of the men of Egypt in the road in this manner about two hundred men.

49 All the men of Egypt saw the evil which the children of Israel had done to them, so all Egypt feared greatly the children of Israel, for they had seen their great power and that not one man of them had fallen.

50 So all the children of Israel returned with joy on their road to Goshen, and the rest of Egypt returned each man to his place.

CHAPTER 65

1 It came to pass after these things that all the counselors of Pharaoh, king of Egypt, and all the elders of Egypt assembled and came before the king and bowed down to the ground, and they sat before him.

2 And the counselors and elders of Egypt spoke to the king, saying,

3 Behold the people of the children of Israel is greater and mightier than we are, and you know all the evil which they did to us in the road when we returned from battle.

4 And you have also seen their strong power, for this power is to them from their fathers, for only a few men stood up against a people numerous as the sand, and struck them at the edge of the sword; of themselves not one has fallen, so that if they had been numerous they would then have utterly destroyed them.

5 Now therefore give us counsel what to do with them, until we gradually destroy them from among us so they don't become too numerous for us in the land.

6 For if the children of Israel should increase in the land, they will become an obstacle to us; if any war should happen to take place, they with their great strength will join our enemy against us, and fight against us, destroy us from the land and go away from it.

7 So the king answered the elders of Egypt and said to them, This is the plan advised against Israel, from which we will not depart,

8 Consider in the land are Pithom and Rameses, cities unfortified against battle; it's best for you and us to build them, and to fortify them.

9 Now go also and act cunningly toward them, and proclaim a voice in Egypt and in Goshen at the command of the king, saying,

10 All ye men of Egypt, Goshen, Pathros and all their inhabitants! The king has commanded us to build Pithom and Rameses and to fortify them for battle; those among you of all Egypt, of the children of Israel and of all the inhabitants of the cities who are willing to build with us, you shall each have his wages given to him daily at the king's order. So go first and do cunningly and gather yourselves to come to Pithom and Rameses to build.

11 And while you are building, cause an announcement of this kind to be made throughout Egypt every day at the command of the king.

12 When some of the children of Israel shall come to build with you, you shall give them their wages daily for a few days.

13 And after they have built with you for their daily hire, drag yourselves away from them daily one by one in secret, and then you shall rise up and become their taskmasters and officers; you shall leave them afterward to build without wages; should they refuse, then force them with all your might to build.

14 And if you do this it will be well with us to strengthen our land against the children of Israel, for on account of the fatigue of the building and the work, the children of Israel will decrease, because you will deprive them of their wives day by day.

15 And all the elders of Egypt heard the counsel of the king, and the counsel seemed good in their eyes and in the eyes of the servants of Pharaoh, and in the eyes of all Egypt; they did according to the word of the king.

16 And all the servants went away from the king; they caused an announcement to be made in all Egypt, in Tachpanches and in Goshen, and in all the cities which surrounded Egypt, saying,

17 You have seen what the children of Esau and Ishmael did to us, who came to war against us and wished to destroy us.

18 Now therefore the king commanded us to fortify the land, to build the cities Pithom and Rameses, and to

fortify them for battle, if they should again come against us.

19 Whoever of you from all Egypt and from the children of Israel will come to build with us, he shall have his daily wages given by the king, as his command is to us.

20 And when Egypt and all the children of Israel heard all that the servants of Pharaoh had spoken, there came persons from the Egyptians and the children of Israel to build with the servants of Pharaoh, Pithom and Rameses, but none of the children of Levi came with their brothers to build.

21 All the servants of Pharaoh and his princes came at first with deceit to build with all Israel as daily hired laborers, and they gave to Israel their daily hire at the beginning.

22 And the servants of Pharaoh built with all Israel, and were employed in that work with Israel for a month.

23 And at the end of the month, all the servants of Pharaoh began to withdraw secretly from the people of Israel daily.

24 And Israel went on with the work at that time, but they then received their daily wage, because some of the men of Egypt were yet carrying on the work with Israel at that time; therefore the Egyptians gave Israel their wage in those days in order that they, the Egyptians their fellow-workmen, might also take the pay for their labor.

25 At the end of a year and four months all the Egyptians had withdrawn from the children of Israel, so that the children of Israel were left alone engaged in the work.

26 And after all the Egyptians had withdrawn from the children of Israel they returned and became oppressors and officers over them, and some of them stood over the children of Israel as task masters, to receive from them all that they gave them for the pay of their labor.

27 And the Egyptians did in this manner to the children of Israel day by day, in order to afflict them in their work.

28 And all the children of Israel were alone engaged in the labor, and the Egyptians refrained from giving any pay to the children of Israel from that time forward.

29 When some of the men of Israel refused to work on account of the wages not being given to them, the exactors and the servants of Pharaoh oppressed them and struck them with heavy blows, and made them return by force to labor with their brothers; thus did all the Egyptians to the children of Israel all the days.

30 And all the children of Israel were greatly afraid of the Egyptians in this matter, and all the children of Israel returned and worked alone without pay.

31 The children of Israel built Pithom and Rameses; all the children of Israel did the work, some making bricks, and some building, and the children of Israel built and fortified all the land of Egypt and its walls. The children of Israel were engaged in work for many years, until the time came when the Lord remembered them and brought them out of Egypt.

32 But the children of Levi were not employed in the work with their brothers of Israel from the beginning to the day of their going forth from Egypt.

33 For all the children of Levi knew that the Egyptians had spoken all these words with deceit to the Israelites, therefore the children of Levi refrained from approaching the work with their brothers.

34 The Egyptians did not direct their attention to make the children of Levi work afterward, since they had not been with their brothers at the beginning, therefore the Egyptians left them alone.

35 And the hands of the men of Egypt were directed with continued severity against the children of Israel in that work, and the Egyptians made the children of Israel work with rigor.

36 The Egyptians embittered the lives of the children of Israel with hard work in mortar and bricks, and also in all manner of work in the field.

37 The children of Israel called Melol the king of Egypt "Meror, king of Egypt," because in his days the Egyptians had embittered their lives with all manner of work.

38 And all the work wherein the Egyptians made the children of Israel labor, they exacted with rigor, in order to afflict the children of Israel. But the more they afflicted them, the more they increased and grew, and the Egyptians were grieved because of the children of Israel.

CHAPTER 66

1 At that time Hadad the son of Bedad king of Edom died; Samlah from Mesrekah, from the country of the children of the east, reigned in his place.

2 In the thirteenth year of the reign of Pharaoh king of Egypt, which was the hundred and twenty-fifth year of the

Israelites going down into Egypt, Samlah had reigned over Edom eighteen years.

3 And when he reigned, he brought forth his army to go and fight against Zepho the son of Eliphaz and the children of Chittim, because they had made war against Angeas king of Africa, and they destroyed his whole army.

4 But he did not engage with him, for the children of Esau prevented him, saying, he was their brother; so Samlah listened to the voice of the children of Esau and turned back with all his forces to the land of Edom, and did not proceed to fight against Zepho the son of Eliphaz.

5 And Pharaoh king of Egypt heard this thing, saying, Samlah king of Edom has resolved to fight the children of Chittim, and afterward he will come to fight against Egypt.

6 When the Egyptians heard this matter, they increased the labor on the children of Israel, that the Israelites should do to them as they did to them in their war with the children of Esau in the days of Hadad.

7 So the Egyptians said to the children of Israel, Hurry and do your work, and finish your task, and strengthen the land, should the children of Esau your brothers come to fight against us, for on your account will they come against us.

8 And the children of Israel did the work of the men of Egypt day by day, and the Egyptians afflicted the children of Israel in order to lessen them in the land.

9 But as the Egyptians increased the labor on the children of Israel, so did the children of Israel increase and reproduce, and all Egypt was filled with the children of Israel.

10 And in the hundred and twenty-fifth year of Israel's going down into Egypt, all the Egyptians saw that their counsel did not succeed against Israel, but that they increased and grew and the land of Egypt and the land of Goshen were filled with the children of Israel.

11 So all the elders of Egypt and its wise men came before the king and bowed down to him and sat before him.

12 And all the elders of Egypt and the wise men there said to the king, May the king live forever; you did counsel us the counsel against the children of Israel, and we did to them according to the word of the king.

13 But in proportion to the increase of the labor so do they increase and grow in the land, and look the whole country is filled with them.

14 So now our lord and king, the eyes of all Egypt are on you to give them advice with your wisdom, by which they may rule over Israel to destroy them, or to diminish them from the land; the king answered them saying, Give your counsel in this matter that we may know what to do to them.

15 And an officer, one of the king's counselors, whose name was Job, from Mesopotamia, in the land of Uz, answered the king, saying,

16 If it please the king, let him hear the counsel of his servant; the king said to him, Speak.

17 And Job spoke before the king, the princes, and before all the elders of Egypt, saying,

18 Behold the counsel of the king which he advised formerly respecting the labor of the children of Israel is very good, and you must not remove from them that labor forever.

19 But this is the advice counselled by which you may lessen them, if it seems good to the king to afflict them.

20 Behold we have feared war for a long time, and we said, When Israel becomes prolific in the land, they will drive us from the land if a war would take place.

21 If it please the king, let a royal decree go forth, and let it be written in the laws of Egypt which shall not be revoked, that every male child born to the Israelites, his blood shall be spilled on the ground.

22 And by your doing this, when all the male children of Israel will have died, the evil of their wars will cease; let the king do so and send for all the Hebrew midwives and order them in this matter to execute it. So the thing pleased the king and the prince; the king did according to the word of Job.

23 The king sent for the Hebrew midwives to be called, of which the name of one was Shephrah, and the name of the other Puah.

24 And the midwives came before the king, and stood in his presence.

25 the king said to them, When you do the office of a midwife to the Hebrew women, and see them on the stools, if it be a son then you shall kill him, but if it be a daughter then she shall live.

26 But if you will not do this thing, then will I burn you up and all your houses with fire.

27 But the midwives feared God and did not listen to the king of Egypt nor to his words; when the Hebrew women brought forth to the midwife son or daughter, then did the midwife do all that was necessary to the child and let it live; thus did the midwives all the days.

28 And this thing was told to the king, and he sent and called for the midwives and he said to them, Why have you done this thing and have saved the children alive?

29 And the midwives answered and spoke together before the king, saying,

30 Let not the king think that the Hebrew women are as the Egyptian women, for all the children of Israel are vigorous, and before the midwife comes to them they are delivered, and as for us your handmaids, for many days no Hebrew woman has brought forth on us, for all the Hebrew women are their own midwives, because they are vigorous.

31 And Pharaoh heard their words and believed them in this matter, and the midwives went away from the king, and God dealt well with them; the people multiplied and increased greatly.

CHAPTER 67

1 There was a man in the land of Egypt of the children of Levi, whose name was Amram, the son of Kehath, the son of Levi, the son of Israel.

2 And this man went and took a wife, namely Jochebed the daughter of Levi his father's sister, and she was one hundred and twenty-six years old, and he came to her.

3 And the woman conceived and gave birth to a daughter, and she called her name Miriam, because in those days the Egyptians had embittered the lives of the children of Israel.

4 She conceived again and gave birth to a son and she called his name Aaron, for in the days of her conception, Pharaoh began to spill the blood of the male children of Israel.

5 In those days Zepho died, the son of Eliphaz, son of Esau, king of Chittim; Janeas reigned in his stead.

6 And the time that Zepho reigned over the children of Chittim was fifty years, and he died and was buried in the city of Nabna in the land of Chittim.

7 And Janeas, one of the mighty men of the children of Chittim, reigned after him for fifty years.

8 It was after the death of the king of Chittim that Balaam the son of Beor fled from the land of Chittim, and he went and came to Egypt to Pharaoh king of Egypt.

9 Pharaoh received him with great honor for he had heard of his wisdom, and he gave him presents and made him a counsellor and praised him.

10 Balaam lived in Egypt, in honor with all the nobles of the king, and the nobles exalted him, because they all coveted to learn his wisdom.

11 And in the hundred and thirtieth year of Israel's going down to Egypt, Pharaoh dreamed that he was sitting on his kingly throne, and lifted up his eyes and saw an old man standing before him; there were scales in the hands of the old man, such scales as are used by merchants.

12 And the old man took the scales and hung them before Pharaoh.

13 And the old man took all the elders of Egypt and all its nobles and great men, and he tied them together and put them in one scale.

14 And he took a milk kid and put it into the other scale, and the kid's weight surpassed all.

15 And Pharaoh was astonished at this dreadful vision, why the kid should surpass all, and Pharaoh awoke and behold it was a dream.

16 Pharaoh rose up early in the morning and called all his servants and related to them the dream, and the men were greatly afraid.

17 And the king said to all his wise men, Interpret I pray you the dream which I dreamed, that I may know it.

18 Balaam the son of Beor answered the king and said to him, This means nothing else but a great evil that will spring up against Egypt in the latter days.

19 For a son will be born to Israel who will destroy all Egypt and its inhabitants, and bring forth the Israelites from Egypt with a mighty hand.

20 Now therefore, O king, take counsel on this matter, that you may destroy the hope of the children of Israel and their expectation, before this evil arises against Egypt.

21 And the king said to Balaam, And what shall we do to Israel? Certainly after a certain manner did we at first counsel against them and could not succeed over them.

22 So now you also give advice against them by which we may succeed over them.

23 Balaam answered the king, saying, Send now and call your two counselors, and we will see what their advice

is on this matter and afterward your servant will speak.

24 And the king sent and called his two counselors Reuel the Midianite and Job the Uzite, and they came and sat before the king.

25 And the king said to them, Behold you have both heard the dream which I have dreamed, and the interpretation thereof; so now give counsel and know and see what is to be done to the children of Israel, whereby we may succeed over them, before their evil will spring up against us.

26 And Reuel the Midianite answered the king and said, May the king live, may the king live forever.

27 If it seems good to the king, let him desist from the Hebrews and leave them, and let him not stretch forth his hand against them.

28 For these are they whom the Lord chose in days of old, and took as the lot of his inheritance from among all the nations of the earth and the kings of the earth; and who is there that stretched his hand against them with punishment, of whom their God was not avenged?

29 Certainly you know that when Abraham went down to Egypt, Pharaoh, the former king of Egypt, saw Sarah his wife, and took her for a wife, because Abraham said, She is my sister, for he was afraid that the men of Egypt should kill him on account of his wife.

30 And when the king of Egypt had taken Sarah then God struck him and his household with heavy plagues, until he restored to Abraham his wife Sarah, then was he healed.

31 And Abimelech the Gerarite, king of the Philistines, God punished on account of Sarah wife of Abraham, in stopping up every womb from man to beast.

32 When their God came to Abimelech in the dream of night and terrified him in order that he might restore to Abraham Sarah whom he had taken, afterward all the people of Gerar were punished on account of Sarah, and Abraham prayed to his God for them, and he was entreated of him, and he healed them.

33 And Abimelech feared all this evil that came on him and his people, and he returned to Abraham his wife Sarah, and gave him many gifts with her.

34 He did so also to Isaac when he had driven him from Gerar, and God had done wonderful things to him, that all the water courses of Gerar were dried up and their productive trees did not bring forth.

35 Until Abimelech of Gerar, and Ahuzzath one of his friends, and Pichol the captain of his host, went to him and they bent and bowed down before him to the ground.

36 They requested of him to petition for them, and he prayed to the Lord for them, and the Lord was entreated of him and he healed them.

37 Jacob also, the plain man, was delivered through his integrity from the hand of his brother Esau, and the hand of Laban the Syrian his mother's brother, who had sought his life; likewise from the hand of all the kings of Canaan who had come together against him and his children to destroy them, the Lord delivered them out of their hands, that they turned on them and struck them, for who had ever stretched forth his hand against them without penalty?

38 Certainly Pharaoh the former, your father's father, raised Joseph the son of Jacob above all the princes of the land of Egypt when he saw his wisdom, for through his wisdom he rescued all the inhabitants of the land from the famine.

39 After which he ordered Jacob and his children to come down to Egypt in order that through their virtue, the land of Egypt and the land of Goshen might be delivered from the famine.

40 So now if it seems good in your eyes, cease from destroying the children of Israel, but if it be not your will that they shall dwell in Egypt, send them forth from here that they may go to the land of Canaan, the land where their ancestors sojourned.

41 And when Pharaoh heard the words of Jethro he was very angry with him, so that he rose with shame from the king's presence and went to Midian, his land, and took Joseph's stick with him.

42 And the king said to Job the Uzite, What do you say Job, and what is your advice respecting the Hebrews?

43 So Job said to the king, Behold all the inhabitants of the land are in your power, let the king do as it seems good in his eyes.

44 And the king said to Balaam, What do you say, Balaam? Speak your word that we may hear it.

45 And Balaam said to the king, Of all that the king has counselled against the Hebrews will they be delivered, and the king will not be able to prevail over them with any counsel.

46 For if you think to lessen them by the flaming fire, you cannot prevail over them, for certainly their God delivered Abraham their father from Ur of the Chaldeans; if you think to destroy them with a sword, certainly Isaac their father was delivered from it and a ram was placed in his stead.

47 And if with hard and rigorous labor you think to lessen them, you will not prevail even in this, for their father Jacob served Laban in all manner of hard work and prospered.

48 Now therefore, O King, hear my words, for this is the counsel which is counselled against them, by which you will prevail over them, and from which you should not depart:

49 If it please the king let him order all their children which shall be born from this day forward to be thrown into the water, for by this can you wipe away their name, for none of them nor of their fathers were tried in this manner.

50 And the king heard the words of Balaam, and the thing pleased the king and the princes, and the king did according to the word of Balaam.

51 The king ordered an announcement to be issued and a law to be made throughout the land of Egypt, saying, Every male child born to the Hebrews from this day forward shall be thrown into the water.

52 Pharaoh called to all his servants, saying, Go now and search throughout the land of Goshen where the children of Israel are, and see that every son born to the Hebrews will be cast into the river, but every daughter you shall let live.

53 And when the children of Israel heard this thing which Pharaoh had commanded, to cast their male children into the river, some of the people separated from their wives and others adhered to them.

54 And from that day forward, when the time of delivery arrived to those women of Israel who had remained with their husbands, they went to the field to bring forth there, and they brought forth in the field and left their children on the field and returned home.

55 And the Lord who had sworn to their ancestors to reproduce them sent one of his ministering angels which are in heaven to wash each child in water, to anoint and swathe it and to put into its hands two smooth stones from one of which it sucked milk and from the other honey, and he caused its hair to grow to its knees, by which it might cover itself; to comfort it and to cleave to it through his compassion for it.

56 And when God had compassion over them and had desired to reproduce them on the face of the land, he ordered his earth to receive them to be preserved therein till the time of their growing up, after which the earth opened its mouth and vomited them forth and they sprouted forth from the city like the herb of the earth, and the grass of the forest, and they returned each to his family and to his father's house, and they remained with them.

57 And the babes of the children of Israel were on the earth like the herb of the field, through God's grace to them.

58 And when all the Egyptians saw this thing, they went forth, each to his field with his yoke of oxen and his ploughshare, and they plowed it up as one ploughs the earth at offspring time.

59 And when they plowed they were unable to hurt the infants of the children of Israel, so the people increased and thrived greatly.

60 And Pharaoh ordered his officers daily to go to Goshen to seek for the babes of the children of Israel.

61 And when they had sought and found one, they took it from its mother's bosom by force, and threw it into the river, but the female child they left with its mother; thus did the Egyptians do to the Israelites all the days.

CHAPTER 68

1 It was at that time the spirit of God was on Miriam the daughter of Amram the sister of Aaron, and she went forth and prophesied about the house, saying, Behold a son will be born to us from my father and mother this time, and he will save Israel from the hands of Egypt.

2 And when Amram heard the words of his daughter, he went and took his wife back to the house, after he had driven her away at the time when Pharaoh ordered every male child of the house of Jacob to be thrown into the water.

3 So Amram took Jochebed his wife, three years after he had driven her away, and he came to her and she conceived.

4 At the end of seven months from her conception she brought forth a son, and the whole house was filled with great light as of the light of the sun and moon at the time of their shining.

5 And when the woman saw the child that it was good and pleasing to the sight, she hid him for three months in an inner room.

6 In those days the Egyptians conspired to destroy all the Hebrews there.

7 And the Egyptian women went to Goshen where the children of Israel were, and they carried their young ones on their shoulders, their babes who could not yet speak.

8 And in those days, when the women of the children of Israel brought forth, each woman had hidden her son from the Egyptians, that the Egyptians might not know of their bringing forth, and might not destroy them from the land.

9 And the Egyptian women came to Goshen and their children who could not speak were on their shoulders, and when an Egyptian woman came into the house of a Hebrew woman her babe began to cry.

10 And when it cried the child that was in the inner room answered it, so the Egyptian women went and told it at the house of Pharaoh.

11 And Pharaoh sent his officers to take the children and kill them; thus did the Egyptians to the Hebrew women all the days.

12 And it was at that time, about three months from Jochebed's concealment of her son, that the thing was known in Pharaoh's house.

13 And the woman hurried to take away her son before the officers came, and she took for him an ark of bulrushes, and daubed it with slime and with pitch and put the child therein, and she laid it in the flags by the river's brink.

14 And his sister Miriam stood afar off to learn what would be done to him, and what would become of her words.

15 And God sent forth at that time a terrible heat in the land of Egypt, which burned up the flesh of man like the sun in his circuit, and it greatly oppressed the Egyptians.

16 And all the Egyptians went down to bathe in the river on account of the consuming heat which burned up their flesh.

17 And Bathia, the daughter of Pharaoh, went also to bathe in the river, owing to the consuming heat; her maidens walked at the riverside, and all the women of Egypt as well.

18 Bathia lifted up her eyes to the river and she saw the ark on the water, and sent her maid to
 fetch it.

19 She opened it and saw the child, and then the babe wept, and she had compassion on him and said, This is one of the Hebrew children.

20 And all the women of Egypt walking on the riverside desired to give him suck, but he would not suck, for this thing was from the Lord in order to restore him to his mother's breast.

21 And Miriam his sister was at that time among the Egyptian women at the riverside, and she saw this thing and said to Pharaoh's daughter, Shall I go and fetch a nurse of the Hebrew women, that she may nurse the child for you?

22 And Pharaoh's daughter said to her, Go, and the young woman went and called the child's mother.

23 And Pharaoh's daughter said to Jochebed, Take this child away and suckle it for me, and I will pay you your wages, two bits of silver daily; and the woman took the child and nursed it.

24 At the end of two years, when the child grew up, she brought him to the daughter of Pharaoh, and he was to her as a son; she called his name Moses, for she said, Because I drew him out of the water.

25 And Amram his father called his name Chabar, for he said, It was for him that he associated with his wife whom he had turned away.

26 And Jochebed his mother called his name Jekuthiel, Because, she said, I have hoped for him to the Almighty, and God restored him to me.

27 And Miriam his sister called him Jered, for she descended after him to the river to learn what would happen to him.

28 And Aaron his brother called his name Abi Zanuch, saying, My father left my mother and returned to her on his account.

29 And Kehath the father of Amram called his name Abigdor, because on his account did God repair the breach of the house of Jacob, that they could no longer throw their male children into the water.

30 And their nurse called him Abi Socho, saying, In his tabernacle was he hidden for three months, on account of the children of Ham.

31 And all Israel called his name Shemaiah, son of Nethanel, for they said, In his days has God heard their cries and rescued them from their oppressors.

32 And Moses was in Pharaoh's house and was to Bathia, Pharaoh's daughter, as a son, and Moses grew up among the king's children.

CHAPTER 69

1 The king of Edom died in those days, in the eighteenth year of his reign, and was buried in his temple which he had built for himself as his royal residence in the land of Edom.

2 The children of Esau sent to Pethor, which is on the river, and they fetched from there a young man of beautiful eyes and handsome, whose name was Saul; they made him king over them in the place of Samlah.

3 And Saul reigned over all the children of Esau in the land of Edom for forty years.

4 When Pharaoh king of Egypt saw that the counsel which Balaam had advised respecting the children of Israel did not succeed, but that still they were prolific, multiplied and increased throughout the land of Egypt,

5 Then Pharaoh commanded in those days that a proclamation should be issued throughout Egypt to the children of Israel, saying, No man shall lessen anything of his daily labor.

6 And the man who shall be found deficient in his labor which he performs daily, whether in mortar or in bricks, then his youngest son shall be put in their place.

7 And the labor of Egypt strengthened on the children of Israel in those days, and if one brick was deficient in any man's daily labor, the Egyptians took his youngest boy by force from his mother and put him into the building in the place of the brick which his father had left wanting.

8 And the men of Egypt did so to all the children of Israel day by day, all the days for a long period.

9 But the tribe of Levi did not at that time work with the Israelites their brothers from the beginning, for the children of Levi knew the cunning of the Egyptians which they exercised at first toward the Israelites.

CHAPTER 70

1 In the third year from the birth of Moses, Pharaoh was sitting at a banquet when Alparanith the queen was sitting at his right and Bathia at his left, and the lad Moses was lying on her bosom, and Balaam the son of Beor with his two sons, and all the princes of the kingdom were sitting at table in the king's presence.

2 And the lad stretched forth his hand on the king's head, and took the crown from the king's head and placed it on his own head.

3 When the king and princes saw the work which the boy had done, the king and princes were terrified, and one man to his neighbor expressed astonishment.

4 And the king said to the princes who were before him at table, What speak you and what say you, O ye princes, in this matter, and what is to be the judgment against the boy on account of this act?

5 And Balaam the son of Beor the magician answered before the king and princes and said, Remember now, O my lord and king, the dream which you did dream many days ago, and that which your servant interpreted to you.

6 Now therefore this is a child from the Hebrew children in whom is the spirit of God, and let not my lord the king imagine that this youngster did this thing without knowledge.

7 For he is a Hebrew boy, and wisdom and understanding are with him, although he is yet a child; with wisdom has he done this and chosen to himself the kingdom of Egypt.

8 For this is the manner of all the Hebrews to deceive kings and their nobles, to do all these things cunningly, in order to make the kings of the earth and their men tremble.

9 Certainly you know that Abraham their father acted thus, who deceived the army of Nimrod king of Babel and Abimelech king of Gerar, and that he possessed himself of the land of the children of Heth and all the kingdoms of Canaan.

10 And that he descended into Egypt and said of Sarah his wife, she is my sister, in order to mislead Egypt and her king.

11 His son Isaac also did so when he went to Gerar and lived there, and his strength prevailed over the army of Abimelech king of the Philistines.

12 He also thought of making the kingdom of the Philistines stumble, in saying that Rebecca his wife was his sister.

13 Jacob also dealt treacherously with his brother and took from his hand his birthright and his blessing.

14 He went then to Padan-aram to the house of Laban his mother's brother, and cunningly obtained from him his daughter, his cattle and all belonging to him, and fled away and returned to the land of Canaan to his father.

15 His sons sold their brother Joseph, who went down into Egypt and became a slave, and was placed in the

prison house for twelve years.

16 Until the former Pharaoh dreamed dreams and withdrew him from the prison house, and magnified him above all the princes in Egypt on account of his interpreting his dreams to him.

17 And when God caused a famine throughout the land he sent for and brought his father and all his brothers, and all of his father's household, and supported them without price or reward, and bought the Egyptians for slaves.

18 Now therefore my lord king behold this child has risen up in their stead in Egypt, to do according to their deeds and to trifle with every king, prince and judge.

19 If it please the king, let us now spill his blood on the ground, that he shall not grow up and take away the government from your hand, and then the hope of Egypt perish after he shall have reigned.

20 And Balaam said to the king, Let us moreover call for all the judges of Egypt and the wise men thereof, and let us know if the judgment of death is due to this boy as you did say; then we will kill him.

21 Pharaoh sent and called for all the wise men of Egypt and they came before the king; an angel of the Lord came among them, and he was like one of the wise men of Egypt.

22 And the king said to the wise men, Certainly you have heard what this Hebrew boy who is in the house has done, and thus has Balaam judged in the matter.

23 Now you judge also and see what is due to the boy for the act he has committed.

24 And the angel, who seemed like one of the wise men of Pharaoh, answered and said as follows, before all the wise men of Egypt and before the king and the princes:

25 If it please the king let the king send for men who shall bring before him an onyx stone and a coal of fire, and place them before the child; if the child shall stretch forth his hand and take the onyx stone, then shall we know that with wisdom has the youth done all that he has done, and we must kill him.

26 But if he stretches forth his hand on the coal, then shall we know that it was not with knowledge that he did this thing, and he shall live.

27 The thing seemed good in the eyes of the king and the princes, so the king did according to the word of the angel of the Lord.

28 The king ordered the onyx stone and coal to be brought and placed before Moses.

29 They placed the boy before them, and the lad endeavored to stretch forth his hand to the onyx stone, but the angel of the Lord took his hand and placed it on the coal, and the coal became extinguished in his hand; he lifted it up and put it into his mouth, and burned part of his lips and part of his tongue, and he became swollen in mouth and tongue.

30 And when the king and princes saw this, they knew that Moses had not acted with wisdom in taking off the crown from the king's head.

31 So the king and princes refrained from slaying the child. Moses remained in Pharaoh's house, growing up, and the Lord was with him.

32 And while the boy was in the king's house, he was robed in purple and he grew among the children of the king.

33 And when Moses grew up in the king's house, Bathia the daughter of Pharaoh considered him as a son, and all the household of Pharaoh honored him, and all the men of Egypt were afraid of him.

34 And he daily went forth and came into the land of Goshen where his brothers the children of Israel were, and Moses saw them daily in shortness of breath and hard labor.

35 And Moses asked them, saying, How is this labor assigned to you day by day?

36 And they told him all that had befallen them, and all the injunctions which Pharaoh had put on them before his birth.

37 And they told him all the counsels which Balaam the son of Beor had counselled against them, and what he had also counselled against him in order to kill him when he had taken the king's crown from off his head.

38 And when Moses heard these things his anger was set ablaze against Balaam, and he sought to kill him, and he was in ambush for him day by day.

39 Balaam was afraid of Moses, and he and his two sons rose up and went forth from Egypt, and they fled and delivered their souls and took themselves to the land of Cush to Kikianus, king of Cush.

40 And Moses was in the king's house going out and coming in; the Lord gave him favor in the eyes of Pharaoh and in the eyes of all his servants, and in the eyes of all the people of Egypt, and they loved Moses greatly.

41 The day arrived when Moses went to Goshen to see his brothers that he saw the children of Israel in their burdens and hard labor, and Moses was grieved on their account.

42 And Moses returned to Egypt and came to the house of Pharaoh, and came before the king, and Moses bowed down before the king.

43 And Moses said to Pharaoh, I pray you my lord, I have come to seek a small request from you, turn not away my face empty; and Pharaoh said to him, Speak.

44 And Moses said to Pharaoh, Let there be given to your servants the children of Israel who are in Goshen, one day to rest therein from their labor.

45 And the king answered Moses and said, Behold I have lifted up your face in this thing to grant your request.

46 And Pharaoh ordered an announcement to be issued throughout Egypt and Goshen, saying,

47 To you, all the children of Israel, thus says the king, for six days you shall do your work and labor, but on the seventh day you shall rest and shall not preform any work, thus shall you do all the days as the king and Moses the son of Bathia have commanded.

48 And Moses rejoiced at this thing which the king had granted to him, and all the children of Israel did as Moses ordered them.

49 For this thing was from the Lord to the children of Israel, for the Lord had begun to remember the children of Israel to save them for the sake of their fathers.

50 And the Lord was with Moses and his fame went throughout Egypt.

51 And Moses became great in the eyes of all the Egyptians, and in the eyes of all the children of Israel, seeking good for his people Israel and speaking words of peace regarding them to the king.

CHAPTER 71

1 When Moses was eighteen years old he desired to see his father and mother and he went to them at Goshen, and when Moses had come near Goshen he came to the place where the children of Israel were engaged in work, and he observed their burdens, and he saw an Egyptian smiting one of his Hebrew brothers.

2 When the man who was beaten saw Moses he ran to him for help, for the man Moses was greatly respected in the house of Pharaoh, and he said to him, My lord attend to me; this Egyptian came to my house in the night, bound me, and came to my wife in my presence, and now he seeks to take my life away.

3 And when Moses heard this wicked thing, his anger was set ablaze against the Egyptian, and he turned this way and the other, and when he saw there was no man there he struck the Egyptian and hid him in the sand, and delivered the Hebrew from the hand of him that struck him.

4 And the Hebrew went to his house, and Moses returned to his home, and went forth and came back to the king's house.

5 And when the man had returned home, he thought of leaving his wife, for it was not right in the house of Jacob for any man to come to his wife after she had been defiled.

6 The woman went and told her brothers, and the woman's brothers sought to kill him, and he fled to his house and escaped.

7 On the second day Moses went forth to his brothers, and looked and saw two men were quarreling; he said to the wicked one, Why do you strike your neighbor?

8 And he answered him and said to him, Who has set you for a prince and judge over us? Do you think to kill me as you did kill the Egyptian? And Moses was afraid and said, Certainly the thing is known?

9 And Pharaoh heard of this affair, and he ordered Moses to be slain, so God sent his angel and he appeared to Pharaoh in the likeness of a captain of the guard.

10 And the angel of the Lord took the sword from the hand of the captain of the guard, and took his head off with it, for the likeness of the captain of the guard was turned into the likeness of Moses.

11 And the angel of the Lord took hold of the right hand of Moses, and brought him forth from Egypt, and placed him outside the borders of Egypt, a distance of forty days' journey.

12 And Aaron his brother alone remained in the land of Egypt, and he prophesied to the children of Israel, saying,

13 Thus says the Lord God of your ancestors, Throw away, each man, the abominations of his eyes, and do not defile yourselves with the idols of Egypt.

14 And the children of Israel rebelled and would not listen to Aaron at that time.

15 And the Lord thought to destroy them, were it not that the Lord remembered the covenant which he had made with Abraham, Isaac and Jacob.

16 In those days the hand of Pharaoh continued to be severe against the children of Israel, and he crushed and

oppressed them until the time when God sent forth his word and took notice of them.

CHAPTER 72

1 It was in those days that there was a great war between the children of Cush and the children of the east and Aram, and they rebelled against the king of Cush in whose hands they were.

2 So Kikianus king of Cush went forth with all the children of Cush, a people numerous as the sand, and he went to fight against Aram and the children of the east, to bring them under subjection.

3 When Kikianus went out, he left Balaam the magician with his two sons, to guard the city and the lowest sort of the people of the land.

4 So Kikianus went forth to Aram and the children of the east, and he fought against them and struck them; they all fell down wounded before Kikianus and his people.

5 He took many of them captives and he brought them under subjection as at first, and he encamped on their land to take tax from them as usual.

6 Balaam the son of Beor, when the king of Cush had left him to guard the city and the poor of the city, rose up and advised with the people of the land to rebel against king Kikianus, not to let him enter the city when he would come home.

7 And the people of the land listened to him and they swore to him and made him king over them, and his two sons for captains of the army.

8 So they rose up and raised the walls of the city at the two corners, and they built an exceedingly strong building.

9 At the third corner they dug ditches without number, between the city and the river which surrounded the whole land of Cush, and they made the waters of the river burst forth there.

10 At the fourth corner they collected numerous serpents by their incantations and enchantments, and they fortified the city and lived therein; no one went out or in before them.

11 Kikianus fought against Aram and the children of the east and he subdued them as before; they gave him their usual tax and he went and returned to his land.

12 When Kikianus the king of Cush approached his city and all the captains of the forces with him, they lifted up their eyes and saw that the walls of the city were built up and greatly elevated, so the men were astonished at this.

13 They said one to the other, It is because they saw that we were delayed, in battle, and were greatly afraid of us; therefore have they done this thing and raised the city walls and fortified them so that the kings of Canaan might not come in battle against them.

14 So the king and the troops approached the city door and they looked up and behold, all the gates of the city were closed; they called out to the sentinels, saying, Open to us, that we may enter the city.

15 But the sentinels refused to open to them by the order of Balaam the magician, their king; they did not allow them enter their city.

16 So they raised a battle with them opposite the city gate, and one hundred and thirty men of the army at Kikianus fell on that day.

17 On the next day they continued to fight and they fought at the side of the river; they endeavored to pass but were not able, so some of them sank in the pits and died.

18 The king ordered them to cut down trees to make rafts, on which they might pass to them, and they did so.

19 When they came to the place of the ditches, the waters revolved by mills, and two hundred men on ten rafts were drowned.

20 On the third day they came to fight at the side where the serpents were, but they could not approach there, for the serpents killed of them one hundred and seventy men; then they ceased fighting against Cush, and they besieged Cush for nine years; no person came out or in.

21 At the time that the war and the siege were against Cush, Moses fled from Egypt from Pharaoh who sought to kill him for having slain the Egyptian.

22 Moses was eighteen years old when he fled from Egypt from the presence of Pharaoh, and he fled and escaped to the camp of Kikianus, which at that time was besieging Cush.

23 Moses was nine years in the camp of Kikianus king of Cush, all the time that they were besieging Cush, and Moses went out and came in with them.

24 And the king and princes and all the fighting men loved Moses, for he was great and worthy, his stature was like a noble lion, his face was like the sun and his strength was like that of a lion, and he was counsellor to the king.

25 And at the end of nine years, Kikianus was seized with a mortal disease, and his illness consumed him, and he died on the seventh day.

26 So his servants embalmed him, carried him and buried him opposite the city gate to the north of the land of Egypt.

27 They built over him an elegant strong and high building, and they placed great stones below.

28 And the king's scribes engraved on those stones all the might of their king Kikianus, and all his battles which he had fought; they are written there at this day.

29 After the death of Kikianus king of Cush it grieved his men and troops greatly on account of the war.

30 So they said one to the other, Give us counsel what we are to do at this time, as we have resided in the wilderness nine years away from our homes.

31 If we say we will fight against the city many of us will fall wounded or killed, and if we remain here in the siege we shall also die.

32 For now all the kings of Aram and of the children of the east will hear that our king is dead, and they will attack us suddenly in a hostile manner; they will fight against us and leave no remnant of us.

33 So now let us go and make a king over us, and let us remain in the siege until the city is delivered up to us.

34 And they wished to choose on that day a man for king from the army of Kikianus, and they found no person of their choice like Moses to reign over them.

35 They hurried and stripped off each man his garments and cast them on the ground, and they made a great heap and placed Moses thereon.

36 And they rose up and blew with trumpets and called out before him, and said, May the king live, may the king live!

37 And all the people and nobles swore to him to give him for a wife Adoniah the queen, the Cushite, wife of Kikianus, and they made Moses king over them on that day.

38 And all the people of Cush issued an announcement on that day, saying, Every man must give something to Moses of what is in his possession.

39 They spread out a sheet on the heap, and every man cast into it something of what he had, one a gold earring and the other a coin.

40 Also of onyx stones, bdellium, pearls and marble did the children of Cush cast to Moses on the heap, also silver and gold in great abundance.

41 And Moses took all the silver and gold, all the vessels, and the bdellium and onyx stones, which all the children of Cush had given to him, and he placed them among his treasures.

42 And Moses reigned over the children of Cush on that day, in the place of Kikianus king of Cush.

CHAPTER 73

1 In the fifty-fifth year of the reign of Pharaoh king of Egypt, that is in the hundred and fifty-seventh year of the Israelites going down into Egypt, Moses reigned in Cush.

2 Moses was twenty-seven years old when he began to reign over Cush, and forty years he did reign.

3 And the Lord granted Moses favor and grace in the eyes of all the children of Cush; the children of Cush loved him greatly, so Moses was favored by the Lord and by men.

4 In the seventh day of his reign, all the children of Cush assembled and came before Moses and bowed down to him to the ground.

5 And all the children spoke together in the presence of the king, saying, Give us counsel that we may see what is to be done to this city.

6 For it is now nine years that we have been besieging round about the city and have not seen our children and our wives.

7 So the king answered them, saying, If you will listen to my voice in all that I shall command you, then the Lord will give the city into our hands and we shall subdue it.

8 For if we fight with them as in the former battle which we had with them before the death of Kikianus, many of us will fall down wounded as before.

9 Now therefore hear this counsel for you in this matter; if you will listen to my voice, then will the city be delivered into our hands.

10 So all the forces answered the king, saying, All that our lord shall command that we will do.

11 And Moses said to them, Pass through and proclaim a voice in the whole camp to all the people, saying,

12 Thus says the king, Go into the forest and bring with you of the young ones of the stork, each man a young one in his hand.

13 And any person disobeying the word of the king, who shall not bring his young one, shall die and the king will take all belonging to him.

14 And when you bring them they shall be in your keeping; you shall rear them until they grow up, and you shall teach them to strike their prey, as is the way of the young ones of the hawk.

15 So all the children of Cush heard the words of Moses, and they rose up and caused announcement to be issued throughout the camp, saying,

16 To you, all the children of Cush, the king's order is that you all go together to the forest and catch there the young stork; each man his young one in his hand and you shall bring them home.

17 Any person violating the order of the king shall die and the king will take all that belongs to him.

18 And all the people did so, and they went out to the wood and they climbed the fir trees and each man caught a young one in his hand, all the young of the storks; they brought them into the desert and reared them by order of the king; they taught them to strike similar to the young hawks.

19 And after the young storks were reared, the king ordered them to be hungry for three days, and all the people did so.

20 On the third day the king said to them, Strengthen yourselves and become courageous men; put on each man his armor and gird on his sword, and each man ride his horse and each take his young stork in his hand.

21 And we will rise up and fight against the city at the place where the serpents are, and all the people did as the king had ordered.

22 And each man took his young one in his hand and they went away; when they came to the place of the serpents the king said to them, Send forth each man his young stork on the serpents.

23 And they sent forth each man his young stork at the king's order, and the young storks ran on the serpents and they devoured them all and destroyed them out of that place.

24 When the king and people had seen that all the serpents were destroyed in that place, all the people sent up a great shout.

25 And they approached and fought against the city and took and subdued it, and they entered the city.

26 There died on that day one thousand and one hundred men of the people of the city, all that inhabited the city, but of the people besieging not one died.

27 So all the children of Cush each went to his home, to his wife and children and to all belonging to him.

28 And Balaam the magician, when he saw that the city was taken, opened the gate and he and his two sons and eight brothers fled and returned to Egyp,to Pharaoh king of Egypt.

29 They are the sorcerers and magicians who are mentioned in the book of the law, standing against Moses when the Lord brought the plagues on Egypt.

30 So Moses took the city by his wisdom, and the children of Cush placed him on the throne instead of Kikianus king of Cush.

31 They placed the royal crown on his head and they gave him a wife Adoniah the Cushite queen, wife of Kikianus.

32 Moses feared the Lord God of his fathers so that he came not to her, nor did he turn his eyes to her.

33 For Moses remembered how Abraham had made his servant Eliezer swear, saying to him, You shall not take a woman from the daughters of Canaan for my son Isaac.

34 Also what Isaac did when Jacob had fled from his brother, when he commanded him saying, You shall not take a wife from the daughters of Canaan, nor make alliance with any of the children of Ham.

35 For the Lord our God gave Ham the son of Noah, and his children and all his descendants as slaves to the children of Shem and to the children of Japheth, and to their descendants after them for slaves forever.

36 Therefore Moses turned not his heart nor his eyes to the wife of Kikianus all the days that he reigned over Cush.

37 Moses feared the Lord his God all his life, and Moses walked before the Lord in truth with all his heart and

soul; he turned not from the right way all the days of his life; he declined not from the way either to the right or to the left, in which Abraham, Isaac and Jacob had walked.

38 Moses strengthened himself in the kingdom of the children of Cush; he guided the children of Cush with his usual wisdom, and Moses prospered in his kingdom.

39 At that time Aram and the children of the east heard that Kikianus king of Cush had died, so Aram and the children of the east rebelled against Cush in those days.

40 Moses gathered all the children of Cush, a people very mighty, about thirty thousand men and he went forth to fight with Aram and the children of the east.

41 They went at first to the children of the east and when the children of the east heard their report, they went to meet them, and engaged in battle with them.

42 And the war was severe against the children of the east, so the Lord gave all the children of the east into the hand of Moses; about three hundred men fell down slain.

43 All the children of the east turned back and retreated, so Moses and the children of Cush followed them and subdued them, and put a tax on them as was their custom.

44 So Moses and all the people with him passed from there to the land of Aram for battle.

45 And the people of Aram also went to meet them; they fought against them and the Lord delivered them into the hand of Moses, and many of the men of Aram fell down wounded.

46 Aram also was subdued by Moses and the people of Cush, and also gave their usual tax.

47 And Moses brought Aram and the children of the east under subjection to the children of Cush; Moses and all the people who were with him turned to the land of Cush.

48 Moses strengthened himself in the kingdom of the children of Cush and the Lord was with him, and all the children of Cush were afraid of him.

CHAPTER 74

1 In the end of years Saul king of Edom died, and Baal Chanan the son of Achbor reigned in his place.

2 In the sixteenth year of the reign of Moses over Cush, Baal Chanan the son of Achbor reigned in the land of Edom over all the children of Edom for thirty-eight years.

3 In his days Moab rebelled against the power of Edom, having been under Edom since the days of Hadad the son of Bedad, who struck them and Midian, and brought Moab under subjection to Edom.

4 And when Baal Chanan the son of Achbor reigned over Edom, all the children of Moab withdrew their allegiance from Edom.

5 Angeas king of Africa died in those days, and Azdrubal his son reigned in his stead.

6 And in those days Janeas king of the children of Chittim died, and they buried him in his temple which he had built for himself in the plain of Canopia for a residence; Latinus reigned in his stead.

7 In the twenty-second year of the reign of Moses over the children of Cush, Latinus reigned over the children of Chittim forty-five years.

8 And he also built for himself a great and mighty tower; he built therein an elegant temple for his residence, to conduct his government as was the custom.

9 In the third year of his reign he caused an announcement to be made to all his skilful men who made many ships for him.

10 And Latinus assembled all his forces, and they came in ships, and went there to fight with Azdrubal son of Angeas king of Africa; they came to Africa and engaged in battle with Azdrubal and his army.

11 And Latinus won over Azdrubal, and Latinus took from Azdrubal the aqueduct which his father had brought from the children of Chittim, when he took Janiah the daughter of Uzi for a wife; so Latinus overthrew the bridge of the aqueduct and struck the whole army of Azdrubal a severe blow.

12 The remaining strong men of Azdrubal strengthened themselves, and their hearts were filled with envy; they courted death, and again engaged in battle with Latinus king of Chittim.

13 The battle was severe on all the men of Africa and they all fell wounded before Latinus and his people, and Azdrubal the king also fell in that battle.

14 The king Azdrubal had a very beautiful daughter whose name was Ushpezena, and all the men of Africa embroidered her likeness on their garment on account of her great beauty and attractive appearance.

15 The men of Latinus saw Ushpezena, the daughter of Azdrubal, and praised her to Latinus their king.

16 And Latinus ordered her to be brought to him; Latinus took Ushpezena for a wife and he turned back on his way to Chittim.

17 It was after the death of Azdrubal son of Angeas, when Latinus had turned back to his land from the battle, that all the inhabitants of Africa rose up and took Anibal the son of Angeas, the younger brother of Azdrubal, and made him king instead of his brother over the whole land at Africa.

18 And when he reigned he resolved to go to Chittim to fight with the children of Chittim, to avenge the cause of Azdrubal his brother and the cause of the inhabitants of Africa, and he did so.

19 He made many ships and he came there with his whole army, and he went to Chittim.

20 So Anibal fought with the children of Chittim, and the children of Chittim fell wounded before Anibal and his army, and Anibal avenged his brother's cause.

21 And Anibal continued the war for eighteen years with the children of Chittim, and Anibal lived in the land of Chittim and encamped there for a long time.

22 Anibal struck the children of Chittim very severely and he killed their great men and princes, and of the rest of the people he struck about eighty thousand men.

23 And at the end of days and years, Anibal returned to his land of Africa, and he reigned securely in the place of Azdrubal his brother.

CHAPTER 75

1 At that time in the hundred and eightieth year of the Israelites going down into Egypt, there went forth from Egypt courageous men, thirty thousand on foot, from the children of Israel who were all of the tribe of Joseph, of the children of Ephraim the son of Joseph.

2 For they said the period was completed which the Lord had appointed to the children of Israel in the times of old, which he had spoken to Abraham.

3 And these men prepared themselves, and each man put his sword at his side, and every man his armor on him, and they trusted to their strength; they went out together from Egypt with a mighty hand.

4 But they brought no provision for the road, only silver and gold, not even did they bring bread for that day in their hands, for they thought of getting their provision for pay from the Philistines; if not they would take it by force.

5 These men were very mighty and bold men; one man could pursue a thousand and two could rout ten thousand, so they trusted their strength and went together as they were.

6 They directed their course toward the land of Gath, and they went down and found the shepherds of Gath feeding the cattle of the children of Gath.

7 They said to the shepherds, Give us some of the sheep for pay that we may eat, for we are hungry; we have eaten no bread this day.

8 And the shepherds said, Are they our sheep or cattle that we should give them to you even for pay? So the children of Ephraim approached to take them by force.

9 And the shepherds of Gath shouted over them so their cry was heard at a distance; all the children of Gath went out to them.

10 When the children of Gath saw the evil doings of the children of Ephraim, they returned and assembled the men of Gath; they put on each man his armor and came forth to the children of Ephraim for battle.

11 And they engaged with them in the valley of Gath, and the battle was severe; they struck from each other a great many on that day.

12 And on the second day the children of Gath sent to all the cities of the Philistines that they should come to their help, saying,

13 Come up to us and help us, that we may strike the children of Ephraim who have come forth from Egypt to take our cattle, and to fight against us without cause.

14 And the souls of the children of Ephraim were exhausted with hunger and thirst, for they had eaten no bread for three days. Forty thousand men went out from the cities of the Philistines to the assistance of the men of Gath.

15 These men were engaged in battle with the children of Ephraim, and the Lord delivered the children of Ephraim into the hands of the Philistines.

16 They struck all the children of Ephraim, all who had gone forth from Egypt, none were remaining but ten men who had run away from the engagement.

17 This evil was from the Lord against the children of Ephraim for they went contrary to the word of the Lord in going forth from Egypt, before the period had arrived which the Lord in the days of old had appointed to Israel.

18 And of the Philistines also there fell a great many, about twenty thousand men, and their brothers carried them and buried them in their cities.

19 And the slain of the children of Ephraim remained forsaken in the valley of Gath for many days and years and were not brought to burial, and the valley was filled with men's bones.

20 The men who had escaped from the battle came to Egypt and told all the children of Israel all that had happened to them.

21 Their father Ephraim mourned over them for many days, and his brothers came to console him.

22 And he came to his wife and she gave birth to a son, and he called his name Beriah, for she was unfortunate in his house.

CHAPTER 76

1 Moses the son of Amram was still king in the land of Cush in those days, and he prospered in his kingdom; he conducted the government of the children of Cush in justice, in righteousness and integrity.

2 And all the children of Cush loved Moses all the days that he reigned over them, and all the inhabitants of the land of Cush were greatly afraid of him.

3 In the fortieth year of the reign of Moses over Cush, Moses was sitting on the royal throne while Adoniah the queen was before him, and all the nobles were sitting around him.

4 And Adoniah the queen said before the king and the princes, What is this thing which you, the children of Cush, have done for this long time?

5 Certainly you know that for forty years that this man has reigned over Cush he has not approached me, nor has he served the gods of the children of Cush.

6 Now therefore hear, O ye children of Cush, and let this man no more reign over you as he is not of our people.

7 Behold Menacrus my son is grown up, let him reign over you for it is better for you to serve the son of your lord than to serve a stranger, slave of the king of Egypt.

8 And all the people and nobles of the children of Cush heard the words which Adoniah the queen had spoken in their ears.

9 All the people were preparing until the evening, and in the morning they rose up early and made Menacrus, son of Kikianus, king over them.

10 All the children of Cush were afraid to stretch forth their hand against Moses, for the Lord was with Moses, and the children of Cush remembered the oath which they swore to Moses, therefore they did no harm to him.

11 But the children of Cush gave many presents to Moses, and sent him from them with great honor.

12 So Moses went forth from the land of Cush and went home and ceased to reign over Cush; Moses was sixty-six years old when he went out of the land of Cush, for the thing was from the Lord. For the period had arrived which he had appointed in the days of old, to bring forth Israel from the affliction of the children of Ham.

13 So Moses went to Midian, for he was afraid to return to Egypt on account of Pharaoh, and he went and sat at a well of water in Midian.

14 And the seven daughters of Reuel the Midianite went out to feed their father's flock.

15 And they came to the well and drew water to water their father's flock.

16 But the shepherds of Midian came and drove them away, and Moses rose up and helped them and watered the flock.

17 And they came home to their father Reuel, and told him what Moses did for them.

18 They said, An Egyptian man has delivered us from the hands of the shepherds; he drew up water for us and watered the flock.

19 And Reuel said to his daughters, And where is he? Why have you left the man?

20 And Reuel sent for him and fetched him and brought him home, and he ate bread with him.

21 And Moses related to Reuel that he had fled from Egypt and that he reigned forty years over Cush, and that they afterward had taken the government from him and had sent him away in peace with honor and with presents.

22 And when Reuel had heard the words of Moses, Reuel said within himself, I will put this man into the prison

house, whereby I shall win over the children of Cush, for he has fled from them.

23 They took and put him into the prison house, and Moses was in prison ten years; while Moses was in the prison house, Zipporah the daughter of Reuel took pity on him, and supported him with bread and water all the time.

24 All the children of Israel were yet in the land of Egypt serving the Egyptians in all manner of hard work, and the hand of Egypt continued in severity over the children of Israel in those days.

25 At that time the Lord struck Pharaoh king of Egypt, and he was afflicted with the plague of leprosy from the sole of his foot to the crown of his head; owing to the cruel treatment of the children of Israel this plague at that time was from the Lord on Pharaoh king of Egypt.

26 For the Lord had listened to the prayer of his people the children of Israel, and their cry reached him on account of their hard work.

27 Still his anger did not turn from them, and the hand of Pharaoh was still stretched out against the children of Israel. Pharaoh hardened his neck before the Lord, he increased his yoke over the children of Israel, and embittered their lives with all manner of hard work.

28 When the Lord had inflicted the plague on Pharaoh king of Egypt, he asked his wise men and sorcerers to cure him.

29 And his wise men and sorcerers said to him that if the blood of little children were put into the wounds he would be healed.

30 Pharaoh listened to them, and sent his ministers to Goshen to the children of Israel to take their little children.

31 And Pharaoh's ministers went and took the infants of the children of Israel from the bosoms of their mothers by force, and they brought them to Pharaoh daily, a child each day, and the physicians killed them and applied them to the plague; thus they did all the days.

32 And the number of the children which Pharaoh killed was three hundred and seventy-five.

33 But the Lord listened not to the physicians of the king of Egypt, and the plague went on increasing mightily.

34 Pharaoh was ten years afflicted with that plague, still the heart of Pharaoh was more hardened against the children of Israel.

35 At the end of ten years the Lord continued to afflict Pharaoh with destructive plagues.

36 And the Lord struck him with a bad tumor and sickness in the stomach, and that plague turned to a severe boil.

37 At that time the two ministers of Pharaoh came from the land of Goshen where all the children of Israel were, and went to the house of Pharaoh and said to him, We have seen the children of Israel slacken in their work and negligent in their labor.

38 And when Pharaoh heard the words of his ministers, his anger was set ablaze against the children of Israel greatly, for he was greatly grieved at his bodily pain.

39 And he answered and said, Now that the children of Israel know that I am ill, they turn and scoff at us. Now therefore harness my chariot for me, and I will take myself to Goshen and will see the scoff of the children of Israel with which they are deriding me. So his servants harnessed the chariot for him.

40 And they took and made him ride on a horse, for he was not able to ride of himself.

41 He took with him ten horsemen and ten footmen, and went to the children of Israel to Goshen.

42 When they had come to the border of Egypt, the king's horse passed into a narrow place, elevated in the hollow part of the vineyard, fenced on both sides, the low plain country being on the other side.

43 The horses ran rapidly in that place and pressed each other, and the other horses pressed the king's horse.

44 And the king's horse fell into the low plain while the king was riding on it; he fell and the chariot turned over the king's face and the horse lay on the king, and the king cried out for his flesh was very sore.

45 And the flesh of the king was torn from him, and his bones were broken and he could not ride; this thing was from the Lord to him, for the Lord had heard the cries of his people the children of Israel and their affliction.

46 And his servants carried him on their shoulders, slowly and carefully, and they brought him back to Egypt, and the horsemen who were with him also came back to Egypt.

47 They placed him in his bed and the king knew that his end was come to die, so Aparanith the queen his wife came and cried before the king, and the king wept a great weeping with her.

48 And all his nobles and servants came on that day and saw the king in that affliction, and wept a great weeping with him.

49 The princes of the king and all his counselors advised the king to cause one to reign in his stead in the land, whomever he would choose from his sons.

50 The king had three sons and two daughters which Aparanith the queen his wife had borne to him, besides the king's children of concubines.

51 And these were their names: the firstborn Othri, the second Adikam, and the third Morion, and their sisters: the name of the elder Bathia and of the other Acuzi.

52 Othri the first born of the king was an idiot, impetuous and hurried in his words.

53 But Adikam was a cunning and wise man and knowing in all the wisdom of Egypt, but of unseemly appearance, thick in flesh and very short in stature; his height was one cubit.

54 And when the king saw Adikam his son intelligent and wise in all things, the king resolved that he should be king in his stead after his death.

55 He took for him a wife Gedudah daughter of Abilot, and he was ten years old; she gave birth to, to him, four sons.

56 And afterward he went and took three wives and had eight sons and three daughters.

57 And the disorder greatly consumed the king, and his flesh stank like the flesh of a carcass cast on the field in summer time, during the heat of the sun.

58 And when the king saw that his sickness had greatly strengthened itself over him, he ordered his son Adikam to be brought to him, and they made him king over the land in his place.

59 At the end of three years the king died, in shame, disgrace, and disgust, and his servants carried him and buried him in the sepulcher of the kings of Egypt in Zoan Mizraim.

60 But they embalmed him not as was usual with kings, for his flesh was putrid, and they could not approach to embalm him on account of the stench, so they buried him in haste.

61 For this evil was from the Lord to him, for the Lord had rewarded him evil for the evil which in his days he had done to Israel.

62 And he died with terror and with shame, and his son Adikam reigned in his place.

CHAPTER 77

1 Adikam was twenty years old when he reigned over Egypt, he reigned four years.

2 In the two hundred and sixth year of Israel's going down to Egypt did Adikam reign over Egypt, but he continued not so long in his reign over Egypt as his fathers had continued their reigns.

3 For Melol his father reigned ninety-four years in Egypt, but he was sick ten years and died, for he had been wicked before the Lord.

4 And all the Egyptians called the name of Adikam Pharaoh like the name of his fathers, as was their custom to do in Egypt.

5 And all the wise men of Pharaoh called the name of Adikam Ahuz, for short it's called Ahuz in the Egyptian language.

6 Adikam was greatly ugly, and he was a cubit and a span and he had a great beard which reached to the soles of his feet.

7 And Pharaoh sat on his father's throne to reign over Egypt, and he conducted the government of Egypt in his wisdom.

8 While he reigned he exceeded his father and all the preceding kings in wickedness, and he increased his yoke over the children of Israel.

9 He went with his servants to Goshen to the children of Israel, and he strengthened the labor over them and he said to them, Complete your work, each day's task, and let not your hands slacken from our work from this day forward as you did in the days of my father.

10 He placed officers over them from among the children of Israel, and over these officers he placed taskmasters from among his servants.

11 And he placed over them a measure of bricks for them to do according to that number, day by day, and he turned back and went to Egypt.

12 At that time the taskmasters of Pharaoh ordered the officers of the children of Israel according to the command of Pharaoh, saying,

13 Thus says Pharaoh, Do your work each day, and finish your task, and observe the daily measure of bricks; diminish not anything.

14 And it shall come to pass that if you are deficient in your daily bricks, I will put your young children in their

stead.

15 And the taskmasters of Egypt did so in those days as Pharaoh had ordered them.

16 And whenever any deficiency was found in the children of Israel's measure of their daily bricks, the taskmasters of Pharaoh would go to the wives of the children of Israel and take infants of the children of Israel to the number of bricks deficient, they would take them by force from their mother's laps, and put them in the building instead of the bricks;

17 While their fathers and mothers were crying over them and weeping when they heard the weeping voices of their infants in the wall of the building.

18 And the taskmasters prevailed over Israel, that the Israelites should place their children in the building, so that a man placed his son in the wall and put mortar over him, while his eyes wept over him, and his tears ran down on his child.

19 And the taskmasters of Egypt did so to the babes of Israel for many days, and no one pitied or had compassion over the babes of the children of Israel.

20 And the number of all the children killed in the building was two hundred and seventy, some whom they had built on instead of the bricks which had been left deficient by their fathers, and some whom they had drawn out dead from the building.

21 And the labor imposed on the children of Israel in the days of Adikam exceeded in hardship that which they performed in the days of his father.

22 The children of Israel sighed every day on account of their heavy work, for they had said to themselves, Certainly when Pharaoh dies, his son will rise up and lighten our work!

23 But they increased the latter work more than the former, and the children of Israel sighed at this and their cry ascended to God on account of their labor.

24 God heard the voice of the children of Israel and their cry in those days, and God remembered to them his covenant which he had made with Abraham, Isaac and Jacob.

25 And God saw the burden of the children of Israel and their heavy work in those days, and he determined to deliver them.

26 Moses the son of Amram was still confined in the dungeon in those days, in the house of Reuel the Midianite, and Zipporah the daughter of Reuel supported him with food secretly day by day.

27 Moses was confined in the dungeon in the house of Reuel for ten years.

28 And at the end of ten years which was the first year of the reign of Pharaoh over Egypt, in the place of his father,

29 Zipporah said to her father Reuel, No person inquires or seeks after the Hebrew man, whom you bound in prison now ten years.

30 So therefore, if it seems good in your sight, let us send and see whether he is living or dead. But her father knew not that she had supported him.

31 And Reuel her father answered and said to her, Has ever such a thing happened that a man would be shut up in a prison without food for ten years, and that he should live?

32 And Zipporah answered her father, saying, Certainly you have heard that the God of the Hebrews is great and mighty, and does wonders for them at all times.

33 He it was who delivered Abraham from the Chaldeans, and Isaac from the sword of his father, and Jacob from the angel of the Lord who wrestled with him at the ford of Jabbuk.

34 Also with this man he has done many things; he delivered him from the river in Egypt and from the sword of Pharaoh, and from the children of Cush, so also he can deliver him from famine and make him live.

35 And the thing seemed good in the sight of Reuel, and he did according to the word of his daughter, and sent to the dungeon to ascertain what became of Moses.

36 He saw, and behold the man Moses was living in the dungeon, standing on his feet, praising and praying to the God of his ancestors.

37 And Reuel commanded Moses to be brought out of the dungeon, so they shaved him and he changed his prison garments and ate bread.

38 And afterward Moses went into the garden of Reuel which was behind the house, and he there prayed to the Lord his God, who had done mighty wonders for him.

39 It was while he prayed he looked opposite to him, and there a sapphire stick was placed in the ground, which was planted in the midst of the garden.

40 He approached the stick and looked, and saw the name of the Lord God of hosts was engraved on it, written

and developed on the stick.

41 And he read it and stretched forth his hand and he plucked it like a forest tree from the thicket, and the stick was in his hand.

42 This is the stick with which all the works of our God were performed, after he had created heaven and earth and all the host of them, seas, rivers and all their fish.

43 And when God had driven Adam from the garden of Eden, he took the stick in his hand and went and tilled the ground from which he was taken.

44 The stick came down to Noah and was given to Shem and his descendants, until it came into the hand of Abraham the Hebrew.

45 And when Abraham had given all he had to his son Isaac, he also gave to him this stick.

46 When Jacob had fled to Padan-aram, he took it into his hand, and when he returned to his father he had not left it behind him.

47 Also when he went down to Egypt he took it into his hand and gave it to Joseph, one portion above his brothers, for Jacob had taken it by force from his brother Esau.

48 After the death of Joseph, the nobles of Egypt came into the house of Joseph, and the stick came into the hand of Reuel the Midianite; when he went out of Egypt, he took it in his hand and planted it in his garden.

49 And all the mighty men of the Kinites tried to pluck it when they endeavored to get Zipporah his daughter, but they were unsuccessful.

50 That stick remained planted in the garden of Reuel until he who had a right to it came and took it.

51 And when Reuel saw the stick in the hand of Moses, he wondered at it, and he gave him his daughter Zipporah for a wife.

CHAPTER 78

1 At that time Baal Channan son of Achbor, king of Edom, died and was buried in his house in the land of Edom.

2 After his death the children of Esau sent to the land of Edom, and took from there a man who was in Edom, whose name was Hadad, and they made him king over them in the place of Baal Channan, their king.

3 And Hadad reigned over the children of Edom forty-eight years.

4 When he reigned he resolved to fight against the children of Moab to bring them under the power of the children of Esau as they were before, but he was not able to because the children of Moab heard this thing, and they rose up and hurried to elect a king over them from among their brothers.

5 Afterward they gathered together a large crowd, and sent them to the children of Ammon their brothers for help to fight against Hadad king of Edom.

6 And Hadad heard the thing which the children of Moab had done, and was greatly afraid of them, and refrained from fighting against them.

7 In those days Moses, the son of Amram, in Midian, took Zipporah, the daughter of Reuel the Midianite, for a wife.

8 And Zipporah walked in the ways of the daughters of Jacob, she was nothing short of the righteousness of Sarah, Rebecca, Rachel and Leah.

9 And Zipporah conceived and gave birth to a son and he called his name Gershom, for he said, I was a stranger in a foreign land; but he circumcised not his foreskin, at the command of Reuel his father-in-law.

10 And she conceived again and gave birth to a son, but circumcised his foreskin, and called his name Eliezer, for Moses said, Because the God of my fathers was my help and delivered me from the sword of Pharaoh.

11 And Pharaoh king of Egypt greatly increased the labor of the children of Israel in those days, and continued to make his yoke heavier on the children of Israel.

12 And he ordered an announcement to be made in Egypt, saying, Give no more straw to the people to make bricks with, let them go and gather themselves straw as they can find it.

13 Also the number of bricks which they shall make let them give each day, and diminish nothing from them, for they are idle in their work.

14 And the children of Israel heard this, and they mourned and sighed, and they cried to the Lord on account of the bitterness of their souls.

15 And the Lord heard the cries of the children of Israel, and saw the oppression with which the Egyptians oppressed them.

16 And the Lord was zealous for his people and his inheritance, and heard their voice, and he resolved to take them out of the affliction of Egypt, to give them the land of Canaan for a possession.

CHAPTER 79

1 Iin those days Moses was feeding the flock of Reuel the Midianite his father-in-law, beyond the wilderness of Sin, and the stick which he took from his father-in-law was in his hand.

2 And it came to pass one day that a kid of goats strayed from the flock, and Moses pursued it and it came to the mountain of God to Horeb.

3 When he came to Horeb the Lord appeared there to him in the bush, and he found the bush burning with fire, but the fire had no power over the bush to consume it.

4 Moses was greatly astonished at this sight because the bush was not consumed, and he approached to see this mighty thing; the Lord called to Moses out of the fire and commanded him to go down to Egypt to Pharaoh king of Egypt, to send the children of Israel from his service.

5 And the Lord said to Moses, Go, return to Egypt for all those men who sought your life are dead, and you shall speak to Pharaoh to send forth the children of Israel from his land.

6 The Lord showed him to do signs and wonders in Egypt before the eyes of Pharaoh and the eyes of his subjects, in order that they might believe that the Lord had sent him.

7 Moses listened to all that the Lord had commanded him, and he returned to his father-in-law and told him these things, and Reuel said to him, Go in peace.

8 Moses rose up to go to Egypt and took his wife and sons with him; he was at an inn in the road, and an angel of God came down, and sought an occasion against him.

9 He wished to kill him on account of his firstborn son because he had not circumcised him and had gone contrary to the covenant which the Lord had made with Abraham.

10 For Moses had listened to the words of his father-in-law which he had spoken to him, not to circumcise his first born son, so he did not circumcise him.

11 Zipporah saw the angel of the Lord seeking an occasion against Moses, and she knew that this thing was because of his not having circumcised her son Gershom.

12 Zipporah hurried and took some of the sharp rock stones that were there, and circumcised her son, and delivered her husband and her son from the hand of the angel of the Lord.

13 Aaron the son of Amram, the brother of Moses, was in Egypt walking at the river side on that day.

14 And the Lord appeared to him in that place; he said to him, Go now toward Moses in the wilderness. And he went and met him in the mountain of God, and he kissed him.

15 Aaron lifted up his eyes and saw Zipporah the wife of Moses and her children, and he said to Moses, Who are these to you?

16 And Moses said to him, They are my wife and sons which God gave to me in Midian; the thing grieved Aaron on account of the woman and her children.

17 Aaron said to Moses, Send away the woman and her children that they may go to her father's house, and Moses listened to the words of Aaron, and did so.

18 Zipporah returned with her children and they went to the house of Reuel, and remained there until the time arrived when the Lord had visited his people and brought them forth from Egypt from the hand at Pharaoh.

19 Moses and Aaron came to Egypt to the community of the children of Israel and spoke to them all the words of the Lord, and the people rejoiced a very great rejoicing.

20 Moses and Aaron rose up early the next day and went to the house of Pharaoh, and they took in their hands the stick of God.

21 When they came to the king's gate, two young lions were confined there with iron instruments; no person went out or came in from before them, unless those whom the king ordered to come, when the conjurors came and withdrew the lions by their incantations, and this brought them to the king.

22 Moses hurried and lifted up the stick on the lions and loosed them, and Moses and Aaron came into the king's house.

23 The lions also came with them in joy, and they followed them and rejoiced as a dog rejoices over his master when he comes from the field.

24 When Pharaoh saw this thing he was astonished at it and was greatly terrified at the report, for their appearance was like the appearance of the children of God.

25 And Pharaoh said to Moses, What do you require? And they answered him saying, The Lord God of the Hebrews has sent us to you, to say, Send forth my people that they may serve me.

26 When Pharaoh heard their words he was greatly terrified before them, and he said to them, Go today and come back to me tomorrow. And they did according to the word of the king.

27 When they had gone Pharaoh sent for Balaam the magician and to Jannes and Jambres his sons and to all the magicians and conjurors and counselors which belonged to the king; they all came and sat before the king.

28 And the king told them all the words which Moses and his brother Aaron had spoken to him; the magicians said to the king, But how could the men come to you, on account of the lions which were confined at the gate?

29 The king said, Because they lifted up their rod against the lions and loosed them, and came to me, and the lions also rejoiced at them as a dog rejoices to meet his master.

30 Balaam the son of Beor the magician answered the king saying, These are none other than magicians like ourselves.

31 So now send for them and let them come and we will try them, and the king did so.

32 In the morning Pharaoh sent for Moses and Aaron to come before the king, and they took the rod of God and came to the king and spoke to him saying,

33 Thus said the Lord God of the Hebrews, Send away my people that they may serve me.

34 And the king said to them, But who will believe you that you are the messengers of God and that you come to me by his order?

35 Now therefore give a wonder or sign in this matter, and then the words which you speak will be believed.

36 Aaron hurried and threw the rod out of his hand before Pharaoh and before his servants, and the rod turned into a serpent.

37 The sorcerers saw this and each man cast his rod on the ground and they became serpents.

38 The serpent of Aaron's rod lifted up its head and opened its mouth to swallow the rods of the magicians.

39 Balaam the magician answered and said, This thing has been from the days of old that a serpent should swallow its fellow, and that living things devour each other.

40 So now restore it to a rod as it was at first and we will also restore our rods as they were at first; if your rod shall swallow our rods we will know that the spirit of God is in you, and if not, you are only a magician like ourselves.

41 Aaron hurried and stretched forth his hand and caught hold of the serpent's tail and it became a rod in his hand; the sorcerers did the same with their rod and got hold each man of the tail of his serpent, and they became rods as at first.

42 When they were restored to rods, the rod of Aaron swallowed up their rods.

43 And when the king saw this thing, he ordered the book of records that related to the kings of Egypt to be brought; they brought the book of records, the chronicles of the kings of Egypt in which all the idols of Egypt were inscribed, for they thought they would find there the name of Jehovah, but they found it not.

44 And Pharaoh said to Moses and Aaron, Behold I have not found the name of your God written in this book, and his name I do not know.

45 The counselors and wise men answered the king, We have heard that the God of the Hebrews is a son of the wise, the son of ancient kings.

46 Pharaoh turned to Moses and Aaron and said to them, I know not the Lord whom you have declared, neither will I send his people away.

47 And they answered and said to the king, The Lord God of Gods is his name; he proclaimed his name over us from the days of our ancestors and sent us, saying, Go to Pharaoh and say to him, Send my people away that they may serve me.

48 Now therefore send us, that we may take a journey for three days in the wilderness and there may sacrifice to him, for from the days of our going down to Egypt, he has not taken from our hands either burnt offering, oblation or sacrifice; if you will not send us, his anger will be set ablaze against you and he will strike Egypt either with the plague or with the sword.

49 And Pharaoh said to them, Tell me now his power and his might. They said to him, He created the heaven and the earth, the seas and all their fish; he formed the light, created the darkness, caused rain on the earth and watered it, and made the herbage and grass to sprout; he created man and beast and the animals of the forest, the birds of the air and the fish of the sea, and by his mouth they live and die.

50 Certainly he created you in your mother's womb and put into you the breath of life, and reared you and placed you on the royal throne of Egypt, and he will take your breath and soul from you and return you to the ground

from where you were taken.

51 And the anger of the king was set ablaze at their words and he said to them, But who among all the Gods of nations can do this? My river is my own, and I have made it for myself.

52 And he drove them from him; he ordered the labor on Israel to be more severe than it was yesterday and before.

53 Moses and Aaron went out from the king's presence, and they saw the children of Israel in an evil condition for the taskmasters had made their labor extremely heavy.

54 Moses returned to the Lord and said, Why have you ill-treated your people? For since I came to speak to Pharaoh what you sent me for, he has greatly ill-used the children of Israel.

55 The Lord said to Moses, Look and you will see that with an outstretched hand and heavy plagues, Pharaoh will send the children of Israel from his land.

56 And Moses and Aaron lived among their brothers the children of Israel in Egypt.

57 As for the children of Israel the Egyptians embittered their lives with the heavy work which they imposed on them.

CHAPTER 80

1 And at the end of two years, the Lord again sent Moses to Pharaoh to bring forth the children of Israel, and to send them out of the land of Egypt.

2 Moses went and came to the house of Pharaoh, and he spoke to him the words of the Lord who had sent him, but Pharaoh would not listen to the voice of the Lord; God roused his might in Egypt on Pharaoh and his subjects, and God struck Pharaoh and his people with very great and severe plagues.

3 The Lord sent by the hand of Aaron and turned all the waters of Egypt into blood, with all their streams and rivers.

4 And when an Egyptian came to drink and draw water, he looked into his pitcher, and behold all the water was turned into blood; when he came to drink from his cup the water in the cup became blood.

5 And when a woman kneaded her dough and cooked her food, their appearance was turned to that of blood.

6 The Lord sent again and caused all their waters to bring forth frogs and all the frogs came into the houses of the Egyptians.

7 And when the Egyptians drank, their bellies were filled with frogs and they danced in their bellies as they dance when in the river.

8 All their drinking water and cooking water turned to frogs, also when they lay in their beds their perspiration bred frogs.

9 In spite of all this the anger of the Lord did not turn from them, and his hand was stretched out against all the Egyptians to strike them with every heavy plague.

10 He sent and changed their dust to lice, and the lice became in Egypt to the height of two cubits on the earth.

11 The lice were also very numerous in the flesh of man and beast, in all the inhabitants of Egypt; also on the king and queen the Lord sent the lice, and it grieved Egypt greatly on account of the lice.

12 Still the anger of the Lord did not turn away, and his hand was still stretched out over Egypt.

13 And the Lord sent all kinds of beasts of the field into Egypt, and they came and destroyed all Egypt, man and beast, and trees and all things that were in Egypt.

14 And the Lord sent fiery serpents, scorpions, mice, weasels, toads, together with others creeping in dust.

15 Flies, hornets, fleas, bugs and gnats, each swarm according to its kind.

16 And all reptiles and winged animals according to their kind came to Egypt and upset the Egyptians greatly.

17 The fleas and flies came into the eyes and ears of the Egyptians.

18 The hornet came on them and drove them away, and they removed from it into their inner rooms, and it pursued them.

19 When the Egyptians hid themselves on account of the swarm of animals, they locked their doors after them, and God ordered the Sulanuth which was in the sea to come up and go into Egypt.

20 She had long arms, ten cubits in length of the cubit of a man.

21 And she went on the roofs and uncovered the raftering and flooring and cut them, and stretched forth her arm into the house and removed the lock and the bolt, and opened the houses of Egypt.

22 Afterward came the swarm of animals into the houses of Egypt, and the swarm of animals destroyed the

Egyptians, and it upset them greatly.

23 Still the anger of the Lord did not turn away from the Egyptians, and his hand was yet stretched forth against them.

24 God sent the pestilence and the pestilence pervaded Egypt, in the horses and asses and in the camels, in herds of oxen and sheep and in man.

25 When the Egyptians rose up early in the morning to take their cattle to pasture they found all their cattle dead.

26 There remained of the cattle of the Egyptians only one in ten, and of the cattle belonging to Israel in Goshen not one died.

27 And God sent a burning inflammation in the flesh of the Egyptians, which burst their skins; it became a severe itch in all the Egyptians from the soles of their feet to the crowns of their heads.

28 And many boils were in their flesh, that their flesh wasted away until they became rotten and putrid.

29 Still the anger of the Lord did not turn away, and his hand was still stretched out over all Egypt.

30 And the Lord sent a very heavy hail, which struck their vines and broke their fruit trees and dried them up that they fell on them.

31 Also every green herb became dry and perished, for a mingling fire descended with the hail, therefore the hail and the fire consumed all things.

32 Also men and beasts that were found abroad perished of the flames of fire and of the hail, and all the young lions were exhausted.

33 And the Lord sent and brought numerous locusts into Egypt, the Chasel, Salom, Chargol, and Chagole, locusts each of its kind, which devoured all that the hail had left remaining.

34 Then the Egyptians rejoiced at the locusts, although they consumed the produce of the field, and they caught them in abundance and salted them for food.

35 And the Lord turned a mighty wind of the sea which took away all the locusts, even those that were salted, and thrust them into the Red Sea; not one locust remained within the boundaries of Egypt.

36 God sent darkness on Egypt, that the whole land of Egypt and Pathros became dark for three days so that a man could not see his hand when he lifted it to his mouth.

37 At that time many of the people of Israel died who had rebelled against the Lord and who would not listen to Moses and Aaron, and believed not in them that God had sent them.

38 And who had said, We will not go forth from Egypt because we'll perish with hunger in a desolate wilderness. They were those who would not listen to the voice of Moses.

39 The Lord plagued them in the three days of darkness, and the Israelites buried them in those days without the Egyptians knowing of them or rejoicing over them.

40 The darkness was very great in Egypt for three days, and any person who was standing when the darkness came remained standing in his place; he that was sitting remained sitting, and he that was lying continued lying in the same state; he that was walking remained sitting on the ground in the same spot; and this thing happened to all the Egyptians until the darkness had passed away.

41 The days of darkness passed away and the Lord sent Moses and Aaron to the children of Israel saying, Celebrate your feast and make your Passover, for behold I come in the middle of the night among all the Egyptians; I will strike all their firstborn, from the firstborn of a man to the first born of a beast, and when I see your Passover, I will pass over you.

42 And the children of Israel did according to all that the Lord had commanded Moses and Aaron, thus did they in that night.

43 It came to pass in the middle of the night that the Lord went forth in the midst of Egypt and struck all the firstborn of the Egyptians, from the firstborn of man to the firstborn of beast.

44 And Pharaoh rose up in the night, he and all his servants and all the Egyptians, and there was a great cry throughout Egypt in that night for there was not a house in which there was not a corpse.

45 Also the likenesses of the firstborn of Egypt which were carved in the walls at their houses were destroyed and fell to the ground.

46 Even the bones of their firstborn who had died before this and whom they had buried in their houses were raked up by the dogs of Egypt on that night and dragged before the Egyptians and cast before them.

47 And all the Egyptians saw this evil which had suddenly come on them, and all the Egyptians cried out with a loud voice.

48 And all the families of Egypt wept on that night, each man for his son and each man for his daughter, being the firstborn, and the tumult of Egypt was heard at a distance on that night.

49 Bathia the daughter of Pharaoh went forth with the king on that night to seek Moses and Aaron in their houses; they found them in their houses eating and drinking and rejoicing with all Israel.

50 And Bathia said to Moses, Is this the reward for the good which I have done to you, who have reared you and made you grow and prosper and you have brought this evil on me and my father's house?

51 And Moses said to her, Certainly ten plagues did the Lord bring on Egypt; did any evil accrue to you from any of them? Did one of them affect you? And she said, No.

52 And Moses said to her, Although you are the firstborn to your mother, you shall not die and no evil shall reach you in the midst of Egypt.

53 And she said, What advantage is it to me when I see the king, my brother, and all his household and subjects in this evil, whose firstborn perish with all the firstborn of Egypt?

54 And Moses said to her, Certainly your brother and his household and subjects, the families of Egypt, would not listen to the words of the Lord, therefore did this evil come on them.

55 Pharaoh king of Egypt approached Moses and Aaron and some of the children of Israel who were with them in that place, and he prayed to them saying,

56 Rise up and take your brothers, all the children of Israel who are in the land with their sheep and oxen, and all belonging to them; they shall leave nothing remaining, only pray for me to the Lord your God.

57 And Moses said to Pharaoh, Behold you are your mother's firstborn, yet fear not for you will not die, for the Lord has commanded that you shall live in order to show you his great might and strong stretched out arm.

58 Pharaoh ordered the children of Israel to be sent away, and all the Egyptians strengthened themselves to send them, for they said, We are all perishing.

59 And all the Egyptians sent the Israelites forth with great riches, sheep and oxen and precious things according to the oath of the Lord between him and our Father Abraham.

60 And the children of Israel delayed going away until night, and when the Egyptians came to them to bring them out, they said to them, Are we thieves, that we should go forth at night?

61 And the children of Israel asked of the Egyptians, vessels of silver and vessels of gold, and garments, and the children of Israel stripped the Egyptians.

62 Moses hurried and rose up and went to the river of Egypt and brought up from there the coffin of Joseph and took it with him.

63 The children of Israel also brought up each man his father's coffin with him, and each man the coffins of his tribe.

CHAPTER 81

1 The children of Israel journeyed from Rameses to Succoth, about six hundred thousand men on foot besides the little ones and their wives.

2 Also a mixed multitude went up with them, flocks and herds, even much cattle.

3 The temporary time of the children of Israel who lived in the land of Egypt in hard labor was two hundred and ten years.

4 And at the end of two hundred and ten years, the Lord brought forth the children of Israel from Egypt with a strong hand.

5 The children of Israel traveled from Egypt and from Goshen and from Rameses, and encamped in Succoth on the fifteenth day of the first month.

6 The Egyptians buried all their firstborn whom the Lord had smitten, and all the Egyptians buried their slain for three days.

7 The children of Israel traveled from Succoth and encamped in Ethom, at the end of the wilderness.

8 On the third day after the Egyptians had buried their firstborn, many men rose up from Egypt and went after Israel to make them return to Egypt, for they regretted that they had sent the Israelites away from serving them.

9 One man said to his neighbor, Certainly Moses and Aaron spoke to Pharaoh saying, We will go a three days' journey in the wilderness and sacrifice to the Lord our God.

10 So now let us rise up early in the morning and make them return; it shall be that if they return with us to Egypt to their masters, then we will know that there is faith in them, but if they will not return then will we fight with

them, and make them come back with great power and a strong hand.

11 All the nobles of Pharaoh rose up in the morning, and with them about seven hundred thousand men; they went forth from Egypt on that day and came to the place where the children of Israel were.

12 And all the Egyptians looked and saw Moses and Aaron and all the children of Israel were sitting before Pi-hahiroth, eating and drinking and celebrating the feast of the Lord.

13 All the Egyptians said to the children of Israel, Certainly you said, We will go a journey for three days in the wilderness and sacrifice to our God and return.

14 So now this day makes five days since you went; why do you not return to your masters?

15 Moses and Aaron answered them, saying, Because the Lord our God has testified in us saying, You shall no more return to Egypt, but take yourselves to a land flowing with milk and honey; as the Lord our God had sworn to our ancestors to give to us.

16 And when the nobles of Egypt saw that the children of Israel did not listen to them to return to Egypt, they prepared themselves to fight with Israel.

17 The Lord strengthened the hearts of the children of Israel over the Egyptians so that they gave them a severe beating; the battle was severe on the Egyptians and all the Egyptians fled from before the children of Israel; many of them perished by the hand of Israel.

18 And the nobles of Pharaoh went to Egypt and told Pharaoh, saying, The children of Israel have fled and will no more return to Egypt, and in this manner did Moses and Aaron speak to us.

19 Pharaoh heard this thing, and his heart and the hearts of all his subjects were turned against Israel; they repented that they had sent Israel, and all the Egyptians advised Pharaoh to pursue the children of Israel to make them come back to their burdens.

20 They said each man to his brother, What is this which we have done, that we have sent Israel from our service?

21 The Lord strengthened the hearts of all the Egyptians to pursue the Israelites, for the Lord desired to overthrow the Egyptians in the Red Sea.

22 Pharaoh rose up and harnessed his chariot; he ordered all the Egyptians to assemble, not one man was left excepting the little ones and the women.

23 And all the Egyptians went forth with Pharaoh to pursue the children of Israel, and the camp of Egypt was a very large and strong camp, about ten hundred thousand men.

24 All of this camp went and pursued the children of Israel to bring them back to Egypt, and they reached them encamping by the Red Sea.

25 The children of Israel lifted up their eyes, and saw all the Egyptians pursuing them; the children of Israel were greatly terrified at them and the children of Israel cried to the Lord.

26 On account of the Egyptians, the children of Israel divided themselves into four divisions and they were divided in their opinions for they were afraid of the Egyptians, and Moses spoke to each of them.

27 The first division was of the children of Reuben, Simeon, and Issachar, and they decided to cast themselves into the sea, for they were greatly afraid of the Egyptians.

28 And Moses said to them, Fear not, stand still and see the salvation of the Lord which He will effect this day for you.

29 The second division was of the children of Zebulun, Benjamin and Naphtali, and they resolved to go back to Egypt with the Egyptians.

30 And Moses said to them, Fear not, for as you have seen the Egyptians this day, so shall you see them no more for ever.

31 The third division was of the children of Judah and Joseph, and they resolved to go to meet the Egyptians to fight with them.

32 And Moses said to them, Stand in your places for the Lord will fight for you, and you shall remain silent.

33 And the fourth division was of the children of Levi, Gad, and Asher, and they resolved to go into the midst of the Egyptians to confound them. Moses said to them, Remain in your stations and fear not, only call to the Lord that he may save you out of their hands.

34 After this Moses rose up from among the people and prayed to the Lord and said,

35 O Lord God of the whole earth, save now your people whom you brought forth from Egypt, and let not the Egyptians boast that power and might are theirs.

36 So the Lord said to Moses, Why do you cry to me? Speak to the children of Israel that they shall proceed, and stretch out your rod on the sea and divide it and the children of Israel shall pass through it.

37 And Moses did so; he lifted up his rod on the sea and divided it.

38 And the waters of the sea were divided into twelve parts, and the children of Israel passed through on foot with shoes, as a man would pass through a prepared road.

39 The Lord displayed to the children of Israel his wonders in Egypt and in the sea by the hand of Moses and Aaron.

40 When the children of Israel had entered the sea the Egyptians came after them, and the waters of the sea covered them and they all sank in the water; not one man was left except Pharaoh, who gave thanks to the Lord and believed in him, therefore the Lord did not cause him to perish at that time with the Egyptians.

41 The Lord ordered an angel to take him from among the Egyptians, who cast him on the land of Ninevah and he reigned over it for a long time.

42 On that day the Lord saved Israel from the hand of Egypt, and all the children of Israel saw that the Egyptians had perished; they beheld the great hand of the Lord in what he had performed in Egypt and in the sea.

43 Then sang Moses and the children of Israel this song to the Lord, on the day when the Lord caused the Egyptians to fall before them.

44 And all Israel sang in concert saying, I will sing to the Lord for He is greatly exalted, the horse and his rider has he cast into the sea, consider that it is written in the book of the law of God.

45 After this the children of Israel proceeded on their journey and encamped in Marah; the Lord gave to the children of Israel statutes and judgments in that place in Marah, and the Lord commanded the children of Israel to walk in all his ways and to serve him.

46 They journeyed from Marah and came to Elim; in Elim were twelve springs of water and seventy date trees and the children encamped there by the waters.

47 They journeyed from Elim and came to the wilderness of Sin, on the fifteenth day of the second month after their departure from Egypt.

48 At that time the Lord gave manna to the children of Israel to eat, and the Lord caused food to rain from heaven for the children of Israel day by day.

49 And the children of Israel ate the manna for forty years, all the days that they were in the wilderness, until they came to the land of Canaan to possess it.

50 They proceeded from the wilderness of Sin and encamped in Alush.

51 And they proceeded from Alush and encamped in Rephidim.

52 When the children of Israel were in Rephidim, Amalek the son of Eliphaz, the son of Esau, the brother of Zepho, came to fight with Israel.

53 And he brought with him eight hundred and one thousand men, magicians and conjurers, and he prepared for battle with Israel in Rephidim.

54 They carried on a great and severe battle against Israel, and the Lord delivered Amalek and his people into the hands of Moses and the children of Israel, and into the hand of Joshua, the son of Nun, the Ephrathite, the servant of Moses.

55 The children of Israel struck Amalek and his people at the edge of the sword, but the battle was very severe on the children of Israel.

56 And the Lord said to Moses, Write this thing as a memorial for you in a book, and place it in the hand of Joshua, the son of Nun your servant; you shall command the children of Israel, saying, When you come to the land of Canaan, you shall utterly wipe out the remembrance of Amalek from under heaven.

57 And Moses did so, and he took the book and wrote on it these words, saying,

58 Remember what Amalek has done to you in the road when you went forth from Egypt.

59 He met you in the road and struck your rear, even those that were feeble behind you when you were faint and weary.

60 Therefore it shall be when the Lord your God shall have given you rest from all your enemies round about in the land which the Lord your God gives you for an inheritance, to possess it, that you shall blot out the remembrance of Amalek from under heaven, you shall not forget it.

61 The king who shall have pity on Amalek or on his memory or on his offspring, behold I will blame him, and I will cut him off from among his people.

62 And Moses wrote all these things in a book, and he advised the children of Israel respecting all these matters.

CHAPTER 82

1 The children of Israel proceeded from Rephidim and camped in the wilderness of Sinai, in the third month from their going forth from Egypt.

2 At that time Reuel the Midianite, the father-in-law of Moses, came with Zipporah his daughter and her two sons for he had heard of the wonders of the Lord which he had done to Israel, that he had delivered them from the hand of Egypt.

3 Reuel came to Moses in the wilderness where he was camped, where the mountain of God was.

4 And Moses went forth to meet his father-in-law with great honor, and all Israel was with him.

5 Reuel and his children remained among the Israelites for many days, and Reuel knew the Lord from that day forward.

6 In the third month from the children of Israel's departure from Egypt, on the sixth day, the Lord gave to Israel the ten commandments on Mount Sinai.

7 All Israel heard all these commandments, and all Israel rejoiced greatly in the Lord on that day.

8 And the glory of the Lord rested on Mount Sinai; he called to Moses and Moses came in the midst of a cloud and ascended the mountain.

9 Moses was on the mount forty days and forty nights; he ate no bread and drank no water, and the Lord instructed him in the standards and judgments in order to teach the children of Israel.

10 And the Lord wrote the ten commandments which he had commanded the children of Israel on two tablets of stone, which he gave to Moses to command the children of Israel.

11 At the end of forty days and forty nights, when the Lord had finished speaking to Moses on Mount Sinai, the Lord gave to Moses the tablets of stone written with the finger of God.

12 When the children of Israel saw that Moses delayed coming down from the mount, they gathered round Aaron and said, As for this man Moses, we know not what has become of him.

13 Now therefore rise up, make to us a god who shall go before us, so that you shall not die.

14 Aaron was greatly afraid of the people, and he ordered them to bring him gold and he made it into a molten calf for the people.

15 The Lord said to Moses, before he had come down from the mount, Go down, for your people whom you brought forth from Egypt have corrupted themselves.

16 They have made to themselves a molten calf and have bowed down to it; now therefore leave me, that I may consume them from off the earth for they are a stubborn people.

17 And Moses sought the countenance of the Lord, and he prayed to the Lord for the people on account of the calf which they had made; afterward he descended from the mount and in his hands were the two tablets of stone which God had given him to command the Israelites.

18 When Moses approached the camp and saw the calf which the people had made, the anger of Moses was set ablaze and he broke the tablets under the mount.

19 Moses came to the camp; he took the calf and burned it with fire, and ground it till it became fine dust and scattered it on the water, and gave it to the Israelites to drink.

20 There died of the people by the swords of each other about three thousand men who had made the calf.

21 The next morning Moses said to the people, I will go up to the Lord, perhaps I may make atonement for your sins which you have sinned to the Lord.

22 And Moses again went up to the Lord, and he remained with the Lord forty days and forty nights.

23 And during the forty days Moses entreaed the Lord on behalf of the children of Israel, and the Lord listened to the prayer of Moses, and the Lord was begged of him on behalf of Israel.

24 Then spoke the Lord to Moses to cut out two stone tablets and to bring them up to the Lord, who would write on them the ten commandments.

25 Moses did so, and he came down and fashioned the two tablets and went up to Mount Sinai to the Lord, and the Lord wrote the ten commandments on the tablets.

26 Moses remained yet with the Lord forty days and forty nights, and the Lord instructed him in standards and judgments to give to Israel.

27 The Lord commanded him respecting the children of Israel that they should make a sanctuary for the Lord that his name might rest therein, and the Lord showed him the likeness of the sanctuary and the likeness of all its vessels.

28 And at the end of the forty days, Moses came down from the mount and the two tablets were in his hand.

29 And Moses came to the children of Israel and spoke to them all the words of the Lord, and he taught them laws, rules and judgments which the Lord had taught him.

30 Moses told the children of Israel the word of the Lord, that a sanctuary should be made for him to dwell among the children of Israel.

31 And the people rejoiced greatly at all the good which the Lord had spoken to them through Moses, and they said, We will do all that the Lord has spoken to you.

32 And the people rose up like one man and they made generous offerings to the sanctuary of the Lord; each man brought the offering of the Lord for the work of the sanctuary and for all its service.

33 All the children of Israel brought each man of all that was found in his possession for the work of the sanctuary of the Lord, gold, silver and brass, and every thing that was serviceable for the sanctuary.

34 All the wise men who were practiced in work came and made the sanctuary of the Lord, according to all that the Lord had commanded, every man in the work in which he had skill; all the wise men in heart made the sanctuary and its furniture and all the vessels for the holy service as the Lord had commanded Moses.

35 And the work of the sanctuary of the tabernacle was completed at the end of five months; the children of Israel did all that the Lord had commanded Moses.

36 And they brought the sanctuary and all its furniture to Moses; like to the representation which the Lord had shown to Moses, so did the children of Israel.

37 And Moses saw the work, and behold they did it as the Lord had commanded him, so Moses blessed them.

CHAPTER 83

1 In the twelfth month, in the twenty-third day of the month, Moses took Aaron and his sons and dressed them in their garments and anointed them, and did to them as the Lord had commanded him, and Moses brought up all the offerings which the Lord had on that day commanded him.

2 Moses afterward took Aaron and his sons and said to them, For seven days you shall remain at the door of the tabernacle, for thus am I commanded.

3 And Aaron and his sons did all that the Lord had commanded them through Moses, and they remained for seven days at the door of the tabernacle.

4 On the eighth day, being the first day of the first month, in the second year from the Israelites' departure from Egypt, Moses erected the sanctuary and put in all the furniture of the tabernacle and all the furniture of the sanctuary, and he did all that the Lord had commanded him.

5 Moses called to Aaron and his sons, and they brought the burnt offering and the sin offering for themselves and the children of Israel, as the Lord had commanded Moses.

6 On that day the two sons of Aaron, Nadab and Abihu, took strange fire and brought it before the Lord who had not commanded them to do it, and a fire went forth from before the Lord and consumed them, and they died before the Lord on that day.

7 Then on the day when Moses had completed erecting the sanctuary, the princes of the children of Israel began to bring their offerings before the Lord for the dedication of the altar.

8 And they brought up their offerings each prince for one day, a prince each day for twelve days.

9 And all the offerings which they brought, each man in his day, one silver charger weighing one hundred and thirty shekels, one silver bowl of seventy shekels after the shekel of the sanctuary, both of them full of fine flour mingled with oil for a meat offering;

10 One spoon, weighing ten shekels of gold, full of incense;

11 One young bullock, one ram, one lamb of the first year for a burnt offering;

12 And one kid of the goats for a sin offering.

13 For a sacrifice of peace offering: two oxen, five rams, five male goats, five lambs of a year old.

14 Thus did the twelve princes of Israel day by day, each man in his day.

15 It was after this in the thirteenth day of the month, that Moses commanded the children of Israel to observe the Passover.

16 And the children of Israel kept the Passover in its season in the fourteenth day of the month; as the Lord had commanded Moses, so did the children of Israel.

17 And in the second month, on the first day thereof, the Lord spoke to Moses saying,

18 Number the heads of all the males of the children of Israel from twenty years old and upward, you and your brother Aaron and the twelve princes of Israel.

19 And Moses did so, and Aaron came with the twelve princes of Israel, and they counted the children of Israel in the wilderness of Sinai.

20 And the number of the children of Israel by the houses of their fathers, from twenty years old and upward, were six hundred and three thousand, five hundred and fifty.

21 But the children of Levi were not numbered among their brothers the children of Israel.

22 And the number of all the males of the children of Israel from one month old and upward, was twenty-two thousand, two hundred and seventy-three.

23 And the number of the children of Levi from one month old and above, was twenty-two thousand.

24 Moses placed the priests and the Levites each man to his service and to his burden to serve the sanctuary of the tabernacle, as the Lord had commanded Moses.

25 And on the twentieth day of the month, the cloud was taken away from the tabernacle of testimony.

26 At that time the children of Israel continued their journey from the wilderness of Sinai, they took a journey of three days and the cloud rested on the wilderness of Paran; there the anger of the Lord was set ablaze against Israel, for they had provoked the Lord in asking him for meat to eat.

27 And the Lord listened to their voice, and gave them meat which they ate for one month.

28 But after this the anger of the Lord was set ablaze against them, and he struck them with a great slaughter, and they were buried there in that place.

29 The children of Israel called that place Kebroth Hattaavah, because there they buried the people that lusted flesh.

30 And they departed from Kebroth Hattaavah and pitched in Hazeroth, which is in the wilderness of Paran.

31 And while the children of Israel were in Hazeroth, the anger of the Lord was set ablaze against Miriam on account of Moses, and she became leprous, white as snow.

32 She was confined outside the camp for seven days until she had been received again after her leprosy.

33 The children of Israel afterward departed from Hazeroth and camped in the end of the wilderness of Paran.

34 At that time, the Lord spoke to Moses to send twelve men from the children of Israel, one man to a tribe, to go and explore the land of Canaan.

35 Moses sent the twelve men and they came to the land of Canaan to search and examine it, and they explored the whole land from the wilderness of Sin to Rechob as you come to Chamoth.

36 At the end of forty days they came to Moses and Aaron, and they brought him word as it was in their hearts; ten of the men brought up an evil report to the children of Israel, of the land which they had explored saying, It is better for us to return to Egypt than to go to this land, a land that consumes its inhabitants.

37 But Joshua the son of Nun and Caleb the son of Jephuneh, who were of those that explored the land said, The land is very good.

38 If the Lord delights in us, then he will bring us to this land and give it to us for it is a land flowing with milk and honey.

39 But the children of Israel would not listen to them, and they listened to the words of the ten men who had brought up an evil report of the land.

40 The Lord heard the murmurings of the children of Israel and he was angry and swore, saying,

41 Certainly not one man of this wicked generation shall see the land from twenty years old and upward except Caleb the son of Jephuneh and Joshua the son of Nun.

42 But certainly this wicked generation shall perish in this wilderness, and their children shall come to the land and they shall possess it. So the anger of the Lord was set ablaze against Israel and he made them wander in the wilderness for forty years until the end of that wicked generation because they did not follow the Lord.

43 And the people lived in the wilderness of Paran a long time, and they afterward proceeded to the wilderness by the way of the Red Sea.

CHAPTER 84

1 At that time Korah the son of Jetzer the son of Kehath the son of Levi, took many men of the children of Israel and they rose up and quarreled with Moses and Aaron and the whole congregation.

2 And the Lord was angry with them and the earth opened its mouth and swallowed them up, with their houses

and all belonging to them, and all the men belonging to Korah.

3 After this God made the people go round by the way of Mount Seir for a long time.

4 At that time the Lord said to Moses, Provoke not a war against the children of Esau, for I will not give to you of any thing belonging to them, as much as the sole of the foot could tread on, for I have given Mount Seir for an inheritance to Esau.

5 Therefore did the children of Esau fight against the children of Seir in former times, and the Lord had delivered the children of Seir into the hands of the children of Esau, and destroyed them from before them and the children of Esau lived in their stead to this day.

6 So the Lord said to the children of Israel, Fight not against the children of Esau your brothers for nothing in their land belongs to you, but you may buy food of them for money and eat it, and you may buy water of them for money and drink it.

7 And the children of Israel did according to the word of the Lord.

8 The children of Israel wandered in the wilderness, going round by the way of Mount Sinai for a long time, and touched not the children of Esau; they continued in that district for nineteen years.

9 At that time Latinus king of the children of Chittim died, in the forty-fifth year of his reign, which is the fourteenth year of the children of Israel's departure from Egypt.

10 They buried him in his place which he had built for himself in the land of Chittim, and Abimnas reigned in his place for thirty-eight years.

11 The children of Israel passed the boundary of the children of Esau in those days, at the end of nineteen years, and they came and passed the road of the wilderness of Moab.

12 And the Lord said to Moses, Besiege not Moab, and do not fight against them, for I will give you nothing of their land.

13 And the children of Israel passed the road of the wilderness of Moab for nineteen years, and they did not fight against them.

14 In the thirty-sixth year of the children of Israel's departing from Egypt the Lord struck the heart of Sihon, king of the Amorites; he waged war and went forth to fight against the children of Moab.

15 And Sihon sent messengers to Beor the son of Janeas, the son of Balaam, counsellor to the king of Egypt and to Balaam his son, to curse Moab in order that it might be delivered into the hand of Sihon.

16 And the messengers went and brought Beor the son of Janeas, and Balaam his son, from Pethor in Mesopotamia; so Beor and Balaam his son came to the city of Sihon and they cursed Moab and their king in the presence of Sihon king of the Amorites.

17 So Sihon went out with his whole army and he went to Moab and fought against them; he subdued them and the Lord delivered them into his hands, and Sihon killed the king of Moab.

18 Sihon took all the cities of Moab in the battle; he also took Heshbon from them, for Heshbon was one of the cities of Moab, and Sihon placed his princes and his nobles in Heshbon, and Heshbon belonged to Sihon in those days.

19 Therefore the parable speakers (wise men), Beor and Balaam his son, uttered these words, saying, Come to Heshbon, the city of Sihon will be built and established.

20 Woe to you Moab! You are lost, O people of Kemosh! Behold it is written on the book of the law of God.

21 And when Sihon had conquered Moab, he placed guards in the cities which he had taken from Moab, and a considerable number of the children of Moab fell in battle into the hand of Sihon; he made a great capture of them, sons and daughters, and he killed their king; so Sihon turned back to his own land.

22 And Sihon gave numerous presents of silver and gold to Beor and Balaam his son, and he dismissed them, and they went to Mesopotamia to their home and country.

23 At that time all the children of Israel passed from the road of the wilderness of Moab, and returned and surrounded the wilderness of Edom.

24 So the whole congregation came to the wilderness of Sin in the first month of the fortieth year from their departure from Egypt, and the children of Israel lived there in Kadesh of the wilderness of Sin, and Miriam died there and she was buried there.

25 At that time Moses sent messengers to Hadad king of Edom, saying, Thus says your brother Israel, Let me pass I pray you through your land, we will not pass through field or vineyard, we will not drink the water of the well; we will walk in the king's road.

26 And Edom said to him, You shall not pass through my country. And Edom went forth to meet the children of Israel with a mighty people.

27 And the children of Esau refused to let the children of Israel pass through their land, so the Israelites left them and did not fight against them.

28 For before this the Lord had commanded the children of Israel, saying, You shall not fight against the children of Esau. Therefore the Israelites went away from them and did not fight against them.

29 So the children of Israel departed from Kadesh, and all the people came to Mount Hor.

30 At that time the Lord said to Moses, Tell your brother Aaron that he shall die there, for he shall not come to the land which I have given to the children of Israel.

31 And Aaron went up at the command of the Lord to Mount Hor, in the fortieth year, in the fifth month, in the first day of the month.

32 And Aaron was one hundred and twenty-three years old when he died in Mount Hor.

CHAPTER 85

1 The king Arad the Canaanite, who lived in the south, heard that the Israelites had come by the way of the spies, and he arranged his forces to fight against the Israelites.

2 And the children of Israel were greatly afraid of him, for he had a great and courageous army, so the children of Israel resolved to return to Egypt.

3 The children of Israel turned back about the distance of three days' journey to Maserath Beni Jaakon, for they were greatly afraid on account of the king Arad.

4 And the children of Israel would not get back to their places, so they remained in Beni Jaakon for thirty days.

5 When the children of Levi saw that the children of Israel would not turn back, they were zealous for the sake of the Lord; they rose up and fought against the Israelites their brothers, and killed of them a great many and forced them to turn back to their place, Mount Hor.

6 And when they returned, king Arad was still arranging his host for battle against the Israelites.

7 Israel vowed a vow saying, If you will deliver this people into my hand, then I will utterly destroy their cities.

8 The Lord listened to the voice of Israel, and he delivered the Canaanites into their hands; he utterly destroyed them and their cities, and he called the name of the place Hormah.

9 The children of Israel journeyed from Mount Hor and camped in Oboth, and they journeyed from Oboth and they camped at Ije-abarim, in the border of Moab.

10 And the children of Israel sent to Moab, saying, Let us pass now through your land into our place, but the children of Moab would not allow the children of Israel to pass through their land, for the children of Moab were greatly afraid that the children of Israel should do to them as Sihon king of the Amorites had done to them, who had taken their land and had slain many of them.

11 Therefore Moab would not permit the Israelites to pass through his land, and the Lord commanded the children of Israel, saying that they should not fight against Moab, so the Israelites removed themselves from Moab.

12 And the children of Israel journeyed from the border of Moab; they came to the other side of Arnon, the border of Moab, between Moab and the Amorites, and they camped on the border of Sihon, king of the Amorites, in the wilderness of Kedemoth.

13 The children of Israel sent messengers to Sihon, king of the Amorites, saying,

14 Let us pass through your land; we will not turn into the fields or into the vineyards; we will go along by the king's highway until we shall have passed your border. But Sihon would not let the Israelites pass.

15 So Sihon collected all the people of the Amorites and went forth into the wilderness to meet the children of Israel, and he fought against Israel in Jahaz.

16 The Lord delivered Sihon king of the Amorites into the hands of the children of Israel, and Israel struck all the people of Sihon with the edge of the sword and avenged the cause of Moab.

17 The children of Israel took possession of the land of Sihon from Aram to Jabuk, to the children of Ammon, and they took all the booty of the cities.

18 Israel took all these cities, and Israel lived in all the cities of the Amorites.

19 All the children of Israel resolved to fight against the children of Ammon, to take their land also.

20 So the Lord said to the children of Israel, Do not besiege the children of Ammon, neither stir up battle against them, for I will give nothing to you of their land; the children of Israel listened to the word of the Lord, and did not fight against the children of Ammon.

21 The children of Israel turned and went up by the way of Bashan to the land of Og, king of Bashan, and Og the king of Bashan went out to meet the Israelites in battle; he had with him many courageous men, and a very strong force from the people of the Amorites.

22 And Og king of Bashan was a very powerful man, but Naaron his son was greatly powerful, even stronger than he was.

23 And Og said in his heart, Behold now the whole camp of Israel takes up a space of several miles. Now will I strike them at once without sword or spear.

24 Og went up Mount Jahaz and took from there one large stone, the length of which was three parsa, and he placed it on his head, and resolved to throw it on the camp of the children of Israel to strike all the Israelites with that stone.

25 And the angel of the Lord came and pierced the stone on the head of Og, and the stone fell on the neck of Og so that Og fell to the earth on account of the weight of the stone on his neck.

26 At that time the Lord said to the children of Israel, Be not afraid of him for I have given him and all his people and all his land into your hands, and you shall do to him as you did to Sihon.

27 Moses went down to him with a small number of the children of Israel, and Moses struck Og with a stick at the ankles of his feet and killed him.

28 The children of Israel afterward pursued the children of Og and all his people; they beat and destroyed them till there was no remnant left of them.

29 Moses afterward sent some of the children of Israel to spy out Jaazer, for Jaazer was a very famous city.

30 The spies went to Jaazer and explored it, and the spies trusted in the Lord; they fought against the men of Jaazer.

31 These men took Jaazer and its villages and the Lord delivered them into their hands, and they drove out the Amorites who had been there.

32 And the children of Israel took the land of the two kings of the Amorites, sixty cities which were on the other side of Jordan, from the brook of Arnon to Mount Herman.

33 The children of Israel journeyed and came into the plain of Moab which is on this side of Jordan, by Jericho.

34 And the children of Moab heard all the evil which the children of Israel had done to the two kings of the Amorites, to Sihon and Og; so all the men of Moab were greatly afraid of the Israelites.

35 The elders of Moab said, Behold the two kings of the Amorites, Sihon and Og, who were more powerful than all the kings of the earth, if they could not stand against the children of Israel how then can we stand before them?

36 Certainly they sent us a message before now to pass through our land on their way, and we would not allow them; now they will turn on us with their heavy swords and destroy us. Moab was distressed on account of the children of Israel and they were greatly afraid of them, and they counselled together what was to be done to the children of Israel.

37 The elders of Moab decided and took one of their men, Balak the son of Zippor the Moabite, and made him king over them at that time, and Balak was a very wise man.

38 And the elders of Moab rose up and sent to the children of Midian to make peace with them, for a great battle and enmity had been in those days between Moab and Midian, from the days of Hadad the son of Bedad king of Edom, who struck Midian in the field of Moab, to these days.

39 The children of Moab sent to the children of Midian and made peace with them, and the elders of Midian came to the land of Moab to make peace on behalf of the children of Midian.

40 And the elders of Moab counselled with the elders of Midian what to do in order to save their lives from Israel.

41 All the children of Moab said to the elders of Midian, The children of Israel shall lick up all that are round about us, as the ox licks up the grass of the field, for thus did they do to the two kings of the Amorites who are stronger than we are.

42 The elders of Midian said to Moab, We have heard that at the time when Sihon king of the Amorites fought against you, when he prevailed over you and took your land, he had sent to Beor the son of Janeas and to Balaam his son from Mesopotamia, and they came and cursed you; therefore did the hand of Sihon prevail over you, that he took your land.

43 Now therefore you send also to Balaam his son for he still remains in his land and give him his wage, that he may come and curse all the people of whom you are afraid; so the elders of Moab heard this thing, and it pleased them to send to Balaam the son of Beor.

44 So Balak the son of Zippor king of Moab sent messengers to Balaam, saying,

45 Behold there is a people come out from Egypt, see how they cover the face of the earth and they are against

me.

46 So now come and curse this people for me for they are too mighty for me; perhaps I shall succeed to fight against them and drive them out, for I heard that he whom you bless is blessed, and whom you curse is cursed.

47 So the messengers of Balak went to Balaam and brought Balaam to curse the people to fight against Moab.

48 And Balaam came to Balak to curse Israel, and the Lord said to Balaam, Curse not this people for they are blessed.

49 And Balak urged Balaam day by day to curse Israel, but Balaam did not listen to Balak on account of the word of the Lord which he had spoken to Balaam.

50 And when Balak saw that Balaam would not accede to his wish, he rose up and went home; Balaam also returned to his land and he went from there to Midian.

51 The children of Israel journeyed from the plain of Moab and camped by Jordan from Beth-jesimoth even to Abel-shittim, at the end of the plains of Moab.

52 When the children of Israel stayed in the plain of Shittim, they began to commit prostitution with the daughters of Moab.

53 The children of Israel approached Moab, and the children of Moab pitched their tents opposite to the camp of the children of Israel.

54 The children of Moab were afraid of the children of Israel, and the children of Moab took all their daughters and their wives of beauty and attractive appearance, and dressed them in gold and silver and costly garments.

55 The children of Moab seated those women at the door of their tents in order that the children of Israel might see them and turn to them, and not fight against Moab.

56 All the children of Moab did this thing to the children of Israel, and every man placed his wife and daughter at the door of his tent; all the children of Israel saw the act of the children of Moab, and the children of Israel turned to the daughters of Moab and coveted them, and they went to them.

57 It came to pass that when a Hebrew came to the door of the tent of Moab and saw a daughter of Moab, and desired her in his heart and spoke with her at the door of the tent that which he desired, while they were speaking together the men of the tent would come out and speak to the Hebrew like these words:

58 Certainly you know that we are brothers, we are all the descendants of Lot and the descendants of Abraham his brother, why then will you not remain with us, and why will you not eat our bread and our sacrifice?

59 When the children of Moab had thus overwhelmed him with their speeches and enticed him by their flattering words, they seated him in the tent and cooked and sacrificed for him, and he ate of their sacrifice and of their bread.

60 They then gave him wine and he drank and became intoxicated; they placed before him a beautiful damsel and he did with her as he liked, for he knew not what he was doing, as he had drunk plentifully of wine.

61 Thus did the children of Moab to Israel in that place, in the plain of Shittim, and the anger of the Lord was set ablaze against Israel on account of this matter; he sent a pestilence among them and there of the Israelites twenty-four thousand men died.

62 Then there was a man of the children of Simeon whose name was Zimri, the son of Salu, who connected himself with the Midianite Cosbi, the daughter of Zur, king of Midian, in the sight of all the children of Israel.

63 And Phineas the son of Elazer, the son of Aaron the priest, saw this wicked thing which Zimri had done; he took a spear and rose up and went after them, pierced them both and killed them, and the pestilence ceased from the children of Israel.

CHAPTER 86

1 At that time after the pestilence, the Lord said to Moses and to Elazer the son of Aaron the priest,

2 Count the heads of the whole community of the children of Israel, from twenty years old and upward, all that went forth in the army.

3 And Moses and Elazer numbered the children of Israel after their families, and the number of all Israel was seven hundred thousand, seven hundred and thirty.

4 The number of the children of Levi, from one month old and upward, was twenty-three thousand, and among these there was not a man of those numbered by Moses and Aaron in the wilderness of Sinai.

5 For the Lord had told them that they would die in the wilderness, so they all died, and not one had been left of them excepting Caleb the son of Jephuneh, and Joshua the son of Nun.

6 And it was after this that the Lord said to Moses, Say to the children of Israel to avenge on Midian the cause of their brothers the children of Israel.

7 Moses did so, and the children of Israel chose from among them twelve thousand men, being one thousand to a tribe, and they went to Midian.

8 And the children of Israel warred against Midian, and they killed every male, also the five princes of Midian, and Balaam the son of Beor they killed with the sword.

9 And the children of Israel took the wives of Midian captive, with their little ones and their cattle, and all belonging to them.

10 They took all the booty and all the valuables, and they brought it to Moses and to Elazer to the plains of Moab.

11 Moses and Elazer and all the princes of the congregation went forth to meet them with joy.

12 And they divided all the goods of Midian, and the children of Israel had been revenged on Midian for the cause of their brothers the children of Israel.

CHAPTER 87

1 At that time the Lord said to Moses, Behold your days are approaching to an end, take now Joshua the son of Nun your servant and place him in the tabernacle and I will command him, and Moses did so.

2 The Lord appeared in the tabernacle in a pillar of cloud, and the pillar of cloud stood at the entrance of the tabernacle.

3 The Lord commanded Joshua the son of Nun and said to him, Be strong and courageous, for you shall bring the children of Israel to the land which I swore to give them, and I will be with you.

4 And Moses said to Joshua, Be strong and courageous, for you will make the children of Israel inherit the land, and the Lord will be with you; he will not leave you nor turn away from you, be not afraid or disheartened.

5 Moses called to all the children of Israel and said to them, You have seen all the good which the Lord your God has done for you in the wilderness.

6 Now therefore observe all the words of this law and walk in the way of the Lord your God, turn not from the way which the Lord has commanded you, either to the right or to the left.

7 And Moses taught the children of Israel rules and judgments and laws to do in the land as the Lord had commanded him.

8 And he taught them the way of the Lord and his laws; behold they are written on the book of the law of God which he gave to the children of Israel by the hand of Moses.

9 And Moses finished commanding the children of Israel, and the Lord said to him, Go up to the Mount Abarim and die there, and be gathered to your people as Aaron your brother was gathered.

10 And Moses went up as the Lord had commanded him, and he died there in the land of Moab by the order of the Lord, in the fortieth year from the Israelites going forth from the land of Egypt.

11 And the children of Israel wept for Moses in the plains of Moab for thirty days, and the days of weeping and mourning for Moses were completed.

CHAPTER 88

1 It was after the death of Moses that the Lord said to Joshua the son of Nun,

2 Rise up and pass the Jordan to the land which I have given to the children of Israel, and you shall make the children of Israel inherit the land.

3 Every place on which the sole of your feet treads shall belong to you; from the wilderness of Lebanon to the great river, the river of Perath, shall be your boundary.

4 No man shall stand up against you all the days of your life; as I was with Moses, so will I be with you, only be strong and of good courage to observe all the law which Moses commanded you; turn not from the way either to the right or to the left, in order that you may prosper in all that you do.

5 And Joshua commanded the officers of Israel, saying, Pass through the camp and command the people, saying, Prepare for yourselves provisions, for in three days more you will pass the Jordan to possess the land.

6 The officers of the children of Israel did so, and they commanded the people and they did all that Joshua had commanded.

7 Joshua sent two men to spy out the land of Jericho, and the men went and spied out Jericho.

8 And at the end of seven days they came to Joshua in the camp and said to him, The Lord has delivered the whole land into our hands; the inhabitants thereof are melted with fear because of us.

9 And it came to pass after that, that Joshua rose up in the morning and all Israel with him, and they journeyed from Shittim; Joshua and all Israel with him passed the Jordan, and Joshua was eighty-two years old when he passed the Jordan with Israel.

10 The people went up from Jordan on the tenth day of the first month, and they camped in Gilgal at the eastern corner of Jericho.

11 And the children of Israel kept the Passover in Gilgal in the plains of Jericho, on the fourteenth day of the month, as it is written in the law of Moses.

12 The manna ceased at that time on the morning of the Passover, and there was no more manna for the children of Israel and they ate of the produce of the land of Canaan.

13 Jericho was entirely closed against the children of Israel, no one came out or went in.

14 And it was in the second month, on the first day of the month, that the Lord said to Joshua, Rise up, behold I have given Jericho into your hand with all the people there; all your fighting men shall go round the city, once each day, thus shall you do for six days.

15 And the priests shall blow on trumpets; when you hear the sound of the trumpet, all the people shall give a great shouting, that the walls of the city shall fall down; all the people shall go up every man against his opponent.

16 And Joshua did so according to all that the Lord had commanded him.

17 On the seventh day they went round the city seven times, and the priests blew on trumpets.

18 At the seventh round, Joshua said to the people, Shout, for the Lord has delivered the whole city into our hands.

19 Only the city and all that it contains shall be accursed to the Lord, and keep yourselves from the accursed thing, that you make the camp of Israel accursed and trouble it.

20 But all the silver and gold and brass and iron shall be consecrated to the Lord, they shall come into the treasury of the Lord.

21 And the people blew on trumpets and made a great shouting, and the walls of Jericho fell down; all the people went up, every man straight before him, and they took the city and utterly destroyed all that was in it, both man and woman, young and old, ox and sheep and ass, with the edge of the sword.

22 And they burned the whole city with fire; only the vessels of silver and gold, brass and iron, they put into the treasury of the Lord.

23 Joshua swore at that time, saying, Cursed be the man who builds Jericho; he shall lay the foundation thereof in his firstborn, and in his youngest son he shall set up the gates of it.

24 And Achan the son of Carmi, the son of Zabdi, the son of Zerah, son of Judah, dealt treacherously in the accursed thing, and he took of the accursed thing and hid it in the tent, and the anger of the Lord was set ablaze against Israel.

25 It was after this when the children of Israel had returned from burning Jericho, Joshua sent men to spy out also Ai, and to fight against it.

26 And the men went up and spied out Ai, and they returned and said, Let not all the people go up with you to Ai, only let about three thousand men go up and strike the city, for the men there are few.

27 And Joshua did so; there went up with him of the children of Israel about three thousand men, and they fought against the men of Ai.

28 And the battle was severe against Israel, and the men of Ai struck thirty-six men of Israel, and the children of Israel fled from before the men of Ai.

29 When Joshua saw this thing, he tore his garments and fell on his face to the ground before the Lord, he with the elders of Israel, and they put dust on their heads.

30 And Joshua said, Why O Lord did you bring this people over the Jordan? What shall I say after the Israelites have turned their backs against their enemies?

31 So now all the Canaanites, inhabitants of the land, will hear this thing and surround us and cut off our name.

32 And the Lord said to Joshua, Why do you fall on your face? Rise, get up, for the Israelites have sinned and taken of the accursed thing; I will no more be with them unless they destroy the accursed thing from among

them.

33 And Joshua rose up and assembled the people, and brought the Urim by the order of the Lord, and the tribe of Judah was taken, and Achan the son of Carmi was taken.

34 Joshua said to Achan, Tell me my son, what have you done, and Achan said, I saw among the spoil a goodly garment of Shinar and two hundred shekels of silver, and a wedge of gold of fifty shekels weight; I coveted them and took them, and behold they are all hid in the earth in the middle of the tent.

35 And Joshua sent men who went and took them from the tent of Achan, and they brought them to Joshua.

36 Joshua took Achan and these utensils, and his sons and daughters and all belonging to him, and they brought them into the valley of Achor.

37 Joshua burned them there with fire, and all the Israelites stoned Achan with stones; they raised over him a heap of stones, therefore he called that place the valley of Achor. So the Lord's anger was appeased, and Joshua afterward came to the city and fought against it.

38 And the Lord said to Joshua, Fear not, neither be dismayed, behold I have given into your hand Ai, her king and her people, and you shall do to them as you did to Jericho and her king, only the goods and the cattle there you shall take for yourselves; lay an ambush for the city behind it.

39 So Joshua did according to the word of the Lord, and he chose from among the sons of war thirty thousand courageous men; he sent them and they lay in ambush for the city.

40 And he commanded them, saying, When you shall see us we will flee before them with cunning, and they will pursue us; you shall then rise out of the ambush and take the city, and they did so.

41 Joshua fought, and the men of the city went out toward Israel, not knowing that they were lying in ambush for them behind the city.

42 Joshua and all the Israelites pretended to be wearied out before them, and they fled by the way of the wilderness with cunning.

43 The men of Ai gathered all the people who were in the city to pursue the Israelites; they went out and were drawn away from the city; not one remained and they left the city open and pursued the Israelites.

44 Those who were lying in ambush rose up out of their places, hurried to come to the city and took it and set it on fire; the men of Ai turned back, and there the smoke of the city ascended to the skies, and they had no means of retreating either one way or the other.

45 All the men of Ai were in the midst of Israel, some on this side and some on that side, and they struck them so that not one of them remained.

46 The children of Israel took Melosh king of Ai alive and they brought him to Joshua, and Joshua hanged him on a tree and he died.

47 And the children of Israel returned to the city after having burned it; they struck all those that were in it with the edge of the sword.

48 The number of those that had fallen of the men of Ai, both man and woman, was twelve thousand; only the cattle and the goods of the city they took to themselves, according to the word of the Lord to Joshua.

49 And all the kings on this side Jordan, all the kings of Canaan, heard of the evil which the children of Israel had done to Jericho and to Ai, and they gathered themselves together to fight against Israel.

50 Only the inhabitants of Gibeon were greatly afraid of fighting against the Israelites that they should perish, so they acted cunningly; they came to Joshua and to all Israel and said to them, We have come from a distant land, so now make a covenant with us.

51 And the inhabitants of Gibeon over-reached the children of Israel, and the children of Israel made a covenant with them, and they made peace with them; the princes of the congregation swore to them, but afterward the children of Israel knew that they were neighbors to them and were dwelling among them.

52 But the children of Israel killed them not; for they had sworn to them by the Lord, and they became hewers of wood and drawers of water.

53 Joshua said to them, Why did you deceive me, to do this thing to us? And they answered him, Because it was told to your servants all that you had done to all the kings of the Amorites, and we were greatly afraid of our lives, and we did this thing.

54 Joshua appointed them on that day to hew wood and to draw water, and he divided them for slaves to all the tribes of Israel.

55 And when Adonizedek king of Jerusalem heard all that the children of Israel had done to Jericho and to Ai, he sent to Hoham king of Hebron and to Piram king at Jarmuth, and to Japhia king of Lachish and to Deber king of Eglon, saying,

56 Come up to me and help me, that we may strike the children of Israel and the inhabitants of Gibeon who have made peace with the children of Israel.

57 And they gathered themselves together and the five kings of the Amorites went up with all their camps, a mighty people numerous as the sand of the seashore.

58 All these kings came and camped before Gibeon, and they began to fight against the inhabitants of Gibeon, and all the men of Gibeon sent to Joshua, saying, Come up quickly to us and help us, for all the kings of the Amorites have gathered together to fight against us.

59 Joshua and all the fighting people went up from Gilgal, and Joshua came suddenly to them and struck these five kings with a great slaughter.

60 And the Lord confounded them before the children at Israel, who struck them with a terrible slaughter in Gibeon, and pursued them along the way that goes up to Beth Horon to Makkedah; they fled from before the children of Israel.

61 And while they were fleeing, the Lord sent on them hailstones from heaven, and more of them died by the hailstones than by the slaughter of the children of Israel.

62 The children of Israel pursued them, and they still struck them in the road, going on and smiting them.

63 And when they were smiting, the day was declining toward evening and Joshua said in the sight of all the people, Sun, stand still on Gibeon, and you moon in the valley of Ajalon, until the nation shall have revenged itself on its enemies.

64 The Lord listened to the voice of Joshua, and the sun stood still in the midst of the heavens, and it stood still six and thirty moments, and the moon also stood still and hurried not to go down a whole day.

65 And there was no day like that, before it or after it that the Lord listened to the voice of a man, for the Lord fought for Israel.

CHAPTER 89

1 Then Joshua spoke this song on the day that the Lord had given the Amorites into the hand of Joshua and the children of Israel, and he said it in the sight of all Israel,

2 You have done mighty things, O Lord, you have performed great deeds; who is like you? My lips shall sing to your name.

3 My goodness and my fortress, my high tower, I will sing a new song to you; with thanksgiving I will sing to you, you are the strength of my salvation.

4 All the kings of the earth shall praise you, the princes of the world shall sing to you, the children of Israel shall rejoice in your salvation; they shall sing and praise your power.

5 To you, O Lord, we confided; we said you are our God, for you were our shelter and strong tower against our enemies.

6 To you we cried and were not ashamed, in you we trusted and were delivered; when we cried to you, you heard our voice, you delivered our souls from the sword, you showed to us your grace, you gave to us your salvation, you rejoiced our hearts with your strength.

7 You went forth for our salvation, with your arm you redeemed your people; you answered us from the heavens of your holiness, you saved us from ten thousands of people.

8 The sun and moon stood still in heaven, and you stood in your wrath against our oppressors and commanded your judgments over them.

9 All the princes of the earth stood up, the kings of the nations had gathered themselves together, they were not moved at your presence; they desired your battles.

10 You rose against them in your anger, and brought down your wrath on them; you destroyed them in your anger, and cut them off in your heart.

11 Nations have been consumed with your fury, kingdoms have declined because of your wrath, you wounded kings in the day of your anger.

12 You poured out your fury on them, your wrathful anger took hold of them; you turned their iniquity on them, and cut them off in their wickedness.

13 They spread a trap and fell therein; in the net they hid, their foot was caught.

14 Your hand was ready for all your enemies who said, Through their sword they possessed the land, through their arm they lived in the city; you filled their faces with shame, you brought their horns down to the ground,

you terrified them in your wrath and destroyed them in your anger.

15 The earth trembled and shook at the sound of your storm over them, you did not withhold their souls from death, and brought down their lives to the grave.

16 You pursued them in your storm, you concumed them in your whirlwind, you turned their rain into hail, they fell in deep pits so that they could not rise.

17 Their carcasses were like rubbish cast out in the middle of the streets.

18 They were consumed and destroyed in your anger, you saved your people with your might.

19 Therefore our hearts rejoice in you, our souls exalt in your salvation.

20 Our tongues shall relate your might, we will sing and praise your wondrous works.

21 For you did save us from our enemies, you did deliver us from those who rose up against us, you did destroy them from before us and depress them beneath our feet.

22 Thus shall all your enemies perish O Lord, and the wicked shall be like chaff driven by the wind, and your beloved shall be like trees planted by the waters.

23 So Joshua and all Israel with him returned to the camp in Gilgal, after having smitten all the kings, so that not a remnant was left of them.

24 And the five kings fled alone on foot from battle and hid themselves in a cave, and Joshua sought for them in the field of battle and did not find them.

25 And it was afterward told to Joshua, saying, The kings are found and there, they are hidden in a cave.

26 And Joshua said, Appoint men to be at the mouth of the cave to guard them, that they not take themselves away. And the children of Israel did so.

27 And Joshua called to all Israel and said to the officers of battle, Place your feet on the necks of these kings, and Joshua said, So shall the Lord do to all your enemies.

28 Joshua commanded afterward that they should kill the kings and cast them into the cave, and put great stones at the mouth of the cave.

29 Joshua went afterward with all the people that were with him on that day to Makkedah, and he struck it with the edge of the sword.

30 He utterly destroyed the souls and all belonging to the city, and he did to the king and people there as he had done to Jericho.

31 He passed from there to Libnah and he fought against it; the Lord delivered it into his hands and Joshua struck it with the edge of the sword, and all the souls there and he did it and to the king there as he had done to Jericho.

32 From there he passed on to Lachish to fight against it, and Horam king of Gaza went up to assist the men of Lachish, and Joshua struck him and his people until there was none left to him.

33 Joshua took Lachish and all the people there, and he did to it as he had done to Libnah.

34 Joshua passed from there to Eglon, and he took that also; he struck it and all the people there with the edge of the sword.

35 From there he passed to Hebron and fought against it and took it and utterly destroyed it; he returned from there with all Israel to Debir and fought against it and struck it with the edge of the sword.

36 And he destroyed every soul in it, he left none remaining; he did to it and the king thereof as he had done to Jericho.

37 Joshua struck all the kings of the Amorites from Kadesh-barnea to Azah; he took their country at once, for the Lord had fought for Israel.

38 And Joshua with all Israel came to the camp to Gilgal.

39 When at that time Jabin king of Chazor heard all that Joshua had done to the kings of the Amorites, Jabin sent to Jobat king of Midian, and to Laban king of Shimron, to Jephal king of Achshaph, and to all the kings of the Amorites, saying,

40 Come quickly to us and help us, that we may strike the children of Israel before they come on us and do to us as they have done to the other kings of the Amorites.

41 And all these kings listened to the words of Jabin, king of Chazor, and they went forth with all their camps, seventeen kings, and their people were as numerous as the sand on the seashore, together with horses and chariots innumerable; they came and camped together at the waters of Merom, and they were met together to fight against Israel.

42 The Lord said to Joshua, Fear them not, for tomorrow about this time I will deliver them up all slain before you, you shall cripple their horses and burn their chariots with fire.

43 And Joshua with all the men of war came suddenly on them and struck them, and they fell into their hands,

for the Lord had delivered them into the hands of the children of Israel.

44 So the children of Israel pursued all these kings with their camps and struck them until there was none left of them, and Joshua did to them as the Lord had spoken to him.

45 Joshua returned at that time to Chazor and struck it with the sword and destroyed every soul in it and burned it with fire; from Chazor, Joshua passed to Shimron and struck it and utterly destroyed it.

46 From there he passed to Achshaph and he did to it as he had done to Shimron.

47 From there he passed to Adulam and he struck all the people in it, and he did to Adulam as he had done to Achshaph and to Shimron.

48 He passed from them to all the cities of the kings which he had smitten, and he struck all the people that were left of them and he utterly destroyed them.

49 Only their booty and cattle the Israelites took to themselves as a prey, but every human being they struck; they permitted not a soul to live.

50 As the Lord had commanded Moses so did Joshua and all Israel, they failed not in anything.

51 So Joshua and all the children of Israel struck the whole land of Canaan as the Lord had commanded them, and struck all their kings, being thirty and one kings, and the children of Israel took their whole country.

52 Besides the kingdoms of Sihon and Og which are on the other side Jordan, of which Moses had smitten many cities, Moses gave them to the Reubenites and the Gadites and to half the tribe of Manasseh.

53 And Joshua struck all the kings that were on this side of Jordan to the west, and gave them for an inheritance to the nine tribes and to the half tribe of Israel.

54 For five years Joshua carried on the war with these kings, and he gave their cities to the Israelites, and the land became tranquil from battle throughout the cities of the Amorites and the Canaanites.

CHAPTER 90

1 At that time in the fifth year after the children of Israel had passed over Jordan, after the children of Israel had rested from their war with the Canaanites, great and severe battles arose between Edom and the children of Chittim, and the children of Chittim fought against Edom.

2 Abianus king of Chittim went forth in that year, that is in the thirty-first year of his reign, and a great force with him of the mighty men of the children of Chittim, and he went to Seir to fight against the children of Esau.

3 Hadad the king of Edom heard of his report, and he went forth to meet him with many people and a strong force, and engaged in battle with him in the field of Edom.

4 And the hand of Chittim prevailed over the children of Esau, and the children of Chittim killed of the children of Esau two and twenty thousand men, and all the children of Esau fled from before them.

5 The children of Chittim pursued them and they reached Hadad king of Edom, who was running before them and they caught him alive, and brought him to Abianus king of Chittim.

6 And Abianus ordered him to be slain; Hadad king of Edom died in the forty-eighth year of his reign.

7 And the children of Chittim continued their pursuit of Edom; they struck them with a great slaughter and Edom became subject to the children of Chittim.

8 And the children of Chittim ruled over Edom, and Edom came under the hands of the children of Chittim and became one kingdom from that day.

9 From that time they could no more lift up their heads, and their kingdom became one with the children of Chittim.

10 Abianus placed officers in Edom and all the children of Edom became subject to Abianus, and Abianus turned back to his own land, Chittim.

11 When he returned he renewed his government and built for himself a spacious and fortified palace for a royal residence, and reigned securely over the children of Chittim and over Edom.

12 In those days, after the children of Israel had driven away all the Canaanites and the Amorites, Joshua was old and advanced in years.

13 And the Lord said to Joshua, You are old, advanced in life, and a great part of the land remains to be possessed.

14 Now therefore divide this land for an inheritance to the nine tribes and to the half tribe of Manasseh, and Joshua rose up and did as the Lord had spoken to him.

15 And he divided the whole land to the tribes of Israel as an inheritance according to their divisions.

16 But to the tribe at Levi he gave no inheritance. The offerings of the Lord are their inheritance as the Lord had spoken of them by the hand of Moses.

17 Joshua gave Mount Hebron to Caleb the son of Jephuneh, one portion above his brothers, as the Lord had spoken through Moses.

18 Therefore Hebron became an inheritance to Caleb and his children to this day.

19 Joshua divided the whole land by lots to all Israel for an inheritance, as the Lord had commanded him.

20 And the children of Israel gave cities to the Levites from their own inheritance, and suburbs for their cattle, and property; as the Lord had commanded Moses so did the children of Israel, and they divided the land by lot whether great or small.

21 They went to inherit the land according to their boundaries, and the children of Israel gave to Joshua the son of Nun an inheritance among them.

22 By the word of the Lord they gave to him the city which he required, Timnath-serach in Mount Ephraim, and he built the city and lived therein.

23 These are the inheritances which Elazer the priest and Joshua the son of Nun and the heads of the fathers of the tribes portioned out to the children of Israel by lot in Shiloh, before the Lord, at the door of the tabernacle, and they left off dividing the land.

24 And the Lord gave the land to the Israelites, and they possessed it as the Lord had spoken to them, and as the Lord had sworn to their ancestors.

25 And the Lord gave to the Israelites rest from all their enemies around them, and no man stood up against them; the Lord delivered all their enemies into their hands, and not one thing failed of all the good which the Lord had spoken to the children of Israel, yes, the Lord performed everything.

26 Joshua called to all the children of Israel and he blessed them, and commanded them to serve
the Lord, and afterward sent them away; they went each man to his city, and each man to his inheritance.

27 And the children of Israel served the Lord all the days of Joshua, and the Lord gave them rest from all around them, and they lived securely in their cities.

28 It came to pass in those days, that Abianus king of Chittim died, in the thirty-eighth year of his reign, that is the seventh year of his reign over Edom; they buried him in his place which he had built for himself, and Latinus reigned in his stead fifty years.

29 During his reign he brought forth an army, and he went and fought against the inhabitants of Britannia and Kernania, the children of Elisha son of Javan, and he succeeded over them and made them subjects.

30 He then heard that Edom had revolted from under the hand of Chittim, and Latinus went to them and struck them and subdued them, and placed them under the hand of the children of Chittim; Edom became one kingdom with the children of Chittim all the days.

31 And for many years there was no king in Edom, and their government was with the children of Chittim and their king.

32 It was in the twenty-sixth year after the children of Israel had passed the Jordan, that is the sixty-sixth year after the children of Israel had departed from Egypt, that Joshua was old, advanced in years, being one hundred and eight years old in those days.

33 Joshua called to all Israel, to their elders, their judges and officers, after the Lord had given to all the Israelites rest from all their enemies round about; Joshua said to the elders of Israel and to their judges, Behold I am old, advanced in years, and you have seen what the Lord has done to all the nations whom he has driven away from before you, for it is the Lord who has fought for you.

34 Now therefore strengthen yourselves to keep and to do all the words of the law of Moses, not to deviate from it to the right or to the left, and not to come among those nations who are left in the land; neither shall you make mention of the name of their gods, but you shall cleave to the Lord your God, as you have done to this day.

35 Joshua greatly encouraged the children of Israel to serve the Lord all their days.

36 And all the Israelites said, We will serve the Lord our God all our days, we and our children, and our children's children, and our offspring forever.

37 Joshua made a covenant with the people on that day and he sent away the children of Israel, and they went each man to his inheritance and to his city.

38 And it was in those days, when the children of Israel were dwelling securely in their cities, that they buried the coffins of the tribes of their ancestors which they had brought up from Egypt, each man in the inheritance of his children; the twelve sons of Jacob did the children of Israel bury, each man in the possession of his children.

39 And these are the names of the cities where they buried the twelve sons of Jacob, whom the children of Israel had brought up from Egypt:

40 They buried Reuben and Gad on this side of Jordan, in Romia, which Moses had given to their children.

41 And Simeon and Levi they buried in the city Mauda, which he had given to the children of Simeon, and the suburb of the city was for the children of Levi.

42 And Judah they buried in the city of Benjamin opposite Bethlehem.

43 And the bones of Issachar and Zebulun they buried in Zidon, in the portion which fell to their children.

44 Dan was buried in the city of his children in Eshtael, and Naphtali and Asher they buried in Kadesh-naphtali, each man in his place which he had given to his children.

45 And the bones of Joseph they buried in Shechem in the part of the field which Jacob had purchased from Hamor, and which became to Joseph for an inheritance.

46 And they buried Benjamin in Jerusalem opposite the Jebusite, which was given to the children of Benjamin; the children of Israel buried their fathers each man in the city of his children.

47 And at the end of two years, Joshua the son of Nun died, one hundred and ten years old, and the time which Joshua judged Israel was twenty-eight years; Israel served the Lord all the days of his life.

48 And the other affairs of Joshua and his battles and his reproofs with which he reproved Israel, and all which he had commanded them, and the names of the cities which the children of Israel possessed in his days, they are written in the book of the words of Joshua to the children of Israel and in the book of the wars of the Lord, which Moses and Joshua and the children of Israel had written.

49 And the children of Israel buried Joshua in the border of his inheritance, in Timnath-serach which was given to him in Mount Ephraim.

50 And Elazer the son of Aaron died in those days; they buried him in a hill belonging to Phineas his son, which was given him in Mount Ephraim.

CHAPTER 91

1 At that time, after the death of Joshua, the children of the Canaanites were still in the land, and the Israelites resolved to drive them out.

2 And the children of Israel asked of the Lord, saying, Who shall first go up for us to the Canaanites to fight against them? And the Lord said, Judah shall go up.

3 And the children of Judah said to Simeon, Go up with us into our lot, and we will fight against the Canaanites and we likewise will go up with you in your lot; so the children of Simeon went with the children of Judah.

4 The children of Judah went up and fought against the Canaanites, so the Lord delivered the Canaanites into the hands of the children of Judah; they struck in Bezek ten thousand men.

5 They fought with Adonibezek in Bezek, he fled from before them, and they pursued him and caught him; they took hold of him and cut off his thumbs and great toes.

6 And Adonibezek said, Three score and ten kings having their thumbs and great toes cut off, gathered their meat under my table, as I have done, so God has rewarded me; they brought him to Jerusalem and he died there.

7 And the children of Simeon went with the children of Judah, and they struck the Canaanites with the edge of the sword.

8 The Lord was with the children of Judah, and they possessed the mountain, and the children of Joseph went up to Bethel, the same is Luz, and the Lord was with them.

9 And the children of Joseph spied out Bethel, and the watchmen saw a man going forth from the city, and they caught him and said to him, Show us now the entrance of the city and we will show kindness to you.

10 And that man showed them the entrance of the city, and the children of Joseph came and struck the city with the edge of the sword.

11 The man with his family they sent away, and he went to the Hittites and he built a city; he called the name there Luz, so all the Israelites lived in their cities, and the children at Israel lived in their cities; the children of Israel served the Lord all the days of Joshua, and all the days of the elders, who had lengthened their days after Joshua, and saw the great work of the Lord which he had performed for Israel.

12 And the elders judged Israel after the death of Joshua for seventeen years.

13 All the elders also fought the battles of Israel against the Canaanites and the Lord drove the Canaanites from before the children of Israel in order to place the Israelites in their land.

14 And he accomplished all the words which he had spoken to Abraham, Isaac, and Jacob, and the oath which he had sworn, to give to them and to their children the land of the Canaanites.

15 The Lord gave to the children of Israel the whole land of Canaan as he had sworn to their ancestors, and the Lord gave them rest from those around them, and the children of Israel lived securely in their cities.

16 Blessed be the Lord forever, amen, and amen.

17 Strengthen yourselves, and let the hearts of all you that trust in the Lord. Be of good courage.

Jasher

ABOUT THE AUTHOR

Joseph Lumpkin has written for various newspapers and is author of over thirty books including, The Lost Book The Bible; Banned From the Bible, The Gospel of Thomas – A Contemporary Translation; Encounter the Warrior's Heart; Dark Night of the Soul – A Journey to the Heart of God, and other works. A complete catalog of the works of Joseph Lumpkin is listed at: www.fifthestatepub.com

22455624R00195

Printed in Great Britain
by Amazon